CW00409927

CHANGING ORDERS

CHANGING ORDERS

The Evolution of the World's Armies,
1945 to the Present

ARMS AND
ARMOUR

For my mother, the Beautiful Helen,
who taught me a love of books.

Arms and Armour Press
A Cassell Imprint
Villiers House, 41-47 Strand, London WC2N 5JE.

Distributed in Australia by Capricorn Link (Australia) Pty.
Ltd, 2/13 Carrington Road, Castle Hill, NSW 2154.

British Library Cataloguing-in-Publication Data: a catalogue
record for this book is available from the British Library

ISBN 1-85409-018-6

Designed and edited by DAG Publications Ltd.
Designed by David Gibbons; edited by Michael Boxall;
printed and bound in Great Britain.

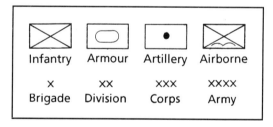

CONTENTS

CONTENTS

PREFACE

From the vantage point of 1992 it is easy to look back upon the period from the Soviet Moscow Victory Parade on 24 June 1945 to the fall of the Berlin Wall on 9 November 1989 as a clearly defined historical era. Rarely have armies grown, flourished and sometimes wilted with such profusion and vigour. As living institutions these armies made a grim but fascinating pageant of the post-war era.

Mercifully, unlike the two previous eras that ended in 1914 and 1939, this post-war era did not terminate in a world war, but it was chock-full of warfare. Also unlike the previous eras, these wars did not consume the strength and substance of the great powers. For once in this century Europe was not the cockpit of the armies. This era's wars, apart from the Greek Civil War and the Soviet suppression of the Hungarian Revolt, were fought almost entirely in the former colonies of the great powers. For it was among the former colonies, now sovereign nations, that new and powerful armies had been born and had won their spurs in battle. Many of the new armies were the creation, and often the agents, of the upheavals that brought their states into being. They were like diamonds shaped by great pressure, hard and brilliant in their ideas and standards – such as the Israeli Defence Force (IDF) and the People's Army of Vietnam (PAVN).

At the same time, the victorious though exhausted armies of the Second World War licked their wounds and then plunged into the new era. Armed now with nuclear weapons, they scared each other to the point where direct conflict was avoided, but was deflected into the arena of the new armies. But their thinking centred around the notion of a great clash of armed hosts in central Europe, and they trained and prepared for the seemingly inevitable replay of the two world wars. By the time the era was ready to die politically, the armies of NATO and the Warsaw Pact had developed the theories and practices of mechanized warfare into high art. Ironically, the NATO half of this competition was able to demonstrate its skills in a dramatic but brief one-act performance in the least likely venue of all – the Arabian Peninsula – seventeen months after the era had actually passed away.

This then was an era of armies. Unlike air forces and navies, whose stories are essentially those of hardware, the story of armies is one of people and institutions. There are only a relatively small number of air forces and navies that have significance in this era, but there are many armies that can claim a place in history. Only a few air forces and fewer navies can claim much combat experience during this era, but the story of the armies is one of much fighting and sacrifice.

This book is organized into chapters by post-war decades to give a snapshot of history. Each chapter then addresses the history and development of the armies in geographical progression from east to west around the world. The same battle or campaign is usually described from the perspective of each of the participants. The purpose is not so much to describe the details of the wars but the performance of the armies that fought them. Because of practical limitations, not all armies are described in each chapter. Usually those that remained major players in the balance of power or experienced a good deal of combat are addressed throughout the book.

For those of us who lived through that era it was in many ways a period of seemingly eternal verities despite the great changes that coursed through the various armies. We knew who our friends were and who were our enemies. The development of our armies, with certain regressions and detours, was generally on a straight-line path of increasing sophistication and complexity. The technological torrent that filled the world's arsenals challenged armies to fashion new doctrines for employing these new tools of war. Yet much of this innovation was locked into the constant strategic relationships of the era. In many ways it was a comfortable military world, with so many of the variables essentially settled. Then the political landscape heaved, and little would be the same again.

December 1993
Alexandria, VA

CHAPTER 1

THE FIRST POST-WAR DECADE, 1945–1955

INTRODUCTION

The first decade after the Second World War was, in many ways, the most remarkable of the entire post-war period. The end of the War in 1945 marked an epochal change in the course of history. It was the great divide that separated nations and their armies from everything that had happened before. That first post-war decade put the armies of the world on a path that would be in most cases a straight line of development to this day.

For the armies of the two great victors, it was a period of indecision. The American and Soviet armies, exhausted by the war effort, placidly digested the lessons of the war and, looking to the past, waited to take a bold step into the atomic era.

The armies of the stricken British and French empires would find their hands full dealing with the disintegration of those empires. In one of the great defeats of modern times the French Army would pass under the yoke at the hands of another new Asian army at Dien Bien Phu in Indo-China. The armies of Germany and Japan had been destroyed root and branch as institutions. They would be reborn to reflect their new governments and societies. Similarly, any remnant of the old Polish army would soon be overpowered and remade as a copy of the Soviet Army. None of these armies, beggared by the economic sacrifice and ruin of their nations during the War, would have the focus or wherewithal to take any bold steps in the development of new doctrine or technologies.

In the Middle East and East Asia, colonialism faded, giving rise to new dynamic armies suckled on wars from birth. Chief among them were the Israeli Defence Force (IDF), The People's Liberation Army of China (PLA), and the People's Army of Vietnam (PAVN). These armies would prove to be the fertile seedbed of new concepts of war. India and Pakistan inherited the stable structure of the British Indian Army. North Korea would have its army moulded and trained by the Soviet Army as would South Korea's be by the United States Army, although the stubborn Koreans north and south would have a strong drive to do things their way. The wars of this first post-war decade would exclusively take place in these areas of the world.

Perhaps the unique feature was the sheer number of new beginnings. No other decade in history had seen the birth of so many new armies, as shown below, either as completely new institutions in existing states or new institutions in new states.

Table 1-1. The New Armies, 1945–1955

State	Official Name	Official Year Of Creation
North Vietnam	People's Army of Vietnam	1945
Poland	Polish People's Army	1945
Yugoslavia	People's Army of Yugoslavia	1945
Syria	The Syrian Arab Army	1946
China	People's Liberation Army	1946

State	Official Name	Official Year Of Creation
North Korea	Korean People's Army	1948
Pakistan	The Pakistan Army	1948
India	The Indian Army	1948
Israel	Israeli Defence Force	1948
South Korea	The Republic of Korea Army	1948
Japan	Japanese Ground Self-Defence Force	1954
South Vietnam	Army of the Republic of Vietnam	1955
West Germany	Bundeswehr	1955
East Germany	Nationalische Volksarmee	1956*

*Note: The NVA was a complete and functioning army well before 1956, the date chosen for its official birthday so as to claim that it was only following the creation of the West German Bundeswehr.

UNITED STATES

In the year of victory, 1945, the US Army numbered more than 8,000,000 men and women in 89 veteran divisions. It was an army that had wrung victory from every front with great skill and ingenuity, but by January 1948, upon his appointment as Chief of Staff of the Army, General Omar Bradley stated with bitter frankness, '... the Army of 1948 could not fight its way out of a paper bag'.[1] Within two years this army was to be engaged in another major land war in Korea under the most severe conditions. A defeat that would have been as humiliating as the victory of five years ago had been exalting, would be avoided only by the narrowest margin. What had happened during these five years? By what alchemy had gold been turned into lead?

The atomic bombs that had destroyed two Japanese cities came close, indirectly, to destroying the US Army as an effective military institution. First, the atomic bomb brought the final victory with such totality that the American people believed that national security had become automatically guaranteed with American monopoly of the secret of the atom. That sentiment turned the army of 1945 from a mighty, skilled host to a shrinking collection of non-combatants. Secondly, the atomic bomb itself revolutionized concepts of warfare to such a degree that there seemed to be no place for the infantryman in an age of instant mass destruction.

DEMOBILIZATION

For the third time in their history, the American people clamoured successfully at the end of a great war to disband a now useless army. Even before the final victory over Japan, the army began to demobilize. On 12 May 1945 the strength of the ground and air forces of the US Army stood at 8,290,000. By the end of 1945 that number had been almost halved to 4,229,000. By the end of June 1946 it had more than halved again to 1,890,000. Within the first nine months of VJ-Day, the army had discharged 6,134,000 troops. By the end of demobilization on 30 June 1947, army strength had been halved yet again to 990,000.[2] In comparison, the Soviet ground and air forces had begun demobilization in the same year from a strength of approximately 9,880,000. They ended their demobilization in 1948 with slightly fewer than 2,500,000.

The decline in combat effectiveness galloped far ahead of the decline in numbers. Within six weeks of the surrender of Japan, the Joint Chief of Staffs estimated that '... a year or more would be required to reconstitute our military position at a

10

fraction of its recent power'. The Deputy Commander, Army Air Forces (AAF) stated that the point had practically been reached 'at which the Army Air Forces can no longer be considered anything more than a symbolic instrument of National Defense'. By 15 November 1945 the Army in Europe was adjudged by its commander to be able to operate in an emergency at *'less than 50 per cent normal wartime efficiency'*, if morale and fighting spirit were not considered for they were non-existent.

General Eisenhower explained part of the cause in December 1945, shortly after he had become Chief of Staff of the Army,

'great groups of officers ... have just quit. Through personal inspections I have encountered this demoralized attitude very, very definitely – a major saying "what the hell, I want to go home. What can you do to me? You can Class B me and throw me out." and that is what he wants.'[3]

In addition to this attitude problem, the sheer mechanics of the departure destroyed the units whose skills and cohesion had been built by years of teamwork. For example, the famed 1st Cavalry Division had suffered a personnel turnover of more than 75,000 men by the end of demobilization. In all the dust of moving men, no trace of the spirit of the old division could have survived. The decline in the technical services was, if anything, even more alarming. Specialists and skilled NCOs had disappeared almost overnight. The lower rate of casualties these groups had suffered gave them the time in service through a points system that gave them a disproportionate priority in demobilization. Major General Gavin, commanding 82nd Airborne Division, the principal strategic reserve during the period of demobilization, recalled:

'Only those present in units at the time will know the disastrous effects of the demobilization program on supply and maintenance activities. Before we were through officers were performing the duties of mechanics and everybody was doing what he could to save the situation...'[4]

In early 1949 General Bradley summed-up the causes and effects of the great demobilization with an unaccustomed edge:

'Many of the Army's difficulties today can be traced to the hasty and hysterical demobilization of the American forces at the end of the war. Instead of dismantling the machine that had made us the most powerful force for peace in the world, the American people chose to wreck it. Even before Hiroshima was cleared, the clamor for instant discharge had disorganized our armies in the field. We chose to view the end of the war as the magic beginning of peace. We put our precious standards of private indulgence before the object that had already cost us 350,000 lives.'[5]

The demobilization was followed by drastic cuts in the peacetime establishment of the army. By February 1948 it had shrunk to 552,000. Half of that number were on occupation duty in Europe and Asia 'serving as policemen and clerks'. The end of the draft and high post-war inflation, which were especially severe on the small, fixed pay of the enlisted ranks, had also served to dry up enlistments.

The crisis in Greece in late 1947 brought the effect of a ruined army on national security into the open. The Joint Chiefs of Staff reported that if it were required to send forces to Greece, a partial national mobilization would be necessary. Shortly after Bradley had assumed his duties, Secretary of State George Marshal informed the National Security Council (NSC) that 'we are playing with fire while we have nothing with which to put it out'.[6] Marshal was later to comment:

'I remember, when I was Secretary of State I was being pressed constantly, particularly when I was in Moscow, by radio message after message to give the Russians hell... When I got back, I was getting the same appeal in relation to the Far East and China. At that time, my facilities for giving them hell – and I am a soldier and know something about the ability to give hell – was 1⅓ divisions over the entire United States. That is quite a proposition when you deal with somebody with over 260 and you have 1⅓rd. We had nothing in Alaska. We did not have enough to defend the airstrip in Fairbanks...'7

The army, supported by President Truman, had pressed for universal military training after the war, but Congress would not act on it. Still, the Communist coup in Czechoslovakia had focused 'some small attention' on the fact that the army's effective combat strength was barely 2⅔ divisions. Congress authorized the renewal of the draft that June for two years and budgeted for an increase of 100,000 in strength. That 'small attention' was quickly superseded by the Administration's desire to economize. In early 1950 Congress again cut army strength which actually fell to 591,000 by June.[8]

By 1950 the army found itself an institution under siege. For the American people and its elected representatives, the army was becoming an irrelevancy. It was a dinosaur that had been shouldered out of its ecological niche by the more technologically advanced military species. The sleek and glamorous new air force, which had evolved quickly from the AAF into its own service, and the incalculable power of the nuclear weapon could incinerate even the finest field force in a flash. Any war would be atomic, and the American monopoly in the hands of the air force would result in an almost automatic victory. Under such conditions the army had to struggle to keep from losing faith in itself.

THE PEACETIME ARMY

Reflecting the needs of a peacetime force, the army made a number of efficient structural changes that were later confirmed by the Army Reorganization Act of 1950. In 1946 the great wartime operating agencies, such as the powerful Operations Division (OPD) were abolished. The General Staff resumed its place, and pre-war Congressionally mandated restrictions on its size were eliminated. The Secretary of the Army was now responsible for setting its size and composition; he also gained authority to determine the number and relative strength of each of the arms and services. The infantry, artillery and armour were recognized as the combat arms. Artillery was a merger of the old field artillery, coast defence artillery and anti-aircraft artillery. Although horses had been long gone, a 'mechanized cavalry' arm had survived but was incorporated now into armour. Army aviation, though neither an arm nor a branch, existed as a 'quasi arm' that was to gradually assume many of the tactical close support missions that the new US Air Force was reluctant to perform. Fourteen service corps were also recognized, among them several for the first time as permanent establishments such as the Transportation and Military Police Corps. The Women's Army Corps had already been recognized by law in 1948, not entirely with the wholehearted concurrence of the army. In the National Defense Act of 1947, the War Department – as did the Navy – lost its status as an executive agent and became a military department subordinate to the new Department of Defense. The War Department also changed its name to the Department of the Army.

DOCTRINE

As early as 1946 the army was beginning to comment on the atomic challenge. General Joseph Stilwell, head of the War Department Board of 1946 on Army equipment, stated that while a war might involve the use of nuclear weapons at some stage, final victory would only come with 'occupation of hostile territory'. In a series of post-war conferences, the army examined its wartime experiences to improve weapons, tactics and organization under the assumption that ground combat would continue to be non-nuclear. The army's statement of doctrine in 1949, Field Manual 100-5, did not even address the subject of tactics on the nuclear battlefield. Instead, doctrine focused on the physical conditions of the future battlefield, such as combat in cities, not on the nature of the future battle. As the Cold War deepened the threat to Europe, the army emphasized the European battlefield which 'reinforced the Army's doctrinal preference for large-scale conventional operations'. In this, for varying reasons, they were much like their Soviet counterparts of the period.[9] With so bleak an institutional future, the past was all too inviting. Nevertheless, the army had begun studying the tactical uses of nuclear weapons and began the development of nuclear-capable artillery in 1949.

The need for close co-ordination of the firepower of field artillery, naval gunfire and tactical air support was one of the major lessons of the War. For this reason the army increased the size of gun batteries, developed more effective fire control methods and initiated with the air force a 'clear doctrine for the tactical air support of ground troops'. The Stilwell Board also came to the conclusion that the '... best anti-tank weapon is a better tank', which arose from dissatisfaction with Second World War anti-tank operations and equipment. The solution was to provide the infantry divisions with enough tanks to fulfil the anti-tank mission. One tank battalion was allocated to each division and one company to each infantry regiment. Little thought was given to providing the infantry with their own primary anti-tank weapons, with the consequence that tanks would be frittered away in the defence rather than massed for offensive penetration and shock. There were alarming similarities to the French outlook of 1940.[10]

Weapons Development

During this period the Soviet Union was making impressive investments in improving existing equipment, designing new weapons systems and creating industrial output adequate for a force five or six times the size of the US Army. By 1950 the US Army was living off the stockpiles of equipment that had been amassed during the War. Little emphasis and fewer dollars were placed on new weapons development and even less on production. Weapons remained those of the Second World War, often designed decades earlier, and included such venerable pieces as the .45 calibre pistol first designed to fight drug frenzied Moro warriors in the Philippines in 1902. The 105mm howitzer and the Sherman tank remained the mainstay of the fighting units. The Pershing tank had made its appearance late in the war, but production had been small, and the Sherman, already inadequate by 1944, was the mainstay of the few armoured units. The US Army would essentially fight the Korean War with these leftovers from the Second World War.

The development of the first generations of post-war tanks is a good example. The army's initial attempt at new tank design was devoted to the development of a new light tank shortly after the end of the War. The M41 'Walker Bulldog' went into production in mid 1951. A new medium tank (T42) was also planned but was not fully ready by the beginning of the war in Korea. The urgency of that war required a new tank, so the army was reduced to the expediency of mating a T42 turret (90mm gun) to an M46 (Pershing M26 refinement) hull and calling it the M47. It was finally accepted for delivery in April 1952. Not until October 1950 had design work begun on a new medium tank, production beginning in April 1952. In contrast, the first Soviet medium tank, the T-54, began production in 1947 and entered service in 1949. Similarly, the first post-war US armoured personnel carrier, the M59, did not go into production until 1954. The first Soviet post-war vehicle, the BTR-152, went into production in 1950.[11]

The Army did lead the way in the development and use of several new weapons and new technologies that had their major operational debut in Korea. The 3.5in rocket-launcher or bazooka replaced the old 2.36in launcher. The infantry also acquired their own artillery with the fielding of the 57mm and 75mm recoilless rifles, 'the greatest innovation in infantry weapons since the Second World War'. Ironically, these weapons resulted in unexpected US casualties. The enemy in Korea ran out of tanks quickly but captured enough of the recoilless rifles to pose a threat to US tanks. The other new technology was the helicopter which 'came of age as the favourite vehicle for local air transportation...' The demand became so great that they were always in short supply. They played an enormously important role in adding a new dimension to the mobility and logistics of ground forces. Unfortunately their potential was only partially realized because of resistance by the US Air Force to allowing Army Aviation to expand beyond narrow limits.

Designing weapons in peacetime is one thing. A sense of urgency in getting them to the fighting forces in peacetime is entirely another. Aside from the recoil-

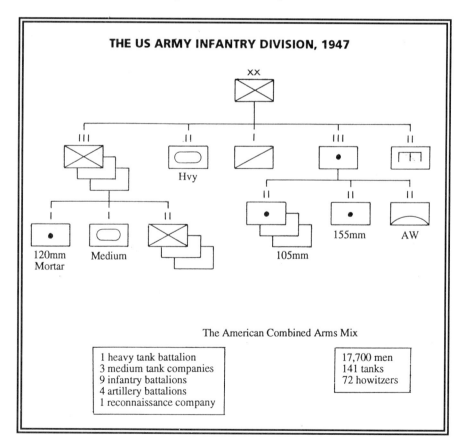

THE US ARMY INFANTRY DIVISION, 1947

The American Combined Arms Mix

1 heavy tank battalion	17,700 men
3 medium tank companies	141 tanks
9 infantry battalions	72 howitzers
4 artillery battalions	
1 reconnaissance company	

less rifle and the helicopter, the army fought the war in Korea with its inventory of Second World War weapons. Heavy weapons, especially tanks and artillery, require long lead times (longer in the West than in the Soviet Union, for some reason). The new generation of tank models hurriedly initiated in 1950 never saw action in Korea.

The material readiness of the army was barely enough to maintain its very limited peacetime programmes far less the demands of war readiness. Since 1945 the army had limited its procurement to food, clothing and medical supplies. Its combat equipment needs were expected to be filled from the surplus of the War. Unfortunately most of that surplus in weapons and ammunition had been disposed of through foreign military assistance programmes, so that the US Army was obliged to operate with worn and obsolete equipment. Although machine-guns and towed artillery existed in large numbers, construction equipment, new radios, modern anti-aircraft artillery, self-propelled artillery and even trucks were in short supply. Maintenance became increasingly difficult as the old equipment 'wore out under constant use or deteriorated in storage depots'. Almost 74 per cent of the 3,457 M24 light tanks and 43 per cent of the 3,202 M4A3 Sherman medium tanks in the United States were unserviceable. Of the new M46 Patton tank, only 319 had been built.[12]

ORGANIZATIONAL CHANGES

In 1950 the army could barely support ten divisions in its table of organization: one armour, seven infantry and two airborne infantry divisions. Four infantry divisions were on garrison duty in Japan and one in Germany. The remaining five were in the United States, the airborne and armour divisions constituting a general reserve. Nine of the ten divisions were seriously under strength with the exception of the 82nd Airborne Division. The infantry divisions were based on the Second World War triangular 'redeployment division' with three infantry regiments and one artillery regiment. Corps and army level assets, such as a tank battalion and an anti-aircraft battalion, were incorporated into the divisions, wartime experience having shown this to be necessary. Unfortunately the pressures for economy overcame experience. The army was able to authorize only the partial establishment of each division, with the exception of the 1st Infantry Division in Germany. Each infantry regiment was allowed only two rather than its three normal battalions, and the battalions were deprived of one rifle company. The result was a tactically anaemic division that should have had 27 rifle companies but had to make do with twelve. To make matters worse, the authorized organic tank battalion was rarely provided. Artillery battalions were equally skeletonized, having only two of the three authorized batteries.[13] No division had its full wartime complement of equipment. Ammunition stocks were minimal. By comparison, a Soviet infantry division was receiving 100 tanks and assault guns and more than 60 pieces of artillery.

More serious than *matériel* or organizational deficiencies was the fact that the army had forgotten that its purpose was to fight. The whole of American society had taken a long rest after the Second World War. No one, including a good many soldiers, thought that there were any real possibilities of combat. This lack of purpose was bad enough, but added to it were the complaisance of an army geared to the pleasant distractions of occupation duties and the constant enervating refrain to economize on operations. Together, these just about knocked any sense of immediacy out of realistic training. Much was also due to a general relaxation of the rigours of army life and discipline. One of the features of the change in social policy was the reform of the military justice system and the introduction of the Uniform Code of Military Justice (UCMJ) applicable to all the services. Its purpose was to soften the severities and harsher aspects of military justice, notably 'discipline, obedience and responsibility', as one officer put it.[14] Whatever the motivations in these policies, they were accompanied by what many veterans considered to be a serious compromise of standards.

THE KOREAN WAR

In June 1950 the North Korean Army delivered a collective slap in the face to the US Army. By the time the Chinese People's Liberation Army (PLA) joined the fray with a stunning roundhouse punch in November, the army had been knocked out of the dreamy unreality of the atomic world and forced back into the mud of infantry combat. And it wasn't ready. Its cumulative deficiencies in training, discipline and armament twice brought it teetering to the brink of disaster in the first six months of the war.

Fortune, at least, did not withhold all favours. The US Army was not faced with an entirely 'new' kind of war, the sort of military revolution brought on by tanks and aircraft in the 1939 or the atomic war that everyone had assumed would be the next war. It was the 'old' kind of war, the basic small-unit war where train-

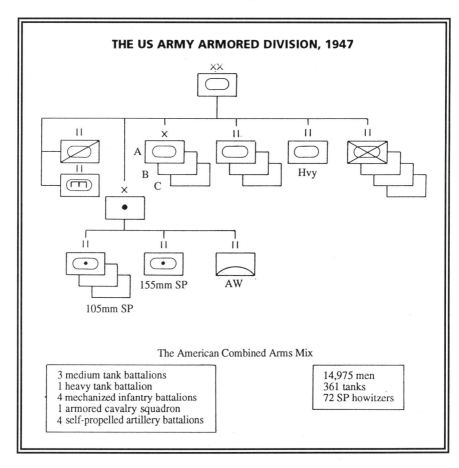

THE US ARMY ARMORED DIVISION, 1947

The American Combined Arms Mix

3 medium tank battalions 1 heavy tank battalion 4 mechanized infantry battalions 1 armored cavalry squadron 4 self-propelled artillery battalions	14,975 men 361 tanks 72 SP howitzers

ing, proficiency, fitness, leadership and cohesion still worked. Ironically, it was the kind of war the army had insisted it would face in the future. The North Koreans and the Chinese had no technological advantage aside from a few tough tanks and tougher infantrymen. The Soviets, who trained and equipped the North Korean Army, only provided equipment they had used during the Second World War, and withheld their post-war designs.

American equipment in the Eighth Army in Japan was of the same vintage as the Soviet weapons in the hands of the North Koreans but had been stocked in almost token amounts. Each division was short of its war strength by the following:

Table 1-2. US 8th Army Shortages per Division

7,000 men	3 rifle battalions
1,500 rifles	6 heavy tank companies
100 90mm anti-tank guns	3 105mm field artillery batteries
205 57mm recoilless rifles	3 AAA batteries

As a result, each division could only deliver 62 per cent of its infantry firepower, 69 per cent of its AAA fire, and 14 per cent of its tank fire.[15] Other equipment in short supply included basic small unit weapons such as .30 calibre machine-guns, mortar components and radios. The few tanks were light M24s. Only thirteen HEAT (High-Explosive Anti-Tank) artillery rounds were to be found in the first artillery battalion sent to Korea. Of the 326 90mm anti-tank guns and 226 57mm recoilless rifles in the peacetime authorization of the 8th Army, only 21 recoilless rifles were available. When the first battalion, Task Force Smith, prepared for departure, other units of its parent regiment stripped themselves to provide the basic table of equipment for it. When K Company joined the task force a week later, it arrived with only incomplete parts for 81mm mortars, and no recoilless rifles. The weapons platoon had one jeep that was the personal property of a private.[16]

FROM TASK FORCE SMITH AND A CYCLE OF DEFEAT

The chickens had come home to roost. Task Force Smith deployed north of Osan, expecting the KPA to run away as soon as they heard that the US Army was in front of them. Instead, on 5 July, supported by infantry, a KPA tank regiment drove right through them guns blazing. The Redlegs quickly expended their entire supply of FIVE anti-tank rounds and then watched their HE (High Explosive) rounds bounce off the enemy tanks. Under pressure from KPA infantry on the flanks, the by-passed Task Force fell back in disorder, abandoning its guns and many wounded. In all, 185 out of 450 men were lost. The shock to the army resounded through four decades. Task Force Smith became the byword for the tragedies of unpreparedness – for which the army only partially blamed the politicians.

The rest of the 24th Infantry Division arrived shortly afterwards and was beaten as badly at Taejon, losing many prisoners. The North Koreans drove the US Eighth Army's three divisions (1st Cavalry, 24th and 25th Infantry) into the Pusan Perimeter in short order. They needed massive replacements. The 24th Division's 21st Infantry Regiment had lost almost 1,500 men, and its 34th more than 1,800. The situation was saved by the hard-fighting Marines, massed field artillery, naval gunfire and tactical air support and by the last incandescent flare of genius from General MacArthur. The landing at Inchon led to the rout of the North Koreans, as Eighth Army, strengthened with replacements and the addition of the 2nd Infantry Division and the British 27 Brigade, burst out of the Pusan Perimeter to hound the

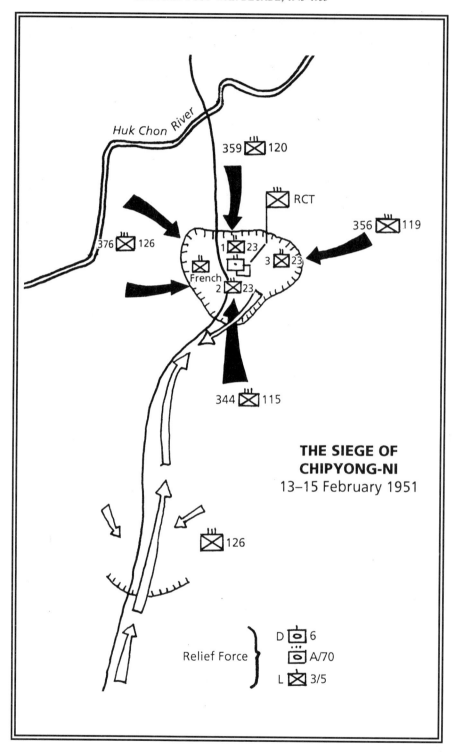

THE SIEGE OF CHIPYONG-NI
13–15 February 1951

KPA in the pursuit toward the Yalu River. During the pursuit they were joined by 3rd and 7th Infantry Divisions and 187th Airborne Regimental Combat Team. By late November when the war seemed over, Eighth Army had lost 27,827 battle casualties – 4,548 KIA or dead of wounds, and 4,834 missing.

On 24 November brilliantly deployed Chinese armies attacked and caught Eighth Army unawares and strung out over Northern Korea. Against tough, veteran Chinese troops in large numbers, the Americans were still too soft. Outmanoeuvred, Eighth Army was forced to fall back. Falling back became a retreat, and retreat often degenerated into flight. 'Bug-out fever' infected too many units, and when they bolted they were often the first to be butchered. Many prisoners were taken, many of them were killed on the spot. Eighth Army continued to fall back, past the 38th Parallel, past Seoul, ever farther south, harried by the swarming Chinese.

MIRACLE OF THE HAN AND MATHEW RIDGWAY

The old virtues saved the army. The institution still had enough of those talents now that crisis had called for them. On the banks of the Han River the army found itself. Leadership re-asserted itself in the person of General Mathew Ridgway as the primal element of war and all else flowed from it. The recovery was phenomenal. There was one more retreat, this time an organized, fighting retreat. Ridgway wielded a scythe to clean out unfit leaders and infused a new confidence and aggressiveness in his men. Then Eighth Army came back, attacking on 5 February. The Chinese struck back and rocked the offensive on its heels, but they broke themselves on the rock of 23rd Regimental Combat Team (with its attached French battalion) at Chipyong-Ni. Surrounded by at least six regiments from four Chinese divisions, the 23rd held on in a bitter fight that left the field strewn with Chinese. Their perimeter penetrated, the 23rd counter-attacked through the Chinese in time to welcome the relieving tank column. Thousands of dead Chinese were counted dead against 355 for the 23rd and another 100 for the relieving column. The army's performance was now measured in terms of units like the 23rd RCT rather than Task Force Smith. Ridgway now knew that the sword would not turn in his hand and launched a series of offensives with names such as 'Killer' and 'Ripper' and was in process of grinding the Chinese to bits when the Truce Talks were declared. The talks ended further decisive offensive operations but not the dying that continued along the still murderous front for almost another two years. When the truce finally came into effect, the army had sustained 27,709 battle deaths and 96,902 wounded. More than 7,000 men had been taken prisoner of whom fewer than 4,000 returned alive.

Curiously, the army did not officially consider that any significant new lessons had been learned in Korea, merely that a few refinements had been made and that lessons had just been re-learned. It was emphatic that changes in doctrine were not necessary. However, 'a subtle but important change had occurred in Army thinking if not in its doctrine'. The army had become further addicted to enormous firepower as a substitute for manoeuvre and offensive action. The enemy was to be devoured by the inexorable attrition of firepower.[17]

The Korean War rescued the army from a state of prolonged penury as the United States undertook a major mobilization of industry to support and expand the services. Within six months of the North Korean attack, the armed forces had been expanded by almost a million men by the call-up of reserves and through the draft. By late 1953 the army would number 1,500,000 men in twenty divisions.

Many of the new divisions had been activated from the National Guard. Much of the increase would be permanent as the war drew attention to the vulnerability of Europe and the need to station a field army there.

SPECIAL OPERATIONS AND NUCLEAR WARFARE

Under pressure of the war, the army had also been indulging in some original thinking in two areas at the opposite ends of the warfare spectrum: the nuclear battlefield and special operations. Beneath the threshold of massive retaliation, the army was looking at the tactical and operational advantages of fighting on the nuclear battlefield as a way to offset Soviet numbers of divisions. By 1953 the 280mm nuclear-capable gun had been fielded, and by 1955 battlefield missiles were being readied. Service schools were already teaching 'atomic tactics', special technical schools had been established, the effects of nuclear weapons on personnel and equipment were being studied, and the problems of organization of ground forces were under close examination.[18]

Although the birth of the army's special operations capability was due to the crisis of the Korean War, it was immediately focused on the defence of Europe. Like the atomic battlefield, it was seen as a means to counter Soviet numbers. Unlike the atomic battlefield, special operations in the form of unconventional warfare were designed to employ the 'indirect approach' of unbalancing the enemy's effort by dislocating his control of the rear.

Special operations did not have much of a tradition within the army prior to the Second World War. The army's association with the OAS had not improved the image. Conventionally trained officers had deep professional apprehensions about the creation of élite units that would drain off quality personnel. Nevertheless the strong support from the Secretary of the Army and the sponsorship of special operations within an existing Army Staff, Psychological Operations, removed the last roadblocks. On 1 May 1952 the US Army Psychological Warfare Center and the 10th Special Forces Group were activated at Fort Bragg, North Carolina.

In January 1953 the army included its 280mm nuclear-capable gun in President Eisenhower's inauguration parade to publicize its work and growing interest in the atomic battlefield. In May the army fired its first atomic shell. 'The resulting explosion not only symbolized the addition of an awesome new weapon to the Army's arsenal, but also symbolized the true beginning of the atomic era for the Army.'[19]

THE NEW LOOK

The advent of the Eisenhower administration in 1953, however, ushered the army into one of the most painful peacetime episodes in its history. President Eisenhower quickly outlined his national security strategy which became known as the 'New Look'. It had two premises: (1) that national defence was based on a strong economy that could be harmed by anything more than the absolutely necessary rather than the 'merely desirable'; and (2) that the real protection of the United States rested on nuclear deterrence.[20]

The air force had the primary role in national defence by its ability to brandish the threat of massive retaliation implicit in the policy of deterrence. Priority of resources went to the air force, and the budget cutters went after the army. Within a few years the air force budget would essentially equal that of the army and navy combined.

Eisenhower's strategic policies left the army with no viable mission. He was frank about the consequences for the army, leaving it only the crumbs of occupation duty and civil defence. General Ridgway, his newly appointed Chief of Staff of the Army, had expressed his great concern for the outnumbered divisions in Europe. Eisenhower stated later that the disparity in numbers was so great that 'only by the interposition of our nuclear weapons could we promptly stop a major Communist aggression in that area. Two more divisions or ten more divisions, on our side, would not make very much difference against the Soviet ground force.'[21] Many officers were to wonder if the President truly considered the Army as 'merely desirable' rather than essential.

Cut loose of any mooring to a realistic mission and savaged by budget and personnel cuts, army morale collapsed. Retention rates for enlisted men plummeted, and junior officers resigned their commissions in record numbers. The level of publicly expressed bitter dismay among general officers reached unprecedented levels. An officer as senior as General Lyman L. Lemnitzer, Chief of Staff 1959–1962, stated that 'today it seems to me that the very survival of the Army... is at stake'.[22] A future lieutenant general expressed the Army's lament in the following stark terms:

'I do not know what the Army's mission is or how it plans to fulfil its mission. And this, I find, is true of my fellow-soldiers. At a time when new weapons and new machines herald a revolution in warfare, we soldiers do not know where the Army is going and how it is going to get there.'[23]

GREAT BRITAIN

The British Army saw the end of the Second World War victorious around the world from the deserts of Africa to the plains of northern Germany to the jungles of Burma. Its nearly 3,000,000 men and women had become a magnificent and highly proficient citizen army. And in the tradition of modern democracy, it was dissolved to a small fraction of its war strength in a series of rapid demobilizations. By 1948 the 3,000,000 had become 400,000.

Nevertheless the British Army was at that time two-thirds the size of the US Army but supported by a population only one-quarter as large. Britain's victories in two world wars had drained her of the treasure of two hundred years of empire, and now that empire was breaking up as well. For the first time in its history the British Army had not only the duties of imperial protector but had assumed the commitment to provide in peacetime major land forces for the defence of Europe. Britain still insisted on the trappings of a great power but had ceased to be able to afford them. The first decade of the post-war period saw the British Army trying to cope with these contradictions.

INDIA

In 1947 India, the great 'jewel in the crown' of the Empire, had been given up amicably in what has been described as an act of ruthless realism. The effect on the British Army was profound. At one stroke it was cut off from its past. India had been 'the Army's spiritual home where it drilled, fought, and lived for over two centuries... planted its roots, formed its traditions, and kept its skill finely honed...' Forty-five battalions of infantry were stationed in India and Burma in 1939. The whole of the British Army would have only 67 in 1949. The loss of India was to dislocate the army for more than twenty years until the Empire had passed and Europe was recognized as the new home.[24]

The actual departure, though, was likened to ripping the backbone out of a living body. Apart from suppressing the immediate and minor post-war mutinies of the Royal Indian Air Force and Navy, British troops had little to fear from the forces of Indian independence. Theirs was the appalling task of first attempting to keep order then withdrawing in the midst of the communal slaughters, 'the great killings' that were to consume millions. Calcutta rioted first at the cost of 14,000 dead and wounded. After restoring order, three British battalions were set the task of body disposal. Gregory Blaxland in *The Regiments Depart* tells of the 'awful 'ush' that greeted the order that the bodies were to be transported respectively to Muslim cemeteries or Hindu burning ghats. 'How the hell do I tell a Moslem from a Hindu when they've all been dead three days?' was the query from the ranks. When no drivers were available to move the rotting flesh, the officers drove – living on cigarettes and gin and reeking of death – unwilling to order their men across this most hideous of beaten zones where only example would do. It was not the end envisaged for Kipling's army.[25]

Much of the death could have been prevented had the army been given a peace-keeping role prior to Independence, but its orders were to disengage. Within these shackled instructions, the remaining units conducted numerous well-received flag marches through the countryside to convey some semblance of order. The crescendo was reached for the British on their departure from the Residency at Lucknow on the night of 13 August, hours before Independence. The Union Jack had flown night and day over the Residency to commemorate its defiance during the siege in the Great Mutiny. In the dark the flag was lowered 'through fear that rioters might next day attempt to make the capture for which so many Indians had striven in vain in 1857. Sappers later blew up the flag-pole and its base to complete the disintegration of this proudest symbol of the British Raj.'[26]

The saddest episode for the army was the treatment of the ten regiments of Gurkhas. No thought had been given to the future of these men whose service had become a byword for fidelity to the British. Less than a month before Independence their fate was hurriedly decided between Field Marshal Montgomery and Nehru. Only eight of the 27 battalions would be transferred to British service. The choice seemed to fall on those conveniently serving already in Malaya. The remainder would stay with India. These battalions were transferred intact, their men given no opportunity to choose. The men of those battalions destined for British service were given a choice; most opted to remain in India. Indian propaganda on the Gurkhas to stay was made potent by confusion over conditions of service and the treatment of their families which the British Army, in its indecision, could not answer.[27]

To add to the army's distress, the loss of India had also dislocated a critical element of British foreign policy. The consequences to the fabric of imperial policy had not been thought through with much clarity. The result was that the British Army was called on to garrison and protect all the imperial possessions that had been acquired over the course of empire precisely to protect the lines of communications to India. In themselves these possessions were economic, political and strategic liabilities. The army would be guarding the road to nowhere.[28]

That road was anything but quiet. The slow retreat that saw one possession after another become a manifest liability also saw the army acting less as an occupation force than as a gendarmerie attempting to keep order in the face of growing unrest, rising national aspirations and the inevitable violence. To its great moral credit, the army saw its way through these nightmares with a dignity and restraint in the face of often enormous provocation and frequent loss of life, that few other armies have matched. In the process it was able to add a few new martial trophies to its collection.

INSURGENCY IN MALAYA

The suppression of the Communist insurgency in Malaya beginning in 1948 was accomplished with a quiet professionalism that put a premium on skill, patience, thoroughness and a good intelligence system rather than material and numbers. The army's instincts were good. There was a natural inclination to rely on what it knew best: solid small-unit leadership, gritty but vital skills of the infantryman, a carefully acquired knowledge of the enemy and a firm but fair treatment of the population. At peak strength the British Army in Malaya numbered 23 infantry battalions with a rifle company strength of approximately 9,000 men, a one-to-one ratio with the guerrilla forces. From 1948 until 1955, 31 of 77 infantry battalions in the British Army rotated through Malaya. In addition, all eight Gurkha battalions and 21 SAS plus three armoured and two artillery regiments also served there. Four additional infantry battalions and one armour and one artillery regiment served thereafter until 1959.[29]

The army spent three years in securing the Chinese population from guerrilla access, then in 1952 went over to the offensive, concentrating on the development of intelligence that allowed the guerrillas to be hunted down methodically. It became a company commander's war. Rather than laager in large base camps, British forces usually occupied individual company camps that were the focal point for local security operations and the endless patrolling that eventually harried and nibbled the insurgents to death. Even this was decentralized. From company strength, the patrols shrank to ten men and two trackers. The army was not shy about securing the help of trackers from unconventional sources either. 'Ferret Force' was created from veterans of Force 136, contracted civilians and Army volunteers, to seek out the enemy in his lairs. An even more exotic effort was the recruitment of 47 Dyak tribesmen from Borneo, expert trackers. 'They were little men with long hair running down their backs like a horse's mane and with disarming smiles, which gleamed incongruously from beside their deadly blowpipes and their fearsome knives adorned with human hair.'[30]

The search for that something extra in the way of special operations skill not normally found in a line battalion led to the rebirth, through the back door, of the Special Air Service (SAS). A jungle warfare expert and SAS veteran, Mike Calvert, was given the task of finding a solution. He concluded that a new force as necessary, one able to live and operate in the jungle far longer than previously thought possible, able to wait and take the patient kills in ambush that are the reward of endurance. He raised a wild and woolly group of local volunteers who were given the title of the Malay Scouts. These were combined with the volunteers from 21 SAS, who carried the battle honours of the Long Range Desert Group, but had languished in the Territorial Army (reserves) since the Second World War. They found natural allies in the Dyaks. It was a deadly combination. The Scouts made a speciality of parachuting into the jungle for extended patrols. It was also the Scouts who developed a special relationship with the aboriginal populations of Malaya, the original and successful 'hearts and minds' campaign. In 1952 the Malay Scouts would become 22 SAS. The SAS was back on the active list to stay.[31]

The counter-insurgency extended into the next post-war decade, but a turning-point was reached in 1954 when the guerrilla leadership fled the country. At a cost of 70 British officers and 280 men and 159 Gurkhas killed, the British Army counted 6,710 enemy dead (countless more perished unknown in the jungles) to its credit. More, it had conducted the classic counter-insurgency operation of the post-war era.

THE KOREAN WAR

The army's next call to action was in Korea, one of the few places in the world where the British soldier had never set foot. Serving at the time in Hong Kong, 27 Brigade was designated to be Great Britain's contribution to the UN Forces. The brigade would take only two of its understrength battalions, the Middlesex (Die Hards) and the Argylls, which were filled up by volunteers from remaining battalions in Hong Kong. The King's Own Scottish Borderers (KOSB, the Kosbies) 'responded on battalion parade as if they had received word of command'.[32]

Landing in Pusan, 27 Brigade took its place in the line on the Naktong River. It participated in the breakout and pursuit of the North Korean Forces and was eventually joined by an Australian battalion north of Pyongyang. This was the beginning of the splendid union of Commonwealth forces first in this brigade then as 1st Commonwealth Division, born on 28 July 1951, by the addition of another British brigade, a Canadian brigade, a New Zealand artillery battalion, and an Indian ambulance company. The performance of the Commonwealth Division was to be a model of multinational co-operation on the battlefield.

That reputation was fairly won on one of the grimmest fields in the experience of the British Army. The British battalions were manned by a mix of regulars,

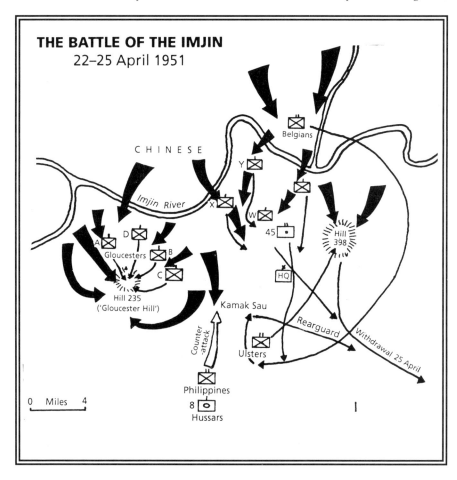

THE BATTLE OF THE IMJIN
22–25 April 1951

24

volunteers and national servicemen, and not all of the latter had been given the choice of volunteering. Yet every battalion lived up to its regular army traditions under incredible conditions. The army had not felt winter privation so badly since the Crimea, nor endured trench warfare as brutal since the Great War.

The last stand of 1st Gloucestershire Regiment (the Slashers) in April 1951 at the Battle of the Imjin River added another selfless epic to the army's honours list and stirred the nation more than any other action since the stand of 'the noble 24th' Foot at Rorke's Drift in 1879. The regiment had more battle honours than any in the British Army, and the men wore a second cap badge at the back of their berets to commemorate their stand back to back at Alexandria in 1801. The regiment had a reputation to uphold. They took the spearpoint of a major Chinese offensive, to give the rest of 29 Brigade time to withdraw. They held the spearpoint and blunted it but were eventually surrounded and overrun. Four officers and 41 men escaped. Seven officers and 51 men were dead or missing; nineteen officers and 505 men were taken prisoner. The Slashers quickly rose from the dead, the old regiment filled with new men and bright honours.[33]

Korea cost the British Army 86 officers and 779 men killed, and 184 and 2,404 wounded. Fifteen infantry battalions, three armoured and three artillery regiments served in rotation in addition to thirteen Australian and Canadian infantry battalions and three Canadian artillery regiments. The 1st Commonwealth Division went out of existence in November 1954; the last British battalion departed in July 1957.

THE MAU MAU IN KENYA

The army conducted the campaign against the Mau Mau uprising in Kenya with the same no-nonsense efficiency that it had acquired in Malaya. The population was controlled and the insurgents were first isolated and then run to ground. Army commanders seemed to have an innate understanding of the need for a unified military and police structure as well as the need to keep separate the civil and military powers of British tradition. The commander of British forces was quite inflexible on this matter:

> 'In operations of the kind we were undertaking there were no prisoners of war since we were not at war and did not give the Mau Mau the rights of a belligerent. On the other hand we often detained people and handed them over to the Civil Power. I made it very plain that the Army did not hold people and certainly did not ill-treat people they detained temporarily. A detained man might be innocent or liable to the death penalty according to the circumstances of his capture. It was for the security forces to provide the evidence and for the Civil Power to bring him to justice.'[34]

The uprising began in 1952 and had been crushed by the end of 1955. Eventually eleven infantry battalions rotated through Kenya, two with service in Malaya and five with Korean War honours.

THE MIDDLE EAST

The failure to reconcile Jew and Arab in Palestine, on the other hand, was quite beyond anyone's power, and the army was roundly criticized for its pro-Arab policies, though they did little more than reflect the prejudices of the British Foreign Office. The army saw action of one sort or another in twenty places on the road back from empire. Its conduct was uniformly witness to its character.

Table 1-3. British Army Casualties 1945–1955

Campaign	Year	Dead	Wounded	Total
Palestine	1945–48	223	478	701
Malaya	1948–60	509	921	1,430
Korea	1950–53	865	2,588	3,453
Kenya	1952–56	12	69	81
Totals		1,609	4,056	5,665

Source: Geoffrey Blaxland, *The Regiments Depart.*

COLD WAR DEVELOPMENTS

As the Cold War deepened into permanent enmity, Britain found herself the linch-pin in the defence of western Europe. A ruined Germany presented a military vac-uum in the centre of the continent that could not be ignored in the face of blatant Soviet hostility. In March 1948 Britain signed the Brussels Treaty and for the first time guaranteed in peacetime the security of nations on the continent, something she had consistently refused to do before 1914 and 1939. Now it would be Britain that would provide in a most critical period the principal ground forces (four divi-sions) for the defence of Western Europe. The Communist attack on Korea was to further focus resources and personnel in support of NATO. In 1954 the Churchill government was to take the momentous step of pledging to station in Europe for fifty years a force of four divisions and a supporting tactical air force. The tradi-tional maritime policy of British defence had been overtly abandoned as the fight-ing heart of the British Army was committed to the continent.

The Korean War provoked the Atlee government into a major re-armament programme that immediately resulted in a steady increase in the size of the British Army. From approximately two divisions in 1948, the army expanded to ten active divisions and ten in the Territorial Army in 1953. Army strength would grow from 360,000 in 1950 to 443,000 in 1954. By 1955 the Churchill government would begin a series of major defence cutbacks paralleling the 'New Look' of the Eisenhower administration in the United States.

Weapons development and production lagged in this decade. The post-war medium tank, the Centurion, had actually been designed in 1944, but the proto-types arrived in Germany too late to see action. They were to receive their baptism of fire in Korea and remain in service throughout the 1960s when they were replaced by Britain's first post-war designed tank, the Chieftain, beginning in 1967. Design of the first British armoured personnel carrier, the Saracen, began in 1948 and it entered production in 1952, being urgently required for the counter-insur-gency programme in Malaya.[35] Tables of organization for British infantry divisions had shown little advance since 1939. The array of mechanized equipment and artillery so noticeable in American and Soviet divisions was distressingly lacking in their British counterparts.[36] The British Army's armoured division, on the other hand, represented a recognition of the value of combined arms learned so painfully in the War. By 1945 the armoured division had come to resemble the flexible com-bined arms structure of the panzer division. The post-war table of organization was a slight modification of the final wartime structure. The division consisted of a tank brigade of three tank and one mechanized battalions, a motorized infantry brigade of four battalions, an armoured car battalion, two self-propelled artillery regiments, and one self-propelled anti-tank regiment. A later modification eliminated one of the motorized infantry battalions and the anti-tank regiment.[37]

PEACETIME CONSCRIPTION

The continuation of conscription after the Second World War was considered necessary to build the large reserve forces which the last two wars had shown were vital
for defence. Field Marshal Montgomery, The Chief of the Imperial General Staff,
was the leading advocate in arguing that conscription was essential. In this he
received little support from the other services but prevailed none the less.[38] About
half the army's strength was made up of conscripts on National Service. By 1954
they were providing 25 per cent of the corporals and 50 per cent of the lance-corpo-
rals; in some skilled trades they made up more than 70 per cent of the men.[39] It was
an unhappy arrangement for the army, and its morale suffered as the transient
nature of National Service broke down the bonds of cohesion that had been so
marked a feature of British Army traditions. That sentiment was tartly expressed by
Lieutenant-General H. B. Martin:

> 'Before the War the Regular Army had most of its goods in the shop
> window. Small though it was, it could yet display a fine array of divi-
> sions, brigades, regiments, battalions – with famous names all...it was
> proud and happy. Today we have gone to the other extreme indeed.

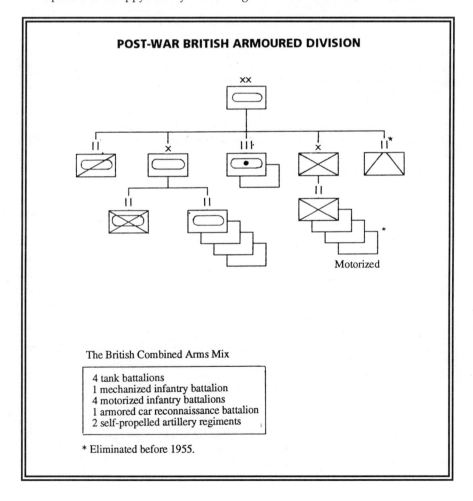

POST-WAR BRITISH ARMOURED DIVISION

Motorized

The British Combined Arms Mix

4 tank battalions
1 mechanized infantry battalion
4 motorized infantry battalions
1 armored car reconnaissance battalion
2 self-propelled artillery regiments

* Eliminated before 1955.

Today a whole-time Army of 400,000 men produces what? – two divisions...There is left to us neither a Regular Airborne division nor yet a Regular armoured division. Half our famous infantry of the line has vanished; the other half is maimed and mutilated. The Regular Army today is little more than an incoherent and uninspiring muddle. For pity's sake let us get our goods into the window again – with the illustrious names back on the labels.' [40]

Heavy overseas commitments and the conscript's two-year period of service required a constant rotation of personnel and the creation of a large training establishment which were further drains on efficiency. At the same time the morale problems of the army inhibited recruiting of long-service personnel which only reinforced the need for National Service. The Government actively attempted to maximize the numbers of regulars recruited because of the concurrent fewer conscripts that would be required. Despite an increase in recruits in 1952, attracted by the performance of the Commonwealth Division in Korea, the failure to attract enough volunteers would plague the army until National Service was finally ended.

THE REGIMENTS

The war's end saw the first of the great post-war convulsions of the army's beloved regimental system. It was holy tradition that a soldier had a 'right' to serve with his regiment in peacetime; many looked forward to the return to that close-knit life. They were to be disappointed. Instead of the regiment as home, the soldier and officer found himself liable to be posted to any regiment in the fifteen large groupings, later brigades, of regiments that were established after the war. Field Marshal Montgomery, as Chief of the Imperial General Staff (CIGS) after the war, was not such an admirer of the regimental system and its tendencies to exaggerate insularity. He quickly quashed a move to split the Royal Tank Regiment (RTR) into eight separate regiments:

'... so far as I am concerned the RTR will be split up over my dead body. The RTR must remain a regiment similar to the Parachute Regiment, officers belonging to the Royal Tank Regiment; they will be posted to units (regiments of the RTR) from time to time in accordance with the needs of the RTR as a whole...' [41]

In late 1946 23 regular battalions were disbanded by the War Office, irrespective of a lineage that for four of them stretched back to the time of King Charles II. Every one of the 64 regiments was reduced to a single battalion. The Foot Guards remained an exception, retaining ten battalions for three regiments, bringing the total number of infantry battalions to 77. The Brigade of Gurkhas added another eight battalions in the four regiments that were allocated to the British Army at the Independence of India in 1948. The Parachute Regiment was not officially allowed a permanent cadre until 1953 for soldiers and 1958 for officers, having to rely on secondment from other units. [42]

The Cold War demands on the British Army brought about a closer identification between the various regiments and their home counties. The need for more battalions allowed fourteen to be released from training roles. Their place was taken by the revival of regimental depots. '... since this was the first time in peacetime that County and Regiment had mutual obligations, the one to provide recruits under the National Service Act, the other to look after them, the relationship between the two became closer than ever'. [43] This reform would outlive conscription and seal the bond between county and regiment.

FRANCE

The French Army that emerged from the Second World War was an institution riven by its own recent history. Of the Western armies, it was to become the most alienated from its society and government and the most politicized. At the same time it was to be the sole Western army to focus intellectually and operationally on an entirely new form of warfare, *la guerre révolutionnaire* or revolutionary war.

Most of the officer corps of the pre-war army in metropolitan France had failed to rally to the Free French under de Gaulle and was permanently discredited. It was the Colonial Army that had filled the ranks of the Free French. Only after the invasion was the French Army increased by large numbers of partisans and volunteers. The colonial element and its outlook was to dominate the post-war army and see itself as the saviour of France. By January 1948 the French Army was being maintained at a strength of 521,000 men including about 160,000 colonial troops, in all almost the number of the US Army, and approximately the same size as the British Army.[44]

The post-war crisis of French democracy under the Fourth Republic led directly to the re-animation of the army's interest in politics and a growing alienation. The first government assault on the corporate sense of the army was a massive post-war discharge, for reasons of economy, of the professional cadres, *'dégagement des cadres'* totalling 45 per cent of the officers and 40 per cent of the non-commissioned officers. Although the number of serving officers far exceeded the army's requirements, they felt that the government had broken the reciprocal obligation undertaken on receipt of the commission. The long-term effects were far more damaging than the initial loss in morale. The growing war in Indo-China drew off a huge proportion of this regular cadre resulting in the rapid decrease in training standards of the conscript forces based in France. It quickly became impossible to recruit NCOs and the quality in their ranks as well as among the officers fell off noticeably as men of talent sought other careers.[45]

That government's bungling of colonial policy set it to pursue one ill-fated venture after another to its further detriment in the eyes of the army's professionals. Beginning in Indo-China in 1946, the government charged the army to restore the authority of France. The role was not supported by the majority of the nation and in the end the government itself was unwilling to support it with sufficient resources or political will. Alienating the army from the population even further was the fact that all Frenchmen serving in Indo-China were from the regular army cadre, French Foreign Legion regiments and colonial troops. This exclusion of conscripts from service in combat further diverted the attention of the French public from the sacrifices of the French Army.

La Guerre Révolutionnaire

As Communist guerrilla insurgencies erupted across the map – from Greece to Indo-China – the theoretical and intellectual nature of French military thought gave rise to a new doctrine of war. The French Army saw in these insurgencies a connected design. In *la guerre révolutionnaire* they believed they had found the effective counter-action. By the time the war in Indo-China had been lost, the French Army had reached some dearly bought conclusions: (1) revolutionary wars are based on a struggle for the allegiance of a people; (2) this struggle culminates in a successful social and psychological effort, not a military one; (3) astute psychological measures could build the cohesive bonds between the guerrillas and the populace; (4) an inferior force could always defeat a modern army if it had the support of the populace;

(5) seemingly conflicting social and education programmes had to be conducted simultaneously with propaganda and psychological programmes to defeat the bonding process. The French developed a formula to explain the dilemma with which they were faced: revolutionary war = partisan war + psychological war.[46]

La guerre révolutionnaire was highly attractive for a host of other reasons. It fed French 'morale and prestige' by emphasizing an alternative to nuclear warfare that did not require vast technological and economic resources. The new doctrine stressed the importance of small-unit leadership, cohesion and initiative and thereby restored the heroic nature of war, a unique national attribute in contrast to the 'atom-intoxicated' British and Americans.[47] The French were able to claim later in 1956 that because of their experience in Indo-China, 'The French Army is practically the only one to have encountered Communism in action in a vast land war of style and amplitude previously unknown. It can, therefore, open broadly the debate on the form of future war.'[48]

INDO-CHINA

Despite their claim, the French Army had relied heavily on the *matériel* and technology of modern armies in its seven-year struggle in Indo-China. The French were to rely on as lavish a scale of equipment as they could afford and the United States was willing to subsidize. The very quantity of *matériel* often played into the hands of their enemies by tying the French to their mechanical means of mobility and the roads. 'The French contended against the jungle while the Vietminh made use of it.'[49] The French regular army was also contending against the indifference of its own society. The refusal of the government to assign conscripts to Indo-China made that war a regular army war. The regulars in Indo-China in 1952 included 54,000 French, 30,000 North Africans, 18,000 Africans, 20,000 Légionnaires and 53,000 natives of Indo-China in addition to the 150,000 men of the Vietnamese National Army. It was not only a war of the regular army but of the colonial army. Of the 92,000 French dead, only 20,000 were natives of metropolitan France, and almost all of these were officers of whom 1,300 were lieutenants. The officer sons of 21 generals and marshals of France were to die in Indo-China. Paul-Marie de la Gorce writes:

> 'Between 1945 and 1954, 800 Saint-Cyr graduates died in Indo-China, 113 of these in the last six months of the war. It has been calculated that, over a period of seven years, one French officer was killed every day. Thus the regular Army bore the brunt of the war, and an appalling burden it was.'[50]

The French woke up to the war in Indo-China with a thunderclap in October 1950. The Vietminh in their first major operation handed the French forces a major defeat and 6,000 casualties. In December, General de Lattre de Tassigny, the famed commander of the wartime First Army, arrived to command in Indo-China, 'just in time to give General Giap a hiding at Vinh Yen' leaving 6,000 to 9,000 dead on the battlefield. His dynamic presence infused new life into the French forces. He chose the most aggressive and daring officers and gave them command of *Groupes Mobiles* (GM), light columns designed to fall upon the Vietminh before they could react. Another successful technique was commando warfare employed since late 1951. The commando force, eventually known as *Groupement Mixte d'Intervention* (GMI), came to control all operations behind enemy lines. They combined the experience of the French *maquis*, the British 'Chindits' and the American 'Merrill's Marauders', but unlike these groups, were organized to remain in enemy territory as guerrilla forces. Only the sick and wounded were flown out. By mid 1954 they numbered 15,000 men supported by 300 tons of airborne supplies a month. Both the mobile groups and commandos were to do great execution, but the war dragged on with the French and Vietminh trading costly victories. It was this very indecisiveness that was slowly working against the French despite the army's frantic efforts.[51]

Despite the successes of the mobile groups and the commandos, the French largely developed their approach to the war on an empirical basis largely at company and battalion level, the lessons of which were never drawn together by the high command. There remained a conventional perspective on pacification as a military operation. 'They implemented no single viable strategy of counter-subversive warfare... The Political and propaganda measures were equally reactive. At no time in the Indo-China War did the French Army really assign a paramount urgency to these tasks or pursue them as an inseparable part of the military problem.' This was the tragedy of the French Army. The officer corps displayed at the tactical level a real ability to improvise, adapt and innovate. Rarely has an army's junior officer corps been so challenged and found so able. Yet this talent was largely wasted by a high command that insisted that there was nothing to learn in Indo-China of either a military or political nature. A totality of view, on the other hand, was the very foundation of the Vietminh's continuing success.[52]

To compensate for this conceptual inferiority, the French had no advantage in numbers over the Vietminh who in turn could count on the determined allegiance not only of all of their combat forces of 300,000 men but also countless support personnel and the Vietnamese population in general. Of the French forces, only the regulars and the Foreign Legion were completely reliable. The North Africans were none too aggressive in a war which they all too soon would emulate, and the Vietnamese troops were only too aware of the sympathies of their own people. Ironically the Legion, which was so reliable and deadly on the battlefield, contained many German veterans of the late world war, as had been the case after 1918. Despite rumours, however, Germans did not dominate the Legion in Indo-China, and never made up more than 25 to 35 per cent of the Legion contingent there. Among the 11,710 officers and men of the Legion who would fall in action, there were many Germans who would earn the tribute 'gestorben für Frankreich' (died for France).[53]

In late 1953 General Navarre, commander of French forces in Indo-China, received the nightmare of every commander, contradictory orders from his government. They enjoined him to protect Laos from major Vietminh forces and yet above everything else, to ensure the safety of our Expeditionary Corps'. No little backbiting in subsequent French history would revolve around Navarre's attempt to reconcile these instructions. He decided to parachute a major force into the interior to establish a major blocking position to hold the Vietminh at bay. It would be at a road junction called Dien Bien Phu.

Both the choice of the tactics and the location were colossal mistakes. Together they irredeemably violated Sun Tzu's rock-bottom dictum to know yourself and know your enemy. The decision to establish a blocking position was taken in ignorance of the terrain which unlike Europe had no developed road system to block. Navarre chose blocking tactics, even though he knew this to be a mediocre solution, because of the 'lack of adaptation of our forces', which unaccountably had adapted themselves quite well to such innovative measures as the mobile groups and commandos. Even more damning, he despised his enemy whom he adjudged incapable of bringing artillery to bear on the defensive positions at Dien Bien Phu from the surrounding mountains. General Giap surprised them by doing exactly that. He swamped the French outposts commanding the base and then proceeded to hammer it to bits with the artillery he was not supposed to have. The Vietminh proved equally inconvenient by displaying a determined and skilled mastery of siege operations that allowed them to reduce the base methodically. All attempts at relief failed. Vietminh gunners closed the airfield, a relief force failed to arrive, 1,530 airborne volunteer reinforcements (50 per cent of them had never jumped before) could not affect the balance, and an attempt at breakout saved only 70 men. Inevitably, the 50,000 brave and well-directed Vietminh overwhelmed the 13,000 brave but badly-directed French defenders. The defeat led to the immediate end of the war and the loss of Indo-China to France; the defeat also was another unbearable mortification for the French Army that would be increasingly at odds not only with its civilian leadership but with the senior leadership of the army itself.

THE KOREAN WAR
Increasingly mired in Indo-China, the French nevertheless determined, for the sake of pride, to send a contingent to fight with the Americans and British in Korea. The single French infantry battalion was commanded by Lieutenant-General Monclar, a veritable Mars, who took a temporary demotion to lieutenant-colonel for the honour of commanding France's contingent. The battalion landed in November 1950 and was attached to the US 2nd Infantry Division. In two months it had distinguished itself in a bayonet charge at Wonju and a magnificent defence of Chip'yong-ni which broke a Chinese offensive. In October 1951 the battalion took the notorious Heartbreak Ridge, and Arrow Head Hill a year later. The battalion finally departed Korea after the armistice in October 1953, leaving behind 261 dead. These losses were only the smallest fraction of the sacrifice offered up in Indo-China, but restored a certain lustre to French arms.[54]

EUROPEAN OBLIGATIONS
After the Second World War the French Army at first seemed ready to re-orient its attention to the conventional Soviet threat in western Europe, and began work on a new series of armoured vehicles, a medium and a light tank, and an armoured car. The medium tank never saw service, but the light tank, the AMX-13, went into production in 1952. By 1948 the army had re-affirmed the traditional concept of 'the nation in arms' attuned to fighting the coalition wars of the twentieth century. General de Gaulle emphasized the point that France was the 'centre and key' to the heart of Europe. Several light but mobile and powerfully armed formations including the 'Javelot Brigade' were created to fight along the whole spectrum from mechanized to nuclear war which General de Lattre de Tassigny, Inspector-General of the Armed Forces, stated would be 'capable of carrying the fight to the enemy or of crushing a large enemy operation at any point in our territory...' Up to this point the thrust of French army thinking had underlined the conventional, *matériel*-oriented defence of Europe. As the war escalated in Indo-China, and later in Algeria, interest waned in face of the waxing obsession with *la guerre révolutionnaire* which overwhelmed the army. There could be no more ironic commentary on this reversal of interest than the departure of the first two 'Javelot'-type divisions to Algeria. Designed to fight on the nuclear battlefield, they would be committed in the mountains of Algeria.

The crushing defeat at Dien Bien Phu in May 1954 closed out the first decade of the post-war period for the French Army. It was an army that had been politicized and then radicalized by the failures of its own government to set and support the missions assigned. It was too an army that drew the lesson that its understanding of *la guerre révolutionnaire* was essentially correct but that its execution had, in the end, been sabotaged by its own government and the indifference of the nation. It was an army that would immediately renew the struggle in Algeria and be willing to strike at its own government in order to succeed.

GERMANY

As the Allies closed in on Germany for the kill, they were determined to destroy the German Army, root and branch. So much so that at Yalta, Stalin slyly suggested to Roosevelt, who thought he was joking, that the victorious Allies execute 100,000 German officers.[55] By the end of May 1945 the German Army and all its institutions had ceased to exist. The symbolic end came in the following month when 200 stands of the German Army's colours were carried in triumph in the Soviet victory parade through Red Square to be hurled on the red granite steps of Lenin's tomb. The Romans could not have done it better. The German Army seemed as dead as that of Carthage after the battle of Zama. Sometimes, however, history has a sense of humour. Within ten years there would be, not one, but *two* German Armies.

The Cold War effected a seemingly permanent division of Germany into two states. As the new inter-German border was also the border of the conflict between the West and the Soviet Union, it was inevitable that these separate halves of Germany be called upon to play their part. The circumstances that brought about the rise of the two armies, however, were significantly different.

EAST GERMANY

Stalin's murderous intentions were qualified in that he had no use for the traditional German Army, but a great deal of use for a Communist German Army under Soviet control. The Soviet decision to build such an army was acted upon almost immediately, in the autumn of 1945, through the device of creating a militarized police force. That this was the origin of the East German Army was later attested by the East German Communist Party:

'Arming of the People's Police was approved by the SMAD (Soviet Military Administration of Germany) on 31 October 1945. This was the moment of birth for the armed forces of the German working class, the armed forces of the first Workers' and Peasants' state in Germany.'[56]

Control was centralized in the East German interior ministry, and by November 1946 the number of People's Police had increased to 45,000. In June 1948 the Soviets instructed the interior ministry to build a training establishment. At the same time, the Soviets began pressuring 1,000 former Wehrmacht officers still in Soviet captivity to serve as the cadre. Recruitment was strictly controlled for reliability; a Soviet military administrative order prescribed that persons would be expelled who had blood relatives in the West, had been prisoners of war of the Western Allies, had been expelled from eastern provinces annexed by the Soviet Union and Poland, were considered politically unreliable, or who had belonged to the police before 1945.[57]

In late 1950, the force, now called the Garrisoned People's Police (*Kasernierte Volkspolizei – KVP*) had grown to 70,000 men exclusive of 80,000 personnel engaged in normal police work. The KVP training establishment now included twelve weapons schools, twelve cadet and five special schools. During the previous year the KVP had already sent its first class of cadres on a 12-month course at the Soviet military academy at Privolsk. The Soviets were very careful to hide these efforts by labelling them as 'police forces' while at the same time attacking the Allies for creating military formations that were genuine police forces. By June 1952 an East German Communist Party conference had laid the first ideological basis for the creation of an East German army:

'... the creation of armed forces in the GDR was the expression of a progressive military policy in harmony with the interests of the entire German nation, whereas the militaristic policy of setting-up a West German army of revenge was reactionary and anti-national in character.'[58]

The fact was that East Germany now had an army in everything but name while West Germany had not taken any concrete steps to establish one.

In 1953 the interior ministry split off the section that exercised the duties of a defence ministry, and the territorial commands and subordinate infantry divisions of the KVP were established. Within that year the new ministry of defence had seven divisions at its disposal. The only setback to this process occurred during the 1953 riots in which the KVP 'failed to fulfil expectations as Party troops', requiring a purge of 12,000 officers and men. Such large numbers of the KVP had refused to act against the rioting civilians that Soviet troops had to be called out. In retrospect it can be seen that this was as close as the army was to get to combat in its history; its moment of glory as the army of a Marxist state would have been to attack the most dangerous enemy of the state, its own people. To its credit, it failed.

Soviet supervision intensified thereafter, but the growth of the KVP was not unduly interrupted. The new army was becoming more and more Soviet in style, methods and organization. Even its new khaki uniforms were Soviet in cut. So effective had these efforts been that by October 1955 the first large-scale multi-division manoeuvres had been conducted.[59] The first soldier was not sworn into the new West German Army until November.

WEST GERMANY

As this last sentence indicates, the story of the West German Army in this decade is not so full as its Communist counterpart. Its origins lay in the increasingly nervous western European and American view of the Soviet threat and in Chancellor Adenauer's determination to restore the prestige of a now democratic Germany. With only a handful of divisions on the continent, it was inevitable that attention be turned not only to Germany's location at the centre of Europe, but to its manpower.

The breaking out of the Korean War sharpened Western apprehensions for the defence of Europe. At that time Adenauer offered West German manpower for a West European army that had been suggested by Winston Churchill. The offer was refused politely, but the door was left pointedly open for future developments. At this time the Allies gave permission for the establishment of 'mobile police formations' at the *Land* (state) level. Adenauer now instructed his military advisers to begin contingency planning for a new German army. This soon led to a confidential conference of former Wehrmacht senior officers at the monastery of Kloster Himmerod.

This conference was to set the moral imprint of the new army. Besides establishing its organizational outline, the members of the conference emphasized the leadership concepts which later became known as *Innere Führung* (leadership from within):

'The basic idea which evolved into Innere Führung not only came from this conference but from professional officers, not civilians. We all knew

that the inner structure of the armed forces had to be changed, simply
because society had changed so much.' [60]

Adenauer soon appointed Theodor Blank, a member of the Bundestag, to head an
office which was the cover for an embryonic defence ministry. Blank assembled a
number of former officers who were known to be reformers and liberals 'determined to revolutionize German military life'. It was this group that refined the
Innere Führung concept.

The most ticklish aspect of German re-armament was the innate distrust of a
re-armed Germany by its neighbours. Blank's successor, Josef Strauss, was to
underline that problem, 'The Bundeswehr is supposed to be strong enough to hold
back the Russians but not so strong as to frighten the Belgians.' Sir John Hackett,
however, voiced the answer to this concern, 'The real value of NATO is that it provides a means whereby West German defence requirements can be met in a system
not dominated by Germans.'[61] Under those conditions, then, the first 101 veteran
officers and NCOs were sworn in as members of the new Bundeswehr on 11
November 1955.

POLAND

The end of the Second World War found liberated Poland with three armies. Of
these the only one with direct links to the pre-war Polish Army was the corps commanded by General Anders with the Western Allies. This body of about 100,000
men was made up largely of former Polish soldiers captured by the Soviets when
they invaded Poland. After Germany attacked the Soviet Union Stalin agreed to create Polish units from the survivors in the camps and allowed them to transfer to the
Western Allies where they served with distinction in Italy.[62] The partisan Home
Army had grown up within Poland during the occupation and was controlled by
the Polish government-in-exile in London. It numbered almost 400,000 but was
badly crippled when the Soviets failed to support its uprising in Warsaw.

The third army, the Polish People's Army (*Ludowe Wojsko Polskie*) consisted of
the two field armies raised from Polish refugees in the Soviet Union. This army of
400,000 men had been created by the Soviets' need for manpower and the desire to
create a counter to General Anders' army, and from it the post-war army of Poland
would claim its descent.

From its inception The Polish People's Army (PPA) bore a clear Soviet imprint
in its organization, training and leadership. Because of a lack of officers, one-third
of the PPA's officer corps would be Soviet by the end of the war.[63] But the refusal of
the army to submerge its Polish nature in a copy of the Soviet Army created a tension that plagued it until 1989. Initial attempts to Sovietize the PPA in 1943 produced a strong counter-reaction among the Poles and led to the introduction of
traditional Polish ranks, uniforms and distinctions.[64] Still, the question, 'Would the
army be Communist or Polish?' would not go away.

The PPA became the sole Polish army with the installation of a Soviet-dominated Communist government in Poland after the war. It was merged with a small
Polish Communist partisan organization, but members of the Home Army and
Anders' army were rejected. The regime, however, demobilized most of the army,
almost 200,000 men, and concentrated on building a large and reliable internal security corps (KBW). This force, rather than the PPA, primarily was used to eliminate
the remnant of the Home Army, units of the anti-Communist underground (NSZ)
and units of the Ukrainian Insurgent Army (UPA). Nevertheless the Polish Army
was also heavily involved, committing 50,000 troops at a cost of 3,000 dead includ-

ing the Vice Minister of Defence and former commander of the Polish Second Army during the Second World War, Karol Swierczewski.[65]

In 1948 the regime decided to rebuild the army. Unfortunately this idea coincided with Stalin's war-level mobilization of the Soviet Army, and the PPA was dragged along in its wake to augment Soviet strength. Conscription was introduced in 1949 to increase army strength to 400,000. A concerted Sovietization of the PPA also began. The Soviet Army transferred officers and NCOs to camps in eastern Poland to train them to assume key positions in the Polish Army. They and their families were ordered to learn the Polish language and customs which measure scarcely betrayed a concern for Polish sensibilities. Their arrival marked a crude attempt to neuter the Polish Army of its special national nature; Soviet drill was introduced, distinctive Polish military caps were eliminated, and political education was intensified. Soviet Marshal Kostantin Rokossovsky, a Soviet citizen of Polish extraction, was appointed Minister of Defence. In 1950 he announced that the Polish Army would be remade on the Soviet model. In the same year the nationalist wing in the PPA was attacked. General Marian Spychalski, Rokossovsky's deputy, and 300 other Polish officers were purged, and three Polish generals were put on trial. Most of the senior staff and command positions within the army, including those of the chief of the general staff, commander of the ground forces, commanders of all military districts, and chiefs of all service branches, were manned by Soviet officers of whom there were now 5,000 in the PPA.[66]

The Soviet takeover of the PPA essentially transformed it into an extension of the Soviet Army. Rokossovsky took his orders directly from Moscow although he was a nominal member of the Polish Party's politburo. So complete was the subordination that Poland and its army were treated as little more than a Soviet military district. Ironically the Soviets did not achieve much in addition to their strength by these measures. The PPA remained structured for mobile defence, not offence; weapons and equipment continued to be inadequate; and combat capability remained low.

SOVIET UNION

Stalin rose from the dinner-table one evening in 1944 and hitched up his trousers like a man ready to fight, 'The war will soon be over. We shall recover in fifteen or twenty years and then we will have another go at it.'[67] Behind Stalin's bravura lay a cold-blooded realism. Long before the guns fell silent in 1945, he had planned for the armed forces needed to ensure the expansion of Soviet power. Unlike the armies of the other two surviving powers, his army would immediately begin a process of directed growth and regeneration. Unfettered by the drain of restive colonies or the indifference of the war-weary electorates of the democracies, the Red Army could respond to the will and direction of one man. Stalin fixed fetters of another kind upon the army, fetters of the intellect that choked off critical inquiry and innovation.

To reforge the battered sword of the Red Army into a strengthened weapon of Soviet power, Stalin directed the peacetime Red Army along four simultaneous lines: (1) demobilization, (2) reorganization, (3) weapons development and production and (4) restoration of political reliability and Party control.[68] The first three resulted in solid accomplishments that genuinely improved the overall capabilities of the armed forces. The last was bound up with the darkest motivations of Stalin's personality and did lasting harm to those forces.

DEMOBILIZATION

Demobilization was an absolute and immediate necessity. As much as mothers and wives wanted their men home, the war-wounded economy cried out even louder. In Stalin's calculations a strong industry ould be the vital forge for the new Red Army. He stated emphatically that, 'Hitler's generals, raised on the dogma of Clausewitz and Moltke, could not understand that war is won in the factories.'[69] Stalin's goal was to restore and strengthen the economy by 1950, and he needed most of the 11,365,000 men then in the armed forces in workers' overalls rather than uniforms to do it. Of that host, the Ground Forces of the Red Army were the overwhelming majority, numbering approximately 9,100,000, as shown in the table:[70]

Table 1-4. Soviet Army by Service 1941–1945

Ground Forces	80.7 – 87.2	per cent
Air Forces	6.2 – 8.7	per cent
Navy	4.5 – 7.3	per cent
National Air Defence	3.3 – 4.8	per cent

These numbers filled an enormous order-of-battle that a nation at peace could not afford and which included:[71]

Table 1-5. Soviet Army Order of Battle at the End of the Second World War

510 infantry divisions/brigades	60 separate tank brigades
34 cavalry divisions	180 tank regiments
20 artillery divisions	150 separate artillery regiments
25 tank corps	125 air divisions
13 mechanized corps	

The losses of the war had been of an even greater magnitude, so horrendous that their true number was kept a state secret until released in March 1990 by the Chief of the General Staff, General M.A. Moiseyev:

Table 1-6 . Soviet Losses 1941–1945

Personnel	Dead	Wounded
Total armed forces	8,668,400	18,000,000
Army and Navy	8,509,300	
Internal Troops	97,700	
NKVD Border Troops	61,400	

Equipment	Number	Percentage of Total
Smallarms	15,500,000	53.0
Tanks/SP artillery	96,500	73.3
Artillery guns, mortars	317,500	50.0
Combat aircraft	88,300	31.8

Source: M.A. Moiseyev, 'The Price of Victory' in *Voyenno-Istoricheskiy Zhurnal*, No. 3, March 1990.

By 1948, 8,500,000 men of 33 separate draft ages had been demobilized in six separate stages with all the older age groups released by 1947. The year 1948 marked the lowest post-war ebb in the strength of the armed forces and the Red Army as numbers fell to 2,874,000 men.[72] The returning veterans found empty places far in excess of their numbers in the shattered villages and cities of the western Soviet Union and the man-starved economy of the whole country. The demobilization released desperately needed men including 250,000 skilled industrial workers, more than 100,000 medical personnel and 46,000 teachers.[73]

But the ghosts of dead men were to haunt the land for generations. In the Ukraine the imbalance between men and women was to remain the widest in the world even if one accepts the 1979 Soviet census. The surviving men found themselves prized and pampered by the women, a natural phenomenon that was to reinforce the certainty that the Soviet Union was a man's world. The female units of the Red Army that had been raised when the manpower pull scraped bottom, and then went on to distinguish themselves, were disbanded. The Red Army, freed of necessity, would again be men's business.

REORGANIZATION

Reorganization of the Red Army was to be thorough and fundamental and would embrace not only its structure but its personnel and their basic military relationships. The reorganization engulfed even the name of the Red Army of Workers and Peasants, so charged with the aura of victory. In 1946 it was changed to the blandly precise 'Soviet Army', a chilling foretaste of what was in store for the army as an institution of living men.

Organizationally the structure of the entire armed forces was rationalized. It was to consist of three services to include the ground forces, air force, and navy. An oddity for the foreign observer is that the 'army' is not included as might be expected. In Soviet general usage, the term 'Soviet Army' basically embraced all elements of the armed forces other than the navy. In that sense, the Soviet use of the word 'army' is far broader than used by most of the rest of the world's armies. The term 'ground forces', on the other hand, is more restrictive in a Soviet context and includes the manoeuvre forces, garrisons and training establishment. For the sake of clarity, 'Soviet Army' will be used in the general sense and 'Ground Forces' when referring to the specific service. The post-war reorganization left air defence, airborne and rear echelons independent of any of the three services. The ground forces was the premier service and held pride of place in the military hierarchy.

Wartime structures of the Soviet Army were quickly eliminated. By February 1946 the army and navy ministries were unified in a single Ministry of the Armed Forces, a year ahead of a similar though less ultimately efficient unification of the armed forces of the United States. Subordinate to the new ministry were the commanders-in-chief of the three services. The wartime field commands of fronts and some armies were transformed rapidly into military district garrisons and headquarters in 1945 as the territory of the USSR was divided into first 33 then 21 military districts along traditional Russian lines. These forces and thereby the territorial structure of the armed forces fell under the authority of the Commander-in-Chief of the Ground Forces for training, administration and readiness. Commands remaining in Germany, Austria, Poland and Hungary were converted to Groups of Forces and were similarly controlled by the Ground Forces. However, peacetime and wartime operational control of the Ground Forces would run through the General Staff to the Ministry of Defence which considerably lessened the prestige and authority of the Commander-in-Chief, surely one of Stalin's primary motives. Until he died, Stalin remained the Minister of Defence or minutely directed his successor, Bulganin. Even the military district commanders, who usually had the rank of marshal, did not have full control of their districts and had to exercise a collective control with a five member military council which included a commissar appointed by the Central Committee of the Communist Party. Lest the 'commander' forget the restricted nature of his command authority, each important decision required the counter-signature of this commissar.[74]

The fighting units of the Soviet Army underwent significant changes stemming from the lessons learnt during the war. Improvements were designed to increase the firepower and mobility of units as well as their ability to operate independently. Large numbers of tanks, artillery and motor transport vehicles were added as well as increased numbers of specialized units such as signals, air defence and engineer troops to provide balanced self-sufficiency. The concept of combined arms, limited by the necessities of the war to comparatively few formations, was to be expanded to include all the Ground Forces manoeuvre units. The combined arms army was to become 'the basic operational field force of the Ground Forces'.[75]

Army corps, which had been dropped from the army structure because of a shortage of staffs early in the war, were reintroduced as the echelon of command and control for rifle or infantry divisions. Henceforth, Soviet armies would consist of several corps of two to three divisions each. Reinforced later by one of the new mechanized divisions, the rifle corps was to become the highest combined arms tactical formation. By 1953 its firepower was seven times that of a wartime rifle corps. The rifle division was transformed into a far more powerful and robust organization than its wartime predecessor. Although still consisting of foot infantry and much horse-drawn transport, the rifle division was beefed-up with approximately 100 tanks and assault guns and 60 artillery pieces. It eventually acquired about 1,488 motor vehicles in the 1948 table of organization (as compared to 419 in the 1944) as horses were replaced, although the infantry were still on foot.[76]

At the same time, in 1946, the wartime tank armies with their subordinate tank and mechanized corps were taken in the opposite direction. The corps were abolished and tank and mechanized divisions were created in their place, directly subordinate to a new mechanized army. As noted by Albert Seaton, both types of division were logical extensions of the successful German SS panzer and panzer grenadier divisions which had been lavishly equipped to a scale that none of the regular German Army panzer and panzer grenadier divisions (with the exception of the Panzergrenadier division *Grossdeutschland*) could ever have hoped to be. Like its German models, the new Soviet tank division was strong in tanks, numbering 180 medium and 60 heavy tanks in three tank regiments and a heavy tank/self-propelled gun (SU) regiment. Additionally there was a motorized rifle regiment. The mechanized division went a step beyond its German model by becoming so strong in tanks as to qualify by most standards as a tank division. Each of its motorized rifle regiments contained a tank battalion. Added to this were both a medium and a heavy tank/SU regiment giving the division about 220 tanks.[77]

Stalin planned for a peacetime force of about 175 divisions of all types. Mobilization plans called for an increase to 300 divisions by 'D-Day plus 40' with another 100 divisions to be mobilized within the following three months. Of the peacetime divisions, there would be 97 rifle, 54 tank or mechanized, eleven artillery, eight airborne and five cavalry divisions. Of these some 50 were to be in a high-readiness category.[78]

The reorganization was also directed at upgrading the quality of the officer corps. The pre-war officer cadre had been decimated first by the purges then brutally winnowed to a small remnant by the war itself. A new regular officer cadre had to be created from the few survivors of the pre-war army and the considerable amount of natural but unschooled and roughshod talent that emerged from the furnace of the war. The officer corps after 1945 was to spend far more of its time in schooling than its Western counterparts. The armed forces could afford to be selective; of the two million serving officers at the end of the war, only 750,000 were retained. Even so, formally schooled officers were so few that 97.5 per cent with higher military, technical or political education were forcibly retained.[79] The compulsion of force was hardly necessary to retain qualified officers. The officer corps had come out of the war with immense prestige and a privileged place in society. And those material privileges were critical in a post-war Soviet Union which passed from scarcity to outright famine in 1946–7. Even among the officer corps, however, there was a gradation of privilege apparently weighted to the line rather than the staff. General Petro Grigorenko recalled in his *Memoirs* that his assignment to the Frunze Military Academy in 1946 almost could have resulted in the starvation of his family. He alone was authorized a small officer's ration but even then he had to join a long colonel's line for it. His family members were rationed to only 44 grams of bread a day each. Only his extra income from writing provided the margin of survival.[80]

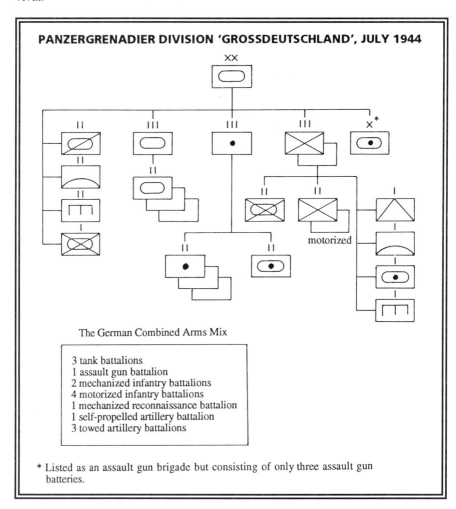

PANZERGRENADIER DIVISION 'GROSSDEUTSCHLAND', JULY 1944

The German Combined Arms Mix

3 tank battalions
1 assault gun battalion
2 mechanized infantry battalions
4 motorized infantry battalions
1 mechanized reconnaissance battalion
1 self-propelled artillery battalion
3 towed artillery battalions

motorized

* Listed as an assault gun brigade but consisting of only three assault gun batteries.

WEAPONS DEVELOPMENT AND PRODUCTION

The lavish tables of organization were supported at first by the excess equipment available from demobilization of the wartime forces. However, Stalin continued to allocate a large part of industry to continued production of armaments. Large investments were made in basic research and design that would lead to important, incremental improvements in the quality and effectiveness of equipment. This effort led to the development and eventual introduction in large numbers into the Ground Forces of such equipment as the T-54 and T-55 tanks, the BTR-40 and BTR-50 amphibious armoured personnel carriers, and the D-48 anti-tank gun, the D-74 122mm gun, the M-46 130mm gun, the M-47 152mm gun and the 240mm mortar as well as a new series of rocket-launchers, the BM-14, Bm-24 and BMD-20, to replace the venerable Katyushas of the war.[81]

The practical development of armoured vehicles is a good example of the support given to the Soviet Army. They were marked not so much by radical innova-

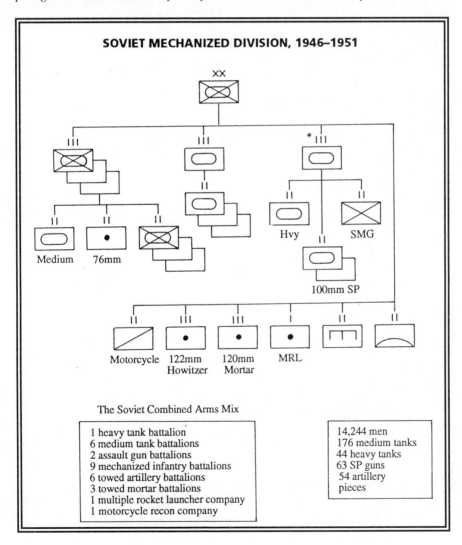

SOVIET MECHANIZED DIVISION, 1946–1951

The Soviet Combined Arms Mix

1 heavy tank battalion	14,244 men
6 medium tank battalions	176 medium tanks
2 assault gun battalions	44 heavy tanks
9 mechanized infantry battalions	63 SP guns
6 towed artillery battalions	54 artillery
3 towed mortar battalions	pieces
1 multiple rocket launcher company	
1 motorcycle recon company	

tion as by incremental and tangible improvements in existing designs. Development of a replacement for the T-34 was continuous during and after the war. The first follow-on was the T-44, a generally unsatisfactory vehicle which went into only limited production. It was soon followed by a further refinement, the T-54, which was completed in 1947 and went into full production in 1949. Not until late 1950 was design work begun on the US Army's first serious post-war medium tank, the M48.[82]

Stalin also invested heavily in the seed corn of the armaments industry; research and design institutes received increases in the 1946 budget 240 per cent over 1945. By 1950 hundreds of new institutes had been created to accelerate the

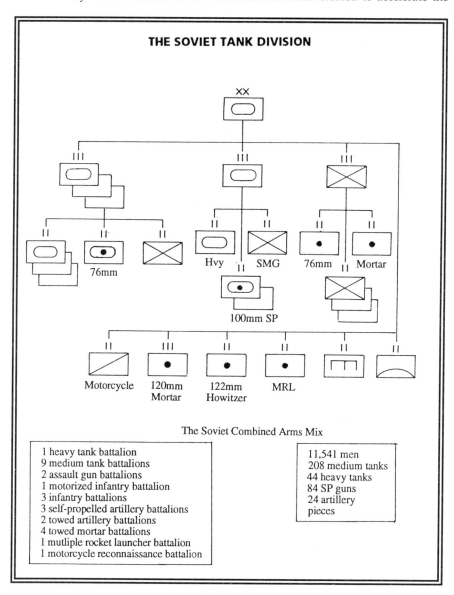

THE SOVIET TANK DIVISION

76mm

Hvy   SMG   76mm   Mortar

100mm SP

Motorcycle   120mm   122mm   MRL
              Mortar   Howitzer

The Soviet Combined Arms Mix

1 heavy tank battalion	11,541 men
9 medium tank battalions	208 medium tanks
2 assault gun battalions	44 heavy tanks
1 motorized infantry battalion	84 SP guns
3 infantry battalions	24 artillery
3 self-propelled artillery battalions	pieces
2 towed artillery battalions	
4 towed mortar battalions	
1 mutliple rocket launcher battalion	
1 motorcycle reconnaissance battalion	

rate of technological development for the arms industry. Hand in hand with increased research and development whole new sectors were added to the economy primarily to support military requirements in advanced electronics, missiles and nuclear weapons. Advances followed quickly. The first battlefield missile, the R-1, was issued to field forces in 1947. Even earlier, in July 1946, an operational missile unit was created as an operational test-bed for the new weapon system. The most dramatic advance was the rapid development and fielding of nuclear weapons. In August 1949 the Soviet Union exploded its first atomic bomb and quickly went into production.[83]

The immediate post-war period saw a remarkable effort both to re-equip the armed forces and to introduce incrementally improved equipment and new technologies. The armed forces had first call on the growing output of a recovering economy but at the cost of terrible privations for the civilian population. Yet the suffering paid the sort of dividends that satisfied Stalin. The armed forces grew steadily more powerful. By 1950, for example, output of the automotive industry was such that half the horse-drawn transport of the Ground Forces had been replaced by motor vehicles.

PARTY CONTROL AND THE CULT OF PERSONALITY

The heart of the Soviet armed forces during the Second World War had been without doubt the Ground Forces. The victory parade in Moscow was a torrent of pride and grateful adulation for the Red Army men. The heroic image of a forest of Nazi banners being hurled at the feet of Lenin's tomb and Marshal Zhukov astride a grey charger, with drawn sabre, acclaimed as *spasitl* ('saviour') by the crowds was a pinnacle of glory few armies have achieved. Yet, like a dark cloud in the corner of a blue sky, Stalin's spiteful and unforgiving face is visible in the background.

Stalin feared Zhukov and his host, yet even more, he was intensely jealous of his fame, or the fame of any general who threatened to cast even the smallest shadow on his primacy, jealous even of the Ground Forces themselves. Trotsky had said of him that he had an asiatic cast of mind assisted by European technique and that, '... everything had to revolve around Stalin as around its axis'.[84] And Zhukov and company were very obviously not revolving around Stalin on that glorious day. For such sins of pride he had struck down the genius of the pre-war army, men of immense talent such as Marshals Tukhachevsky, Uborovich and Yegorov. The shouts of 'Ura' that fell like flowers on Zhukov fed the paranoia. Zhukov and the generals were an affront to him as they demonstrated an institutional pride and self-respect earned on the battlefield that seemed to have no need to credit much of anything to Stalin. According to Khrushchev, '... Stalin excluded every possibility that services rendered at the front should be credited to anyone but himself'.[85]

The army as an institution was also an object of this jealousy. During the latter part of the war:

'... a terrific esprit de corps had blossomed within the Red Army, which was bursting with pride at its achievements. Soldiers walked with heads held high in confident, not to say, jaunty manner, their pride in their profession manifest.'[86]

Stalin wasted little time in draining that animating spirit and replacing it with the obedience that comes from fear. As early as February 1946, he stated pointedly that, '... it would be a great mistake to say that we won only because of the gallantry of our troops'. Zhukov, the *spasitl*, was soon stripped of his post as Commander-in-Chief of the Ground Forces and relegated to the command of the second-rate

43

Odessa Military District from which he was later transferred to a fifth-rate assignment in the Urals. By the following year Stalin was openly belittling the military reputation of Lenin and presenting himself as the 'mastermind' of victory.[87] The new Defence Ministry was almost immediately saddled with an institutional political watchdog, the Main Political Administration, the Party's faithful sentinel of reliability. The Ground Forces received their own version. 'Marshal Zhukov's removal was designed to frighten the military into absolute silence... In this it succeeded: from late 1946 to 1953 the Soviet Army High Command was paralyzed by fear of Stalin and the NKVD.'[88] Field Marshal Montgomery was to remark on a visit to Moscow how the marshals and generals of the Soviet Army High Command were as quiet and timid as mice in Stalin's presence.

Stalin also diffused the authority of lower and middle grade commanders through the workings of military councils dominated by commissars. The new education programme for officers was heavily political in content. Unit identification and cohesion were crippled by the mass transfer of officers from the units with which they had served during the war. Camaraderie withered. The enlisted ranks were alienated as brutal discipline, more formalized than at any time since that of the Tsarist Army, was reintroduced to replace the excellent officer-soldier relationships based on respect and shared experiences, that had flourished in the veteran combat formations.

> 'The Aim of the Soviet rulers seems to be to replace the obedient and
> comradely forces of the Second World War with some type of re-incar-
> nation of the grenadiers of Frederick the Great, regardless of its inappro-
> priateness to modern war.' [89]

The officers were isolated from their men and from one another and found it safer to retire within a shell of aloof self-interest.

Stalin struck the Soviet Army a second blighting blow at the same time, by paralyzing its intellectual vigour and its ability to conduct critical analysis of the nature of modern war. As the 'mastermind' of victory, he was by definition the source of all knowledge of strategy. This was not a new tendency; his pernicious attitude had been evident before the war. Marshal V.D. Sokolovskiy was to write after the war that, 'The cult of Stalin had a very harmful influence on the development of Soviet strategic thought in the pre-war period... Creative investigation of problems of military theory was replaced by a dogmatic repetition of statements made by Stalin.' Harriet Fast Scott has also pointed out the comments of another Soviet general, N. Pavlenko, who stated:

> 'In 1935 at the Frunze Military Academy, a military history department
> was formed. According to the department head, a 32-hour course of lec-
> tures was envisaged on the theory of strategy. The Deputy Comman-
> dant, in looking over the programme, asked: 'What is this strategy
> course? Strategy is Comrade Stalin's personal occupation and is not any
> of our business.' [90]

This situation obtained to an even greater degree during the post-war period that ended with Stalin's death in 1953. While the lessons of the war were carefully analysed with regard to tactics and operational art, the world of strategy remained 'Stalin's personal occupation'. He identified five 'permanently operating factors' that neatly summarized his understanding of the essence of strategy. They were (1) stability of the rear, (2) morale of the army, (3) quality and quantity of divisions, (4) armament of the army and (4) organizing ability of command personnel. Rather than being the theory of war, they were in fact, Stalin's way of explaining victory in the last war and were very much a part of his own performance. They specifically served to rationalize the colossal blunders of the first half of the war. They helped to explain that he was not caught unprepared by the German invasion but only sought to lure the enemy deep into the interior in order to destroy him.[91] They were particularly irrelevant to the advent of nuclear weapons and missile delivery systems which could reach deep into the Soviet Union by surprise and achieve in a few hours what the Wehrmacht 'almost accomplished in a few months'.[92] Tragically they demanded a level of readiness that the war-ravaged Soviet economy could not bear and contributed directly to the famine of the late 1940s.

Combined with the Cult of Personality, the 'Stalin-Strategy' as it became known, utterly smothered any original thinking or objective appraisal of the war. Lessons from the war were limited to the fields of tactics and operational art and were merely refinements on a successful theme. Increasingly they lapsed from critical analysis to simple but safer commentary. Grigorenko gives a description of the type of officer that flourished under these conditions:

'I knew Markov from my work on the faculty. He thought and spoke in clichés. Possessed of a remarkable memory, he knew all the statutes and directives. During those years, when all real ideas were being suffocated, his talent for smoothly formulating his thoughts gave him fame as a theoretician. He had the ability to take any text and make it read relatively smoothly, even though it might not contain a single living thought. Though his work imparted no knowledge whatsoever, it also did not arouse objections from the "party-thinking" censors – an extremely important fact at the time. For these reasons Markov was simultaneously editor of a military scientific work and chief of the Scientific Research Branch. His jobs were to write a theoretical work that contained no military theory and to transform the Scientific Research Branch into an organ that would plug up all the cracks and crevices through which the academy's vital military scientific thought might slip.'[93]

Stalin very pointedly derided the strategic effect of nuclear weapons:

'I do not believe the atomic bomb to be as serious a force as certain politicians are inclined to regard it. Atomic bombs are intended to intimidate the weak-nerved, but they cannot decide the outcome of a war, since atomic bombs are by no means sufficient for this purpose.'[94]

At the same time – paradoxically – he devoted massive resources to their rapid development. Apparently this was an effort to make a virtue of necessity while only the United States possessed such weapons. 'Stalin's main recourse in the military field lay in making the threat of Soviet land power against Europe the counterpoise to US nuclear power.'[95] In this he was largely successful; the memoirs of the highest American political and military figures give ample testimony that this threat was taken with the utmost seriousness as not only a real possibility but an imminent one. Perhaps he was only waiting for a delivery system to add nuclear weapons to his arsenal. If so, a matter of timing was all that prevented him. They were deployed shortly after his death in March 1953.[96]

Only death ended the stranglehold on the development of strategic theory. Ironically, his reorganization and re-equipping of the Soviet Army and his parallel investment in research and industrial production capacity would combine to pay huge dividends to his successors. Freed of Stalin-Strategy, they would launch the Soviet Army on an entirely new and dynamic course of development by 1955.

This new course was to be inextricably bound up with the re-emergence of Marshal Zhukov. Stalin had already partially rehabilitated him by 1950; his talents suddenly had become valuable again in light of American rearmament and mobilization for the Korean War. This put Zhukov near the centre of power in the struggles for succession after Stalin's death. His role was decisive and ensured Khrushchev's eventual triumph in 1954. Zhukov threw his support behind Khrushchev in response to cuts in the army's budget made by Premier Malenkov based on his belief that nuclear weapons made war highly unlikely. In February 1954 he was rewarded by appointment as Minister of Defence; but even by late 1953 he had initiated the renaissance in Soviet military thinking that had begun to unleash a torrent of critical comment and analysis on the problems and nature of future war.

GREECE

Of the European armies destroyed by the Germans, none had a more dramatic or more demanding rebirth than the Greek or Royal Hellenic Army. The tiny remnant that had escaped the fall of Greece in 1941 to serve with the British would be the basis on which the army was rebuilt in the midst of a ruinous and vicious civil war.

The Royal Hellenic Army in the twentieth century has ridden a roller-coaster of triumphs and tragedies. Victorious in the Balkan Wars of 1912 and 1913 against the Turks and Bulgarians, it fulfilled the nation's destiny to reclaim the Greek lands in Europe. The Army was the agent of the *Megali Idea*, the Great Idea, the dream to reclaim all the Greek lands bordering the Aegean to recreate the Byzantine Empire. To this day the Greek officer corps sees itself as the protector of modern Hellenism, meaning that of Christian Byzantium. During the First World War Russian greed for Constantinople and the Straits denied it the priceless opportunity to intervene decisively at the onset of the Gallipoli campaign in 1915. There can be little doubt that the tough little army could have rolled up the peninsula in conjunction with the British and marched into Constantinople to reconsecrate the Hagia Sophia Cathedral for Orthodox Christianity. Instead the army was to serve in the mountains against Bulgarians, a grinding campaign of small gains. The breakup of the Ottoman Empire in 1918 saw the Greek nation and army seize this last chance to recover the Greek lands of Anatolia. The field army conquered large parts of western Anatolia and marched on Ankara in 1921. In a great three-day battle outside the city, the Greeks and Attaturk's new army fought to a draw. Stretched to breaking-point, the Greek supply lines collapsed, squeezed off by a British and French naval blockade. Much of the army was destroyed in the retreat to the sea where the survivors were evacuated. This was the great Catastrophe of modern Greek history. The remnant of the army returned to hang a number of politicians and its own generals.

SECOND WORLD WAR

The Royal Hellenic Army next saw combat in 1940 when the Italians invaded Greek Epirus from Albania. The army numbered barely 65,000 men, equipped much as the First World War had left it, but it was well-trained, hardy and eager to close with the Italians. A timely mobilization strengthened forces in Epirus. The invasion was stopped cold and thrown back across the border. The lavishly equipped Italians, who also enjoyed complete air superiority and a numerical superiority of at least three to two, could barely hold on to Albania. Even the German newspapers were asking when would the Greeks march on Rome! The Greek soldier displayed a rugged fortitude amid the agonies of mountain fighting in winter, and a ferocious will to get at the enemy with the bayonet, attributes he would again have need of in the Civil War and in Korea. The Germans attacked through the Bulgarian passes in early April 1941. The small forts of the Metaxas Line held under repeated assaults which cost the Germans 15,000 casualties. In a rare show of respect, the Wehrmacht presented arms to the garrisons that surrendered later under the general capitulation. The Germans then side-stepped across the unfortified Yugoslav border. The bulk of the Greek Army, 140,000 men, were trapped in Epirus and Albania by the German armour thrusts to central Greece and were forced to surrender. Following the fall of Athens, Hitler announced to the Reichstag that in recognition of its gallant conduct the Greek Army would be allowed the honour of being disbanded rather than marched off to prison camps:

> 'For the sake of historical justice I feel obligated to testify that amongst our adversaries the Greeks fought equally with reckless courage and supreme contempt for death. They capitulated only when further resistance became impossible and therefore futile.'[97]

Greek resistance continued with the few regiments, mostly in training, that were stationed in Crete and attached to the British garrison. Their spirited role and that of the native Cretans in the defence of the island has been largely overlooked by Western, particularly British, historians. More than a few German paratroop companies were overrun with the bayonet. Having botched the defence of the island, the British withdrew hurriedly, failing even to notify the Greek units still fighting as a covering force for the British.[98]

No Royal Hellenic Army units of any size escaped the German conquest of Greece. Eventually a sufficient number of individuals made their way through the islands to Cyprus and thence to Alexandria to form an infantry brigade and a commando unit called the Sacred Band. The brigade served with the British Eighth Army from North Africa to Italy while the commandos operated in the Aegean Islands. The brigade earned the honorific 'Rimini' for its spirited action there. While this small remnant of the Royal Hellenic Army was fighting the Germans across the Mediterranean, the Greek Communists organized themselves as a guerrilla force whose first priority was the elimination of non-Communist Greek guerrilla forces. The Germans suddenly evacuated Greece in 1944; the Communists immediately stepped into the vacuum to seize power. Only the quick dispatch of British forces and the Greek contingents to Athens frustrated the initial attempt. In December 1944 the Communists attacked British and Greek forces in Athens, but the battle for the city was a disaster for the Communists whose units, in fierce street fighting, were broken and driven out.

THE CIVIL WAR

By February 1945 the Communists had been largely disarmed although several thousands of their cadres had crossed the border into Yugoslavia and Bulgaria. By late 1946 they had formally re-entered Greece as the Democratic Army of Greece (DAG) and had begun the Civil War. The Royal Hellenic Army had barely begun the task of re-forming itself as a national army. Although its strength had been raised to 100,000 through the recall of veterans, it was woefully equipped with weapons and transport. Its effectiveness was further undermined by the endemic political paralysis of the government. Politicians ensured that their own areas would be garrisoned which effectively tied the army down to a static defence, which was precisely the wrong tactic to employ in counter-insurgency operations

47

where mobility was essential. The newly re-established general staff, chronically vulnerable to political influence, showed little flexibility and exerted far too much control over the deployment of formations; divisional commanders could not even move their subordinate units without general staff permission. All the initiative and mobility rested with the DAG.[99]

Compounding these problems was the inability of the ruined Greek economy to support its armed forces. The British had initially been able to meet most of the immediate needs of the Hellenic Army to the point where Greek troops were generally clad in British battledress, webbing, boots and greatcoats, and about 50 per cent had British smallarms. Originally the British had hoped that the Greeks could be self-supporting by early 1946, but continuing economic and political chaos made that impossible, and the British agreed to continue their support until March 1947. Even so, this support was extremely limited because of Britain's own considerable economic problems. British assistance would not supply the necessary trucks and heavy weapons needed to fight a major counter-insurgency. By April 1947 the depth of Democratic Army inroads and the inadequacy of British assistance persuaded the Greek government to ask the United States for assistance.[100]

Within a very short space of time the DAG had become dangerously effective as a guerrilla force, operating in bands throughout the country. Supplied from secure bases on the Yugoslav, Albanian and Bulgarian borders and commanded by the brilliant General Markos, it quickly spread its control to some 80 per cent of the country, using classic guerrilla tactics to isolate towns and cities and their garrisons. They also employed the classic techniques of terrorism. The ruthlessness of the Greek commissar was indistinguishable from that of his Chinese and Vietnamese contemporaries. This immediate resort to terror speedily alienated most of the Greek people, limiting the number of volunteers to the DAG's ranks to the relatively few committed believers. Additional recruits, both men and women, had to be press-ganged from captured villages. Propaganda, relentless supervision and draconian punishments were necessary to keep them in the ranks. The Communist battle-cry 'By fire and axe!' typified the remorseless nature of their struggle. There was little alternative to the impressed peasant. Markos' tactics had the Royal Hellenic Army cornered. It was spread too thinly in defending too many locations, demoralized by its lack of direction and *matériel*, loss of initiative and an omnipresent fifth column within its ranks.

In April 1947 the Royal Hellenic Army shook off its lethargy and emerged from its garrisons to conduct a major operation against the guerrillas in their mountain strongholds. It pursued the Communists through snow and hail and inflicted heavy casualties, then returned exhausted to its garrisons. For months afterwards, no more than eight infantry battalions could be scraped together for further offensive operations. DAG morale recovered while that of the Royal Hellenic Army sank.

At this nadir in their fortunes, US aid began to arrive. Weapons, equipment and supplies soon began fleshing out the firepower, mobility and sustainability of Greek units. The United States also sent a military mission of 250 officers, most of whom assisted in the retraining of the Royal Hellenic Army with fifty assigned as advisers to the General Staff. While the Americans worked closely with the Greeks, it was the Greek officer corps that commanded and the Greek soldier that fought. Once properly equipped and supported, the Royal Hellenic Army would rise to its task and bring home its own victory.[101]

For almost a year Markos was able to limit the gains of the reviving army. Heavy fighting across the mountains of northern Greece had inflicted severe casualties on both sides, but had not given the army any hope for eventual success. At last, all military authority was vested in a single commander-in-chief, General Papagos, who had commanded the Greek forces so successfully against the Italians in 1940–1. He urged an expansion of the army to 150,000 men; order of battle was eight divisions, three independent brigades, and four commando groups.[102] Papagos added that jolt of brilliance and natural leadership which the army needed if it were to recover its balance as a fighting force. He moved immediately to shake up the Army's command structure. He surrounded himself with trusted subordinates from the Greco-Italian War and immediately weeded out the ineffectives from the General Staff down to brigade level. He had the invaluable ability to put the right man in the right job. With an icy objectivity that weighed only an officer's abilities, he was not loath to remove old friends and promote personal enemies. Equally important, the actions of the army and government had succeeded by early 1949 in breaking up the Communist intelligence and sympathizer networks, isolating them from the population and protecting the population from their terror.

OPERATION PYRSOS

At that time the Communists presented the Hellenic Army with a priceless opening. Markos was replaced by his rival, Nikos Zakhariades, who immediately converted the DAG to a conventional force of five divisions. This was the cardinal mistake of the war. Conventional war entailed losses that the DAG could not replace in the long run against a newly equipped, aggressive and relentless Royal Hellenic Army which had revived the battle-cry of the Greek Revolution – 'Freedom or death!' Papagos moved quickly to clear the Peloponnese of the DAG, and having secured southern Greece, pushed his clearing operations northwards. The great border battles of 1948 were repeated, but this time the DAG was badly cut up. Only the ability to slip across the border into Communist sanctuaries saved the shrinking remnant of the DAG. Finally even these bolt-holes closed as political alignments changed.

The last battle of the war, the Battle of the Frontiers code-named Operation 'Pyrsos' (Torch), 2–30 August 1949, concentrated two-thirds of the Greek Army – ten Greek divisions of the newly formed First Army, against the last DAG strongholds in the mountains along the Albanian border on Mount Grammos and Mount Vitsi, held by 7,000 and 5,000 men respectively. The DAG expected that the army would attack the weaker Grammos redoubt first, as in the past. Papagos had something else in mind. Operation 'Pyrsos' was conducted in three phases. In the first, beginning on 2 August, a strong attack was delivered on the Grammos redoubt as a feint. Then on 10 August the second phase began with a massive surprise attack on the Vitsi redoubt. The Communists fought for every yard, but the army could smell victory and clawed its way through with pack artillery up front to give direct fire support, and the stronghold had been overrun by 15 August. Four thousand DAG fighters, including wounded, fled into Albania where the fit were sent to reinforce Grammos. First Army had suffered 1,682 casualties of all types but counted 1,182 DAG dead. The DAG now offered the Royal Hellenic Army another gift – it determined to fight it out and not retreat into Albania, hoping to hold on until bad weather halted operations. In the third phase, beginning on 25 August, the First Army turned on Grammos which was softened first by an intensive air attack. Fixing the enemy's attention with heavy attacks in the centre, the army sent two pincers from the north and south along the Albanian border. At this point the Albanian government got cold feet and announced that it would intern any Greek who crossed the border. The sanctuary had shut down. DAG defences were overrun one by one, and DAG's political leaders thought better of its do-or-die stance and, for the last time, slipped across the border with the survivors. DAG's back was broken; it had lost 2,280 dead and 3,000 wounded in addition to 1,632 prisoners and deserters, to the Hellenic Army's 3,960 casualties of all types.

In October Alexandros Papagos, victor in the Greco-Italian War and Civil War, was rewarded by his nation with the rank of field marshal, the only Greek officer ever to hold that rank. He had twice moulded and commanded superlative Greek armies the fighting men of which developed an unparalled talent for aggression and tenacity under the rigours of winter and mountain fighting. The record of the Greek soldier during those terrible nine years from 1940 to 1949 was one of valour and ability. He was inured to hardship, innately aggressive in combat, capable of initiative and leadership at the lowest levels, and able to master the modern technologies and methods of war. His officers' command and staff skills were high by Western European standards. That the cost of the Civil War had been so high is attributable to the very same characteristics among their fellow Greeks in the DAG.

Table 1-7. Greek Casualties in the Civil War 1944–46

	Dead	Wounded	Prisoners
Hellenic Army	12,777	37,732	
Gendarmerie	1,579	2,329	
DAG*	36,839	unknown	41,684

*Since the DAG carried away many of its dead and wounded, figures were much higher. Other Greek losses included 165 priests and 4,123 civilians executed by the Communists.

Source: Evangelos Averoff-Tossizza, *By Fire and Ax*, p. 355.

THE KOREAN WAR

The embers of the Civil War had scarcely cooled when the Greek government dispatched a battalion to fight alongside the United Nations forces in Korea. Raised from volunteers recruited from three infantry divisions, the battalion received its war flag from King Paul at the Monument to the Unknown Soldier in Athens in November 1950 and arrived in Korea in December. Its first significant combat was in January in defence of Hill 381 north-east of Inchon. Struck by a Chinese regiment, the battalion held against repeated assaults that finally exhausted its ammunition and reduced the defenders to hand-to-hand combat with bayonets, knives, rifle butts and bare fists. The Chinese were thrown off the hill, leaving 800 dead and wounded on the blood-streaked snow.[103] The Greeks had arrived – skilled in winter and mountain fighting; with the bayonet and with a taste for Communists. The battalion was eventually attached to the US 15th Infantry Regiment of the 3rd Infantry Division with which it would serve until the armistice. It was a good relationship symbolized by the shared colours of light-blue and white for the Greek flag and the 3rd Infantry Division's famous Rock of the Marne shoulder patch. The Greek contingent were already familiar with American procedures and equipment from their service in the Civil War, and became a valued element of the division. The battalion saw a great deal of combat, distinguishing themselves during the final spasm of the war in the Battle for Harry Hill. Casualties for the war were 174 dead and 543 wounded; by 1955 4,441 Greeks had served in Korea. Of the enemy casualties that could be counted, the Greeks were credited with 1,218 dead and 208 prisoners.[104]

With the armistice in July 1953, the combat record of the Royal Hellenic Army came to a halt. Halfway round the world from ancient Hellas lies the monument to this last combat. On a hill near Inchon, beneath fluted columns, a tablet in Greek, Korean and English reads: 'Happiness Consists in Freedom, and Freedom in Valour'.

ISRAEL

AN ARMY BEFORE A STATE

In 1945 the 'birth' of the Israeli Defence Force (IDF) was still three years away, but the forces that would coalesce into that army were already growing in experience and organization. Those forces sheltered under the Haganah, the Jewish community's self-defence force. Chief among them was the Palmach, the Hebrew acronym for 'strike companies'. The Palmach was founded in May 1941 by the Haganah as an élite, special operations strike force to resist an Axis advance into Palestine. They were to provide 4,000 men as officer cadres for the new army in the War of Independence. There were an additional 27,000 Palestinian Jewish men and women who had served in the British Army during the Second World War.[105] By 1945 the Haganah had at its disposal a large number of men with valuable military experience.

But a collection of men is no more an army than a pile of building materials is a house, as Socrates had observed almost twenty-five hundred years before. The Haganah's decision in 1945 to begin a 'struggle' for independence against the British garrison of Palestine would mould those men into an army during the next two and half years. By late 1947, when the United Nations voted for the partition of Palestine, the Haganah had transformed itself into an effectively organized though unconventional and poorly armed military force. So poorly armed that the Haganah's carefully hoarded weapons reserve amounted to fewer than 5,000 rifles, and they had no tanks or artillery.

The lack of artillery and the Israelis' by-hook-or-by-crook methods of acquisition are an example in miniature of their desperation and their resourcefulness. The first weapons that could loosely be called artillery had begun their military careers as Ottoman guns which, in retirement, had been placed as trophies of the First World War outside the Jewish Legion veterans' club hall. In the dark of night, the Haganah carried them off to their hidden workshops where their barrels were sawn into segments to make mortars nicknamed 'Davidkas'. So desperate were they that the Chief Rabbi of Jerusalem granted dispensation to the workers who laboured to complete them on the Sabbath. Ammunition was improvised from water pipes stuffed with explosives, nails and metal scrap. The first authentic piece of field artillery was the audacious gift of a British soldier who had thrown in his lot with the new Israel. He asked what he could bring with him when he deserted and was told a cannon would be nice. Whereupon he drove a crane into the British artillery depot in Haifa, announced that the Jerusalem Command had lost a 25pdr in a ditch and needed a replacement. The general commanding the depot cheerfully waved at his guns, 'Help yourself!'. Five minutes after he had left the depot, 25pdr in tow, the Haganah had its first serious artillery.[106]

Much of the credit for the spirit motivating the leadership cadres of the Haganah and primarily the Palmach at this time can be laid at the door of the British officer, Captain (later General) Wingate of Burma campaign fame. Wingate arrived in Palestine in the 1930s at a formative time for the Haganah. A passionate Zionist from his fundamentalist Christian beliefs, he provided invaluable assistance to the Haganah's counter-guerrilla operations. His personal example, leadership and teaching made tremendous lasting impressions among a whole generation of the Haganah who were to form the cadre for the Palmach. These lessons were inculcated into the Israeli military ethos where they survive and thrive to this day. Chief among these gifts to the future leaders of a new army was the personal example of the commander; the demand for meticulous operational discipline; careful planning; the inclusion of subordinates as partners in thought and action, 'whose readiness and comprehension had to be won before the start of an operation'; exploitation of surprise and mobility; the importance of ideological inspiration in war; and a deadly appreciation of and taste for night operations.[107]

The War of Independence, 1948–1949

Well after the fighting had started in Israel's War of Liberation, the Haganah was officially transformed into the first independent Jewish army since the Revolt of Bar Kochba in the Second Century. On 20 May 1948 the army of the new Israel was born, named Zahal, the acronym for Israeli Defence Force (*Zavah Haganah Le Yisrael*). By the beginning of the last stage of the war, in June 1948, Zahal consisted of ten infantry brigades (seven Haganah and three Palmach) and one small, miserably equipped armoured battalion. The infantry brigades had been adequately equipped with Czech and French weapons, but the artillery, though improved, was unable to provide full support. By now the forces numbered more than 60,000 men and women and would climb to about 100,000 – practically every able-bodied adult male – by the war's end. New weapons included some tanks (ten ancient French H-35s, two British Cromwells and one US Sherman), halftracks, improvised armoured cars, trucks, and a few aircraft. Despite these organizational and *matériel* improvements, Zahal was still much inferior in numbers and equipment to its Arab enemies. Its superiority lay in organization, discipline, fighting spirit, unity and that ultimate weapon described by General Yigal Allon as 'the sense of no alternative'.[108]

The War of Independence showed the IDF's penchant for the use of the classic strategy of the 'indirect approach'. The finest example of this was Operation 'Yaov' ('Ten Plagues') which drove the Egyptian Army out of the Negev. In the IDF's post-war analyses, General Yadin, the new Chief of Staff, wrote:

'There is no doubt that the strategy of the indirect approach is the only sound strategy ... To exploit the principles of war ... so as to determine the issue of the fighting even before the fighting has begun, it is necessary to achieve the three following aims: (a) to cut the enemy's lines of communications, thus paralysing his physical build-up; (b) to seal him off from his lines of retreat, thus undermining the enemy's will and destroying his morale; (c) to hit his centres of administration and disrupt his communications, thus severing the link between his brain and his limbs.' [109]

It is no surprise that Yadin had been a student of Liddell Hart's theories and had used his book, *Strategy of the Indirect Approach* as a textbook for the courses he taught in the Haganah during the years 1940–3. General Allon was also a disciple of Liddell Hart and dedicated a book to him, *The Theory and Practice of War: Essays presented to Captain B. H. Liddell Hart on His Seventieth birthday.* [110] A second though invalid lesson had also been learned, one that was to influence the tactics and equipment of the IDF until 1956.

In Operation 'Yaov' the fledgling tank battalion of the IDF had been committed in the attack on a fortified village and had failed completely, losing all but one of its tanks. This setback confirmed the IDF opinion that tanks should be used only for infantry support and that the primary offensive arm was mechanized infantry.

A third lesson, this one fundamentally sound, absorbed by the IDF, was on the nature of the wars Israel could expect to fight against its Arab neighbours. Such wars would probably be short and subject to rapid United Nations interference. Under such conditions, surprise was a vital asset in seizing territory from Arab armies. Since Israel could not afford more than one such Arab bite, the IDF developed a doctrine of the 'anticipatory counter-attack'. Allon stressed that the only counter to a threatened attack would be 'an overall initiative on the part of Israel, if necessary a pre-emptive counter-attack, having as its object the destruction of the enemy's forces,' before they themselves were ready to attack. Future wars would be short and decisive and, above all, would take place on the enemy's territory. [111]

As an institution, the IDF came out of the war with its character indelibly fixed by that experience. It had acquired a military ethos upon which it would build an unparalleled reputation for battlefield lethality. In the words of Allon, the IDF had acquired:

'... a habit of deeply-rooted purposefulness, idealism, and belief in voluntary service; a spirit of comradeship and mutual responsibility, among units and ranks as well as individuals ... The freedom from obsolete army tradition that had been so conspicuous a feature of the Haganah passed, virtually unchanged, into the new army. As far as military forms and conventions were concerned, it adopted only the minimum necessary for securing discipline and efficiency.'[112]

Zahal had also come out of the war with a deep sense of its role in a democratic society and with exceptionally close bonds to the new society and nation of which it was so much a part.

An Army for a New State

The demobilization in 1949 of most of the 80,000 men recruited during the war almost completely dismantled the new army. Most disruptive was the loss of virtually the entire officer cadre. The overwhelming majority of them had never had any intention of pursuing a military career and returned to the more attractive challenges of civilian life. The experienced cadres of the Palmach were actively discouraged by the government from remaining in the army because of the Palmach's élitist attitudes and identification with the Mapam Party and its leftist political agenda. The almost wholesale departure of Palmach officers left the IDF in the hands of those officers whose formative military experience had been with the British Army and who were considered politically less obstructive.

This brought about an attempt to introduce a stricter, more formal discipline, an 'external' school of discipline as opposed to the Palmach leaders who championed the completely internal and self-imposed discipline of the Palmach. Although the army was built on British models of discipline for the next several years, it was not a permanent conversion, and much of the Palmach style eventually returned to the army.[113]

By the end of 1949 the new Chief of Staff, General Yadin, had initiated a complete re-appraisal of the basis of the IDF based on Israel's strategic situation. The central fact to emerge from this review was that Israel's small population could not support the traditional types of military organization, such as large conscript or regular armies, that would be necessary to defend the country. With barely 30,000 conscripts per year available, Israel had no hope of meeting Arab numbers with an army manned by such means. The solution was an original one, realistically based on Israel's population and economic constraints yet designed to wring the maximum combat effectiveness out of the entire nation. The decision was made that the reserve forces would be the most important and vital component of the IDF, not its regulars or its conscripts. The IDF would fight primarily with reserve brigades committed to immediate combat. The small regular cadre would be devoted to providing support in peacetime to the reserves and to training the conscripts to pass them into the reserves. Reserve units would be regionally based and train together as units. The crux of the problem was whether reserve formations could ever achieve and maintain the proficiency necessary for immediate front-line duty.

The question of proficiency was solved first by giving conscripts a long and thorough period of training of two to three years. Secondly reservists, particularly officers, were given frequent periods of refresher training to bring their proficiency up to that of full-time regulars. The enlisted reservist was obliged to fulfil thirty-one days' reserve training a year plus an extra one day per month. Officers and NCOs had to put in even more time. No other society has asked for and received so much of itself. Yadin was reputedly to say, 'Every civilian is a soldier on eleven months' annual leave.'[114]

This absolute integration of Zahal with society was one of the key objectives for both Prime Minister Ben Gurion and Yadin. To Ben Gurion, the educational role of the army in helping Israel absorb and socialize the huge waves of oriental and occidental Jewish immigrants was of equal importance to its combat readiness mission. Another facet of the integration was the conscription of women which found its origins in the egalitarian, frontier nature of Israeli society and the numerical limits of its 'man' power. However, contrary to myth, Israeli women are shielded from combat, though they receive weapons training for self-defence. Primarily they perform the unglamorous but vital support and administrative tasks, with the exception of menial work, that would in other armies absorb large numbers of men. The egalitarian thread runs broadly throughout Zahal in many other ways. There are no gentlemanly roads to a commission. All officers serve first in the ranks as conscripts. Merit is the road to success, and success is rewarded with rapid advancement which keeps the leadership of the IDF young, vital and sharp.

COMBAT ORGANIZATION: TANKS AND PARATROOPS

The next problem addressed by the 1949 review was the combat organization of the IDF. It was determined that the traditional structures of the forces of the major powers, colonial battalions and conventional divisions, did not meet the IDF's needs. Again, an original solution was devised. The self-contained brigade, made up of three battalions with service and support units, was created. Such a unit was ideal for the rapid offensive deep into the enemy's rear. By late 1952 the IDF still consisted almost entirely of infantry with two infantry brigades, one partly-armoured and one paratroop brigade in the regular forces and eight infantry brigades in the reserve forces. Small-arms consisted of bolt-action rifles and submachine-guns in equal numbers. Vehicles consisted of about 50 Sherman tanks and 200 M.3 halftrack infantry carriers; the artillery consisted of British 25pdrs. Personnel strength was estimated at 35,000 conscripts and regular cadre and 80,000 reservists.[115]

The early 1950s also saw the rise of the two élite branches of the IDF that were to play such prominent roles in all the wars that followed – the Armoured Corps and the Paratroops. Ironically both started from very lacklustre beginnings.

The 1949 reorganization called for each brigade to have its own tank contingent, but lack of vehicles prevented this for some time. Considerable thought was given to the future role of tanks, but under the influence of infantry-minded chiefs of staff such as Yadin and Moshe Dayan, whose opinions of tanks were formed by the failure of the tanks in Operation 'Yaov', the tank would be relegated to a support role even at the beginning of the 1956 Sinai campaign.

Nevertheless, the destiny of the armoured corps of the IDF was to be rescued from even deeper anonymity by the action of two men. The first was Lieutenant-Colonel Ben-Ari, deputy commander of 'S' Tank Brigade. During the 1952 manoeuvres, Ben-Ari drove the brigade more than 80 miles into his opponent's rear area. He had disrupted the entire timetable of the exercise; a red circle was drawn around his unit's position on the map from which it was forbidden to move. The 'S' Brigade's performance drew a stiff rebuke from General Yadin. Apparently that was only an encouragement for Ben-Ari who repeated the feat in the 1953 manoeuvres. This time the brigade overran an infantry battalion which fled in panic from the sight of the on-rushing tanks. Watching from the roadside was David Ben Gurion, the Prime Minister and Minister of Defence. From that moment the Armoured Corps began to grow as it was rapidly promoted in the list of priorities.[116]

The destiny of the paratroops was also rescued by the aggressive personality of one man, a young lieutenant-colonel named Ariel Sharon. In 1953 he was selected by the new chief of staff, Moshe Dayan, to lead a special formation, Unit 101, outside the formal command structure of the IDF, to conduct reprisal raids against Arab villages from which terrorist raids into Israel had been launched. The regular battalions of the IDF had proven uniformly unsuccessful. In Unit 101 he created, in effect, a small, private army which revived the IDF's lost skills in night operations, infiltration and field craft, and was ruthlessly effective. So much so that the international outcry almost led to the disbandment of his unit. Instead, Dayan merged Unit 101 with the paratroop battalion. That battalion had sunk into mediocrity and not lived up to the high expectations normally associated with paratroops. Things changed under Sharon's command. Although the members of Unit 101 were a small minority in the new combined battalion, their hard-nosed attitude and dash devoured the timid spirit of the paratroops. The General Staff soon had a unit that could be trusted in the most difficult operations and was to set the standards for the rest of the army. Moshe Dayan took a special interest in the paratroop battalion and used it as a tactical school for all the infantry, and required all officers to undergo paratroop training. By 1956 he had enlarged it to a brigade. Edward Luttwak writes that, 'The infantry brigades of the standing forces, and later reserve units as well, responded to this "imitative pull" of the paratroopers, and even attempted to compete with them.'[117] Sharon was the living embodiment of the old motto, 'Who dares wins'. His was the rarest of accomplishments – to transfer an essentially individual trait into the living traditions of an institution, the IDF.

The first decade of the post-war era ended for the IDF in the middle of Dayan's tenure as Chief of Staff. His accomplishments were to prove crucial for the decisive battlefield edge which the IDF would demonstrate in the future. Yet he built upon the work of a remarkable collection of talented men. His predecessor, General Yadin, had constructed the reserve system and established much of the combat organization of the IDF and its strategic outlook. The Armoured Corps, thanks to Ben Ari's impudence and Ben Gurion's farsightedness, was expanded sufficiently to be able to show its potential in 1956. Sharon created the Paratroops in his own lethal image. To Dayan's credit goes the return to the more informal and enlightened Palmach attitudes towards discipline and motivation that so much more naturally suited Israel's fighting traditions and society. To him also goes the credit for the rejuvenation of the infantry and its morale through his support of the paratroops as role models, as well as many other improvements that set the stage for the victory of 1956.

EGYPT

The Egyptian Army bitterly sat out the world wars of the first half of the twentieth century. Kept on a short leash by the British occupation forces, the Egyptians watched helplessly as two epic campaigns were staged from their country. In 1946 the British lion finally departed, but after almost a century of subordination, the Egyptian eagle was a scrawny bird, debilitated by corruption, neglect and pervasive incompetence. It was not a promising beginning for the second half of the century. Yet in less than thirty years the eagle would fight six wars and conduct one of the masterpieces in the history of military operations.

British military influence began to wane immediately after the departure of the British occupation forces when the last British presence, an advisory military mission, left Egypt in 1947. But Egyptian officers continued to attend British military schools until 1956. A century of British military advice had done little for the efficiency of the Egyptian Army. Reflecting its society as much as the scandalously incompetent and greedy government of King Farouk, the officer corps put its self-interest above duty. The vast social gulf between officers and men never allowed a sense of mutual trust to grow; care of the troops and equipment was badly neglected. As a result, neither operated well in the 1948 war with Israel. With a strength of 50,000, the army initially fielded barely 10,000 men in its first major war of this century, although by the end of the year there were 40,000 men in the field including foreign volunteers. Although numbers gave the Egyptians a few minor victories, the smaller Israeli forces were clearly the victors by February 1949.

The seeds of change, however, had been sown as early as 1936 when sons of the middle class had been allowed entry into the Egyptian Military Academy. The graduates of the classes of 1938–40 were a new breed – patriotic, aggressive and thoroughly disgusted by the incompetence and corruption both in the army and government. After the war they formed the secret Free Officers' Movement which overthrew the Farouk regime in July 1952 and abolished the monarchy in June 1953. The new head of state was the conservative older General Muhammad Neguib. The younger elements of the Movement overthrew Neguib and replaced him with his deputy, Colonel Gamal Abdul Nasser in November 1954.

After the war the army sought non-British foreign military advisers and eventually hired up to 60 former German officers headed by General Wilhelm Fahrmbacher. The Germans remained in Egypt from 1950 to 1957. The most flamboyant of them, General Gerhard Mertins, trained the parachute and commando units. He is vividly remembered for his command, 'Over the pyramids! Quick march!' in which he concluded a desert march by leading his Egyptian charges up one side and down the other of the Great Pyramid of Khufu. The new Nassar regime took definite steps to recast the army out of its British mould by turning to Czechoslovakia as a major arms supplier when the British finally evacuated the Canal Zone in 1954–5.[118] The Czechs, however, were merely a proxy. Nasser had turned to the Soviets in order to rebuild the army with equipment, training and doctrine on modern lines.

SYRIA

In their new Syrian colony after the First World War, the French organized a colonial security force, the Syrian Legion, in 1919 and set the tone for the future army by their divide-and-rule policy of recruiting this colonial force from the minority populations normally excluded from positions of power: Alawi, Kurds, Circassians and Armenians.

At the end of the Second World War the British, who were then in occupation of Syria, reorganized the Syrian Legion and sent many of its officers to Egypt for advanced military training. Shortly thereafter, in 1946, Syria was granted independence and the Syrian Legion was transformed into the Syrian Army. It had inherited some armoured vehicles, mostly French, from the Vichy and later Free French forces. It was this army of barely 8,000 men that attacked into the Galilee from the Golan Heights on the day after Israel's declaration of independence in 1948 and inflicted considerable casualties on the Israelis at Semach and Mishmar Hayarden before being stopped and thrown back over the border. Disputes with Israel over the terms of the armistice resulted in constant tension with localized exchanges of artillery and rocket fire continuing until 1967.

The defeated Syrian Army under its commander, General Husni az Zaim, enraged by revelations of corruption and profiteering by political leaders, overthrew the government in March 1949. This coup would be the first of many to punctuate Syrian history for the next twenty years. Two more coups followed closely on the heels of the first, the latter led by Colonel Adib Shashakli who retained power until 1954. While Shashakli, like most other senior Syrian officers, had close ties with the majority Sunni élite, most of the junior officers were from the minority populations of Syria, particularly the Alawites. Attendance at the miliary academy at Homs had let them drink deeply from the Arab nationalist ideology that prevailed there. They were also strongly influenced by the example of Nasser in Egypt and by the prevailing anti-colonial and socialist movements in the Arab world. In 1954 officers from this background overthrew Shashakli and ushered in the era that would prevail until 1989.

BRITISH INDIA – THE RAJ

Partition of the British Indian Army

The bands played 'Auld Lang Syne' as the 2nd Battalion of the Royal Norfolk Regiment boarded ship in Bombay on 17 August 1947 to depart India for ever. Two days earlier the British imperial possession of India had achieved independence, broken into two states, Hindu India and Muslim Pakistan, and the 200-year relationship between the British Army and the army of the Indian Raj had passed into history. The Indian Army of the Raj had fought around the world in the service of the British crown and had acquired a distinguished reputation. Now it too would be split along the religious and geographic lines that had split the subcontinent itself.

As early as the First World War the Indian Army had left its mark as an army of international service and reputation. It provided an entire corps for service in the trenches on the Western Front, holding as much as one-third of the entire British sector of the front within a year of the start of the war, thereby giving the British Army the necessary time to mobilize a modern mass army. Indian troops served in East Africa, Egypt, Mesopotamia and Gallipoli. More than 1,000,000 men of the expanded army were sent overseas, and 100,000 were killed.[119] The Indian Army came of age during the Second World War and again played a distinguished even vital role in the operations of the forces of the British Empire. It had begun the war with a peacetime strength of 189,000 men and 2,800 officers (2,300 British and 500 Indian) and expanded to 2,644,000 and 22,000 officers (13,500 British and 8,500 Indian). Its contribution to the campaigns in North Africa and Italy were critical to British success. Its contribution to the defence of India and the reconquest of Burma were primary.[120] The war had provided two essentials for the creation of the armies of the modern independent states: a military industrial capacity it had not had before, and a large number of native Muslim and Hindu officers.

At the time of Partition in 1947, the Indian Army was a single, seamless institution. With the exception of the ten Gurkha and eight wholly Hindu regiments, all formations were mixed Hindu and Muslim. Strength at Independence was 11,800 Indian officers and 450,000 men. The army's physical infrastructure of bases, schools, depots and ordnance factories was spread throughout the subcontinent without regard to Muslim or Hindu demography. Partition would require this institution to tear itself into two unbalanced halves. As a purely military operation, the partition of the army would at any time have been appallingly difficult; undertaken in the midst of the creation of two new states and the bloody and chaotic exchange of populations numbering more than 8,500,000 and resulting in a million deaths, it would be a remarkable, almost miraculous, achievement. It is a testament to the professionalism and esprit of the old Indian Army that during this wrenching separation, there was no strife among comrades who had worn the same uniform.

On 30 June 1947 the procedure for the division of the forces of the army, armaments, ordnance factories, stores, training centres and schools was agreed by the Partition Council. The division of the army between Pakistan and the Union of India was to be accomplished on a communal basis and movable stores had to be divided by the same ratio: 64 per cent and 37 per cent. By late September details of the split had been finalized and promulgated. The division of the units of the army was agreed to as shown here:[121]

Table 1-8. Division of the Regiments of the Indian Army

	Pakistan	India
Combat Arms:		
Infantry Regiments	8	15
Gurkha Regiments	0	6
Armoured Regiments	6	14
Artillery Regiments	8	40
Engineer Groups		
Support Services:		
Pioneer Companies	2	10
Garrison Companies	8	15
Army Service Corps units	60	97
Ordnance units	28	61
Medical units	14	32

Of the two new armies, the Pakistan Army was the one most hurt by the division. The Indian Army had received intact the eight all-Hindu regiments and the six Gurkha regiments. Only seven of the Indian regiments but all eight of the Pakistani regiments were mixed units. After the assignment of the regiments, each man made his own choice of armies. The loss of large numbers of Sikh and Hindu soldiers was a blow to all the Pakistani regiments, whereas only one-third of the regiments assigned to India were similarly disrupted. Exchange resulted in the eight Pakistani regiments being under-strength by 8,000 men. During the personnel exchange, 64 Hindu companies from these regiments were exchanged for only 29 Muslim companies. The assignment of support units was similarly unbalanced, these being stripped in many cases of most of their men. The home training stations of the various regiments suffered the least disruption, having fallen with three exceptions (two Pakistani and one Indian) in their new homelands.[122]

In the division of infrastructure, the Pakistan Army suffered first from the realities of geography. Of the large and balanced training establishment, it had located on its territory only eight of 46 formations. Of these the only combat arm school was the Anti-Aircraft Artillery School. The staff college at Quetta was probably the most valuable for the long-term development of the army. In the division of depots and their supplies, India was the major beneficiary. During the war the reconquest of South-east Asia had been based out of eastern India which logically now contained the great war-built logistics system of depots. The three small depots located in Pakistani territory contained general engineering equipment and static machinery such as pumps and generators. Additionally all seventeen ordnance factories were located in the territory of the Union of India. At the insistence of India, Pakistan agreed to accept compensation in place of a share of the factories. The agreed division of assets involving the transfer of stores was not fulfilled anywhere near the ratio. For example, Pakistan's share of ordnance stores was 160,000 tons; it received 23,225. Pakistan was to have as its share 40–60,000 tons of ammunition, 249 tanks and 1,461 trucks, but only 74 of the trucks were received.[123]

The Partition Council had also decided that each country would have operational control of its share of the original army by Independence on 15 August 1947. Overall control was to be maintained under a Supreme Commander, Field Marshal Auchinleck, of the British Army. It was a much constrained command, having largely administrative authority involving the division of the army until 1 December 1948 when its task was scheduled to be finished. At the insistence of the Indian government that the work of division had been substantially completed, the Supreme Command was dissolved on 30 November.[124]

One last mission remained to the old Indian Army after Independence. The vast Punjab had been split by Partition and now formed the new border and had become the flashpoint of communal strife and bloodshed as civil order collapsed and the local police force disappeared. A large number of the 8,500,000 refugees crossing the border in both directions were passing through the Punjab. The Army had established the Punjab Border Force (PBF) to control the exodus and restore order which it did as well as possible under the circumstances. Despite the increase in tensions among Muslim and Hindu troops aroused by the communal bloodletting, no violence broke out within the PBF. The PBF had been disbanded by 1 September 1947 as responsibility for keeping order passed into the hands of the new governments. The old army was a thing of the past, but its passing had not left its twin sons with the mark of Cain.

RECONSTITUTION

The two armies had effectively separated themselves by late 1947 and set about the task of reconstituting complete and balanced armies while at the same time engaging in their first war over Kashmir. At this point, the histories of the separate Indian Army and Pakistan Army begin.

INDIA

The Indian Army had inherited about 260,000 officers and men of the old army, most of the training facilities, depots and stores, and all the ordnance factories. Only one-third of its infantry regiments, the combat heart of the army, had been disrupted by the division of the old army. It was in far better shape to reconstitute itself as a balanced force than the Pakistan Army. The Indian Army also absorbed the small armies of the autonomous states that had existed within the Raj but which now had been incorporated into the Union of India. The survivors of the Indian National Army which had been recruited by the Japanese during the Second World War from anti-British Indians and Indian POWs captured in Malaya were not accepted into the new army.

The Indian government was a firm supporter of the army and considered it an important element in furthering social change and nation-building in India. On 1 February 1949 the Ministry of Defence abolished class and caste requirements in the army to make it 'representative of all nationals in the country'. Traditionally the army's recruitment policy had been based on preference for the 'martial races' over the 'unmartial' races of India, e.g., choosing Sikhs rather than Bengalis. A new Brigade of Guards, modelled after the British Brigade of Guards, was established as an 'all class mixed' infantry brigade and was intended to be the test-bed for integration, but the first attempt at complete integration would not be made for another twenty years. The army was extensively used in disaster relief work and other social campaigns as proof that it was now the army of the nation.

As of late November 1947 the Indian Army had had 1,204 British officers on its rolls; these were given three months' notice terminating their services, but the government recognized that it still had a critical need of a number of British officers in technical and advisory capacities to help the army through its reconstitution difficulties. Although the native officer corps had been rapidly increased during the Second World War and after, it still did not have the necessary depth. There were only 93 officers of lieutenant-colonel rank and above with thirteen to twenty years' service, of whom 26 were general officers. The government offered to accept British officers and other ranks for temporary service of one year; 418 were accepted, including nine general officers, one of whom, General Sir Roy Bucher, served as Chief of the Army Staff and Commander-in-Chief, Army, for the next year. On 15 January 1949 General Bucher was succeeded by General Cariappa, the first Indian officer to reach the rank of full general, thus ending the 200-year line of British commanders of the Indian Army. As evidence of the successful process of the indianization of the officer corps, the event had such significance that the date has since been observed as Army Day. The last senior British officer left the Indian Army in 1955; a year later there were only six British officers remaining in Indian service.

The army quickly began to remodel its structure to meet the balanced requirements of a sovereign state. A new defence academy to train jointly officers of all the services was established in 1949, based on the concept of inter-service co-operation whose importance had been demonstrated during the Second World War. A National Cadet Corps and a Territorial Army were also created in that year. The aim of the Cadet Corps was to provide military training for students in colleges and secondary schools and it quickly became a popular institution. The Territorial Army's mission was to relieve the regular army of internal security missions. In 1950, with the establishment of the Republic of India, the army removed all designations of 'Royal' and crown emblems, established a new system of decorations, and retired all the King's Colours from the regiments in a sentimental ceremony accompanied by 'Auld Lang Syne' and 'God Save the King'. The army valued its heritage, and as the Defence Minister stated, the ceremony represented, 'the end of a glorious chapter in the history of these regiments', and 'the beginning of a new one'[125] However, one tradition was dropped quickly: the old term *sepoy* for an Indian soldier was replaced by *jawan* which remains in use to this day.

A defence policy of self-reliance was enunciated by Prime Minister Nehru in 1953, 'the first thing to realize is that defence does not merely consist of the armed forces... more and more, it consists of the strength behind the armed forces... the industrial capacity of the nation...' In 1955 he stated, 'We prefer to have – if I may use the word – the second-rate weapons that we can produce rather than the first-rate weapons for which we have to rely on somebody else.' This policy was to reap a great harvest in later decades as the production of a large and capable defence industry was to make possible the expansion of the power and size of the Indian Army.[126]

The Indian Army's combat experience during this decade was limited to the Kashmir War with Pakistan, but the army was active internationally, sending numerous peace-keeping missions at the request of the United Nations and suppressing a Communist revolt in Nepal at the request of the Nepalese government. The most important of these was the support of the UN Forces in the Korean War. The army sent a hospital unit and later contributed a significant element to the Neutral Nations Repatriation Commission in 1953. Altogether 5,230 officers and men of the Indian armed forces, mostly the army, served in Korea. India contributed also to the peace-keeping commission in Vietnam beginning in 1954.[127]

PAKISTAN

The act of tearing the old Indian Army apart had done far more damage to the one-third allotted to Pakistan. The new Pakistan Army began life as a thoroughly disrupted and seriously unbalanced organization. There were gaping holes not only in the fighting formations but, even more alarmingly, in the training and support establishments. The ordnance production establishment was simply not viable.

Although many of the men allotted to the Pakistan Army were veterans of Second World War combat, the army's share of senior officers was minute: one major-general, two brigadiers and six colonels.[128] The immediate problem with reconstitution was to organize the units and all the officers and men that had arrived as individuals from the territory of India. It was daunting task because 40 per cent of the units allotted to Pakistan had originally been stationed in what was to become the Union of India. The re-assignment of units and individuals was rapid despite the chaos that surrounded such massive dislocation. It was given added impetus by the outbreak of fighting with Indian forces in Kashmir. It would be difficult to find in the annals of history an army that had to deal both with the chaos of reconstitution and combat simultaneously.

The old army deployments and stations in the territory of Pakistan had not been based on 'operational' considerations given the security of the frontiers of the old Raj. Pakistan found a more acute security situation immediately with the outbreak of fighting in Kashmir. The army moved immediately to rationalize the deployment of its reconstituting forces to meet these new 'operational' requirements. Five divisions and one armoured brigade were created. It was also decided to abandon the British 'forward deployment' policy on the north-west frontier by withdrawing the area from military control as an act of good faith to the Pathan tribes. This freed considerable forces to bolster the redeployment.[129]

The combat arms were relatively the easiest elements to reconstitute. Most of the infantry regiments had their training establishments located in Pakistan. The armoured regiments were not so lucky, only two of six being in Pakistan; the other four had to take over facilities and equipment (often sabotaged) left by Hindu regiments. Of the combat arms, the artillery was the easiest to reconstitute with the help of British officers who agreed to stay behind. New regiments were raised to reflect the national obligations of the army. Traditionally, only men from West Pakistan had served in the army; the government of Pakistan now saw the necessity of raising a regiment in East Pakistan from the native Bengalis who, like their Indian relatives, had not been considered one of the 'martial races.' It was also considered good policy to raise a Pathan regiment for the first time. Both regiments were raised to give these peoples their first opportunity to serve their country under arms.[130]

Far more damaging than the disorder in the combat arms was the wholesale ruin of the service units assigned to the army. Exceptions were few. The engineers survived the division as intact companies and, with their 'proverbial ingenuity' managed to squirrel away through India their fair share of stores and equipment. The transport service also came away intact. The other services had not survived the division as organized units but rather as a mass of individuals. The imbalance of skills left great gaps in the vital support structure. For example, the Signal Corps survived with only 98 officers and 6,766 men who had to be reorganized into new regular units as they arrived from India. With the exception of the few schools and training centres described earlier, the army had to create its training establishment from scratch with the small Muslim elements of the India-based schools. The most immediately dangerous element of the reconstitution effort was the almost complete loss of ordnance stores and other supplies. This shortfall was eventually eased by emergency purchases overseas. The most potentially dangerous long-term element was the loss of all ordnance production factories and machinery. The Union of India would not agree to divide these assets but provided monetary compensation amounting to less than 13 million dollars.

By 1951 the problems of Partition had settled down. Under the direction of General Mohammad Ayub Khan, the first Pakistani Commander-in-Chief, operational planning and training were systematized and greatly improved. Much emphasis was placed on realistic training, especially on the ability to operate without the lavish support that experience during the Second World War had taught many officers to expect. In 1954 a milestone was achieved with Exercise 'November Handicap' in which 50,000 troops were deployed. Despite the success of the exercise General Khan recognized that the army structure inherited from the British was out-of-date and inadequate for Pakistan's defence needs. In 1953 and later in 1955 a planning board was set up to determine a complete reorganization of the army. New ideas were encouraged on a positive and informal basis by the board which passed the word, 'If you have any time to waste, come and waste it here.' The board's efforts resulted in significant economies, vital to an army whose resources were slender, and equally significant increased efficiency in training, organization and effectiveness, all leading to improved morale. These reforms would provide the basis of the future development of the Pakistan Army whose commander recognized that though Pakistan could not meet the physical resources of India, his army, at least, could match its battlefield efficiency.[131]

VIETNAM

PEOPLE'S ARMY OF VIETNAM (PAVN)

The People's Army of Vietnam (PAVN) has the distinction of having seen more combat than any other army since 1945. In fact its history has been one of practically continuous fighting. During its short existence it has defeated two major Western armies, one on the battlefield and the other on the home front, given the Chinese People's Liberation Army a bloody nose, and driven Pol Pot's monsters from their bone-strewn lair in Cambodia. PAVN has justly swept up more laurels on the battlefield than any other army save the IDF and rightly earned the backhanded epithet of 'the Prussians of Asia'.

There is more truth in that title than might seem feasible at first glance. The Vietnamese are a small, delicately built people who do not appear to be the stuff of warriors, yet they are as truly one of the 'martial races' as were the Prussians. Douglas Pike draws a vivid portrait:

'The alarums and excursions of war echo like an endless drum-roll down the corridor of Vietnamese history. In vast and rhythmic cycles the Vietnamese experience for two thousand years has been invasion, siege, occupation, rebellion – interspersed with lesser moments of dissidence, covert militant opposition and other forms of social sabotage. Mentally the Vietnamese always have lived in an armed camp.'[132]

From its very beginning the PAVN was the child of the fledgling Vietnamese Communist Party and its creator, Ho Chi Minh. The womb that carried the child was the Vietminh united front of Vietnamese nationalists determined to expel the French colonial authority. Although the Party was only one element of the Vietminh, it was the decisive element and was eventually to place the military arm of the movement tightly under its control.

As early as 1940 the Vietminh were being trained in guerrilla warfare by the Chinese Nationalists in Kweilin, China. Under the guidance of Vo Nguyen Giap, the nucleus of a guerrilla force was established in a sanctuary zone just inside the Chinese border north of Hanoi in Cao Bang province. The caves of Cao Bang were to become part of the founding epic of Communist Vietnam and a national shrine, in emulation of the Mao Zedong's experience in the caves of Yennan.

By 1945 Giap had created the sound organizational structure for a military force built upon Ho's theoretical concepts of a vast mobilization of support among the Vietnamese people. Giap's Party Armed Propaganda Teams spread through the country with the slogan, 'Political action is more important than military action; propaganda is more important than fighting.' The drumbeat theme was the crash mobilization and motivation of the human resources. In May all the anti-French elements were united in a Vietnam Liberation Army, renamed in August the Vietnam National Defence Army, with Giap as commander-in-chief. In September Ho created a general staff for the new army. By the time the French returned to Indo-China in 1946, the army had grown to about 1,000 men in thirteen infantry companies. An attempt to oppose the French resulted in defeat, and the small army was driven into the hills.[133]

Within a year of this defeat Giap's genius as a military manager had increased the army to 60,000 men. He had incorporated experienced soldiers from the French Union Forces and the Japanese-controlled Nationalist Army. Equipment came initially from surrendered Japanese and captured French and American stocks. Later the Chinese PLA was to provide large amounts of weapons as well as training. The new army was renamed, for the last time, People's Army of Vietnam. Giap organized it in three segments: local militia units engaged in reconnaissance, logistics and battle reinforcements; regional forces engaged in day-to-day, low-level attacks and harassment of French forces; and the regulars employed in battles of strategic importance. In 1949 the first PAVN infantry division, the Vanguard Division, was formed. Five more 10,000-man divisions rapidly followed in 1950. The provision of artillery created 'heavy divisions' along the lines of Soviet artillery divisions for the PAVN. Many of these divisions were manned along ethnic or regional lines. By the end of the war in 1954 the PAVN numbered 380,000 including 120,000 regulars.[134]

The equipping of PAVN regular divisions is particularly interesting. By the beginning of 1952 they had been completely equipped with new PLA equipment as well as US equipment captured in Korea. The Vietminh would maintain the US weapons with spare parts and ammunition captured from the French who were also receiving US equipment. Frequently the Vietminh would be the recipients of US equipment manufactured in 1950–51 while the French were outfitted with similar items manufactured at the beginning of the Second World War. For example, the Communists were equipped with captured US 75mm recoilless rifles while the French had only the much less effective 57mm model.[135]

PAVN tasted first blood in October 1950 when they crushed the string of French posts along the Chinese border, employing fourteen regular and three artillery battalions. The French lost 6,000 men and abandoned enough stocks to equip another PAVN division in their greatest colonial catastrophe since Montcalm's regiments were shattered on the Plains of Abraham two centuries earlier. In January 1951 the PAVN went over to the offensive with 81 regular battalions. It was the set-piece battle the new French commander, General de Lattre de Tassigny, had been seeking and cost PAVN 6,000–9,000 dead outside Hanoi at the battle of Vinh-Yen. Giap profited from the lesson. Isolated French units were targeted for destruction, and the French were not to be given the opportunity to marshal the firepower meatgrinder that had been so successful at Vinh-Yen. Only in late 1953, with the siege of Dien Bien Phu, would Giap reverse this policy and accept decisive engagement, but under favourable strategic conditions that prevented the French from effectively deploying airpower and firepower.

Dien Bien Phu ranks with the PLA's defeat of the UN forces along the Yalu River as the premier battle of the first post-war decade. It marked the maturity of the PAVN as a first-class military organization able to compete successfully with one of the best armies in the world. PAVN success owed a great deal to Chinese training and equipment, but was based primarily on the ability of the Vietnamese to create, train and manage a complex military organization in the space of a few years, learn the arts of war, and execute them with a tactical and strategic finesse only equalled by their mentors, the Chinese. The PAVN had no technological superiority over the French, no airpower and no modern transportation or logistics system. What they had was a firm grasp of strategic realities, sound organization and motivation. They also had a keen grasp of the enemy's strengths and weaknesses, particularly the French tendency to under-estimate the enemy. Giap summarized this success:

> 'The (French) Expeditionary Corps was surprised because it did not believe that we would attack – and we attacked; and it was tactically surprised because we had succeeded in solving the problems of concentrating our troops, our artillery and our supplies... We did construct our supply roads; our soldiers knew well the art of camouflage, and we succeeded in getting our supplies through.'[136]

With the regrouping process called for in the peace accords, approximately 80,000–90,000 troops moved from the south to North Vietnam. Another 10,000 were left behind as a cadre for the eventual war of re-unification.[137]

THE VIETNAMESE NATIONAL ARMY (VNA)

The First Indo-China War was as much a Vietnamese civil war as a war against French colonialism. By 1954 the Vietminh were fighting more than 400,000 Vietnamese either in French uniform as part of the French Union Forces or of the fledgling Vietnamese National Army under the Bao Dai government. Founded with some promise by the French Marshal de Lattre de Tassigny in 1951, the Vietnamese National Army suffered from a fundamental morale problem, the lack of an inspiration to fight. The Vietminh fought for independence, but the VNA seemed to serve only the French and Bao Dai.[138]

For all that, the growth of the VNA from scratch was fairly rapid. By 1952 it had reached a strength of 80,000, and by 1953 had almost doubled to 150,000. However, this should be compared to the 200,000 Indo-Chinese troops serving with the French Union Forces in 1952. A military academy for Vietnamese officers had been started in 1949 and was beginning to provide officers at an increasing rate, though by the end of the war in 1954 only 2 per cent of the Vietnamese troops were officers. By 1954 most of the VNA's service schools and service commands had been created and were functioning. The VNA was able to field several of the Groupes Mobiles that had proven so effective for the French, had its own paratroops, marines and an embryo navy. A United States Military Advisory Group (MAAG) also arrived in July 1950, but the priority of the Korean War prevented any large-scale US armament of the VNA. Instead the Vietnamese received French castoffs which did little for an already fragile morale. As it was the VNA was badly under-equipped, completely lacking, for example, the recoilless rifles that the Vietminh had in plenty, and radios below battalion level.[139]

Nevertheless there were glints of steel through the tarnish. One third of the French garrison at Dien Bien Phu was Vietnamese, and of the 1,530 volunteers that parachuted into the dying fortress, almost 800 were Vietnamese.

CHINA

Surprise is a principle of war. When employed tactically in an ambush it is deadly to a small unit. When employed strategically it results in sudden reversals in the course of wars. Twice since the Second World War it has been used on the strategic plane with consummate skill. The second achievement was the crossing of the Suez Canal in October 1973 by the Egyptian Army. The first was the undetected movement of 250,000 Chinese troops across the Yalu River in late 1950. This attack was to shatter the UN forces and hurl them south by 1951.

In many ways the Chinese achievement was more arduous. Obstacles of terrain, weather and distance that did not challenge the Egyptian Army were overcome by the Chinese.[140] As an institution the PLA demonstrated a skilled and practised understanding of tactics, operations and strategy, the three levels of the art of war. Communist China had been in existence for barely a year and yet its army, although weak in a *matériel* sense, in many ways displayed the maturity of far older military organizations.

That army had emerged in 1945 with 21 years of accumulated combat experience, with a distinctly original and effective doctrine, a sound sense of institution, a system that guaranteed the morale and reliability of its members and a profound sense of purpose. Mao Zedong (Mao Tse-tung) was the animating genius of the PLA, a brilliant theoretician and strategist and man of practical action. It is not surprising that the PLA became his creation.

In moulding that creation, he had designed and created a training system for the leadership cadre of the PLA whose roots were to be found in the Soviet military academies, attended by members of the Chinese Communist Party, and the Whampoa Military Academy in the 1920s. He built on that experience by creating a system of schools, the *Kangda* (in its Chinese acronym) academy which had trained 100,000 leadership cadres by 1945. Training emphasized doctrine and strategy. Much of Mao's writings on warfare were prepared as lectures for the *Kangda*. These schools produced a leadership cadre '...with a military ethic that was distinctly different from Western armies and distinct even from its model, the Red Army of the Soviet Union', in its fiercely egalitarian sense.[141]

Another aspect of this military ethic, and one that permeated the entire organization, was the emphasis on the willing self-discipline that grew out of the PLA's long experience as essentially a guerrilla organization. Mao Zedong identified this sense of discipline as integral and essential to the decentralized nature of guerrilla warfare:

'A revolutionary army must have discipline that is established on a limited democratic basis. In all armies, obedience of the subordinates to their superiors must be exacted. This is true in the case of guerrilla discipline, but the basis for guerrilla discipline must be the individual conscience. With guerrillas, a discipline of compulsion is ineffective... (It) must be self-imposed, because only when it is, is the soldier able to understand completely why he fights and how he must obey. This type of discipline becomes a tower of strength within the army, and it is the only type that can truly harmonize the relationship that exists between officers and men.'[142]

The PLA aimed to build in miniature within itself the type of revolutionary society that was envisaged for the whole of China. The soldier was not merely trained but socialized too. Failing this, other methods of coercion were employed. The PLA intended that the basis of small group cohesion be distinctively that of political identification and loyalty animated with the zeal of a Crusade.[143]

This consistent emphasis on the human element reflected the fact that the PLA was making a virtue of necessity. Its enemies in the Kuomintang and the Japanese had always had a vast *matériel* superiority. Mao sought to counter that advantage with the fervour and skill of his human resources:

'Weapons are an important factor in war, but not the decisive factor; it is people, not things that are decisive. The contest of strength is not only a contest of military and economic power, but also a contest of human power and morale.'[144]

However original Mao's moulding of the human element, his employment of strategy was firmly founded in the Chinese military classics, particularly Sun Tzu's *The Art of War*. Much of what he said was either paraphrased or directly quoted from the old master of the fifth century BC, which as events continue to show, is probably the best distillation ever written of the immutable principles of war. He was especially fond of Sun Tzu's dictum: *Chih-ti, Chih-chi; Pai-chan, Pai-sheng* – 'Know the enemy and know yourself; in a hundred battles you will never be in peril'.[145] This sound appreciation for focusing on the enemy's weaknesses was inculcated in the PLA.

THE CIVIL WAR

By 1946 the PLA had grown into an army of 1,300,000 men with a militia reserve of 3–5,000,000. Although the Soviets turned over to the PLA large stocks of surrendered Japanese weapons, it remained largely a foot mobile, light infantry army sorely lacking in artillery, communications, logistics and transportation. By October 1948 the PLA was beginning to acquire the specialists in supporting arms that a more conventional army needed. PLA divisions were organized on a triangular basis, and strength now averaged 6,000. Small artillery divisions had been formed the year before, and the number was now increased by the swelling captures of Nationalist guns and the defection of their gunners. PLA commanders were quick to appreciate the value of the new arm which rapidly achieved proficiency. The infantry division also acquired a small but efficient unit of engineers. The PLA had even acquired a few tanks, though commanders were far less confident in their use than with artillery.[146]

In a series of decisive and skilful campaigns ending in 1949, the PLA destroyed the Nationalist Army and drove its remnant on to Formosa. The decisive battle of the Civil War was the Battle of Hsuchow which lasted from November 1948 until January 1949. The bewildered Nationalists lost 550,000 men as the PLA commanders manoeuvred skilfully around them on the battlefield. The PLA picked up a rich harvest from the battlefields of the Civil War, much of it the lavish but wasted result of massive American military aid to the Nationalist Army of Chiang Kai-shek: 319,000 light and heavy machine-guns, 54,400 artillery pieces, 1,000 tanks and armoured cars, 20,000 motor vehicles, 189 aircraft and the vast miscellany of equipment acquired by armies.[147]

With victory came a decision to remodel the PLA into a copy of the Soviet Army. The final strength of the PLA at the end of the Civil War was in excess of 5,000,000. A major demobilization released large numbers of the less reliable and left a hard core of experienced dependable troops. Under the terms of the 1950 treaty of mutual assistance, Stalin provided 3,000 Soviet Army advisers and technicians to modernize the PLA along conventional lines. In the short time available before the outbreak of the Korean War, the Soviets achieved some solid accomplishments in improving infantry, armour, artillery, engineers and transportation. They organized twelve-gun artillery battalions for many of the infantry divisions which were also increased in strength. Tank tactics and tank-infantry co-operation were taught. An officers' training establishment that included numerous academies and other facilities was begun as well as a centre for higher military studies.[148]

THE KOREAN WAR

The re-organization was incomplete when Chinese armies were sent into Korea under the guise of the Chinese Volunteer Army (CVA). The PLA massed 850,000 men in Manchuria; in three weeks ending in early November, General Lin Biao led 300,000 men in ten armies in secrecy across the border of the Yalu River into Korea. The subsequent defeat of General MacArthur's UN Command was set in motion by this great strategic deception and brilliantly executed by Lin Biao and half-frozen veterans. The UN defeat was confirmed by the faithful execution of Sun Tzu's admonition to strike weakness. What had been formulated in the Era of the Warring States in China *c*. 500 BC was to prove lethally effective in the Atomic Age. The PLA attacked the weaknesses of the UN Forces, not their strengths, using their foot mobility over terrain abandoned as too difficult by the enemy to envelop and isolate him. In the greater expanses of northern Korea, the PLA's ability to manoeuvre

67

around unsupported UN Forces, with certain notable exceptions[149] first demoralized them, then caused them to flee south. These tactics had worked well against the Nationalist Army. Now they worked equally well against the flawed US Army forces and the poorly trained and equipped South Koreans. But there was a difference this time – the firepower commanded by the Americans. The PLA discovered for the first time the truth of Pétain's dictum, 'Fire kills!'

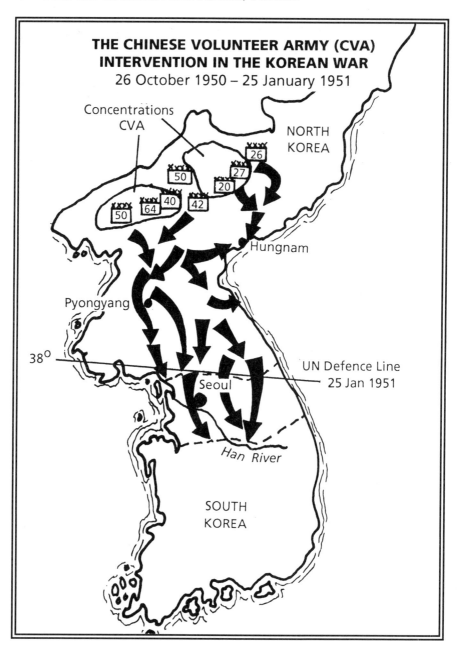

THE CHINESE VOLUNTEER ARMY (CVA)
INTERVENTION IN THE KOREAN WAR
26 October 1950 – 25 January 1951

The Chinese were stunned by the volume of fire that the enemy could call down upon them. Unlike the Nationalists, the Americans knew how to co-ordinate the delivery of massed machine-gun and artillery fire as well as air strikes and naval gunfire. The Chines were equally distressed by the immense losses among their hard-to-replace quality formations. It had been a Pyrrhic victory for the PLA; losses were so heavy that the Chinese could not pursue UN forces that managed to break contact. Operations could only continue with a fresh infusion of PLA divisions. As the war moved south to the narrows of the peninsula, it lost its mobile character and became even more a war of firepower and now one of position. The PLA was fixed under the lash of firepower which burned out its offensive capability and air strikes that crippled its logistics.

By now the PLA had also run into a new commander of the UN forces, General Mathew Ridgway, a general of the first rank who also understood *Chi-ti, Chih-chi; Pai-chan, Pai-sheng*. His leadership instilled new discipline and aggression into the US and ROK forces. The Chinese were forced to resort to the only resource in which they were rich – manpower. Mass attacks had to substitute for firepower and manoeuvre, but quickly lost their effectiveness. UN forces reported a new battlefield phenomenon, 'trigger fatigue'. 'The trigger finger became exhausted with killing, and ... men finished up by pulling the triggers with the third, fourth and little fingers.'[150] For the first time the PLA were fixed by a competent enemy at the company level, denied the ability to manoeuvre, and wilted under the storm of fire.

The experience was to have two long-term effects on the PLA. It immediately led to a downgrading in the fighting formations of the importance of the commissars. They had no ideological response to US firepower and no propaganda and mobilization role amid an alien population. Secondly, a concentration on the *matériel* aspect of war was seen as the only counter to the firestorm that was shredding the army's ability to fight. The beginning of truce talks in June 1951 gave the PLA a desperately needed respite and saved them from the inevitable consequences of inexorably effective UN offensives.

Despite this last-minute save, the performance of the PLA had been truly impressive. They had accomplished their mission in a major war with a great power, an epitaph any army would relish. Great efforts had been made to overcome matériel deficiencies, although the PLA would never be adequately equipped; Soviet equipment in relatively small amounts did not start to reach the PLA forces in Korea until August 1951, well after the major campaigns had been fought. The Chinese had diligently worked to increase the numbers of their artillery and showed a surprising talent for gunnery as to merit the professional respect of US Army artillerymen, a hard bunch to impress. Less bold was the PLA's use of Soviet-supplied tanks which were used primarily as mobile artillery support. The PLA's morale was undamaged, but it had gained a sobering appreciation of the realities of modern warfare. The butcher's bill had been more than 900,000 combat casualties and untold numbers from weather and disease. The experience served to confirm the Chinese in their decision to continue modernization on the Soviet model.

POST-WAR DEVELOPMENTS

For the first time in their history the PLA would have to transform itself into a peacetime army. Under the guidance of an increased Soviet military mission and with increasing amounts of Soviet equipment, the PLA would begin another major reorganization in 1954 aimed at modernization and take the first steps at mechanization. Conscription was introduced for the first time as well as the formal recognition of the existence of officers and fixed ranks. The creation of an increasingly traditional structure aroused the growing hostility of those who feared that they were set on the corrupt path of the Kuomintang in which machines would supplant men as the foundations of war, an unpalatable refutation of the PLA's origins and ideological lodestone.[151] This controversy would feed on itself with growing divisiveness for the next twenty years.

KOREA

In 1945 Korea suffered the fate of Germany, to be divided between the Soviet Union and the United States in separate zones of occupation. Unlike Germany, Korea had no strong, recent national military traditions or institutions to resurrect. Fifty years of Japanese occupation had erased most memory of the small and antiquated army of the old Korean kingdom. Neither did the Korean people have a strong martial outlook like the Vietnamese despite hard-fought and successful resistance to Chinese and Japanese conquests centuries before. Each half of the divided land would begin to build a modern army in the model of its mentor and establish the martial traditions of a stubborn nation in a war of epic ferocity.

NORTH KOREA

The North Korean People's Army (KPA) was born out of the loveless marriage of two Korean Communist organizations after the Second World War. One group, the *Kapsen Ban* (*ban* is defined as a power-holding group) was led by Kim Il Sung and was Soviet-sponsored and trained. Kim had been an anti-Japanese Communist guerrilla forced to seek refuge in the Soviet Union where he joined the Soviet Army, fought at Stalingrad and was decorated for valour. The second group, the *Yenan Ban*, also known as the Korean Volunteer Army (KVA), was trained and supported by the Chinese PLA and was largely recruited from ethnic Koreans living in Manchuria. The KVA functioned as an integral part of the PLA in the wars against the Japanese and the Chinese Nationalists.[152]

Each group not only reflected the interests of its sponsor but also its concepts of war. The *Kapsen Ban* was trained in the Soviet styles of conventional and partisan warfare. The *Yenan Ban* concentrated, in the spirit of Mao Tse-tung, on the mobile guerrilla warfare learned in long years of fighting during the Second World War and the Chinese Civil War as part of the PLA. Needless to say, the Soviet occupation authorities clearly favoured the *Kapsan Ban* forces by providing them with immediate access to their zone of occupation to establish their organization. KVA forces that attempted to enter Korea from Manchuria were given the choice by the Soviets of being disarmed or returning to assist the PLA in the Chinese Civil War. Kim Il Sung's cadres were able to secure an advantage which they would never lose.

In the late spring of 1946 the Soviet occupation authorities began assembling the cadres for the new army of a Communist Korea. Initially disguised as a constabulary called the Korean Preservation Corps, the army would be renamed the Korean People's Army (KPA) and officially recognized on 8 February 1948, seven months before the establishment of the North Korean state. The KPA was a large baby, numbering 60,000 on the date of its birth. Training centres staffed by Soviet officers were established in North Korea for Korean veterans of the Soviet Army and KVA.[153] Between 1945 and 1948, 10,000 Koreans were to receive military training in the Soviet Union. By June 1950, 3,000 Soviet officers were training and advising the KPA with as many as fifteen officers serving on the staff of each Korean division. By then the KPA had been increased to at least 135,000 men and possibly as many as 200,000. The KPA was augmented by the Border Constabulary (BC), the military arm of the Communist internal security forces. They were trained and equipped as light infantry with mortars and anti-tank guns, organized into five brigades and totalled more than 18,000 men.[154]

Following the departure of Soviet occupation forces from North Korea in 1948, the Soviets stepped up training and equipment deliveries to the KPA. Organization and doctrine were modelled on the Soviet Army. The force structure that emerged from this intensive process included eight full-strength infantry divisions, two at half-strength, and an armoured brigade. Divisional strength totalled 89,000 men.[155] The infantry divisions were triangular, numbering about 10,000 men at full strength; Second World War artillery was lavishly supplied – 44 guns including twelve self-propelled guns. In contrast, the ROK Army's table of organization for a fully equipped division called for only twelve guns. Tanks were the sturdy T-34/85, with 120 in the armoured brigade and 30 more in one of the infantry divisions. The ROK Army had no tanks.[156]

Both the Soviets and the Chinese actively prepared the KPA for invasion of the South. In the spring of 1950 the Soviets made very large deliveries of weapons and supplies and put each KPA division one at a time through a rigorous training course across the border in the Soviet Union. The Chinese released large numbers of ethnic Koreans from PLA units to join the KPA; in effect they were just transferred from one flag to another. Such was this contribution, in addition to veterans from the KVA, that five infantry divisions and the armoured brigade were especially well-trained and manned with large numbers of experienced troops. A total of 40,000 men were veterans of the KVA and PLA, and 10,000 were either Soviet veterans or had been trained as officers and technicians by the Soviets.[157]

Table 1-9. Ethnic Korean Units of the PLA Transferred to the KPA

PLA	becomes	KPA
164th Division (3 inf regts)		5th Division
166th Division (10,000 men)		6th Division
139th, 140th, 141st, 156th Divisions		7th Division
Other PLA Units		1 Regt of 1st Division
Other PLA Units		1 Regt of 4th Division

Upon arrival in North Korea, all PLA veterans were re-equipped with KPA uniforms and Soviet weapons, and were retrained in Soviet conventional tactics.[158]

Well trained, well equipped and experienced, the KPA attacked South Korea on 25 June 1951 in what it would call the Fatherland Liberation War. After several weeks the lighter ROK Army collapsed and the KPA went on to maul the US 24th Infantry Division. The victorious rush south soon became plagued by the inability of the KPA's logistics system to support mobile operations in the face of increasingly effective resistance by escalating US forces, particularly the deployment of airpower. By the time the KPA had penned US and South Korean forces inside the Pusan Perimeter, casualties had reduced the combat strength of the fighting divisions from 89,000 to 58,000 men. Conscription of peasants in the north and south was to keep strength at 100,000 but at diminishing levels of effectiveness and reliability. The landing of US forces at Inchon forced the withdrawal of the KPA which turned into a rout as whole divisions disintegrated. Perhaps as few as 25,000 men would actually escape across the 38th Parallel.[159]

71

The ruin of the KPA was completed as UN forces chased its shrinking remnant north to the Chinese border. Only the surprise intervention of the PLA saved KPA survivors from seeking refuge in China and the Soviet Union. So thorough had the decimation of the KPA been that they would play only a minor part in the remaining three years of the war, the brunt of which would be borne by the PLA. During that time the KPA was 'rebuilt from the ground up'. China trained the personnel and the Soviet Union re-equipped them. By July 1951 strength had reached 210,000, and the KPA was regaining some of their edge as evidenced by several well-fought engagements. Nevertheless the PLA relegated them to a relatively inac-

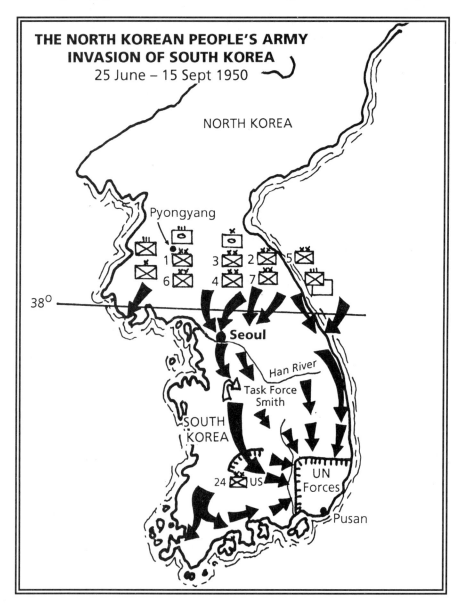

THE NORTH KOREAN PEOPLE'S ARMY
INVASION OF SOUTH KOREA
25 June – 15 Sept 1950

NORTH KOREA

Pyongyang

38°

Seoul

Han River

Task Force
Smith

SOUTH
KOREA

24 US

UN
Forces

Pusan

tive role as a general reserve, perhaps because of the horrendous losses among the cadres. American estimates of KPA dead for the entire war amounted to 500,000.[160]

A unique feature of the KPA from its inception was the emphasis on special operations in the enemy's rear, an understandable characteristic given that the army had sprung from two guerrilla movements. Tension between the *Kapsen Ban* and *Yenan Ban* was evident as special operations units tended to conduct operations according to the experience of their individual commanders who had been schooled in Soviet partisan operations or in the PLA's guerrilla warfare. As Kim Il Sung's shattered forces attempted to rebuild themselves, the *Yenan Ban* seized the ascendancy within the KPA and modelled their considerable special operations behind UN lines on Chinese techniques and doctrine. That dominance lasted only as long as the war. With the superior organizational skills of the *Kapsen Ban*, Kim Il Sung fixed blame for the defeat on the Yenanites and began the purge that would culminate in his complete control of the KPA by 1958.[161]

SOUTH KOREA

The Republic of Korea (ROK) Army also had its origins in the post-war occupation of Korea. US forces had formed a constabulary in January 1946 with the intention of supplementing the normal police structure in the maintenance of internal security. The organization grew slowly to 5,000 men over the next sixteen months. Initial training and support by the US Army was limited, and the constabulary, armed only with light Japanese weapons, were forced to rely on experience gained in the Japanese and Chinese armies. Despite a tendency to launch Banzai attacks on enemy positions, this experience had its positive side. 'They were not bound by road nets, nor did they expect much in the way of organic transportation; the Japanese- and Chinese-trained officers were satisfied with horses and human carriers. In the rugged Korean terrain this attitude was important.'[162]

The growth of North Korean forces and the imminent departure of the US occupation forces in 1948 prompted the South Korean administration to begin planning for armed forces to ensure internal security and protect the borders of the independent state. While MacArthur hesitated to recommend the transformation of the constabulary into an army, the South Koreans had quietly increased its strength to 50,000 men by March 1948. Six months after the KPA was officially recognized, the South Korean constabulary became the ROK Army in August 1948.

The new army was severely tested in October when Communist elements of the 14th Infantry Regiment instigated a mutiny and spread insurrection in surrounding areas. The ROK Army suppressed the mutiny and gained valuable experience in the deployment of fairly large formations.

In January 1949 it had been increased to 60,000 men who were equipped by the United States with smallarms and mortars. By the time of the KPA's attack in late June 1950, the ROK Army had increased to 98,000 men, 66,000 of whom were in eight infantry divisions. Although their order-of-battle matched that of the KPA in number of divisions, the South Korean force was far weaker as shown in Table 1-10. The divisions were only formed in the very month of the KPA attack.

Table 1-10. Fighting Strengths of the Two Korean Armies, June 1950

KPA		ROK Army	
1st Division	11,000	1st Inf Division	9,715
2nd Division	10,838	2nd Inf Division	7,910
3rd Division	11,000	3rd Inf Division	7,059

KPA		ROK Army	
4th Division	11,000	5th Inf Division	7,276
5th Division	11,000	6th Inf Division	9,112
6th Division	11,000	7th Inf Division	9,698
7th Division	12,000	8th Inf Division	6,866
10th Division	6,000	Capital Inf Division	9,561
13th Division	6,000		
15th Division	11,000		
12th Regiment	2,000		
766th Regiment	3,000		
105th Tank Bde	6,000		
BC 1st Brigade	5,000		
BC 2nd Brigade	2,600		
BC 3rd Brigade	4,000		
BC 5th Brigade	3,000		
BC 7th Brigade	4,000		
Total KPA	130,438	Total ROK	64,697

Only five of the divisions had three regiments; the remaining three had only two regiments. Only four divisions were near their authorized strength of 10,000. Only the four divisions stationed along the 38th Parallel and the Capital Division in Seoul were fully equipped with US weapons. However, their authorizations included only one 15-gun artillery battalion per division. These 105mm M3 howitzers were out-ranged by the KPA divisional artillery of 44 guns. The ROK Army had no tanks, no medium artillery, no 4.2in mortars, no recoilless rifles and no air support. The remaining three divisions were armed with mostly Japanese light weapons and were engaged in counter-guerrilla operations far south of the 38th Parallel. Ammunition stocks would be exhausted in a few days of combat, and the initial stocks of spare parts provided to the ROK Army had already been exhausted before the invasion.[163]

> 'While the United States in 1946 was hedging about the terms national defense and internal security in South Korea, the Communists were sending thousands of North Koreans to the USSR for specialized training. While a handful of US military advisors were nursing the South Korean Constabulary through the years 1946–49, each North Korean division trained under scores of Soviet advisors. Where South Korean armament was limited to a few light howitzers and armored cars, with no combat aircraft or tanks, the North Korean forces boasted fighter planes, medium armor, and artillery of far greater range than that employed by the Republic of Korea forces.'[164]

The KPA smashed the ROK Army in a few weeks, inflicting losses of 40,000 men and 70 per cent of equipment. Upon entering the war, the US Army intended to rebuild the ROK Army quickly; it was done too quickly. The divisions that crossed the 38th Pparallel in October were still poorly trained and equipped. They received the special attention of the PLA in its November and December offensive and again crumbled under the same pressure that also shattered better equipped and led US Army units.[165]

By the middle of 1951 the US Army had embarked on a comprehensive and thorough rebuilding programme for the ROK Army and eventually increased the strength of the Korean Military Advisory Group (KMAG) to 1,800 men. The first phase emphasized a great expansion of the military school and training centre system in order to train the cadres and specialists. Military schools closed by the invasion were re-opened. The Korean Military Academy re-opened on a West Point model; the Korean Command and General Staff College also re-opened to begin training senior officers. Particular emphasis was given to officer training and leadership.[111][86] The second phase concentrated on the refitting and retraining of the ROK divisions. Each was rotated out of combat and given a 5–9-week intensive refresher course. To provide the fire support so conspicuously lacking earlier, the amount of artillery authorized for each division was increased from one battalion to four, and tank companies were introduced.

The last phase involved the expansion of the army to 20 divisions. In 1952 ROK strength had increased to 250,000. By the war's end in 1953, sixteen divisions were in the field amounting to 75 per cent of front-line UN forces. Some of the last major Chinese attacks of the war were directed against the reorganized ROK Army in the summer of 1953. The South Koreans initially gave ground in a disciplined manner and then counter-attacked. The army had come of age. Although problems remained in leadership and ability to handle complex operations, the intensive training, increased discipline and professionalism had paid off. So well had the training foundations been laid that within a year of the end of the war, the ROK Army could be expanded to 650,000 men.[167]

JAPAN

The ruin of Japan in the Second World War had also thoroughly ruined the reputation of the disbanded Imperial Japanese Army in the eyes of the Japanese people. Only in West Germany was such a deep martial tradition so completely rejected by the nation.

So great was the revulsion against the very concept of soldiering and war that the post-war constitution even renounced 'war as a sovereign right of the nation and the threat of the use of force as a means of settling international disputes'. In an excess of idealism this was even taken to imply the inadmissability of self-defence by many Japanese despite General MacArthur's protestation that the constitution 'by no sophistry of reasoning could be interpreted as a complete negation of the inalienable right of self-defense against an unprovoked attack'.[168] This tension between idealism and reality was to become a permanent fixture in the relationship between Japan's new army and a large segment of the nation.

The Japanese government, however, had determined that Japan's long-term strategic interests in light of the deepening Cold War lay in a mutual security arrangement with the United States. Prime Minister Yoshida believed that the Soviet Union would attempt to break Japan away from its growing identification with the West by instigating labour unrest and even insurrection, a serious threat in light of the considerable Communist-inspired labour violence at the time. Further pressure on Japan was foreseen as a Soviet threat to invade Japan's northernmost main island, Hokkaido. To rely entirely upon American arms to ensure Japanese internal and external security would be intolerable for Japan's future. Yoshida envisaged a mutual defence agreement which included the creation of a paramilitary centralized police force to ensure internal security and the stationing of US troops in Japan to ensure external security. In 1947 he proposed such an arrangement to the United States.

The US government and General MacArthur, Supreme Commander Allied Forces, were very comfortable with the current arrangement and showed no interest – until the outbreak of the Korean War upset US security arrangements in the Far East. The almost immediate transfer of 75,000 men of the US Eighth Army to Korea prompted MacArthur to authorize the creation of a National Police Reserve (NPR) of 75,000 men to 'cope with internally fomented Communist insurrection'.[169] Initially recruiting was limited to men with no prior active military service so as to avoid any taint with the dead Imperial Japanese Army. At first only IJA reserve officers were permitted to apply for commissions, but so few recruits came forward that this restriction was dropped, and the NPR quickly reached its allocation by the enlistment of many old army veterans.

Now the United States was even eager for the creation of Japanese military forces far beyond anything that Japan's economy or public opinion would bear. In January 1951, during the talks on new security arrangements, the US Secretary of State stated that he expected Japan to create a 300,000-man army in order to look to its own defence. Yoshida refused but supported a compromise which led to the formal recognition of the NPR with both an internal and external security mission. The NPR was then reorganized in 1952 under the new name of the National Safety Force (NSF) and increased to 100,000 men. It was equipped with surplus US Second World War era equipment (light weapons to include machine-guns, mortars, recoilless rifles and halftracks) and quickly deployed to Hokkaido to replace the US 1st Cavalry Division which was sent to Korea.[170]

In 1954 the new Japanese army was formally acknowledged in law by the Diet with the passing of the Defence Agency Establishment Law and the Self-Defence Forces Law. This legislation created a ministry of defence, the Japan Defence Agency, and its subordinate Self-Defence Force which included three services: the Ground Self-Defence Force (GSDF), Maritime Self-Defence Force (MSDF), and the Air Self-Defence Force (ASDF). The awkwardness of these names showed the still tenuous nature of national acceptance of the armed forces. The new Japanese army was not even allowed to call itself an army or be described as a military organization as this might imply that it was not solely for 'defence'. There was a definite design to mark a complete break with the Imperial army; martial traditions and customs were not revived, and in the most symbolic gesture of all, the sword, for the first time in Japanese history, was forbidden as a military symbol or article of dress. From the moment of its birth, the GSDF would learn to walk on eggshells.

AUSTRALIA

Few nations breed more aggressive and natural fighting men than Australia. Yet, even more than their American cousins, the Australians are the first to scorn the profession of arms in peacetime. After the Second World War Australia quickly dismantled its veteran army in which 727,000 men had served out of a population of barely seven millions. Almost one-third, 219,000 men, had become casualties. According to the 1947 5-year defence plan, it was intended that the 6-division force fielded during the war be shrunk to a 19,000-man Australian Regular Army of which the main fighting element would be a single brigade group of three infantry battalions and a small armoured force. At the same time, the organized reserves upon which Australia had traditionally relied was renamed the Civilian Military Force (CMF) and, like the Australian Regular Army (ARA), recruited on a volunteer basis.[171]

The regular brigade was a sharp break with Australian traditions, being the first establishment of regular combat forces in peacetime. After the First World War a small, regular establishment of 1,536 men had been retained to train the reserve forces and conduct planning. The new regular infantry units were designated 1st, 2nd and 3rd Battalions, Royal Australian Regiment (RAR). Unfortunately, by 1949 the brigade group's strength was barely 1,000 of the 3,000 infantrymen authorized. The government's refusal to improve pay and housing crippled recruiting. Equipment consisted of increasingly obsolete Second World War stocks. A further burden on the tiny regular force was the training requirements for the conscripts assigned to the Civilian Military Force reserve structure who underwent an all too brief period of training. The military value of the CMF was nil because Australian law permitted only volunteers to be assigned outside Australian borders.

THE KOREAN WAR

The Communist invasion of South Korea on 25 June 1950 glaringly illuminated Australia's military deficiencies. When called upon to contribute ground forces to resist aggression, Australia could only offer the single half-strength battalion (3 RAR) on occupation duty in Japan. So in need of training, numbers and equipment was this battalion, that it was not immediately committed to action, sparing the Australians the humiliation suffered by the Americans' Task Force Smith which had also arrived straight from the same soft and carefree occupation duty. The 3 RAR was only brought up to strength by stripping its two Australia-based sister battalions and by special recruiting. After intense training and re-equipping, 3 RAR was sent to Korea in late September to be brigaded with the British 27 Brigade, later to be dubbed the Commonwealth Brigade. They arrived in time to join the pursuit of the North Koreans in flight from the dislocation of their strategy by the Inchon landings. The Australians were often in the van of the pursuit up the eastern side of the peninsula. As the Chinese intervention reversed the fortunes of war, the Australians often found themselves the rearguard, a recognition of their steadiness and professionalism when so many other UN forces were dissolving in rout. In April 1951, when the UN lines stabilized south of Seoul, the Commonwealth Brigade fought its most decisive action when it crippled an attacking Chinese division at the Battle of Kapyong and frustrated the enemy's 5th Phase Offensive to drive the UN Command back into a coastal enclave.

American demands for a greater Australian commitment of ground forces finally forced the Australian government to dispatch a second battalion (1 RAR). Bringing the original 3 RAR up to strength during the previous year had badly strained the army's resources. Only by further stripping 2 RAR and by recruiting in Britain could 1 RAR be filled out and sent in March 1952. The crisis of the war had caused the government to reintroduce a limited form of conscription, but it did little good for the RAR. National Servicemen were not liable for duty outside Australia. Despite the penury of their government, the Australian regulars maintained and burnished the nation's martial traditions. For an army of barely three paper battalions in 1950, Korea had been a very heavy commitment. Between 1950 and 1955, 10,657 men of the regular Australian Army served in Korea and suffered 1,526 casualties that included 276 KIA and seventeen other deaths, 1,210 wounded and 23 POWs.[172]

THE ART OF STRATEGY

If strategy is 'the art of distributing and applying the military means to fulfill the ends of policy' as defined by Liddell Hart, one must ask how successfully did the major armies of the world perform this mission in the ultimate testing ground of war? Within in this question, certainly is the relation of policy to the practicable.

A mixture of post-war force reductions and retrenchments and the advent of the Atomic Bomb were massive complications for most of the established armies of the world. Perhaps the British Army in its long but orderly rearguard action at the end of empire performed the best. Here policy was practicable, if only barely keeping ahead of cheese-paring economics. For the French who would not relinquish empire there was a gulf between the means available to the French Army and the policy. The bloodbath of the First Indochina War resulted. The US Army suffered from being ignored to the point of irrelevance by policy that relied more and more on the Atomic Bomb. The result was the near catastrophe in Korea. The army that had become the faintest shadow of its might of half a decade before was found wanting in the most elemental military means.

Among a number of states freed from colonialism such as Egypt, Syria, Pakistan, and India, relatively stable military structures evolved at first. None of them had been born in the evolutionary supercharger of revolution. The first two would stumble at first because gap between policy and the practicable was masked by an abiding institutional corruption that quickly revealed itself in the stress of war. The armies of India and Pakistan were far more healthy institutions that luckily did not undergo that stress of war in this decade of restructuring.

The strategies of the armies of a group of new states were generally successful because they bore a close relationship between the military means at hand and the practicable. Israel in its war of independence, North Vietnam in the First Indochina War, and China in its Civil War were uniformly successful in the development and application of military strategies to fulfill policy. interestingly, all of these armies developed in revolutionary contexts which emphasized the strengths of man over machine. Unlike the older, established armies, they exhibited a healthy and dynamic sense of adaptability and were highly receptive to new ideas. Of these new armies, only China approached a breakdown between means and policy. Its initial entry into the Korean War had been masterful and fulfilled the traditional Chinese policies of limited defensive forays beyond its borders. Once locked into a war of attrition against an entirely new kind of enemy that had relearned the rules of modern war, Chinese military means based on revolutionary war barely escaped a severe defeat.

NOTES

1   Omar N. Bradley and Clair Blair, *A General's Life.* (New York: Simon and Schuster, 1983), p. 474
2   John C. Sparrows, *History of Personnel Demobilization in the United States Army*, DA Pamphlet 20-210. (Washington, DC: Department of the Army, 1952), p. 265.
3   Sparrows, ibid., pp.268–273.
4   Ibid., pp. 271–74.
5   Omar Bradley, July 1949, cited in a *Military Review*, July 1949, p. 49.
6   Ibid.
7   *Remarks by the Secretary of Defense at the National Preparedness Orientation Conference, 30 Nov 50*, cited in Sparrow, ibid., p. 283.
8   Russell F. Weigley, *History of the United States Army*.(Bloomington, IL: University of Illinois Press, 1984), pp. 497–502.
9   Robert A. Doughty, *The Evolution of US Army Tactical Doctrine, 1946–1976* (Fort Leavenworth, KS: Combat Studies Institute, US Army Command and General Staff College, 1979), pp. 2–3.
10 Doughty, ibid., pp. 4–5.
11 Foss, Christopher F., *Jane's World Fighting Vehicles* (New York: St. Martin's Press, 1976), p. 306.
12 James F. Schnabel, *United States Policy in the Korean War, Policy and Direction: The First Year* (Washington, DC: Officer of the Chief of Military History, 1972), pp. 45–6.
13 Weigley, ibid., p. 503; Matloff, ibid., p. 542.
14 Weigley, op. cit., p. 503.
15 Schnabel, op. cit., p. 54.

16   Roy K. Flint, 'Task Force Smith and the 24th Division,' in Eds., Charles E. Heller and William Stofft, *America's First Battles* (Lawrence, KS: University Press of Kansas, 1986), p 274.

17   Doughty, op. cit., p. 12.

18   Jack J. Wagstaff, 'The Army's Preparation for Atomic Warfare,' *Military Review*, May 1955, pp. 5–6.

19   Doughty, op. cit., pp. 13–4.

20   Dwight D. Eisenhower, *Mandate for Change, 1953–1956: The White House Years* (Garden City, NY: Doubleday & Co., 1963), pp. 447, 451.

21   Eisenhower, ibid., p. 453.

22   A. J. Bacevitch, *The Pentomic Era: The U.S. Army Between Korea and Vietnam* (Washington, DC: National Defense University, 1986), pp. 20–1.

23   John H. Cushman, 'What is the Army's Story,' *The Army Combat Forces Journal* 5 (October 1955), p. 49.

24   Terry Gander, *Encyclopedia of the Modern British Army* (Cambridge: Patrick Stephens, 1982) p. 12.

25   Gregory Blaxland, *The Regiments Depart: A History of the British Army 1945–1970* (London: William Kimber, 1971) p. 19.

26   Ibid., pp. 21–2.

27   Bryon Falwell, *The Gurkhas* (New York: W.W. Norton & Co., 1984) pp. 250–54.

28   Correlli Barnett, *Britain and Her Army, 1509–1970* (New York: William Morrow and Co., 1970), p. 481.

29   Gregory Blaxland, *The Regiments Depart: A History of the British Army 1945–1970* (London: William Kimber, 1971) pp. 73–115; and Richard L. Clutterback, 'Communist Defeat in Malaya: A Case Study, *Military Review*, September 1963, pp. 63–64.

30   Blaxland, ibid., p. 81.

31   Tony Geraghty, *This is the SAS: A Pictorial History of the Special Air Service Regiment* (London: Arms & Armour Press and New York: Arco Publishing Inc., 1982) pp. 40–41.

32   Blaxland, op. cit., pp. 136–7.

33   Blaxland, op. cit., pp. 172–8.

34   General Sir George Erskine, 'Kenya – Mau Mau,' *Journal of the Royal United Service Institution*, November 1955, p. 14.

35   Christopher F. Foss, *Jane's World Armored Fighting Vehicles* (New York: St. Martin's Press, 1976), pp. 43–44, 243.

36   Special Correspondent, 'A Visit to the B.A.O.R.,' *The Fighting Forces*, January 1950, p. 222.

37   Richard M. Ogorkiewicz, 'British Armored Divisions,' *Military Review*, October 1958, p. 84; digested from *Revue Militare Generale*, February 1958.

38   Major Gerald Whitely, 'The British Experience of Peacetime Conscription,' *The Army Quarterly and Defense Journal*, July 1987, p. 321.

39   'Army Notes,' *Journal of the Royal United Service Institution*, May 1955, p. 3126.

40   H. B. Martin, 'The Army and the Crisis,' *The Fighting Forces*, December 1948, pp. 230–3.

41   Nigel Hamilton, *Monty: Final Years of the Field Marshal* (New York: McGraw-Hill Book Co., 1986) p. 671.

42   Blaxland, op. cit., pp. 6–9.

43   Blaxland, op. cit., p. 212.

44   'France and the Union of West Europe,' *Military Review*, March 1949, pp. 73–76; digested from the *Irish Defence Journal* (Eire), October 1948.

45   Paul-Marie de la Gorce, *The French Army: A Military and Political History* (New York: George Braziller, 1963), pp. 352–3.

46   Donn A. Starry, '*La Guerre Revolutionnaire*,' *Military Review*, February 1967, pp. 61–3.

47   George Armstrong Kelly, *Lost Soldiers: The French Army and Empire in Crisis, 1947–1962* (Cambridge, MA: The M.I.T. Press, 1965), p. 10.

48   Colonel Nemo, 'La guerre dans le milieu social.' *Revue de Defense Nationale*, May 1956, p. 606., cited in Kelly, ibid.

49   Marshall Andrews in forward to Bernard Falls, *Street Without Joy* (Harrisburg, PA: The Stackpole Co., 1967), p. 11.

50   De La Gorce, op. cit., pp. 376–7; Bernard Fall, *Street Without Joy* (Harrisburg, PA: The Stackpole Co., 1967), pp. 17, 45.

51   Geoffrey Bocca, *La Legion* (New York: Thomas Y. Crowell Co., 1964) p. 165; and Fall, op. cit., p. 269.

52   Kelly, op. cit., pp. 90–3.

53   Geoffrey Bocca, op. cit., 1964.

54   Nigel Thomas and Peter Abbot, *The Korean War 1950–53* (London: Osprey Publishing, 1986) p. 22.

55   Stalin was not entirely cheated of his suggestion; most of the 2,000,000 German POWs held by the Soviets in 1945 were worked to death in the next ten years.

56   Thomas M. Forster, *The East German Army: The Second Power in the Warsaw Pact* (London: George Allen & Unwin LTD, 1980) p. 20.

57   'The East German Army,' *Military Review*, April 1962, p. 22; digested from *Soldat und Technique*, February 1962.

58   Ibid., pp. 22–6.

59   Forster, *The East German Army: A Pattern of a Communist Military Establishment* (London: George Allen & Unwin, 1967), p. 26.

60   Walter Henry Nelson, *Germany Rearmed* (New York: Simon and Schuster, 1972), pp. 31–2.

61   Nelson, ibid., p. 33.

62 The Soviets captured over 180,000 Polish officers and soldiers in 1939. Of the 14–15,000 officers, almost 5,000 were murdered by the NKVD in the Katyn Wood; most of the rest are believed to have been also murdered. It should be noted that of the total taken captive, the 75,000 that joined Anders' corps were almost all of the survivors.

63 *Voenno-istoricheskii zhurnal* (Moscow: July 1974), p. 63, cited in Ross Johnson, et al, East European Military Establishments: The Warsaw Pact Northern Tier (New York: Crane Russak, 1980).

64 Lezek K. Stachow, 'Poland,' in Gabriel, ed., *Fighting Armies: NATO and the Warsaw Pact*, (Westport, CT: Greenwood Press, 1983), p. 228.

65 Zdazislaw Stapor and Julian Kaszmarek, 'Fundamental Problems of the Polish People's armed forces in the years 1942–1975,' in Polish. *Wojskowy Przeglad Historyczny* (Military Review of History) no. 4 (74) (November–December 1975, p. 38; cited in Edmund Walendowski, *Combat Motivation of the Polish Forces* (New York: St. Martin's Press, 1988) p. 22.

66 Joachim Georg Goerlich, 'The Development of the Polish People's Army, *Military Review*, January 1967, pp. 31–2 (originally published in *Wehrkunde*).

67 M. Djilas, *Conversations with Stalin* (London: Rupert Hart–Davis, 1962), p. 106.

68 Edgar O'Ballance, *The Red Army* (London: Faber and Faber, 1964), p. 189.

69 S. M. Shtemenko, *The General Staff in the Years of the War*, (Moscow: Progress Publishers, 1973), p. 504.

70 M. V. Zakharov, ed., *50 Let Vooruzhennykh Sil SSR (Fifty Years of the Armed Forces USSR)* (Moscow: Voyenizdat, 1968), p. 464; cited in Harriet Fast Scott and William F. Scott, *Soviet Military Doctrine: Continuity, Formulation, and Dissemination.* Boulder, CO: Westview Press, p. 19.

71 O'Ballance, op. cit.

72 That figure was to be short-lived. As a result of the Berlin Blockade crisis and later the Korean War, Stalin began, in effect, a war mobilization that was to increase the size of armed forces to almost 5,763,000 men, a figure cited by Albert Seaton, *Stalin as Military Commander* (New York: Praeger Publishers, 1976), p. 268.

73 S. A. Tyushkevich, *The Soviet Armed Forces: A History of Their Organizational Development*, (Moscow: Voenizdat, 1978), pp. 371–2; Published under the auspices of the U.S. Air Force.

74 Albert Seaton and Joan Seaton, *The Soviet Army* (New York: The New Library, 1987), pp. 150–1.

75 Ibid., p. 388.

76 Ibid., pp. 388–9; Seaton, op. cit., pp. 152–154; and O'Ballance, op. cit., p. 191.

77 Seaton and Seaton, op. cit., pp. 152–6.

78 O'Ballance, op. cit., pp. 190–1.

79 Tyushkevich, op. cit., p. 193

80 Petro Grigorenko, *Memoirs.* (New York: W.W. Norton Co., 1982), p. 207.

81 P. A. Rotmistrov, 'Poslevoyennoye stroitel'stvo tankovykh voysk,' *Vremya i tanki (Time and Tanks)*, (Moscow: Voyenizdat, 1972) reproduced in *Selected Soviet Military Writings 1970–1975*, a selection of articles from the Soviet military press published under the auspices of the US Air Force, Washington, DC, 1976, pp. 250–51; and Tyushkevich, op. cit., p. 381.

82 Christopher F. Foss, *Jane's World Armoured Fighting Vehicles* (New York: St. Martin's Press, 1976), pp. 67, 100.

83 Tyushkevich, op. cit., pp. 378–81.

84 Leon Trotsky, *Stalin: An Appraisal of the Man and His Influence.* (New York: Harper & Brothers Publishers, 1941), pp. 393–4.

85 Otto Preston Chaney, Jr. *Zhukov* (Norman, OK: University of Oklahoma Press, 1971), p. 341.

86 O'Ballance, op. cit., pp. 192–3.

87 Roman Kokowicz, *The Soviet Military and the Communist Party* (Boulder, CO: Westview Press, 1985), p. 72.

88 Malcolm Mackintosh, *Juggernaut: A History of the Soviet Armed Forces* (New York: Macmillan Co., 1967), p. 276.

89 B. H. Liddell Hart, ed., *The Red Army* (New York: Harcourt, Brace and Co., 195?), p. 206.

90 Both quotations are cited by Harriet Fast Scott in her editor's comments to V. D. Sokolovskiy, *Soviet Military Strategy.* 3rd ed. (New York: Crane, Russak & Co., 1975), p. 118. Sokolovskiy's comment was contained in the 2nd edition but dropped in the 3rd. Pavlenko's statement was drawn from *The Military History Journal*, No. 6, 1967.

91 It is no wonder then that Soviet military historians refurbished the reputation of General Kutuzov who was credited with the same strategy of luring the enemy, Napoleon, deep into the country in order to destroy him.

92 William T. Lee and Richard F. Staar, *Soviet Military Policy Since World War II* (Stanford, CA: Hoover Institution Press, 1986) pp. 15–16.

93 Grigorenko, op. cit., p. 218.

94 Stalin in a notorious answer to a letter written by the Soviet military historian, Colonel E.A. Razin, in *Bolshevik*, Moscow, No. 3, February 1947, pp. 4–8.

95 Thomas J. Wolfe, *Soviet Power and Europe, 1945–1970.* (John Hopkins Press, 1970), p. 34.

96 Lee and Starr, ibid., p. 13.

97 Alexandros Papagos, *The Battle for Greece 1940–1941* (Athens: The J.M. Scazikis 'Alpha' Editions, 1949) pp. 358, 392.

98 G. C. Kiriakopoulos, *Ten Days to Destiny: The Battle for Crete* (New York: Franklin Watts, 1985) pp.

355, 358.

99   Edgar O'Ballance, *The Greek Civil War 1944–49* (New York: Frederick A. Praeger Publishers, 1966) p. 129.

100 O'Ballance, op. cit., pp. 130, 137.

101 Evangelos Averoff-Tossizza, *By Fire and Ax: The Communist Party and the Civil War in Greece, 1944–49* (New Rochelle, NY: Caratzas Brothers Publishers, 1978) p. 191.

102 O'Ballance, op. cit., pp. 187–8.

103 *The History of the United Nations Forces in the Korean War* (Seoul: The Ministry of National Defense, Republic of Korea, 1974) pp. 292–4.

104 Ibid., pp. 283–4.

105 Martin Levin and David Halevy, 'Israel,' in Richard A. Gabriel, ed., *Fighting Armies, Antagonists in the Middle East, A Combat Assessment* (Westport, CT: Greenwood Press, 1983), pp. 7–8.

106 Larry Collins and Dominique Lapierre, *O Jerusalem* (New York: Simon and Schuster, 1972), pp. 152–3, 392–3.

107 Yigal Allon, *The Making of Israel's Army* (New York: Universe Books, 1970), pp. 10–11.

108 Allon, ibid., pp. 36–7; and Charles Messenger, *The Blitzkrieg Story* (New York: Charles Scribner's Sons, 1976), p. 221.

109 Yigal Yadin cited in B.H. Liddell Hart, *Strategy* (New York: Frederick A. Praeger, Publisher, 1967), p. 397.

110 Allon, op. cit., Preface.

111 Allon, op. cit., pp. 64–65.

112 Allon, op. cit., p. 44.

113 Edward N. Luttwak and Daniel Horowitz, *The Israeli Army 1948–1973* (New York: Abt Books, 1983), pp. 82–3.

114 Ibid., pp. 76–7.

115 Ibid., pp. 102–3.

116 Shabtai Teveth, *The Tanks of Tammuz* (New York: The Viking Press, 1968), pp. 43–5.

117 Luttwak and Horowitz, op. cit., pp. 110–117.

118 John Laffin, *Arab Armies of the Middle East wars 1948–73*, (London: Osprey Publishing, 1987).

119 C. W. S. Brodsky, 'India and Pakistan,' in Richard A. Gabriel, ed., *Fighting Armies: Nonaligned, Third World, and Other Ground Armies – A Combat Assessment* (Westport, CT: Greenwood Press, 1983), p. 8; and Richard F. Nyrop, et al, *Area Handbook for Pakistan*, (Washington, DC: American University, 1975), p. 372.

120 V. Longer, *Red Coats to Olive Green: A History of the Indian Army 1600–1974* (Bombay: Allied Publishers, 1974), p. 216.

121 Fazal Muqeem Khan, *The Story of The Pakistan Army* (Karachi: Pakistan Branch, Oxford University Press, 1963), p. 29.

122 Khan, ibid., pp. 30, 51; and Nyrop, op. cit. The area of Pakistan provided half of the 1,000,000 British Indian Army volunteers to go overseas in the First World War, and one-third of all volunteers for service in the Second World War.

123 Khan, ibid., pp. 24–6.

124 Longer, op. cit., p. 274.

125 Longer, op. cit., pp. 284–5, 324–7.

126 Longer, op. cit., p. 330.

127 Longer, op. cit., pp. 333–339.

128 Nyrop, op. cit., p. 373.

129 Khan, op. cit., pp. 48–51.

130 Khan, op. cit., pp. 51–2.

131 Khan, op. cit., pp. 137–148.

132 Douglas Pike, *PAVN: People's Army of Vietnam* (Novato, CA: Presidio Press, 1986), p. 9. The Vietnamese have not always been victims. In their drive south they exterminated the Cham kingdom and drove the Cambodians from the Mekong Delta during the Middle Ages.

133 Ibid., pp. 32–3.

134 Bernard Fall, *Street Without Joy* (Harrisburg, PA: Stackpole Co., 1964), pp. 32–3; Pike, op. cit., pp. 39–40.

135 Fall, op. cit., pp. 55–6.

136 Ibid., p. 106.

137 Daniel F. O'Brien, 'Vietnam,' in Richard A. Gabriel, *Fighting Armies – Nonaligned, Third World, and Other Ground Armies: A Combat Assessment* (Westport, CT: Greenwood Press, 1983), p. 56; Pike, op. cit., p. 41.

138 Phillip B. Davidson, *Vietnam at War: The History 1946–1975* (Novato, CA: Presidio Press, 1988) p. 16.

139 Bernard Fall, *The Two Vietnams: A Political and Military Analysis* (New York: Frederick A. Praeger Publishers, 1967) pp. 219–220.

140 This is not to denigrate the achievement of the Egyptian Army which, unlike the Chinese, had to achieve surprise against an enemy with which they were in contact behind a formidable well-prepared fortification not to mention the primary obstacle of the Suez Canal.

141 Paul H. B. Goodwin, *The Chinese Communist Armed Forces* (Maxwell Air Force Base, AL: Air University Press, 1988), p. 14.

142   Alexander L. George, *The Chinese Communist Army in Action: The Korean War and its Aftermath* (New York: Columbia University Press, 1967), p. 25.
143   Ibid., pp. 26–7.
144   Mao Tse-tung, 'On Protracted War,' *Selected Military Writings* (1938), p. 217
145   Samuel B. Griffith, II, *The Chinese People's Liberation Army* (New York: McGraw-Hill Book Co., 1967) p. 83.
146   Edgar O'Ballance, *The Red Army of China: A Short History* (New York: Frederick A. Praeger, Publisher, 1963), pp. 169, 173.
147   Ibid., p. 103.
148   Gerald H. Corr, *The Chinese Red Army: Campaigns and Politics Since 1949* (New York: Schocken Books, 1974), pp. 75–6.
149   Significantly, Chinese tactics failed against the US 1st Marine Division in its anabasis from the Chosin Reservoir to the sea. The Marine Corps had suffered none of the peacetime softening that had crippled the Army.
150   Corr, op. cit., p. 89
151   Michael Carver, *Twentieth Century Warriors: The Development of the Major Military Nations in the Twentieth Century* (New York: Weidenfeld & Nicolson, 1987), pp. 420–1.
152   Joseph S. Bermudez, Jr., *North Korean Special Forces* (Coulsdon, Surrey: Jane's Publishing Co., Ltd., 1988), pp. 14–17.
153   Ibid.
154   Roy E. Appleton, *United States Army in the Korean War: South to the Naktong, North to the Yalu* (Washington, DC: Department of the Army, 1961), p. 8.
155   The armour brigade consisted of three tank regiments and one mechanized regiment and numbered 6,000 men. It was raised to the status of a division at the end of June upon the capture of Seoul.
156   Appleton, op. cit., pp. 10–1.
157   Fredrica M. Bunge, ed., *North Korea: A Country Study* (Washington, DC: The American University, 1981), p. 222.
158   Appleton, op. cit., pp. 10–11.
159   Larry Niksch, 'North Korea,' in Gabriel, ed., *Fighting Armies: Nonaligned, Third World*, op. cit., pp. 103–4.
160   Ibid., pp. 105–6; Bunge, ibid.
1681   Bermudez, op. cit., pp. 24–5.
162   Robert K. Sawyer, *Military Advisors in Korea: KMAG in Peace and War* (Washington, DC: Department of the Army, Office of the Chief of Military History, 1962), p. 25.
163   Appleton, op. cit., pp. 13–7. The Soviet 76mm gun in the KPA's divisions easily outranged the ROK Army's short-barrelled 105mm M3 gun by 14,000 to 8,200 yards.
164   Sawyer, op. cit., p. 106.
165   Niksch, 'South Korea,' in Gabriel, ed., *Fighting Armies: Nonaligned, Third World. . .*, op. cit., pp. 139–40.
166   Sawyer, op. cit., pp. 178–81. So closely was the Korean Military Academy modelled on West Point that the dress uniform of 18th Century grey and white uniform with shako was adopted.
167   Niksch, op. cit., pp. 140–41.
168   John S. Pustay, 'The Rearming of Japan,' *Military Review*, November 1962, pp. 41, 45.
169   Malcolm MacIntosh, *Japan Re-armed* (London: Francis Pinter, 1986), p. 31.
170   Joseph N. Flanz, 'Japan,' in Richard A. Gabriel, ed., *Fighting Armies: Nonaligned, Third World, and Other Ground Armies – A Combat Assessment* (Westport,CT: Greenwood Press, 1983), p. 154.
171   John Keegan, *The World's Armies*, (Detroit: The Bale Research Co., 1983), p. 27.
172   Jeffrey Grey, *A Military History of Australia* (Cambridge: Cambridge University Press, 1990), p. 207.

CHAPTER 2

THE SECOND POST-WAR DECADE

1955–1965

INTRODUCTION

If the preceding decade had been one of bloody birth for many of the world's new armies, this next decade was one of growth and expansion. The patient training and building of military establishments occupied this, the most peaceful of the post-war decades. The new armies relied in many cases on new or old patrons to provide military assistance in the form of training, advisory groups and equipment. The Soviet Union actively supported its new-found allies as did the United States and Great Britain with old allies and former colonies of their own or other broken empires. The two defeated Axis powers were allowed to have three new armies but these were controlled within the victors' own alliance systems. Creating new armies when national martial traditions had been discredited became a lasting problem for all three armies.

The armies of the four victors of the Second World War spent much of this decade painfully coping with the political realities of the Cold War. For each of them it was a traumatic time of retrenchment, cutbacks and reorganization. In both the United States and the Soviet Union, the armies were treated as poor cousins, pride of place being given to the new nuclear wonder weapons. In tamdem, General Ridgway and Marshal Zhukov were sacked for standing up for the traditional roles and capabilities of their services. Great Britain and France continued gradually to relinquish their empires while the Soviet Union consolidated a new empire and the United States a new leadership. The two older European powers suffered the demoralization of massive cutbacks, the French after Algeria and the British with the Sandys Reforms.

Wars in the conventional sense were relatively few and minor. Most were among the new armies themselves: Israel thrashed the Egyptians (1956) and China pushed the Indian Army off the Himalayan borders (1962). The British and French fought rearguard actions in their remnants of empire, the British successfully. The British Army saw the most varied active service in Cyprus (1955–60), Suez (1956), Oman (1957), Aden (1955–8, 1963–7) and Borneo (1963–66) while the French packed everything into Algeria (1955–62). The great Communist powers fought a few nasty campaigns of empire consolidation: the Soviets in Hungary (1956) and the Chinese in Tibet (1958–61). All in all, it was a decade of preparation for greater things to come.

UNITED STATES

General Ridgway's rearguard action against 'The New Look' came to an end in June 1955 when President Eisenhower pointedly refrained from asking this incomparable soldier to serve another term as Chief of Staff. Like Zhukov two years later, he had become inconvenient in his opposition to the political authority's obsession with the economically convenient strategy of nuclear war. His successor, General Maxwell Taylor, was equally opposed to 'The New Look' but had profited from Ridgway's failure. He embraced deterrence as a political reality but was determined to work within this strategy to build an army that would be able to fight if deterrence failed.

In an address to The Army War College in August he stated that the army 'decline[d] to accept civil defense ... as a primary mission'.[1] To the contrary, he staked out a posture for the army that was a real break with tradition. If the army was to play a role as a deterrent force, it had to be prepared for combat at a moment's notice. Previous US experience had allowed for a mobilization period in which to train an expanded army. Such a shift would call for unprecedented training and operational tempos. This effort had to be directed to a specific concept of war, but the army believed that it might be faced with any of a number of types of war – nuclear, conventional, counter-insurgency. Obviously they could not afford to develop separate forces for each type, a dilemma General Taylor resolved by endorsing the concept that the army must attain a dual capability to deploy both nuclear and non-nuclear weapons. As A.J. Bacevich noted:

> 'Army leaders decided that conventional war simply was a lesser included case of nuclear conflict. Nuclear war was the "worst case" – though not necessarily the most probable. If the Army could develop techniques to fight a nuclear war successfully, other less-demanding conflicts would be manageable.'[2]

While the army opposed strategic nuclear warfare as having all the utility of suicide, it saw tactical nuclear warfare as the enhancement of traditional forms of combat. Tactical nuclear weapons were simply a much more effective form of artillery support to ground tactical operations. Such weapons were enthusiastically adopted because they fitted easily within the traditional US reliance on technological solutions and preference for increased firepower on the battlefield. Technology and firepower would redress the imbalance in numbers that faced the US Army in any one of its likely areas of deployment.

THE PENTOMIC EXPERIMENT

Of course, the enemy would also have his nuclear artillery, a reality that would make traditional concentration and linear alignment of forces fatal. The division would manoeuvre on a cellular rather than linear model. Dispersion, flexibility and mobility were characteristics vital to any force that wanted to survive on such a battlefield. 'Concentrate to fight – Disperse to live', summarized the army's approach, and this would lead to one of its most radical yet ultimately unsuccessful experiments – the Pentomic Division.

The Army concluded that it required formations that were (1) too small to offer a good target for nuclear weapons; (2) sufficiently balanced to survive if isolated; (3) logistically self-supporting to preclude long, vulnerable trains; and (4) sufficiently streamlined in its command and control to speed the flow of information and decisions. The resulting 'Pentomic' (the acronym for 'penta' (five) and 'atomic') infantry and airborne divisions were built on five battle groups rather than the traditional three infantry regiments. The battle group replaced both the regiment and the battalion as the divisional building block. Larger than a battalion but smaller than a regiment, the battle group's proclaimed advantage was the elimination of the battalion level of command. In effect, however, the battle group was an oversized battalion eventually consisting of five large rifle companies, a headquarters and service company, a 4.2in mortar battery, and the command and reconnaissance elements of the regiment. The army changed even the organization of the squad, which grew from nine to eleven men and so enabled it to adopt the Marine Corps' fire and movement tactics. Division could provide additional support in the form of one tank company, one 105mm howitzer battery and one engineer company to each battle group. Important advances were made in mobility as well. For the first time transport helicopters and armoured personnel carriers in large numbers were added to the US infantry division.[3] The Pentomic infantry division numbered 11,486

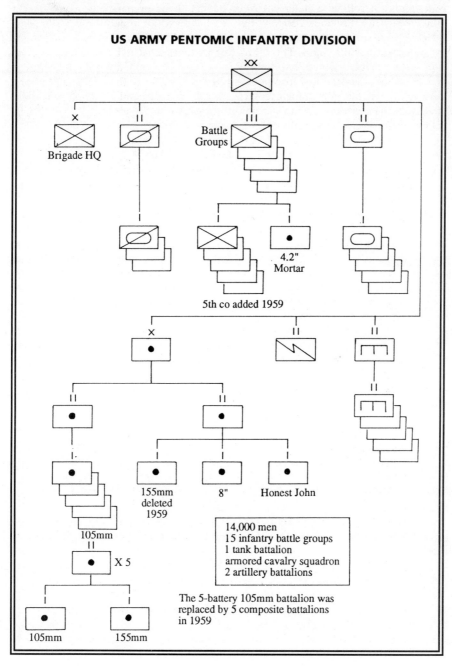

US ARMY PENTOMIC INFANTRY DIVISION

Brigade HQ

Battle Groups

4.2" Mortar

5th co added 1959

155mm deleted 1959

8"   Honest John

105mm

X 5

105mm   155mm

14,000 men
15 infantry battle groups
1 tank battalion
armored cavalry squadron
2 artillery battalions

The 5-battery 105mm battalion was replaced by 5 composite battalions in 1959 as against the 17,000 men of the old infantry division, the cuts coming largely from command and control and combat service support in order to increase the relative 'foxhole' strength.

In practice a number of glaring problems became evident. Fire support was increased by one composite artillery battalion for each battle group; the battalion consisting of one 105mm and one 155mm battery. Training, maintenance, ammunition supply and fire control for the two weapons produced as many problems as their addition solved. The elimination of the battalion produced similar difficulties by all too successfully increasing the span of control for division and battle group commanders to the point of overload. The addition of a transportation battalion of armoured personnel carriers turned out to be an awkward half measure. The battalion could only transport one battle group at a time; being a separate organization, its drivers were not integrated into the battle group and this did little for training or cohesion. At a time when the Soviet Army was rapidly mechanizing its entire infantry force, this was indeed a meagre gesture. The armoured divisions managed to avoid this experiment and retained their Second World War structure of two combat commands of four tank and four armoured infantry battalions. One of the successful offshoots of the Pentomic experiment was the organization of the armoured cavalry regiment with true combined arms formations at both squadron and troop level, which integrated tanks, artillery, infantry and scouts.[4]

The Pentomic concept was introduced in late 1956. By the beginning of the 1957–58 academic year at the Command and General Staff College (CGSC) the previous emphasis on the conventional battlefield had been completely reversed in favour of the atomic battlefield. The army had never before experienced such a fundamental peacetime change in its doctrine and organization. Yet it was a short-lived experiment. The Pentomic concept, so clever in theory, could not in practice overcome its basic organizational flaws and lack of resources. It was an evolutionary dead end, and by 1959 the aarmy was already looking for a replacement system. One general voiced the institutional opinion when he said, 'Ground commanders everywhere breathed a sigh of relief when they were no longer faced with the grim possibility of having to employ it in combat.'

THE ARMY AND THE MISSILE AGE

Despite the failure of the Pentomic concept, there were other stars in the army's crown, none shining more brightly than the army's entry into the missile age – an entry which proved a far more effective adaptation to the nuclear age than the mating of nuclear weapons and ground combat. Missile technology coupled with nuclear weapons, however, was an even more successful breeding programme which produced heretofore undreamed of improvements in the range, accuracy, reliability and destructiveness of weapons. Missile technology held the key to three exciting new fields: space exploration, long-range attack with surface-to-surface missiles (SSMs) and air defence with surface-to-air missiles (SAMs), but these were fields that the air force had staked out for their own. The counsel of the chief of the army's missile programme, Major General John B. Medaris, was both prescient and practical in encouraging the army to muscle-in on this rich field of opportunities:.

> 'If you put all your energy and effort into justifying these conventional weapons and ammunition ... I think you are going to get very little money of any kind. It is far easier to justify a budget with modern items thatare popular ... Why don't you accentuate the positive and go with that which is popular, since you cannot get the other stuff anyway?' [5]

The army enthusiastically took up the challenge. The gage was thrown in the air force's face, sparking one of the bitterest inter-service contests of the post-war period, and for a change the army was to carry away most of the laurels.

The army took an early lead in space exploration and kept it throughout the fifties. A series of impressive feats followed one after another, such as the 3,000-mile Redstone shot in 1956 and the Explorer I orbit in 1958 which put the United States back into the space race after the acute embarrassment of losing the lead to the Soviet Sputnik I. The army's clear lead in missile technology growing out of its space programme was quickly applied to the development of SSMs and SAMs. It was the range of these new systems that confused the Key West agreement of 1948 which had defined the missions of the services. Missions determined by the puny range of field – and air – defence artillery were increasingly irrelevant in the face of continent-ranging missiles. The 75-mile range of the army's first battlefield SSM, Corporal, exceeded the army's battlefield mission responsibility which extended only 50 miles beyond contact with the enemy. This beginning was eventually parlayed into the Thor-Jupiter intermediate-range ballistic missile (IRBM) programme, a strategic weapon that could not be easily squared with the army's battlefield mission. Their early lead in SAMs with the fielding of the NIKE-Ajax involved a similar contentious dispute with the air force. Although the air force had the air-defence 'mission', the army's capabilities actually enabled it to field a continental defence system. Finally both SSM and SAM disputes were resolved in late 1956 by Secretary of Defense Wilson. His decision acknowledged the army's usurpation of the air-defence mission by giving them responsibility for all point defence which effectively put the air force out of the SAM business for good. He also directed that the IRBMs come under air force control and that the army would be limited to SSMs of 20 miles' range. Although the inter-service score now seemed to be even, the army was not out of the SSM business. Wilson's successor approved the army's request to conduct a feasibility study on a 500-mile SSM. His approval of this narrow request was all that the army needed to begin to put together a programme that eventually was fielded as the highly successful Pershing missile.[6]

The ROAD Reorganization

The election of John F. Kennedy in 1960 was a watershed for the army. In the young president they found a friend and a booster who saw the need for an army able to respond to the many types of armed conflict short of nuclear war that seemed to be characterizing the post-war era. These spanned the spectrum from guerrilla to mechanized fighting in environments as diverse as the jungles of the Third World and the plains of northern Europe. The arrival of the Kennedy management team headed by Secretary of Defense Robert McNamara saw the eclipse of the atomic enthusiasm and the arrival of the concept of 'flexible response', a more pragmatic, aggressive and conventionally-oriented strategy. As such, it was a windfall for the much-neglected army.

The army's studies of alternatives to the Pentomic Division were quickly approved by the new administration and announced on 25 May 1961. The Reorganization Objectives Army Division (ROAD, pronounced 'Row-ad') was quickly introduced. The ROAD concept was a hardy balance between the stability of the old triangular divisions and the flexibility sought in the Pentomic Division. Unlike the Pentomic experiment, ROAD restructured all the army's divisions, including the armoured divisions. All divisions would have a common base which included three brigade headquarters, divisional artillery (DIVARTY), a cavalry reconnaissance squadron, an engineer battalion, an air-defence battalion and a divisional support base (DISCOM). The ROAD division would deploy three brigades, but these commands would be 'task organized' with anything from two to seven infantry and tank battalions to add a level of flexibility found in the old armoured division's combat commands. In a lesson learned from the Pentomic Division, the battalion, again formed of three like companies, became the largest fixed-manoeuvre formation with its own reconnaissance, mortar and service support units. In turn, battalions were to be cross-attached to form combined arms teams and task forces to suit a specific mission. While task organization presented great flexibility, its down side was poor co-ordination and above all the loss of that great lubricant of efficiency, knowledge of the men with whom one had to work and fight. In compensation, commanders tended always to cross-attach or task organize with the same units. The ROAD reorganization was to prove one of the most successful in the army's history and was to form the firm basis for subsequent reorganizations throughout the post-war period.[7]

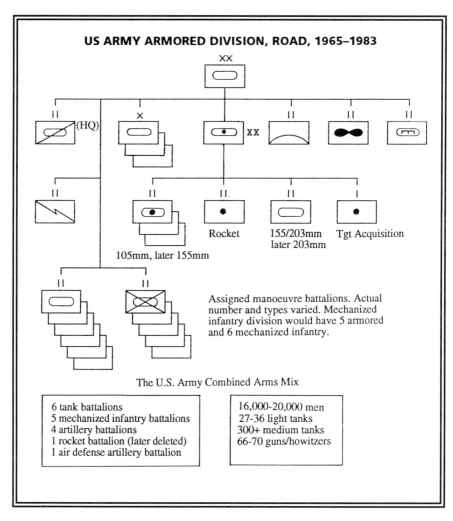

US ARMY ARMORED DIVISION, ROAD, 1965–1983

105mm, later 155mm

Rocket

155/203mm later 203mm

Tgt Acquisition

Assigned manoeuvre battalions. Actual number and types varied. Mechanized infantry division would have 5 armored and 6 mechanized infantry.

The U.S. Army Combined Arms Mix

6 tank battalions 5 mechanized infantry battalions 4 artillery battalions 1 rocket battalion (later deleted) 1 air defense artillery battalion	16,000-20,000 men 27-36 light tanks 300+ medium tanks 66-70 guns/howitzers

In addition to this new organizational efficiency, the army profited from generous new scales of equipment which greatly increased its mobility and mechanization. Numerically it grew from 875,000 men in eleven divisions to 1,000,000 in sixteen divisions. The administration based the decision to increase mechanization and size partly on the requirements of a potential European battlefield in the hopes that a successful defence would at least postpone the necessity of using nuclear weapons.

Table 2-1. ROAD Mechanization

Division	Battalion Type: Infantry	Mech Inf	Armoured
Armoured		5	6
Mechanized		7	3
Infantry	8		2
Airborne	9		1

Because divisions were tailored to meet tactical requirements, it was seldom that any two were alike in their battalion mix. Divisions were expected to be able to con-

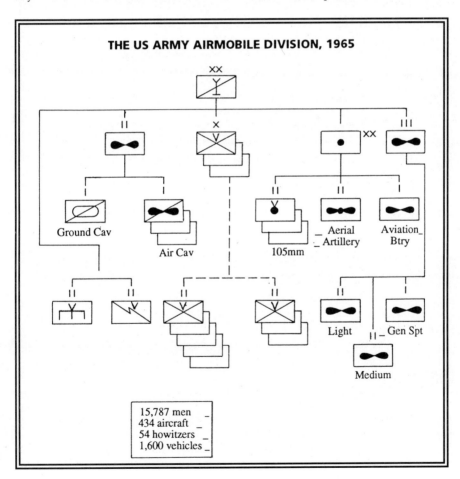

THE US ARMY AIRMOBILE DIVISION, 1965

Ground Cav

Air Cav

105mm

Aerial Artillery

Aviation Btry

Light — Gen Spt

Medium

15,787 men
434 aircraft
54 howitzers
1,600 vehicles

trol up to five brigades and fifteen battalions. Armoured and mechanized divisions were basically the same and designed one way or the other to preserve armour and infantry lineages. The first divisions to be reorganized were the 1st Armored and 5th Infantry (Mech) Divisions in early 1962. Airborne divisions were not converted until 1964.

THE RISE OF ARMY AVIATION AND AIR ASSAULT

The rich promise of army aviation seen in the Korean War had not been exploited because of the army's fear of being seen as usurping an air force mission which went so far as to forbid army helicopters to fly in formation. The Marine Corps had led the way in developing ground forces aviation for mobility and tactical use. However, the Chief of Army Aviation, Major General Hamilton Howze, had made this period one of fruitful experimentation. With Kennedy in the White House, bold and innovative ideas were eagerly sought. At McNamara's direction the historic Howze Board was convened in 1962 to explore the possibilities.

After extensive tests Howze recommended the establishment of several air assault divisions and air cavalry brigades which would be completely airmobile and dependent solely upon army aircraft. After a short but sharp internal fight, the Department of Defense authorized the creation of a test formation, the 11th Air Assault Division. From 1963 to 1965 this small division laid the groundwork often from scratch for one of the major innovative means and forms of combat in the post-war era. There was far more to this innovation than airmobility. The helicopter created an entirely new medium for combat operations.

'The division's air cavalry squadron combined elements for aerial observation, insertion and recovery of ground reconnaissance teams, and
armed helicopter "gunships" within each air cavalry troop. The air cavalry conducted the traditional cavalry missions of reconnaissance,
screening, and raids, almost entirely from the air.'[8]

At the same time a parallel but combat test for army aviation was being conducted in South Vietnam. Shortly after Kennedy's decision to expand military aid to South Vietnam in December 1961, 300 army pilots in 'Eagle Flights' arrived there to begin ferrying ARVN troops. Personnel and lessons flowed between the 11th Air Assault Division and aviation units in South Vietnam to build a solid body of experience. By 1964 army aviation and South Vietnamese infantry units had formed small air assault units. By the summer of the following year the aviation tests of the 11th Air Assault Division had been declared successful. The test division converted to 1st Cavalry Division (Airmobile) and deployed to Vietnam.

THE RISE OF SPECIAL FORCES

The rise in Communist insurgencies during the late 1950s gradually shifted the focus of the army's Special Sorces (SF). Training guerrilla forces in the enemy's rear during conventional operations in NATO gave way to training friendly Third World armies to fight guerrillas during counter-insurgency operations. The army's only two special forces groups, 10th and 77th stationed in Germany, were augmented by the creation of the 1st in Okinawa in 1957. As early as 1957 1st SFGA teams were training the nucleus of the future South Vietnamese SF at Nha Trang. The 77th, later designated 7th Special Forces Group (Airborne) (SFGA) in 1960, began training operations in Laos in 1959.

Special forces seized their big chance in October 1961 when President Kennedy visited the Special Warfare Center at Fort Bragg. The 7th SFGA's demonstration of prowess and techniques thoroughly impressed the young President who quickly concluded that SF provided the right tool for the counter-insurgency dilemma and ordered its immediate expansion. He also authorized the wearing of the celebrated green beret. The beret had been worn without official permission for four or five years, having been banned by the animosity of a general officer whose forces had been ostentatiously disrupted by the SF during manoeuvres. The wearing of the beret had become a court-martial offence, but had survived in out of the way training areas and back-of-beyond deployment areas such as Laos. With the daring that typified the SF, Colonel William Yarborough, Commander of the Special Warfare Center, wore the beret for Kennedy's visit. The President took to the beret immediately; in a message after his return to Washington, he described it as the 'symbol of excellence, the mark of distinction, the badge of courage'. It was not long before army regulations detailed its size, shape, badges, colour and manner of wearing it.[9]

The enemies of special forces, those supporters of bland uniformity – the sort who delighted in starching the cotton field uniform to the consistency of a board, were completely frustrated by the SF's new patron and were reduced to the petty spite of referring to them as 'Jacqueline Kennedy's Own Rifles'. Kennedy sensed a resonance in the SF with his own concept of manly service to the nation. His patronage quickly followed his visit. Two months later a third SFGA was activated to support training missions in South-east Asia to be followed by three more groups in 1963. The three original groups were quadrupled in size to 1,500 men each. Nine groups were organized for the reserve components in 1961.

The Administration made special forces the cutting edge of its counter-insurgency strategy and exposed them to the cooing adulation of the press. Secretary McNamara pointedly informed the West Point Class of 1962 that membership was the road to success. The resulting stampede quickly overwhelmed the ability to train personnel up to standards. So great was the requirement to fill the new units that quality suffered as well. Previously, attrition had been carefully used in training to weed out the unsuitable. Training attrition in 1961 had been 90 per cent; by 1962 it was 70 per cent, and by 1964 it had fallen to an ominous 30 per cent. Special forces were suffering the fate of all small élite units when rapidly expanded. Nevertheless they continued to attract recruits of substantially higher quality than the rest of the army. Each man still had to be a triple volunteer – for the army, the airborne, and the special forces.

As the numbers of SF escalated so too did their active mission in South Vietnam where the government was finding it increasingly difficult to cope with the Vietcong. The SF's major success was the creation of the Civilian Irregular Defense Group (CIDG) programme composed of non-Vietnamese mountain peoples (Montagnards) paid directly by the Special Forces. Missions of the CIDG strike force camps included border security, infiltration, trail interdiction, local village security, civic action, local medical care, and intelligence collection. By the end of 1963 the SF controlled 18,000 CIDG strike force personnel and 43,000 hamlet militia. On the personal and professional level it was a highly successful relationship. Out of this mutual respect and loyalty came an increasingly effective organization that was tasked with ever more aggressive missions. Within its counter-insurgency sphere, the CIDG was a great practical and professional success, but the war was becoming more and more conventional; by 1964 it was surging over the parameters of counter-insurgency and was set to bring down the entire structure of South Vietnam.

THE BERLIN CRISIS 1961 AND REORGANIZATION OF THE RESERVES

The army's most tense moment since the Korean War came in August 1961 when the Soviets tried to wrest Berlin from the West by a series of provocations culminating in the building of the infamous Berlin Wall. Robert Kennedy advised the Soviet Ambassador that the President, 'believed that the Berlin issue was worth going to war over'. Unfortunately President Kennedy had inherited an army that had been sadly neglected by the Eisenhower administration and did not constitute a credible threat. He immediately began to build up the army's conventional capabilities. The ROAD reorganization and the support given to army aviation and special forces were only some of the long-range improvements that sprang from this crisis. To deal with the crisis at hand, though, he was forced to mobilize army reserve and National Guards units to replace active divisions sent to Europe from the Strategic Reserve. In late September 46,000 reservists were called-up followed in the next month by two divisions and an armoured cavalry regiment. These National Guard divisions were found to be at only 70 per cent strength and in need of several months' training to reach combat readiness. Bringing these units up to strength with the proper specialities was a major difficulty. Particularly galling to Secretary McNamara was the number of reservists who attempted to evade call-up.

The mobilization was credited with helping to cool the crisis, but McNamara was determined to reorganize the reserve components so that they would be effective and timely additions to US military power in future crises. In 1963 he pruned the overall size of the National Guard to 467,000 and the Army Reserve to 375,000, the realistic size to which they were likely to be recruited, a force of 29 line and thirteen training divisions. He ensured that readiness and manning levels would provide the strategic reserve with six divisions, some of which would be deployable within four weeks. Gradually two-thirds of the reserves would be trained and equipped up to a higher priority status that would allow the army to increase its Strategic Reserve by 60 per cent in eight weeks.[10]

McNamara also attempted to combine the two parallel army reserve components, the federally controlled army reserve and the state controlled, army National Guard. He felt, with considerable justification, that to have two structures was anachronistic. The Army Reserve had been created out of fears of state control of the National Guard, but the two world wars and Korea proved that state control in peacetime was no bar to their federal control in times of crisis and war. McNamara concluded that the Army Reserve could be efficiently subsumed in the National Guard and in 1965 obtained President Johnson's approval for the amalgamation. Neither man had reckoned with the fact that the Army Reserve had sunk roots as deep in their local communities as the National Guard. Congress was far more alive to local political sensitivities; the ensuing Congressional outcry effectively and permanently shelved the plan. The parallel reserve structures, though streamlined and more efficiently integrated with the regular army, would survive throughout the post-war era as a monument to local politics.

The army began the decade as a neglected service, relegated to insignificance in the national defence, a period of institutional anguish aptly known as its 'Babylonian Captivity', but ended as a favoured service with a vital role. By 1965 it had been reorganized, expanded and re-equipped so as to be relevant to modern warfare. It was for such an army that Generals Ridgway, Taylor and Gavin had sacrificed themselves.

GREAT BRITAIN

The British Army of the second decade of the post-war period almost immediately walked into a one-two punch. These blows, the Suez fiasco and the Sandys White Paper, cost little in blood but were to send the army into convulsions that neither the jungles of Malaya nor the mountains of Korea had been able to induce.

SUEZ, 1956

On 27 July 1956 the Prime Minister directed the Chiefs of Staff to re-occupy the Canal Zone after its seizure by Egypt's President Nasser. The intervening three months until the operation were to demonstrate that the British armed forces had largely forgotten how to conduct a major expedition and worse, had failed to maintain the necessary resources and organization. The entire episode was to be an excellent example of how quickly hard-won wartime skill in organization and teamwork can wither away in peacetime. These were not the skills of the British soldier in battle; the Tommy gave an excellent account of himself as usual. After all, the British infantry had been campaigning hard in a number of small wars since 1945. What had atrophied were the unglamorous skills of the planner and logistician and especially the knack for combined operations. Financial resources had dwindled, as had the government's war skill, steadfast support of its war aims and an understanding of the soldier's tasks.

It was to be an operation of limited objectives and limited forces. No more than a reinforced division was to be employed. Yet the British Army, numbering at the time more than 400,000 men, was obliged to call-up 23,000 reservists, an amphibious warfare expert from as far away as South Africa, and seek assistance in the form of French military participation. The only element of which the army had more than enough was infantry, a unique moment in British military history, two divisions having just rotated back to England from Egypt. Armour was a different story. Nothing could be taken from NATO commitments so the general staff contemplated the calling-up of a territorial regiment. Instead two regiments on territorial training assistance duty were designated. They had to mobilize a large number of reservists, receive and train on an entirely new tank, the Centurion, and receive special ammunition and preparation to face the Stalin tanks in the Egyptian inventory. The 16th Paras, designated for the airborne landing, had been chasing Greek Cypriot guerrillas so long that its battalions had to be flown back to England one at a time for refresher training.[11]

Even more daunting was the emaciated logistics infrastructure and its bare larder of supplies and equipment. Successive waves of economy had so reduced available landing craft that there remained a sufficient number to lift only two battalions of infantry and one squadron of tanks, and most of these had been mothballed since the war. The largest command ship available was designed to support a brigade. Transport aircraft were antiquated and in short supply. In these shortages, the army could claim innocence, the aircraft coming within the province of the Royal Navy and RAF. The army of an island nation is the only service that must depend completely on the others to get it to the fighting. The army had problems enough of its own. Operational and administrative district chains of command were inexcusably muddled. No one seemed to know the cargo capacities of designated shipping; peacetime port regulations on loading were in force and varied from port to port causing some elements of the 3rd Division to travel the length of Britain and back looking for a berth. Worse still, transport drivers and stevedores were working to snail-like union rules. The final indignity was the necessity to haul the Centurions by commercial furniture removers to their ports of embarkation. In all this confusion it is little wonder that vehicles were not combat loaded; the vehicles that needed to be landed first had not been embarked last. The army was lucky to be embarked at all. The inevitable footnote was written at Port Said when the first vehicle to be unloaded of the 2,000 afloat was the officers' mess truck of the Life Guards, which had been dropped from the operation's order of battle six weeks earlier.[12]

Mercifully, the fighting to seize Port Said was brief. The 3rd Paras and French paratroops dropped into Port Said supported by an amphibious landing of the tank-supported Royal Marines 3 Commando Brigade. The port was cleared in a short, sharp action that left three paras killed and 32 wounded and eight killed and 60 wounded among the Marines. British estimates of Egyptian losses were put at 650 killed and 900 wounded. It had been ascertained that the Egyptian Army had no more than a mixed brigade of regulars and national guards supported by a few tanks and guns at the port; the rest were being pulled back to Cairo from their defeat in the Sinai at the hands of the Israelis. For the British this was unalloyed good luck. Port Said had been chosen as the main target because of its control of the Canal – the primary political goal of the operation. For military reasons it had been originally dismissed out of hand because it dangled at the end of a 26-mile causeway to the mainland. The memory of the single road to Arnhem in 1944 was still fresh as well as General Horrocks' bitter advice, '... never try to fight an entire Corps off one road'.[13] The British planners had dreaded the prospect of a single gun or tank blocking the causeway. As it happened, there was nothing to stop further advance to the mainland except the British government's own ceasefire. The best epitaph was written by Correlli Barnett, 'There was something awfully familiar

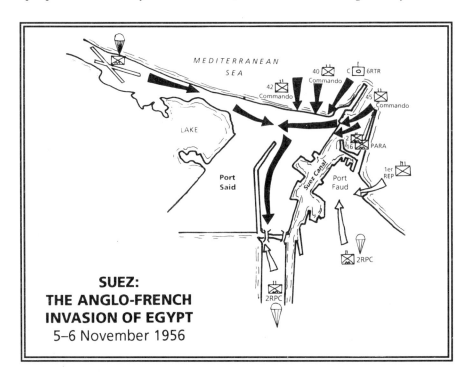

**SUEZ:
THE ANGLO-FRENCH
INVASION OF EGYPT**
5–6 November 1956

about the Suez operation: shades of York's operations in Flanders, of the Crimea, of Gallipoli, of Tudor landings in France or Spain.'[14]

THE SANDYS WHITE PAPER, 1957

Suez was the British Empire's last military operation. The military unpreparedness and mobility difficulties had exposed Britain's pretensions to great power status as being economically untenable. The government concluded that Britain could no longer afford its surviving imperial political or military commitments. In April 1957, Minister of Defence Duncan Sandys released his Defence White Paper which was to have such traumatic consequences for the army. He reasoned that the chief Cold War threat was not a direct nuclear or conventional attack by the Soviet Union but an assault through the Third World in the form of limited wars. At the same time Britain had to conserve its economic energies for the long haul. Finally, Britain did not have to prepare to fight an independent global war but would fight as a member of the NATO alliance; the first duty of an ally was 'to remain solvent'.[15] To do so required deep and painful cuts in the armed forces, particularly the swollen National Service army.

National Service had long since lost support in the Royal Navy and RAF; their complements were 90 and 70 per cent regulars respectively. By 1957 the army had had enough as well, but its recruitment problem was severe. It had never forgotten that the heart of the army was its regular cadres; yet the requirements of training large numbers of conscripts discouraged regular recruitment.[16] In 1957 the army numbered 400,000 and only 164,000 were regulars of whom only 80,000 were on enlistments of more than three years. The Sandys White Paper proposed to end conscription by January 1960 and set the strength of the post-National Service army at 165,000, a figure derived more from the logic of economy than the arithmetic of commitments. Sir Gerald Templer, Chief of the Imperial General Staff, held that a minimum of 200,000 was needed. By 1963 strength had fallen to 163,000 with the discharge of the last National Servicemen. Britain was fortunate in that the relative calm of this period put no pressure on the army as it struggled to become a regular army again for the first time since 1939.[17]

A REGULAR ARMY AGAIN

The end of conscription had been long awaited in the army, particularly at battalion level by those who had to deal with the constant high turnover of personnel and the loss of so many senior NCOs to basic training duties. Conscription had not been an unalloyed problem though. It had brought a vigorous cross-section of the nation into the army, the same cohorts of British youth that had triumphed in 1918 and 1945 and had gone on to serve so ably in Malaya, Korea, Kenya and the scores of other crises of that decade. More importantly for the army as an institution, it had propped up the traditional regimental structure. Without the manpower provided by conscription, the number of regiments could not be maintained. The Sandys White Paper reforms would bring the army from a strength of 375,000, excluding Gurkhas, in 1957 to 163,000 in 1963.

The easiest cut was within the depot training establishment which would need far fewer men to train regulars than conscripts; its complement was reduced from 42 to 35 per cent of the total force. Headquarters and housekeeping billets were also cut so that the 165,000-man force envisaged by Sandys concentrated more than 25 per cent of its strength in the infantry, the highest percentage since 1939. That still entailed the reduction in the number of infantry battalions from 77 to 60;

the Gurkhas and 22 SAS remaining intact. Armoured battalions fell from 30 to 23 regiments. The Royal Artillery suffered the deepest cuts, losing twenty field and fourteen air-defence regiments as the role of nuclear weapons edged aside the traditional role of the gunner.[18]

Among those corps of the army that shared a common cap badge, such as the Royal Artillery, Royal Engineers and Royal Signals, the loss of regiments was merely a matter of transfer of personnel within the corps with which they identified. In the Royal Armoured Corps (RAC) and the infantry, it provoked a primal scream. The regiments of these corps were distinct military communities, brotherhoods of distinct traditions, histories and battle honours. The prospect of mass extinctions was appalling. The practical alternative of creating a single Corps of Infantry or Armour could not survive the pull of regimental loyalties, although the RAC had gone halfway down that road with a homogeneous Royal Tank Regiment of eight numbered regiments within which soldiers could be easily posted, in addition to its traditional cavalry regiments. Regimental loyalty was enough to counter the experience of the Second World War which had shown the regiment to be a poor base from which to create the flexible battle groups the Germans used so well.

The only palatable alternative was amalgamation. The RAC divided its seven amalgamations among the twenty former Cavalry of the Line (four) and the eight of the Royal Tank Regiment (three). The two Household Cavalry regiments were left untouched. As Geoffrey Blaxland noted, 'the cavalry spirit was almost as strong as the regimental and the interchange of officers and men was readily accepted as a fact of life'. The infantry, on the other hand, had no such sense of corps or even brigade. The regiment was the infantryman's life. The anguish was apparent in a letter quoted by the Queen from a private, posted away from his regiment, to his colonel:

> 'You will see from the above address that disaster has overtaken me. I feel something like a man awakened from an operation to find himself minus a limb. They have taken my cap badge away and with it the great love of my life. The traditions of my county regiment are in my blood, and to be known as a Forester was an estate of which I was deeply proud.' [19]

The infantry cuts fell most easily on the Foot Guards who lost two of ten battalions; The Parachute Regiment retained all three of its battalions and the Gurkhas kept their eight. That left fifteen amalgamations to be apportioned among infantry of the line. These changes were to be made in the larger context of structural reorganization of the brigade system. The single-battalion infantry regiments were grouped into brigades which consolidated their regimental depots. The brigades being geographically located in the county, their recruiting potential became the driving consideration for the selection of regiments for consolidation. Ireland and Wales, with strong recruiting grounds, avoided loss of regiments. England surrendered thirteen; Scotland, which was over-represented, lost two. The amalgamations were conducted in a good spirit born of inevitability by the regiments which became healthy crossbreeds exhibiting the best of both parents. The only controversy came from Scotland where the Highland Light Infantry was torn from the Highland Brigade and amalgamated with The Royal Scots Fusiliers as part of the Lowland Brigade. The prospect of losing the right to wear the kilt, the prerogative of the Highland regiments, provoked a storm of protest resulting in marches in Glasgow and appeals from Members of Parliament. Eventually even this mix of Highland and Lowland settled down into the solid The Royal Highland Fusiliers though not without one last protest:

'This occurred when [Field Marshal] Templer was explaining the reason for the HLI and the Fusilier amalgamation by going over the alternatives. He mentioned the Gordon Highlanders, and at this there was a crash. One of the pictures of his predecessors, on the wall behind him, had fallen to the ground. It was of Sir Archibald Murray, CIGS in 1914 and Colonel of the Gordons, and the glass was cracked diagonally from corner to corner.'[20]

The army that happily crawled back into its pre-war regular army mould was a curious mixture of change and continuity. The social composition of the pre-war army quickly re-asserted itself, the ranks were filled by the working class and the officer corps by the 'gentlemen' of rural gentry background. 'Professionally it was more serious, more keen, more skilled, than the polo players of the 1930s – it was master of sophisticated modern weapons and techniques of administration.'[21]

Other changes saw the modernization of weapons and equipment. The venerable Lee-Enfield rifle, Vickers machine-gun and the Bren gun were replaced by the NATO standard Belgian FLN automatic and the general-purpose machine-gun. The new Chieftain tank was accepted for service in 1963. Its excellent armour and 120mm gun, the first use of that calibre anywhere, made it one of the most advanced and formidable tanks in the world. The Saladin armoured car reconnaissance vehicle armed with a 76mm gun went into production in 1958 and the FV 432 series armoured personnel carrier in 1963 to supplement the Saracens rushed into production during the previous decade. The FV 430 basic chassis also gave rise to the FV 433 Abbot 105mm self-propelled gun.[22]

The structure of the division also underwent drastic changes, some for the worse initially. According to Richard Orgorkiewicz, the 1955–6 armoured division suffered a regression to the 'all tank' ideas that had been discredited by the experience of the Second World War. The tank division shrank to little more than a glorified brigade of four tank and one armoured infantry battalions plus one battalion each of armoured cars, medium artillery and engineers. Ogorkiewicz argued that the ratio of tank to infantry should have been closer to one to one. Subsequently the division structure was changed to create a single type of division, dropping the title Armour or Infantry. These divisions were powerful combined arms formations consisting of brigade groups of four battalions with a ratio of three to one infantry or armour and an integral artillery regiment and engineer squadron. A nuclear capable regiment of mixed howitzers and Honest John rockets was added to the divisional artillery.[23]

The emphasis on a strong combined arms structure and battlefield nuclear capability accented the British Army's re-orientation to its NATO responsibilities and to the Soviet Ground Forces as its primary opponent. Even so, the echoes of imperial commitments were to see its primary operational experience in engagements in Cyprus, Oman, Aden and Borneo, and not the North German Plain. Yet from 1954 to 1967 the British Army would commit to these operations 146 fighting battalions, 98 of which were infantry. Although many of the infantry battalions were rotated through several of these areas, the amount of operational experience gained during this period was immense. It was a rare infantryman that could not boast of experience of active operations in at least one of these areas. Although total casualties did not exceed 1,700 killed and wounded, these operations demanded skills that were the British infantryman's bread and butter – small unit leadership, independent manoeuvring, tactical and weapons proficiency, a sense for civil affairs – and grit.

CYPRUS

Ceded to Britain in 1878 by the Turks, Cyprus became the headquarters for British forces in the Middle East in 1954, just in time to counter the newly formed guerrilla movement, EOKA, which was determined to achieve *enosis*, or union, with Greece. Only the British Army stood in the way. But this was the rare pacification effort in which the British Army did not have at least the passive support of the population. Fortunately, Cyprus is a small island, half the size of Wales, and it was easily isolated. For once the British Army had sufficient troops with the evacuation of Egypt and the winding down of operations in Kenya. Thirty-five infantry battalions were rotated through the island over the space of four years with eighteen being the largest number present at any one time. A good intelligence system, integrated planning and operations, constant patrolling, and strict population control were eventually to squelch EOKA by 1959, only to have the government grant independence in 1960.

OMAN

In 1957 the Sultan of Oman, faced with a growing rebellion, appealed for aid from Britain. Elements of several battalions of infantry, armoured cars and the SAS were quickly dispatched. Combined British and Omani forces advanced upon rebel strongholds in the mountains. The climax of the operation came when a squadron of 22 SAS climbed the almost sheer face of the mountain dominating the rebel position and the terrified rebels fled into Saudi Arabia. This exploit clinched the survival of the SAS Regiment which had been marked for dissolution by the Sandys reforms.

ADEN

The British Army played twice in Aden during this period. The first time (1955–8) to suppress belligerent tribes from the interior egged on by Yemen and later Egypt, drunk with hatred over Suez, trying to disrupt the peace of the Protectorate. The climax of the campaign was something out of Kipling and the North-West Frontier. The British resident political officer was besieged in a mountain fortress at As Sarir by Yemenis and tribesmen; attempts at relief by the Protectorate Levies failed. A combined force of 1st King's Shropshire Light Infantry and 1st Buffs, supported by 13th/18th Hussars and the guns of 33rd Parachute Field Regiment stormed the surrounding heights to relieve the fort.

The second act in Aden – beginning with the Radfan War – was far more grim and ultimately thankless. The Rafdan was the mountain fastness of the Quteibi tribe which in 1963 began aggressively preying upon the areas controlled by the new State of Aden, again encouraged by Yemen and Egypt. Aden appealed to Britain for assistance in suppressing this redoubt of the Quteibis. Although the army was heavily committed in Borneo, Cyprus and Africa, elements of Commando, SAS, Parachute, RTR armoured car, and field artillery battalions, and one line infantry battalion were scraped together under an improvised brigade headquarters. Between April and October 1964, the Rafdan strongholds were stormed and the tribes were subdued in operations that put a premium on close co-ordination of all arms and once again the special operations skill of the Commandos, SAS and Paras.

The war then took a deadlier turn for the British during the next two years as terrorists, guerrillas and mutinous local police and troops took a far heavier toll of British lives than had the storming of the Rafdan. The steady wastage came to an end in 1967 when Britain abandoned Aden.

BORNEO

As in Aden, the British Army found Borneo a two-act performance. In both acts inter-service co-operation was vital; in both acts the Gurkhas played the lead. The first saw the army suppress a local rebellion against the Sultan of Brunei in 1962. The second and more arduous (1963–6) was played against Indonesian-inspired and resident Chinese Communist guerrillas in the territories of Borneo that had chosen to join Malaya in the Federation of Malaysia. Henceforth the British Army would fight in support of its ally and in the field with Malaysian troops. By the end of 1963 this new threat had also been crushed. Determined to annex the whole of Borneo, Sukharno of Indonesia committed regular troops to the fighting from 1964 until 1966. It was a form of limited warfare, designed to bleed and discourage the British without provoking a more violent response. The Indonesians were more formidable opponents than the guerrillas, experienced against the Dutch, well-armed and in large numbers. In 1964 British forces were consolidated into a full divisional structure, the 17th Gurkha Division, which consisted of five Gurkha, three Malay and one each of line infantry, SAS and Commando battalions. Eventually all eight Gurkha battalions, 23 infantry and SAS, three armoured car and fourteen artillery regiments in addition to the Federal Malaysian forces and several Australian and New Zealand battalions were to serve in Borneo. It was a war that swirled around company strongpoints with heavy patrolling along jungle mountain borders. Artillery played a stronger part than in any of the other post-war colonial operations. Frequent reliefs of units kept fresh troops in the field. In one instance the system of reliefs left the 1st Scots Guards with an attached company of 1st Irish Guards and an attached platoon of 1st South Wales Borderers, 'a rare Celtic union'.[24] In 1966 the steam went out of the war when the Chinese Communist coup in Indonesia failed and dragged Sukharno down with it.

Table 2-2. British Army Operational Experience 1955–1967

Area	Inf	Battalions Rotated: Gurkha	Armour	Arty
Cyprus	35	–	3	12
Aden 1955–8	11	–	3	1
Aden 1964–7	27	–	6	5
Oman	2 –	–	3 –	–
Borneo	23	8	3+	14
Totals	98	8	18	32

Source: Geoffrey Blaxland, *The Regiments Depart.*

Table 2-3. British Army Casualties 1954–1967

Area	Year	Dead	Wounded	Total
Oman	1957–9	7	8	15
Aden	1955–8	5?	10?	15?
Aden	1963–7	92	669	761
Suez	1956	11	92	103
Borneo	1962–6	75	164	239
Totals		269	1,387	1,656

Source: Geoffrey Blaxland, *The Regiments Depart.*. Note: Casualties in Aden 1955–8 are totalled from numbers in Blaxland's narrative and may not be complete. Figures for Suez and Borneo also include losses of Commandos serving with the army.

FRANCE

The French Army reeled out of its Indo-China defeat directly into another colonial insurgency in Algeria, the precious jewel of the French Empire and the spiritual home of the army. The struggle to keep Algeria French so estranged the army from the government of France as to provoke civil war. The crisis would tear the army away from its colonial past and set it firmly again in Europe.

THE ALGERIAN WAR, 1954–1962

On 1 November 1954, less than four months after the Indo-China armistice had been signed, the Algerian *Front de la Libération Nationale* (FLN) attacked French posts in the Aures Mountains. The French garrison of Algeria then numbered 57,000 men, only 3,500 of whom were available for operations. Almost immediately, the 25th Parachute Division was transferred directly from Indo-China. By February 1956 the garrison had grown to 200,000, almost all veterans of Indo-China. The cutting edge of the garrison consisted of the paratroop units, and of these the toughest were the paratroopers of the Foreign Legion. Also by February 1956, the French government had taken the fateful step of assigning conscripts and reservists to the forces in Algeria, and the garrison grew to 500,000 men.[25] Algeria was the 10th *Département* of France, an integral part of the nation, and not a colony in French eyes – especially not in the eyes of the army. Algeria was to the French Army what India had been to the British Army.

As late as 1954 the French military establishment in metropolitan France persisted in refusing to recognize much of professional value to be gained from the experience in Indo-China. The shock of defeat, the return of embittered veterans seething with discontent, and the outbreak of the Algerian War, quickly reversed this attitude.

The concept of *la guerre révolutionnaire* had deeply influenced the generation of officers who served in Indo-China and their return to France marked its triumph as both military theory and policy.[26] 'Against *la guerre révolutionnaire*, the French sought to bring the most touted Communist weapons of psychological action and political indoctrination in the context of a general war common to Marx-Lenin-Mao. To complement their action programme, they developed *action psychologique* – a theory of psychological action.'[27] The first effect was the creation of large psychological warfare and administrative services. In early 1955 the first psychological warfare school was established in Paris, later followed by training offices in Algeria designed to teach soldiers the political and social aspects of the new war. In the spring of 1956 a seventh arm of the service for psychological and propaganda operations was established, the first companies being fielded a few months later. In the summer of 1957 new staff elements, the *5ème Bureaux* or G5, were added to division, corps, army and military region staffs. The following year G5 was added to the General Staff to 'direct and co-ordinate the psychological action of national defence'.[28] G5's many responsibilities came to embrace psychological action, psychological warfare, morale – civilian and military – troops and public information, chaplain activities and civil affairs. Thus armed with theory and structure, the French Army went to war in Algeria.

As early as 1957 the theory and structure were put to the test when the FLN created a liberated zone in the Arab quarter of Algiers. General Massu's 10th Parachute Division, 'fresh from the frustration of Suez', took the FLN apart in a ruthless demonstration of the new techniques. *La guerre révolutionnaire* and *action psychologique* had worked.

A war in Indo-China was one thing, a war in metropolitan France quite another, even to the government of the Fourth Republic. The Territorial Army, located in France itself, would be liable to service as much as if the war were in the Department of the Loire. At its height the war drew into Algeria 60 per cent of the French Army and required not only masses of conscripts but the call-up of large numbers of reserves. The army swelled to 830,000 men by 1957, but its conventional capabilities actually shrank as it focused exclusively on colonial insurgent warfare. The three new Javelot mechanized divisions were transferred to Algeria and broken up for security duties; only 50,000 troops were left in Germany.[29] More than 300,000 men of the Territorial Army, 80 per cent conscripts, were used to garrison the numerous small security districts into which Algeria had been divided. Another 30,000 men formed the Réserve Générale consisting of paratroops, Foreign Legion infantry and paratroops, and Marine commandos. The Legion was 100 per cent professional, but the army paratroops included a large percentage of conscripts. Nevertheless the Réserve Générale overall was about 60 per cent professional.[30] Within this exclusive company were the 1st and 2nd Foreign Legion Parachute Regiments (*1er* and *2ème Régiments Etrangers de Parachutistes* – REP). Withdrawn from Algeria temporarily as part of the 10th Parachute Division for the Suez operation, these regiments had impressed their British allies with their dash and professionalism. Each regiment numbered about 1,300 men in the lethal combined arms formation shown in figure 2-4. There were actually few parachute operations; the paras operated more as airmobile forces, actively exploiting the considerable value of the helicopter in guerrilla warfare. The French Army was eventually able to lift two battalions at a time.[31]

For this élite was reserved the special strike operations against the FLN in support of Territorial Army garrisons. Located in the politically charged atmosphere of Algiers and including many bitter veterans of Indo-China, this force was keenly receptive to the lure of *la guerre révolutionnaire*. It was soon apparent that

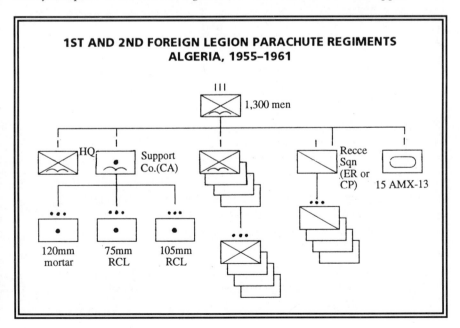

**1ST AND 2ND FOREIGN LEGION PARACHUTE REGIMENTS
ALGERIA, 1955–1961**

1,300 men

HQ

Support Co.(CA)

Recce Sqn (ER or CP)   15 AMX-13

120mm mortar   75mm RCL   105mm RCL

France had two armies in Algeria – the largely conscript Territorial Army on garrison security duty and the Réserve Générale which quickly styled itself an élite, an élite that burned with the bright blue flame of a warrior's code and a passionately held mission.

Moreover it was this élite that was doing most of the fighting. All too often Territorial Army units would pull back upon contact to 'wait for the Paras'. There came to be no correlation between the number of men in the field and the number of combat effectives. A former para described the effect on the élite minority:

'The spearhead is blunted in ceaseless combats, almost always successful. But when it achieves a victory at one point, the enemy takes over the lightly defended zones, where he need fear no serious resistance ... This perpetual circulation of the "general reserves" ... wore out the paras and the Legion during the entire Indo-Chinese war, when they were deployed to the four corners of the country. ... So its military competence does not confer on the élite corps a superiority sufficient to outweigh the numerical inferiority. They are not conquered, but they are lost in the crowd.' [32]

Such was the division between the armies, between apathy and passion, between dull garrison duty and warrior spirit, that a mutual hostility inevitably festered. Yet the more the paras became the embodiment of the primal warrior ethos, the more they excited the envy and admiration of the 'other army'. It was an irresistible appeal captured in the prayer of the paras:

'Give me, my God, what you still have
Give me what no one asks for

I do not ask for wealth
Nor for success, nor even health
People ask you so often, my God, for all that
That you cannot have any left
Give me, my God, what you still have
Give me what people refuse to accept from you

I want insecurity and disquietude
I want turmoil and brawl
and if you should give them to me, my God
Once and for all
Let me be sure to have them always
For I will not always have the courage
to ask for them.' [33]

The self-image of the paras was every bit as powerful as described by the para archetype, the renowned Colonel Bigeard of the 3rd Colonial Paras: 'The men of the regiment are handsome, proud and courageous ... Our *paras*, we make real men out of them; healthy sporting types, humane and well-bred.' In their touchy pride, spirit, courage and instinct for the kill, they resembled heroes of *The Iliad* more than 20th-century soldiers.

Initially these élite forces were frittered away in penny packets with mixed results in hunting down the armed units of the FLN. By the middle of 1957 a more coherent use for them was found. By September the Algerian borders with Morocco and Tunisia had been sealed from the sea to the Sahara by 'a broad barrier of electrified wire, mines and radar sensors'. French mobile forces were deployed along these barriers to pounce quickly on FLN cross-border reinforcement operations. This 'battle of the frontiers' lasted seven months and cost the FLN 6,000 dead before it gave up this tactic of infiltration. The French then turned their attention to the hidden refuges of the FLN within Algeria and systematically hunted them out in a series of major operations that lasted until December 1960. They were models of professional expertise. French 'hunting commandos' would make contact with FLN forces and hold on at all costs while the troops of the Réserve Générale were summoned to the kill. They methodically cordoned and strangled each FLN unit in a district one by one. It became a war of sharp, hard firefights at platoon and company level. In this war casualties were relatively light compared to Indo-China. The 1st REP suffered 775 casualties in all, 2nd REP 741. The latter unit killed more than 3,650 FLN and captured 538. The paras developed the use of the helicopter, to the point where it became almost second nature, for moving troops quickly around the battlefield in response to rapidly shifting intelligence. On the anniversary of the Battle of Austerlitz, in an appropriate climax to a campaign fought with a rare combination of speed, co-ordination and flexibility, the last FLN company was run to earth in a wild fight up and down wooded mountains.[34]

The paras were active on more than just the battlefield; they had drunk deeply of *la guerre révolutionnaire* and been infused with a political outlook that led many of their leaders to envisage a new social order based on reconciliation with the Muslim population. This ability both to fight and empathize with the natives of Algeria arose from sensitivity to the role of the population instilled by *la guerre révolutionnaire* and from the paras' own warrior code which had become both egalitarian and indifferent to race. So few Frenchmen had volunteered for the regular army paras during the war in Indo-China that they had accepted numerous Germans, North Africans and Vietnamese. The Legion and its para regiments, of course, was already closed to French citizens except for officers. This growing political awareness led the forces of the Réserve Générale increasingly to usurp the civil administration of Algeria as it implemented *la guerre révolutionnaire*. From this total commitment, it was a logical step to playing a part in the coup of 13 May 1958 which brought down the Fourth Republic and persuaded General de Gaulle to return from retirement and again save France. The sin of the Fourth Republic was the suspicion that it was on the brink of negotiating with the FLN at the moment of military success. The army believed that de Gaulle had given his word as a soldier that Algeria would remain French; it would learn to its bitter regret that he had given his word as a politician.

Over the next three years it became distressingly obvious that de Gaulle was coming to accept the inevitability of Algerian independence. For the paras it was too much. They were by now dangerously politicized and had had the taste of one broken government in their mouths. The realization that they had fought yet another futile war, and this time to victory, and would be abandoning more than a million French settlers and countless loyal Algerians was an outrage they were not prepared to tolerate. On 22 April 1961 three para regiments, including 1st REP and 14th and 18th RCP (Régiments Chasseurs Parachutistes) of the regular army, staged a coup in Algiers, but their leaders had little idea what to do next. It mattered little because de Gaulle punctured what little support they had and rallied the rest of the army to him in one of his superb radio speeches. Punishment followed immediately. Many para officers were dismissed from the service or sentenced to prison to languish until the amnesty of 1968. The 1st REP was disbanded and its enlisted men scattered to other units. The coup brought about the very abandonment of Algeria that the paras had sought to prevent by destroying any French bargaining position with the FLN. By 1963 the French were gone.

SUEZ, 1956

So intense was French anger at Egyptian support of the Algerian rebels that they willingly swallowed the pill of subordination to overall British military command. The French had no qualms about dipping into their NATO designated forces and committed General Massu's hard-bitten 10th Parachute Division to be backed up by 7ème Mécanique Rapide with its fast new AMX tanks. The 10th was fresh from Indo-China and had not lost its edge. Its major units were *1er Régiment Etranger Parachutistes* and *2ème Régiment de Parachutistes Coloniaux*. Deployed to Cyprus for staging, the 10th's professionalism and equipment made a positive impression on the British as did the colourful array of berets – green for the Legion, red for the colonials, blue for the units from metropolitan France.

The British had every reason to be impressed; the French paras were more experienced and better equipped. Most of them were long-service professionals and had been serving continuously since 1945 in Indo-China and Algeria. Scarcely one of them had made fewer than 160 jumps, and they had made numerous regimental jumps under combat conditions whereas the last such British drop had been in 1945. The paras also conducted monthly regimental (1,300 men) training jumps; the British could expect only one annual brigade jump. The paras were supported by more modern transport aircraft than the British, and French jump techniques had been better honed. Their small-arms had been designed specifically for paratroops so that when a French para hit the ground he was ready for combat unlike his British counterpart who had to retrieve his weapon from a container. In the drop on Suez both French and British paras landed on dug-in Egyptian infantry who fired up at them. The French aerial infantry's return fire effectively silenced the Egyptians. One British para, on the other hand, was reduced to throwing a weapons container at an Egyptian before attacking with his jack-knife.[35]

The two French para regiments played an important role in the assault on Port Said. The 2nd Colonial dropped precisely on its objective to seize the Egyptian garrison's escape route while the 1st Foreign Legion supported by AMX tanks made an amphibious landing on the other side of the Suez Canal to seize Port Faoud. A French innovation was the battle management executed by General Gilles, the French Commandant de l'Operation Aéroportée. Circling 1,000 feet above Port Said in his aerial command post, he deftly directed his own forces and the supporting Corsairs from the carrier *Lafayette*.

The performance of the French forces lived up to their reputation. At a cost of ten dead and 22 wounded, they had conducted one of the most professional 'forced entry' operations of the post-post-war period. Like the Romans, the French professional army found constant war made them very, very good.

'THE ARMY OF TOMORROW'

De Gaulle had long determined to renew the lustre of French grandeur in the councils of the great powers. The events of 1961 gave him the opportunity to reshape the army as a contribution to that end. That army was spiritually spent after twenty-one years of soul corroding defeats and exhausting recoveries. Since 1945 almost all its energies had been poured into colonial wars that left it neither technologically nor doctrinally equipped to take its place again in the European big leagues. With a clean, swift cut de Gaulle severed the army's ties to its colonial past and repositioned it in Europe facing east. His instrument was the defence reorganization of 1961. The government would now exert tighter control than ever before in order to preclude another coup and at the same time provide the structure for a major conversion of the army to its primary role of European defence. It was not a happy time for the French Army. The G5 and psychological warfare staff organizations and units were abolished. With the reduction in size, the cadres suffered another large pruning which did much to demoralize the remaining forces. A large element of distrust continued to permeate the relationship between the army and the government. Tank ammunition was strictly controlled and issued only at firing ranges and all rounds were strictly accountable. General Massu, for instance, as a military region commander, was followed everywhere by a government security detachment. Ironically in 1968 it was Massu, then commander of French forces in Germany, that de Gaulle visited personally to be assured of his support during the anarchy of the student riots of that year.

Under this cloud the reforms of 1961 were implemented. There was to be a new technological orientation to heavily mechanized forces, but the primary emphasis would be on the army's planned battlefield nuclear weapons which were scheduled for fielding by 1970. By 1963 French forces were already armed with the US supplied Honest John rocket, although the warheads remained under US control. For the first time France would not count the strength of the army solely in the number of divisions but in the technical quality of its equipment and personnel. The end of the Algerian War and the expense of the new mechanized forces would mean a cut in army strength from 700,000 to 450,000. The proportion of officers was to be raised in the 'Army of Tomorrow'. The reorganization also created a new service, the *force de frappe*, the nuclear delivery capability of which would pay France's way into the exclusive club of nuclear powers. The event was crucial to the army's future. For the first time in its history the army would no longer be France's premier service and would have to compete in the future for priority in resources.[36]

By 1964 the Chief of Staff of the French Army, General Le Puloc, had described the shape of an army that emerged from a three year study on how to adapt to the nuclear age. The new army now would consist of territorial forces to safeguard the rear into the depth of metropolitan France, and manoeuvre forces, most of which were armoured. Manoeuvre forces would be focused on the nuclear battlefield but be capable of all levels of conflict below that level. Manoeuvre forces acting as part of the NATO covering force were to be kept at 100 per cent strength. The army would also contribute forces at 100 per cent strength (infantry and paratroops) to the national intervention force designed for use 'wherever French interests or commitments require ...'. Army strength was fixed at 350,000. Manoeuvre forces were organized into two army corps of five mechanized divisions and one intervention division (two paratroop and one marine brigades), nine territorial, and overseas forces (Foreign Legion). Personnel policy was also altered to increase the number of volunteers necessary for an adequate enlisted cadre base. French national opinion retained its support for conscription, but the army required a large number of career NCOs to maintain professional and technical standards. After the debâcle in Algeria and the reorganization of the army, enlistments had fallen to a dangerous low of 3,600 against a requirement of 16,000 in 1963. Hurried efforts were made to make enlisted careers more attractive by increasing technical training opportunities and opening a career path to the officer corps. A sharp improvement in enlistment soon began to alleviate, although not solve, the problem. The junior officer corps was also re-oriented to the more technical demands of modern war, as Le Puloch happily observed:

'It has also been necessary to lift the sights of our young officers beyond the field of battle of a psychological war toward other disciplines, such as social and technical sciences. The results have been more than we hoped. These warriors of the jungles who dreamed of nothing but swamps and forests – and who had plenty of those – threw themselves with the same ardour and the same intelligence into this new field of activity.'

Le Puloch was also quick to point out that the French Army would 'not succumb to the slogan of the push-button war. We believe that for a long time to come, the virtues of the fighting man will have their place in war.' The deep strain of the warrior avocation or the 'Damascus Path' was still strong in the French Army.[37] The paratroop spirit which rejoiced in the 'rejection of materialism, the exaltation of asceticism, violence and risk, of action for action's sake', was shared to a large degree by the traditional French officer and was to remain a feature of the French officer corps throughout the post-war era. Such was its influence that para standards of training, stressing physical and moral toughness, were incorporated into general army training policy. The policy emphasized, particularly from officers and NCOs, 'sustained physical conditioning and willingness to set the example'.

This continued emphasis on traditional themes was balanced at the other extreme by the creation of the army's first battlefield nuclear capability with the arrival of US Honest John rockets by 1963. The warheads remained under US control.

THE FOREIGN LEGION AFTER ALGERIA

The Foreign Legion marched out of the Algerian War without a home, tarred by the participation of 1st CAP in the coup, and the likely target of disbandment now that France had liquidated her empire. Indo-China had been costlier to the Legion, 10,483 dead – Algeria had claimed only 1,855 lives but had delivered a more nearly lethal wound to the Legion as an institution. In the end the Legion had saved itself by refusing to follow the wayward 1st CAP, though at the price of a severe pruning of its strength by 20,000.

When the French Army left Algeria, it returned to its original home. When the Legion left, it abandoned its first and only home, the historic *Maison Mère* at Sidi-bel-Abbes, around which so much romantic legend had grown. An era had truly come to a close, but another had started. The Legion, with a new home in the South of France, would look to the future without forgetting where it came from. Even the calendar seemed to acknowledge the shifting of epochs. The move to the Legion's new home came just in time to celebrate the 100th Anniversary of Cameron Day (1863), the moment of glory in Mexico when the Legion's legend of heroism was born. The monument built to commemorate the Legion's 100th anniversary had also been moved and re-assembled stone by stone in its new home.[38]

The Legion's home may have been relocated to the South of France, but the regiments were quickly scattered to garrison the shreds of empire that France still retained in Djibouti, Madagascar and in the Pacific islands. It was both a convenient and fortunate decision. The complications of garrison duties in metropolitan France were avoided. At the same time, France retained a small but effective force for the maintenance of French prestige in areas of French influence around the world without having to risk its citizen soldiers abroad. The Legion had found its niche, and a useful one it would be to France during the next two decades.

WEST GERMANY

The German Army was reborn in the garage of the Erkmekeil Barracks on 12 November 1955. In an austere, almost penitent ceremony, 101 men were sworn into the new army (das Heer or officially das Bundesheer – the Federal Army) against the backdrop of two symbols of German history that for the first time were to form a healthy partnership. The new defence minister, Theodor Blank, addressed the assembled army's first officers and NCOs backed by a gigantic Iron Cross flanked by the red, gold and black German national flag. The Iron Cross represented the German military tradition going back to the wars of liberation against Napoleon; the flags represented the 'historic flag of German parliamentary democracy'. The message was unmistakable; for the first time in modern German history the army would be fully subordinate to the elected representatives of the nation.

Nevertheless the date of the army's incorporation had been carefully chosen to underline continuity with a 'positive' military tradition – the two hundredth anniversary of the birthday of General Gerhard Johann David von Scharnhorst, the great military reformer of Prussia's army after the defeats of 1806. The choice symbolized the great dilemma of the new army – to what extent was German military tradition acceptable to the army of the new German democracy, given the horrors of 1939–45? Blank was clear on this point; the reforms of Scharnhorst had ultimately failed; those of the new armed forces would not.[39] But the larger question of the valid military tradition of the new army would continue to be a contentious issue throughout the post-war period.

Reforging the Broken German Sword

The new army had its work cut out. Chancellor Adenauer, perhaps optimistically, had promised his NATO allies that West Germany would field twelve divisions by 1959. In November 1955 the German Army had no facilities of any kind, no armaments industry, no logistics system, no training schools and only an embryonic staff to deal with the monumental planning necessary to start an army possessing nothing except ability. This last was the crucial element. Douglas MacArthur stated the case well when defending the US Army from budget cuts in the 1930s:

> 'Skilled officers like all other professional men, are products of continuous and laborious study, training, and experience. There is no short cut to this peculiar type of knowledge and ability they must possess. Trained officers constitute the most vitally essential element in modern war, and the only one that under no circumstances can be improvised or extemporized.'

Essential perhaps, but it was also a perishable element. The veteran Wehrmacht officers who answered the call had been civilians for the last ten years; many of the best could not be enticed away from dynamic and well-paid careers. Had a longer period elapsed far fewer suitable men would have been available; the ageing veterans were increasingly unable to render useful military service. The ten years of enforced 'civilianhood' had been enormously beneficial in ridding them of their sense of almost reclusive and contemptuous isolation as a class from society. They successfully applied their skills to the challenges of rebuilding Germany and developed an empathy and political sophistication that made them firm supporters of the new German democracy.

By the end of 1956, despite a great deal of public hostility, 265,000 men had volunteered for the Bundesheer although the intake requirement for that year was only 70,000. The great majority were Wehrmacht veterans. To ensure that the army harboured no Nazi or other anti-democratic elements, two commissions were established by the Bundestag to screen the applicants. Those considered for recommissioning in officer ranks up to lieutenant-colonel were screened by the Annahmeorganissationen (acceptance organizations) while those considered for the rank of colonel and above were investigated by the PGA (Personalgutachterausschuss) board. Those who had committed crimes against humanity or held the rank of colonel or general in the Waffen SS were not even considered. While it was not impossible for Waffen SS veterans to obtain a commission, the required standard was as stringent as that faced by the camel attempting passage of the eye of the needle. If a veteran could prove that he had been forced into the Waffen SS against his will, only the normal screening for any applicant was applied. Veterans who had transferred from the Wehrmacht or police had to provide an adequate explanation for this. All Waffen SS veterans had to make an 'active disavowal' of National Socialism. By the end of 1956, only 566 men, less than 1 per cent of the 67,000 men of the Heer, were Waffen SS veterans. Of that number only 45 were commissioned of the 299 accepted. The personal approval, unlikely as it might seem, of the defence minister was required for the commissioning of certain other categories such as former members of the following groups:

1. Allgemeine SS (the camp guards and Gestapo);
2. Sicherheitsdienst (SD), Gestapo intelligence;
3. Reactionary veterans' groups such as Stahlhelm;
4. French Foreign Legion;
5. Sentenced by foreign courts;
6. Served foreign intelligence organizations;
7. National Committee for a Free Germany.

The last category were those German soldiers who had been taken prisoner by the Soviets and had collaborated with them. German military tradition had a strong aversion to surrender and disloyalty to comrades; these men had been guilty of both as well as being tainted as present security risks by their association with the Soviets.[40]

Of the 117,000 deemed 'acceptable' in the initial screening, 53,000 were not Wehrmacht veterans. In the rank of major and above, 72 per cent of veteran officers were found acceptable, but of all ranks only 58 per cent were considered qualified. Of the latter, a large number were rejected solely because of age and not attitude.[41] On the senior screening board a critical part was played by the former General der Panzertruppe Frido von Senger und Etterlin. A Wehrmacht general officer and an avowed anti-Nazi during the war, he had won a reputation as a superlative tank general of the first order and as a chivalrous Christian gentleman. He had ensured the highest standards of moral conduct by the troops under his command, and as a member of the PGA screening board he had equally ensured the exclusion of any of those former Wehrmacht officers who had not met these standards. Upon his death in 1963, he was described by a colleague:

'He was the very man who influenced the Screening Committee's work in a decisive way for the good ... He was never reticent about his opinions and gave them to the committee unembellished ... it was one of the reasons why he was not exactly adored by everybody on the Board.' [42]

Von Senger's obstinate sense of justice and chivalry reflected living German military traditions that had been almost extinguished by the horrors of the twentieth century. The men who were chosen by Adenauer to plan and then organize the Bundeswehr were in that same tradition. They were the moral bedrock upon which it was founded. Von Senger expressed that spirit in a letter to the officers of his regiment in February 1941:

'From earliest times when troubadours sang chivalrous ballads in Provence, to the time when Prussia perfected the ideal of the 'perfect professional officer', and our enemy of today that of the 'perfect gentleman officer', the one guiding principle was that the feudal lord or the officer, the man set in authority, should devote himself to the protection of the weak. Your subordinates are placed there by the authority that the state has entrusted in you. They are placed there in your protection and they are totally dependent on your judgement, your care and your decisions. They are the weak – just as are they who inhabit the lands on which you now stand as a conqueror.' [43]

The embryo army now began to grow. It was a time of firsts. The first organized formation, a training company, was established on 1 January 1956. The first 1,500 officers and NCOs were inducted that month as the cadre for the first combat units. They began their work at the Bundeswehr's first depot, at Andernach, a small town between Bonn and Koblenz. They soon had the assistance of 9,572 volunteers who had transferred from the Bundesgrenzshutz (Federal Border Guard). It soon became apparent that recruitment of cadres was not the primary manpower problem; The army was short of privates. The prevailing anti-military attitude of German youth typified in the expression, *'ohne mich'* (without me) caused recruitment to lag seriously. Now, the wearing of a uniform, which had been treated with great respect in the past, often provoked public abuse. In 1956 the government was forced to resort to conscription at no little political cost, but it solved the manpower problem. The first conscripts were inducted on 1 April 1957. By the end of that year Bundeswehr strength had climbed to 134,000 doubling from the 67,000 at the end of 1956. However successful, conscription was the child of a compromise. The prospect of riots had been so grave that the new minister of defence, Franz Josef Strauss, had allowed only those eligible men who 'voluntarily' accepted military service to be conscripted.

The army's structure grew rapidly as well as its numbers. The first three of the twelve divisions promised to NATO had been raised by 1957, four in 1958 and one more in 1959. By the end of that year the Bundeswehr numbered 235,000 men of whom 144,000 were in the Bundesheer. Another 13,000 were in the Territorial Defence Command. Eight divisions had been formed and committed to NATO command, a remarkable organizational achievement. By 1960 the army had grown to ten divisions, the eleventh was added in 1963, and the twelfth was finally raised in 1965. The army has kept that number as being the maximum that German manpower and resources can support.[44] These twelve divisions were all assigned to NATO command and designated the Field Army (das Feldheer).

The Germans initially proposed to raise all twelve divisions as Panzer divisions. The armour-heavy force was designed to fight under the conditions of the nuclear battlefield and to provide forces for manoeuvre and counter-attack, but the United States requested a more balanced force structure so as to coincide with overall NATO requirements. The Germans adopted these considerations in their first army structure design (Heerstruktur I) for 1955–8 in which it raised the initial seven divisions (three infantry (Jäger), two armoured (Panzer), one mountain (Gebirgs) and one airborne (Luftlande)). The armoured and infantry divisions were based on three combat commands of four battalions each. The armoured commands consisted of two armoured and two motorized infantry battalions; the infantry commands of one armoured and three motorized infantry battalions.[45]

From 1958 until 1967 the Bundesheer drastically reorganized its divisions under Heerstruktur II to meet the requirements of both the nuclear and the post-nuclear battlefield. The changes cast the Field Army into the structure it was to retain throughout the remaining decades of the post-war era. The Jäger divisions were reorganized into Panzergrenadier (mechanized) divisions. When the twelfth division was finally raised in 1965, the Field Army consisted of three Panzer, seven Panzergrenadier, one Gebirgs, and one Luftlande divisions. Combat commands were eliminated and replaced with brigades of which each division had three. Brigades were robust, well-armed formations; the Panzergrenadier brigade had two Panzergrenadier, one Panzer and one towed artillery battalion. The Panzer brigade reversed the mechanized and tank mix and had a battalion of self-propelled guns. Both types of brigades had a mixed combat service support battalion to promote operational independence and self-sufficiency.[46]

In order to field as much combat power as possible, Heerstruktur I and II concentrated most of the assets of the army into its divisions and combat support elements. To facilitate this construction, the US Army agreed to provide most of the Bundesheer's combat service support as well as recognize in principle the need for the creation of a German Territorial Army that would assume rear area security and logistics functions in the future.[47]

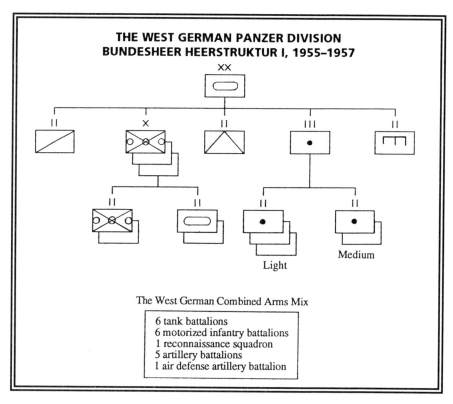

THE WEST GERMAN PANZER DIVISION
BUNDESHEER HEERSTRUKTUR I, 1955–1957

Light

Medium

The West German Combined Arms Mix

6 tank battalions
6 motorized infantry battalions
1 reconnaissance squadron
5 artillery battalions
1 air defense artillery battalion

Equipping this army was a more difficult proposition. The cadre of veteran officers and NCOs was the only direct military resource available to West Germany. The country had ceased arms production in 1945, and would require military aid from allies until such time as arms production could be resumed. Neither France nor Britain had the economic strength for a major military aid programme. The United States immediately responded. The Assistant Secretary of Defense, Frank Nash, headed a team that reviewed German requirements and compiled an inventory for the twelve divisions. This 'Nash List' was quickly approved; the first arms were delivered on 15 May 1956. Total US military assistance had reached $900 million by 1961.[48]

By 1963 the army's size and scale of equipment were impressive though by no means complete. Reconnaissance equipment included the US M24 Chaffee and M41 Walker Bulldog light tanks. The medium tank inventory numbered 2,500 including 1,500 M47 and 1,000 M48 Patton tanks. The United States had also supplied the M44 155mm self-propelled howitzer. German industry was now producing an armoured personnel carrier in quantity, the HS-30 with its 20mm cannon, and had delivered more than 1,000 to the army. Despite the numbers, few of the German divisions had their complete table of equipment. This was symptomatic of the growing pains throughout the army's structure. For example, the determination to field twelve divisions as quickly as possible assigned a lesser priority to the support forces. In 1963 the Bundesheer division slice was only 27,000 men. Added to this uneven growth was the relatively short, 18-month, conscription term and a continuing

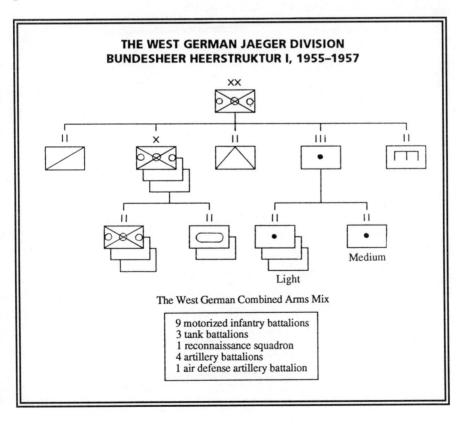

**THE WEST GERMAN JAEGER DIVISION
BUNDESHEER HEERSTRUKTUR I, 1955–1957**

The West German Combined Arms Mix

9 motorized infantry battalions
3 tank battalions
1 reconnaissance squadron
4 artillery battalions
1 air defense artillery battalion

shortage of 25,000 junior officers and NCOs both of which put a severe strain on the training establishment.[49]

STAATSBÜRGER IN UNIFORM

The manning and equipping of the Bundesheer were major accomplishments by any standard. A more profoundly difficult task was the creation of a new concept of service – one that ran counter to much of German military tradition, not to mention that of its democratic allies – that of the Staatsbürger in uniform (citizen in uniform). In the words of the original reformers of the Blank Amt, 'the inner structure of the armed forces in a free society must be such that young soldiers can complete their military training without a fundamental break with their civilian environments.' Unlike his counterparts in other major NATO armies, the soldier of the Bundesheer does not lose his political status during military service. He can run for any political office and if elected will be allowed to resign to take his seat. He can, if a regular or volunteer, belong to the servicemen's union or a civil service union; conscripts can retain their membership of a union. The creators of the armed forces were fully alive to the centrality of discipline to any military organization. At the same time, they were painfully aware of the visceral reaction within the German population to things military and the need for a practical accommodation of these

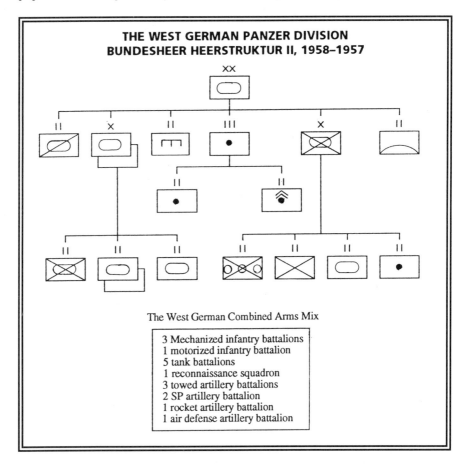

THE WEST GERMAN PANZER DIVISION
BUNDESHEER HEERSTRUKTUR II, 1958–1957

The West German Combined Arms Mix

3 Mechanized infantry battalions
1 motorized infantry battalion
5 tank battalions
1 reconnaissance squadron
3 towed artillery battalions
2 SP artillery battalion
1 rocket artillery battalion
1 air defense artillery battalion

realities. Their goal was 'not a democratic army, but an army to serve a democratic society'. It was a tightrope that few soldiers have ever had to walk.

The working mechanism of the 'citizen in uniform' policy was the concept of *Innere Führung* which emerged from the initial planning for the new army among the leading military reformers, all Wehrmacht veterans. It was a soldiers' creation, not that of suspicious civilian officials in the defence ministry. *Innere Führung* means literally 'inner leadership', but it has a myriad connotations that emphasize the moral responsibilities of each soldier as a member of a democratic society. Through its lens all military relationships would now be viewed. One of the founders of the Bundeswehr and high priest of *Innere Führung*, Count Wolf von Baudissin, described the intent in late 1955, 'A secularized "soldier's honour" which describes obedience, duty, hardihood and readiness for action as unquestioned and absolute concepts abandons the soldier blind and helpless to the whim of criminals and charlatans.'[50] By May 1956 the concept had been was embodied in the *Innere Führung Handbuch*, a brief collection of short essays that, as Walter Nelson described:

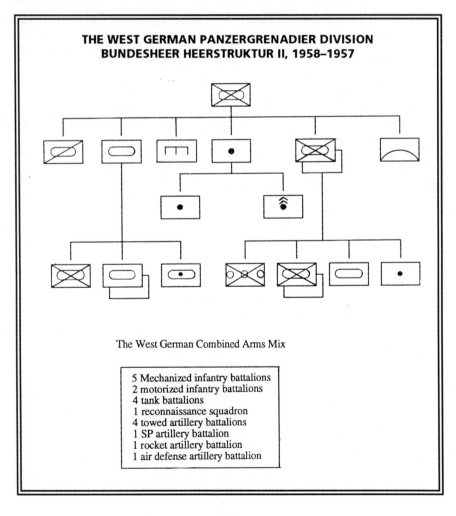

**THE WEST GERMAN PANZERGRENADIER DIVISION
BUNDESHEER HEERSTRUKTUR II, 1958–1957**

The West German Combined Arms Mix

5 Mechanized infantry battalions
2 motorized infantry battalions
4 tank battalions
1 reconnaissance squadron
4 towed artillery battalions
1 SP artillery battalion
1 rocket artillery battalion
1 air defense artillery battalion

'tried to tackle the agonizing problem of tradition, covered the relationship between officers and men, discussed and analyzed the concept of the citizen-in-uniform and his obligations as well as his rights, laid down the principles governing a decent and humane treatment of troops, and explained the limits to be set on military obedience.'[51]

Innere Führung represented less of a break in the tradition of military obedience than it appeared. Prussian and German military tradition had overtly encouraged the development of initiative at all levels to the point of disobedience if necessary. The concept was immortalized in the reply of the renowned Prussian general von Seydlitz to Frederick the Great on a battlefield of the Seven Years War. He had received instructions from the king that betrayed a misunderstanding of the situation. Von Seydlitz sent the royal messenger back with the statement that his head belonged to His Majesty any time he wanted it, but so long as it remained on his shoulders, he would continue to use it in the king's service. The 1911 German Army Field Service Regulations required 'every officer, under all conditions, to exercise initiative to the maximum extent, without fear of the consequences. Commanding officers must encourage and require this.'[52] A former Wehrmacht general on the PGA board, Fabian von Schlabrendorff, noted that it was the Hitler period that created the aberration: 'The so-called "blind obedience" of the German Army was a purely Hitlerian creation and there cannot be the slightest doubt that it is invalid from both the ethical and military point of view.' The object of the creators of *Innere Führung* was to ensure that every soldier was aware of and determined to exercise the moral initiative in both its ethical and military dimensions.

An institutional mechanism was added to the conceptual one of *Innere Führung* to safeguard the army's allegiance to its role in a democratic society. The Bundestag created The Parliamentary Commissioner for Military Affairs as its own military watchdog who is independent of the executive functions of the government. The commissioner's role combines that of inspector-general and military ombudsman. He has no direct authority whatsoever, but relies on the considerable 'prestige of his position and his powers of persuasion to redress grievances' in the protection of soldiers' civil rights and the principles of *Innere Führung*. In practice, the commissioner will investigate a complaint and either advise the minister of defence or the appropriate commanding officer of the need to take action. In extreme cases he can refer the matter to the federal criminal courts; the army has no courts-martial system, and military justice is handled through the federal court system. By 1964 the commissioner's net had widened far beyond the initial responsibilities of the office. In that year, he investigated 1,696 cases within the army, of which only 12 per cent related to the protection of civil rights. The great majority of complaints fell within two groups – career concerns such as promotion, pay, education and training; and welfare, especially relating to family life.[53]

THE THORN OF TRADITION

No problem was to torment the Bundesheer so much as the question of the maintenance of military tradition (*Traditionsphlege*). By tradition was meant customs, events and the ethos of the past that are inextricable from a nation's experience and give meaning and purpose to the present. For the army this represented an enormous dilemma. Considering the memories of two world wars, what were the valid traditions of the German Army? The fact that von Scharnhorst's two hundredth anniversary was chosen as the army's founding day showed that there was a keen appreciation of the importance of tradition. Yet, at the same time, there was a sharp reluctance on the part of the government to permit German military traditions full rein. Minister of Defence Blank was quite clear in his opinion that the military's fondness for tradition and its pageantry was 'a burden in the age in which techno-logical progress of armies and modern weapons placed ever greater demands on the soldier's abilities'. The Bundeswehr did not need, 'the *Pathos* of parades and military pageants, but the sobriety with which one does the most essential thing without too many big words'.[54]

Blank's viewpoint underscored the dilemma faced by the army. Soldiering is not clerking. Soldiering is an emotionally intense profession that demands the deepest moral and physical efforts from its practitioners; it cannot be reduced to the spiritual anonymity of clerking – unless the nation wishes to throw good money after bad to support an army that will collapse when called upon to fight. Count von Baudissin argued that the maintenance of spiritual and ethical values were the essence of tradition, not the common fixation on the 'externals, rituals and symbols of military life'.[55] Man, however, lives by symbols, the German soldier as much as anyone. Draw a line in time and tell the British or French Armies that they are to pick only lightly from the traditions on the far side of the line, then watch the life and vigour pour out of those centuries old institutions. There is a bond over cen-turies that still animates performance on the battlefield, however much the typical civilian may scoff.

The most obvious failure in this regard was the miserable selection of the new uniform, a baggy and shapeless double-breasted suit of 'gray sacking' that was intentionally chosen as a break with German tradition. American-style collar insignia and helmets, new rank badges and webbing belts did exactly that. The uni-form was chosen apparently because a group of young soldiers liked it. It was met with derision in public and was an acute embarrassment to wear for the veteran soldier.[56] More embarrassment was in store; at a reception hosted by the British Army, the German officers could only stare in pained silence at the resplendent dress uniforms of their hosts. The British commander inquired politely why the German officers were not wearing their combat and service ribbons and was told that the French had objected. He whispered to his aide. The British officers filtered out of the reception and returned without their ribbons. It was a mark of respect and sensitivity for the soldierly spirit that the new German Army had thirsted for and found only at the hands of a former enemy.

The thirst for tradition found other forms. There was an intensely negative reaction, for example, to adoption of the American position of attention with fists along the seams of the trousers, referred to as the 'peeing stance' or 'SPD stance', rather than the traditional flat hands along the seams. The troops also reintroduced the old traditional salute. The issue of unit lineages and honours quickly arose as the Bundesheer began to expand. Permission was increasingly asked to reintroduce the von Seekt system of lineages and honours adopted in 1921 in which company-level units of the Reichswehr had preserved continuity with regiments of the old imperial army. A plan was initially devised which would allow garrisons to revive local traditions. 'Tradition has everything for itself in a specific garrison: the mem-ory of the population (and) the (presence of) buildings and monuments'. A plan was to be drawn up to identify the units that had been stationed in Bundeswehr garrisons until 1914, after 1918, and up to 1933. Before it could be implemented the army was faced with the initiatives of local commanders. For example, in February 1958, Panzer Battalion 2 in Hemer, Westphalia, formally assumed the lineages of the three imperial hussar regiments (including the Blücher Hussars and the Death's

Head Hussars of Danzig) and the Reichswehr and Wehrmacht 5th Cavalry Regiment of Stolp in Pomerania, the unit which had in its turn first assumed the lineage of the Death's Head Hussars. The troops responded positively to the assumption, and the commander asked permission to name their barracks after Marshal Blücher of Waterloo fame. By the end of 1958 the army had developed a plan of assigning unit lineages up to 1939 to take effect in 1961 with the proviso that no action be taken until the decree was issued. But the implementing decree was steadily postponed as units increasingly assumed the lineages associated with their garrisons and, as with the hussars, with units whose garrisons were now in East Germany or Poland. The acts of affirmation were greeted with no little enthusiasm by the troops, veterans groups, and the civilian populations of the garrison towns. Finally in 1965, at the behest of the government, a new decree was issued. The assumption of lineages according to the Reichswehr convention was strictly forbidden.[57]

EAST GERMANY

The Nationale Volksarmee (NVA) marked its official foundation on 18 January 1956, an event supposedly arising from the 'spontaneous' reaction to the events surrounding the founding of the Bundeswehr the previous November. It was a clumsy fiction; the NVA had already completed its first major phase of expansion and development. In January 1956, when the first cadres reported to the first Bundeswehr company, the NVA strength stood at 120,000 men in seven divisions.

Although East Germany was vociferous in its outrage over the number of former Wehrmacht officers in the Bundeswehr, the NVA had also been founded of the same material although the vetting had had somewhat different priorities. As early as 1952 15,000 former officers and 30,000 former NCOs had been pressed into service to form the basis for the NVA's major expansion. The defence minister, Willi Stoph, a politician, held the rank of colonel-general but was assisted by Lieutenant-General Vincenz Müller, formerly of the Wehrmacht, in the same rank, and a former member of the National Committee for a Free Germany.[58]

The East German government was even more desperate than the Federal Republic had been to generate the support of its population for the new army. The Wehrmacht uniform was reintroduced with only minor changes. The Nazi eagle was gone, and a new style helmet was developed. Even the uniform colour was the same, although the NVA was at pains to explain that the colour was actually *steingrau* (stone grey) and not *feldgrau* (field grey), a distinction lost on civilian and veteran alike. Even the branch colours going back to the imperial army were retained. The NVA found itself impaled on the same dilemma of tradition as did the Bundeswehr. In fact the NVA situation was even thornier. It had not only carefully to pick and choose over the field of German military traditions, it also had to do so under the glaring eye of Communist ideology, what would be called a basic marketing error in the West. There was no question of reintroducing the von Seekt convention for unit lineages; after all, the DDR had proclaimed all ties broken with the past state structures of Germany. The NVA was to be the army of the working class; it was also to be primarily the instrument of the Communist Party of East Germany. The acceptable military tradition began with the Peasants Revolt of the Middle Ages. As with the Bundeswehr, the safely distant Scharnhorst and the other military reformers of the wars against Napoleon were enshrined. Much was made of the alliance of Prussia and Russia. After that the field became even thinner. The mantle of modern German military tradition fell almost entirely on the revolutionaries of 1848, the Red soldier and sailor revolutionaries of 1918, the Germans who had served with the Spanish Loyalists, and the collaborators of the Committee for a Free Germany.

With the formation of the Warsaw Pact, all the forces of the NVA were subordinated to the Pact's Unified Command. In 1958 the last major changes were made in the structure of the NVA prior to its disintegration in 1990. The 6th Motorized Rifle Division was disbanded, and the remaining six divisions divided into two equal military districts of one tank and two motorized rifle divisions each.

Despite a determined recruitment campaign that often descended to coercion and terror, the NVA remained so unattractive that it could not meet its strength goals. By the time of the building of the Berlin Wall at the end of 1961, 24,300 soldiers and police had fled to the West. The Wall helped staunch the flow of deserters and gave the DDR the excuse to begin conscription in August 1962, confident that it would not cause a stampede of young men westward.[59]

The organization and equipment of the NVA were close copies of Soviet models and adapted in tandem to the changes in Soviet doctrine. For example, in the early 1960s, the proportion of infantry was reduced in favour of artillery and armour to fight on the nuclear battlefield. The major difference with the Soviet models was the lower personnel strengths in the NVA; tank divisions averaged 7,200 men and motorized rifle divisions 9,250. Soviet units had twice the supporting units and more field and anti-aircraft artillery. Soviet equipment was more modern. Training was hard, more than one-third taking place at night; wartime requirements and privation were stressed together with frequent exercises and deployments.[60]

With the building of the Berlin Wall, the NVA claimed the dubious honour of being the first German army since 1945 to acquire real operational experience – of an odious sort. The NVA deployed to cut off West Berlin and stand guard as the Wall was built.

POLAND

THE POLISH OCTOBER

In June 1956 Polish workers rioted in Poznan, and Polish soldiers refused the orders of their political officers to fire on them. The internal security troops were not so squeamish and inflicted hundreds of casualties. The resulting revulsion throughout the nation precipitated the fall of the Stalinist government and the return to power of Wladyslaw Gomulka in October. In the face of a Stalinist coup and the movement of Soviet divisions on Warsaw, the Polish Army was split between its Soviet generals and Polish officers supportive of Gomulka and remained confined to barracks. Reform-minded internal security, air force and navy units, however, did prepare to defend the capital, and the Soviet Union backed down.

RE-NATIONALIZATION

The return to power of Gomulka marked a return to Polish national themes rather than slavishly copied Soviet forms. The army, which had failed to support the Polish cause, was rapidly 'de-Sovietized' and 're-nationalized'. Soviet Marshal Rokossovsky, the Defence Minister of Poland, and his contingent of Soviet officers were thanked and sent home. Grudgingly one Soviet officer was left in a critical position as chief of the general staff. General Spychalski, who had been purged in 1948, was made defence minister. Another purge victim, General Zarzycki, was made head of the Main Political Administration. A number of other purged Polish officers and even a few who had served in the pre-war army were recalled.[61]

The official position of Soviet forces in Poland was put on a more equitable basis in December when a status-of-forces agreement was signed which specifically included a statement of Soviet 'non-interference' in Polish internal affairs.[62]

Polish national military traditions were re-introduced in uniforms, insignia, flags and ceremonies. The most notable return was to the distinctive CZAPKA headgear based on the nineteenth-century lancer's cap. Polish eagle cap badges identical with those worn by the troops of the Grand Duchy of Warsaw, minus only the crown, were reintroduced.[63] Indestructible Polish notions of romantic chivalry also re-appeared in the commissioning ceremony in which an officer touches the kneeling officer aspirant on the shoulder with his sabre. Another feature unique within the Warsaw Pact was the official presence in the PPA of Catholic chaplains. Although their presence represented the regime's grudging acknowledgement of the Polish people's devotion to Catholicism, the PPA limited both the number of chaplains and the scope of their duties.

The Polish Army quickly discovered that there were limits to its re-nationalization, some things the Soviet Union and the Polish Communist Party would not tolerate. The denunciations of Stalin at the 22nd Soviet Party Congress encouraged Polish officers to demand an accounting of the massacre of Polish officers in the Katyn Forest. The Polish Party immediately forced the resignation of 500 officers including the Chief of the Main Political Administration, General Zarzycki. A few Soviet generals were even returned for service in the Polish Army. This only reinforced the hostility towards the Soviets of large elements of the Polish Army. As late as 1963 the Chief of the Main Political Administration, General Jaruzelsky, stated that the prestige of the West remained high and that a certain coolness persisted in Polish attitudes to other members of the Warsaw Pact, particularly the Soviet Union.[64]

Despite re-nationalization the Polish Army continued to suffer from the low prestige caused by Soviet domination prior to the Polish October. In 1958 a survey of Warsaw secondary school youth showed that its ranking had fallen to 21st place, below office workers. Officer recruitment became very difficult, the artillery academy being able to fill only 40 per cent of its class of 1957–8.[65]

Re-nationalization also diminished the power of the political apparatus in the Polish Army. The activities of the Main Political Administration were severely curtailed and political officers were removed from company level. The result was a strengthening of the professional officer corps in relation to the Communist Party. Party authority was represented largely by Party organizations in the army that had authority only over Party members, but loyalty to the Party was never questioned by the army's élite which had long become attuned to Soviet military thought and were willing to marry Polish national security to Soviet military imperatives. The consequence was full Polish participation in the Soviet conceptualized 'Revolution in Military Affairs' that emerged in the late 1950s. The Polish Army developed its own double component in this new doctrine. This argued that the Polish Army would have to fight on both external and internal fronts. The first was offensive action against NATO; the second was defence against nuclear strikes on the Poland itself.

Beginning in 1960 Polish divisions were restructured on the Soviet model and began modernizing with considerable Soviet assistance and with domestic commitments that badly strained the Polish economy. By 1965 the Polish Army was second only to the Soviet Union in the Warsaw Pact in size and modernization. Its 200,000 men filled fourteen divisions including four tank, nine motorized rifle and one airborne. The Soviet presence within the army persisted, with Soviets filling the posts of third deputy defence minister and Chief of the Main Political Administration. Another Soviet general commanded the Warsaw Military District, and Soviet officers commanded all Polish rocket units. The pre-war officer cadres had almost all been retired; by the middle 1960s all but 2 per cent of the officer corps had received their training in the Communist army.[66]

In 1963 the faction of the officer corps made up of former Communist wartime partisans worked its way into the top leadership levels of the army. This faction maintained that Poland did not solely owe its liberation to Soviet forces. The Sino-Soviet rift caused a number of these officers to advocate that Poland turn the dispute to its advantage in the example of Rumania to slip out from under Soviet vassalage. Although by 1965 the influence of this group had been reduced by Gomulka, they were responsible in that year for again raising the issue of an accounting of the Katyn Massacre. It was an issue which Gomulka was able to suppress only with great difficulty.[67]

SOVIET UNION

During the previous decade the Soviet Army had recovered its strength and repaired the damages of purges and war. It emerged improved and re-armed, but was still only a few short steps from the army of 1945. The new decade would be an evolutionary leap as the army adopted a new doctrine and drastically reorganized itself. The new decade would also see the army's first entry in the political struggles of the CPSU and its first major combat, in Hungary, since 1945.

ZHUKOV, THE KINGMAKER

Marshal Zhukov and his fellow generals had been well rewarded by Khrushchev for their moral support in his power struggle for leadership of the Party. In February 1955 Zhukov was made minister of defence and eleven generals were promoted to the rank of Marshal of the Soviet Union (MSU). Like a spring that had been compressed for twenty years, the army sprang forward to re-assert itself as an institution and as a major player at the highest level of Soviet politics.

The new vigour that coursed through the army emanated from the confident and aggressive personality of Zhukov. The hero of the nation and the darling of the army, hailed as 'today's Suvorov', and 'the military genius of our time', Zhukov quickly moved forward on three fronts to right three of the military's most deeply held grievances: (1) the stultifying political controls by which the principle of unity of command was violated as the commander was forced to share authority with military councils and political officers; (2) the deadly embrace of Stalinist military doctrine; and (3) the denigrating and condescending treatment of the army's role in Soviet history which assigned the essential credit for victory to Stalin and the Party.[68]

Zhukov rapidly began to dismantle those Party controls that most interfered with the commander's authority and contributed least to military efficiency and professionalism. He played down the role of military councils and abolished company and battalion level *Zampolits* (political officers), insisting that those at regimental level confine their work to educational and morale support activities, preferably in the soldiers' leisure time. Commanders could substitute combat for political training, and officers' political and ideological training was made voluntary. Time given to the teaching of Marxism-Leninism was drastically shortened as Zhukov bluntly stated that it was necessary 'to abolish aimlessness and abstract instruction ...' Finally, to the great satisfaction of the officer corps, the detested public criticism sessions which commanders had to endure were abolished.[69]

The military also began to insist that the histories of the war be rewritten to reflect accurately the army's contribution to victory, and properly to assign (after the 20th Party Congress in 1956) the blame for the initial great defeats of Soviet arms to Stalin. There was also a campaign to encourage Soviet writers and film makers to portray the Soviet officer in a more positive light. One of the most remarkable results was a film script published by the celebrated war novelist, Konstanin Simonov, which portrayed favourably Soviet prisoners of war who had previously been excoriated as traitors.

The Army had broken free for the time being. With the KGB humbled after the revelations about Stalin's butcheries, there was no choice for the Party but to swallow the army's new self-assertion. The years 1955 to 1957 saw the army's brief heyday of professionalism in which the fetters of political control and interference seemed to melt away under Zhukov's glare. In June 1957 Zhukov played kingmaker, the first time in Soviet history that a sword had been thrown on to the political scales to mark the winner. A Party faction had attempted to remove Khrushchev as First Party Secretary. Zhukov's timely support in the name of the army at the Central Committee showdown ensured Khrushchev's victory. His gratitude was of the order of Justinian's to Belisarius. Fearing that the man who had made him this time could be the man who deposed him the next, in October 1957 he removed Zhukov from all his posts in the army and the Party. Zhukov was broken as thoroughly as the army's brief affair with professional independence. Political controls were reimposed, and stewardship of the army was put in the hands of Marshal Malinovsky whose chief characteristic was obedience.

With Zhukov dismissed, the Party rushed in to liquidate his reforms and reintroduce every stultifying element of political control. The political officers were reinstated with their power and authority re-affirmed. The whole of 1958 was a year of witchhunts. Every officer who had publicly supported Zhukov's reforms was identified and denounced in the military press. Their fate was either retirement, transfer or a speedy recantation followed by enthusiastic political work among the troops.[70]

THE REVOLUTION IN MILITARY AFFAIRS

The ferment in Soviet military theory encouraged by Zhukov survived his fall. In 1958 a series of general staff seminars was conducted to review problems of military art and the nature of future war. The participants concluded that nuclear weapons and the missile had worked a fundamental change in the very nature of warfare, such that the very basis of Soviet military thought would have to be rebuilt from its foundations. Based on these seminars, Khrushchev ordered a major study of this issue by the army's senior officers and theorists. They confirmed the initial thesis from which the Party leadership concluded that nuclear weapons and missiles would be the decisive factors of modern war. The Party had thus fulfilled its responsibility to approve doctrine, which in Soviet terms is the determination of the nature of future war.[71] These conclusions were distilled in Marshal V.D. Sokolovsikiy's book, *Soviet Military Strategy* which was to remain the bible of Soviet military theory for almost twenty years.

This doctrine became so thoroughly embedded in Soviet military practice and theory through a massive education and information campaign that it easily survived Khrushchev's fall in 1964. This in itself is testimony to the firm grip on the army held by the Party. The implementation of the doctrine caused immense turmoil and hardship within the army. Khrushchev had set the stage for this when he announced that the firepower of nuclear weapons had replaced mass armies. In his view the role of the Ground Forces was to 'prolong' the effect of the initial nuclear strike. He believed in a short war scenario in which the role of the Ground Forces was clearly auxiliary to that of the nuclear missile forces. The days of the Ground Forces as the premier service seemed over. Pride of place was given to the new Strategic Rocket Forces.

The Ground Forces brooded over the consequences of Khurshchev's decisions. The demobilizations were personally insulting to the army; the doctrinal shifts were professionally even more disquieting. While the role of nuclear weapons was not resisted, there was a great deal of unease over Khrushchev's insistence on a short war scenario which had very real consequences for the army's size, equipment and training. The position he had taken was an alarming contradiction of a deep theoretical tradition that insisted that no one weapon or system was a war-winner; he attempted to paper over this problem by supporting the doctrine of the combination of the various arms as the only way to seal success, though the missile forces remained the key. That approach allowed particular weapons within the Ground Forces to be called into question for their utility. Even the sacrosanct tank was challenged.[72]

> 'When I went out on to the training field and saw the tanks attacking and how the anti-tank artillery hit these tanks, I became ill. After all, we are spending a lot of money to build tanks. And if – God forbid, as they say – war breaks out, these tanks will burn even before they reach the line indicated by the commands.'[73]

In 1964 Khrushchev even abolished the headquarters of the Ground Forces and re-subordinated it directly to the general staff. A few years earlier the *shefstvo* (patronage) policy, first practised in the 1930s, was reimposed on the Ground Forces. *Shefstvo* essentially told off troops to a factory, state or collective farm as general labour. Military considerations were rarely taken into account; troops were especially needed during the peak planting and harvest times in spring, early summer and autumn which unfortunately were also the Ground Forces' prime training periods. The system became another Soviet institutional prop to an inefficient economy. By the early 1970s 55,000 military trucks and drivers alone were assigned to support agriculture in Kazakhstan. The days of the Ground Forces as the premier service surely seemed over. There was no doubt that pride of place had been given to the new Strategic Rocket Forces.

THE GREAT DEMOBILIZATIONS: THE ARMY IS MUGGED AGAIN

Between 1955 and 1961 the Soviet armed forces suffered three major traumatic reductions. The demand of Soviet industry for labour forced the initial massive reduction between 1955 and 1957. From a strength of 5,763,000, 1,840,000 men were demobilized. In 1958–9 another 300,000 men were cut followed by 600,000 in 1960–1. A fourth reduction of 600,000 slated for 1964 was forestalled by Khrushchev's ousting in 1964. A total of 2,740,000 men were released from 1955 to 1961.[74] By the early 1960s the Soviet armed forces had fallen to about 2,400,000 men of whom 1,600,000 were in the Ground Forces. Industry's demand for labour was a symptom of a fundamentally intractable problem. The horrors and privations of the war years and the famines of the early post-war years had resulted in a dramatic fall in the birth rate. By the early sixties there simply would not be enough young men available for conscription to fill an armed force numbering almost six million. From a high of 6,915,000 males between the ages of 18 and 21 in 1961, the number would fall to 3,164,000 by 1964.[75]

The demobilization was so incompetently conducted that it resulted in what one author called 'disorder bordering on sabotage'. The almost three million demobilized men included well over a quarter of a million officers, most of whom had neither a pension nor another calling to fall back on. The treatment of these cadres was so shabby that the scar became an indelible part of the army's institutional memory that would chill support for Gorbachev's reductions at the end of the Cold War. Barely 35 per cent of these released officers found jobs of comparable position and salary. The rest sank from privileged professionals to under-privileged labourers. Oleg Penkovskiy recounted the plight of a dismissed general, a veteran of two wars and thirty years' service, reduced to raising strawberries. For accepting the help of a collective farm worker, he was denounced as an exploiter and stripped of his meagre pension. The remaining cadres recoiled in horror, anxious at any cost to avoid such a fate. Part of the cost was the need scrupulously to toe the Party line. The political officers also used it gleefully as an opportunity to glean the few stalks of wheat that had shown sufficient spirit or independence to be noticed above the rest.[76]

Adding insult to injury, Khrushchev began an economy campaign that cut pay, pensions and privileges of the active forces and was to blame Zhukov for the idea in his memoirs though it was Zhukov who had remonstrated with him to defend the dignity of the officer corps, 'I do not want my officers to become beggars. If they become beggars, they will not fight; indeed, nobody will be able to recognize them as officers. An officer must be well fed and be able to provide more or less adequate support to his family.' Khrushchev had his own opinions, 'They have become fat! We cannot and must not raise such intelligentsia and capitalists.' The pensions of the officer corps were reduced between two and two and a half times. Even the pensions for the families of fallen officers were reduced by 50 per cent. After Zhukov's fall, even the marshals Konev, Sokolovskiy and Timoshenko who had excoriated him in order to curry favour with Khrushchev, opposed his military personnel policies. 'The reductions among the middle-level army officers will reduce them to a state of pitiful vegetation.'[77]

The military's detestation of Khrushchev grew with each ruthless reduction. Morale collapsed. The army had been brutalized to a degree only surpassed by Stalin's massacre of the officer corps in 1937–8. For good reasons Khrushchev began to fear for the army's reliability in a conflict. In time-honoured fashion he attempted to buy off the military's leadership by a wholesale promotion of 373 marshals and generals on Victory Day, 9 May 1961. Now, with crises in Cuba and Berlin beginning to fester, he needed the army. When Berlin finally erupted later in 1961, Khrushchev asked that Zhukov and other prominent but retired marshals return to active duty to show their support. Marshals Konev and Sokolovskiy agreed, but Zhukov refused. For this old soldier, enough was enough.[78] When Brezhnev engineered Khrushchev's removal on 14 October 1964, the military leadership understandably failed to offer him any help. In fact, the military had been informed of the impending action and approved.

COMPLETE MECHANIZATION
Although this decade was marked by the Soviet army's foray in and out of politics and the fearful turmoil of demobilization, it is perhaps more appropriately to be remembered for the transition to complete mechanization. Tukhachevsky's dream

of a fully mechanized combined arms team was realized. The Second World War had validated that dream and Soviet industry had been bent to its realization. Zhukov set this process in motion in 1955 and by 1957 was able to see the work largely accomplished. For the first time in history a major power would prepare its entire army to ride to war.

By the end of 1955 the ground forces' horse transport had disappeared. Infantry (rifle) divisions shrank in strength as the armoured forces were expanded in size to provide a complete armoured complement as the mechanization of the infantry progressed. By 1957 rifle divisions and the post-war mechanized divisions were converted to motorized rifle divisions equipped with either wheeled or tracked armoured personnel carriers, although a number of lower category readiness divisions were to rely on truck transport for their infantry into the late 1980s. The motorized rifle division became a formidable combined arms team, possessing more tanks than a Second World War mechanized corps and acquiring anti-tank guided missiles, powerful new artillery and new engineer equipment. Personnel were largely armed with automatic weapons.[79]

The tank troops had also been reorganized by 1957, becoming the main striking arm of the Ground Forces. A reorganized tank division now had more tanks than a wartime tank corps. The emphasis on the tank was based on its unique role on the nuclear battlefield.

> 'Because of their new organization, great striking power, mobility, and low vulnerability to nuclear weapons, tank troops were able extensively to exploit the results of nuclear weapons use and to inflict crushing blows on the enemy, developing an uninterrupted offensive at great speeds and to great depth. '[80]

By 1955 the airborne forces of the VDV (Vozdushno-Desantnyye Voisk) had become the élite of the armed forces and expanded to seven divisions within their own command directly subordinated to the ministry of Defence. With the fall of Zhukov, they lost independent status and were resubordinated to the Ground Forces from 1956 to 1964. Their role was limited to supporting nuclear strikes with tactical and operational landings.[81]

Mechanization allowed the number of divisions to be reduced from about 175 to 140, some 20 of which would be maintained at a low-strength cadre status. The new tank and motorized infantry divisions were now grouped into more streamlined groupings. The tank army consisted of three to four tank divisions, while the combined arms army (CAA) was made up of two to three motorized infantry divisions and one tank division. The combined arms army was generally designed for the breakthrough effort and the tank army for exploitation and pursuit. A combination of two to three armies was called a front. Both armies and fronts were supported by new nuclear-capable missile brigades.

By 1965 the tank and motorized rifle divisions had assumed – with some modifications – the basic form they were to retain until the present time. Each type of division was built on four manoeuvre regiments split 3 to 1 between tank and motorized rifle regiments. The tank division had three tank regiments and one motorized rifle regiment; the latter had included one tank battalion giving the division ten tank battalions or about 300 tanks. The motorized rifle division had three motorized rifle regiments, each with one tank battalion, and a tank regiment, giving it six tank battalions of about 180 tanks. Both types of division were supported by a 3-battalion artillery regiment. The design of the divisions reflected the lessons learned from the Great Patriotic War about deep operations; they were everything that Zhukov had wished he had had. The tank division was a flexible, easily controlled formation capable of exploiting the fluid battlefield, but it lacked staying power, the ability to operate in difficult terrain and to hold ground; characteristics that were not lacking in the motorized rifle division with its three motorized rifle regiments. At the same time, it had the tank strength of a western tank division.[82]

To meet the demands of mechanization Soviet industry produced a number of new types of armoured equipment. Pride of place was held by the T-62 tank, a follow-on development of the T-54/55. Production began in 1961 and continued until 1971–2, although it did not make its first public appearance until 1965. The T-62 displayed many innovations in tank technology such as a 115mm smoothbore gun fully stabilized in both horizontal and vertical axes. An automatic loading mechanism for the main gun was another innovation, though less of a success as indicated by the number of Soviet jokes about soprano gunners and devoured loaders. Another feature befitting its origin after the Revolution in Military Affairs was the PAZ nuclear defence system which sealed the vehicle against airborne contaminants by use of air filters, hatch liners, and an overpressure system. The T-55 stayed in production until 1981 and remained the mainstay of the Soviet tank force.[83]

To support the tanks new scout vehicles and armoured personnel carriers were also produced in large numbers. The BRDM-1 wheeled scout vehicle was developed in the mid-1950s and entered production in 1957. The wheeled 8 x 8 BTR-60P series APC was also developed in the mid-1950s and went into production in 1961. The first Soviet tracked APC, the boxy BTR-50P series, was seen even earlier, in 1958. The wheeled BTR-60P series was designed to equip the motorized rifle divisions while the tracked BTR-50P series was allocated to the infantry regiment of the tank divisions. The first versions of both APCs were open topped making the occupants vulnerable to artillery and requiring exit over the sides as a consequence of the rear-mounted engines, a rather risky business when in combat. Later models provided overhead armour protection, but the infantry had to wait for the BMP series for a less hazardous dismount. Both vehicles were also amphibious with waterjet propulsion systems and both were equipped with NBC protection systems.

BATTLE HONOURS: BUDAPEST, 1956; NOVOCHERKASSK, 1962
The Soviet Army shed a great deal of proletarian blood during this decade, once against its Hungarian ally in the newly proclaimed Warsaw Pact, and once against its own starving citizens in Novocherkassk.

The Hungarian Revolt planted a sharp slap in the face to the Soviet Army. The two divisions initially sent into Budapest to support the Communist regime were severely mauled and forced to withdraw by an aroused populace. More disturbing was the brittle reliability shown by many of the troops. Many of the troops were reluctant to fight people whom they had come to know. Many defected and joined the Hungarians. In one incident, a Soviet tank officer ordered the guns of his unit turned on the Hungarian Communist security troops who had fired into a peaceful crowd and killed a child in its mother's arms. The embarrassed withdrawal of these troops was followed by Zhukov's commitment of 220,000 fresh troops and 2,500 tanks. These troops had no such ties to the local population and many of the tanks were the new T-54/55s. Budapest was pounded into submission with great brutality but at the cost of an estimated 8,000 Soviet casualties.

In 1962 the people of Novocherkassk in the Caucasus region of the Soviet Union rioted in desperation over conditions of near starvation. General Shaposhnikov, commander of the troops sent to the scene was ordered to fire into the crowd; he refused and was immediately replaced by an officer who eagerly gave the order. Hundreds of civilians were killed, and General Shaposhnikov was dismissed from the service.[84]

ISRAEL

Sinai 1956 – The Stallions' War

If wars have military patron saints, the Sinai Campaign of 1956 surely had two who perched in spirit on the shoulder of the IDF – Liddell Hart and Lord Nelson. Hart and his strategy of the indirect approach had already been a favourite of the self-made leaders of the IDF. That was evident in Moshe Dayan's concept of the operation, 'To confound the organization of the Egyptian forces in the Sinai and bring about their collapse ... we have no interest in killing a maximum number of his troops.' Throw the enemy off balance so that he falls of his own weight. Isolate Egyptian fortified areas so that they would be abandoned as useless. It was an intelligent approach for an army needing a quick and as bloodless a victory as possible.

Nelson's contribution was to complicate things a bit. His order before Trafalgar was prophetic of this campaign as well: 'But in case signals can neither be seen nor perfectly understood no Captain can do very wrong if he places his Ship alongside that of an Enemy.' The senior battlefield leadership of the IDF was in many ways a new Nelsonian 'band of brothers', attuned to a common insight of war, an energetic blend of aggression, adaptability and impudent initiative.

With a force of ten brigades the IDF destroyed four well-equipped and well-entrenched Egyptian brigades in less than eight days, mastering an area of the Sinai three times larger than Israel at the cost of 180 Israeli dead and 3,000 Egyptian dead and 7,000 prisoners.[85] Rather than the desperate, close-run victory of 1949, the IDF gave a performance reminiscent of the lethal dash of Guderian and Rommel's panzers. Nevertheless, for the IDF, the glow of victory did not obscure the appearance of serious problems; rather they provoked a wide range of reforms.

The most glaring deficiency was in the mobilization system. Mobilization had been delayed too long resulting in insufficient preparation time. Seven of the ten Israeli brigades were provided by the reserves, but in the interests of security and surprise most had had no refresher training; four of them were not mustered until D + 2. As a result many reservists were sent into battle with only a few hours of preparation. Most of them had served on active duty either during the War of Liberation or before Dayan revitalized the army. The performance of the three conscript brigades (1 Infantry 'Golani', 7 Armoured and 202 Parachute) was everything that could be expected. That of the reservists was far more uneven. Two of the seven brigades failed in their missions while three were exemplary.[86]

During the vehicle call-up the army received far fewer trucks than it had expected. Many were in poor working order, poorly equipped and often not matched with their civilian reservist drivers. It was found that Ariel Sharon's parachute brigade had been promised 153 trucks but only received 46. 'And in the entire column there was not a single spanner to fit the wheel nuts of the vehicles with front-wheel drive, so that any truck with a punctured tyre had to be abandoned.'[87] These problems were evidence of widespread administrative and logistics management failures that plagued the IDF.

At the operational level the IDF's flexible and decentralized command and control system proved very effective. As Edward Luttwak has written:

> 'The brigades operated as virtually independent forces under loose control of divisional headquarters while the control of the Area Command

... and GHQ in Tel Aviv was looser still. Without having to follow detailed plans prepared in advance or being subject to a continuous flow of orders from above, brigade commanders and their staffs were free to make their own tactical decisions.' [88]

In practice higher headquarters limited themselves to ensuring that the tactical units adhered to guidelines that had established only 'objectives, targets and timetables'. The problem with this system lies in the abdication of higher headquarters responsibilities to co-ordinate the various formations to take advantage of strategic and operational opportunities. After the decentralized command system had been modified, an 'optional control' feature allowed higher headquarters to intervene to take control of an operation when a 'broad picture' approach was required. The decentralized approach fitted Moshe Dayan's informal style of leadership. It should have been no surprise to him when two of his commanders disregarded his orders and made their own decisions on the battlefield. That they were ultimately correct decisions is a tribute to the personalities Dayan had cultivated in the IDF's leadership.

Ariel Sharon commanded 202 Parachute Brigade whose mission was to link up with the parachute battalion dropped near the Mitla Pass. He was to stop short of the pass, but in the words of S. L. A. Marshall:

'All tactical logic has a utilitarian ambivalence which works to the advantage of the imaginative commander on the spot, as in Sharon's case. If he wishes sufficiently to resume an offensive enterprise, he can almost invariably find a defensive reason for doing so.'[89]

His reason was to reconnoitre the pass which was under threat from an approaching Egyptian brigade. His advance elements were ambushed in the pass by two enemy battalions. In the costliest fight of the campaign (34 Israeli and 211 Egyptian dead), the pass was cleared.

The second instance of disobedience wrecked Dayan's campaign plan but led to a stunning victory on the northern Sinai front. Dayan, an infantryman at heart, had little time for the tank; he intended that the infantry brigades break open the Egyptian defences and then allow 7 Armoured Brigade to pass through. The front commander, General Assaf Simchoni, disregarded that plan and sent Uri ben Ari's tanks in as the spearhead a full day earlier than planned and before the infantry had breached the Egyptian defences. While the Israeli infantry attacked the Egyptian positions from the front, the tanks destroyed their perimeter from the opposite end, deep in the rear at Abu Agheila. Without pause 7 Armoured continued the attack and seized the whole of central Sinai within 24 hours.

To Dayan's credit he preferred to see these acts of disobedience as evidence of intelligent and aggressive initiative, traits which will in the end always profit an army. His attitude was summed-up in his comment, 'better to be engaged in restraining the noble stallion than in prodding the reluctant mule'.

THE POST-WAR ARMY

The 1956 War had proved a fertile seed-bed for the IDF; not only had its morale and self-esteem been given a psychological shot in the arm, but much of its fighting style and technique had been validated. But the war had also pointed the way to a host of improvements that would eventually lead to the even more profound victory of 1967.

Without doubt the tank had won the laurels of the battlefield and Dayan was now fully alive to its potential. The Armoured Corps was expanded and made the

IDF's chief striking arm on the ground. Quality officers were assigned to the corps and modern British Centurion and US Patton tanks were purchased. Major-General Israel Tal succeeded Ben Ari as the leader of the corps and set the direction for the development of the IDF for the next fifteen years. Tal completely reversed the poor technical performance of the Corps by a thorough training programme that emphasized and demanded high standards in maintenance, gunnery and crew training. So effective was the insistence on high standards that Armoured Corps personnel soon began to be noted for their punctilious style in the wearing of the regulation uniform. 'As Tal had predicted, technical discipline went hand in hand with formal, "external" discipline.'[90]

Tal also made a major break with accepted international concepts of combined arms operations. He concluded that tank-infantry combined arms formations were unnecessary in the prevailing conditions, that concentrated tank formations could easily counter the existing short-range anti-tank weapons with accurate gunnery. The lack of cover in the region gave the advantage to long-range tank gunnery. This was to hold true during the 1967 Six Day War, but the problem had been overcome with the advance of anti-tank technology by the time of the 1973 War. At the same time Tal recognized the need of battlefield mobility – movement in the presence of the enemy; he insisted that a well-armoured tank could survive longer in combat and continue to advance against the enemy long after a faster but lighter tank had been destroyed. This conclusion would stand the tests of both 1967 and 1973.

EGYPT

In 1956 events converged to bring Egypt its second war and second defeat. Nasser's government had been actively supporting terrorist operations out of Gaza against Israel and now planned to go beyond that with an outright conventional attack in concert with Jordan and Syria. In this Nasser over-estimated the capability of the army which was attempting to digest new Soviet equipment and doctrine. At the same time, Nasser nationalized the Suez Canal to finance the Aswan Dam, throwing Britain and France into the arms of an alliance of convenience with Israel.

Egypt's enemies struck first. The Israelis attacked Egyptian forces in the Sinai on 29 October. At this time, the mobilized strength of the Egyptian Army was 100,000 men in eighteen brigades: ten infantry, one medium machine-gun, three armoured (one training), one coastal defence, and three anti-aircraft. Most manoeuvre units were either in the Sinai (30,000 in two divisions) or guarding the Canal Zone (one division), and most were in the midst of transition from British or American to Soviet equipment. The Egyptians in the Sinai never had a chance. The Israelis seized and held the operational initiative throughout the campaign and quickly destroyed the Egyptian defences. All the fragile seams in the Egyptian Army snapped. The Egyptians could not operate at similar high operational tempos; cohesion, never very strong, evaporated as many officers shamelessly abandoned their men. In a few instances, at the Mitla Pass and at Abu Agheila, the defence was well-laid out and stubbornly conducted, but was eventually overcome. Nasser ordered a retreat which the Israelis turned into a route to the Canal. On 5 November the British and French air landings began in the Canal Zone followed by sea landings the next day; by the 7th the fighting had stopped.

The cost in blood, arms and pride had been high for the Egyptians. Against 700 Israeli and 166 Anglo-French casualties, the Egyptians had lost 3,000 dead, 7,000 taken prisoner and almost all the new equipment in the Sinai and Canal Zone. In the Canal Zone alone losses had been 750 dead and 2,100 wounded. The fragile sense of *esprit de corps* which Nasser had tried to nurture in the army had withered in the blast of war. Public esteem for the armed forces, never very high in Egyptian society, relapsed into its traditional contempt.

Politically, Nasser retrieved the battlefield disaster when the United Nations supported by the United States and Soviet Union put pressure on the Israeli and Anglo-French forces to evacuate Egyptian territory. Firmly established as Egypt's patron, the Soviet Union began in earnest what it had done only by Czech proxy previously – rebuild, retrain and re-equip the Egyptian Army, leaving an imprint that would last more than twenty-five years.

In 1962 Nasser sent an Egyptian expeditionary force that eventually numbered 65,000 men to Yemen to support the new socialist republican regime that followed the Egyptian-engineered overthrow of the monarchy. Royalist forces were supported by the Saudis, and a bloody guerrilla war ensued that would last until 1967. Although the Egyptians used gas, they were never able to inflict any significant damage on the royalists; on the other hand, they suffered no significant defeats. Institutionally, however, the Egyptian Army was being badly weakened by the requirement to keep such a large force overseas. Units in Egypt were stripped of qualified personnel and the training base was degraded just as the army was beginning to enjoy the benefits of Soviet military aid and training.

SYRIA

The new radical military regime that took power in 1954 found a ready patron in the Soviet Union. It was a unique opportunity that threw the Syrians and Soviets into each others' arms. The new Syrian leadership was being pressured into joining the Baghdad Pact which was aimed at the Soviets, but they resisted. The Soviets found their opening and offered diplomatic support in 1955 and then began to provide the modern arms that the West had refused to sell in any quantity. Soviet and Czech equipment and Soviet military advisers arrived that year. The following year the relationship deepened when the Soviets provided guarantees to Syria during the Israeli–Anglo–French attack on Egypt.

Despite the Soviet connection, the Syrian Army did not make significant improvements until the March 1963 coup that brought officers of the Ba'ath (Renaissance) Party to power. The Ba'ath, in the words of John Keegan, 'had a political doctrine and a party framework which allowed them to survive. This doctrine ... combined pan-Arabism with a rather incoherent version of Marxist socialism'. The Ba'athists first eliminated all other factions in the armed forces and then destroyed the traditional Sunni political and economic élites.[91]

Fighting flared between Syria and Israel in November 1964 in the 'Water War' when Syria attempted to block the waters of the Rivers Jordan and Yarmouk in order to disrupt Israeli agriculture. The Israelis struck back with air attacks on Syrian engineering works, and the Syrian Army responded by attacking Israeli settlements with its Soviet T-34/85 tanks. The approach of Israeli Centurion tanks armed with 105mm guns forced the Syrians to retire. It was a fortuitous retreat for the Syrians because it triggered a major re-armament effort by the Soviets. T-54/55s and BTR-152s soon began arriving in large numbers.[92]

PAKISTAN

The development of the fledgling Pakistan Army was strongly influenced by the country's entry into the US-created web of anti-Soviet alliances – CENTO and SEATO – in 1954. A USMAAG (US Military Assistance Advisory Group) arrived shortly thereafter to assist the Pakistan Army in a major modernization and expansion effort. Pakistan received the equipment to field one armoured division, one brigade and seven infantry divisions. Large investments were made in facilities and infrastructure, and the army's reserves were also strengthened.

Overshadowing the large amounts of US equipment was the impression left on the Pakistani Army by American training, attitudes and military style, summed-up by a senior Pakistani officer:

'The Americans affected everything – the scales were completely different, hundreds of our officers went to America, and we had new standards of comparison. Also, the experience the Americans gained in the Second World War and Korea, it couldn't have been bought, it was offered to us on a plate. We wouldn't have done so well in '65 without – not just the material aid, but the training.' [93]

The expansion of the army coincided with the emergence of a generation of Pakistani officers who had had no experience of the old Indian Army or the British Army. Two hundred Pakistani artillery officers alone attended US schools from 1955 to 1958. Many more attended from other combat arms and support services where exposure not only to US methods but to the thousands of officers from other countries gave the Pakistani officer corps a broad, international perspective. The US style of fighting, with its heavy emphasis on mechanization, firepower and its offensive-mindedness couldn't have made a greater contrast with cautious and conservative Indian Army and British traditions.

A brake on modernization was the army's reliance on a conservative peasant society for its manpower. Emphasis was placed on making the recruit a member of his regimental family guided by a firm paternalism rather than severity. To compensate for the lack of technical ability and equipment, discipline and motivation were stressed. Most recruits tended to be Punjabis, in continuance the martial tradition of the region inherited from the Indian Army. Other ethnic groups, particularly the Bengalis from East Pakistan, were severely under-represented. Conversely, this led to the belief in an innate superiority over the Indian Army which had consciously decided to recruit from its so-called 'unmartial' races as well as traditionally 'martial' groups.

1958 – COUP AND MILITARY GOVERNMENT

In the middle of this transformation, the Pakistan Army was dragged into politics by the corruption that paralyzed the nation's so-called parliamentary democracy. As Pakistan slipped into political chaos, it was obvious that the army was the only stable and efficient arm of government that was able to stay above the miasma. By late September 1958 the army's leadership had decided that it must displace the civil leadership that had brought the country to ruin. Martial law was declared on 7 October by the President who further co-operated on 27 October by resigning and leaving the country. Ayub assumed the dual role of president and martial law administrator. It was a bloodless and popular coup. Ayub promptly purged and co-opted the civil service in support. Although the military remained in overall control of the government, Ayub insisted that the day-to-day business be left in the hands of the civil service. He further insisted that the army continue to stay out of politics as much as possible and concentrate on its professional duties. Ayub's regime was relatively tolerant, executing not political opponents but a number of important reforms. The period of martial law ended with the adoption of a new constitution in 1962 based on indirect representation in which Ayub was elected president.

INDIA

The Indian Army had confirmed itself in the eyes of the nation by its defence of Kashmir in 1947, but the following fourteen years saw it languish under the studied indifference of a national leadership piously committed to non-violence and non-alignment. The 1961 military occupation and annexation of Portuguese Goa, while bloodless, revealed serious logistics failures. The only active service seen by the army from 1947 to 1962 was in suppressing the revolt of Naga tribesmen on the Burmese border.

THE SINO-INDIAN WAR, 1962

Harsh reality burst upon India on 20 October 1962. In a succession of well-prepared attacks in the disputed areas of the Himalayas (the Aksai Chin Plain in the west and the North-East Frontier Agency (NEFA) in the east), the Chinese administered a severe drubbing to the Indian Army. Goaded by their own inflexible demands for the disputed areas, the Indian government resorted to military action to settle the issue. A lack of seriousness at senior levels of government and army characterized the initial attempt by an Indian brigade on 10 October to shoo the Chinese off a ridge in the NEFA. The Chinese lashed out with mortars and a swift downhill counter-attack which swept the Indians away. The gape-jawed Indian theatre commander blurted out, 'Oh, my God, you're right. They mean business.' In one month of fighting before declaring a ceasefire, three Chinese divisions gutted the five brigades of the Indian 4th Division. Similar attacks in the western sector resulted in a similar Indian defeat, but Indian commanders withdrew with far more skill than those in the NEFA débacle. Indian losses were 3,079 dead and missing, and 3,968 prisoners. While the Indian Jawan had upheld the honour of the army, those charged with his doctrine, training and equipment had not. Indian weapons were found to be outclassed and at least one generation behind those of the Chinese. Indian troops had not been trained or equipped for cold weather and mountain fighting, nor were they acclimatized to the altitude. Waves of vigorous, warmly clad Chinese with AK-47s, supported by tanks and artillery, easily overran altitude sick and frostbitten Indian units armed with Lee-Enfield rifles and clothed in thin cotton. Miserable generalship and staffwork added to the Jawans' miseries.

Their suffering was not without ultimate purpose. The shock to India was such that official indifference to the army became a dead letter. The attack was a defining moment, not just for the Indian Army, but for the nation. Prime Minister Nehru immediately elevated the priority of national defence and received wide popular support. From this day forward the Indian people would not stint expenditure on defence. Resources were poured into the army, which was almost doubled in size to 825,000 men, and modern equipment was purchased. Ten new mountain divisions were created and the tempo and standards of training were raised. In a large-scale house-cleaning, many incompetent officers were removed. Nehru also initiated a serious re-examination of India's defence problems which concluded that India would have to be prepared to fight conventional wars on two fronts – against China and Pakistan. The first five-year defence plan for ordered growth dates from this time. From this volte-face can be truly measured the birth of the modern Indian Army.

Britain and the United States had promptly filled India's military assistance requests made during the Chinese attack but were not willing to support her subsequent re-armament. The Soviet Union was immediately willing to support all phases of the ambitious Indian re-armament programme. By 1964 the Soviet Union was India's largest arms supplier, a position it would maintain throughout the remainder of the post-1945 period. Soviet support was doubly acceptable because it favoured India's policy of eventual self-sufficiency in defence production. The Soviet Union was willing to assist in the development of an Indian arms industry which was greatly accelerated after 1962.

Finding the manpower for the expanded army was not a problem in populous India, and this enabled the Indian Army to continue its volunteer traditions. Recruitment remained high and continued to emphasize the traditional 'martial races' such as the Gurkhas, Rajputs, Sikhs, Gorgras, Marathas, Jats and Punjabis, despite government attempts after independence to integrate units. In contrast to the Pakistan Army, the Indian Army has played down religion as a unifying factor and encouraged a more neutral attitude which, given India's plethora of religions and sects, is in itself a unifying factor. Again, in contrast to the Pakistan Army and most other post-colonial armies, the Indian Army continued to abstain rigorously from any involvement in politics and this did much to strengthen the army's professionalism as well as the co-operation between army and government. This position was facilitated by the relative stability of Indian domestic politics, which had sunk deep democratic roots, and the strong leadership of Prime Minister Nehru.

SOUTH VIETNAM

The Vietnamese National Army shared the defeat of the French in 1954 but survived, transformed into the Army of the Republic of Vietnam (ARVN). Strangely, for an army that had been so closely tied to that of its colonial mentor, it cut itself off from all the frequently distinguished traditions of Vietnamese military accomplishment in league with French arms. The Vietnamese burned their French rank insignia in a 'symbolic bonfire'. The only tie retained from the past was the paratroops' red beret.

The United States quickly replaced France as the military patron of South Vietnam. With that status came advice, mostly bad, on how to organize and equip the army. The American experience in the Korean War was superficially transferred to the situation existing between North and South Vietnam. Taken by surprise in 1950, they would not be taken unawares again in Asia – forgetting that surprise rarely takes the same form twice. The ARVN was designed to counter a major, conventional cross-border attack; and this definition of its role was to prove fatal. The situation was described by Bernard Fall:

> 'Unmindful of the bloody lessons of the Indo-China War, the new South Vietnamese Army was trained to be a field force ready to face its North Vietnamese rivals in the kind of set-piece battle they had refused to the French for eight long years: mobile groups were merged into light divisions, light divisions into full-sized field divisions, and the latter topped off by full-fledged army corps. The valuable Dinassaut were largely disbanded since the French had invented them and there was no equivalent in American manuals, and were soon followed into oblivion by the commando forces. No attempt whatever was made to reconstitute anything approaching the GCMAs until 1962.'[94]

The South Vietnamese themselves seemed helpless to break out of this mould, tied to the umbilical of US aid and increasingly addicted to ruinous corruption. Yet they were all too aware of the consequences (of only the aid, unfortunately). The British military attaché noted: 'Vietnamese officers were heard to talk about the "American-type of war we train for and the Indo-China war we will have to fight".'[95]

That war was already in the making as the cadres left behind in the south by the Communists began to rekindle the insurgency in the countryside as early as 1958. Here again the emphasis on the conventional attack across the DMZ distracted attention from the actual beginnings of a very different sort of war. The Vietnamese needed a paramilitary force to ensure internal security. What they got was eight conventional divisions. By early 1960 the Communist guerrillas were confident and able enough to overrun a regular infantry battalion. In that year 3,000 to 4,000 local officials were murdered, unprotected by an army that was not trained or equipped to contest the allegiance of the populace in every village and hamlet.

NORTH VIETNAM

The victory of 1954 saw the 200,000-strong PAVN become the professional army of an independent state and the complete creature of the Party as the mask of the Viet-minh national front was discarded. Ho Chi Minh boasted of the professionalization and the adding of naval and air arms, 'Before we had only the night and the jungle. Now we have the sky and the water.'[96] At the 12th Party Plenum in 1957 the decision was made to initiate a general reorganization to transform the PAVN into a balanced modern army within the resources of North Vietnam. To that end military assistance was sought and obtained from China, the Soviet Union and other Warsaw pact countries.

Unlike its Vietnamese counterpart in the South, PAVN made rapid progress. There were two reasons for this. First, PAVN had an efficient strategy. As a later PAVN commander-in-chief, Senior General Van Tien Dung, was to define:

'War is the highest, most comprehensive test of a nation and its social system. War is a contest that not only tests the skill and strategy of two adversaries, but also their strength and will. Victory goes to the side which has the correct military strategy, which makes the best use of the art of military science and which most successfully limits the war-making capacity of its adversary.'[97]

That strategy, *dau tranh* (struggle) perhaps known better in the West as Revolutionary War, consisted of two inseparable and reinforcing aspects, the armed and the political which are portrayed as hammer and anvil. Armed *dau tranh* was the 'revolutionary violence programme' while political *dau tranh* was the 'systematic coercive activity'. Douglas Pike describes it in operation:

'The pincers of dau tranh close on the enemy. They represent the complete strategy. All actions taken in the war – military attack or guerilla ambush, propaganda broadcast or official statement at the conference table, every mission abroad, every decision taken from the Party cell to the Politburo in Hanoi – all come within the scope of the two dau tranhs. There is nothing else.'

The PAVN recruit was immersed in this concept which permeated and coloured all training and indoctrination. It became second nature to the soldier and a major source of dedication and inspiration.[98]

Secondly, General Giap would see it done. Despite the Party's insistence on using the army for internal labour, Giap accomplished a miracle of organization. He realized that the next war for unification of the South would entail combat against the lavish American use of *matériel*, especially air power. For such a struggle he needed an officer corps that was thoroughly schooled in the profession of arms; the empirical experience acquired in the war against the French, as able men rose through the ranks of an informal guerrilla organization, would not be enough. A system of military schools for the infantry, artillery and staff was created; the first instructors were Chinese. An officer training establishment was vital to provide the leadership for the rapidly expanding PAVN which almost doubled in size between 1955 and 1965, from 210,000 to 400,000. The officer corps grew even more, from 20,000 to 50,000 during that period. Belying its Communist stamp, the officer corps was recruited overwhelmingly from the traditional leadership elements of Vietnamese society: 73 per cent of bourgeois background, 19 per cent gentry and only 8 per cent proletarian. Unit training was accomplished with numerous small manoeuvres and combined arms exercises.[99]

Giap realized that the strength of the army would be in its infantry and made high standards of rifle marksmanship a priority. Artillery training emphasized massed and indirect fire. Even a modest tank corps, initially based on the light Soviet PT-76 tank, was begun in 1959. Giap also organized a logistics system, but in this he was less successful. He had even less success with the introduction of a regularized system of administration and the army continued to be run with the loose informality of a guerrilla force. Many old veterans refused to wear the new uniform and insignia issued to them.[100]

The PAVN's first operational deployment occurred even before the reforms had been fully implemented. A North Vietnamese peasant revolt, ignited by the excesses of the Communist land reform programme, exploded in the province of Nghe An, Ho Chi Minh's birthplace. Spreading rapidly, it overwhelmed the local militia. On Ho's orders, Giap promptly and decisively suppressed it, 325th Division reportedly killing thousands.

It was a prophetic bloodletting. Within a few years, PAVN would be actively supporting Hanoi-directed insurgents in the South to cut another bloody swathe through Vietnamese history. In late 1960 Hanoi ordered its Communist cadres in South Vietnam to create what was known as the National Liberation Front (NLF), its military headquarters being the Central Office for South Vietnam (COSVIN). Although COSVIN controlled guerrilla operations in South Vietnam, there was no doubt that PAVN controlled COSVIN. COSVIN's indigenous independence was a cherished fiction of the West's ever gullible Left. COSVIN's military arm was the People's Liberation Armed Forces (PLAF), also known as the Vietcong. By June 1961 PAVN had sent 1,500 men (including sixty captains and ten majors) south to assist in its expansion to two regular battalions by early autumn. By the beginning of 1964 three VC regiments had been formed in the South, and the South Vietnamese were shuddering from blow after blow, but all but one of PAVN's six divisions were still stationed in the Red River delta. By that summer Hanoi made the fateful decision to send PAVN divisions south to accelerate the conquest of South Vietnam. Four of the regular divisions sent their regiments south while retaining cadres to replace new divisions. Rather than assign new divisional and regimental numbers, the new units retained the old numbers of their parent units and affixed a letter.[101] Hence it was the 325B Division that would face the Americans of the 1st Cavalry Division (Airmobile) in the jungle of the Ia Drang valley a year later.

CHINA

The post-Korean War decade for the People's Liberation Army (PLA) witnessed a painful metamorphosis. The revolutionary war concepts of its first twenty-eight years of existence were being transformed, often under the influence of Soviet models, to meet the more traditional requirements of an army of an established state. The Sovietization of the PLA was enthusiastically supported by Marshal Peng

Dehuai who had replaced the legendary Chu Te in 1954. The Korean War had also exposed an entire generation of leaders to the demanding technological and leadership requirements of modern conventional warfare. Against this tide of modernization, a stubborn rearguard action was fought by the followers of the concepts of revolutionary people's war, now cast in the conservative role, their once-new ideas now become dogma.

One of the first changes was the establishment in February 1955 of a defined hierarchy of ranks, closely resembling the Soviet pattern, and a system of military orders and honours. Heretofore the PLA had had no traditional rank system but rather emphasized the equality and personal responsibility of each soldier in a specific situation. As Paul Godwin observes:

'... one of the principal norms of the Chinese Communist military ethic – equality – was removed. The establishment of rank structure based on the Soviet model complemented the organization and technical modernization being pursued under Soviet direction.'

The Korean War experience also broke down the political commissar system, so effective in a revolutionary war context but dysfunctional to rapid decision-making in foreign conventional wars. The political officers and Party committees rapidly lost power and were largely ignored in many PLA units. A third pillar of the revolutionary war PLA was its interaction with the civil population as an economic work force. Here again the impetus of modernization was at work. A fourth pillar was the reliance on a large militia to reinforce the PLA, the guarantee that the ultimate defence of China rested with the people. The PLA in the 1950s came to see 'militia training as an unnecessary distraction from its major task – the creation of a modernized combat-ready military establishment'. The rapid professionalization of the newly defined officer corps was the engine pulling the PLA away from its traditions. The attention of the new professionals was focused primarily on the combat capabilities of the PLA, what Mao Zedong condemned as the 'purely military viewpoint'. For Mao, these very connections with the civil population were the means of maintaining the healthy relationship between the army and the people. The development of a separate and distinct military subculture was a threat to that relationship.[102]

Into this doctrinal fray the question of nuclear warfare fell like a boulder into a pond. The 'New Look' of the United States presented the prospect of crushing nuclear strikes followed by invasion. For Mao the choices were clear. China could not generate the economic growth to match the United States on its own terms. The PLA's goals of across the board modernization were not attainable, especially since the Soviet arsenal was not proving to be the bottomless well the PLA had anticipated. In 1959 a suspicious Soviet Union had also abrogated a 1957 agreement to supply China with its own nuclear weapons. Mao concluded that the PLA's modernization would be along the one narrow direction it could afford – the development of a nuclear capability. For the rest, the PLA would have to rely on its traditional light infantry and the people, much as in the war against Japan.

The withdrawal of Soviet aid in 1960, and the catastrophes of the Great Leap Forward and the bad harvests of 1959–61 brought these issues to a head. Adherents of professionalization, including Marshal Peng, were purged as Mao attempted to re-establish the traditional values of the PLA. A set of 'General Principles' – people's army and people's war – that enshrined Mao's thoughts as doctrine was promulgated in 1961. Marshal Lin Biao, one of China's most distinguished soldiers, was charged with the execution of this new line. In his first important policy speech, in September 1959, after becoming defence minister, he left no doubt of the upcoming reversal of direction:

> 'Some comrades take the view that modern warfare differs from warfare in the past, that since the weapons and equipment available to our army in the past were inferior we had to emphasize dependence on man, on his bravery and wisdom ... They say that modern warfare is a war of technique, of steel and machinery, and that in the face of these things, man's role has to be relegated to a secondary place ... Contrary to these people, we believe that while equipment and technique are important, the human factor is even more so.'

During the next five years Lin forced the PLA to repudiate most of the progress made during the period 1953 to 1956. He rebuilt the political control system within the PLA, emphasized the nuclear programme to the neglect of the modernization of conventional forces, and re-established the equal relationship of the militia with the conventional forces. Political work was focused at company level, and a number of intensive ideological campaigns rippled through the PLA based on the principle that Lin enunciated at a 1960 Military Affairs Committee special session: 'human factor first; political work first; ideological work first; and living thought first'. By 1964 the PLA was being depicted as a politically correct paragon for the civil population. Military cadres were lent to civil institutions to guide them in the creation of new political departments. Perhaps the most symbolic change was the abolition of the system of ranks in May 1965, justified as a return to fundamental traditions of 'close relations between the officers and men, between the higher and the lower levels, and between the army and the people'. Together with the abolition of ranks, all insignia and uniform differences were done away with. Everyone wore the same simple uniform with its red cap badge and red collar tabs. Soldiers were addressed, as before 1955, as for example, Company Commander Wang or Fighter Lee.[103]

Throughout this decade the PLA went on a roller-coaster ride between professionalization and People's War, both designed to fight against the United States and its allies in the Pacific. Ironically, during this period the PLA would be called upon to fight a major guerrilla campaign and a conventional campaign on its south-eastern border – on the Roof of the World in the Himalayas – against a primitive indigenous people and against an erstwhile friend – India.

THE TIBETAN REVOLT, 1956–1960

In 1950 the Chinese evoked traditional claims to Tibet and occupied the country, provoking a vicious guerrilla war with the native mountain nomadic tribes that cost the PLA more than 10,000 casualties in less than a year. By the spring of 1950 an accommodation had been reached that recognized Tibetan autonomy. By 1956, however, Chinese colonization and increasingly high-handed attempts to 'reform' traditional Tibetan culture sparked a great uprising.

The mountain tribes again were the muscle of the revolt that eventually spread throughout the country, including the capital, Llasa, by 1959. Rebel groups massacred numbers of PLA garrisons and outposts, one nomad column overruning fourteen such positions in one sweep. Chinese soldiers and civilians were suffering thousands of casualties. At this point, Beijing decided to absorb Tibet thoroughly into China. The PLA garrison of 250,000 men was given unequivocal orders to destroy the Tibetan insurgency at whatever cost. With these firm directives, the PLA broke the risings in Llasa by reducing the rebel-held monasteries with artillery. They relentlessly ground down the mountain tribes by patiently boxing them into smaller and smaller areas while they hunted them from the air. By 1960 the revolt had been extinguished.

The Sino-Indian War, 1962

In October 1962, a long simmering border feud between China and India over the Aksai Chin plain in the west and the North-East Frontier Agency (NEFA) in the east exploded into a short but bitter fight on the high slopes of the Himalayas. The indistinct borders were a legacy of British unilateral map-making which no Chinese government had agreed. Chinese road-building in the Aksai Chin plain and military presence on its side of the British-drawn border were considered a provocation by the Indian government which worked itself and the nation into a fit of pique over the matter. Troops were dispatched to the NEFA and deployed on the Chinese side of the old border to eject the Chinese from the Thag La Ridge in an attack on 10 October.

The Indian government had given its army an operationally impossible task made worse by the assumption that the Chinese would allow themselves to be pushed out of the way. The Indians had no way to be supplied except by air and were unused to altitudes of 15–16,000 feet. The Chinese troops had been in these high altitudes for years and were fit. A network of roads behind the front kept them well-supplied. Indian military intelligence was practically non-existent while that of the Chinese was meticulously accurate. They had been carefully watching the laborious activities of the Indians for months and knew the day of their attack. On 10 October as the Jawans of 7 Brigade were moving forward to seize Thag La Ridge, the PLA greeted them with a heavy mortar barrage followed by a sharp downhill counter-attack which shredded the Indians and threw them back.

Three days later the Indians were ordered again to take Thag La Ridge and were slapped back down almost as soon as they had left their positions. By now the Chinese leadership decided that decisive action was required to wake up the Indians. Winter was coming, and the Chinese enjoyed the advantages of superior numbers and heavier equipment. Reinforcements from Tibet quickly raised the size of the Chinese force to three divisions.

They struck on the morning of the 20th, infantry racing behind a heavy barrage. They lapped around the flanks of the too widely spaced Indian positions and the isolated strongpoints were crushed one by one. By nine in the morning the Indian brigade had been swept away. Far to the west, the Chinese had also attacked across the wastes of the Aksai Chin Plain or the Ladakh Sector as it was called. There too the PLA's tactics had swamped the Indians, but the main weight of their offensive was still in the NEFA.

The Indians had fallen back to defend the Se La Pass where they concentrated five brigades. The Chinese did not pursue them immediately, but carefully built a supply road to the area which they saturated with patrols. On 17 November the Chinese fixed the attention of their enemy by assaulting the pass with great loss, but like the Persians at Thermopylae, the Chinese found a mountain trail around it. Fifteen hundred Chinese overwhelmed the Indian brigade sent to stop them. 'Panic, brother to blood-stained rout' spread through the Indian troops guarding the pass. The Chinese followed a withdrawing battalion into its positions and poured fire on the neighbouring units which broke. Other Indian positions were infiltrated and units were ambushed all along the front, including the single Indian divisional headquarters attempting to control the battle. The remnant fled. In short order the Chinese reached their objective of Chaku, the gateway to the Assam Plain.

Two days later China announced that it would withdraw. Its objective had been accomplished with the drubbing administered to the Indian Army. Indian losses were 3,079 killed and missing and 3,968 prisoners. Chinese losses may have been about the same. The Indians had fought well when they could, but had been badly deployed and handled; the Chinese fought well consistently because they had been well-led throughout the operation. Perhaps the best evaluation of the PLA's performance was by an Indian officer, Brigadier J. P. Dalvi, 7 Brigade's commander:

'The most impressive display of Chinese training was their uncannily accurate artillery barrages ... The real Chinese success can be attributed to their high command. They had manoeuvred the Thaglar incident with cunning; and the Chinese soldier had delivered the coup de grâce with skill and fanaticism.[104]

NORTH KOREA

The Korean People's Army (KPA) had been badly mauled in the Korean War and survived only because of overt Chinese and covert Soviet intervention. Until 1958 emphasis was placed on rebuilding the infantry core of the army and on the acquisition of new weapons and equipment. The Chinese Volunteer Army (CVA), which was finally withdrawn in October of that year, provided a shield while the KPA was rebuilt.

The two rival military factions remained within the KPA, the *Kaspan Ban* dominated by North Korea's dictator, Kim Il Sung, and the *Yenan Ban* comprised of Korean veterans of the Chinese Civil War. In 1958 the *Yenan Ban* attempted to overthrow Kim Il Sung and failed despite the presence of the *ban*'s Chinese patrons. Kim's purge of the Yenanites and the departure of the Chinese gave him undisputed control of the KPA. He would keep that grip throughout the remaining decades of the post-Second World War era and beyond; rarely has an army been so closely associated with a single individual for so long.

Kim had already begun a major reorganization and reconstruction campaign in 1956 which released thousands of men and women from military service to rebuild the war-shattered economy. While the KPA grew smaller, its combat capability increased as units were consolidated and thousands of personnel training in China and the Soviet Union returned home. In 1956 the voluntary system of recruitment was abandoned in favour of universal military service for five to six years, the longest in the world. Large-scale Chinese and particularly Soviet military assistance in the 1950s provided a vital base to the effective reorganization of the KPA.

That base was threatened when North Korea was pressured to take sides in the growing hostility between China and the Soviet Union. A Soviet assistance treaty signed in 1961 was suspended the next year when Kim sided too much with the Chinese. The suspension of conventional military assistance from the Soviet Union and the missed opportunity to take advantage of the May 1961 coup in South Korea persuaded Kim to seek a more indirect approach to unify the peninsula. In December 1962 he unveiled his new policy of the Four Great Military Lines of self-reliance:

1. The whole people will be armed.
2. The whole country will be fortified.
3. All soldiers will be trained as cadre. Each person will be capable of performing the duties of his immediate superior.
4. All arms will be modernized.

The new policy had three purposes: (1) to construct a military power base that reflected North Korea's situation; (2) to devise an independent Korean strategy; and (3) to build defences that could withstand retaliation following a KPA attack on South Korea: 'Kim advocated a politically aware "army of cadres" (revolutionary agitators), the arming of his entire populace, completion of nationwide military industrialization, and modernization of his conventional armed forces. Rejecting his army's almost wholly conventional Soviet-style doctrine, the DPRK premier directed an emphasis on irregular warfare drawn from studies of his own operations against the Japanese during the Second World War...' [105]

The new doctrine coincided with the reorganization of the KPA's intelligence and unconventional warfare forces tailored to conditions on the Korean Peninsula.

SOUTH KOREA

The Korean War had revealed that the single greatest weakness of the Republic of Korea Army (ROKA) had been its training, and a firm training foundation for the first post-war decade was laid down. Large numbers of officers attended military schools in the United States, and the army's own academies such as the Korean Military Academy (KMA) began graduating well-trained junior officers. Higher-level schools such as the Command and General Staff School at Chinhae:

'laid great emphasis not only on modern management procedures but on concepts of patriotism, spirit of service and avoidance of politics. In addition, courses of the National Defence College introduced officers to economics, political science, national development and the broader terms of the Army's role in world strategy and national defence.' [106]

The experience of war and the intensive post-war training and education programme produced in the officer corps a truly national outlook and an institution that was the most modern in the Republic of Korea. Universal conscription ensured that this institution would have a powerful effect on the entire nation.

Outwardly the ROK Army closely resembled its US mentor in organization, uniforms, insignia, tactics and equipment. But the spirit of the army owed little, if anything, to American influence. Korea's Confucian culture was stony soil for the growth of a martial tradition. The Japanese conquest, however, had incorporated a number of Koreans in the police and lower ranks of the Imperial Army, and those veterans founded the ROK Army, and transmitted many attitudes learned from the Japanese. They included rigorous and often harsh levels of discipline. The striking of a soldier by an officer for a minor infraction became a common feature, much as it was in the old Imperial Army. Ironically, such methods are anathema in the post-war Japanese Army. Other features included the rigid sense of hierarchy and perquisites of rank, a more sacrosanct command authority, and less tolerance for individual initiative. All in all, however, they contributed to a corporate identity that would allow the army to be of unique service to the nation. [107]

THE 1961 COUP AND MILITARY RULE

By 1960 the autocratic rule of President Rhee had failed to produce either the stability or growth the nation expected. The army pointedly stood aside as civilian disturbances toppled him from power. After a year of chaotic government, the military intervened. A group of middle-grade officers and young generals led by Major-General Chung Hee Park quietly seized power, in a move that came as a surprise to the rest of the army. The commander of First Army refused to act against Park because he feared splitting the army into warring factions.

Park and his confederates constituted themselves a Supreme Council for National Reconstruction. Of its 30 members, 25 were from the army, three from the marines and one each from the air force and navy. The striking feature of the Council was its lack of preconceived plans; in hindsight this was a virtue. Park and his associates were pragmatic, interested only in effective solutions to national ills. The most successful of these evolved into a programme of modernization which led to rapid and sustained economic growth. Park also had a pragmatic approach to democracy, believing that in poorer Asian countries, the people 'are more frightened of poverty and hunger than totalitarianism'. Democracy in the American sense would have to wait until Korea was rich enough to afford it. Unlike many military regimes that outlive their usefulness, Park's found a continuing justification among the Korean people, not only because of its continuing economic success but most importantly because of the constant threat from North Korea.

JAPAN

The first decade (1955–65) of the new Japanese army, the Ground Self-Defence Force (GSDF), was one of rapid professionalization and growth, especially during the first Defence Build-up Plan (1958–1961). Recruitment was not particularly easy in post-war, pacifist Japan. By 1961 the GSDF's authorized strength had been increased to 170,000 from 150,000 in 1955, but actual strength fluctuated from 162,684 in 1958 to a low of 142,320 in 1961, the lowest percentage (83) of intake in the history of the GSDF.[108] Six divisions, four combined brigades, three tank groups, and supporting artillery, signals and engineer units had been equipped and fielded. The combined brigades consisted of an infantry regiment of three battalions and an artillery battalion. The divisional manoeuvre elements consisted of four battle groups of five companies each, an echo of the unfortunate American experience with the Pentomic system. The following year the number of divisions was increased to eight, and to thirteen by 1963, which number it would hold until 1990. Manpower remained fairly constant, and the increased number of divisions was managed by lowering the strength authorizations. Ambitious plans to establish an airborne division would not be realized, and the GSDF would eventually field only an airborne brigade.[109]

This was also a period in which many of the GSDF schools were established. The Defence Academy, which was established to provide officers for all three services, graduated its first class in 1957. Upon graduation officer cadets served a year as sergeants. The GSDF was still suffering a shortage of junior officers by mid-decade, Japan's post-war anti-militarism making the profession of arms a low-status occupation. At this time most officers, especially senior ones, were Imperial Army veterans, as were most warrant officers and senior sergeants.

The shock of defeat in the war had provoked a severe re-appraisal of traditional Japanese military professional and social attitudes. In 1961 the Japan Defence Agency published a set of ethical principles by which the services were to be guided. 'Patently idealistic in tone and content, they constitute an appeal for patriotism that recognizes the debt owed to past generations and future ones, too, and the need to protect the fatherland. Solidarity, discipline and a sense of responsibility are stressed.' There was also a very untraditional emphasis on individualism and the isolation of the soldier from any political involvement which was actually embodied in the oath of service. As evidence is the use of polite and even informal forms of the language between officers and men and the complete ban on any physical punishment that was so pervasive in the old Imperial Army.[110]

In the first part of the Defence Build-Up Plan, emphasis was laid on the defence of Japan in conjunction with US forces, against external threats, particularly from the Soviet Union. That orientation explained the priority given to the defence of the main island of Hokkaido which was within striking range of Soviet-held Sakhalin Island and the Kuriles. By the time the GSDF's order of battle had expanded to its full thirteen divisions, the four strongest divisions were stationed in Hokkaido. The internal security mission was played down until the occurrence of the massive demonstrations and riots instigated by the Left to overthrow the government in its opposition to the 1960 security treaty with the US. Since that time, internal security has been a high priority of the armed forces, especially the GSDF, and has been tackled with great thoroughness.

AUSTRALIA

In 1959 Australia abandoned the National Service conscription in force since 1951 which freed 3,000 men of the Australian Regular Army (ARA) from training duties to expand and re-equip combat formations. The vehicle for this programme was the reorganization of the army into the new Pentropic Division, similar to the US Army's Pentomic Division. In the Australian version, the division would consist of five battle groups of five battalions each. The army reasoned that this system would meet the demands of the new strategic environment, particularly a limited war in south-east Asia. Unfortunately, the ARA began introducing the Pentropic Division in 1960, just as the Americans were about to abandon the unwieldy five-sided concept. By 1964, the ARA came to the same conclusion, dropped the Pentropic Division, and returned to the tested and sturdy triangular system of organization of combat units. Cadres released from the latest reorganization allowed the ARA to expand to six infantry battalions. Late in the same year conscription was reintroduced on a selective basis. This time, National Servicemen were fully integrated into operational units and were liable for overseas deployment.

MALAYA, 1956–1964

By 1956 the last of the ARA's two battalions had been removed from Korea. The tiny 3-battalion army was immediately presented with a new mission – supporting the British Army's counter – insurgency operations in Malaya. For most of the decade, the ARA maintained a battalion, an artillery battery, and support troops in Malaya as part of 27 Commonwealth Brigade, rotating these forces every two years. Australians were integrated into the British headquarters in Malaya as well as into the brigade. Although the crisis of the campaign had passed before the Australians were committed, they still saw a great deal of small unit action in rooting out the last of the Communist guerrillas. The constant patrolling and the emphasis on the ambush taught a new generation of Australian fighting men the arts of jungle warfare. The Australians also learned priceless lessons in separating the guerrillas from the civilian population. As late as 1964, an ARA battalion was patrolling the Thai border as the last embers of the insurgency were dying. Australian losses were relatively light during eight years of service in Malaya: thirteen KIA, 24 WIA and 21 non-combat deaths and 111 injuries. The losses may have been light, but the education had been first-rate, as events were to prove.

THE ART OF STRATEGY

The struggle between means and policy fundamentally broke down for the US Army in much of this decade. Eisenhower's New Look, despite the evidence of the

Korean War that conventional warfare was applicable to the new Atomic Age, relegated the army to a civil defence/civil affairs role. The army struggled under successive chiefs of staff to match means and policy by carving out a nitch on the Atomic battlefield. A more balanced approach was only adopted under President Kennedy and his administration's policy of Flexible Response. The Army was strengthened and given the means to fulfill policy.

In a strange tandem with the US Army, the ground forces of the Soviet Army were afflicted with a similar national policy emphasis on the strategic nuclear forces. That emphasis seemed to exclude the ground forces from serious participation in the fulfillment of national policy. This was no better demonstrated than by Khrushchev's drastic reductions of force and the awarding of pride of place to the new Strategic Rocket Forces. Again in tandem with the United States, a change of power in 1964 initiated a relook at policy that resulted in a more balanced approach under Brezhnev.

The British Army was only partially able to fulfill the missions imposed by national policy in this second decade of the post-war era. As in the first decade, most British military commitments involved an progressive though sometimes bloody divestiture of its shrinking empire. British commitment to NATO was the first British peacetime commitment of major land forces on the continent. In this, military means and policy separated, a gap luckily never tested by war. The French repeated the disaster of Indochina again in Algeria. At the same time, their commitment to NATO was as inherently hollow as the British.

Outside of NATO and the Warsaw Pact, Israel's defeat of Egypt in the 1956 War and China's drubbing of India in 1962 were the best wartime applications of matching the military means to policy. For Israel, which geography left no second chances, the strike first strategy was the only option. For China, which geography made invulnerable, the strike out of the Himalayas was a well-calculated stroke of realpolitik made doubly effective by its restraint and limited scope.

NOTES

1   Maxwell Taylor, remarks at The Army War College, 22 August 1955, Box 5, The Papers of Maxwell D. Taylor, National Defense University, Washington, DC, in A. J. Bacevich, *The Pentomic Era: The US Army Between Korea and Vietnam* (Washington, DC: The National Defense University, 1986), p. 49.
2   Bacevich, ibid., p. 63.
3   Jonathan M. House, *Toward Combined Arms Warfare: A Survey of 20th–Century Tactics, Doctrine, and Organization* (Fort Leavenworth, KS: The US Army Command and General Staff College, 1984), p. 155.
4   Ibid., pp. 155, 157.
5   John B. Medaris, *Countdown for Decision* (New York, 1960), p. 65.
6   Bacevich, op. cit., pp. 73–92.
7   House, op. cit., p. 158.
8   House, op. cit., p. 161.
9   Charles M. Simpson III, *Inside the Green Berets: The First Thirty Years* (Novato, CA: Presidio Press, 1983), pp. 32–3.
10   Russell F. Weigley, *History of the United States Army* (Bloomington, IN: Indiana University Press, 1984), pp. 531–3.
11   Gregory Blaxland, *The Regiments Depart* (London: William Kimber, 1971), pp. 236–8.
12   Ibid., pp. 238–9, 262.
13   James M. Gavin, *On to Berlin: Memories of an Airborne Commander 1943–46* (New York: The Viking Press, 1978), p. 170.
14   Correlli Barnett, *Britain and Her Army 1509–1970* (New York: William Morrow & Co., 1970), p. 486.
15   Wyn Rees, 'The 1957 Sandys White Paper: New Priorities in British Defense Policy?', *Journal of Strategic Studies*, Vol 12, No. 2, June 1989, pp. 215–222.
16   'Army Notes,' *Journal of the Royal United Service Institution*, Vol XCIX, No. 594, May 1954, p. 304.
17   Rees, op. cit; Gerald Whiteley, 'The British Experience of Peacetime Conscription,' *The Army Quar-*

terly and Defense Journal, Volume 117, No. 3, July 1987, p. 327.

18 Blaxland, op. cit., p. 332.

19 Blaxland, op. cit., pp. 330–1, 333–4.

20 Blaxland, op. cit., pp. 236–8.

21 Barnett, op. cit., pp. 487–8.

22 Christopher F. Foss, *Jane's World Armoured Fighting Vehicles* (New York: St. Martin's Press, 1976), pp. 37, 238.

23 Richard Orgorkiewicz, 'British Armored Divisions,' *Military Review*, October 1958, pp. 84–5; Blaxland, op. cit., p. 341.

24 Blaxland, op. cit., p. 406.

25 Michael Carver, *Twentieth Century Warriors* (New York: Weidenfeld & Nicolson, 1987), p. 79.

26 The last time the French Army had become so enamoured over an all embracing military theory was before the First World War when Foch was the expositor of the offensive spirit as the decisive key to success. That success was to be measured in two sets of figures: The French class of 1914: 640,000; the class of 1939: 340,000.

27 Don A. Starry, 'La Guerre Révolutionnaire,' *Military Review*, February 1967, pp. 64–5.

28 Peter Paret, 'The French Army and La Guerre Révolutionnaire,' *The Journal of the Royal United Services Institute*, No. 613, Vol CIV, February 1959, pp. 62–3.

29 Michel L. Martin. *Warriors to Managers: The French Military Establishment Since 1945* (Chapel Hill: The University of North Carolina Press, 1981), pp. 64–5.

30 George Armstrong Kelly, *Lost Soldiers: The French Army and Empire in Crisis 1947–1962* (Cambridge: The M.I.T. Press, 1965), pp. 176–8.

31 Martin Windrow and Wayne Braby, *French Foreign Legion Paratroops* (London: Osprey Publishing, 1985), pp. 17–20.

32 Paul-Marie de la Gorce, *The French Army: A Military-Political History* (New York: George Braziller, Inc., 1963), pp. 483–4.

33 Ibid., p. 484.

34 Windrow and Braby, op. cit., pp. 20–24.

35 A. J. Barker, *Suez: The Seven Day War* (New York: Frederick A. Praeger, Publishers, 1965), pp. 112–13.

36 Pierre Messmer, 'The French Military Establishment of Tomorrow,' *Orbis*, Summer 1962, pp. 205–6 and 'France's Military Policy.' *Military Review*, August 1963, p. 28.

37 L. J. Le Puloch, 'The Future of the French Army,' *Military Review*, November 1964, pp. 40–9; digested from an article in *L'Armée*, May 1964.

38 Patrick Turnbull, 'The French Foreign Legion: 1945–1981,' *RUSI*, Volume 127, No. 2, June 1982, pp. 51–2.

39 Walter Henry Nelson, *Germany Rearmed* (New York: Simon & Schuster, 1972), pp. 21–2.

40 Ibid., pp. 64–5.

41 Ibid., p. 69.

42 Letter from Freiherr von Boeselager to von Senger's widow on 18 January 1963, cited in Ferdinand von Senger und Etterlin, 'Senger,' ed. Correlli Barnett, *Hitler's Generals* (New York: Grove Weidenfeldt, 1989), p. 389.

43 Ibid., p. 385.

44 Norman C. Walpole, *Area Handbook for Germany* (Washington, DC: US Government Printing Office, 1960), p. 927.

45 Phillip A. Karber and John H. Milam, 'Developments in the Front-Line States: The Federal Republic of Germany,' Jeffery Simon, ed., *NATO – Warsaw Pact Force Mobilization* (Washington, DC: The National Defense University Press, 1988), pp. 247–8.

46 Ibid., pp. 249–50.

47 Ibid., p. 248.

48 John A. Reed, Jr., *Germany and NATO* (Washington, DC: National Defense University Press, 1987), p. 70.

49 Neville Brown, 'The Armies in Central Europe,' *RUSI*, November 1963, p. 344.

50 Hermann Renner, 'NPD-Bazilus in der Bundeswehr?' *Die Welt*, 29 October 1968; cited in Nelson, op. cit., p. 161.

51 Nelson, op. cit., p. 162.

52 Hugo von Freytag Loringhoven, *The Power of Personality in War*; cited in *The Art and Practice of Military Strategy*, p. 458.

53 Paul R. Shirk, 'The German Defense Commissioner,' *Military Review*, February 1967, pp. 55–60.

54 Donald Abenheim, *Reforging the Iron Cross: The Search for Tradition in the West German Armed Forces* (Princeton: Princeton University Press, 1988), p. 83.

55 Ibid., p. 153.

56 Ibid., p. 153.

57 Ibid., pp. 175–184.

58 Thomas A. Forster, *The East German Army: A Pattern of a Communist Military Establishment* (London: George Allen & Unwin, 1966), p. 28.

59 'Die 'Nationale Volksarmee'– Entstehung, Aufbau, Gliederung und Kraefteordung', *Soldat und Technik*, February 1962.

60 'Die 'Nationale Volksarmee', ibid.

61 Joachim Georg Goerlich, 'The Development of the Polish People's Army, *Military Review*, January 1967, p. 31; digested from 'Polens Volksarmee – Entwicklung und Innere Struktur', *Wehrkunde*, May 1966.

62 A. Ross Johnson, Robert W. Dean, and Alexander Alexiev, *Eastern European Military Establishments: The Warsaw Pact Northern Tier* (New York: Crane Russak, 1982), p. 14.

63 John Keegan, *World Armies*, 2nd ed. (Detroit: Gale Research Co., 1983), p. 481.

64 Georlich, op. cit.

65 Johnson, et. al., op. cit., pp. 22–3.

66 Goerlich, op. cit., p. 31.

67 Goelrich, op. cit., pp. 31–3.

68 Roman Kolkowicz, *The Soviet Military and the Communist Party* (Boulder, CO: Westview Press, 1985), p. 116.

69 Georgi Zhukov, *Krasnaya zvezda*, April 16, 1956, cited in Kolkowicz, ibid., p. 130.

70 Malcolm Mackintosh, *Juggernaut: A History of the Soviet Armed Forces* (New York: The Macmillan Co., 1967), p. 296.

71 Harriet Fast Scott and William F. Scott, *The Armed Forces of the USSR* (2nd ed.), (Boulder, CO: Westview Press, 1979), p. 42.

72 John Erickson, Lynn Hansen, and William Schneider, *Soviet Ground Forces: An Operational Assessment* (Boulder, Co: Westview Press, 1986), p. 29.

73 N. S. Khrushchev, *Pravda*, 22 September 1964.

74 Jeffery Record, *Sizing Up the Soviet Army* (Washington, DC: The Brookings Institute, 1975), pp. 5–6.

75 Scott and Scott, op. cit., p. 43.

76 Edgar O'Ballance, *The Red Army* (London: Faber and Faber, 1964), pp. 199–200.

77 Oleg Penkovskiy, *The Penkovskiy Papers* (New York: Doubleday and Co., 1967), p. 229.

78 Penkovskiy, ibid., pp. 223–231.

79 S.A. Tyushkevich, *The Soviet Armed Forces: A History of Their Organizational Development* (Moscow: Voenizdat, 1978), p. 418; published under the auspices of the US Air Force.

80 Tyushkevich, ibid.

81 Mark L. Urban, 'The Strategic Role of Soviet Airborne Troops', *Jane's Military Review*, Ian V. Hogg, ed., 1985, pp. 238–9.

82 Albert Seaton, *The Soviet Army: 1918 to the Present* (New York: New American Library, 1986), p. 183.

83 Christopher F. Foss, *Jane's AFV Recognition Handbook* (London: Jane's Publishing Co., 1987), pp. 70–73; Steven J. Zaloga, *Modern Soviet Armor* (Englewood, NJ: Prentice-Hall, Inc., 1979), p. 20.

84 V. Molchanov, 'Before and After Midnight', Interview with General Leonid I. Shershnev, *Moscow Television Service*, 2000 GMT 26 May 1990.

85 R. Ernest Dupuy and Trevor N. Dupuy, *The Encyclopedia of Miliary History* (New York: Harper & Row, Publishers, 1970), p. 1239.

86 Edward Luttwak and Dan Horowitz, *The Israeli Army* (New York: Harper & Row Publishers, 1975), pp. 156–7.

87 Moshe Dayan, *Diary*, p. 81; cited in Luttwak and Horowitz, p. 147.

88 Luttwak and Horowtiz, ibid., p. 161.

89 S.L.A. Marshall, *Sinai Victory* (New York: William Morrow and Co., 1958), pp. 71–2.

90 Luttwak and Horowitz, op. cit., pp. 189–91.

91 John Keegan, *World Armies*, 2nd Ed., Detroit: World Research Company, 1983), p. 562.

92 John Laffin, *Arab Armies of the Middle East Wars 1948–73* (London: Osprey Publishing, 1985), p. 17.

93 Stephen P. Cohen, *The Pakistan Army*, (Berkeley, California: 1984), p. 65.

94 Bernard Fall, *Street Without Joy* (Harrisburg, PA: The Stackpole Co., 1967), pp. 343–4.

95 H. C. B. Cook, 'Shaky Dike Against a Red Flood', *Daily Telegraph* (London), reprinted in the *Bangkok World*, 15 March 1962; cited in Bernard Fall, *The Two Vietnams: A Political and Military Analysis* (New York: Frederick A. Praeger Publishers, 1967), p. 328.

96 Ronald J. Cima, *Vietnam: A Country Study* (Washington, DC: American University, 1989), p. 253.

97 Cited in Douglas Pike, *PAVN: People's Army of Vietnam* (Novato, CA: Presidio Press, 1986), frontispiece.

98 Pike, op. cit., pp. 215–17.

99 Ibid., pp. 190–91.

100 Phillip B. Davidson, *Vietnam at War, The History 1946–1975* (Novato, CA: Presidio Press, 1988), pp. 285–6.

101 Ken Conboy, Ken Bowra, and Simon McCouig, *The NVA and Viet Cong* (London: Osprey Publishing Ltd, 1991), pp. 8–9.

102 Paul H. B. Godwin, *The Chinese Communist Armed Forces* (Maxwell Air Force Base, Alabama: Air University Press, 1988), p. 16.

103 Donald P. Whitaker, et al, *Area Handbook for the People's Republic of China* (Washington, DC: US Government Printing Office, 1972), pp. 616–18.

104 Goodwin, op. cit., p. 32.

105 Daniel P. Bolger, *Scenes from an Unfinished War: Low-Intensity Conflict in Korea, 1966–1969*, Leavenworth Papers No. 19 (Fort Leavenworth: Combat Studies Institute, 1991), p. 3.

106 Kenneth G. Clare, et al, *Area Handbook for the Republic of Korea* DA Pam 550–41 (Washington, DC: US Government Printing Office, 1968), p. 428.

107 Edward A. Olsen, 'The Societal Role of the ROK Armed Forces', in Olsen, ed., *The Armed Forces in Contemporary Asian Societies* (Boulder: Westview Press, 1986, pp. 91–2.
108 James H. Buck, *The Modern Japanese Military System* (Beverley Hill, California: Sage Publications, 1975), p. 76.
109 Edgar O'Ballance, 'The Armed Forces of Japan', *Military Review*, September 1961, pp. 22–27.
110 James H. Buck, 'The Japanese Self-Defense Forces', *Military Review*, March 1968, p. 21–24.

CHAPTER 3

THE THIRD POST-WAR DECADE

1965–1975

INTRODUCTION

This third decade of the post-war period saw most of the major conflicts of the era. These were not the wars that the great armies of the NATO and Warsaw Pact alliances had been so diligently preparing for, but they were excellent laboratories for them. The previous decade had been spent in growth and preparation for the new armies. Now they were ready to feed the ambitions and policies of their political masters.

Israel and its Arab enemies fought two quick but deadly wars (1967 and 1973) that seemed to re-define and re-define again the verities of modern armoured warfare. In doing so, they became the surrogates for the US and Soviet armies both of which painstakingly studied and analysed the lessons of those wars. Pakistan and India similarly fought two sharp wars (1965 and 1971) though with less world impact. The bloodbath of the era, though, was in South-east Asia. The quick kill expected by North Vietnam over South Vietnam in 1965 was postponed for ten years of carnage by the intervention of the United States (1965–73) and its Australian and South Korean Allies. That war saw the post-war era's only utter destruction of a major army when the North Vietnamese extinguished both the state and army of its southern brother. The US Army reeled out of that war, not wounded from battlefield defeats but from its own internal failures. One of the world's great armies drank the cup of humiliation to the dregs. Another great army, the Chinese People's Liberation Army (PLA), nearly broke down in the lunacy of the Great Cultural Revolution. The Soviet Army and its Warsaw Pact allies, smug and self-confident, expanded in size and sophistication of equipment and doctrine, poised for the great thrust to the Pyrenees that would never come.

UNITED STATES

LEAPING INTO THE ABYSS: VIETNAM

As South Vietnam tottered toward collapse in early 1965, President Johnson determined to do something decisive to redeem the situation. That 'something' was the commitment of US ground forces. In this, the army leadership was fully supportive, the army being in confident mood. The vast sums spent on its expansion and modernization had allowed it to slip into a comfortable groove worn smooth by generations of successful US armies stretching back a full hundred years to the Civil War. One historian has described that groove as 'The Army Concept'.

The Army Concept of war is, basically, the army's perception of how wars *ought* to be waged and is reflected in the way the army organizes and trains its troops for battle. The characteristics of the Army Concept are two: a focus on mid-intensity, or conventional, war and a reliance on high volumes of firepower to minimize casualties – in effect, the substitution of *matériel* costs at every available opportunity so as to avoid payment in blood.[1]

Despite the recent emphasis on counter-insurgency, the army committed large ground forces to Vietnam with every intention of fighting in the same the way that it had done from Spotsylvania to Pork Chop Hill. It would 'close with and destroy the enemy by fire and/or manoeuvre', the rigid mantra of the infantry. In the North Vietnamese concept of People's War, it would find an opponent of great subtlety and flexibility.

On 5 May 1965 the first manoeuvre unit of the US Army, the 173rd Airborne Brigade, began arriving in South Vietnam. In June they saw combat in attempting to clear a VC stronghold known as the Iron Triangle. Estimates of the size of forces needed to stem the Communist offensive escalated. By 5 June the commander of US forces in Vietnam, General William Westmoreland, decided that the planned thirteen battalions were not sufficient and called for 44. Ten days later the army's new airmobile test division was alerted for deployment and designated 1st Cavalry Division (Airmobile).

First Battle – The Ia Drang

The core of the army's strategy was to find the conventional combat units of the Vietcong and People's Army of Vietnam (PAVN), fix them and pound them to bits with firepower, thereby allowing the South Vietnamese to regain control of their population, 90 per cent of whom were distributed throughout the coastal provinces. The army's timing was perfect because the Communists had recently accelerated their struggle into the final and conventional phase of their insurgency. General Giap had sent the first full PAVN division, 325B Division, into South Vietnam to cut the country in two. The pride of the US Army, the 1st Cavalry Division (Airmobile), had just arrived in Vietnam in mid-September as the first full US division and was spoiling to show its stuff. In a remote valley in the Central Highlands both strategies would collide and fix the nature of the war.

The PAVN made the first move on 19 October when they besieged Plei Mei which sat astride communications to the provincial capital of Pleiku. They hoped to lure another Army of the Republic of Vietnam (ARVN) relief force into ambush. This force unexpectedly fought well, supported by artillery carried forward by US Chinook heavy lift helicopters. The PAVN retreated into what had been the sanctuary of the Ia Drang valley. This time they were followed by the prowling helicopters of 1st Cavalry. On 27 October General Westmoreland ordered them to begin search and destroy operations. Now it was the PAVN that was harried with unrelenting surprise as the air cavalry exploited their mobility in a new environment.

The PAVN withdrew into the Ia Drang valley which was inaccessible to heavy ground formations but no bar to the air cavalry. The PAVN division was being concentrated for the first division-level attack of the war, to be thrown at Plei Mei. Sensing the presence of PAVN formations, 1st Bn, 7th Cavalry, the regiment of Custer fame, was deployed to a landing zone (LZ) code-named X-ray on 14 November. The battalion was commanded by the blond Kentuckian, LTC Harold G. Moore, affectionately known to his men as 'Yellow Hair', in a nod to regimental history and his own aggressiveness. The 1/7th would need the advantage of good leadership; it was going into battle with 457 men, barely two-thirds of its establishment. When the first company landed, a prisoner revealed the presence of three PAVN battalions above them in the Chu Pong Massif who wanted very much to kill Americans. Moore immediately pushed a force forward that immediately ran into a large PAVN force coming to ambush the LZ. As the day wore on Moore spread his incoming companies in a semi-circle to the west of the LZ, effectively blocking the NVA's attempts to outflank the Americans. For three days and two nights the PAVN attacked around the perimeter attempting to 'close with' the Americans to negate the crushing firepower delivered by artillery and air, but the Americans

146

pounded back and still called in the firepower. Moore's battalion was reinforced beginning on the second day with companies of the 2/7th and 2/5th Cavalry until most of 3rd Brigade was in action. It was none too soon – his battalion was rapidly wasting away under the incessant attacks as the fighting flared and lapped around the LZ. So were the North Vietnamese. One of men of 2/5th Cavalry was stunned at the sight of the battlefield as his battalion entered the fray. 'My God, there's enemy bodies all over this valley. For the last 30 minutes we've been walking around, over, and through bodies.' The 1st Cavalry were up against a first-class opponent – valiant, aggressive and intelligent. Every effort was made to outflank or find cracks between the American units or just to break over them. The enemy's handling of small units was skilful. Fire was accurate and heavy. Luckily, they did not have the heavy anti-aircraft machine-guns that could have taken a greater toll of the Cavalry's helicopters.

Late on 16 November the fighting died down as the PAVN quit the field and slipped away, leaving an estimated 1,300 dead. Although outnumbered by at least two to one, American losses were only 79 killed and 121 wounded. The equalizer had been just what the Army Concept had prescribed – firepower. During the action at LZ X-ray, the artillery had fired 18,000 shells; helicopter gunships had fired 3,000 2.75in rockets; 400 air sorties had been flown in close support; and for the first time in history, B-52s had flown in close support, on the Chu Phong Massif, sometimes as close as 5,000 metres.[2]

The 1/7th Cavalry was flown out while 2/7th and 2/5th Cavalry marched out to two other LZs on 17 November. The march of 2/5th was tactically sound, but that of the 450 men of the 2/7th towards LZ Albany was vulnerable to ambush, its companies being strung out in column. Their commander delayed to question a prisoner, and this gave his unit, 8th Bn, 66th Regiment, enough time to set up an L-shaped ambush. The US commander had called forward all his company commanders and most of the first sergeants shortly before the North Vietnamese struck; only one officer made it back to his company. The lead and tail companies were crushed while the PAVN charged through the centre of the column. The action disintegrated into countless desperate individual and small group fights. Survivors managed to crawl into a perimeter for the night as they listened to the enemy shooting their wounded. Had it not been for air support, every company would have been annihilated. At daybreak the PAVN were gone. The 2/7th Cavalry had been gutted as badly as at the Little Big Horn, with 151 killed and 121 wounded.

Although the 325B Division had been badly hurt at LZ X-ray, it had had the last deadly word in the Ia Drang battle at LZ Albany. Understandably the US Army chose to emphasize the former rather than the latter action. Nevertheless, the Ia Drang battle had been decisive. It had frustrated the final push of the final conventional phase of the war in the South. Defeat had been staved off. What use the US Army and its ARVN ally would make of the second chance was in the long run even more decisive. The army was also pleased with the performance of the 1st Cavalry Division. The unit had proved itself to have mastered airmobile operations, and the men had shown themselves aggressive and tactically proficient. Small unit leadership had been excellent, and the disaster at LZ Albany was put down, probably rightly so, to a new and inexperienced battalion commander.

1965–1968

If the battle of the Ia Drang had been a victory for the United States, in the long term it was a strategic victory for the PAVN whose strategy was to lure the Americans into the interior *away* from the population, the control of whom was the real strategic battle ground. In this General Giap was to succeed during the next three years as General Westmoreland's Military Assistance Command Vietnam (MACV) sought out his main force VC and regular PAVN units in the interior. Earlier Westmoreland had come to the conclusion that if US units were broken down into smaller components to fight the pacification struggle in the populated areas, they would be destroyed in detail as the ARVN had been on several occasions. Giap was only to happy to feed this conclusion. The Communists also rachetted the war down from the phase 3 'conventional' level to phase 2 after the arrival of the US. troops. Battalion-level attacks had fallen from 9.7 to 1.3 per month between the final quarters of 1965 and 1966. Yet 90 per cent of insurgent initiated incidents continued to occur in the 10 per cent of the country that was inhabited by 80 per cent of the population.[3]

Forbidden to seek a battle of annihilation in North Vietnam and unable easily to get to grips with the enemy in South Vietnam, the adherents of the Army Concept found a solution in attrition. Such strategy needed large forces, and these poured over from the United States so profusely that all that remained of the the strategic reserve was the 82nd Airborne Division.

Table 3-1. The Arrival of US Army and Marine Ground Forces in South Vietnam 1965–1967

1965 1st Cavalry Division (Airmobile)
1st Infantry Division
3rd Marine Division
173rd Airborne Brigade
1st Brigade, 101st Airborne Division
1966 4th Infantry Division
9th Infantry Division
25th Infantry Division
1st Marine Division
11th Armored Cavalry Regiment
196th Infantry Brigade
199th Infantry Brigade
1967 101st Airborne Division
23rd Infantry Division

The Army spent much of 1966 re-aligning these forces and settling them into their areas of responsibilities, in preparation for the serious fighting of late 1966–7. Then the strategy of attrition could be set in motion. Over time, large-scale search and destroy operations would wear down the enemy's combat forces faster than they could be replaced until the insurgency collapsed. The period 1966–7 was punctuated by these multi-division operations: ATTLEBORO (September-November 1966), CEDAR FALLS (January 1967) and JUNCTION CITY (February-May 1967). Yet the enemy was never really hurt by these operations and continued to draw replacements and supplies from the population for whom they waged the real strategic though undramatic struggle. The US troops continued to be drawn into the interior and border areas of South Vietnam where the ferocious Battles of the Highlands and Dak To were fought against the PAVN. Despite the overwhelming American presence, it was this enemy that continued to hold the tactical initiative. For example, during JUNCTION CITY, only one engagement was not initiated by the enemy. After the end of the Battles of Highlands, the 4th Infantry Division's after action report stated ruefully:

'The most difficult tactical problem found in fighting the NVA in large areas of difficult terrain is finding the enemy. That is, finding him without having tactical units shot up and pinned down by automatic weapons and snipers ... at close range.'[4]

The PAVN was also turning the attrition weapon back upon their enemy. By 1967, despite the big battles with the PAVN, 96 per cent of all army engagements were fought by companies or smaller units. On this more equal footing, the army's firepower and numerical advantages were often checked as the army began to bleed from a thousand cuts. It was not only casualties that reduced strength in the line units. Huge numbers of troops were tied down in rear echelon duties and could be prized out only with the greatest determination. Although divisions were above their authorized strengths, their infantry battalion strengths were chronically short. Rifle battalions of the 1st Cavalry Division, for example, with establishments of 920 men, could field less than 550.

The army began the Vietnam experience at the height of its Kennedy-inspired renaissance. Happy to be back in its conventional tradition, flush with new equipment and increased in size, it was a good army, technically and tactically proficient. It also had a professional NCO corps and well-trained junior leaders. The units that went to Vietnam were effective and cohesive. As US strength, mostly army, built to almost 550,000 men during these years, a number of misguided policies broke down the levels of proficiency, the standards of leadership, and unit cohesion. Forbidden to call-up any of the Reserve Components for political reasons, the army for the first time in this century had to fight a major war with only its regular cadre and draftees. Individuals and not units, unlike the Australians, were rotated for tours that were barely twelve months. Almost every shoot of institutional memory was nipped by this constant rotation. Unit cohesion waned as unit composition changed on a daily basis. Battalion and higher commanders were rotated through their commands at an even faster rate of six months, a measure generated ostensibly to spread combat experience as widely as possible. The driving force was far more banal. Promotion depended upon command, and command in combat was even better. The result of this notorious 'ticket-punching' policy was to ensure that the men were constantly paying in blood to provide commanders with experience that was barely learned before it was put on the shelf. By 1968 the professional NCO corps was being used up by combat casualties and the exhaustion of repeated tours. Heavy casualties among experienced junior officers meant that the junior leadership was thinning in quality. Second lieutenants were promoted captain in two years. The combat ranks were increasingly filled with draftees as volunteers and better educated draftees had some choice of speciality and branch of service. These draftees in combat units increasingly were lower class and minority as middle and upper class youths sought every deferment available. Casualty rates for draftees were 3.1 per cent KIA and 20.3 per cent WIA, while volunteers suffered only 1.7 and 12.0 per cent.

The effects on other army units around the world was even more crippling as they were repeatedly levied for experienced officers and NCOs and starved of funds for maintenance of equipment and facilities. In Germany, companies were not infrequently commanded by second lieutenants. The army made the best of a tragic incident at tank gunnery one year when the battalion commander died of a heart attack on the first range. The next senior officer was a first lieutenant, a rank reached after one year's service. The fact that he led the battalion to qualify was a testament to his personal abilities and not the challenging circumstance the army had created for him.

The army's record was not one long nightmare as this catalogue of stupidities might make it seem. Despite them the army excelled in, if not initiating, a number of advances. The best of these was the transformation of the helicopter into a magnificent weapon of war. The American soldier took to the helicopter as the Plains Indians took to the horse and extracted every bit of mobility, firepower and flexibility it could offer. The two airmobile divisions, 1st Cavalry and later 101st Divisions and the airmobile squadrons of the other divisions, turned airmobility into a military art form. The artillery grew in expertise and technique, and its accurate and quick responses saved countless lives in desperate jungle fighting. The artillery also developed fire support co-ordinators to integrate the increasing number of weapons supporting the ground forces.[5] The logistics effort to supply so large a force was a remarkable feat by any measure, and the army accomplished it with great efficiency. Logistics is an American forte and did not fail the soldier or the strategist. If anything it was too successful, producing such comfort in the rear echelons as to act as a magnet for the troops. Its own scale ended up diverting many troops to its support that could have been more efficiently used in the line battalions. A generation later in Operation 'Desert Storm', such skill coupled with an effective strategy and stern self-control, was to produce a dramatic victory.

RIF in the Rubber

Most of the army's units, despite these handicaps, continued to be effective and proud fighting formations. Army traditions and the quality of the troops pulled most units through the ordeal, as for example, the performance of the 11th Armored Cavalry 'Black Horse' Regiment and the 1st Cavalry Division. The reconnaissance in force (RIF) at Loc Hoa in November 1968 was an example of combat performance to the highest degree. An armoured cavalry troop, C Troop, 1st Squadron, 11th ACR, commanded by CPT William Hansen, was attached to 2nd Bn, 12th Cavalry, 1st Cavalry Division and teamed with B Company, commanded by CPT W. Witt, to form a task force to operate out of Loc Ninh, a district capital seven kilometres from the Cambodian border. Both units were integrated to take advantage of the Cavalry's mobility and firepower and the Aircavalry's security and close combat capability. Both units saw the advantages and quickly developed a close and friendly relationship.

Intelligence identified a PAVN unit at the village of Loc Hoa, on the edge of a rubber plantation north of the Loc Ninh. Aero scouts verified the report, and the task force, with the aircav troopers riding atop the Black Horse's ACaVs, was dispatched to find the enemy. A stream running south of the rubber planation initially blocked the task force, but another culvert was found one kilometre to the northwest. The task force then moved quickly to the new crossing site. As luck would have it they had stumbled upon an observation post of the 3rd Bn, 141st Regiment, which quickly oriented its defence to the TF's first attempted crossing site. As the TF reconnoitred the crossing, PAVN observation posts were flushed, and the ACaVs immediately pursued. They then began to take fire from their east flank. The TF quickly turned in this direction and attacked. The first attack did not succeed in breaking the enemy's bunkered defence line, and air and artillery strikes were called in. The second attack successfully ground through the defences. A PAVN attempt to flank the Americans by sending a company up the stream bed was thwarted by the TF's firepower and security. Then the Black Horse's armoured vehicles formed a blunt wedge followed by the airmobile infantry on foot. The ACaVs kept the North Vietnamese pinned down and crunched over the bunkers and spider holes. The following infantry grenaded the bunkers and shot any PAVN that attempted to shoot the cav troopers from the rear. Fifty-eight PAVN were killed at the cost of fifteen US wounded. The next few days saw the TF gut the remainder of the 141st Regiment with equally small casualties.[6] This TF's tactical prowess and professionalism were models of which any army would be proud. Had the overall strategy of the war matched the intelligence and ingenuity of the tactics and leadership shown by this TF and countless other such units, history would surely have scoured a different path.

THE TET OFFENSIVE – 1968

By January 1968 the army believed it was still on the right track with its attrition strategy although the situation had not noticeably improved in the last year. MACV's attention was still focused on the border regions, where the PAVN had engaged in a number of battles since October 1967, and on the Marines in the Khe Sanh area in the north. The diversion of even more forces to the borders just before the late January Tet holidays was cancelled as the intelligence picture rapidly worsened. Still no responsible American or ARVN general expected a major country-wide offensive on the professional grounds that it would be idiocy. But, 'One never attributes folly to his enemy – but then, of such stuff are surprises made.' Now the storm of the Tet Offensive burst upon the allies. On 30–31 January, 84,000 VC and PAVN attacked Saigon, 36 of 43 provincial capitals, five of six autonomous cities, and 64 of 242 district capitals. Almost every large city was penetrated. The brunt of the fighting fell upon the ARVN, many of whose soldiers were home on leave. Although a number of US installations were attacked, the enemy's goal was to crack the ARVN and provoke an uprising that would make the American position untenable. They accomplished neither. The South Vietnamese held and fought.

For the US Army the Tet Offensive was a godsend. For two years the enemy had not succumbed to the attrition strategy and had always eluded the Cannae the Americans had planned for them. Now they had thrown themselves into the jaws of the Army Concept in the pitched battles the army had lusted after. And the army wrought havoc among them. The allies killed 37,000 and took 6,000 prisoners as opposed to 4,000 American and 8,000 AVRN casualties of all types. In most cases, the allies quickly defeated the enemy. The VC infrastructure had revealed itself and been destroyed together with most of the mainforce VC battalions. It was one of the most ghastly blunders since Terrentius Varro convinced himself that he had Hannibal's number.

1968–1973

The Americans, however, were no more able to take advantage of their Vietnamese Cannae than were the Carthaginians 2,200 years before. As the army congratulated itself on its victory, support on the home front evaporated. The army's rosy projections since 1966 that the enemy was increasingly on the ropes had been refuted by the images of Tet. Westmoreland's request for another 250,000 troops seemed to be the last straw. By May the US's focus had shifted from winning to transferring the conducting of the war to the South Vietnamese and withdrawing US forces.

After Tet Westmoreland was kicked upstairs to become Chief of Staff and was replaced by General Creighton Abrams. By early 1969 Abrams had crafted a One

War Concept which decreed an end to the war of the big battalions and merged the conventional and pacification efforts into a single plan. US ground forces had reached their peak on 1 January with 359,313 soldiers and 80,716 Marines in 110 infantry and tank battalions. The US Army was now in a supporting role to ARVN which received vast amounts of new equipment and intensive training. Combat missions were reduced as many units began to prepare to stand down. Numerous officers and NCOs were transferred from remaining line units to the pacification effort.

By the end of 1969 army morale in Vietnam had sagged badly and worsened during the next two years. Now that the withdrawal had begun, no one wanted to be the last man to die. The hostile and vocal activities of the anti-war movement corroded morale, particularly the activities of prominent Democrat members of Congress and the previous administration. Arousing particular hatred among the troops were the celebrity supporters of the Communists, such as the notorious 'Hanoi Jane' Fonda. Anti-war activists went so far as to throw excrement on flag-draped coffins returned from Vietnam.[7] Drugs and racism, which had not been serious problems until now, poisoned relationships and unit effectiveness as the propaganda of the civil rights and anti-war movements and the counter-culture seeped into Vietnam with every new replacement. Serious disciplinary problems spread as officers and NCOs who were too aggressive or too willing to maintain discipline were increasingly defied or even fragged. The drain-off of officers and NCOs to the pacification programme stripped the army of its first-line of discipline just when it was most needed. The army that had performed with skill and courage for three years was going soft, and it was to get worse in 1970-2 as withdrawal accelerated.

By this time an even more pervasive poison had entered the army's blood-stream. The officer corps was breaking down as a moral and professional entity. As General H. Norman Schwarzkopf relates:

'That summer of 1970, the Army war College issued a scathing report – commissioned by General Westmoreland who was now chief of staff – that explained a great deal of what we were seeing. Based on a confidential survey of 415 officers, the report blasted the Army for rewarding the wrong people. It described how the system had been subverted to condone selfish behavior and tolerate incompetent commanders who sacrificed their subordinates and distorted facts to get ahead. It criticized the Army's obsession with meaningless statistics and was especially damning on the subject of body counts in Vietnam.'

A prevalent example of this sort of behaviour were the lies told to subordinates about their confidential efficiency reports. At this time a rating officer did not have to show the rated officer his efficiency report. It became all too common to tell the rated officer that he had been given a good report when in fact it had been damaging. The officer could only see the original report if he went to Washington to review his official personnel file.[8] An officer corps that regularly lies within itself and exhibits such base behaviour will inevitably fail in its role as moral leaders. Rather than exhibit the moral courage required of their rank, the general officer corps collectively seemed to lose its nerve in the face of cascading internal problems. These problems were particularly acute in the majority of the army stationed outside Vietnam, in the United States and Germany. To combat indiscipline, they resorted to the classic tactics of bankrupt leadership and let slip the bonds of discipline even further in the pathetic hope that the ranks could be bought off. They

sharply curtailed the authority of company grade officers and NCOs, often elevat-
ing decisions normally reserved for platoon sergeants to battalion commanders. By
1971 there seemed to be an organized campaign to portray the traditional NCO as a
stupid Neanderthal brute incapable of leading the so-called finest generation America had ever put into uniform. Insulted by its senior leadership and stripped of
authority, the NCO corps gradually stopped functioning. The development of
junior officers by their seniors also seemed to wither. In a loathsome corruption of
the concept of Nelson's band of brothers, senior officers regularly relieved junior
officers for minor reasons, blasting their careers, in what seemed to be a cult of
ruthlessness and cover up. The prospect of having to go with this tide of selfish
incompetence for the rest of their lives caused many of the army's best young officers to leave the service. Race had become such a politically correct issue that many
commanders allowed their units simply to break down into hostile camps rather
than endanger their careers by confronting escalating black radicalism in the ranks.
They were equally at a loss to confront the growing violence within the ranks
although one brigade commander in Germany in 1970 went so far as to bring tanks
into the barracks area to shine their searchlights across the buildings at night to
keep the muggers indoors.

By 1970 most US forces were either standing down or working overtime to get
the ARVN into shape so that they could go it alone. As a result casualties continued
to fall as the troops concentrated on their own security. There was to be one last
large operation, a joint US-ARVN strike at the vast PAVN support facilities across
the Cambodian border. Immense quantities of stores were captured, but the PAVN
simply withdrew. The logistics disruption of the enemy may have given the South
Vietnamese another year. It was the last hurrah for many of the participating units,
including the 1st Cavalry Division and 11th ACR, which they executed with all the
spirit of their first years in country. By March 1972, when the PAVN conducted a
major invasion in the north, the only US ground forces permitted to take part were
army and marine helicopters. Eighteen army advisers volunteered to stay with
ARVN units in Quang Tri City.

On 22 August 1972 the last army combat unit furled its colours and departed
South-east Asia. Ironically, it was the 1st Bn, 7th Cavalry, the unit that had triumphed at LZ X-ray in November 1965. After the Paris Accords were signed, the
last American soldiers left South Vietnam by the end of March. The army came
home as a stream of individuals, not as units marching triumphantly with their
colours. There were no parades and no official thanks. They were just forgotten. It
was to be almost twenty years before the Vietnam veterans were given the mod-
icum of respect they deserved. The cased colours came home to be given to new
men in new places. The living threads with the past that makes a battalion a formidable and almost holy thing, had been snapped.

Table 3-2. US Army and Marine Corps Casualties in South-east Asia 1964–1973

	Army	Marine Corps
Serving	4,368,000	794,000
Casualties		
Killed in action	30,907	13,082
Other deaths	7,274	1,754
Wounded	96,802	51,392
Total casualties	134,983	66,228

Source: *Defense 91*, September-October 1991.

No better description of the army's failure in Vietnam has been expressed than in the exchange between LTC Harry Summers and his NVA counterpart during the release of US POWs from North Vietnam. Summers belligerently informed his counterpart that PAVN had never beaten the US Army in the field. The North Vietnamese answered matter-of-factly that that was true but irrelevant. The bottom line was that PAVN had defeated the army's strategy, which was more important.

THE SECOND KOREAN CONFLICT, 1966–1969

As US deployment to Vietnam was quickening in 1966, rumbles were heard on the Korean DMZ. The North Korean dictator, Kim Il Sung, had decided that the time was fortuitous for fomenting an insurgency in South Korea that would disintegrate the ROK government and allow his armies to finish the job. He reckoned that the Americans would not be able to respond, their army being hip deep in South Vietnam.

His method was to slip highly trained special operations troops through the DMZ to establish guerrilla bases in the interior. At first he had an easy mark. The two divisions of the US Eighth Army were in deplorable condition. Stripped of qualified officers and NCOs to boost units in Vietnam, their tactical abilities, discipline and morale were low. A 13-month rotation period also relentlessly broke down cohesion. The KPA highlighted this on 3 November 1966 during a visit of President Johnson to Seoul, when they ambushed a US patrol in the DMZ and killed eight men. The KPA special operations troops were masters at infiltration and the savage ambush. A rising US death toll in the DMZ confirmed that.

The new commander of the United Nations Command and Eighth Army, Lieutenant General Charles Bonesteel, quickly thought through the problem. Discovering a doctrinal void, he devised his own methods: traditional patrolling techniques allied to the prevention of infiltration by new techniques. He advised the ROK on internal security policy, but refused to take over sovereign responsibilities of the ROK. His patient efforts eventually paid off. The KPA remained superior at patrolling in the DMZ and able to continue infiltration, but the US troops and their ROK counterparts narrowed their edge enough to make infiltration increasingly difficult and costly. ROK internal security measures eventually made the south a deadly destination for the KPA. By 1969 Kim had recognized failure and called off the effort. The 317 US (mostly army) casualties made this relatively unknown second Korean Conflict the third costliest campaign for the US Army since the end of the Second World War – but it was a victory.

THE ARMY SURVIVES

Opposition to the Vietnam War had become so intertwined with the draft, that one of the casualties of the withdrawal was conscription itself which was ended by Congress in late 1972. The army began 1973 as an all-volunteer force for the first time since 1940. Worldwide the army had already been shuddering from the accelerated release of draftees which made training often impossible and reduced much of the army to caretakers of property and equipment.

Table 3-3. US Army Strength 1965–1975

1965	969,066	1968	1,570,343
1966	1,199,784	1969	1,512,169
1967	1,442,498	1970	1,322,548

1971	1,120,822	1974	780,464
1972	807,985	1975	781,316
1973	788,177		

The army's first years with the volunteer system were not promising. The endeavour to attract recruits of quality was a depressing succession of defeats made worse by a failure of pay and benefits to keep pace with the cost of living. After the Vietnam War, military service was not a popular career especially with the better educated middle class. The army tried to use the term 'Volar' to describe the changes, but the word only became an epithet of derision among the troops. An initial reliance on gimmicks to attract volunteers was typified by the army's recruiting slogan, 'The Army Wants to Join You'. In a search for bodies to fill the ranks the army rapidly expanded the Women's Army Corps (WAC). If quality males could not be attracted, quality females could. The WAC always had higher recruiting standards than the rest of the army and grew from 0.9 per cent in 1964 to 2.4 per cent in 1977 and 6.7 per cent by 1977. Women were broken out of the strict job limitations of the past and integrated into much of the army apart from the combat arms. In its rush to integrate women, every applicable lesson learned from the Second World War was ignored. Nevertheless the army discovered that the old WAC had produced excellent soldiers who now had a wider stage on which to show their talents. If recruitment for the active force had become difficult, it collapsed for the Reserve Components which no longer had the draft and the war to fill their ranks.

General Abrams had returned from Vietnam to succeed Westmoreland as Chief of Staff. He found an army morally and institutionally exhausted. Before he died of cancer, he initiated a number of reforms that began the long process of recovery for the army. Foremost among them was the creation of the Training and Doctrine Command (TRADOC), commanded by the brilliant General William DePuy whose mission was to start from scratch to re-think both training and fighting concepts. Abrams also decided increase the number of divisions from thirteen to sixteen without an increase in strength. Support services were streamlined, and thousands of experienced NCOs were culled from support branches and retrained for the combat arms. The Reserve Components provided the third or 'roundout' brigades of many active divisions.

Even more important was the fruit of the severe introspection and self-examination undergone privately and professionally by thousands of army officers stunned and embittered by the nation's defeat in Vietnam. Particularly painful were the morale and leadership failures of the officer corps which had become obsessed with careerism and was intellectually sterile. The best of the junior officer corps, the institution's seed corn, was being driven out of the army by this wretched example and by the common, ruthless practice of destroying the careers of subordinates for minor failures. As the dust of the war settled, young field grade officers such as H. Norman Schwarzkopf resolved that the army would never again create the same follies they had endured.

GREAT BRITAIN

With the abandonment of Aden, the British Army marched out of an era. The last serious imperial commitment had been shed. The Sandys reorganizations and amalgamations had finally been completed; a happier balance had been achieved between missions and resources. The army could now concentrate fully on the Soviet Threat from across the North German Plain. Or so it thought. There would be distractions, and both would originate, for once, close to home. Across the Irish Sea, Northern Ireland would destabilize as bitterly as had the Punjab in 1948, and in London an increasingly leftist Labour Government under Defence Minister Healy would take a meat axe to the army in the name of cost effectiveness.

ANOTHER AMALGAMATION

The first blow came in 1965 and was directed against the reserve system. The Territorial Army (TA) and the Army Emergency Reserve (AER) were to be combined into a single organization, the Army Volunteer Reserve (AVR), and reduced from 120,000 to 50,000 men. Strong political pressure saved most of the battalions as a sort of home guard while thirteen were earmarked for wartime reinforcement of the BAOR. The reserve system had virtually been destroyed, leaving the army with a weaker wartime reserve than it had had in 1914 or 1939.[9]

The next swing of the axe struck the active force in 1967, the continuing trouble in Aden and Borneo having prevented even a labour government from dragging the army to the chopping-block straight away. Strength which had grown to 237,000 by 1966 was steadily reduced to 166,500 by 1975. Infantry battalions would be trimmed from 66 to 50 (not counting the 22 SAS and Paras), armoured regiments from 22 to 19, and artillery from 27 to 23. The BAOR would take seventeen infantry battalions and thirteen armoured regiments; nine battalions and one regiment would suffice for overseas duties, leaving 22 battalions and five regiments for duty in Britain, the highest number at home since 1948. The drastic cuts in the number of infantry battalions and armoured regiments meant another hideous round of amalgamations of regiments that had barely healed from the earlier Sandys surgeries. In the end, in place of the old Corps of Infantry bugaboo, six infantry divisions replaced the old brigades that sheltered the regiments. Within a few of the divisions, large regiments of several battalions absorbed the traditional single-battalion regiments, though the old regimental traditions and hybrid names survived. Regiments that shared designations such as 'fusilier', 'light infantry', or 'rifle' were obvious choices for consolidation into these large regiments, becoming known as The Royal Regiment of Fusiliers, The Light Infantry, and The Royal Green Jackets. Only the Brigade of Gurkhas and The Parachute Regiment would not be swallowed up by the division system, though the Gurkhas were to lose three of their eight battalions. Table 3-4 shows the structure of the British Army as it settled down in 1971; with slight modifications this was the army that would carry on until the withering of the Soviet Empire set in motion another convulsion.

Table 3-4 . The British Army – 1971

	Battalions/Regiments
Armoured	
Household Cavalry	2
Royal Armoured Corps	17
Supporting Arms	
The Royal Regiment of Artillery	29
The Corps of Royal Engineers	
The Royal Corps of Signals	
Infantry	
The Guards Division	7
The Scottish Division	6
The Queen's Division	9

Battalions/Regiments	
The King's Division	8
The Prince of Wales's Division	9
The Light Division	6
Airborne	
The Parachute Regiment	3
22 Special Air Service Regiment	1
The Brigade of Gurkhas	5

Source: Geoffrey Blaxland, *The Regiments Depart*.

The army's reaction, particularly among the infantry, was predictably sour; re-enlistment rates fell dangerously. The public also sensed this disquiet, and enlistments of recruits noticeably declined. In its alarm the government petulantly suggested that if a better face were not put on the transition, it might provoke the abolition of the regimental system and its substitution by that old bugaboo, the faceless Corps of Infantry. Although this threat was never followed through, opposition within the army and outside was intense.

Again, it was Scotland that would not go quietly, despite sneers of tribalism from the left. The Council of Scottish Colonels decided that not another Scottish regiment would suffer amalgamation. The Cameronians paraded into extinction on 14 may 1968, on one last march 'to their ancestral stronghold at Castle Dangerous where they had first mustered as a regiment 279 years before'.[10] The Argyll and Sutherland Highlanders, on the other hand, would not to go without an argument. They gave it a good shot, collecting a million signatures to the cry 'Save the Argylls!' and were eventually, by dint of hard fighting, to win a reprieve. A similar though less successful cry of 'Save the Royal Scots Greys!' was heard when Scotland's only armoured regiment was to be fused with the 3rd Carabiniers to become The Blues and Royals.[11]

In 1969 a concession was made to the regimental system by allowing infantry regiments to wear their own cap badges which they had not done since 1957 when every man had to wear his brigade badge. Of 64 regimental cap badges worn in 1957, there were now only eight that could be worn by regiments that had survived the two great amalgamations. The remaining regiments could wear new badges designed around their new hybridized regiments. Ultimately, this was the wisest of the changes. No other symbol represents the regimental tradition and its animating spirit so much as the cap badge. Men live by symbols, and the British Army regimental cap badge among men of war has few rivals in this age. Recruiting, which had soured under the pain of the new amalgamations, picked up again when the cap badges came back, a tangible bow to the power of symbols.[12]

Looking back on this latest convulsion, Correlli Barnett observed that Britain had completed the great three centuries expansion and contraction of empire:

'Britain again stood where she had stood in the reign of Elizabeth I – a second class, perhaps a third class, power in terms of relative economic strength, population, and warlike capability, living precariously in the face of keen trade rivalry and sandwiched between the superpowers.'

As a result the army was to find itself as the proverbial square peg in a round hole. It had been created to meet imperial needs that no longer existed. Britain was now a European power with a much truncated imperial army. The labour government had just destroyed the reserve system that every other European power found vital to its defence, while the previous conservative government had abandoned the other feature of European armies, conscription. The damage to the reserve system would have been immediately crippling in time of war. Only by calling-up every reservist in the United Kingdom could the army have been brought up to its war establishment. Not a replacement would have been available. 'That army was therefore capable of fighting for no more than a week or so before wasting away from want of sleep and reinforcements.' The government tried to justify its lack of foresight by claiming that a future war would rapidly go nuclear. There would be only the briefest if any conventional phase, so investment in the sustaining ability of the army was a waste of money. The army faced the ultimate nightmare – the nation's defence was in the hands of a committee of hostile sophists and accountants.[13]

NORTHERN IRELAND

The army now had its gaze fixed on its European commitments only to have the next crisis erupt at its back in Northern Ireland. The garrison in Northern Ireland had been considered a good source for reinforcement overseas in the 1950s and 1960s, at times being allowed to shrink to only one battalion. In August 1969 seething tension between Catholics and Protestants caused three battalions to be sent to Londonderry and Belfast to relieve the police and re-establish the even hand of the law in keeping the Queen's Peace. Soon more than half the army's strategic reserve was committed to protect the Catholic minority. In late September the army suffered almost fifty wounded as it held Protestant mobs at bay in Belfast. During the first months of the violence the garrison peaked at fifteen infantry battalions and two armoured regiments, which was the same manning level as the garrison in Cyprus at the height of the guerrilla war.

By 1977 the continued unrest necessitated a large permanent garrison which in the summer of 1972 had peaked at 22,000, being augmented by units sent from the United Kingdom and BAOR on a rotation system ('roulement'), each serving 4 and later 4½-month tours of duty. It was essentially infantryman's work, but the strain on the battalions was so great that armour, artillery and engineer regiments and even service units as well as TA units were trained as infantry for security duty, and were inter-changeable. Units that draw recruits from Northern Ireland, such as the Irish Guards, are not required to serve in the Province.[14]

Peacekeeping in Northern Ireland was to be the longest continuous operation of the British Army since 1945. Begun in 1969, it was still under way in 1990, though at a much reduced level. The initial goal of protecting the Catholic minority was to change quickly to upholding British sovereignty as the Irish Republican Army reappeared (as the Provisional Irish Republican Army – PIRA), animated from the grave by Marxist incantations. Determined to unite all of Ireland, this 'Gaelic Khmer Rouge' found in the British Army a mortal enemy, one that had acquired most of its operational experience around the world from Borneo to Cyprus in preventing similar nasty minorities from seizing power by violence. The army found that not all of this experience was transferrable and that it would have to break some very new ground. The most remarkable task was to supplant and retrain the civil police, the Royal Ulster Constabulary, which was both hopelessly ineffective and partisan. The army crossed this threshold with great reluctance; no British soldier has entertained the idea of assuming police powers with any enthusiasm since Cromwell's Army set such a lasting and virulently negative impression on the nation. Happily it was only a temporary measure until the army could retrain the police, in particular, to employ military methods of intelligence gathering and analysis. Another measure was to abolish the brutal RUC reserves and replace them with a new organization, The Ulster Defence Regiment (UDR). Rather than a police reserve, the UDR is a British Army regiment of unique type. Its mission is to assist the reorganized RUC in the protection of the lives and property of the people of Northern Ireland. Established in 1970, it is both the youngest and largest regiment in the army, totalling some 7,500 men and women by 1975. The UDR is unique in that its personnel are a mix of regular army, and full- and part-time cadres. In 1985 the Regiment consisted of four categories of soldier: 100 Regular, 2,500 Permanent Cadre (PC), 3,250 Part Time (PT) and 650 Greenfinches (women). The UDR provides military support to the RUC with the PC permanently on duty supplemented by the PT at weekends and evenings.[15] The army was to suffer more casualties in Ireland than in any of the imperial efforts; by 1983 they had lost 271 dead and 3,025 wounded. By 1986 the death toll had climbed to 381, the Ulster Defence Regiment losing 149, and the Royal Ulster Constabulary 212.[16]

Keeping the peace in Northern Ireland was in many ways more difficult for the army than it had been in the colonies. Martial law has never been declared so the soldier is subject to the observance of all the rigorous safeguards of Anglo-Saxon common law and the authority of civil government. A watchful press armed with television is there to record any indiscretion committed under great pressure. Hunting EOKA terrorists in Cyprus was so much easier. In the end, the result was very similar; patient efforts suppressed much but not all terrorist activity. There was another dividend that the army would cash in during the Falklands War. Peacekeeping put a premium on small unit leadership:

'The basic tactical unit is the four-man 'brick' led by a junior officer or NCO, who can often find himself in a position where he has to make a split-second decision, knowing that if he acts wrongly he can bring trouble not just to himself but to the image of the Security Forces as a whole.'[17]

AN IMPERIAL EXCEPTION – DHOFAR
Having ostentatiously shed its last imperial commitment, Britain found herself making an important exception to defend the Sultanate of Oman from a Marxist insurgency operating out of the Dhofar region and materially supported by South Yemen. Oman lies opposite the Gulf of Hormuz, the throttle on the West's oil supply. The SAS were dispatched in July 1970 to assist the new Sultan Qaboos who had replaced his corrupt and despotic father by a coup. The SAS rarely had more than one squadron in country at a time, but their deft approach was worth several divisions of regular troops. Liddell Hart would have been delighted with the Regiment's innate understanding of the 'indirect approach' which allowed it carefully to turn the much abused population away from the guerrillas. The most innovative approach was to enlist guerrilla deserters as SAS auxiliaries. These were men the SAS civil affairs programme had weaned away from the guerrillas in the first place. The Dhofar campaign ended successfully in a negotiated peace in October 1976. It had been a unique experience for the SAS; for the first time since the Second World War they had met an enemy armed with artillery and multiple rocket-launchers. In the final battle at Sarfait, one SAS troop reportedly came under heavier fire than anything experienced since Korea.[18]

THE EUROPEAN BATTLEFIELD
The commitment to Northern Ireland tended to obscure the fact that the British Army had, at last, made the full transition from an imperial to a European army.

Except for nine battalions in Hong Kong, Brunei, Belize and Cyprus (all five Gurkha battalions), the entire army was either in Germany as part of the BAOR or in the United Kingdom where it served as either home defence or reinforcement for the Rhine Army. The focus was firmly on its NATO role as an element of an alliance. No longer were the British armoured divisions in Germany the only manoeuvre forces barring the Soviet Army's way as in the late 1940s. In 1974 BAOR held 59 of the 109 fighting battalions of the British Army. In that year, it numbered 55,500 men in three divisions which had dropped the titles Infantry or Armoured. Divisional organization continued to evolve in order to reach the right combined arms mix. Brigade groups of four regiments in a relation of three to one of either armour or mechanized infantry were allotted their own subordinate artillery regiment and engineer squadron (company). By 1974 the division had two large brigades of four regiments each, usually two armoured and two mechanized with artillery and engineers subordinate to division. A fourth division (the 3rd Division) was remodelled as an airportable infantry formation and located in the United Kingdom as the Strategic Reserve.[19]

The decade 1965–75 saw a major improvement in the equipment of the British Army. The introduction of the 105mm Abbot SP gun in 1966 finally allowed the BAOR's divisional artillery to be entirely self-propelled. The first full-service Chieftain tanks were introduced in 1967, and by 1974 the tank fleet of 900 vehicles was to consist of all Chieftains. The Scorpion light tank went into production in 1972, and

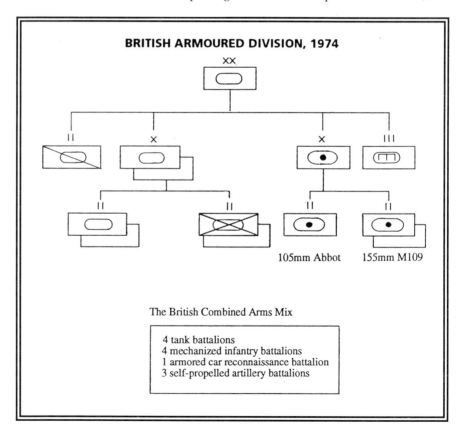

BRITISH ARMOURED DIVISION, 1974

105mm Abbot   155mm M109

The British Combined Arms Mix

4 tank battalions
4 mechanized infantry battalions
1 armored car reconnaissance battalion
3 self-propelled artillery battalions

Above: The British Centurion tank was developed near the end of Second World War, and 4,423 were produced for the British army and export. The Centurion was one of the better Western early post-war tanks and saw considerable action in Korea and the Arab-Israeli and Indo-Pakistan Wars of the 1950s and 1960s.

Below: The Soviet T-54, armed with a rifled 100mm gun, was the first of the post-war era's main battle tanks. With its T-55 variant, it was the most numerous tank produced in the post-war period and saw service in at least 46 countries. Its small size was an advantage in the flat plains of Eurasia but forced storage of fuel and ammunition in the crew compartment with the result that any hit by a comparable tank had a fifty percent chance of destroying the T-54/55 by fire and/or explosion.

Above: A US M46 Medium Tank engaged in fire support in Korea. The mountainous nature of the Korean Penin-sula precluded armour from being more than a supporting arm to the infantry armies of both sides. The M46 was a refinement of the M26 introduced in the last few months of the Second World War.

Below: Just as enthusiasm for the atomic bomb had written off conventional ground forces, the US army found itself in an old-fashioned infantry war in Korea in the summer of 1950. The ground war was fought, by both sides, with Second World War inventories, and with traditional close-fighting and leadership skills.

above: The first Soviet tracked armoured personnel carrier, the BTR-50 series was first seen in public in 1957 and was designed for its cross-country capabilities and assigned to motorized infantry regiments in tank divisions. The TR-50 was an innovative vehicle for its time with an amphibious capability, propelled by two water jets. Initially it ad an open-topped troop compartment, but later models were fully enclosed and NBC protected. (US Army)

elow: The Soviet T-62 tank was a further development of the T-54/55. Its greatest innovation was a 115mm moothbore gun. At one time the Soviets experimented with an automatic loader that reduced the crew to three, ut this proved to be unsuccessful.

Opposite page, top: The 1960s and 70s saw constant, incremental growth in the Soviet ground forces. Motorized rifle regiments, such as the one shown here, were increased from 66 BTR-50 armoured personnel carriers in 1967 to 141 BMP infantry combat vehicles in 1982. However, as numbers and equipment grew, training itself degenerated into rote, carefully rehearsed exercises in which the art of tactics withered. (Department of Defense)

Left: The first German designed and produced tank since 1945, the Leopard 1 Main Battle Tank, was developed in the late 1950s with first production models delivered to the Bundesheer in 1965. Its design emphasised speed, manoeuvrability and the importance of the gunnery system. Eight NATO allies and Australia quickly recognized its excellent qualities and purchased it for their armies.

Above: Troop A, 1st Squadron, 11th Armored Cavalry Regiment in Vietnam, December 1970. The 'Black Horse' regiment compiled one of the most distinguished combat records in Vietnam from its arrival in 1966 to its departure in 1971. Organized and equipped as combined arms teams, Black Horse operations were characterized by speed, aggressiveness and intelligence, as shown by the C Troops 1968 RIF (recon in force) in the 'Rubber' operation. (US Army)

Above: Although most of the technology used by the North Korean People's Army is from the 1950s and 1960s, they have been inventive in creating numerous armoured hybrids using existing vehicles and weapons systems as shown here in this military parade in Pyongyang. (Department of Defense)

Below: The Soviet 16-tube, 220mm BM27 multiple rocket launcher was an advanced system developed for high intensity war in central Europe. It was capable of firing high-explosive conventional rounds, scattering mines and delivering chemical warheads as far as 40km. The BM27 was widely used in Afghanistan.

Right: The North Korean People's Army maintains a strong special operations force capability and pose a serious multifaceted threat to the Republic of Korea's army and the US army. However, the special operations campaign waged against South Korea in 1966–69 was a complete failure and succeeded only in strengthening the bond between the South Korean people and their government and the army.

Below: Geumsa Ri, South Korea. A Republic of Korea Army M47 tank advances past personnel of the 1st Battalion, 5th Infantry, 25th Infantry Division, during the joint US/South Korean exercise Team Spirit '85. By the late 1980s the ROK Army had advanced from the M47 of 1950s vintage to its own domestically produced version of the M1 Abrams. (US Army)

Above: The Egyptian Army's performance during the 1973 war with Israel earned it great respect not only at home but internationally as well. Egypt's subsequent break with its Soviet mentor and its new relationship with the United States resulted in an infusion of Western equipment and in a growing professional relationship as shown by the joint Egyptian–US Bright Star exercises. Here Egyptian troops participate in an assault with an OT-62 APC during Bright Star '85. (US Air Force)

Below: Soviet built BTR-60 armoured personnel carriers destroyed by US Army Rangers during operation Urgent Fury on the first day, 25 October 1983. Shouting 'Rangers, be hard!' the commander of the 1st Battalion, 75th Ranger Regiment, led the battalion combat jump on Salinas airfield, Grenada. A Cuban counterattack across the airfield with three BTR-60s was shot to pieces by the anti-tank weapons of the 2/75.

Above: The mainstay of the Soviet tank fleet at the end of the post-war period, the T-72 main battle tank, had a great reputation within armies worldwide, which made it eagerly sought after by Third World countries. The Indian and Iraqi armies acquired large numbers. The Iraqi Republican Guard made efficient use of them in its final victories over the Iranians in 1988. However, in the Gulf War in 1991 they were called 'Pop-top' tanks by American tank crews because of the way they suffered complete destruction by one round from the M1 Abrams. (Defense Intelligence Agency)

Below: The Soviet BMP-2 Infantry Fighting Vehicle, shown here at the memorial to the Great Patriotic War in Kiev, was first seen in 1982. Its armament included a 30mm cannon and a Spandrel ATGM launcher (not shown).

Top left: A British Warrior Mechanized Combat Vehicle. With a crew of three, the Warrior can carry an infantry section. This well designed vehicle, with its 30mm Rarden cannon, entered service in the mid-1980s to complement the Challenger tank, both of which performed well in the 1991 Gulf War. (GKN)

Left: The Challenger was originally a development of the Shir 2 Main Battle Tank developed for Iran. The first production run was delivered to British tank battalions in 1983. Protected with Chobham armour and armed with a 120mm rifled gun, it was to prove the equal of the vaunted American M1 Abrams in the Gulf War. (Ministry of Defence)

Above: The British Abbot 105mm self-propelled gun was employed by close support regiments of the Royal Artillery. It has been superseded in the British army by 155mm armed vehicles but is still in service with the Indian army. (Vickers)

Left: The US army M2 Bradley Infantry Fighting Vehicle was the final result of a lengthy programme to replace the M113 Armoured Personnel Carrier. With its 25mm Chain Gun cannon and TOW 2 anti-tank missile system, the fighting vehicle marked a major change from a carrier to an actual fighting vehicle that could not only keep up with the M1 Abrams tank but also accompany it into battle. (Department of Defense)

Below: Unique in the training developments of the post-war period was the US Army's National Training Center (NTC) at Fort Irwin, California. For the first time a professional opposing forces organization was formed that was modelled on a likely enemy. While enough Soviet built APCs were available, T-72s had to be created by visually modifying US Army Sheridans. (US Army)

Above: A column of OPFOR Vismod (Opposing Force Visually Modified) vehicles at the NTC. The first vehicle replicates a Soviet T-72 tank, the second a ZSU-23-4 air defence vehicle, and the last four 2S1 self-propelled 122mm howitzers. The tactical expertise of the US Army in the Gulf War was attributed directly to this training process. (US Army)

Below: Through most of the post-war era, the US army was seriously deficient in air defence weapons. That weakness was largely rectified in the 1980s with introduction of a number of systems, the most advanced of which was the Patriot. So versatile was Patriot, that programing modification allowed it to also serve as an anti-missile defence, as dramatically proved in the 1991 Gulf War. (Department of Defence)

Left: The US Army's M1 Abrams Main Battle Tank was the ultimate tank of the post-war era, a technological wonder that was amply demonstrated in the Gulf War when it easily destroyed its greatest rival, the Soviet T-72, without serious loss. Its Chobham armour proving highly effective against the T-72 gun ammunition. (General Dynamics)

Below left: The first prototypes of the French Leclerc AMX40 Main Battle Tank were completed in 1983 but never went into production owing to a lack of foreign customers and perennial underfunding of the French army. By the late 1980s, the French army had fallen behind its major NATO allies two full tank generations with the Leclerc not scheduled for production until 1992.

Below: The French amphibious AMX-10RC is a versatile reconnaissance vehicle that packs a substantial punch with its 105mm cannon. The first prototype was completed in 1971 and the first production vehicles were delivered to the French Army in 1978.

Left: The East German Nationale Volksarmee was probably the best of the Warsaw Pact satellite armies. Asked whether the NVA was any good, a senior Bundeswehr officer retorted, 'They are an excellent army. They are a German army. They train like we used to in the old army!' They also won an embarassing number of military competitions with their Soviet mentors.

Left: Polish combat vehicle crewmen with the colours of Communist Poland. No other Warsaw Pact army retained so many symbols of its pre-communist past such as the Polish Eagle, instead of a red star. Another such symbol was the existance of a Chaplains Corps, the only one in the Warsaw Pact.

180 were in service by 1974. The Fox reconnaissance vehicle began production in 1973 and was with the forces by 1975. That the human element of the army had been neglected cannot be denied; its equipment had fared better.[20]

FRANCE

By 1965 the French Army had successfully shed its Janus-faced organization between colonial and territorial armies. The army of 1965 was that of a European continental power despite the few antique garrisons of the Foreign Legion. The de Gaulle reforms embodied in the 1961 defence reorganization became the foundation of the modern French Army.

This new French Army was divided into a Territorial Army (*Organization Territoriale*) and the Standing Army (*Force Permanente*). The Territorial Army supported conscription, training, mobilization and internal security. The Standing Army embodied the fighting elements of the army and was further divided into three parts. Its chief striking power had become the *Force de Manoeuvre* (FM) which included the First Army of 58,000 men in two corps of five mechanized divisions,

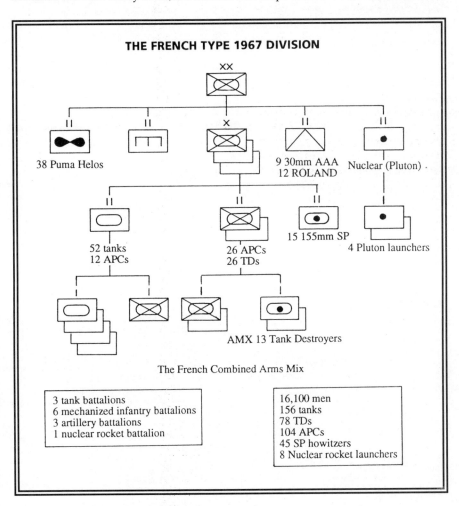

THE FRENCH TYPE 1967 DIVISION

38 Puma Helos

9 30mm AAA
12 ROLAND   Nuclear (Pluton)

52 tanks
12 APCs

26 APCs
26 TDs

15 155mm SP

4 Pluton launchers

AMX 13 Tank Destroyers

The French Combined Arms Mix

3 tank battalions 6 mechanized infantry battalions 3 artillery battalions 1 nuclear rocket battalion	16,100 men 156 tanks 78 TDs 104 APCs 45 SP howitzers 8 Nuclear rocket launchers

and a brigade in Berlin. One of the corps, with two divisions, was stationed in Germany. An additional three divisions in France and the Legion garrisons rounded out the FM. The second element of the Standing Army was the *Forces àvocation de Défense Operationelle du Territoire* (DOT), made up of separate non-divisional units for reinforcement of the FM. The DOT could expand 25 infantry battalions to 80 upon mobilization. The third element was the *Force d'Intervention*. Although France was firmly committed to its role as a continental power, de Gaulle's vision of France also included the determination to retain the image if not some of the reality of a great power. That could only be achieved by the creation of the capability to intervene outside Europe with credible ground forces. The *Force d'Intervention* filled that requirement. Assigned to it were 11th Parachute Division and 9th Brigade. The 11th Parachute Division contained two fully air-droppable or transportable brigades fully supported by their own organic armour, artillery and engineers. Included in 9th Brigade were marines, infantry, light armour and artillery, it being designed to be deployed overseas as an amphibious landing or air-transportable force.[21]

The 'Type 1967' division represented a major restructuring of the French mechanized division. It was a heavy division of three all-arms brigades numbering 16,100 men (figure 3-2). Eventually the division was to replace its US Honest John rockets with French built Pluton nuclear rockets; each division received a regiment with four launchers.

By 1975 French combat arms had become more specialized into clearly defined sub-elements than those of any other army (table 3-5). For example, the infantry was subdivided into four categories by equipment and mission; armour into three. Organizations such as the paras, marines and Foreign Legion that would normally be lumped with the infantry in many other armies were recognized as individual arms.

Table 3-5. French Combat Arms 1975

Arm	*Mission*
Infantry	
Régiments mécanisés	Equipped with tracked APCs to operate with armoured forces
Régiments motorisés	Equipped with wheeled APCs for mobility and use in difficult terrain
Régiments d'Infanterie	Dismounted local defence units
Unités spécialisées	Alpine and paratroop units
Armour (*l'Arme blindée et Cavalerie*)	
Régiments de Chars de Bataille	Equipped with medium tanks for shock
Régiments mécanisés	Equipped with light tanks to operate with mechanized brigades
Régiments de reconnaissance	Descended from horse cavalry; gather intelligence and screen forces.
Airborne (*Unités de Parachutistes*	Lightly equipped with armoured cars, ATGW; a main element of *Force d'Intervention*
Artillery	Field artillery, air defence, and nuclear artillery, rockets
Marines (*Troupes de marine*)	Surviving colonial formations transformed into marines in 1968; amphibious element of *Force d'Intervention*

Arm	Mission
The Foreign Legion (*La Légion Etrangère*)	Garrisons overseas in French dependencies
Army Aviation (*L'Aviation légère de l'Armée de Terre*)	Anti-tank, liaison, supply, reconnaissance
Gendarmerie Nationale Française	Protection of French borders and maintenance of public order

Source: Otto von Pivka, *The Armies of Europe Today* (London: Osprey Publishing Ltd., 1974)

Since the early 1960s the French Army had been working on integrating other arms into the basic structure of the infantry battalion to achieve an effective combined arms mix. The result was the unique 'tank-infantry' battalion within the mechanized brigade of the Type 1967 Division. The new battalion combined two light AMX-13 tank destroyer companies (four tank platoons and an ATGM platoon each) with two mechanized infantry companies (three mechanized infantry platoons each). Battalion also controlled reconnaissance and mortar platoons. Platoons were freely cross-posted between companies which led to the need to intensify training of junior officers to help them cope with commanding three types of platoon. This, in turn, led to the reduction in the size of French platoons to three vehicles, to reduce the junior officer's span of control to the most effective minimum. The experiment in combined arms structure was too successful, an example of the workings of the Law of Unintended Consequences. The 'tank-infantry' battalion had sacrificed too much of its organic infantry strength to support the armoured brigades of the division which, in turn, resulted in the addition of a mechanized infantry company to the armoured brigade.[22]

The Foreign Legion had recovered from its transplanting out of Algeria and had taken root around the world. Surprisingly, by 1975 half the Legion's regiments besides its depot regiment were located in metropolitan France: one in Orange and two in Corsica.

Table 3-6. The Foreign Legion 1975

1st Foreign Regiment (depot regt)	Aubagne (Legion Home)
2nd Infantry Regiment	Corsica
2nd Parachute Regiment	Corsica
3rd Infantry Regiment	Madagascar
1st Cavalry Regiment	Orange
13th Demi-Brigade	Djibouti
5th Infantry Regiment	Pacific Islands

By the early 1970s the French Army was equipped with a full range of modern domestically produced equipment. Unfortunately, the production of equipment was in chronically inadequate numbers. Although the French arms industry had undergone a major expansion as a world's arms supplier, the industry had remained oriented to the export market. The resulting economy of scale could not be translated into sufficient budgetary resources to equip the army to its table of organization. So far behind had the French Army slipped in its equipment that it lagged behind every other continental army of similar size. In 1973 its medium tank inventory (850) alone was weaker in medium tanks than West Germany's (3,300), East Germany's (2,000), Italy's (1,500), Poland's (3,400) and Czechoslovakia's

(3,400). Even tiny Israel had a larger and more modern tank fleet (1,700), not to mention Egypt (1,850).[23] This concentration on the export market frequently, according to complaints of French officers, meant that the army was given equipment that did not thoroughly meet its needs. The army had been put on budgetary half-rations to provide the resources necessary not only for the modernization of the air force and the navy, but primarily to develop the French strategic nuclear arsenal. Even this priority did not hasten the equipping of the army with its Pluton battle-field nuclear rockets; they began slowly to reach the field in 1974. Nevertheless, during the decade 1965–75 the army did receive a wide if shallow array of major combat equipment as shown in Table 3-7.

Table 3-7. Equipment Received by the French Army 1965–75

AMX-30 Main Battle Tank	1966
AMX-13 DCA SPAAG	1968
Crotale SAM	1971
Roland SAM 1	1972
AMX-10P Infantry Combat Vehicle	1973
Berliet VBX-170 APC	1973
Pluton Tactical Nuclear Missile	1974

Source: Christopher F. Foss, *AFV Recognition Handbook* (London: Janes, 1987).

If the French Army had not been able to equip itself as it had wanted, it made great strides in expanding and strengthening the NCO corps which in the 1970s made up 17 per cent of the manpower. The reorganization after 1961 had opened a career ladder into the commissioned ranks for NCOs. From 1967 to 1973 30 per cent of the officers were former NCOs who had attended special officers' schools, and another 15 per cent had been promoted directly from the NCO corps. By now the social origins and education levels of the French NCO tended to be more white- than blue-collar, attesting to the army's success in attracting quality professional cadres.[24]

The influence of the NCO corps became more pervasive as more of their sons joined the officer corps directly. As the proportion of officers of NCO origin climbed to 45 per cent by 1973, the proportion of graduates of St. Cyr military academy who were sons of soldiers grew dramatically. Before the Second World War they had never represented more than 25 per cent of any class; by 1971 the figure was 52 per cent. Before the war there had been five times more officers' than NCOs' sons, but from 1968 to 1976 the proportion had shifted to 28 per cent officers' sons and 18 per cent NCOs' sons. The proportion was actually more as many of the officer fathers had been NCOs at one time.[25]

The decade 1965–75 was a period of rest and recuperation after the first two tumultuous decades of the post-war era. For the first time since 1940 French troops were not involved in significant combat anywhere in the world. The single exception was the intervention in Chad in 1969 when the fledgling government of the former French colony collapsed. Elements of the Legion's 2nd CAP (1,000) and the *Troupes de Marine* (900) subdued rebel forces and were able to depart by late 1971 at a cost of eight dead and 30 wounded.

The re-orientation to a European battlefield, the production (albeit in small quantities) of new equipment, and the strengthening of the professional cadre were all products of this decade of quiet. With the issuing of new disciplinary regulations in 1966, the army (and other services) attempted yet another major act of renewal. Clearly influenced by the new West German Army's concept of *Innere Führung*, which liberalized military discipline and stressed the need of initiative and self-discipline in the ranks, the new French regulations were an attempt to replace the harsher elements of the traditionally rigid standards of discipline by a regime that encouraged intelligent initiative on the part of all ranks. The highly technical nature of the air force and navy proved ideal climates for the success of the new regulations, but the army provided a less conducive medium. It had not been exposed to the full force of technical modernization as had the other services, having been consistently short-changed by the government's allocation of resources. Additionally, the percentage of conscripts was far higher than in the other services. The conscript's one year's service and the constant rotation of classes were scarcely conducive to the introduction of a more liberal system of discipline.[26]

WEST GERMANY

The second decade of the Bundesheer's existence saw the effects of its fast and uneven growth made more difficult by the appearance of the iconoclastic generation of the late 1960s and early 1970s. This decade also saw the army weather these problems and emerge as the most sophisticated and well-armed army in either western or eastern Europe.

HEERSTRUKTUR III 1967–1980

In 1967 the Bundesheer, in response to NATO's change of policy to 'Flexible Response', began its third major evolutionary restructuring in twelve years. For the German Army this meant emphasizing a defence as far forward as possible and the capability to deter or defeat a conventional attack. As a result two Panzergrenadier divisions were converted to Jäger divisions. Their heavy equipment allowed the creation of independent tank regiments assigned to each corps as a reserve.[27] By 1974 the three army corps of the Field Army (Feldheer) had the following structure:

Table 3-8. Das Feldheer – 1974

I Corps:
- 1st Panzergrenadier Division
- 3rd Panzer Division
- 6th Panzergrenadier Division
- 7th Panzergrenadier Division
- 11th Panzergrenadier Division
- Panzer Regiment 100

II Corps:
- 4th Jäger Division
- 10th Panzer Division
- 1st Gebirgs Division
- Panzer Regiment 200

III Corps:
- 2nd Jäger Division
- 5th Panzer Division
- 12th Panzer Division
- 1st Luftlande Division

Heerstruktur III represented a steady continuity with previous restructuring by strengthening the operational capabilities of the army. This was done by (1) creating a Territorial Army to support the Feldheer by providing rear area security and a host of logistics functions; and (2) more efficiently organizing manpower pools to provide fillers for cadre units, low-strength active units, and for replacement battalions to make good wartime losses. These reforms allowed a transfer of 10,000 men from support to combat positions. By 1975 the Bundesheer had reached its maximum strength of 345,000 and was able optimally to man its formations by using the following peacetime strength levels:[28]

Corps level units	50 per cent
Division level units	75 per cent
Brigade level units	95 per cent

In 1975 reserves numbered 1,056,000 and these, on mobilization, would expand the Bundesheer to more than 1,400,000 men as shown in Table 3-9.

Table 3-9. Das Bundesheer – 1975

	Active	Conscript	Reserves
Feldheer	282,000	147,000	615,000
Territorial Army	63,000	30,000	441,000
Totals	345,000	177,000	1,056,000

Source: IISS *The Military Balance 1975–1976.*

German reserves are not organized into reserve formations as in the United States' reserve components. Reservists are assigned as individual fillers to bring active formations to wartime strength. Although the twelve divisions of the Feldheer were assigned to NATO command in peace and war as part of the price of German rearmament, the forces of the Territorial Army remain under the control of the Federal Republic.

EQUIPMENT

By 1975 heavy combat equipment had grown considerably in both quantity and sophistication. Most of the equipment was now of German manufacture and of excellent quality. The British, French and US arms exporters were spared deadly competition by the provision in German law that forbade arms exports. The most impressive pieces of equipment were the Leopard tank and the Marder APC, which upheld the German reputation for the design of armoured vehicles. The armoured vehicle inventory alone numbered 4,820 medium tanks, armoured anti-tank vehicles and 7,710 tracked APCs. With approximately the same number of men in its army, France at this time had one-quarter the number of tanks and one-eighth of APCs; more than half the French tanks were light, and most of the APCs were wheeled. The German Army, backed by a strong economy and a defence-minded government, had ensured that the German soldier would fight in the best equipped army in Europe.[29]

Table 3-10 . Equipment of the Bundesheer – 1975

Tanks

M-48A2	1,400
Leopard I	2,300

AT Vehicles

Jagdpanzer w/90mm gun	770
Jagdpanzer w/SS-11 ATGW	350

APCs

Marder	2,100
HS-30	660
Hotchkiss PZ 4-5	1,600
M-113	3,350

Artillery

Towed 105mm Howitzer	280
Towed 155mm Howizter	80
SP 155mm Howitzer	600
SP 203mm Howitzer	80
SP 175mm Gun	150
LARS 110mm MRL	210

Anti-Aircraft Artillery

20mm	1,000
40mm	310
30mm SP AA gun	500

Rockets

Honest John	70
Sergeant	20

Source: IISS *The Military Balance 1975–1976.*

GROWING PAINS

By the late 1960s the army was experiencing serious problems as a consequence of its rapid expansion. Growth had so outpaced the recruitment of junior professional cadres that there was a shortage of 26,000 NCOs and 2,600 junior officers. Existing cadres were increasingly overworked. Added to the strain were the growing complexities and frustrations of small-unit leadership in the context of *Innere Führung*. A British observer captured the essence of the burden:

'In theory the Inner Guidance [Innere Führung] calls for a standard of intellectual leadership in the armed forces which would be almost unattainable, certainly at NCO level. While most armed forces subscribe to a hazy concept of leadership which becomes less and less intellectual the lower the rank, the Germans have made their own system more complicated by codifying their idea of leadership in military legislation which is itself enshrined in the Basic Law (the constitution) ... Officers concede that the answer would lie, ideally, in a higher calibre of NCO, but they find themselves in a vicious circle. The regulations governing complaints and military discipline are so precisely drawn that they make the position of an NCO unenviable, with the result that there is a shortage of high-calibre NCOs.'[30]

A German junior officer pointed out a major flaw in the theory:

'the object of Innere Führung is to treat the average soldier as a responsible adult, in the hope that he will then act in a responsible adult manner and develop a willingness to obey orders. The problem we face on the company and platoon level is that the average soldier all too often isn't an adult at all and won't respond in an adult manner ...'[31]

The complexities of *Innere Führung* resulted in junior leaders hesitating to apply discipline, and middle-grade officers afraid to back them up when they did. The final straw seemed to be the arrival in the late 1960s and early 1970s of a new generation of aggressively rebellious conscripts, countless barrack-room lawyers willing to contest every order. The crisis went public in April 1971 when 30 combat arms company commanders of the 7th Panzergrenadier Division sent a critical memorandum over the chain of command directly to Defence Minister Helmut Schmidt. While supporting *Innere Führung* in principle, captains stated that they did not have the moral, legal or material means to discipline or train their troops and would no longer answer for such conditions. For these officers the issue was not simply an overly complex theory of leadership and its absurdities, but the whole issue of tradition and the military calling.

> 'The integration of the soldier into society is judged to be a higher good than his value as a fighting man. The effort to make the self-image of the soldier more civilian obscures that which is specific to the soldier. He is denied the unique image of his profession, this in contrast to all other careers.'[32]

The 'Captains of Unna' as the 30 captains came to be called, were well received by their peers. Of the 9,000 captains in the army, 800 wrote in direct support of their efforts. They were also lucky that a man as astute as Helmut Schmidt was Defence Minister. He brought to the situation the perspective and insight of a reserve officer and a willingness to take practical measures. He persuaded the SPD government to remedy many of the problems brought to light by the 'Captains of Unna' including a streamlining and clarification of *Innere Führung* guidelines, alleviation of the shortage of NCOs and junior officers, improvement in barracks and training facilities, and a tightening of training. All of these measures eased the burden of junior leadership and did much to bring peace to the ranks. As the 1970s progressed, the spirit of rebellious youth mellowed, and the German soldier became more and more accepted as a valued member of society.[33]

The cry from the heart from the 'Captains of Unna' was indicative of both the deep professionalism of the German officer and his sense of avocation for the soldierly life. This was evidence that the traditional virtues of the officer corps -service, self-denial and self-sacrifice, and a rigorously stern sense of honour – had survived the war and had sent up healthy, vigorous shoots. These were the virtues historically associated with the legendary *Preussens Gloria* (Prussia's glory), but Prussia had disappeared in the wake of Polish and Soviet annexations. Prussia's people, however, had not. Millions fled to West Germany during and after the war where they retained this ingrained sense of service and duty. It is not surprising that a comprehensive survey taken in 1967 showed that 49.7 per cent of all Bundeswehr officers were of Prussian origin; 55.2 per cent of all generals, and the biggest eye-opener, 61.2 per cent of the lieutenants. The greatest change is the watering down of the traditional military aristocracy. In the imperial army 70 per cent of generals were of aristocratic origin; in 1967 the figure had fallen to less than 10 per cent and the overall representation of the aristocracy had fallen to 2.7 per cent of the officer corps. In fact, an officer was twice as likely to be of working class than aristocratic origin. By this time the officer corps was being recruited from a much wider and more representative segment of German society than ever before.[34]

EAST GERMANY

The decade 1965–1975 saw the maturation of the NVA from a distrusted member of the Warsaw Pact to one of its star pupils, highly proficient and eager to march at the Soviet Army's side. By the end of this decade thousands of NVA officers had attended Soviet military schools and 25 per cent of its own military instructors had been trained by the Soviets. But the pupil was increasingly besting the master. All too often the NVA would carry away the prizes in East German-Soviet military competitions.

The improvement in the NVA's reputation was in part a consequence of the strengthening of the professional qualities of its officer and NCO corps as it entered its second decade. The SED was even more solicitous of the cadres' political qualities; it was clear to the SED that one of the chief pillars of its power was the NVA. By the middle 1970s 85 per cent of the officer corps and 50 per cent of the NCO corps were SED members.

In a sharp departure from its Soviet model, officer education stressed the provision of both a military and a general education. One of the very un-Soviet features of this military education was the development of the ability to deal with rapid change on the battlefield. By 1971 80 per cent of NVA officers were the product of three or four years' at training schools; by 1973 25 per cent of the officer corps had earned academic degrees compared to 10 per cent in the Bundeswehr. NVA officers were also expected to master two technical specialities so that battlefield losses could be replaced.[35]

From its beginnings the NVA NCO corps, like its Bundesheer counterpart, suffered from a lack of authority which, in this case, stemmed from its creation on the Soviet model of conscript sergeants. During the middle 1960s, in sharp departure from Soviet methods, the NVA recreated its NCO corps along traditional lines; the NVA NCO being fully integrated into the command and leadership structure, receiving status, respect, prestige and authority. He was a long-service professional, much like his predecessors in earlier German armies, enlisting before the age of 26 for an initial 10-year hitch; most continued to serve until retirement at the age of 65. NCO training stressed technical and military proficiency; an NCO could expect to serve his entire career in the same technical speciality.[36]

Training was thorough and, physically and emotionally, far more exacting than in the Bundesheer. One-third of training was conducted at night following Soviet norms; privation and hardship were themes persistently stressed.

Despite its trumpeted claims to be the 'army of the working class', the NVA consciously re-introduced the most exaggerated standards of drill, discipline and obedience from the Wehrmacht and imperial armies. These were the very standards that the West German people had so strenuously resisted in the creation of the Bundeswehr. The NVA gave enormous importance to close-order drill, allotting 25 per cent of basic training to it, twice the Bundeswehr standard; it was an emphasis that was continued throughout the soldier's service. The most eye-catching element of drill was the re-introduced goose-step, the very symbol of German militarism. The NVA also tried to develop an almost 18th-century mystique of the battleflag and issued a dazzling array of at least fifty medals and decorations, to develop *esprit de corps*.

However proficient the officers and NCOs and however extensive the revival of traditional military symbols, the loyalty of the enlisted ranks continued to remain doubtful. The moral foundations of the NVA represented the worst of the old armies mixed with an indigestible political system. Relations between the leaders and the led were in the stiff and formal manner of a bygone era with none of the genuine paternalistic concern of those times. There was certainly none of the informality of the West German armed forces. The conduct of the NCO was often petty and authoritarian in the notorious mould of Corporal Himmelstoss in *All Quiet on the Western Front*. The blatant material rewards of political loyalty and the often vicious and irrationally hysterical punishments for transgression created a deep cynicism in the ranks. This author remembers being told in 1972 of the fate of a young East German border guard who had fired and missed at civilians escaping to the West. The boy's father explained that his son was sentenced to five years in the Bautzen prison camp. The reasoning was that he could only have missed deliberately since he was a registered expert marksman. Only the voluntary enlistment of a younger brother shortened the sentence.

Behind the façade of flags and Prussian drill and the efficiency of its professional officers and NCOs, the NVA remained a hollow army. Its emptiness was prophetically described by a former conscript in the early 1970s:

> 'All of that is a lot of shit. We all have to play along with this on the surface, but I can assure you of one thing: if that wall ever fell down, our frontier guards would have to climb up the nearest tree to escape being trampled to death by the people heading west.'[37]

THE INVASION OF CZECHOSLOVAKIA, 1968

In 1968 the NVA again beat the Bundesheer in achieving an historical first. It was to be the first German army since 1945 to set foot on foreign soil as an aggressor. The East German Communist leader, Walter Ulbricht, eagerly offered the NVA to the Soviets as a tool for the suppression of the Prague Spring's challenge to the heirs of Stalinism. They assigned two NVA divisions to the operation, the 11th Motorized Rifle Division to the Soviet First Guards Tank Army and the 7th Tank Division to the Twentieth Guards Army. The Soviets did not allow the NVA to participate as a separate national contingent as did a Polish army. It was quickly apparent that the use of German troops had been a blunder that threatened to drive the usually self-controlled Czechs to violence. It was also quickly apparent that the NVA troops were not as reliable as expected. Too many Czechs spoke good German for the NVA troops to be able to remain ignorant of exactly what it was they were doing. The two NVA divisions were kept out of sight in the Bohemian forests and allowed to travel only at night. In a few days they were withdrawn and replaced by Soviet troops.

POLAND

The decade 1965–1975 was a period of constant turmoil within the Polish People's Army (PPA). Events followed quickly one after another to purge the army of various groups and severely damage its prestige within the Polish nation. These events would also finally produce a professional and Polish officer corps, but one increasingly autonomous of the Communist Party.

THE SIX-DAY WAR 1967

The wave of satisfaction demonstrated by many Polish officers at the defeat of the Soviets' Arab client states in the Six-Day War was a not so subtle criticism of Soviet doctrine and equipment. The Air Defence Command was particularly outspoken. Upon it fell the immediate wrath of the Party which relieved its entire leadership. The faction within the army's leadership made up of former partisans from the Second World War used this opportunity to demand that the army's 200 Jewish officers sign a statement condemning Israel. In the words of a former Polish officer, '... those who refused were dismissed immediately; while those who signed were dismissed six months later'. The resulting purge of fourteen generals and 200 colonels, most of whom were Jewish, seemed to secure the power of the Partisan faction. Actually, it did not result in the placement of Partisan officers in the new vacancies.

Rather they were filled by younger, less factionally political and more quietly professional men. Chief among this group was General Jaruselski who became Minister of Defence in 1968.

THE INVASION OF CZECHOSLOVAKIA, 1968

A Polish contingent of two divisions participated in the Soviet-initiated invasion of Czechoslovakia in 1968 at the direction of the Polish Communist Party. The Party leader, Wladyslaw Gomulka, the one-time Polish nationalist and hero of the Polish October had particularly feared the liberalization of the Prague Spring. In contrast, the Polish troops showed a remarkable apathy and passivity. Polish divisions were markedly slower in encircling Czechoslovak Army garrisons than Soviet divisions. Such was their performance that they had to be quickly withdrawn and replaced by Soviet troops. Although this attitude was sharply criticized, the invasion was considered an 'unforgivable mistake' on the part of the country's political and military leadership.[38] The event caused such embarrassment within the armed forces that all historical trace of it seems to have disappeared into an institutional black hole. Official histories only mentioned manoeuvres around Czechoslovakia at the time and fail to address the subject of the invasion at all.[39]

THE BALTIC RIOTS, 1970

The suppression of rioting Polish workers in the Baltic ports in December 1970 introduced the PPA to the new and detested role of internal security, the forces responsible for which being unable to control the situation. The PPA's subsequent participation was seen as limited and half-hearted, though more recent information cited by Les Griggs indicates that its role was far greater and harsher. Acting on direct orders from the Party chief, Wladyslaw Gomulka, Defence Minister General Jaruselski, ordered the army to fire on the crowds, but with a proviso: '... after warning shots into the air, after a repeated warning and warning shots into the ground'. Only then could the troops fire at the most aggressive rioters and should aim only at the legs. But 44 people were killed and 1,165 wounded. Apparently the PPA employed the equivalent of a field army – more than 61,000 troops with 1,700 tanks and large numbers of helicopters.[40]

The implications for the army were enormous whatever the scale of its involvement. For an army that prided itself on being the protectors of the Polish people, it had shed Polish blood, and in fact had been the first eastern European army to be employed against its own people in a police role. The prestige of the military withered in the eyes of the nation; added to the shame of the Czechoslovakian adventure, it caused the flow of applicants to officer schools to dry up. The demoralization and resentment of the officer corps was profound. Jaruselski admitted that a 'difficult morale problems had arisen ... public opinion has turned against the military'.[41] The trauma of its involvement firmly established the precedent that the army would never be so used in a similar situation. A further implication for the future was found in Jaruselski's reported reply to a Soviet offer to use Soviet troops to put down the workers – he could not guarantee their safety if Polish soldiers saw Soviet soldiers in the area.

THE PROFESSIONALIZATION OF THE OFFICER CORPS

By 1973 the army had entered a period of stability marked by the growing professionalism and homogeneity of the officer corps. Jaruselski had succeeded in removing most of the members of the Partisan faction and replacing them with younger officers who, like himself, had been soldiers or junior officers in the war, who had managed the modernization of the Polish Army that had begun in 1960, who had received advanced training in the Soviet Union, and who had remained relatively aloof from political factionalism. This final purge marked the end of the period that had begun in 1945. Gone now were the Soviet officers, the reformist Communists who supported Polish autonomy, the old 'Muscovite' Communists who included many political officers, and the Partisan faction that consisted of security officers for the most part.

With the departure of the Russo-Poles and the purge of the entire Jewish component, the officer corps became purely Polish and was now far better educated and more thoroughly professional. By 1974 the proportion of officers with academic degrees had increased to 40 per cent compared to 17 per cent in 1958, and half the members had engineering or technical qualifications. A new career management programme was established, and there were now fourteen officers' academies that were degree-granting institutions in which the curriculum increasingly stressed military rather than political considerations. The growing emphasis on professional training and qualifications caused the Party no little apprehension because modernization was creating a condition of autonomy outside the Party's grasp.[42] In an attempt to re-assert control, the Party tried to emphasize the role of the political officer while at the same time increasing benefits for the officer corps in a bid to buy its loyalty. The events of the next decade were to show how well-founded were the Party's apprehensions.

SOVIET UNION

THE BREZHNEV RECOVERY

The years 1964 to 1967 were ones of careful re-appraisal of the organization and role of the Ground Forces by the new political leadership that had removed Khrushchev. The re-establishment of the Ground Forces as a separate command in 1967 sounded the end of the service's painful twilight existence. John Erickson concluded that in the end, Brezhnev:

'rejected the concept of "one-variant" – nuclear war and nothing short of it – on the grounds that it imposed unacceptable inflexibility on Soviet policy and was based on the unrealistic assumption that conventional Soviet military means were incapable of attaining Soviet objectives. The "nuclearizing" of the Soviet Ground Forces, when carried to extremes, would leave them dangerously deficient in all-round capabilities. The possibility of the Ground Forces in a nuclear straightjacket disquieted many senior Soviet commanders, but, in fact, Brezhnev had no such intention. Rather, he developed for the first time a genuine dual capability within the Ground Forces.' [43]

These policies prevailed throughout the 1970s and set the stage for a major transformation of the Ground Forces. First, the prestige of the Ground Forces was re-established. Marshal Grechko, who succeeded to the post of Minister of Defence in 1967, restored much of the Ground Force's self-esteem by improving pay and conditions for the officer cadres. Secondly, resources were redirected to realize a robust dual capability that emphasized combined arms in order to provide Soviet policy makers with a more flexible and realistically useful tool. From this point on there was a more precise matching of capabilities with objectives. To ensure that the Ground Forces could implement its share of the combined arms effort, numerous new weapons systems were introduced to include five new tactical air defence systems, five artillery systems, three new tracked infantry combat vehicles, and improved tactical engineering and logistics systems.[44]

Ground Forces' capabilities were improved by the gradual addition of more personnel, equipment and new units to the standard tank and motorized rifle divisions shown in figures 3-3 and 3-4. This packing of existing forces allowed greater and greater combat power to reside in the same number of divisions. Most of such packing went on in the groups of forces and western military districts that would provide the initial forces in a war against NATO. The tank battalions of motorized rifle regiments increased from 31 to 40 tanks. This process of packing units continued throughout the rest of the post-war period as is shown by the evolution of the motorized rifle regiment more typical of these forward areas.

Table 3-11 . The Motorized Rifle Regiment 1967–1976

	1967	*Early 1970s* *BTR*	*1976* *BM*	*1982* *BMP*
Personnel	1,800	2,400	2,300	2,225
Medium Tanks	31 T-54/55	40 T-62	40 T-72	40 T-72
Light Tanks	3 PT-76	3 PT-76	5 PT-76	-
BMP	-	-	102	141*
BTR-152	66	-	-	
BTR-60	-	105	28	
BRDM	10	34	28	9

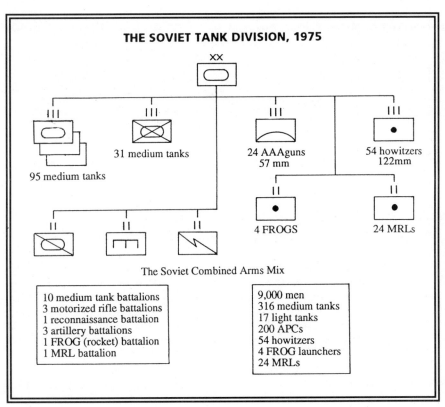

THE SOVIET TANK DIVISION, 1975

31 medium tanks

95 medium tanks

24 AAguns 57 mm

54 howitzers 122mm

4 FROGS

24 MRLs

The Soviet Combined Arms Mix

10 medium tank battalions 3 motorized rifle battalions 1 reconnaissance battalion 3 artillery battalions 1 FROG (rocket) battalion 1 MRL battalion	9,000 men 316 medium tanks 17 light tanks 200 APCs 54 howitzers 4 FROG launchers 24 MRLs

	1967	Early 1970s	1976	1982
		BTR	BM	BMP
Artillery	NIL	18 122mm	18 122mm	18 122mm
	towed	SP	SP	
Mortars	9 82mm	18 120mm	18 120mm	18 120mm
Air Defence	NIL	4 ZSU-23	4 ZSU-23	4 ZSU-23
			4 SA-8	4 SA-9

*Includes 30 recon BMPs. Sources: John Erickson, *et al.*, *The Soviet Ground Forces: An Operational Assessment*, p. 32; Defense Intelligence Agency, *Soviet Divisional Organization Guide*, DDB-1100-333-82, July 1982, p. 28.

The Ground Forces continued to represent the cutting edge of the army despite post-Khrushchev improvements in logistics and engineering support. Jeffery Record calculated that the proportion of fighting strength to overall strength was higher in the Soviet Army than in any army of its potential Western opponents.

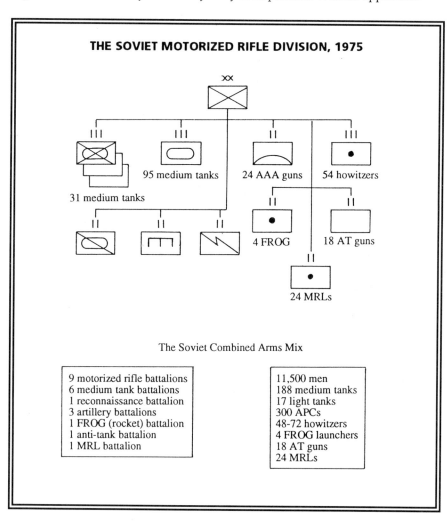

THE SOVIET MOTORIZED RIFLE DIVISION, 1975

95 medium tanks · 24 AAA guns · 54 howitzers

31 medium tanks

4 FROG · 18 AT guns

24 MRLs

The Soviet Combined Arms Mix

9 motorized rifle battalions
6 medium tank battalions
1 reconnaissance battalion
3 artillery battalions
1 FROG (rocket) battalion
1 anti-tank battalion
1 MRL battalion

11,500 men
188 medium tanks
17 light tanks
300 APCs
48-72 howitzers
4 FROG launchers
18 AT guns
24 MRLs

Table 3-12. Ratio of Medium Tanks to Men – 1974

	Mechanized/MRD	Tank Div
Soviet Ground Forces	1:64	1:29
United States Army	1:75	1:51
Bundeswehr	1:62	1:48
British Army	1:63	1:63

Source: Jeffery Record, *Sizing Up the Soviet Army* (Washington, DC: The Brookings Institution, 1975)

This decade also saw an overall growth in the size of the Ground Forces from about 1,600,000 to 1,825,000 and in the number of manoeuvre divisions (tank, motorized rifle and airborne) from 147 to 167. Until 1968 the general diminishing of the Ground Forces had continued, but from 1969 to 1974 the force expanded rapidly with the raising of 24 new divisions. The majority were motorized rifle divisions (nineteen MRDs to five TDs). These increases largely stemmed from the necessity to station a new group of forces in Czechoslovakia after 1968 and to bolster the forces on the Chinese border. In addition to these manoeuvre divisions, a substantial number of artillery and air defence divisions were created.

Table 3-13. The Growth of the Soviet Ground Forces 1965 – 1974

	MRD	Tank	AB	Total
1965	90	50	7	147
1966	90	43	7	140
1967	86	43	7	136
1968	88	45	7	140
1969	90	50	7	147
1970	100	50	7	157
1971	102	51	7	160
1972	106	51	7	164
1973	107	50	7	164
1974	110	50	7	167

Source: IISS, *The Military Balance, 1965–1975*

An important part of the combined arms role fell to the airborne and air assault forces of the VDV. Almost immediately after the removal of Khrushchev in late 1964, the VDV was removed from the control of the Ground Forces and re-established as an independent command directly subordinated to the Ministry of Defence. In 1966 their new potential within the dual capability force was announced with the statement that:

> 'An airborne force transported to the deep rear of the enemy must be able to conduct military operations without counting on linking up with the ground troops. The force itself or in conjunction with other such landing forces will constitute a unique operational group ... the troops which constitute the force need to have the same qualities which are inherent in the troops attacking from the front: a high degree of manoeuvrability and the possession of all types of weapons, equipment and matériel means necessary to conduct long-range military opera-

tions, both in the conditions of the use of nuclear means by both sides and without such conditions.'[45]

The missions inherent in this statement included destruction of enemy nuclear weapons (primary mission) and command and control centres, and the seizure and retention of key terrain to disrupt enemy reserves and facilitate the forward advance of the Ground Forces. The announcement was greeted with scepticism until the airborne forces proved themselves first in the invasion of Czechoslovakia in 1968 when almost two divisions seized critical objectives in advance of the Ground Forces, and in operations along the Chinese border shortly thereafter in 1969. In the Far East, it was the mobility of the airborne forces alone that could provide the only swift reaction force between widely separated Ground Force garrisons. Vital to the realization of the airborne's potential were the beginnings of the complete mechanization of the airborne division. The new BMP infantry fighting vehicle was modified for the airborne as the BMD.[46]

Soviet industry was increasingly turned to the production of modern systems for the Ground Forces. The T-64 tank with its smoothbore 125mm gun entered production in 1966. It was never exported even to the Warsaw Pact. In 1971 another new tank, the T-72, also armed with a 125mm smoothbore gun, went into production and was exported to the Warsaw Pact and most Soviet client states. The most significant combat vehicle to enter the inventory, however, was the tracked BMP-1, which made its first public appearance in 1967. It was the world's first true infantry fighting vehicle (IFV) and not an armoured personnel carrier or battle taxi. With the BMP, the Soviet motorized infantry had a vehicle that was a genuine partner of the tank, able to keep up over difficult terrain and able to provide infantry support. The BMP's armament also made it a lethal anti-tank system with the Sagger AT missile and the 73mm smoothbore, low-velocity anti-tank gun. Additional tracked vehicles were the

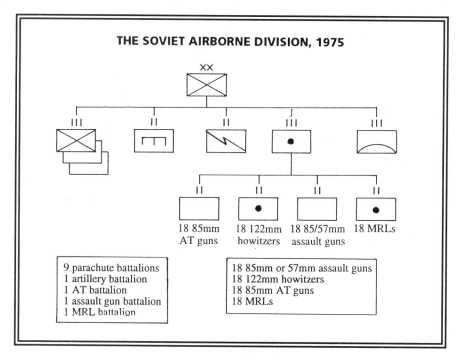

THE SOVIET AIRBORNE DIVISION, 1975

18 85mm AT guns 18 122mm howitzers 18 85/57mm assault guns 18 MRLs

9 parachute battalions	18 85mm or 57mm assault guns
1 artillery battalion	18 122mm howitzers
1 AT battalion	18 85mm AT guns
1 assault gun battalion	18 MRLs
1 MRL battalion	

airborne's BMD derivation of the BMP, and the MTLB, developed in the late 1960s, which was originally a tracked artillery mover but became the prime personnel carrier in the difficult terrain of the Soviet Far East and elsewhere. The BRDM-2 amphibious scout car replaced the BRDM-1, and was first seen in public in 1966. The BRDM-2 also came in an anti-tank variant mounting the Sagger AT missile.

Field artillery broke with its tradition of towed guns and introduced three self-propelled guns and mortars in the early and mid-1970s. The fielding of the 122mm SP howitzer (2S1) and the 152mm SP gun/howitzer (2S3) provided the tanks and motorized rifle troops with mobile artillery that could accompany them rapidly and provide timely support. Air defence weapons were also mechanized beginning with the lethal ZSU-23-4 quad 23mm (Shilka) air defence system which represented an international major advance in traditional air defence artillery which the US Army has not been able to effectively match to date. Production lasted from 1965 to 1983 and it has been widely exported. The wheeled SA-9 Gaskin low-altitude SAM was developed in the 1960s and was fielded in 1968 followed by the wheeled SA-8 Gecko SAM first seen in 1975. It filled the gap between the SA-8 and the manportable SAM-7 Grails. The tracked SA-4 Ganef medium- to high-altitude SAM became operational in the late 1960s. The tracked low- to medium-altitude SA-6 Gainful SAM was seen first in 1967. By the early 1970s Soviet planners had provided the Ground Forces with a fully mobile and overlapping air defence envelope of guns and missiles.[47] The new BMP-1 IFV, self-propelled artillery, and self-propelled air defence AAA and missiles in combination with the traditional tank had at last created a completely mobile combined arms force.

The 1967 War and the Yom Kippur War of 1973 saw thousands of Soviet tanks deployed by the Arabs in the most intense tank battles since the Second World War. These wars provided an opportunity for the West to evaluate the quality of Soviet military technology and industry. As described by an Israeli authority, the T-55 was found to be

> 'a good tank with excellent automotive capabilities riding on one of the world's best suspension and track systems, its heavy armour but low weight adding survivability. That tank had an extremely low silhouette, and was fast even over rough terrain and sand. Its powerpack was fairly reliable and simple to maintain.'[48]

There were major drawbacks with the internal fuel and ammunition stowage which were stored together in the right front of the crew compartment. So vulnerable was this arrangement that the US Army determined that any hit had a 50 per cent chance of completely destroying the tank by fire and/or explosion. The crew's positions which aligned the driver, gunner and commander made casualties more likely. The human engineering, or almost complete lack of it, of Soviet tanks was probably the greatest weakness. Crew spaces were cramped for even small men in the T-55, a condition that actually worsened with the T-62, T-64 and T-72. Bad ventilation caused fatigue and exhaustion. 'In fact, Arab tank crews, overcome by deadly fumes and heat stress under severe climatic conditions, often abandoned their tanks, which were picked up perfectly intact'. The T-62 featured a left-handed load arrangement for the main gun, so physically awkward for the loader that it quickly reduced the firing sequence.[49]

THE 1967 LAW ON UNIVERSAL MILITARY SERVICE

The Brezhnev recovery of the Ground Forces was not confined to doctrine, organization and equipment, but contained a vital manpower acquisition and training element that was embodied in the 1967 Law on Universal Military Service which replaced the regulations in effect since 1939.

The demographic echoes of the low birthrates of the war years had finally bottomed out in 1962 when the 18-year-old cohorts fell below one million. As shown in the graph, the figures began steadily to rise, passing 1,500,000 by 1965. By 1967 there were more than 2,000,000, the figures reaching almost 2,500,000 by 1975. The Soviet armed forces were faced with a dilemma. Conscription swept up about 80 per cent of eligible 19-year-old males for three years in the Ground Forces. At this rate the the armed forces would soon balloon to more than 6,000,000 including cadres. The general staff arrived at a solution embodied in the 1967 Law on Universal Military Service which would solve a number of pressing problems. The term of service was reduced from three to two years in the Ground Forces, and the age of conscription was reduced from nineteen to eighteen. University bound students were deferred but were required to serve one year after graduation; most became reserve officers. A twice yearly call-up in the spring and autumn replaced the annual call-up.[50]

These changes achieved several important objectives: (1) the armed forces could be kept at a reasonable level; and (2) the shorter term of service allowed almost the entire growing generation to be trained, thus retaining universal military service. There were sound strategic reasons for the second point as noted by Marshal V. D. Sokolovskiy in *Soviet Military Strategy*, 'it is well known that the shorter the period of service in the army, the greater the number of men with military training discharged every year into the reserves'. The original 1962 edition contained the additional qualification subsequently omitted from the 1968 edition, '... however, the quality of the training and consequently the combat readiness of those discharged is correspondingly reduced'.[51] The difference was rationalized by arguing that the Soviet conscript aged eighteen upon completion of ten years of schooling was better educated and more technically adept than previous generations. He could be well trained in two instead of three years. The lamentations from the regimental officers actually charged with training these 18-year-old paragons indicated otherwise.

In reality the Ministry of Defence knew that the lost year of training had to be at least partially made up in some way. Attendant upon the 1967 Law, major changes were made in two programmes that would transfer some military training to the civilian education system and to the extra-curricular activities of the general population. A significant degree of basic military training (140 hours) was to be conducted in the nation's secondary schools in the Beginning Military Training (NVP) programme. NVP was officially under the auspices of the Ministry of Education but was made the direct responsibility of the Commander-in-Chief, Ground Forces. Control was exercised through the military commissariats. Training courses consisted of the inevitable political indoctrination, marksmanship, light weapons, basic tactics, topography, map reading and NBC protection. In addition to decreasing the training burden on the active forces, the programme was also intended to ease the speed of transition into military life by familiarizing the conscript with the basic duties, skills and customs of the service.[52] With the expansion of the programme in the late 1960s, 50,000 military instructors entered the nation's secondary school system. Most were reserve officers, many with war experience, although reserve sergeants were more the norm in rural areas.

The second programme to undergo change was DOSAAF (*Dobrovol'noye Obshchestvo Sodeystiviya Armii, Aviastsii i Flotu*) the Volunteer Society for Co-operation with the Army, Aviation and the Fleet. Until this time, DOSAAF had been a genuinely voluntary association for the sports enthusiast. The 1967 Law turned it into a mass organization to complement NVP. The voluntary aspect lingered only in its title; the Society had been transformed into a mass organization numbering 70,000,000 members by the middle 1970s and 100,000,000 by the early 1980s. The entire secondary school population and working population, including women, was eligible. Although technically not within the jurisdiction of the Ministry of Defence, it was put in the charge of a marshal of aviation with a substantial military staff.

DOSAAF eventually established 350,000 local organizations in almost every school, factory, farm and office in the country, its mission being to train specialists in many of the more than 400 military specialities required by the armed forces. Technical specialities included radio-electronics, motor vehicle driving and mechanics, and even helicopter, fixed wing and jet aircraft training. Military-applied sports were also stressed and included parachuting, scuba diving, marksmanship and even hang-gliding. This kind of adventure training did much to make the programme attractive, and there was no private alternative to DOSAAF monopoly. Every year more than 2,000,000 young men learned a military skill through DOSAAF. Eventually 75 per cent of conscripts selected for parachute units were already jump qualified through DOSAAF training. Most pilot trainees were already flight-qualified. According to Soviet claims, one third of each conscript class already had a DOSAAF certified military speciality. Reservists were also encouraged to participate in DOSAAF to keep their military skills fresh.

Despite the impressive statistics, serious problems developed in both programmes. Local authorities frequently gave lukewarm support. Factory and school officials showed an understandable lack of interest in spending resources on basically non-productive military training. Training that supported the economy was far more popular with local managers and the students themselves. Supporting the economy through training specialists was an additional DOSAAF mission. Many NVP instructors were found to be unqualified. Claims that 90 per cent of young men met national fitness standards were belied by the military's growing complaints over the number of physically unfit conscripts. NVP was particularly unpopular in the non-Slavic republics because it was seen as a means to russification. Russian was the language of instruction, and the need to learn it for military service was often used as an excuse to increase the level of mandatory Russian in place of the local native languages. Consequently, DOSAAF and NVP became increasingly hollow the farther they operated from the Slavic heartland. The Balts simply refused to participate; the Central Asians reported intensive efforts and did almost nothing.[53]

A MATTER OF CORRUPTION

As the Brezhnev expansion of the Ground Forces continued, other features of the Brezhnev era, corruption and a dangerous intellectual incuriosity, began seeping pervasively through the army. General officers were all too often selected for their political and family connections. Entire chains of patronage struggled against one another, rising and falling with the fate of their particular patron. Fulfilling the military training plan and putting on a good show at choreographed manoeuvres, these modern Soviet military Potemkin Villages, replaced serious training for war. At the general staff level, the consequences were potentially horrific. The brilliant general staff officer who developed the correlation of forces concept described his analysis of the paralytic effects of even a few nuclear weapons on the European battlefield. The response of a deputy minister of defence for whom the analysis was made was to order him to recalculate his figures until he arrived at a 100-kilometre Soviet advance rate per day. Later the staff officer mused that too much of the general officer corps was simply 'untrainable'.

THE INVASION OF CZECHOSLOVAKIA, 1968

Alost immediately after the transformation of the Ground Forces had been undertaken, they were called upon to mount the single largest operation since 1945 – the invasion of Czechoslovakia on 20 August 1968. It was a solid professional performance. Exercises in May and June prepared many of the forces designated for the operation. Military commissariats had sufficient time to call-up reserves to fill out low-readiness category divisions within the Soviet Union although some units were called-up seemingly at the last minute and had no time for training. The initial invasion force numbered about 200,000 men which were drawn from the Warsaw Pact allies, the Soviet groups of forces in eastern Europe and the western Soviet military districts. Ultimately between 400,000 and 500,000 troops of the Warsaw Pact were employed to suppress the Prague Spring, of whom fewer than 100,000 were non-Soviet.[54]

The smooth success of the operation was a consequence of the excellent performance of the airborne forces in seizing key objectives ahead of the Ground Forces' divisions, and the simple fact that the Czech Army and people offered no more than passive resistance. As it was, the arguments of the Czech people, in Russian, caused widespread confusion, bewilderment and shock among hitherto carefully sheltered Soviet troops. As in Hungary in 1956, the first exposure to a non-Soviet reality resulted in serious morale problems. Under more stressful conditions the reliability of Soviet forces might have been seriously shaken. Reports indicated that many of the invasion troops were kept closely isolated from the Soviet civilian population upon their return home.

THE SINO-SOVIET BORDER

With the breakdown in relations between China and the Soviet Union beginning in 1960, the border became the scene of thousands of tit-for-tat incursions and minor reprisals. The situation crossed a major threshold on 2 March 1969 when the Chinese wiped out a small Soviet garrison on Damansky Island in the River Ussuri near Khabarovsk in the Soviet Far East. On 15 March the Soviet Army replied with a sledgehammer blow that obliterated the Chinese now defending the island. The Chinese had made a major miscalculation. The Soviet response was far more vigorous than they had anticipated. During the rest of the summer the Soviet Army carried out hundreds of punitive operations along the border. The Chinese were scared into a massive nuclear shelter building programme, but Soviet coercion had had its desired effect, and an agreement to defuze the situation had been reached by September.[55]

Even before 1969 the Soviets had been increasing their garrisons along the Chinese border. Beginning in 1965 divisions were brought to a higher state of readiness and received more modern weapons. In 1966 Moscow obtained the legal right to station troops in Mongolia, and these were to become a force of four to five divisions. By 1975 the Soviet Army along the Chinese border numbered 43 divisions (seven tank and 36 MRD). About a third were kept at the highest readiness category.[56]

ISRAEL

For Israel this decade was war upon war – three wars jammed into the middle seven years of the decade – the June War of 1967, the War of Attrition of 1968–70 and the October War of 1973. During these seven years the IDF would go full circle from pride in as perfect a victory as is possible in 1967 – to the frustration of a static war of attrition – and to the demoralization of the near disaster of 1973.

THE SIX DAY WAR, 1967

Variously called the Six Day War, the Lightning War, and the June War, the victory of 1967 began the decade with a stunning triumph that established the IDF as one of the great armies in skill and fighting spirit. Tested and improved by the Sinai Campaign of 1956, the IDF's operational, leadership and organizational skills had been honed to a razor's sharpness. Seldom in history has an army been better prepared to fight the right war in the right place at the right time. Israeli doctrine was founded on the irrefutable logic that war must come at the time and circumstances of Israel's choosing. Her enemies were too strong and too many to afford them the priceless advantage of the first blow. Therefore as in 1956, Israel must attack first and by surprise to reduce the odds. The IDF was built and trained for just such a task.

Unlike 1956 the IDF would attack not on a single front but on three – against Egypt in the Sinai, against Jordan on the West Bank, and against Syria on the Golan Heights. As against the nine brigades that saw action in 1956, the IDF would commit 24–26 brigades in 1967. At full mobilization the IDF ground force would number approximately 250,000 of whom conscripts and regulars amounted to only 71,000. In place of the single armoured brigade of 1956, the IDF would now field eleven. The single provisional parachute brigade of 1956 had become four. There were also 9-11 infantry brigades. The armoured corps fielded 800 tanks (250 Centurions, 200 Patton M48s, 200 modified Shermans with new engines and a new 105mm gun dubbed 'Ishermans', 150 obsolete French AMX-13s). The armoured brigades fielded two tank and one mechanized battalion, the latter still equipped with the venerable M3 halftrack.[57]

This time the mobilization worked like a well-oiled machine and was accomplished in 77 hours, a world's record. There were no embarrassing organizational failures as in 1956. Each brigade column was supported by sufficient transport to carry a 72-hour supply of fuel, ammunition and spare parts. Civilian mechanics had been called-up with their own equipment and vehicles to form maintenance units complete with recovery vehicles, winches and workshop tools. Reservists had been encouraged to bring their own cars to ensure that enough transportation was available which explains why one of the first vehicles into El Arish was a red Mustang.[58]

Most impressive were the zeal and self-discipline with which the reservists rushed to the colours. Every man knew his place and duty. It was that rare moment in history when a nation willingly acts as one determined man. The spirit was typified in the description of one of the most terrible punishments to be inflicted in any army. A reservist had unwittingly revealed his location to his wife:

'The man was summoned before his commanding officer and charged with a breach of security ... The sentence was severe. "Go home," said the officer. "We have no place for the likes of you." The man slunk out but he did not go home. He began instead a sit-down strike by the camp gate. He begged everyone who entered to plead with his C.O. to reconsider his sentence and take him back. He was still at the gate in the morning. In the evening the C.O. relented. The soldier refused after that to answer any question put to him by his comrades. He would not even tell anyone the time.'[59]

One of the greatest weapons the IDF brought to the war was the self-confident mental agility and flexibility of its commanders and their willingness to act on their own responsibility without question. This was nowhere better demonstrated than in the planning for the Sinai attack. The decision to attack had been triggered by the deployment of dangerously large Egyptian forces to the eastern Sinai. The IDF devised its plans on a crash basis to fit the evolving situation. Three *ugdahs* (divisional groups designed for specific missions) would break the Egyptian defences and penetrate into the Sinai during the first stage of the operation. No plans were formulated beyond that point; they would be made as the situation developed. Brigadier-General Tal, the forger of the armoured corps after 1956, worked out the key flanking movement of his brilliantly successful attack the night before it began. Tal's divisional column and that of Brigadier-General Ariel Sharon delivered the two blows that sent a shudder through the Egyptian Army and ensured that subsequent operations were in effect a grand pursuit to the Suez Canal. Both employed

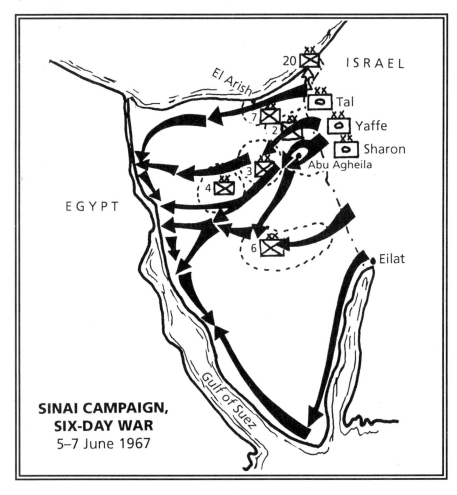

**SINAI CAMPAIGN,
SIX-DAY WAR**
5–7 June 1967

the indirect approach to infiltrate armoured columns across difficult ground and deep into the enemy rear, yet each operation was different in substance, being crafted to the situation. Tal achieved a clean massed tank breakthrough of a series of Egyptian defences 40 miles deep in half the 24 hours that had been estimated. Sharon fought an intricate set-piece night battle to overcome a single massive fortified perimeter around Abu Agheila.

Flexibility was also required on the central front when Jordan unexpectedly entered the war in an attack towards Tel Aviv. A paratroop brigade boarding transports for a combat drop in the Sinai was rushed in civilian buses to Jerusalem where it was reinforced by an *ugdah* assigned initially to the Syrian front and a reserve armoured brigade. Holes were punched through the Jordanian line and tanks poured through to seize key communications points in the enemy's rear. On the northern front the Syrian positions on the Golan heights had secured flanks but were reduced by a combination of attrition and surprise. A 100-hour barrage allowed careful penetrations through which armour passed to the rear to paralyze communications.

Israeli tactics in 1967 were a blend of concepts devised by the three great chiefs of staff, Yigal Yadin, Moshe Dayan and Itzhak Rabin. Yadin, the first Chief of the General Staff from 1949 to 1951, developed the triple concept of outflanking, bypassing and surprising. Dayan, 1954–58, originated the concept of 'assault by willpower' 'which stresses that all officers, no matter what rank or what position they hold, must, at all times, move in front of their men, setting a personal example for the troops'. The concept also obtained in combat where everyone goes 'without sleep or normal food for days until the enemy is crushed'. One side has to crack under the strain. Rabin, who commanded in 1967, evolved the 'human steamroller' concept. He maintained that the victory is only complete when the enemy has been utterly broken. The infantry was trained to assault enemy positions from the front with submachine-guns, grenades and demolition charges.[60]

Tactics, however, can only reach their potential when combined with skill at arms. The IDF's emphasis on gunnery whether by air or by ground forces was repaid a thousandfold. The deadly precision of IDF tank gunnery proved decisive again and again. Israeli gunners were usually able to get off two or more rounds before their opponents fired at all. By then the Israelis were on target. Egyptian anti-tank guns were picked off at extreme ranges; commanders had a favourite expression, 'Then I called on my snipers', special gunners who could hit anything at a reasonable range.[61]

Animating these techniques were the principles that have always proven to be the distilled essence of the art of war:

> 'psychological shock which stuns the enemy command, unexpected moves at unexpected times in unexpected directions, freedom of decision and fullest operational initiative to commanders in the field, and constant pushing without rest or intermissions. From the moment the Israeli forces moved into action, officers and men did not pause for sleep until the war was over.'[62]

The brilliant successes of the IDF did not entirely obscure serious problems. A price had been paid for the creation of the élite armoured corps and paratroop brigades. The best men had been siphoned off resulting in an inevitable watering down of the quality of the infantry brigades. The very successes of the tank brigades had reinforced the opinion that they were invincible as single-arm formations. The relatively small artillery complement had been efficient, but too few in numbers; the tanks had provided most of the close-support artillery. What artillery there was had a minimal long-range capability.

The great disparity in Israeli and Egyptian losses underscored the success of the mix of flexibility, and the skill and motivation of the Israeli soldier. The Israelis lost fewer than 700 dead and 3,000 wounded while inflicting 13,500 – 15,500 Arab dead and perhaps 27,000 wounded.

Table 3-14 . Losses in the June 1967 War

	Egyptian Front		Jordanian Front		Syrian Front	
	KIA	WIA	KIA	WIA	KIA	WIA
Israeli	275	800	299	1,457	115	306
Arab	10–12,000	20,000?	1,000	2,000	2,500	5,000

Source: Luttwak and Horowitz, *The Israeli Army*, p. 282

S. L. A. Marshall got it right when he summed-up the IDF's performance in the June War, one of the most perfectly conducted campaigns in history.

'It would be too much to extract from this campaign the lesson that audacity always pays off. It is enough to say, rather, that Israel's army believes that it does, most of the time. That it paid off handsomely in June 1967 is beyond dispute.' [63]

THE WAR OF ATTRITION, 1968–1970

The War of Attrition bound the IDF to the rock of the fixed defence, the very situation the army had done everything to avoid in 1965 and 1967. Guerrilla raids often supported by the Syrian and Jordanian armies marked operations on Israel's northern and eastern borders. The greatest threat lay in the west along Israel's new border of the Suez Canal.

After 1967 the Egyptian Army was massively re-equipped by the Soviet Union and by late 1968 had decided upon a strategy of attrition to dislodge the IDF from the Canal. The thin line of outposts along the Canal, their patrols and soft logistics support were especially vulnerable to Egyptian commando raids and artillery barrages from hundreds of heavy guns, howitzers and mortars. The Egyptian strategy had placed the IDF in the worst possible situation. Its vaunted skill and flexibility counted for little since it was fixed by geography and politics to the Canal. The Egyptians even outclassed the IDF in the two chief features of the conflict – their heavy artillery, which clearly outmatched the IDF's, and their willingness to suffer far heavier casualties. The Egyptian strategy struck at the IDF's weakness and exposed itself to none of its strengths. Two can read about Liddell Hart's indirect approach.

The Israelis side-stepped this neat trap by changing the rules. The IDF delivered its firepower from the skies with air raids that savaged the Egyptian artillery and air defences to force their efforts away from the Canal in March 1969. Commando raids taught the Egyptians that no place was safe from the IDF's reach. The first raid, by paratroops in late October 1968, sabotaged a major new power transformer hundreds of miles from the Canal as well as two important bridges over the Nile. The raid quietened the Egyptian artillery for more than four months during which time the IDF rebuilt the Canal outposts into reinforced strongholds that came to be known as the Bar-Lev Line (after the Chief of the General Staff). In late 1969 two raids were especially humiliating for the Egyptians. In September an Israeli armoured column consisting of captured Egyptian tanks was landed south of the

Canal on the Gulf of Suez. Thrusting their way south through numerous Egyptian installations without hindrance, they re-embarked 30 kilometres south of their landing point. In December a commando raid seized a new Soviet P-12 radar station near Ras Gharib and dismantled it in one of the intelligence coups of the decade.

The air war escalated to the point where Israeli aircraft were shooting down Soviet fighters. This prompted a ceasefire in August 1970 jointly recommended by the United States and the Soviet Union. The War of Attrition had cost the IDF 594 dead and 1,959 wounded on all fronts from June 1967 to August 1970, 86 and 76 per cent respectively of their losses in the June War. On the Egyptian front, the losses were 244 dead and 699 wounded. Egyptian casualties were estimated to have reached 30,000 chiefly due to the airborne artillery of the IAF.[64] Although the war ended without the Egyptians achieving any tangible gains, they had set in motion a process that would pay great profits in the next war. Despite the Israelis' airpower and commando raids, the Egyptians had forced the IDF to adopt static defences and start to think in terms of positional warfare. The Egyptians had unwittingly ensured that the next blow they would strike would be against a fixed target.

THE IDF TRANSFORMS ITSELF, 1967–1973
The years between the major conventional wars of 1967 and 1973 were years of remarkable transformation for the IDF. Rigorous lessons had been learned from the June War and the War of Attrition and were thoroughly applied throughout the IDF. During these years it was both re-equipped and retrained in light of the lessons learned, and new and more complex technologies and systems were assimilated.

The ordnance workshops of Israel turned out an increasing array of new weapons and equipment, and remodelled or refurbished foreign and captured *matériel* to higher standards than the original designs. US M48 Pattons, British Centurions and 100 captured Soviet-made T-54/55s (designated TI-67) were re-engined with US diesels and up-gunned with British 105mm guns. Soviet-made BTR-152 armoured personnel carriers, BTR-40 reconnaissance vehicles, 122mm and 130mm guns, and multiple rocket-launchers were incorporated into the inventory with only a little refurbishing. By 1972 the IDF had received its first new factory-fresh tanks in its history, the US M60, already armed with the 105mm and the new diesel engine. All previous tanks had been 'used' and sold off by other armies. From the US also came the M113A1 armoured personnel carrier, nicknamed 'Zelda' by the IDF. Artillery was also significantly improved as a consequence of the War of Attrition. The largest addition were the Israeli-made 160mm and 120mm SP mortars mounted on the old Sherman M4 chassis. An SP 155mm gun was also developed by combining the Soltam 155mm gun and the durable M4 chassis. Long-range SP artillery in the shape of the popular 175mm 107 and the 203mm M110 was purchased from the United States.[65]

Table 3-15 . The IDF in 1973

Armoured Vehicles		*Order of Battle*
Tanks	1,700	10 Armoured Brigades
M60	150	9 Mechanized Brigades
M48	400	9 Infantry Brigades
Ben Gurion*	250	5 Paratroop Brigades
Centurion	600	3 Artillery Brigades
Isherman	200	

Armoured Vehicles		Order of Battle
TI-67	100	7 (2 armoured, 3
APCs	1,450	infantry, 2 para) at full
M113A1	450	strength; 5 (1 armoured,
M2/M3	1,000	4 mechanized) at 50 per cent;
Other AFVs	1,550	rest at cadre strength
Artillery	1,250+	11,500 regulars, 83 conscripts
105/155mm SP	350	including 12,000 women; 275,000
120/160mm mortar	900	on mobilization
175/203mm	unknown	
122/130mm gun	unknown	

*Centurion with French 105mm gun.

Source: IISS *The Military Balance 1973–74*

The force-building effort was complicated by the omnipresent fact that throughout much of the 1967–73 period Israel was still fighting its middle war of the decade, the War of Attrition. Although not the full-blown high-intensity war of the two that bracketed it, it still required high operational tempos of both active and reserve formations that competed with training time. The interruption was serious because training was so often needed in the new defensive tactics that were being emphasized. In some cases, as with the artillery for example, training could be combined with actual operations. Training courses for the infantry garrisons in the occupied West Bank were simply transferred from central Israel to the well-appointed former camps of the Arab Legion. The IDF was able to overcome these problems by an overall higher level of activity driven by the necessity to re-arm and retrain in accordance with the lessons of the June War. Conscript service was increased from 30 to 36 months. Reservists accumulated far more time on active duty from 1970 to 1973 than in all the years from 1949 to 1967. In many ways it was a much better army that rushed to arms again in 1973.[66]

Yet it was an army that had made fundamental errors in analysing and applying the lessons of the June War. Chief among them was the failure to appreciate the fact that the IDF had attacked an enemy that had been hastily deployed to the Sinai. As Haim Herzog observed, 'Israeli commanders had emerged from it thinking that it was possible to accomplish everything with a tank and a plane and so built their armed forces in an unbalanced manner.' The Egyptians had correctly analysed their mistakes and concluded that a hefty anti-tank defence and a dense, layered air-defence umbrella would counter the IDF's emphasis on the aircraft and the tank. In this they were to prove correct. The IDF's infatuation with these two weapons led to the neglect of the infantry and the artillery. In 1967 the halftracks had often failed to keep up with the tanks so the the infantry had become increasingly disregarded. The IDF had relied largely on its own tanks and the IAF for its direct and close artillery support because its own meagre field artillery had not reached the battlefield until the third and fourth day because of the lack of transporters. That lesson had been learned too well. Despite the addition of more and heavier field artillery, the IDF still had a much smaller artillery component than most modern armies, 33 manoeuvre brigades to three artillery brigades, a ratio of eleven to one. Night fighting, once the special forte of the IDF, was also neglected because it was not an activity in which the tank and aircraft excelled; the Arabs on the other hand were actively exploiting its possibilities. The IDF's anti-tank assets had been sharply reduced because the tank was considered the best anti-tank weapon; the enemy's anti-tank capability was discounted. The danger of the systematic use of ATGMs such as the Soviet-made Sagger was completely overlooked.[67]

THE OCTOBER WAR, 1973

The Arab surprise attack on the afternoon of 6 October 1973 was a classic demonstration of skill, intelligence and subtlety. The other side of this coin was the equally classic failure of IDF intelligence and senior command to determine from the mass of information available that an attack was imminent. Such a failure was inevitable given the basic assumption against which the information was sifted; that the Arabs were either unwilling or unable to attack. The Israelis' error was not realized until shortly before the attack; mobilization was not ordered until 8.30 that morning. The sixth of October was Yom Kippur (The Day of Atonement), the holiest day of the Jewish calendar. While its choice certainly added to the element of surprise, it actually facilitated mobilization. Not a vehicle was on the roads to clog military traffic, and practically the entire population was at home where they could be easily notified.

The IDF desperately needed that small advantage because it had just lost the key element inherent in its mobilization capability – the minimum time of three to four days to mobilize in an organized and thorough manner. Instead the IDF had to improvise on a grand scale. The tank transporters were unavailable so many units had to travel rapidly to their positions in their tanks, many of which broke down. IDF units were reaching the front with vehicles in need of maintenance and with fatigued crews. In many instances tank guns were not zeroed and still packed in protective grease. So desperate was the situation on the Syrian front that tank crew integrity was destroyed as individual crewmen were married up as they arrived in new crews and sent often in single tanks to reinforce the fighting units. Major-General Avraham (Bren) Adan, who commanded in the Sinai, described the chaos that attended the mobilization of his division:

' ... I learned that getting Aryeh's brigade ready had become very complex. One of his battalions was supposed to be composed of regular troops, but it had been sent to the Golan Heights prior to the outbreak of war. Thus he was now short almost a full battalion of tanks and men – nearly a third of his strength. Other tank crews belonging to his brigade were caught up in the so-called "operational employment". These were reserve crews who had been called-up for a limited period to augment regular units along the borders and were now deployed in widely scattered locations from Sharm el-Sheikh in the far south to Mount Hermon in the north. As a result, Aryeh now had to assemble tanks and crews from other sources that Armoured Corps placed at his disposal. Nevertheless, I was pleased that while his deputy was remaining behind to complete the rebuilding of the brigade, Aryeh himself intended to move to the front at midnight with about half a brigade.'[68]

In this seeming chaos, hundreds of thousands of acts of initiative, selflessness and flexible thinking revealed the hard core of the national character of Israel and its armed forces and the inherent soundness of the mobilization system. A system designed to come on line in a minimum of three days was supplying fighting replacements within hours to the units holding on by their fingertips to the Golan Heights. Commanders and staffs sorted out men and equipment from what was available and moved to the front. Men whose units had not been called-up joined others that had as they moved out. As a result of the high standard of training the new tank crews on the Golan showed no fall off in performance. The mobilized strength of the IDF did not enter the fight in the order planned, but it got there when it mattered.[69]

The IDF was faced with two simultaneous blows on two distant fronts. The Egyptians crossed the Suez Canal with five infantry divisions supported by two

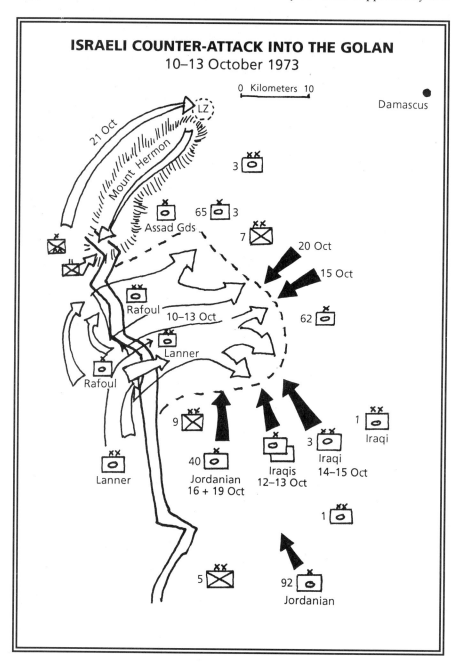

ISRAELI COUNTER-ATTACK INTO THE GOLAN
10–13 October 1973

armoured divisions; the Syrians attacked the Golan Heights with three infantry divisions in the first wave followed by two armoured divisions. The Syrian threat was the more serious; Israel had the whole of Sinai between itself and the Egyptians, but there was no buffer against the Syrians. That deadly fact immediately established the strategic priority, propelling reinforcements north to the Golan Heights battles. The IDF would concentrate first on defeating the Syrian Army then turn its forces south against Egypt.

The first shock to the IDF was the failure of the air force as airborne artillery. The Arabs' dense air-defence envelopes inflicted heavy air force casualties and left the ground forces with only their meagre complement of field artillery. Many of these units were mobilizing later than the armoured brigades that now desperately needed their support. Close air support only became a factor later in the war when a combination of air and ground force attacks on air-defence systems managed to tear a hole in the air-defence umbrellas of the Arab armies.

On the Golan Heights 930 tanks of the three Syrian first-wave divisions supported by 115 artillery batteries struck two Israeli tank brigades. Within 24 hours the second and third echelons of 800 tanks joined the attack. The southernmost Israeli brigade was eventually overrun. The northern 7 Brigade held on in well-prepared defences that allowed a swift concentration of long-range fire, as Tal had advocated, to destroy an estimated 300 Syrian tanks. The commander, Colonel Yanush, attributed their success to 'good ground, guts and gunnery'. The Syrians' southern attack was eventually held and crushed just short of the bridge into the Galilee by the individual tanks and small units of the reserves who had been rushed to that sector. Numerous small outposts had been bypassed by the Syrians and survived; had they been better armed with anti-tank weapons they could have done even greater damage to the passing Syrian units than they did.

By 8 October the IDF had three armoured divisions on the Golan front and began its counter-attack to re-establish the original pre-war front line. This was followed by an offensive which ended on 13 October, having penetrated to within 30 kilometres of Damascus. By the end of the campaign the equivalent of three more Arab divisions from Iraq, Jordan and Morocco, had been committed. The two Iraqi divisions were essentially destroyed. The Syrians left more than 1,150 tanks and thousands of other vehicles on the Golan Heights of which 867 tanks were recovered, many in good running order; the Iraqis lost far more than 100 tanks, and the Jordanians 50. Estimates of Syrian casualties varied from 3,500 dead cited by Haim Herzog to 12,000 dead cited by Edward Luttwak. Israeli casualties were 772 killed, 2,453 wounded and 65 prisoners. The IDF never had more than 400 operational tanks on that front at any one time. Some 250 tanks were hit of which 100 were a total loss; the rest were quickly repaired and sent back into battle.[70]

Despite the initial surprise, the fighting on the Golan had played to Israeli strengths in gunnery and flexibility. While the Syrian soldier was much better trained and far more effective than in 1967, his command and control system was still rigid and repeatedly failed to take advantages of opportunities. The waves of Syrian armoured vehicles that attacked had been struck down in their masses by the master gunners and skilful commanders of the IDF. The Syrians and their allies had fielded the equivalent of more than eight divisions on this front and seen them thrashed to near destruction by three IDF divisions operating this time with minimal close air support.

The Egyptians were not to be nearly so accommodating as the Syrians and posed a much more serious challenge to the IDF. Egyptian planners had an objective understanding of their enemy and the limitations of their own army and designed their attack around this kernel of common sense. By 1973 the Bar-Lev Line was nothing more than an outpost line; its garrison of 436 men in positions eight miles apart were supported by 70 guns; the IDF garrison of the Sinai consisted of one armoured division with some 277 tanks. The Egyptians seized the Canal and overwhelmed the Bar Lev Line in a meticulously planned and rehearsed operation supported by 2,000 guns and mortars, and immediately established a layered infantry anti-tank defence of hand-held RPG-7s and Sagger ATGMs. Within 24 hours all the Egyptian infantry divisions had crossed the Canal and second-echelon units were following. By now 150 of the 240 attacking Israeli tanks had been knocked out in piecemeal tank versus tank fighting. The infantry and artillery were still mobilizing and had not reached the front. More counter-attacks by arriving reserve divisions were equally fruitless. On 8 October Adan's division delivered the first counter-attacks and was reduced to fewer than two dozen tanks by the end of the day.[71]

From pain comes wisdom. By 12 October, Egyptian intelligence reports were stating that the IDF had abandoned tank only operations and were now attacking as combined arms formations replete with infantry and artillery. Israeli reinforcements from the Syrian front were arriving as the Egyptians massed their own armour on the Israeli side of the Canal for a major offensive. The ensuing battle pitted 1,000 Egyptian against 600 Israeli tanks in the largest tank battle since 1945. For the first time the Egyptians advanced beyond their anti-tank screen and outside the air-defence umbrella. The Israelis were waiting in hull-defilade positions and destroyed 264 Egyptian tanks for the loss of six of their own. General Bar-Lev observed wryly, 'It has been a good day. Our forces are themselves again and so are the Egyptians.'[72]

Next day the IDF executed the plan for crossing the Canal which had been advocated by Major-General Sharon, commanding one of the reserve armour divisions. He ferried a small force across the southern end of the Canal to the west bank; his men split up into raiding parties that wrought havoc among Egyptian installations, particularly the air-defence sites whose destruction opened an air corridor for the IAF to deliver close air support. But a major battle on the east bank of the Canal, the Battle of the Chinese Farm,[73] raged for two days; 360 Egyptian tanks were destroyed before a strong bridgehead could be established late on 17 October. By 21 October 50 per cent of the IDF tanks in the Sinai had crossed to the west bank. By 24 October the IDF had swung south down the west bank and trapped the 20,000 men of the Egyptian Third Army on the east bank as the final ceasefire concluded the war. More than 8,300 Egyptians had been taken prisoner.

The war had lasted eighteen days and had cost Israel 2,680 killed, 7,000 wounded and more than 500 prisoners. Proportionally the death toll exceeded US losses in the First World War. Peace threw the nation and the IDF into a frenzy of recrimination over the handling of the war – 'the blunder of October'. Senior IDF officers engaged in bitter disputes about one anothers' conduct during the war, often along political party lines. A board of inquiry, the Agranat Commission, headed by the Chief Justice of the Supreme Court resulted in the resignations of many senior officers, including the chief of staff, the chief of intelligence, and the commanding officer of Southern Command. The commission made enforceable suggestions to restructure both military intelligence and the IDF to prevent the mistakes of 1973 being repeated in the future. The chief casualty of the war had been Israel's sense of unquestionable superiority over the Arabs. Despite the numerous organizational and tactical changes generated by the shock of the war, the most important fact to emerge was that quality was not enough; a quantitative improvement was needed. The years after 1973 would see a major expansion in the size, mechanization and firepower of the IDF.

EGYPT

This decade was momentous for Egypt with its two wars in 1967 and 1973. The first war would see a third humiliating defeat for Egyptian arms; the second would begin with an initial world-class military operation, ending in a military draw but a moral victory.

THE 1967 WAR

Ten years of Soviet assistance had re-equipped the Egyptian Army on an impressive scale. The inventory included more than 1,000 tanks of which about 250 were modern T-54/55s, 350 armoured personnel carriers, 430 Soviet 120mm and 122mm mortars and artillery pieces as well as fifty 100mm self-propelled guns (SU-100). Peacetime strength was 100,000 regular army personnel and 50,000 national guardsmen who could be mobilized to 250,000. The field forces consisted of five infantry and two armoured divisions. All seven divisions were committed to the Sinai with their armour assets close to the border. Nasser was provoking war with Israel again in concert with Syria and Jordan and believed that a forward deployment would hold the Israelis. The Israelis had other plans. They attacked on 5 June and shattered the Egyptian front in three places, plunging deep into the Sinai. The Egyptian high command ordered a retreat to the Canal which degenerated into a rout as the Israelis harried them on the ground and from the air. Within six days the Egyptian Army had disappeared as a fighting force in an uncanny repeat of 1956. Aggressiveness and initiative were lacking at all levels. Officers did not lead from the front or show any spirit of self-sacrifice, and their casualties were much smaller in proportion than among the men subordinate to them. The butcher's bill was enormous for a bare six days: 15,000 dead, 12,000 prisoners; there would have been more prisoners, but the Israelis released thousands of captured enlisted men and sent them towards the Canal. The Red Cross and Red Crescent counted 15,000 stragglers crossing the Canal at Qantara alone. Many had thrown away their boots to escape all the more quickly; how many more died of exposure in the Sinai is unknown. Egypt had drunk the cup of humiliation to the dregs.

After the war, attempts to reorganize the army were slowed down by a purge of more than 800 senior officers. Nevertheless by the end of 1967 the army's order of battle had been re-assembled and most of its equipment replaced by the Soviets. Generous with equipment though the Soviets had been, they were disinclined to throw it away a third time, and were now determined to exert a more militarily productive influence on the Egyptian Army after the débâcle. Defeat had made the Egyptians more receptive to control and guidance. By the end of October 1967, 2,500 Soviet advisers had arrived in Egypt; by mid-1970 the number had soared to 15,000. With the new equipment and advisers also came an unprecedented level of control. The Soviets encouraged a reorganization of the high command along Soviet lines and a restructuring of the field army into three Soviet-type armies, each with two infantry and one armoured division. Nassar even authorized the Soviet advisers to simply take over the training of the Egyptian armed forces, Egyptian officers, even of higher rank, being obliged to obey their mentors. The Soviets were not known for their cultural sensitivity and did little to make the galling situation easy for the Egyptians who came to detest them for their arrogance and crudity. But they had an important effect:

'The Russians insisted that the Egyptian officers work harder and longer with their men, and many Egyptian officers discovered for the first time that the fellaheen could be good soldiers if properly led.'[74]

While the Soviets did play an important role in the reorganization of the Egyptian Army, probably too much can be made of it. In the end it was the Egyptians who reformed themselves. The officer purge and the rise of more competent men impelled by the spur of defeat appears to have set in motion a vital regeneration.

Between the 1967 and 1973 wars was fought what was known as the War of Attrition (1968–70), an affair of raids and artillery. The Egyptian commandos gave a good account of themselves in numerous cross-Canal raids. The air-defence forces and the artillery also were heavily engaged in those years. Although it is considered that Egypt got the worst of this little war, the price was less one-sided than before, and a whole generation of leaders had acquired vital operational experience.

THE 1973 RAMADAN WAR

Planning for the counter-attack against Israel began in 1968. Although Egypt had 800,000 men under arms, it was a deceptive figure upon which to base offensive operations. As large a proportion as 58 per cent of this figure was tied down in security missions protecting:

'hundreds of isolated bridges over the Nile and its tributaries; an intricate and vulnerable irrigation system on which our agriculture depends; water lines spanning hundreds of miles of desert with pumping stations and reservoirs en route; telephone systems strung over like distances; petrol lines; plus the usual strategic targets such as railways, roads, electricity plants, government buildings and the like.'[75]

The vulnerable Red Sea coastline also siphoned off its multitudes. Another drain was the expanded training system which was working overtime to pump out the trained officers and men needed for the assault across the Canal.

Even so, Egyptian strategic planning rightly concluded that it would barely achieve parity with available Israeli forces in the Sinai when actual manoeuvre forces were balanced. For that reason, the planners carefully matched Egyptian missions to resources and capabilities. They chose to make a limited attack to 'cross the Canal, destroy the Bar-Lev Line, and then take up a defensive position. Any further, more aggressive moves would need different equipment, different training and a lot more preparation'. The Egyptian Chief of Staff, General Saad el Shazly, based this on four factors: 1. The air force was too weak to support deep operations; 2. The effective SAM system was not mobile and could only operate over the Canal; 3. The Israelis had to be denied the opportunity to fight the battle under their own terms; and 4. A limited operation would increase combat experience of the army without decimating it. He would be proved correct on each point.[76]

Having addressed the strategic dimension, el Shazly concentrated his efforts on the tactical training of the individual soldier and small unit which had been seriously neglected in the past. A major effort was made not only train the soldier but to inform him of his tasks in what was to be known as the Great Crossing. El Shazly poured out a stream of directives and pamphlets that went directly to the men who would execute them. He was later to write:

'One of the happiest moments of my career came at the Suez front on October 8, two days after our crossing. Wherever I went, the troops

192

cheered and shouted: "Directive 41, we did it!" In Directive 41, I had
laid down how our infantry divisions would cross the Canal.'[77]

Soviet equipment kept arriving in huge quantities to equip the army. From May
1971 to October 1973, the Egyptian armed forces expanded from 800,000 to
1,200,000 men; the officer corps grew from 36,000 to 66,000. Even before the expansion, the army was short of 15,000 officers. The solution was to create the new rank
of 'War Officer', trained in 4–5 months to accomplish just one task, usually to lead a
platoon. Conscripted college graduates were pressed into this programme which
allowed the creation of hundreds of new units. By October 1973 the army's order of

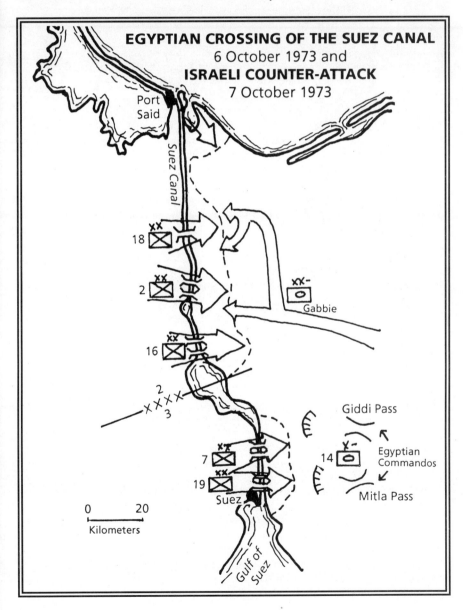

EGYPTIAN CROSSING OF THE SUEZ CANAL
6 October 1973 and
ISRAELI COUNTER-ATTACK
7 October 1973

battle listed nineteen infantry, eight mechanized, ten armoured and three airborne brigades in addition to an amphibious and an SSM brigade. Its weapons inventory included 1,700 tanks, 2,500 APCs, 2,000 artillery pieces, 1,500 AT guns, 700 AT missiles and thousands of RPG-7 AT rockets.

Planning for the crossing was painstakingly thorough and included large doses of ingenuity, traits not surprisingly found in the descendants of the men who built the pyramids. The high sand banks of the Bar-Lev Line were to be washed away with high-pressure water hoses. Replicas of the Canal were built and crossed in more than 300 exercises beginning in 1968. A careful deception plan lulled the Israelis into carelessness. The Israelis had convinced themselves that a crossing was impossible and the Egyptians fed that attitude. As they made their final preparations and crept silently towards their jump-off positions, it was a new Egyptian Army that was waiting to be born.

When they struck in the afternoon of 6 October, the Egyptians achieved the near impossible in war: complete strategic and tactical surprise. Two thousand guns smothered the Bar-Lev Line as thousands of anti-ank gunners paddled across the Canal to work their way a few miles inland. The first Israeli counter-attacks were stopped cold by the Sagger AT missiles and RPG-7 anti-tank rockets. The second waves overran the separate positions in the Bar-Lev Line; tank and mechanized units crossed rapidly on numerous bridges thrown across the Canal through holes cut in the great sand berms by the water hoses. Within two hours 15,000 engineers had crossed the Canal. Five infantry divisions reinforced by 800 tanks deployed across the Canal within ten hours. The Israelis responded with unsupported tank attacks that impaled themselves on the anti-tank hedges, littering the desert with burning Israeli tanks. At the same time frantic Israeli air attacks were shattered on the air-defence umbrella. For two weeks the war was fought on Egyptian terms as the Israelis raged uselessly. Then Sadat ordered a major advance beyond the original limited objectives. The Syrians were being badly defeated and begged for the Egyptians to take pressure off them by staging an offensive. Fighting a battle of manoeuvre outside their air umbrella resulted in a sharp reverse. Then the Israelis were upon them, crowding into the seam between the Egyptian Second and Third Armies. Under the redoubtable Sharon, the Israelis widened the gap, crossed the Canal and attacked north and south in the relatively unprotected Egyptian rear. The Third Army was cut off on the east bank of the Canal. Further reverses were prevented by a US–Soviet-imposed ceasefire.

Technically, the Israelis won the last round of the fighting, but they had suffered grave strategic and moral defeats at the hands of the new Egyptian Army. Never again would the Israelis look with casual contempt to easy victories. They, the victors on points, were convulsed with self-doubt and recriminations after the war. Sharon paid the Egyptian Army its finest compliment when he said, 'I have been fighting for 25 years, and all the rest were just battles. This was a real war.'[78] The Egyptians had recovered their credibility in what was known as the Battle for Honour. Peace was to follow, the ultimate measure of success for any army.

SYRIA

THE 1967 WAR

The Syrian Army in alliance with Egypt and Jordan prepared for war against Israel with far more enthusiasm than its operational efficiency warranted. Almost twenty years of politicization had resulted in an officer corps that was not conspicuous for operational efficiency, and with the emergence of a radical neo-Ba'athist regime in

1966, this trend kicked into high gear. Loyalty became not the most important consideration for promotions and assignments but the only consideration. At the same time, the Soviet Union rewarded the radicalism of the new regime with a more lavish supply of modern equipment, almost doubling the Syrian tank force from 400 to 750. Its military judgement impaired by its addiction to politics, the Syrian Army and regime easily confused numbers with lethality on the battlefield.

The result was a débâcle after barely thirty hours of combat beginning on 9 June 1967. Having allowed its two allies to be destroyed as it watched from the Golan Heights, the Syrian Army then received the concentrated attention of the Israeli Defence Force. Deployed for a set-piece defence and conventional attack carefully taught them by their Soviet advisers, the Syrian forces collapsed almost everywhere in a panic started by their own government's premature announcement that the provincial capital had fallen. In many instances officers led the race for Damascus. The exception was the stout defence of the heavily fortified positions at Tel Faq'r which had to be crushed in hand-to-hand fighting. The Syrian losses were about 1,000 dead, 600 prisoners, and 80 tanks.

Although the Soviets made good Syrian losses, the real improvements in the Syrian Army only began after the 1970 coup which put the commander of the Air Force, General Hafiz al Assad, into power. The precipitating event was the regime's support of the PLO in its attempt to seize power in Jordan. Unsupported by its own air force, which Assad kept grounded, Syrian tank units sent into Jordan were badly shot up by Jordanian ground and air forces. The regime lost face, and Assad struck successfully in November. Although he headed another faction of the Ba'athists, Assad was relatively moderate and moved to professionalize the officer corps. Although loyalty was a basic requirement, it now had to be accompanied by basic competence and efficiency. Officers whose only attainment was political correctness were purged, though Assad carefully placed fellow-Alawites and low-profile Christians or Sunnis in all important positions. Assad also developed an even closer relationship with the Soviet patron which initiated a major re-equipment and retraining campaign. Tank strength doubled to 1,500, and Soviet advisers were assigned down to battalion level. The size of the army was doubled to 120,000 men and included two tank and three infantry divisions, ten independent brigades and a lavishly equipped Praetorian Guard tank brigade known as the Assad Republican Guard.

THE 1973 WAR

As Assad prepared for war with Israel, the Syrian Army gave two disturbing performances. The 1972 winter's exercise on the Golan had not been impressive. Even worse was the débâcle that ensued when he ordered the 5th Infantry division to invade Jordan in September 1973. Syrian T-55s were severely handled by an even smaller force of Jordanian Centurion tanks.[79]

Any satisfaction the Israelis may have felt were wiped out when the Syrians attacked on 6 October, achieving complete tactical, operational and strategic surprise – a professional accomplishment of high order. The Syrians then proved that they had learned far more than the art of surprise. The Syrian attack on the two Israeli brigades defending the Golan Heights was a classic Soviet twin-echelon breakthrough. Their combined arms assault completely disrupted the Israelis' line, crushed one brigade and threw a second into a desperate defence. The Syrian Army was poised to burst over the Jordan and into the Galilee. Victory beckoned then faded as rigid, Soviet-style command and control broke down amid the chaos of the fighting. Now it became a battle of quick wits and initiative. Assad's reforms had not gone so far as to encourage either trait. Israeli reserves stopped the Syrians, then concentrated to counter-attack. The Syrians wilted and sagged but fought back. The Afrika Corps they were not, but they were well-trained and cohesive. Units did not collapse and flee as in 1967, but withdrew in good order from one defensive position to another or fought and died. Nevertheless the Syrians would not have been able to stabilize the front eventually had they not been aided by three factors: (1) they received significant reinforcements of three tank division equivalents from the Iraqis and Jordanians, the latter the more important from a qualitiative standpoint; (2) the Israelis were unwilling to incur the inevitable casualties of a continued attack, especially given the prospect of fighting within the huge urban sprawl of

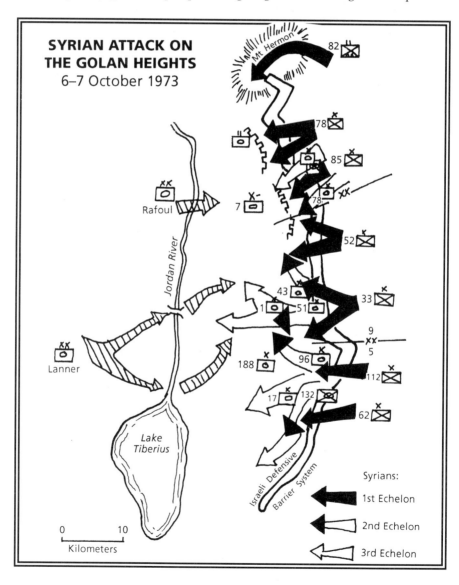

Damascus; and (3) the Israelis were unwilling to commit the forces necessary for a *coup de grâce* when they still had to contend with two Egyptian armies entrenched in the Sinai.

Nevertheless the intensive effort since 1967 to professionalize the Syrian Army had paid off. The 24 October ceasefire found the Israelis within artillery range of Damascus, facing a battered but still feisty Syrian Army which had lost 7,000 dead, 21,000 wounded, and 867 tanks. Significantly the Israelis had taken barely 370 prisoners.[80] Although Syria accepted the ceasefire, sporadic fighting continued on the Golan Heights until the disengagement agreement was reached the following March.

PAKISTAN

By 1965 the accelerating Indian re-armament programme and the large scale of Soviet arms shipments had seriously alarmed the Pakistan Army. Indian military superiority was now a real prospect.

THE 1965 WAR

The precipitating cause of the 1965 War was again Kashmir. In late December 1964 India abolished Kashmir's special status and incorporated it into India as a full state. The Pakistanis responded by introducing guerrillas into the region, expecting Indian responses to be hamstrung by their deployment of large forces in the Himalayas watching the Chinese. The Indians were unexpectedly decisive. They responded with regular forces which pinched off a 250 square mile bulge of Pakistani territory. The conflict quickly escalated and transferred to the border area south of Kashmir where three corps-sized operations flared for a month of intensive fighting which ended with both sides approaching logistics exhaustion. Although intense, the campaign had been essentially a draw. The Pakistan Army had acquitted itself quite well, especially its artillery. (See this chapter's section on India for a complete description of the fighting.)

THE 1971 WAR

The government of General Ayub Khan fell in 1968 to a wave of popular protest and was replaced by another military regime headed by the current Commander-in-Chief of the Army, General Agha Muhammad Yahya. His attempt to remove the army from politics and restore a representative government led to an electoral victory for a new popular assembly that would allow East Pakistan for the first time to dominate West Pakistan. The victor favoured a drastic decentralization of Pakistan which the Punjabi leadership viewed as treasonous. On the advice of his prime minister, Zulfiqar Ali Bhutto, Yahya refused to convene the newly elected assembly. In response, East Pakistan declared itself independent as Bangladesh. By then the single division in East Pakistan had been reinforced by three more from the west. The leader of the opposition was arrested, and the army embarked on a campaign of brutal repression directed against the Bengali élite and the large Hindu minority. Ten million refugees, mostly Hindus, fled to India. From them the Mukhti Bahini (People's Liberation Army) was formed; India provided arms and base camps from which to operate. In the ensuing guerrilla campaign, the army was encouraged to be merciless to this 'kafir' (pagan) enemy and is estimated to have killed at least 300,000 Bengalis.

When the Indians attacked into Bangladesh on 4 December, 50,000 Mukhti Bahini intensified their efforts to hold down the Pakistani garrisons. Greatly outnumbered by the Indians, beset by guerrillas, and despised by the civilian population, the Pakistan garrison attempted to defend far too much of the country and was spread too thinly. The army had intended to hold a series of strongpoints and river crossings, but were continually bypassed by the Indians who reached the Pakistani fallback positions first. Indian control of the air and sea completely cut off the Pakistani garrison from relief or escape. Despite a number of sharp engagements, the outcome was inevitable. With the fall of Dacca on 16 December, the Pakistani forces surrendered.

The Indian invasion had been awaiting the appropriate moment which was provided by Pakistan. Seemingly without a plan, a pre-emptive strike was ordered on Indian airfields in north-west India for 3 December, hoping to reproduce the Israeli 1967 surprise raids on Egypt. The Indians had read about the strikes, too, and their countermeasures not only frustrated the Pakistani purpose, but they were able to strike back and achieve air superiority in 24 hours. Pakistan Army ground attacks made only small gains in the Punjab and Kashmir and were easily held by the Indian Army which counter-attacked further south, capturing almost 3,000 square miles of territory. Upon the fall of Dacca, the Indian Government initiated a unilateral ceasefire which the Pakistanis were glad to accept the following day. The Indians counted 56,998 regular military and 18,287 paramilitary personnel as prisoners in the fighting. Estimates of Pakistani dead reach as high as 8,000 of whom 2,980 were killed in East Pakistan.[81]

The Pakistani disaster had at least four causes. Although morale had been high at the beginning of the war, that only masked a serious professional deficiency. The army had neglected to make the vigorous efforts necessary to match the Indian Army's professional growth following the 1965 War. The military's involvement in politics had in fact seriously debilitated the professional functioning of the upper levels of command. The concentration of power at the top broke down inter-service and intra-service communication so badly that the Chief of the Naval Staff only heard about the Pakistani strikes on India over the radio. For days before the air strikes the Army Chief of Staff had tried to contact Yahya and had no idea of what strategy to pursue. Secondly, the Pakistanis had seriously miscalculated the degree of force necessary to suppress Bengali nationalists. This led to the appalling situation of attempting to defend one half of a bifurcated country while in conditions of civil war.

AFTERMATH

General Yahya was dismissed and replaced by Bhutto who attempted to rebuild and rehabilitate the defeated army. The loss of East Pakistan did not seriously rend the army since 60 per cent of recruits were Punjabis and a further 35 per cent Pathans from the North-west Frontier. Less than two years later, the army was again actively engaged in another disaffected region of the country, Baluchistan, which, like East Pakistan, provided very few recruits to the army. Bhutto concentrated 80,000 troops who waged a difficult and costly counter-insurgency operation that was to cost the army as many as 3–6,000 dead and wounded by 1976 when the situation had stabilized.

INDIA

THE 1965 WAR

The Indian Army was feeling the positive effects of its re-armament programme and expansion when it was committed to its second major combat in three years.

Confrontation over Kashmir had again led to open conflict with Pakistan, but unlike the 1947 fighting over Kashmir and the 1962 fight in the Himalayas with the Chinese, this time the Indian Army would be fighting several corps-sized operations over a wide front.

By 1965 the army had been expanded to 850,000 men in a force of 20 divisions, some of which were still forming. The reforms following the 1962 débâcle had revitalized morale and improved training. Although still largely an infantry army, the Indian Army possessed about 1,000 armoured fighting vehicles, a large number of which were British Centurion tanks. The artillery relied on the 25-pounder, and there were even some self-propelled guns. Although heavily outnumbering the Pakistan Army, the odds were surprisingly even given that India was maintaining a large number of divisions in the Himalayas against the Chinese. The army was able to commit at least eleven divisions to the theatre of which five were in Kashmir.

The first move was India's. In late August an Indian brigade lopped off a 250 square mile Pakistani bulge in the border opposite Kashmir. Kashmir, the source of the trouble, then slipped into the background as the fighting shifted to the south. The Pakistan Army landed the first blow on 1 September by throwing two armoured brigades across the border in the direction of Jammu. Light Indian infantry formations were forced back, but the area was poor tank country, and the Indians were eventually able to slow the attack with anti-tank weapons. On 6 September, to relieve this pressure, the Indians launched a corps-sized attack at Lahore which was stopped by determined resistance on the Ichhogil Canal. The Pakistanis transferred their tank bridges from the Jammu fighting to the relief of Lahore. Heavy Pakistani armoured counter-attacks the next day merged into the Battle of Asal Uttar in which the Indians effectively employed an anti-tank defence in the cane fields and soggy areas around the canal. On the 9th the Indians again attempted to force the canal but failed.

On the 8th, the Indians kicked off their main offensive south from Jammu in the direction of Sialkot with a strong corps consisting of two infantry divisions and the 1st Armoured Division. The Pakistan Army intercepted the Indians barely ten miles into Pakistan with its own 6th Armoured Division. Strangely both divisions outstripped their infantry and hit each other in a great tank engagement. The succeeding fifteen days of fighting was the largest tank battle since the Second World War. Beginning on the 10th, a number of tank engagements blurred into what was to be called the Battle of Phillora. By now the fighting was on such a scale that both armies were stripping their depots and repair facilities of tanks to throw into the fighting. The last spasm of tank engagements flared on 14–17 September in the Battle of Chawinda.

By the 23rd both sides agreed to a ceasefire that was becoming a necessity since stocks of ammunition and vehicles had been badly depleted. Casualties had been heavy on both sides but conflicting claims are hard to reconcile. India admitted to 2,212 killed, 7,636 wounded, 1,500 missing and 128 tanks lost. Pakistan admitted to 1,030 killed, 2,171 wounded, 630 missing and 165 tanks lost. Each side claimed to have accounted for almost 480 of the other's tanks, perhaps a more reliable figure given the intensity of the fighting and the concentration on tank killing.[82]

Several features of this war were remarkable. Both sides were essentially infantry armies, yet concentrated on tank fighting though the tank deployment was reminiscent of stationary infantry attrition models; little or no manoeuvre or deep penetrations, but attrition through gunnery from relatively stationary positions. In these gunnery duels neither side made much use of infantry for consolidation and anti-tank support. The lack of sufficient motorized infantry on both sides may have been a limiting factor that prevented an effective combined arms approach. Nevertheless both armies had demonstrated high professionalism in their handling of large formations and the fighting skills of their *jawans*, and the leadership of regimental officers was excellent. But the senior leadership of both sides repeatedly threw away opportunities to catch unsupported tanks in co-ordinated killing grounds by rushing their own unsupported tanks pell-mell into action. There was little evidence of deception and deployment at the operational level.

The Indian Army emerged from the war with its morale high and its reputation restored. It had engaged a comparable foe on fairly even terms with considerable skill, a testament to the vast improvements carried out in the three short years since the humiliation in the Himalayas.

THE 1971 WAR

If the 1965 War with Pakistan had been a draw, the 1971 War was as unambiguous a victory as they come. The reforms following 1962 had matured and deepened as the army grew both in size and expertise. The civil war in East Pakistan had driven more than a million refugees into India in 1971 and inexorably drew the Indian Army into conflict with Pakistan. The army shifted four of its ten mountain divisions from the Himalayas to the border of East Pakistan, the snow in the passes preventing any Chinese intervention. These divisions joined four others and were assembled in five corps. The four Pakistani divisions had been seriously distracted by a brutal guerrilla war and were badly deployed to defend the lengthy borders of East Pakistan.

Pakistan precipitated the fighting by launching a pre-emptive strike on India from West Pakistan. Its raid on Indian airfields on 3 December was a failure as was a ground attack the next day. On the 4th the Indian Army invaded East Pakistan in 20 columns. Movement was fast assisted by the imaginative use of helicopters and paratroops The Indians avoided frontal attacks and manoeuvreed around the Pakistanis, reaching the Pakistani fallback positions before them. Pakistani morale collapsed. By the 16th all fighting ended as the last of 75,275 Pakistani regular and paramilitary troops surrendered. The fighting had cost the Pakistanis 2,980 dead and 4,314 wounded.

In the west, the Indian advantage did not appear so great, thirteen Indian to twelve Pakistani divisions, but the Indians had an actual 3:2 advantage in troops and 2:1 in tanks (1,270 to 700). The Indian air force gained air superiority within 24 hours of the Pakistani strike on its bases. The Indians easily contained enemy ground attacks and then went on to overrun almost 3,000 square miles of Pakistani territory to the south in Sind. In West Pakistan the situation deteriorated almost as rapidly though not so completely as in East Pakistan. On the day of the surrender in the east, India declared a unilateral ceasefire which the Pakistan government accepted the next day. Pakistani losses of 8,000 dead and 246 tanks greatly outweighed India's 3,238 killed, 8,559 wounded, 310 missing, 617 prisoners, and 73 tanks.[83] The 1971 campaign had lasted a bare thirteen days but had achieved a decisive victory that firmly established Indian military pre-eminence in South-west Asia.

SOUTH VIETNAM

By early 1965 the Vietcong had the Army of the Republic of Vietnam (ARVN) on the ropes. Trained and equipped by its American patrons to fight a conventional invasion, and crippled by its own internal corruption, it was being broken a battalion at a time by a masterfully conducted three-stage insurgency that was now ready to move in for the kill.

The arrival of the Americans in force in the summer staved off defeat; but it was only a temporary reprieve. ARVN had been given a poisoned opportunity of sorts. The very scale of the American involvement in South Vietnam pushed the ARVN into the background so far as the defence of the country was concerned. The United States felt that they could not demand direct command of South Vietnamese forces lest they be branded as colonialists, but they brought hosts of planners and advisers with their staffs. This indirect control achieved the worst of both worlds. It crushed the already low esteem and self-confidence of ARVN without being able to get at the root of its massive leadership and corruption problems.

By early 1966 the South Vietnamese had become passively resigned to letting the Americans assume responsibility for the main burden of the war. At that time ARVN numbered 264,000 men in ten divisions supplemented by a Regional Force of 120,000, the Popular Force at village level of 140,000, and 25,000 men in the Irregular Defence Group, mostly mountain tribesmen. It was decided that the American operations would concentrate on the destruction of the VC's main force and large NV units while ARVN conducted pacification operations. ARVN's role was codified in the Combined Campaign Plan of 1967; its performance was poor. Some ARVN units took the opportunity to train effectively, the excellent Dong De NCO School being a case in point, but most took the respite as a chance to loaf. Many military schools were staffed by uninspired political appointees teaching outdated US Second World War doctrine. Corruption, however, was the all-destroying cancer eating away at the ARVN. President Thieu's rise to power gave the official imprimatur to the spoils system that pervaded even the better new units such as the Ranger battalions. Morale suffered as the soldier saw massive amounts of US aid stolen by his own leaders, aid that was meant to support the soldier and his family. Despite relegation to the pacification mission, ARVN did participate in a number of large operations and saw sufficient fighting to lose about 10,000 dead a year until 1968.

By early 1968 ARVN had grown by one airborne division which was rated as an élite unit for its aggressiveness, skill and cohesion. The marine corps added another good division to the ground order of battle. Of the regular divisions, two were rated as good, three as adequate and improving, two as barely effective, and three as problem prone or ineffective. Regional Forces had been slightly expanded to 151,376 and Popular Forces to 148,789 while the Civilian Irregular Defence Groups (CIDG) now numbered 42,000. Some 12,000 Americans served as advisers with the ARVN, 300 per division, and each battalion was assigned a 3–5 man advisory team whose superior radio communications could easily bring in US fire support. At this time, ARVN was poorly equipped and outgunned by the VC and, especially, by the NVA whose common firearm was the fully automatic AK-47. In contrast, only the airborne, marines, one army regiment, and a few Ranger battalions had the comparable US M-16.

Debilitating the ARVN's effectiveness was the endemic level of corruption in which posts were bought and sold in both the government and army. The fall of President Diem in 1964 had badly disrupted an already weak system, but the coup after coup that followed paralysed any attempt at reform. In October 1967 fateful national elections made General Nguyen Van Thieu president. He ruled with the support of an oligarchy of corrupt generals and officials. This support made it impossible for him to root out the very corruption that guaranteed his immediate political survival. Corruption could be likened to a military variety of AIDS which destroyed the army's ability to stave off attacks on efficiency and professionalism.

THE TET OFFENSIVE, 1968

For the Vietnamese, the Lunar New Year or Tet was a celebration of such importance that it seemed above any political differences. The South Vietnamese declared the usual 48-hour truce which they expected the Communists to honour, and most units granted generous leave to more than half their men. ARVN's 7th Division sent 3,500 of 7,500 men on leave. As the celebrations began, 84,000 VC and NVA assault troops were moving into position for one of the greatest surprise attacks of modern military history. Their target was the regime, and in particular, ARVN. They had identified the South Vietnamese army as the allied centre of gravity. If it could be broken in one rush, the regime would collapse, and the Americans would be trapped in a hostile country, able only to negotiate their withdrawal. Making ARVN even more vulnerable was the absence, at South Vietnamese insistence, of American combat units in the larger cities and towns. Little in ARVN's previous conduct indicated that this was anything other than a logical strategic decision.

On the morning of 30 January, the Communists struck at five of six autonomous cities, 36 provincial and 45 district capitals, and 50 villages. The blow fell mostly, as intended, upon ARVN's regular garrisons and regional force units. Saigon, with a garrison of ten battalions, mostly Ranger and marine, was targeted by 35 enemy battalions. There was only one US military police battalion in the city although there were 23 other battalions in the region around Saigon.

To the shock of the Communists, ARVN not only did not fall apart from their roundhouse punch, but stood its ground and fought. South Vietnamese troops frustrated many VC infiltration efforts by simple acts of initiative. Two of ARVN's four corps commanders failed miserably, but their commands held on through the efforts of subordinate leaders and American firepower. Other generals did not hesitate to take the decisive action that saved the day. In the Central Highlands, the commander of the 23rd Division, Colonel Dao Quang An, acted immediately on capturing a VC battleplan before the attack. He cancelled all leave and set patrols to ambush the VC. The resulting edge in the battle for Ban May Thuot just made the difference. As it was, the fighting raged for nine days as the 23rd slugged it out with enemy in bitter house-to-house fighting. In the Delta, the Mobile Riverine Force (MRF) fought for 30 days without rest and earned a US Presidential Unit Citation and General Westmoreland's praise, 'The MRF saved the Delta'. The battle for Saigon was essentially an ARVN victory with heavy US firepower assistance. US forces around the city intercepted and beat many enemy formations. Elsewhere it was US communications, mobility and firepower in support of Vietnamese garrisons that often made the difference.

The most vicious fighting, however, was in the ancient capital of Hue. Essentially an undefended city, Hue was overrun by two reinforced NVA regiments that besieged the headquarters of ARVN's 1st Division which was defended by one recon company. The division's commander, the redoubtable BG Ngo Quang Truong, had deployed his battalions in the hinterland, believing Hue's status as an open city would protect it. But his compound and a MACV compound on the other side of the city both held and attracted reinforcements. As the US Marines fought their way into Hue from the south, the ARVN's 1st Division's battalions reinforced by airborne and armoured cavalry units fought through one stiff ambush after another to reach the beleaguered city. They broke in and even stormed the gate of the great moated, 3-square-mile brick citadel only to be dislodged by a counter-attack. For the next two weeks, supported by US firepower, a mixed force of 1st Division and airborne battalions gnawed their way into the citadel as the US Marines broke in from the opposite direction. On 24 February, as the Allied forces mopped-up the last resistance, ARVN hauled down the VC colours and raised its own in the citadel. ARVN losses had been 384 dead and 1,830 wounded. Together with the US Marines, they had accounted for an estimated 5,000 enemy dead.

With the relief of Hue, the last flicker of the Tet Offensive winked out. The South Vietnamese centre of gravity had held. ARVN losses were some 4,000 to 8,000 dead against 40,000 enemy dead. The US forces suffered 4,000 casualties. ARVN had won a victory by keeping its nerve and holding on while US firepower eventually shred much of the enemy force.

VIETNAMIZATION, 1969–1971

Despite the objective military victory won by the allies, the political will of the United States had snapped under the shock. Determined to withdraw from the war, they decided to buy themselves a decent interval in which to train and equip the South Vietnamese to take over. Thus was born the Vietnamization programme. Although they didn't realize it, for the corrupt leadership of ARVN it was a last chance. The US Army's senior intelligence officer under Westmoreland and Abrams, Lieutenant General Phillip Davidson, observed:

'In 1969, the South Vietnamese missed the vital point that Vietnamization was more than modernization and expansion ... it was a strategy for United States withdrawal, leaving the South Vietnamese to defend themselves ... regardless of their capacity to do so. This sombre fact they never grasped – at least, not until it was too late. The South Vietnamese were convinced almost to the end that the United States would support them in whatever way was necessary until they could clearly go it alone.'[84]

The first phase of the programme saw the ground combat burden of the war shifted to ARVN, but with US air and naval support. The second phase saw an increase in ARVN's supporting arms such as artillery. The final phase would see the US role limited to the presence of advisory personnel who would then be withdrawn. The programme lurched ahead, beset by countless problems. The Regional and Popular Forces were greatly expanded so as to release the regular divisions from their static garrison duties. Divisions and corps received more artillery battalions, and 500 helicopters were received. The rapid expansion of the ARVN simply overwhelmed the training and logistics infrastructure. There were not enough qualified cadres to provide the thousands of new officers and NCOs necessary for the expanded force. The fundamental, almost Spartan, efficiency necessary for such a national transformation was completely beyond the capabilities of the Thieu government which ruled by dint of the spoils it could dispense. Corruption siphoned off resources destined for the troops who by 1970 were deserting at the rate of 100,000 a year. Commanders found it profitable to cover the desertions and pocket the pay and subsistence of these 'ghost soldiers'. Corruption extended even to siphoning off the subsistence for those troops who remained with the colours, reducing them and their families to poverty if not starvation. Incredibly, progress, though fragile and uneven, was made. By 1970 all regular and most Regional/Popular Forces troops were armed with the M16 rifle. By 1972 the armed forces numbered more than 1,000,000 evenly divided between regular and Regional/Popular Forces. By 1971 the enemy had been largely confined to ten provinces where only a quarter of the population lived. Part of ARVN's success was due to the decimation of VC forces and cadres during the Tet Offensive and part to a pacification programme that was aimed at the needs of the peasantry and which had essentially crippled the insurgency by 1971.

Vietnamization, however, suffered a gory test in early 1971. The previous year, ARVN units had participated successfully in the invasion of Cambodia to clean out the enemy's vast support infrastructure. A more ambitious operation entitled 'LAM SON 719' was intended to strike into the mountains of Laos and sever the Ho Chi Minh Trail. The best regular ARVN divisions, the 1st and the Airborne, reinforced by armour, marines and Rangers battalions (17,000 men) were assigned the mission. The United States supplied both air transport and air support. Things went wrong quickly. Bad weather limited the air support and slowed the advance. Nevertheless the objective was reached, but the force was too small to stay there without reinforcement while the PAVN closed in with a numerical advantage of two to one. The ARVN expedition fought well, but was too far out on a limb, too heavily outnumbered and not so well supported as it should have been. President Thieu played a disastrous role by repeatedly interfering in the operation. Rather than commit more forces, Thieu, in probably his only rational decision, ordered a withdrawal to save the army's élite units for more serious fighting ahead. The PAVN closed in for the kill and succeeded in mauling many ARVN units in bitter fighting before they could be withdrawn. ARVN's losses were 7,683 (1,764 KIA) while US losses were 1,402 (215 KIA) against an estimated 20,000 PAVN dead, most of which were inflicted by B-52s. Despite the lopsided butcher's bill, ARVN knew it had suffered a defeat. Glaring weaknesses had been exposed. ARVN's mobile

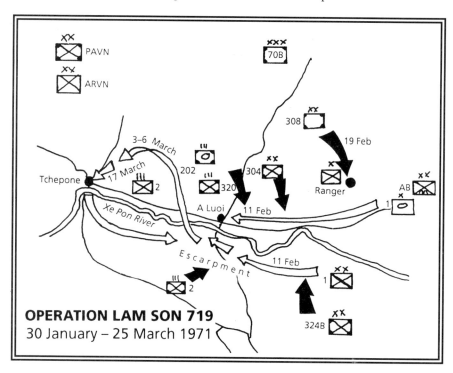

OPERATION LAM SON 719
30 January – 25 March 1971

strategic reserve, which consisted of the airborne and marine divisions was inadequate in size and capabilities. Thieu's refusal to reinforce the operation was based on the inability of any other regular army division to engage in mobile operations. Even élite ARVN units had relied on their American advisers for too many of the nuts and bolts command, co-ordination and staff skills and now found themselves seriously deficient when they were on their own.[85]

THE EASTER OFFENSIVE, 1972

The Cambodian and Laotian operations had bought another year for South Vietnam, and forced the PAVN to move their major offensive back to early 1972. When it came, at the end of March, it was a massive conventional cross-border invasion spearheaded by tanks and supported by masses of heavy artillery. The first blow simply disintegrated the newly raised 3rd Division in the DMZ and rolled on to Quang Tri City. I Corp commander's conduct of the defence was a model of incompetence that compressed his surviving forces into Quang Tri City from which they fled in disorder as the NVA were about to encircle it from the south. The panic was sown by that deadly weakness of almost all ARVN divisions, the presence of the families of the troops who were desperate to take them to safety rather than stay and fight. It was a futile wish, for the mass of those fleeing was savaged by NVA fire that left thousands of dead. The corps commander was replaced by MG Truong, the hero of Hue in Tet 68. Truong took hold of the ARVN forces and organized an effective defence east and north of Hue. By June he was commanding ARVN's three best divisions (1st, Airborne, and Marine) and was ready for a counter-offensive that recaptured Quang Tri City in September. He had stopped and rolled back the major three PAVN attacks and had saved South Vietnam.

In the Central Highlands, the NVA blow routed two of 22nd Division's regiments and converged on Kontum. The 23rd Division, under another aggressive professional, Colonel Ly Tong Ba, and, significantly, unburdened by fear for the safety of their families, reached the city first, and held it under desperate siege and counter-attack while B-52s pounded the besiegers. The third and southern NVA attack also placed an ARVN force under siege at An Loc on the road to Saigon. This time ARVN skillfully employed reserves to thwart the NVA and took quick advantage of several intelligence windfalls. As the offensive dried up, the South Vietnamese were aware how close they had come to disaster. Overall, however, ARVN had done well. Thieu had been forced to replace two incompetent corps commanders with professionals. Excellent officers like Truong and Ba were the right men at the right place at the right time. The NVA had also made some critical mistakes. Truong summed-up the critical ingredient in ARVN's survival: 'Quang Tri City could not have been retaken, nor could ARVN forces have held Kontum and An Loc, had it not been for the support of the United States Air Force.'

FINAL DEFEAT, 1975

The Paris Peace Accords of 1973 not only saw the departure of US air and artillery support for ARVN but also brought a drastic reduction in *matériel*. ARVN had been built on the US model of being able to rely on ample spare parts, ammunition and fuel, and when these were reduced ARVN was seriously crippled. This knowledge delivered the *coup de grâce* to ARVN morale, already devastated by the suicidal corruption of its leadership. Hanging over everything, said one South Vietnamese officer, was 'everyone's conviction that the enemy would never give up'.[86] Taken together with its other infirmities, the effect was mortal.

Despite the Accords, the NVA maintained 300,000 troops in South Vietnam. These forces, with a higher ratio of combat personnel, had greater mobility than ARVN who were tied to regional defence roles and weighed down with dependents. One ARVN general estimated that of a paper strength of 1,100,000 troops, barely 100,000 were 'fighters'.[87]

In 1975 the writing was on the wall when the NVA for the first time captured an entire province, isolated Phuoc Long, north of Saigon, and ARVN did not have the reserves to contest the loss. But this was merely a try-out. The great NVA offensive kicked off on 10 March with an attack on Ban Me Thuot in the Central Highlands, and a series of disastrous decisions led to the collapse of the entire corps. The proximity of military dependents was again a crucial weakness. A Ranger relief force attempting to fight its way into the city was diverted to evacuate dependents. Troops of the 23rd Division deserted *en masse* to evacuate their families when helicoptered into the city for a counter-attack. The division commander fled to a hospital because he had a scratch on his face. Stirring this chaos was President Thieu whose contradictory orders destroyed any chance of a coherent defence. His eventual order to evacuate the Central Highlands precipitated the final disaster. A mob numbering more than 500,000 ARVN troops, dependents and refugees were hurriedly moved down an inadequate highway towards Da Nang on the coast. Barely 20,000 of 60,000 troops and 100,000 civilians got through. Most of Military Region II was lost and South Vietnam was cut in two.

Thieu then pulled the rug out from under I Corps by withdrawing the Airborne Division to Saigon to protect himself from a coup. He held up the re-deployment plans of Lieutenant-General Truong, who had saved the province in 1972, until it was too late. PAVN had isolated the coastal strongpoints which fell one by one as ARVN morale collapsed during attempts at seaborne evacuation. By 30 March Military Region I was entirely lost. The rest of Military Region II followed as South Vietnam passed the point of no return. With a few exceptions, senior commanders had fled first, abandoning their commands which then collapsed. 'From Thieu on down, ARVN leadership reaped the whirlwind which eventually befalls the inflexible, the incompetent and the cowardly.'[88]

The NVA with four corps closed on Saigon for the kill. ARVN had only the three divisions organic to Military Region III plus remnants of other units that had escaped the débâcles to the north. Ironically this was ARVN's best fight. The 18th Division, which had been rated combat ineffective in 1968, fought one of the epic battles of the entire war at Xuan Loc, holding off an entire corps in a hammer-and-tongs fight. After three days the battered 18th withdrew, having lost most of its infantry but having killed 5,000 NVA and destroyed 37 tanks. Xuan Loc had shown what the South Vietnamese soldier, with proper leadership, could do – and was to be an eternal reproach to the clique that had ruined their country. Fittingly, Thieu fled to Taiwan the day before the 18th had to give up the unequal struggle on 22 April. The end came quickly as the NVA began its assault on Saigon on 26 April. In four days it was over. The NVA had won a complete victory. ARVN and the state it had served passed into history.

NORTH VIETNAM

THE UNITES STATES ENTERS THE WAR

With the arrival of the Americans in large numbers in 1965, the war in South Vietnam reached a new intensity that saw PAVN gradually absorb the PLAF. The VC organized three of its four regiments into its first division, the 9th. The 5th Division was formed next year with mixed VC and PAVN cadres. In 1967 the 7th Division was formed largely from two PAVN regiments. By the time of the Tet Offensive of January 1968, American intelligence estimated that 50 per cent of the 197 VC main force battalions, some 60,000 men, were comprised of North Vietnamese regulars and that an additional 50,000 regulars in seven divisions were in the South. This offensive decimated the VC's fighting forces and resulted in their wholesale replacement by PAVN regulars.

The first PAVN division to enter the South, the 325B, moved into the Central Highlands in 1965 with the intention of cutting the country in two. They were pounced upon by the newly arrived US 1st Cavalry Division (Airmobile) in October when the PAVN unit attempted to overrun the ARVN base at Plei Mei. The US helicopters hounded and harried the 325B back into the refuge fastness of the Ia Drang valley and followed them to trigger the first major battle for the PAVN and the US Army. Both were eager to take the other's measure, and for both the ensuing slaughter was a mutually cruel test. The Americans played their mobility and firepower cards to the maximum. The North Vietnamese equally demonstrated their impressive light infantry skill. The first phase of the battle wrecked two PAVN regiments with at least 1,300 dead. The Americans held off superior numbers of the well-handled PAVN in close combat while their artillery and airpower hammered the attackers. After three days of fighting, the 325B Division slipped away. In the second phase, a PAVN battalion caught a withdrawing US battalion and ripped it apart in a hasty but deadly ambush.

The battle set a pattern for much of the rest of the war. 'When the Americans entered the war, we spent all our time trying to figure out how to fight you. The incredible density of your firepower and your mobility were our biggest concerns.' PAVN units' with their superior foot mobility, usually initiated actions against the Americans and were equally able to break them off and withdraw when it suited them, cloaked in the invisibility of the dense vegetation and often mountainous terrain. This ability helped to counter US superiority in firepower. As one PAVN general explained:

'Our mobility was only our feet, so we had to lure your troops into areas where helicopters and artillery would be of little use. And we tried to turn those advantages against you, to make you so dependent on them that you would never develop the ability to meet us on our terms – on foot, lightly armed, in the jungle.'

Another general stated later:

'The way to fight the American was to grab him by his belt, to get so close that his artillery and air power was useless.'

Nevertheless, one North Vietnamese veteran estimated that artillery and air strikes accounted for 70–80 per cent of their casualties in the war. PAVN units were structured with this in mind. They were essentially well-trained light infantry whom, the Americans quickly learned, fought with courage, tenacity and intelligence. The Americans had another dose of it in the terrible Battles of the Highlands and Dak To later that year. Nevertheless, all the light infantry skill in the world was at best a close match for the Americans' mobility and firepower, for which the Communists retained a healthy respect.

Despite the techniques formulated to cope with the Americans, PAVN and the VC suffered heavy losses throughout 1966 and 1967. The Americans thought their attrition strategy was working, unaware that PAVN had an unlimited human expense account with 200,000 young men reaching military age every year. Unlike the Americans, the North Vietnamese soldier was in the fight for the duration, knew it and accepted it. The Americans were also unaware of more subtle North Vietnamese strategies; PAVN was tying down most of the US forces in the interior and border areas of South Vietnam. But the population was the real strategic goal of the North Vietnamese, and 80 per cent of it was huddled along the coastal lowlands. As PAVN drew the Americans deep into the interior, the VC cadres and local forces were fighting, often successfully, to control the population.

General H. Norman Schwarzkopf mentions his incredulity when the following statement by Ho Chi Minh, outlining a further subtle strategy, came to light in 1965:

> 'I know you're facing more and more Americans right now, but don't worry. We're going to win the war against America the same way we won the war against the French: not on the battlefield, but in the enemy's homeland. All you have to do is hang on. The American people are not tough enough to see this war through and we are. We have fought for twenty years; we can fight another twenty years; before then, they will give up and not support their troops anymore, and we will win.'[89]

The political line of this statement resonated with the individual soldier. He believed it and continued with stoic endurance against every setback and loss. The PAVN soldier may have been in for the duration as was his ARVN counterpart, but he had one enormous advantage over the ARVN – his family was in relative safety in the north while ARVN's was living with him in his garrisons. Families in combat are distractions that a soldier can do without, as later events were to underline. As an army, PAVN had a similar advantage – they were not obliged to dissipate their strength protecting the human and physical infrastructure of the state, as the ARVN had to. This advantage gave him mobility and enabled him to take the initiative.

THE TET OFFENSIVE, 1968

Nevertheless, by late 1967 the American attrition strategy was at least achieving a grinding stalemate. Frustrated, Hanoi determined to upset this bloody balance with a strike at the Americans' centre of gravity, the weakness of their South Vietnamese allies. The head of COSVN, the remarkable General Tran Van Tra, devised an offensive plan to bring down the army and government of South Vietnam in a *coup de main* that would leave the Americans stranded and able only to negotiate a withdrawal. Tra explained that the purpose of the offensive was to:

> '... rapidly undermine the enemy so that he no longer possesses the will and capacity to resist or counter-attack, thus leading him to total collapse, total defeat ... This coup de main does not necessarily mean the destruction of the bulk of enemy vital forces but only certain parts of them. It also means the occupation of certain localities with strategic significance ...'[90]

The strategic locations were five of six autonomous cities, 36 provincial and 64 district capitals, and 50 villages. The VC would lead most of the attacks to preserve the fiction of their autonomy in order to provoke an uprising. Before the offensive PAVN would draw more American units into the interior and in the defence of Khe Sanh in the north. On 31 January 1968, the 84,000 VC and PAVN troops attacked right across South Vietnam during a national holiday when many ARVN units had relaxed and allowed thousands of men go home on leave. Saigon was the primary target against which COSVN allotted 35 battalions, eleven of which with 4,000 men were to strike targets in the city centre. Surprise was complete as VC sappers blew their way into the US Embassy compound, the Joint General Staff (JGS) compound and other vital targets.

These successes were repeated in many places. PAVN units in the north attacked Quang Tri City and were repulsed, but captured most of Hue in two hours. Then the plan started to come apart. Reinforcements did not arrive for many units, such as those in central Saigon. Worse still, to the Communists' surprise, the people did not rise, and the ARVN fought back hard. And the Americans were on them like a hammer, jubilant that their elusive enemy had come out into the open. Within a week the Communists had been driven from all their gains with great loss, although the fighting dragged on for weeks. COSVN ordered all units to disengage on 21 February except for the PAVN defenders of Hue. Their defence crumbled that same day as almost a month of ferocious city fighting came to an end when the ARVN 1st Division and US Marines overran the Imperial palace and hauled down the VC flag. The battle for Hue had been the longest infantry battle of the war. PAVN lost about 5,000 dead but only 89 prisoners. ARVN losses were 384 dead and 1,800 wounded; American Marines and soldiers suffered 216 killed and 1,364 wounded.

As a military operation, the Tet Offensive had been a disaster for the Communists. Forty to fifty thousand men had been killed and 5,000 taken prisoner. ARVN losses were 8,000 killed; the Americans suffered 4,000 killed and wounded. The VC had been disembowelled as a military organization and did not recover. The empty ranks were filled by more North Vietnamese replacements. The six training divisions and two groups in North Vietnam were stamping them out at the rate of 6–8,000 men per division and 6,000 per group every three months. These were the replacements that fleshed out the three decimated VC divisions and turned them in everything but name into PAVN units.

Post-Tet 1968 Operations

The next year was spent licking wounds as it dawned on Hanoi that the military disaster of Tet had wrecked American domestic support for the war. After the war, one PAVN general remarked, 'In all honesty, we didn't achieve our main objective, which was to spur uprisings throughout the South ... As for making an impact in the US, it had not been our intention – but it turned out to be a fortunate result.'[91] The Americans may have been on the way out, but they were still dangerous. As a parting gift to the ARVN, the Americans raided the Cambodian sanctuaries of the Communists in 1970 and destroyed vast facilities and stores. Simultaneously, a new and hostile Cambodian government also attacked them. The setback may have given the South Vietnamese another year, as thousands of PAVN troops were drawn into fighting the Cambodians. The ARVN and Americans aimed another blow the following year in Operation 'Lam Son 719' which attempted to sever the Ho Chi Minh Trail in Laos by a large ARVN force with US air support. For the first time, the PAVN organized and operated a corps (70B) which forced the ARVN eventually to withdraw after bitter fighting.

The Easter Offensive, 1972

The PAVN successes in 'Lam Son 719' led the North Vietnamese to conclude that they could conduct a large multi-division conventional operation. PAVN massed large forces (fourteen divisions and 26 separate regiments) equipped with armour and artillery in the DMZ and attacked during Easter 1972. This time there was no attempt to win over the population; the PAVN would blow their way into population centres. But their forces were dissipated in four separate offensives instead of concentrating for one powerful strike, although the strongest attack came across the DMZ. Large numbers of anti-aircraft guns and SAMS in the DMZ discouraged air attacks. Quang Tri City quickly fell as other offensives kicked off in the Central Highlands and towards Saigon. Then the operation faltered when the PAVN paused for three weeks. When it resumed towards Hue, the North Vietnamese were held and then counter-attacked with US air support; eventually most of the lost territory was retaken. Once out of their air-defence envelope along the DMZ, American and South Vietnamese air attacks had taken a heavy toll. Symbolically, the ARVN drove the PAVN out of Quang Tri City in a bloody fight in September. In the Central Highlands, ferocious fighting erupted around An Loc which the North Vietnamese besieged. Tank attacks into the city were unsupported by infantry and were wiped out. Here too incessant US air support, particularly by B-52s, was the decisive element. A captured PAVN document revealed North Vietnamese understanding of their margin of defeat: 'Saigon's infantry = American Fire Power = National Liberation Front's Army.'[92] Everywhere the North Vietnamese had shown a poor understanding of combined arms operations which resulted in the loss of more than 600 armoured vehicles. More than 190,000 troops had been killed or taken prisoner by the time the Easter Offensive petered out in September with the recapture of Quang Tri by the South Vietnamese.

THE HO CHI MINH CAMPAIGN, 1975

When the last Americans left South Vietnam shortly after the Paris Accords were signed on 27 January 1973, there were still 160,000 PAVN troops in country. By the end of 1974, 180,000 more had reinforced them to flesh out weakened divisions. Hanoi tested the US resolution not to return when a PAVN corps overran the

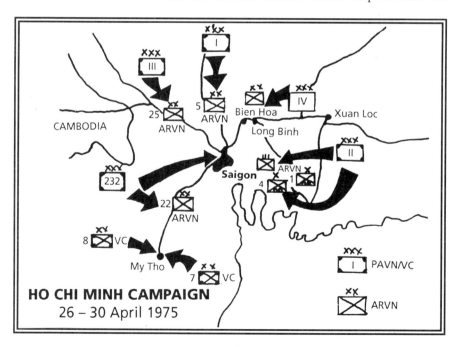

provincial capital of Phuoc Long in January 1975 as part of a 1975-6 campaign plan to reduce the whole of South Vietnam. When Washington did nothing, the North Vietnamese could plan their next operation without fear of being flailed from the sky. The NVA prepared well and had a strong logistics system in place to support sustained operations.

This time PAVN would not strike with an open hand by spreading its offensives too thinly. On 10 March a corps crushed the ARVN at Ban Me Thuot in the Central Highlands with superior numbers. South Vietnamese President Thieu ordered a withdrawal from the area that turned into a rout. The PAVN quickly pursued the enemy out of the Highlands and cut South Vietnam in two. Then a PAVN corps crossed the DMZ and attacked Quang Tri City. Thieu's orders again sowed disaster, and the defence of the North collapsed and along with it ARVN's best divisions.

By the beginning of April the victories had exceeded the wildest expectations of the North Vietnamese Politburo which, however, did not hesitate to accelerate its campaign plan. The final push was named the Ho Chi Minh Offensive. With a name like that, no PAVN soldier would dare fail. Morale was sky high. Five PAVN corps now raced for Saigon, crushing the remnants of a demoralized ARVN. By early April Hanoi had committed 300,000 men in eighteen divisions to the offensive. A final battle was fought against the surprisingly spirited ARVN 18th Division at Xuan Loc north of Saigon. For three days the NVA threw four divisions against 18th Division. The exhausted enemy finally withdrew on 21 April as the North Vietnamese rushed south to the capital for the kill. Saigon fell on the 30th as PAVN tanks rode into the city and administered the *coup de grâce* by crashing through the gates of the Presidential Palace. It was all over at last. The NVA victory was complete; the government and army of South Vietnam were destroyed in the most total victory of the post-Second World War period – at a cost of at least 750,000 PAVN and Vietcong dead.

CHINA

By late 1965 Mao Zedong could take satisfaction from the purification of the People's Liberation Army (PLA). The first victims in the purge of adherents to professionalization had been executed in 1959. During the ensuing six years, his new defence minister, the fanatic Lin Biao, had thrown the PLA full reverse into its revolutionary pre-Korean War past. The ideological will embodied in 'Red' had triumphed over the 'Expert', and the PLA had been held up as the paragon of the nation.

In 1965 supporters of professionalization were given a new and pressing argument. Growing American involvement in the Second Indo-China War was seen as a real threat to China's security. Alienated from the Soviet Union, China was clearly outclassed should the United States attack. This group found its spokesman in the PLA's Chief of Staff, Marshal Lo Ruiquing, who advocated a *rapprochement* with the Soviet Union and a de-emphasis of revolutionary war which was irrelevant to China's current security dilemmas. Patching up the rift with the Soviets was paramount for Lo; China could not develop its own nuclear deterrent quickly enough and would need the Soviet nuclear umbrella for the foreseeable future. Mao and Lin argued that people's war was the 'spiritual nuclear bomb', for China, one that would adequately deter the United States from any protracted war in China. Lin's exaltation of will over material had by now become an arrogant dogma expressed in his September statement:

211

'Guerrilla forces have ultimately defeated regular armies. "Amateurs" who were never trained in any military school have eventually defeated "professionals" graduated from military academies.'[93]

Lo's stand came at a time when Mao was preparing his catastrophic Great Cultural Revolution in which he intended to sweep away the Party structure which in its own way preferred to be 'Expert' rather than 'Red'. Just before the New Year, Lo and his followers were swept away in the first gusts of the coming hurricane.

THE PLA AND THE GREAT CULTURAL REVOLUTION

Having assured himself of the PLA's loyalty, Mao was content to let it stand aside while he attempted to instil the same 'Red' attitudes in society. At first the PLA was an active participant in the propaganda and education effort, sending cadres into the institutions of civil society. But to break the hold of the Party and government bureaucracies, Mao and Lin had recourse to a blunter instrument – the fanatical Red Guards, viciously indoctrinated youths, who embarked on an orgy of social deconstruction. The ostensibly pure PLA became a horrified bystander. Armies, after all, are based on order and hierarchy, and have an instinctive revulsion to disorder, especially the mindless hooliganism of the Red Guards. Lin cautioned the PLA not to become involved against them:

'Many men and women have committed suicide, and many others have been murdered. Production has fallen ... but our losses are not as great as they were during the war against the Japanese or the civil war against the Kuomintang! ... You must take no action without clearing it with higher authority. But you must pay no attention to the provincial committees of the Party. They are all rotten!' [94]

Lin's previous attempts to return the PLA to its People's War roots had required intense efforts to break up the army's traditions of autonomy as an institution and matrix of regional and personal loyalties. Despite massive transfers of officers and promotion of the those whose sole qualification was their 'Redness' (Mao's orderly was promoted to command a division), the PLA was not sucked completely into the madness. By June 1967 Red Guards were raiding arsenals, which the PLA was belatedly given permission to defend, and looting arms shipments to Vietnam. Despite Lin's warning not to stand in the way of the Red Guards, many regional PLA commands were taking the initiative to stand between the Red Guards and more conservative elements of society. Such action tended to support the latter. Local commanders, under orders not to oppose the Red Guards, secretly formed their own 'mass organizations' of conservative Red Guards who struggled against the radicals, often in pitched battles with machine-guns, artillery and tanks. One of the most notorious incidents broke out in Wuhan where the local military district commander, Ch'en Tsai-tao, formed his 'Million Heroes' from large numbers of conservative peasant militia and used them and local troops to crush the radical Red Guards. Lin sent in the Air Force's 15 Airborne Corps, and more fighting erupted. Lin went further, and called all regional commanders to Beijing where he attempted severely to curtail their authority. This move was a signal to the radical Red Guards to attack military headquarters throughout China. At the same time, Lin was lecturing the regional commanders to humble themselves before and learn from the very young thugs they had been fighting. Lin's attack on the PLA leadership was almost the undoing of the army and the nation. Thousands of soldiers were killed in attempting to stop battles or were murdered outright by Red Guards. By August the country was at a standstill; fighting had broken out in all of China's

26 provinces. Now PLA units were fighting one another. In Szechcuan they fought with tanks, heavy artillery and even gunboats. Civil war loomed. At this point Foreign Minister Chou En-lai's heroic efforts to mediate among commanders may have prevented the final descent into war; the radical leadership in Beijing blinked. Although fighting continued in many places until early 1968, the radicalization of the PLA was officially halted on 5 September 1967.[95]

For the next three years the radical leadership lionized the PLA as it attempted to restore order. It had no alternative, having been so successfull in wrecking China's governing institutions and discrediting its élites. The PLA was the only remaining efficient organization. Throughout China the PLA found it had to replace the wrecked Party and government structures to hold society together. The PLA moved into the shattered school systems to restore order with political and military training. PLA cadres also replaced civilian managers in vital positions in the civil economic infrastructure. By 1971 the PLA was responsible for most police functions. Most critically, the PLA cadres had assumed pivotal positions within the devastated Party structure. To combat civil strife, main force units had been spread thinly throughout the country. More than a million regional force personnel, almost its entire strength, had been committed to reinforcing local governing and economic structures. Chao En-lai admitted at this time that the PLA had suffered hundreds of thousands of casualties in the Great Cultural Revolution.[96] Unintentionally, Mao had created the conditions that negated the very order of army-Party relations he himself had established: 'The Party commands the gun, and the gun will never be allowed to command the Party.'

THE CONFRONTATION WITH THE SOVIET UNION, 1969–73

Sino-Soviet relations had soured badly during the early sixties when Soviet aid had been cut off. They had worsened as both countries competed for ideological leadership of the Communist world and as Chinese demands for return of territories in the north annexed by Russia in the last century became strident. The Soviet Union rapidly built up its forces in Mongolia and its military districts opposite China from Central Asia to the Far East as a response. These moves and the Soviet invasion of Czechoslovakia in 1968 aroused Chinese fears of invasion as relations between the two countries practically ceased. The radical movement was just the right tinder for these fears. The Soviet Union quickly became the new main enemy in place of the United States. The militants seemed even eager to suck the Soviet mechanized armies into the death of a thousand cuts of People's War. The tinder ignited on 2 March as Chinese border guards attacked and wiped out a Soviet border guard detachment on Zhenbao Island (Damansky Island in Soviet geography) in the River Ussuri, 100 miles south of Khabarovsk. Who started the fighting has never been clearly established, but the Soviets retaliated with a major operation on 14 March that inflicted heavy losses on the Chinese in the contested area. Clashes began to ripple and flare along the immensely long Sino-Soviet border. From April until the end of June fighting erupted in Xinjiang and again in August. In June and July there had been more incidents near Khabarovsk.

Beijing put the crisis in the starkest terms by ordering preparations for 'a People's War against aggression'. The PLA received its new marching orders when the *Liberation Army Daily* stated 'we should not think that by putting politics in command military affairs can be neglected'. The PLA quickly switched to a war footing; political training gave way to renewed emphasis on light infantry skills which had remained at high levels. They were the very skills enshrined in the PLA's People's

War traditions. For that reason Lin, even before the crisis, had ensured that military training still occupied 60 per cent of a soldier's time as opposed to 25 per cent for political training. The militia or regional forces were expanded and minimum age was lowered to fourteen.[97] Eventually the immediate crisis was defused, but China settled down for a long-term confrontation with its main enemy to the north. As a result, the PLA received a large increase in the defence budget of 1969 and 1970. By 1971, not only was it piecing a shattered society together, but it had become the shield of the nation in a true crisis. It had reached the pinnacle of its political influence.

THE FALL OF LIN BIAO

The redefinition of the main enemy as the Soviet Union had not sat well with Lin Biao. For him that honour still belonged to the United States although he was also willing to view the Soviets as a second enemy. Mao, on the other hand, was convinced of the need for a *rapprochement* with the United States as a balance against the Soviet Union. Lin's opposition in this matter and other domestic issues made it clear to Mao that not only was the political power of the PLA too great, but that under Lin's leadership it could no longer be controlled. Although the details are clouded, Lin apparently was plotting Mao's overthrow, but, believing his planned coup had been compromised, he fled by air on 12 September 1971, making for the Soviet Union. His aircraft crashed or was shot down in Mongolia. On his death, Mao purged the PLA of his supporters and firmly subordinated it to the reviving civil authorities he had done so much to destroy in the Great Cultural Revolution.

NORTH KOREA

In 1965 Kim Il Sung possessed a powerful conventional force in the Korean People's Army (KPA). Soviet aid had resumed in 1964. The KPA's leadership was experienced and professional and, unburdened by a commissar system, could exercise far more initiative. Years of intensive propaganda had inculcated a martial spirit in the population. More lavishly equipped with tanks and artillery than the South Koreans, the KPA was designed for a rapid knockout blow. There lay the rub. Richer and more prosperous, South Korea would have the advantage in a war of attrition. But a KPA *Blitzkrieg* would stumble over US air and naval power, not to mention the two US infantry divisions of I Corps. The national unity of the Republic of Korea had to be undermined to negate its advantages. As explained by Daniel Bolger: '... a well-orchestrated LIC [low-intensity conflict] effort might spark the insurgency necessary to divert US-ROK forces and give the edge to Kim Il Sung's conventional military units.'[98]

Kim's tool in this regard was his small but splendidly trained special operations forces, most of whom were subordinated to the Reconnaissance Bureau. KPA special operations troops were equally adept at infiltration, demolition, land navigation, small unit tactics and political agitation. In 1967 two special units were created, the 127th and 283th Army Units, about 1,000 strong each, and all hand-picked officers.

THE SECOND KOREAN CONFLICT, 1966–1969

Kim's campaign exploded during President Lyndon Johnson's 1966 visit to Seoul. On 2 November KPA infiltrators ambushed US and ROK patrols at opposite ends of the DMZ, killing eight Americans and two ROKs. In 1967 KPA attacks escalated, killing sixteen US and 100 ROKs as well as 75 civilians. The North Koreans quickly revealed themselves as masters of infiltration, able to seep through the DMZ almost at will. US forces were particularly inept as opponents, professionally hamstrung by the stripping of their units of experienced cadre for Vietnam and by the short one-year rotation period. ROK units were better because of their greater cohesion and longer periods of duty. KPA efforts, however, seemed unfocused. They killed ordinary soldiers but did little against sensitive targets, especially those that might alienate the Americans and South Koreans from each other. Nor did they have the strength to mount a serious LIC operation. In fact, the KPA campaign was pushing the ROK into many of the very nation-building efforts that would throttle an insurgency in its cradle. The UN Command was also building barrier systems along the DMZ and intensifying patrolling to make infiltration more difficult.

The creation of the two special army units that year heralded a more directed effort. The 124th Army Unit mounted two large special operations in 1968. The more audacious of these was assigned to a 31-man detachment to 'cut off the head of Park Chung Hee', in the presidential Palace, the Blue House. Slipping through the DMZ within 30 metres of a US outpost on 17 January, they entered the ROK and, adding insult to injury, made camp within a few kilometres of the US 2nd Infantry Divisional Headquarters. They were discovered by South Korean wood-cutters whom they quickly seized, harangued then released with warnings to say nothing. The woodcutters immediately notified the police who sent out a major alert. Even so, the KPA team was able to infiltrate Seoul, dressed as ROK troops, on 20 January. Eight hundred metres from the Blue Palace they were stopped by suspicious ROK police. A gun battle began and they fled. Eventually, 28 were killed, one was captured and two could not be found. Their skill as fighters was evident in the 68 dead and 66 wounded ROK soldiers and civilians left in their wake. President Park put the nation-building programme into high gear and organized an armed militia to which the populace flocked. He had been saved by the loyalty of four woodcutters. The message was not lost on him.

The 124th's next operation was the infiltration of a 120-man unit at eight locations on the east coast of South Korea on 30 October in the Ulchin-Samchok landings. They headed into the Taebaek Mountains to organize guerrillas in an area noted for its hostility to the ROK government, unaware of the fact that the ROK had been conducting aggressive nation-building efforts in that very region. The next day they occupied a few villages. To their confusion, they found only blank looks rather than the jubilant welcome they had expected. True to form as Communists, they promptly beat a man to death as an example, but the alarm had already been spread by many villagers. The ROK forces quickly mobilized 70,000 men and ran the North Koreans to ground within two weeks, killing 110 and capturing seven for a loss of 40 ROK soldiers, police and militia, and 23 civilians killed.

The Ulchin-Samchok landings marked the collapse of the KPA effort. An enraged Kim Il Sung purged a wide swathe of KPA officers who had participated in the effort to destabilize the South. But the blame really lay at Kim's own door. His generals had only been reacting to his demands for quick, sensational results and had insufficient forces to conduct an LIC. Kim seized upon the latter excuse to initiate a major reorganization of his special operations forces by creating an overall command, VII Special Purpose Corps, which had reached a strength of 15,000 by 1970. An expansion of airborne and amphibious forces followed in the early 1970s. By 1975 there were 20 special operations regiments and brigades. Kim Il Sung still hungered for his guerrilla war in the South as he built more and more cadres. It never dawned on him that four woodcutters in 1968 had invalidated it forever.

SOUTH KOREA

The first decade after the Korean War was a period of intensive growth for the ROK Army. The second decade was an extended combat graduation test. During that decade the army simultaneously sent a major expeditionary force to Vietnam and fought an intensive struggle at home against a determined North Korean special operations campaign. It passed both courses with flying colours.

A KOREAN EXPEDITIONARY FORCE, 1964–1973

As South Vietnam began to shudder under Vietcong attacks in 1964, the South Korean government offered the assistance of military medical teams and martial arts instructors in July. In December the South Koreans organized an engineer construction group to support the ARVN's pacification efforts. Nicknamed the Dove Unit, the Republic of Korea Military Assistance Group, Vietnam, numbering 2,416 men arrived between February and July of 1965 and immediately went to work building bridges, schools and medical dispensaries and treated 30,000 patients.

In May the ROK government at the request of the United States agreed to send a full division to South Vietnam. The only alternative, as the Americans suggested, would be to send one of the US divisions from South Korea. The ROK valued the continued strong American presence too much to balk. By the beginning of November the 18,212 men of the ROK Capital Division, also known as the Tiger Division, had deployed to South Vietnam, one of its three regiments having been replaced by the ROK Marine Corps 2 Blue Dragon Brigade. The Koreans were assigned the VC hotbed of Bin Dinh Province for their area of operations. In less than a year, they were joined by a second ROK division, the 9th or White Horse Division of 23,665 men, bringing the Korean expeditionary force to a strength of 47,872. After the United States, the ROK's was the largest foreign contingent to fight in support of the Republic of Vietnam.

The ROK Army's mission was largely one of security since the South Koreans generally lacked the air, artillery and re-supply assets to engage in the mobile big sweep operations the Americans were employing. Nevertheless they conducted a number of joint operations with the US Army. Their own aggressive nature also ensured that they would see their own fair share of the fighting. In one of the first joint operations along the Cambodian border in August 1966, an ROK company was ambushed by the NVA 101st Regiment and immediately formed a hasty perimeter. Outnumbered four to one, it fought off the attackers who left 182 dead around their position at the cost of three Koreans killed. In an ROK operation the following July and August, they battered the 95th NVA Regiment in Phu Yen Province, killing 638 North Vietnamese and losing fewer than 30. In January of the following year they destroyed another NVA unit, killing 278 for the loss of eleven Koreans. In November they destroyed an entire battalion of the 18th NVA Regiment, killing 382 of the enemy for practically no loss. The secret of ROK success was careful, almost excruciatingly careful, planning and great patience, and an orthodox by the book cordon and search technique. Their American mentors may have looked askance at the plodding nature of Korean operations, but they could not argue with its success. General Westmoreland considered them fully on a par with US divisions. The best judgement of all, was that of the enemy; a captured document stated that 'contact with the Koreans is to be avoided at all costs unless a victory is 100 per cent certain'.[99]

For the remainder of the war, the ROK Army was engaged in pacification, not the most happy mission for the naturally aggressive and straight-forward South

Korean troops. The ROKs were happy to drive the VC and NVA out of an area, but evinced little interest in the civil affairs aspects of pacification as was shown by their occasional penchant for brutal acts of reprisal against villages that supported Communist attacks on them.

The ROK expeditionary force stayed longer in South Vietnam than the US Army. At the end of 1972 there were still 36,760 ROK troops in country while the American contingent had shrunk to a mere 24,000. Unlike the US Army, the ROK Army had acquired great prestige at home by its record in South Vietnam. More than 300,000 ROK troops had rotated through combat to disseminate their experience throughout the army. The army suffered 4,407 killed and nearly 10,000 wounded, a sacrifice that was proportionally almost as great as that of the US Army.

THE SECOND KOREAN CONFLICT, 1966–1969

No sooner had the second ROK division been dispatched to South Vietnam, than North Korea's dictator, Kim Il Sung, unleashed what has been called the Second Korean Conflict. Unlike his conventional invasion of 1950, Kim sought to start a revolution in the South through a special operations campaign while the Americans were pre-occupied elsewhere and while a large part of the ROK Army was deployed out of the country.

The first KPA raids struck both American and ROK patrols in the DMZ on the very day that President Johnson was visiting Seoul. Initially the Korean Government seemed eager for the United Nations Commander, LTG Bonesteel, to direct all counter-measures to the KPA campaign, even those in the interior of the country. But, while offering ideas and resources, Bonesteel emphasized UN responsibility for the DMZ and the ROK's sovereign responsibility for interior security. At first South Korean responses to KPA special operations had been on an *ad hoc* basis, among the army, police and KCIA; whoever was nearest would take action. Over time this proved inadequate to deal with the well-trained infiltrators of the KPA. In late 1967 President Park brought some order to the ROK's response by issuing ROK Presidential Instruction No 18 which established a national co-ordinating council, determined clear chains of command for all types of incident, created eight (later ten) ROK Army counter-insurgency battalions, and expanded the Combat Police. Intensive ROK Army and American patrols and other barriers in the DMZ slowed down the rate of KPA infiltration and engaged in numerous small ambushes and firefights. Fearing the riots that had toppled a previous government, he hesitated to create the next logical element of the plan, an armed militia.

Park's attitude changed in late January 1968. A 31-man detachment of KPA commandos who had been detailed to 'cut off the head of Park Chun Hee', got to within 800 metres of the Presidential Palace, the Blue House, before they were discovered. Within weeks he had approved the creation of a people's militia, the Homeland Defence Reserve Force (HDRF), and at a stroke, had cut the Gordian Knot. It was a widely popular move. Within six months, two million South Koreans had volunteered and were organized into 60,000 platoons and companies around a corps of ROK Army veterans. He next organized a series of new 'Reconstruction Villages' just south of the DMZ, peopled by intensely anti-Communist ROK veterans and their families. The villages functioned just like the Israeli *kibbutzim* as barriers to infiltration. The ROK Army then launched an intensive civic action programme in the countryside and especially in the backward villages of the mountain ranges that were prime KPA infiltration routes. Their efforts were quickly successful in building trust between the people and the army, and instilling a flinty anti-Communist spirit and a new-found sense of ROK patriotism.[100]

The test for the ROK came in October when 120 men of an élite KPA special operations unit landed on the east coast of South Korea and headed into the mountains to create guerrilla bases – as it turned out, among the very villages that had benefited greatly from ROK Army civic action. The populace reported their presence and soon 70,000 troops had mounted a counter-operation; 110 of the KPA infiltrators were killed and seven captured.

In 1969 the ROK Army created two tough Ranger brigades of ten battalions to prowl the mountain infiltration routes while forces along the DMZ and along the coasts constricted KPA infiltration even more. Most importantly, the ROK Army redoubled its civic action programmes. Infiltration fell off dramatically. That year Kim Il Sung threw in the towel, and purgd numerous senior officers involved in the campaign. He had created the very unified ROK people and government he had hoped to strangle in its cradle. The effort had cost the ROK 299 dead and 550 wounded, but 397 KPA troops had been killed, twelve captured and 33 had been persuaded to desert. Another 2,462 agents and collaborators were arrested thanks to the enthusiastic work of the militia.

The ROK had won the Second Korean Conflict in a patient and subtle effort that few armies could emulate. At the same time, the ROK Army expeditionary force in Vietnam was giving a splendid performance that won the praise of allies and enemies alike. The ROK Army had come of age.

JAPAN

During its first full decade (1955–65), the Japanese Ground Self-Defence Force (GSDF) had been organized, trained and equipped. In its second the GSDF found its greatest problem to be the recruitment and retention of manpower. Japan's lingering Second World War hangover kept the profession of arms a low prestige occupation. The economic expansion of Japan also put the military in direct competition for manpower, a contest the SDF invariably lost. Periods of greatest economic growth were also those of poorest SDF recruitment.

Although Japan went to greater lengths than Germany in ensuring that its new army had no continuity with its Second World War predecessor, recruitment in Japan as in Germany continued to come disproportionately from those districts with old martial traditions. A 1973 study on recruitment into the GSDF showed that the Islands of Kyushu and Hokkaido were heavily over-represented. For example Kyushu, with about 10 per cent of Japan's population, provided 25 per cent of the cadets at the Defence Academy.

Table 3-16. Origins of Members of the SDF, 1973

Prefecture	Officers	Warrant Officers	Enlisted	Totals	% SDF	% Pop
Kyushu						
Kagoshima	2,101	143	11,555	13,799	6.0	2.0
Kuamomoto	1,919	103	11,095	13,117	5.6	2.0
Hokkaido	1,724	220	18,884	20,878	9.0	5.3
Honshu						
Tokyo	2,469	68	4,194	6,731	3.0	12.0
Osaka	503	26	2,003	2,352	1.0	8.0

Source: Buck, ed., *The Modern Japanese Military System*, 1975, pp. 72–75.

Kyushu's martial traditions go back many centuries. SDF recruiters are welcomed in high schools unlike most of the rest of Japan where they are strictly excluded. Hokkaido's history, on the other hand, is short, it having been colonized only after Perry opened Japan. Hokkaido, though, does have the reputation of being Japan's frontier, and its population being of a more independent character. Both Kyushu and Hokkaido are rural communities, the traditional seed-bed of soldiers.

Despite the martial traditions of a few prefectures, recruitment into the GSDF became increasingly difficult in this decade, the GSDF, unlike the other services, rarely reaching 90 per cent of its authorized strength (falling as low as 78 per cent in 1970). In fact by the end of the decade, 90 per cent of recruits were 'persuaded' rather than 'pure' volunteers who overtly sought to join.

The Japanese government was not overly concerned with filling its military vacancies. It preferred to put its money into modern, high-tech equipment and facilities that would economize on manpower. But in this the Maritime and Air Self-Defence Forces continued to receive priority.

AUSTRALIA

The third decade of the post-war period was one of almost continuous military operations for the Australian Regular Army (ARA). It would draw heavily on its counter-insurgency experiences in Malaya and add new honours to Australian arms.

THE CONFRONTATION, 1965-1967

In an attempt to wrest control of Malaysia's territories in Northern Borneo, the Indonesian Army initiated a campaign of small-unit incursions into those areas in 1964. Australia provided one infantry battalion and elements of its exceptional Special Air Service (SAS) Regiment in January 1965 to the Commonwealth force deployed to counter the Indonesians in what became known as the 'Confrontation'. The Australians were very much at home in this campaign of small units stalking one another in the jungle. As in Malaya, it was a ceaseless routine of patrolling and ambushing against a persistent foe who rarely appeared in formations larger than a platoon. The ARA repaid the Indonesians in their own coin by mounting secret cross-border operations, code-named 'Claret'. Confrontation subsided in late 1965 when Indonesia was shaken by the attempted Communist coup and its army became preoccupied with internal security. ARA losses were light: seven KIA and six WIA, ten dead and fourteen injured in non-combatant accidents. If Malaya had been a long schooling in counter-insurgency warfare for the ARA, Confrontation was the final examination.

VIETNAM, 1965-1972

The ARA's involvement in Vietnam began in July 1962 when the Australian Army Training Team Vietnam (AATTV) of 30 junior officers and NCOs was dispatched to assist the Army of the Republic of Vietnam (ARVN). Operating under the US advisory system, the AATTV grew to 80 men by 1964 and began to accompany ARVN units on operations.

In 1965 the Australian government agreed to send an infantry battalion at the urgent request of the South Vietnamese government engineered and heavily endorsed by the United States. The timing was fortuitous. Conscription was permitting the rapid expansion of the ARA. By 1967 there would be nine infantry battalions in the army.

In June 1965, 1RAR and support units arrived in South Vietnam and were brigaded with the US Army's 173 Airborne Brigade (Separate) in Bien Hoa. The Americans provided all support except for items of specific Australian issue such as weapons and uniforms. The arrangement proved to be awkward. The Australians' experience with small-unit jungle warfare in Malaya and North Borneo had taught them the value of constant and intensive patrolling and the art and utility of the ambush. However effective, it was a patient, professional and altogether too indirect and unglamorous approach for the US Army whose training was for the conventional battlefield and whose taste was for the direct approach and the application of overwhelming firepower. Adding to the difficulties of the Australians was the scandal of their equipment issue. An overly officious Australian supply system had issued them with Second World War boots that fell apart in a few days, worn out radios, and 20-year-old obsolete automatic weapons. These experiences convinced them that their force needed to be separate and self-supporting. In March 1966 two new battalions (5 and 6RAR) and a support group (now named 1st Australian Task Force – 1ATF) relieved 1RAR and was deployed to Phuoc Tuy, a coastal province that could be easily supplied and a self-contained geographic unit with which the Australians could be identified. The deployment of the 1st Australian Logistic Support Group was a historic achievement for the ARA. '... for the first time in its military history Australia was forced not merely to field an expeditionary force but largely to supply and maintain it also.'[101]

The operational history of 1ATF can be divided into three periods. The first, from mid-1966 to December 1967, witnessed the Australians' major action of the war. Initially 5RAR and 173 Airborne Brigade saw heavy fighting in May and June 1966 in clearing the Nui Dat area before 1ATF could move into its base camp. Once settled, the PAVN sent a welcome to the neighbourhood in the form of a mortar attack in which 23 Australians were wounded. The TF commander, Brigadier G.D. Jackson, dispatched 'D' Company, 6RAR as a thankyou note to hunt down the mor-

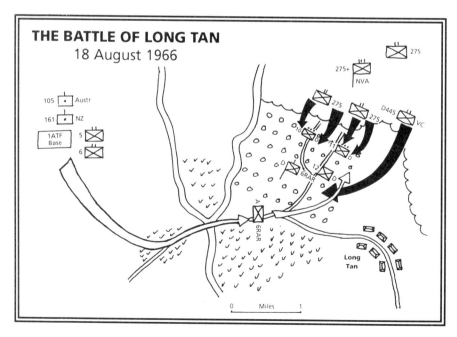

THE BATTLE OF LONG TAN
18 August 1966

tar teams near the village of Long Tan, four miles from Nui Dat. 'D' Company's 108 men were commanded by Major Harry Smith, a veteran of Malaya. Smith deployed two platoons up, on a 400-metre front, with one platoon back as the company moved through a rubber plantation near Long Tan. Coming towards them and unaware of their presence were three battalions of the PAVN 275th Regiment and the VC D445 Battalion, some 2,500 men on an approach march to assault 1ATF's new base camp. A classic but lopsided engagement exploded as the first Australian platoon reached the edge of the plantation. The PAVN immediately attacked but met a well-directed return fire. Manoeuvring for an envelopment, they ran into the second platoon. The fighting now rippled and flared along 'D' Company's entire front as the PAVN commander sent wave after wave of his infantry against the Australians. 'D' Company's forward observer, Captain Maury Stanley, called in fire from 1ATF's two Australian and New Zealand artillery batteries. A consummate artilleryman, Stanley directed his fire with precision to strike and sear each PAVN attack.

Despite the artillery, numbers began to count. The lead Australian platoon finally had to exfiltrate its survivors back to a consolidated company strongpoint in the rear. The entire company was now fully committed and fighting for its life. At this point the NVA commander was convinced that he had located the extent of his enemy's position and sent the D445 Battalion to get round the Australians' right flank and take them in rear. Simultaneously, Brigadier Jackson sent 'A' Company, 6 RAR , to the rescue, mounted on M113 APCs. They arrived just in time to attack directly through the advancing D445 Battalion. It was the second encounter of the battle as 'A' Company, firing from their APCs, sliced through the black pyjama-clad VC formations. 'A' Company may have been infantry, but this day they were cavalry, albeit makeshift, as they cut through the VC and then turned round to ride through their ranks again and again. The VC were as broken as any infantry ever ridden down by curassiers. As night fell 'A' Company laagered around the survivors of 'D' Company. The next morning they found the enemy gone, having left 245 dead on the field. Many more dead were found on a sweep of the area. Wounded were estimated at 500. Australian losses were sixteen killed and 21 wounded from 'D' Company, a ratio of 20 to 1. The Australian victory decided the nature of their fighting for the remainder of the war. In the short term, the battle mangled a reinforced NVA regiment and saved 1ATF's base camp from a surprise assault. In the long run, the deadly reputation earned by the Australians that day persuaded the NVA to avoid them like the plague.[102]

In the second phase of Australian operations (January 1968 to mid-1969), a third battalion was added to 1 ATF, bringing its strength to 8,300. This phase was one of intense patrolling and ambushing, route clearance, search and destroy operations, village cordon and search, and civic action. Several large engagements were fought, the most serious being during the Tet Offensive when the PAVN overran part of a battalion defensive position, losing 76 KIA to the Australians' 23. The third phase lasted until December 1971 when the last of 1ATF was withdrawn. Although the Australians had driven VC main force and PAVN units out of Phuoc Tuy and pacified it by day, a hardcore cadre remained to contest the night.

As with their American cousins, Australia's Vietnam veterans came home to shabby treatment at the hands of the general public and the newly elected Labour Government whose platform had opposed the war. Of the 46,000 Australian soldiers who served in Vietnam, 3,504 had become casualties. Only in 1988 did Australia, in an act of national catharsis, hold its Vietnam veterans' parade.

Table 3-17. Australian Army Losses in Vietnam 1962–1972

	To April 1966	ARA	NS	CMF	Total
KIA, died of wounds	28	200	184	1	413
MIA, presumed dead	1		1		2
Non-combatant deaths	7	42	15		64
WIA 154	986	880	6	2,026	
Other	30	567	399	3	999
Totals	220	1,795	1,479	10	3,504

Source: Central Army Records Office, and Australian Archives A1945, file 48/I/I as presented in Grey, *A Military History of Australia*, 1990, p. 238.

The new government abolished conscription in 1972 and abandoned the forward defence policy which had committed troops to the anti-Communist struggles in South-east Asia. By 1974 forces had been reduced to a level that would hold steady until the end of the Cold War.

Table 3-18. Australian Army 1972–1990

	1972	1974	1990
Tank Regiment	1	1	1
Cavalry Regiment	3	1	1
Infantry Battalions	9	6	4
Mechanized Infantry Bn	0	0	1
Parachute Battalion	0	0	1
Special Air Service (SAS)	1	1	1
Medium Artillery Regiment	1	1	1
Field Artillery Regiment	3	2	3
AA Artillery Regiment	1	1	1
Aviation Regiment	1	1	$1^{1/3}$
Troop Strength	47,760	31,185	31,300

Source: IISS *The Military Balance 1972–3, 1974–5* and *1989–90*

Conditions of service declined; the government's priority was to reduce defence expenditures, not increase them. Traditional Australian disdain for peacetime service further reduced the attractiveness of military life. This disdain is a strange contradiction in a people who define themselves as a nation by their glories in wartime. Despite these problems and the perennial shortage of modern equipment, the warrior's spark burned bright enough for Australia to maintain, man for man, one of the most professional, well-trained and best-led armies in the world.

THE ART OF STRATEGY

This third decade of the post-war era demonstrated some of the most telling examples of the mismatch between the military means and policy. The greatest by far was the U.S. Army's disastrous experience in Indochina. Here both means and policy were at loggerheads. Policy was unclear and indecisive in the hands of Lyndon Johnson, arguably the worst war Leader in American history who effectively destroyed public support by his inability to articulate a clear national interest. The army's own approach to the war was also fundamentally flawed by its inability to decide which kind of war it wanted to fight, the thunderous war of the big battalions or the patient war of counterinsurgency. It conducted the former, along the well-worn path of its own hitherto successful martial traditions. The failure shook the institution to its core.

The Americans recoiled from Vietnam defeated by a flexible and tenacious interaction between North Vietnamese policy and military means. So effective was this union that it was able to survive a number of grave operational misjudgments such as the 1968 Tet Offensive and the 1972 Easter Offensive.

The near defeat of Israel in 1973 was another great example of a sudden failure of strategy. Success in 1956 and 1967 and in the War of Attrition had bred in the Israelis a supreme and increasingly uncritical assumption of the innate superiority in both the Israeli fighting man and the tank and airplane combination. Infecting policy, this attitude further assumed that the Egyptians and Syrians would learn nothing from their defeats and thereby were not serious threats. But they were indeed. Defeat concentrates the military mind wonderfully. The Arabs, particularly the Egyptians, under this goad fashioned a strategy that was a close join between military means and policy: cross the Suez Canal and hold it. To this policy end the Egyptian army prepared itself, carefully and objectively applying its resources to this clear and attainable mission. The correctness of this approach was validated in the first week of the 1973 War when the goals of policy were resoundingly accomplished. Then overweening political influence forced the army to go beyond its military means with a major offensive operation. By this time the Israelis had recovered from their initial drubbing. Imminent defeat had concentrated Israeli minds as well, in record time to revise the application of military means to the needs of the battlefield. However, even subsequent Israeli tactical and operational battlefield successes could not repair the initial strategic failure. Events ensured that the soundness of Egyptian strategy would prevail. In the end it was Israel that abandoned the Sinai.

NOTES

1   Andrew F. Krepinevich, Jr. *The Army and Vietnam*. (Baltimore: The John Hopkins Press, 1986), p. 5.

2   George C. Herring, 'The 1st Cavalry and the Ia Drang Valley 18 October – 24 November 1965,' in Charles E. Heller and William A. Stofft, eds., *America's First Battles, 1776–1965* (Lawrence: The University of Kansas Press, 1986), p. 319.

3   Krepinevich, op.cit., p. 188.

4   Selby L. Stanton, *The Rise and Fall of an American Army: US Ground Forces in Vietnam, 1965–1967* (Novato, CA: Presidio Press, 1985), p. 164.

5   Bruce Palmer, Jr., *The 25-Year War: America's Military Role in Vietnam* (New York: Simon & Shuster, 1984), pp. 156–7.

6   Manuscript, by CPT William W. Witt and CPT William W. Hansen, 'RIF in the Rubber,' provided to the author in 1970 by CPT Hansen at the ROTC, University of Utah.

7   As this book is being written, the United States has electied to the presidency one such antiwar activist. It will be interesting to see how the mantle of commander-in-chief is worn by one who boasted of his hatred and loathing of the very military he will presume to send in harm's way.

8   H. Norman Schwarzkopf with Peter Petre, *It Doesn't Take a Hero* (New York: Bantam Books, 1992), p. 178.

9   Geoffrey Blaxland, *The Regiments Depart: A History of the British Army 1945–1970* (London: William Kimber, 1971).

10 David Griffin, *Encyclopedia of Modern British Regiments* (Wellingborough: Patrick Stephens, 1985), p. 186. Also on 14 May 1968, The 1st York and Lancaster Regiment paraded for the last time.

11 Blaxland, op.cit., pp. 470–74.

12 Blaxland, op.cit., p. 476. The Roman legionnaire's devotion to his eagles might come close.

13 Barnett, op.cit., p. 493.

14 Gander (3rd ed.), op.cit., pp. 93–4; Blaxland, op.cit., pp. 477–8.

15 Terry Gander, op.cit., p. 82.

16 Gander (3rd ed.), op.cit.; Richard A. Gabriel, *Fighting Armies: NATO and the Warsaw Pact, A Combat Assessment* (Westport, CT: Greenwood Press, 1983), p. 67.

17 Charles Messenger, *History of the British Army*, (Novato, CA: Presidio Press, 1986), pp. 212–3.

18 Tony Geraghty, *This is the SAS: A Pictorial History of the Special Air Service Regiment* (London: Arms & Armour Press, 1982; New York: Arco Publishing Inc., 1982), pp. 68–74.

19   Otto von Pivka, *The Armies of Europe To-Day* (London: Osprey, 1974), pp. 63–4; *The Military Balance 1974–1975* (London: International Institute for Strategic Studies, 1974), pp. 18–19; Gander (2nd ed.), op.cit., p. 18; Blaxland, op.cit., p. 341.

20   *The Military Balance*, ibid.; Gander (3rd ed.), ibid., pp. 164–86.

21   Otto von Pivka, *The Armies of Europe To-Day* (London: Osprey Publishing, 1974), pp. 169–70.

22   Jonathan M. House, *Combined Arms Warfare: Survey of 20th-Century Tactics, Doctrine, and Organization* (Fort Leavenworth, KS: U.S. Army Command and General Staff College, 1985), pp. 170–1.

23   *The Military Balance 1973–1974* (London: The International Institute for Strategic Studies, 1974).

24   Michel L. Martin, *Warriors to Managers: The French Military Establishment Since 1945* (Chapel Hill: The University of North Carolina Press, 1981), pp. 244–5.

25   Martin, op.cit.., pp. 290–7.

26   Ibid, p. 233.

27   Phillip A. Karber and John H. Milam, 'The Federal Republic of Germany,' ed., Jeffrey Simon, *NATO – Warsaw Pact Force Mobilization* (Washington, DC: The National Defense University Press, 1988), p. 252.

28   Ibid., pp. 252–3.

29   *The Military Balance 1975–1976* (London: The International Institute for Strategic Studies, 1975), pp. 20–23.

30   Charles Douglas-Home, 'Complex Rules Impede German Forces', *The Times*, London, July 14, 1969; cited in Walter Henry Nelson, *Germany Rearmed* (New York: Simon and Schuster, 1972), pp. 172–3.

31   Nelson, ibid., p. 170.

32   Donald Abenheim, *Reforging the Iron Cross: The Search for Tradition in the West German Armed Forces* (Princeton: Princeton University Press, 1987), pp. 249–250.

33   Ibid., pp. 253–4.

34   Nelson, op.cit., pp. 72–4.

35   Dale R. Herspring, 'Detente and the Military,' in Lyman H. Leytes, ed., *The German Democratic Republic* (Boulder, CO: Westview Press, 1978), p. 204; cited in William C. Martel, 'East Germany' in Richard Gabriel, ed., *Fighting Armies – NATO and the Warsaw Pact: A Combat Assessment* (Westport, CT: Greenwood Press, 1983), p. 207.

36   Martel, ibid., p. 208–9.

37   Nelson, op.cit., p. 286.

38   Les Griggs, 'The Polish People's Army,' in Jeffery Simon, ed., *NATO – Warsaw Pact Force Mobilization* (Washington, DC: The National Defense University Press, 1988), p. 363.

39   A. Ross Johnson, Robert W. Dean, and Alexander Alexiev, *East European Military Establishments: The Warsaw Pact Northern Tier* (New York: Crane Russak, 1982), pp. 50–51.

40   Griggs, op.cit., p. 364.

41   Johnson, et. al., op.cit.

42   Johnson, et. al., op.cit., pp. 48–9.

43   John Erickson, Lynn Hansen, and William Schneider, *Soviet Ground Forces: An Operational Assessment* (Boulder, CO: Westview Press, 1986), p. 30.

44   Ibid.

45   K. Andrukhov and V. Bulatnikov, *Military Thought*, July 1966; cited by Mark Urban, 'The Strategic Role of Soviet Airborne Troops,' *Jane's Military Review 1985*, ed., Ian V. Hogg (London: Jane's, 1985), p. 139.

46   Urban, ibid., pp. 138–40.

47   Christopher F. Foss, *Jane's AFV Recognition Handbook* (London: Jane's Publishing Co., 1987), pp. 66, 68, 109, 284, 287, 326, 370, 371, 398, 400, 423, 441, 443, 458, 460.

48   David Eshel, 'Soviet Tanks: An Israeli View,' *Armor*, May–June 1988, p. 75.

49   Ibid., pp. 16–17; *Tips for Tankers: Defeating Soviet Armor*, TC-17-12-1, Washington, DC: US Government Printing Office, 30 May 1973, p. 15.

50   Harriet Fast Scott and William F. Scott, *The Armed Forces of the USSR*, 2nd ed. (Boulder, CO: Westview Press, 1979), pp. 303–6.

51   V. D. Sokolovskiy, *Soviet Military Strategy*, 3rd ed., Harriet Fast Scott, ed. (New York: Crane, Russak & CO., 1975), pp. 309, 406.

52   Peter G. Tsouras, 'Where the War Toys Are Real,' *How They Fight*, US Army Intelligence and Threat Analysis Center, April–June 1988, pp. 23–4.

53   Ibid., pp. 25–6.

54   Alex P. Schmid, *Soviet Military Interventions Since 1945* (New Brunswick (USA): Transaction Books, 1985), pp. 31–2.

55   Ibid., pp. 36–7.

56   Ibid., pp. 36–7; and IISS, *The Military Balance 1975–76* (London: IISS, 1975), p. 9.

57   N. Safran, *From War to War*; cited in Edward Luttwak and Dan Horowitz, *The Israeli Army* (New York: Harper & Row Publishers, 1975), p. 217.

58   Leo Heiman, 'War in the Middle East: An Israeli View,' *Military Review*, September 1967, p. 62.

59   W. Byford-Jones, *The Lightning War* (New York: The Bobbs-Merrill Co., Inc., 1967), p. 52. Legend tells of a survivor of Thermopolae, shunned by everyone, who threw away his life by leaping into the Persian ranks at Platea in order to recover his pride. Alexander's army knew no more dreaded punishment than that meted out by the king himself to an unprepared soldier pushed out of the ranks

before a battle as unworthy of his army.
60   Heiman, op.cit., pp. 64–5.
61   Marshal, 'The Army of Israel,' *Military Review*, April 1968, pp. 6–7.
62   Heiman, op.cit., pp. 62–3.
63   Marshall, op.cit., p. 9.
64   Luttwak and Horowitz, op.cit., pp. 321, 327.
65   Steven J. Zaloga, *Israeli Tanks and Combat Vehicles* (London: Arms and Armour Press, 1983), pp. 55–60; Luttwak and Horowitz, op.cit., pp. 329–330.
66   Luttwak and Horowitz, op.cit., pp. 334–5.
67   Chaim Herzog, *The War of Atonement* (Boston: Little, Brown and Co., 1975), pp. 270–1.
68   Avraham (Bren) Adan, *On the Banks of the Suez* (Novato, CA: Presidio Press, 1980) pp. 13–14.
69   US Army Command and General Staff College, *Selected Readings in Tactics: The 1973 Middle East War*, RB 100–2, Vol I (Fort Leavenworth, KS: USACGSC, 1980), p. 5–21.
70   Herzog, op.cit., p. 145; Luttwak, op.cit., p.392.
71   USACGSC, op.cit., p. 4–11.
72   Herzog, op.cit., p. 206.
73   A Japanese research station had been located in the area, and the Israeli soldiers had mistaken Japanese for Chinese inscriptions.
74   John Laffin, *Arab Armies of the Middle East Wars 1948–1973*, (London: Osprey Publishing, 1987).
75   Saad El Shazly, *The Crossing of the Suez*, San Francisco: American Mideast Research, 1980, p. 22.
76   Ibid., p. 25.
77   Ibid., p. 45.
78   John Keegan, *World Armies*, 2nd ed., (Detroit: Gale Research Company, 1983), p. 167.
79   Samuel M. Katz, *Arab Armies of the Middle East Wars (2)*, (London: Osprey Publishing, 1988), p. 14.
80   Thomas Collelo, ed., *Syria: A Country Study*, Washington, DC: Federal Research Division, Library of Congress, 1988, p. 242; Chaim Herzog, *The War of Atonement*, (Boston: Little, Brown, and Co., 1975), p. 145. The number of tanks cited is the number recovered by the Israelis from the battlefield.
81   V. Longer, *From Red Coats to Olive Green, A History of the Indian Army, 1660–1974* (Bombay: Allied Publishers, 1974), p. 500.
82   Edgar O'Ballance, 'The India-Pakistan Campaign, 1965' *RUSI*, November 1966, p. 334.
83   V. Longer, op.cit, pp. 500–1.
84   Phillip B. Davidson, *Vietnam at War: The History 1946–1975* (Novato: Presidio Press, 1988), p. 604.
85   Ibid., pp. 650–54.
86   Stephen T. Hosmer, et al, *The Fall of South Vietnam* (New York: Crane, Russak and Co., 1980), p. 127.
87   Ibid., p. 132.
88   Davidson, op.cit., p. 774.
89   H. Norman Schwarzkopf, *It Doesn't Take a Hero* (New York: Bantam Books, 1992), p. 181.
90   Hung P. Nguyen, 'Communist Offensive Strategy and the Defense of South Vietnam,' *Parameters*, Winter 1984, pp. 10–11.
91   Timothy J. Lomperis, 'Giap's Dream, Westmoreland's Nightmare', *Parameters*, June 1988, p. 24.
92   Stephen T. Hosmer, et al, *The Fall of South Vietnam* (New York: Crane, Russak and Co., 1980), p. 135.
93   Morton H. Halperin and John Wilson Lewis, 'Communist China: Army-Party Relations,' *Military Review*, February 1967, p. 77.
94   Robert S. Elegant and Sidney C. Liu, 'Red China's Divided Army,' *Military Review*, November 1967, pp. 33–34.
95   Harlan W. Jencks, *From Muskets to Missiles: Politics and Professionalism in the Chinese Army 1945–1981* (Boulder: Westview Press, 1982), pp. 94–100.
96   Ibid., p. 104.
97   Gerard H. Corr, *The Chinese Red Army* (New York: Shocken Books, 1974), pp. 127–8.
98   Daniel P. Bolger, *Scences from an Unfinished War: Low-Intensity Conflict in Korea, 1966–1969* (Fort Leavenworth: Combat Studies Institute, 1991), p. 15.
99   Dale Andrade, 'Tigers, Blue Dragons and White Horses', *Vietnam*, Leesburg, VA, December 1989, pp. 52–3.
100 Daniel P. Bolger, *Scenes from an Unfinished War: Low-Intensity Conflict in Korea, 1966–1969* (Fort Leavenworth: Combat Studies Institute, 1991), p. 83.
101 Jeffrey Grey, *A Military History of Australia* (Cambridge: Cambridge University Press, 1990), p. 234.
102 Grey, ibid., pp. 234–5; Lex McAulay, 'Long Tan Battle Royal,' *Vietnam*, October 1992, pp. 39–45.

CHAPTER 4

THE FOURTH POST-WAR DECADE
1975–1985

INTRODUCTION

This was the second of the two great central killing decades of the post-war era. In ghastly symmetry, three costly and interminable wars began in 1979 and 1980 and ground on grimly into the final period to end in 1988 and 1989: The Vietnamese invasion of Cambodia, the Soviet invasion of Afghanistan, and the Iraqi attack on Iran. The Vietnamese conquest of Cambodia actually spawned another but short war with China in 1979. The Soviets must have looked jealously on the two short, tidy and victorious campaigns waged by their enemies – The British in the Falklands (1982) and the Americans in Grenada (1983). The Israeli Defence Force (IDF) certainly intended its invasion of Lebanon (1982) to be short, tidy and successful and got exactly the opposite.

The worlds' armies continued to increase in size, sophistication and weapons inventories. The armies of Iraq, India, North Vietnam and North Korea elbowed their way at least into the anteroom of the clubhouse of the great armies. In size, and size of tank fleets, for example, all four outnumbered the British and French Armies which struggled to maintain themselves on budgetary starvation diets. The US Army, on a much more generous diet, began its own great Post-Vietnam reform that would overhaul it thoroughly and create the splendid fighting force that would make Desert Storm in the next decade look so easy.

UNITED STATES

Defeat is the best teacher of armies, and in this decade the US Army would be a rapt pupil. Vietnam had been a strange defeat with no surrendered swords and colours and no great battlefield defeats. Yet the army had come close to suffering a systemic collapse in its inability to bring off its image of victory. Most tragically it had lost faith in itself and saw at best an indifference in the rest of the nation. Worst of all was the clear perception that the army's most serious wounds had been self-inflicted.

Recognizing this, the army began a long process of renewal that would change just about every way things were done. The most serious problem was making the All-Volunteer army work. However, for the first half of this period the army was in the position of making bricks without straw. Congress and the Administration had gladly promised to increase pay and benefits to attract quality volunteers when the draft was abolished, but did little. By late 1979, 32 per cent of the enlisted personnel were drawing less than the federal minimum wage. The number of personnel applying for food stamps became a scandal. Although economic recession in the Carter years improved enlistment, it did little to retain the best soldiers especially in the senior NCO grades. The situation only improved with the generous pay rises initiated by the Reagan Adminstration in the early 1980s.

A more serious problem was the moral issue of what standards would be maintained. Since the late sixties, drugs and other disciplinary problems had been rampant. While the end of the draft certainly bled off some of the pressure, these problems frustrated efforts to re-establish unit cohesion and high professional standards. There was a tendency to tolerate trouble-makers and sub-standard performers simply because recruitment and retention were such problems. This was getting the army nowhere. Finally, in the late 1970s, firm action was taken with a relentless zero drug tolerance programme monitored by strict urinalysis and an expedited discharge programme. The effects were quickly positive. The drug culture was eventually driven out of barracks, and the more positive environment fostered good soldiering.

The officer corps also saw its reforms. The huge reductions in force (RIFs) as Vietnam wound down, had winnowed out many incompetent officers. Unfortunately the archaic division of the officer corps into Regular US Army and Reserve Army of the United States (AUS) halves had resulted in only the AUS half being winnowed. Eventually, the unthinkable came to pass when the Regular half underwent its first RIF in the late 1970s. By this time Congress had taken a hand by introducing the Defense Officer Personnel Management Act (DOPMA) which eliminated the division of the officer corps and integrated all officers in the Regular Army by the tenth year of service if not earlier.

As the personnel side of the house was being cleaned up, the training side was also undergoing major changes. The Training and Doctrine Command (TRADOC) had developed and implemented a comprehensive concept of training to uniform standards and training to overcome weaknesses. For the first time, the achieving of training standards was directly tied to promotion. At the higher levels planning, TRADOC was wrestling with the re-emphasis of Europe as the major future battlefield. It would have been easy for the army to have slipped back into the attrition model of the Army Concept. At least the European battlefield was a conventional one. But it was hard to miss the obvious equation that attrition did not work with an enemy whose equipment and military art were at least equal to one's own and who had a great numerical advantage to boot. The conclusion stated in the 1976 edition of Field Manual 100-5 *Operations* was revolutionary though necessary: in the next major war, 'The US Army must prepare its units to fight outnumbered and to win.' This edition emphasized that an 'active defense could exploit the lethality of modern weaponry to destroy a major portion of the enemy's armed forces before the transition to an American offensive should occur'. Such an active defence is in itself an attrition model but without the profligate use of material and personnel. It was attrition based on skill. The 1982 edition was an even bolder step forward by its emphasis on manoeuvre 'as the indispensable foundation for any successful combat by inferior against superior numbers', which would 'unhinge the enemy's psychological and physical balance and thereby permit possession of the initiative to shift'.[1] This emphasis clearly was a reflection of the new intellectual vigour of the officer corps triggered by a more creative and thoughtful military education system and an institution eager for new solutions. Clearly the planners were reading the classic texts of their profession – Sun Tzu, Liddell Hart, Clausewitz, *et al.*

AirLand Battle Doctrine

The army was on a roll and quickly moved beyond even the 1982 FM 100-5 by developing jointly with the air force the AirLand Battle Concept which eventually became doctrine in the 1986 FM 100-5. AirLand Battle doctrine put the best of the army's post-Vietnam thinking about the nature of war, operational art, leadership and integration of technology into a coherent synthesis.

AirLand Battle describes the army's approach to generating and applying combat power at the operational and tactical level. It is based on securing or retaining the initiative and exercising it aggressively to accomplish the mission ... Success on the battlefield will depend on the army's ability to fight in accordance with four basic tenets: *initiative, agility, depth* and *synchronization* ... The ten imperatives of AirLand Battle are:

1 Ensure unity of effort.
2 Concentrate events on the battlefield.
3 Concentrate combat power against enemy vulnerabilities.
4 Designate, sustain and shift the main effort.
5 Press the fight.
6 Move fast, strike hard and finish rapidly.
7 Use terrain, weather, deception and OPSEC.
8 Conserve strength for decisive action.
9 Combine arms and sister services to complement and reinforce.
10 Understand the effects of battle on soldiers, units and leaders.[2]

AirLand Battle caused particular concern within the Soviet Army by its emphasis on the integration of intelligence and reconnaissance means to conduct deep operations aimed specifically at disrupting the careful commitment of its operational and strategic echelons. It was an effective counter to Warsaw Pact mass. The new doctrine sought to destroy first the strategy of that mass, a lesson as old as Sun Tzu.

THE NATIONAL TRAINING CENTER (NTC)

A sophisticated doctrine is not automatically translated into tactically and operationally efficient fighting formations. Equally sophisticated training is called for. The army developed exactly such a mechanism in the National Training Center (NTC) at Fort Irwin, California, in the late 1970s and early 1980s. The concept was based on the creation of large professional opposing forces (OPFOR) units that would employ the doctrine of the anticipated enemy. In a startling innovation, the army configured an armoured and a mechanized infantry battalion into the 32nd Guards Motorized Rifle Regiment, an accurate replica of a Soviet unit. A large quantity of Soviet equipment was provided by anonymous donors, some vehicles still bearing the traces of battle damage.[3] Unfortunately the donors could not provide the large numbers of T-72 tanks necessary, and an efficient makeshift was found by plastic visual modifications (VISMOD) to US M551 Sheridan light tanks.

The army fielded one more innovation that amounted to a training revolution that kept the NTC from being just a glorified 'Bang! Bang! You're dead!' exercise. This was the multiple integrated laser engagement system (MILES), a weapon scoring technology. Individual and crew weapons are fitted with an eye-safe gallium arsenide laser transmitter that simulate the strike of a projectile when a blank is fired. The laser strikes where the weapon is pointed. The targets, both troops and equipment, are fitted with receptors that will instantly record hits, near misses and, more importantly, whether the kill is realistic. A rifle fired at a tank turret is a hit but not a kill; a rifle fired at an exposed tank commander is both a hit and a kill.[4] The information from brigade-sized exercises is recorded by computer and then played back and analysed by the NTC staff and by the brigade in training. From the brigade commander to the lowest private, every man learns exactly when, why and how he killed or was killed, and how his performance fitted into the overall operation. The opportunity for absorbing hard lessons was unparalleled in military training. As Commander of the 24th Infantry Division (Mechanized), Major General H. Norman Schwarzkopf, admonished his troops, 'The NTC is the National *Training* Center – not the National *Testing* Center. I *expect* you to make mistakes. I want you to use your initiative. I'd rather have you fall on your ass in peacetime than in war, because in peacetime it doesn't cost lives.'[5]

Eventually the army was able to rotate approximately fourteen brigades a year through the NTC for three weeks of intensive training. This rate allowed every armour and mechanized brigade in CONUS to train there about every two years. Such a cycle allowed commanders to train their brigades there twice in a command tour; the first visit identified weaknesses which the commander could address in his subsequent training programme and then judge the results in his second. Complete battalion equipment sets are maintained at Fort Erwin for the use of these units. The army has been careful to observe the results of training by brigades with heavy or light configurations of armour and mechanized battalions in order to reveal operational strengths and weaknesses. A smaller OPFOR programme was developed at the army training center at Grafenwöhr, Germany, in which two battalions are matched against each other using the Miles systems. The OPFOR is not a permanent force as at the NTC.

Training at the NTC resulted in a real improvement in the combat capabilities of the army's heavy forces that became readily apparent over the years as brigades steadily improved their performance. In the early years, they were regularly made hash of by the 32nd Guards. By 1985 they were offering tougher and tougher competition. The greatest achievement was the deepening professionalism and knowledge of the individual soldier to the point where it pervaded the combat manoeuvre arms. As one observer noted:

'They've spent about two intense weeks in the closest thing to combat that peacetime will permit. Each soldier and each leader has lost something and won something. Each has been involved in losing battles and each has probably lost his life – at least once and perhaps many times – and by losing has gained some realistic insights into the nature of his chosen profession and the risks and consequences of failure. Each has gained some realistic appreciation of the effectiveness of his unit and the unit's role in the greater plan of the parent units above. Each also gained some sense of his unit's ability to react, learn, survive, and inflict damage on the enemy. Each soldier, leader, and commander comes away wiser in the ways of conflict in general and armored combat in particular ...'[6]

The Reagan Administration's re-armament policy began delivering in large quantities the new equipment that had been in the planning stage for a number of years. The army was largely re-equipped with a series of excellent new armoured fighting vehicles such as the M1 Abrams Tank and the M2 Bradley Infantry Fighting Vehicle (IFV) and its reconnaissance variant, the M3 Cavalry Fighting Vehicle (CFV). Innovative Fire support weapons such as the Multiple Launch Rocket System (MLRS) and air-defence weapons such as the Patriot missile were also entering service.

Table 4-1. Fielding of New US Army Armoured Vehicles 1979–1989

	1979	1980	1981	1982	1983	1984
M1 Tank	0	152	151	300	1,229	1,483
M2/M3 IFV	0	0	–	–	450	1,100

	1985	1986	1987	1988	1989
M1 Tank	2,883	4,798	4,500	5,290	5,994
M2/M3 IFV	2,150	3,492	3,600	4,013	4,883

Source: IISS *The Military Balance, 1979–90*

OPERATION 'URGENT FURY' – INTERVENTION IN GRENADA, 1983

In late October 1983 the bloody internal coup by the Marxist ruling group on the Caribbean island of Grenada presented the army with its first combat since the withdrawal from Vietnam ten years before. As the situation deteriorated, the Reagan Adminstration agreed to intervene at the request of the Organization of Eastern Caribbean States, no doubt relishing the opportunity to pull a Marxist regime out by the roots. The United States had concerns of its own about Grenada. The unusually large airport being built there by a large Cuban contingent would become a Cuban and Soviet strategic threat in the region. There were also almost 1,000 American students and faculty at a medical college. Luckily, two navy task forces were in the region, one with a Marine Amphibious Unit (MAU) of 1,700 men, but these would be insufficient to overpower the several thousand men of the People's Revolutionary Army (PRA) and its Cuban advisers.

The commander of the joint operation (Joint Task Force 120) was the commander of the Second Fleet, VADM Joseph Metcalf III. The army would supply most of the ground forces for the operation: 1st and 2nd Battalions, 75th Rangers; 82nd Airborne Division; and 1st Special Operations Command elements. Warning orders

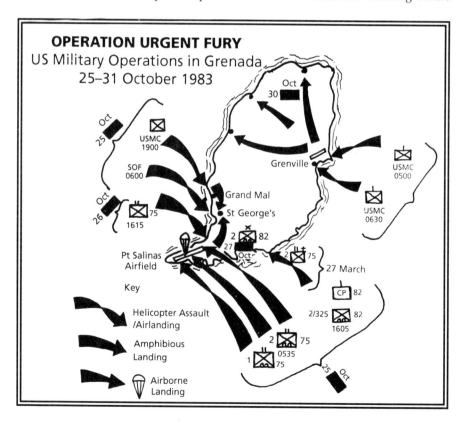

went out to these units on 21 October. D-Day was to be the 25th, which meant an incredibly short time in which to put together a *coup de main*, given that there was no prior planning to fall back on. To ensure that the navy handled the ground forces correctly, Metcalf was assigned a tough army major general named H. Norman Schwarzkopf and promptly made him his deputy and commander of ground operations.

The army's part of the operation began with the Ranger paratroop assault on Salinas airfield. The attack went in at dawn, later than planned because of equipment failures aboard their aircraft, and promptly ran into strong anti-aircraft fire from the Cubans and PRA. The initial drop by 1/75th Rangers was aborted so that Spectre gunships could suppress the AAA. Unfortunately the battalion command group's aircraft was the only one that failed to receive the message. They jumped and went into action. The following 2/75th jumped in after them. The commander, LTC Ralph Hagler, shouted to his men, 'Rangers, be Hard!' as he led the jump. The Rangers quickly cleared the airfield, removing obstacles placed by the Cubans including metal stakes set in the runway which they flattened with a bulldozer. The Rangers then attacked the Cuban camp. Ranger snipers killed or wounded eighteen Cubans who were trying to fire their mortars. The camp and 175 Cubans surrendered. A Cuban company attempting to withdraw from its beach defences also surrendered after a sharp firefight with 1/75th. A Cuban assault across the airfield with three BTR-60 APCs was shot to pieces by anti-tank weapons of the 2/75th. That afternoon elements of the 82nd began arriving.

On the second day Rangers in Marine helicopters rescued medical students at Grand Anse. There wasn't enough room for everyone, and twelve Rangers volunteered to stay behind. They evaded the PRA, stole a small boat, and were later picked up by the Destroyer *Caron*. That afternoon the 82nd's 2nd 'Falcon' Brigade attacked with two battalions and cleared a warehouse complex near the airfield, killing sixteen and capturing 86 Cubans. Reinforced with a third battalion, the Falcons next day moved north, encountering mostly snipers as the PRA and Cubans shed weapons and uniforms to hide among the population. To the army's surprise, the local population greeted the Americans with a delight not encountered since France in 1944. The Civil Affairs detachment proved its value by preventing the large numbers of civilians that had been passed to the rear from impeding the military operations. The only casualties were to friendly fire when a navy A7, given a misidentified target, strafed and wounded sixteen paratroopers. Later that day a major airmobile assault, with 2/75th and one company of 1/75th Rangers, was launched on Calivigny Barracks which was thought to house a 600-man Cuban and PRA garrison. This became a chapter of accidents. The second UH-60 Blackhawk helicopter to land crashed into the first. Shattered helicopter blades scythed through the dismounted Rangers, leaving three dead and twelve wounded. The 30-man garrison put up a good fight then surrendered. Six of eight Blackhawks and an OH-58 had been damaged and three more men were wounded.

The victory in Grenada, for all its tiny dimensions, was a tonic for the army. It was a quick, clean-cut fight, and the Rangers and 82nd Airborne had done well. The greatest gratification for the army was the realization of the public's overwhelming support. The self-congratulations were not allowed to go to anyone's head. The army keyed in on the weaknesses and failures of the operations: little or no accurate military intelligence of the enemy; failure of inter-service communications; and inter-service rivalries[7], among others. These deficiencies would be conspicuously absent in subsequent operations in Panama and Kuwait.

GREAT BRITAIN

The British Army marched into its fourth post-war decade with the experience of myriad counter-insurgency operations under its belt. But apart from Korea and the brief action at Port Said, it had precious little experience in the type of conventional operations to which it was now entirely dedicated as a member of NATO. The army also carried with it the bitter experiences of successive force reductions, regimental amalgamations, and economies that would have crippled other armies. Ministers and accountants have destroyed more armies than a host of conquerors and are far more persistent. Sadly, the army could look forward to more of these debilitating economies and to continued peace-keeping operations in Northern Ireland. Neither would do the army's conventional fighting abilities much good.

Unexpectedly, the army was to march out of the decade heads up, intact, and proof (at least until 1990) against the dry rot of economies. There were two obvious reasons – the persistence of the running sore in Northern Ireland and the close-run victory in the Falklands War.

Certainly the decade had not begun well. The Labour victory in 1974 re-introduced a government determined not only to eliminate all non-NATO commitments but to cut back on those to NATO itself. Cuts fell heavily on the Royal Marines and the Royal Navy's amphibious warfare capability, both of which had come to be integral to army operations whether in NATO or around the world. The Royal Marine Commando units had served with the army in most of the post-war

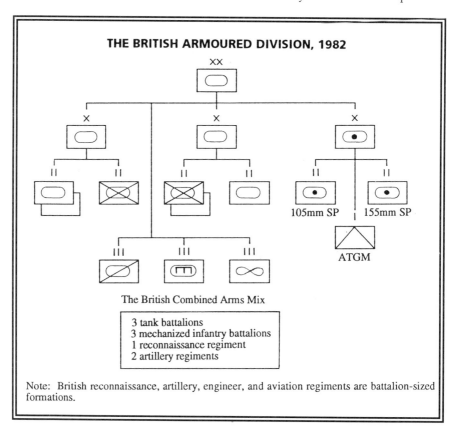

THE BRITISH ARMOURED DIVISION, 1982

105mm SP ¦ 155mm SP

ATGM

The British Combined Arms Mix

3 tank battalions
3 mechanized infantry battalions
1 reconnaissance regiment
2 artillery regiments

Note: British reconnaissance, artillery, engineer, and aviation regiments are battalion-sized formations.

counter-insurgencies and in Korea. A truly positive symbiotic relationship was being torn apart. Army special operations forces were also targets. The Airborne Joint Task Force and 16 Parachute Brigade were eliminated in 1974. Of the three paratroop battalions, only one was to remain on active service. Mobile reserves in the UK were to be cut from two brigades to one. The army was slated for a man-power cut of 15,000, almost 10 per cent. Some of these cuts were justified by the fur-ther games played with reorganizations of the BAOR, a device in continuous use since the 1950s to disguise economic motivations by a tactical sleight of hand. The government also withdrew from a number of joint ventures nearing completion such as long-range artillery with Germany and helicopters with France.[8]

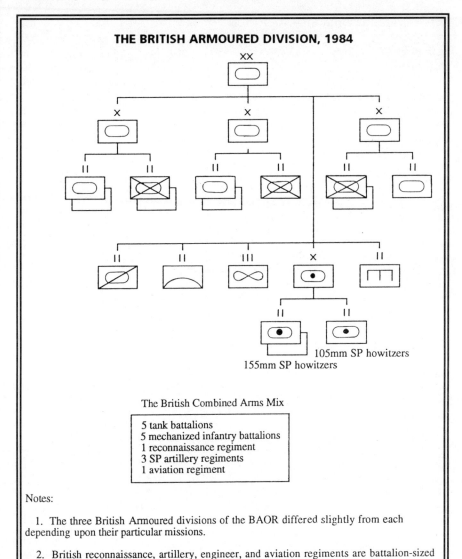

THE BRITISH ARMOURED DIVISION, 1984

155mm SP howitzers
105mm SP howitzers

The British Combined Arms Mix

5 tank battalions
5 mechanized infantry battalions
1 reconnaissance regiment
3 SP artillery regiments
1 aviation regiment

Notes:

1. The three British Armoured divisions of the BAOR differed slightly from each depending upon their particular missions.

2. British reconnaissance, artillery, engineer, and aviation regiments are battalion-sized formations.

The Conservatives returned to power in 1979 to find an army that could not sustain further cuts. Labour had only been able to cut four artillery and two engineer regiments, and 1 Royal Marine Commando. There had actually been another infantry battalion authorized, and all three paratroop battalions had been saved. Defence expenditures were allowed to rise to relieve the most onerous burdens of the previous decade. The TAVR was enlarged and eventually returned to its cherished old name of Territorial Army (TA). As Tables 4-2 and 4-3 show, army strength remained stable until the late 1980s when manpower reductions were made in both the Regular Army and TA, although the number of regiments was not appreciably reduced.

Table 4-2 . British Army Strength 1974–89

	1974	1979	1986	1989
Personnel	178,300	163,681	162,100	155,500
women	5,700	5,817	6,600	6,500
enlisted outside UK	7,900	7,500	9,450	8,900
(of which Gurkhas)	?	?	8,100	7,600
Armoured regiments	13	10	14	13
Armoured recon regiments	5	9	5	5
Infantry battalions	47	48	47	47
Gurkha battalions	5	5	5	5
Para battalions	3	3	3	3
SAS battalions	1	1	1	1
SSM regiments	2	1	1	1
Artillery regiments	25	18	18	17
SAM regimentst	1	3	3	3
Engineer regiments	14	9	13	13
Aviation regiments	2	6	4	4

Source:IISS *The Military Balance 1974–5, 1979–80, 1986–7, 1989–90.*

Table 4-3. British TAVR/TA Strength 1979–1989

	1979	1982	1986	1989
Personnel	58,900	70,200	77,000	72,800
Armoured regiments	0	0	2	2
Armoured recon regiments	2	2	3	3
Infantry regiments	38	38	40	41
SAS battalions	2	2	2	2
Artillery regiments	0	5	3	3
Light Air Defence regiments	7	3	4	4
Engineer regiments	7	7	7	8
Aviation squadrons	0	1	1	1

Source: IISS *The Military Balance 1979–80, 1982–3, 1986–7, 1989–90.*

Inevitably, BAOR was reorganized yet again. By 1981 the Nott reorganizations (Defence Minister John Nott) reduced BAOR from four to three armoured divisions and one infantry division. Two armoured divisions now had two armoured brigades of three battalions each, and another 3-battalion armoured brigade held by Army for commitment to the division in wartime. The third armoured division would remain in reserve with its own two armoured brigades and an infantry brigade attached from Army. The infantry division would be distributed as needed along BAOR's front. Under this structure the term brigade was replaced by 'task force', a rather poorly understood term that may have been more window dressing than substance.[9] A subsequent change produced a new triangular division structure in BAOR by 1985, one that remains current. Each armoured division contains three armoured brigades of three armoured and mechanized battalions. This organization is purely administrative. On the battlefield the brigades are flexibly task-organized into a number of combined arms 'battle groups' supported by divisional engineers, signals, artillery, etc., as the situation requires.[10]

The Falklands War, 1982

Perhaps only the Israeli campaigns of 1956 and 1967 compares with the British experience in the Falklands as textbook cases of exemplary professionalism and dash crowned with success. Not even the Israeli efforts, though, were conducted against such numerical odds and at the fraying tip of a logistics lifeline 8,000 miles long.

The initial expeditionary force assigned to contest the Argentinians' capture of the Falklands was primarily a Royal Navy show. The Royal Marine 3 Commando Brigade of three battalions was augmented with 2 and 3 Paras of 5 Brigade, the army's 'out of area' force assigned to operations outside north-west Europe. The remaining battalion was 1/7th Duke of Edinburgh's Own Gurkha Rifles. The two Para battalions were replaced by 1st Battalion Welsh Guards and 2nd Battalion Scots Guards, both public service battalions and both coming off long stints of ceremonial duties when the decision was made to expand the land forces of the expedition. Both were mechanized infantry battalions that had not been trained up to the high physical endurance standards of the Commandos and Paras. Their transfer reflected the Defence Ministry's opinion that 5 Brigade would act only as support for 3 Brigade.[11] Had the Ministry realized the demands that would be made of the foot infantry, a more thoughtful choice might have been the Green Jackets battalions which maintained a reputation for physical fitness. Additionally, the staff of 5 Brigade was new and had not had time to settle down to the easy efficiency that comes of old relationships. There was only time for one field exercise to shake down the brigade. Wales was chosen for the similarity of climate to the Falklands' wet and chilly heaths and rocks, only to respond with a heat wave. That 5 Brigade and the Guards battalions were able to overcome these obstacles, not of their own making, is testimony to the power of the regimental spirit.

In addition to the five battalions, the army's contribution to the campaign escalated to include two squadrons of the SAS, two recce troops (platoons) of The Blues and Royals, an air-defence battery and troop, a field artillery battery, and a helicopter squadron. Including the Royal Marines, the total landing force numbered about 9,000 men against an Argentinian garrison of more than 12,000. The preparation and embarkation of the expeditionary force was anything but a repetition of the Suez fiasco. Bureaucratic red tape dissolved as the British services worked closely together to get the force to sea ready for combat. For once since 1945, pinchbeck economy was not a drag on operations, as was incredulously expressed by a senior defence ministry official, 'It made us rather light-headed. We didn't ask the Treasury for anything. We just told them.' Even so, there was a major miscalculation in assigning 5 Brigade to such a minor role. As a result, the brigade was to be badly short-changed both in the support units it normally would have had and in the equipment necessary for combat under conditions in the Falklands.[12]

From the initial landings at San Carlos Bay to the final storming of the hills around Port Stanley, the British Army responded like a supple beast of prey, animated by a vigorous energy, suffused with determination, and having as much advantage as daring and ingenuity could devise. It needed every ounce of advantage for it was fighting two enemies – the Argentinians and the Falklands terrain itself. Of the two, the islands were to prove the greater obstacle, featuring none of the familiar infrastructure of a well-populated and developed area such as northwest Europe. No roads and no shelter from the elements. Cold and wet, foot-slogging through its soggy peat and stony heath was appallingly arduous. An immediate demand was made on the health and vigour of the infantry. The Commandos and Paras 'yomped' across the terrain to reach their objective. 'Yomping' was a term picked up in Norwegian exercises for crossing cold and difficult terrain on foot carrying heavy loads. The only alternatives were insertion by helicopter or end runs by sea. The too few helicopters were fully occupied in the insertion of SAS teams, and ferrying artillery, supplies and casualties.

The first major action of the land campaign was the night attack on Goose Green by 2 Para. Odds of one to one had been anticipated, but in fact the enemy outnumbered 2 Para by three to one. Well dug-in, the Argentinians stoutly defended their positions, actively supported by air and artillery. After two days of fighting, 2 Para had killed 55 and wounded 80–100 of the enemy and captured 1,400 at a cost of sixteen dead and 36 wounded. Among the booty were as many heavy weapons as had supported 2 Para itself. Neither *matériel* nor numbers had been critical to success; 2 Para had done it in the old-fashioned way, through leadership and traditional infantry skills.

By the time 5 Brigade landed at San Carlos Bay, 3 Brigade was conducting its epic yomp across the north of East Falkland Island. All available helicopters were supporting 3 Brigade which had a number of invaluable tracked Volvo Land Rovers unavailable to 5 Brigade. Despite this support, the Commandos and Paras had to march carrying loads of 80 to 120 pounds. Lacking this support, the Guards in 5 Brigade attempted a similar yomp across the equally wretched terrain of the southern part of the island, but this had to be abandoned after twelve hours because the troops were exhausted. With the land route unfeasible, the Guards were inserted by sea at Fitzroy, south of Port Stanley. It was there, in one of the inevitable bad breaks of war, that the Argentinian Air Force caught the Welsh Guards still on board. For the army the strike was catastrophic; it left both landing ships on fire and 38 Guardsmen dead and 85 wounded. Other army and RN casualties brought the total to almost 200, which would prove to be be almost 20 per cent of all casualties for British forces in the campaign.

The Fitzroy disaster was the culmination of the problems and miscalculations faced by the British Army in the Falklands, and these concentrated on 5 Brigade like filings flying to a magnet. They stemmed from the Ministry's failure to appreciate that a unit sent into harm's way may have to fight. From the less than optimum choice of battalions to fill out 5 Brigade, to the failure to provide sufficient supporting units and equipment, to the failure to appreciate the imperatives of amphibious operations, these misjudgements placed the Welsh Guards at the point of maximum vulnerability.[13]

The marvel of this account is not that a series of mistakes led to a disaster. That is a commonplace in war. The marvel lies in the fact, that despite all these difficulties, the Guardsmen of 5 Brigade surmounted them and went on to beat a more numerous, well-equipped and well-entrenched enemy at every encounter. While there are a handful of armies in the world whose élite forces could have done as well, there are probably only one or two whose line battalions, even if they hadn't become stale from ceremonial duties, could have matched this feat. There was little to distinguish the combat performance of 3 and 5 Brigades. The victory of 2 Para at Goose Green was matched by the action of 2nd Scots Guards at Mount Tumbledown. In all the engagements there was a striking similarity that seemed to run through all units like a broad bright-red thread. It was a spirit of excellence that suffused not only the battalions but the supporting arms as well. The history of the land campaign comprises one account after another of soldiers at every level, under stamina-bleeding conditions of weather and terrain, doing their utmost. And that utmost was of a very high professional order. As one American commentator noted, the British had an obsession with time, making the best of it, and using it to achieve and maintain the momentum of operations. They had an innate understanding of speed, surprise and initiative, the mark of superior armies throughout history, and were undaunted at the thought of having to attack a numerically superior and entrenched enemy. He also observed that

> 'The courage and professionalism demonstrated by the British were no accident. Their training instills pride, discipline and responsibility to others at the outset. It emphasizes operations in all weathers and conditions. One does not win battles if he has left his aircraft on the ground, his ships in port and the troops in barracks during large periods of their training cycles.' [14]

The night is one such condition from which most armies shy away in their training; the extent to which an army trains at night is a good indicator of its effectiveness. By that standard, the British Army is very good. Its penchant for night operations became a critical advantage in the Falklands.

Yet good training is achieved only in a conducive medium. In this case the medium was the cohesion of the regimental system in a professional army, and it paid off handsomely. Opportunities for leadership and initiative, in such a system, are seized eagerly; corporals left in command of leader-stricken platoons, led them aggressively. Even sacrifice is willingly grasped as the price of leadership and initiative. The Victoria Cross was thus awarded twice, to Lieutenant-Colonel Herbert Jones, Commanding Officer of the 2nd Battalion, The Parachute Regiment, at Goose Green, and to Sergeant Ian McKay, 3rd Battalion, at Mount Longdon. The following excepts from their citations speak for themselves and for the whole army:

Lieutenant-Colonel Herbert Jones

'In his effort to gain a good viewpoint, Colonel Jones was now at the very front of his battalion. It was clear to him that desperate measures were needed in order to over-come the enemy position and rekindle the attack, and that unless these measures were taken promptly the battalion would sustain increasing casualties and the attack perhaps even fail. It was time for personal leadership and action. Colonel Jones immediately seized a submachine-gun, and, calling on those around him and with total disregard for his own safety, charged the nearest enemy position. This action exposed him to fire from a number of trenches.

'As he charged up a short slope at the enemy position he was seen to fall and roll backward downhill. He immediately picked himself back up, and again charged the enemy trench, firing his submachine-gun and seemingly oblivious to the intense fire directed against him. He was hit by fire from another trench which he outflanked, and fell dying only a few feet from the enemy he had assaulted. A short time later a company of the battalion attacked the enemy, who quickly surrendered. The devastating display of courage by Colonel Jones had completely undermined their will to fight further.'

Sergeant Ian John McKay

'The enemy fire was still both heavy and accurate, and the position of the platoons was becoming increasingly hazardous. Taking Sergeant McKay, a corporal and a few others, and covered by supporting machine-gun fire, the platoon commander moved forward to reconnoitre the enemy positions but was hit by a bullet in the leg, and command devolved upon Sergeant McKay.

'It was clear that instant action was needed if the advance were not to falter and increasing casualties to ensue. Sergeant McKay decided to convert the reconnaissance into an attack in order to eliminate the enemy positions. He was in no doubt of the strength and deployment of the enemy as he undertook this attack. He issued orders, and taking three men with him, broke cover and charged the enemy position.

'The assault was met by a hail of fire. The corporal was seriously wounded, a private killed and another wounded. Despite these losses, Sergeant McKay, with complete disregard for his own safety, continued to charge the enemy position alone. On reaching it he despatched the enemy with grenades, thereby relieving the position of beleaguered 4 and 5 Platoons, who were now able to redeploy with relative safety. Sergeant McKay, however, was killed at the moment of victory, his body falling on the bunker.' [15]

The bill for the campaign was 255 killed and 777 wounded (including non-battle casualties) for the entire expeditionary force. The army's share was approximately half. The Argentinians variously claimed between 800 and 1,000 dead. The British took more than 11,000 prisoners.

Admittedly, the Argentinian Army had severe training, leadership and morale problems, but a prolonged conflict against a lesser opponent would have made them better given time. That much could be said about most armies today. Even the Argentinian Army was a tough opponent in the defence. But an army such as the British, that does it right the first time, doesn't give the amateur armies a second chance to become veterans.

FRANCE

By the time of the inauguration of President Valerie Giscard d'Estaing in 1974, the conversion of the old half-colonial French Army into a modern integrated fighting force had been completed. The decade 1975–1985 would see further refinement to the needs of the modern battlefield as well as the deft performance of the French Army in a series of minor operations in Africa and the Middle East.

THE 1977 REORGANIZATION

The 1977 reorganization was built on four principles:
1. Standardization according to mission. The army quickly abandoned the division into 'three armies' that characterized the reforms initiated in the 1960s. The distinction between Territorial Army, Manoeuvre Force and Intervention Force was done away with, and units were expected to be 'polyvalent' or liable to commitment to

whatever mission their organization and equipment permitted.

2. Simplification of command. Operational and territorial chains of command were merged wherever possible. There were no competing operational and administrative chains of command. The same man would command both the major military formation in the district in wartime and administer the military district in peacetime.

3. Suppression of the brigade level. The brigade concept was abandoned in the structure of the Type-1977 division. 'To promote versatility', the 20 brigades that had divisional elements were reorganized into fifteen small, so-called divisions. The eight armoured divisions were little more than US or German armoured brigades.

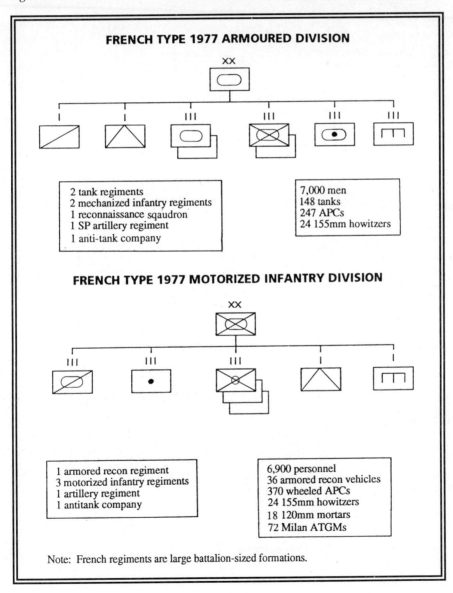

FRENCH TYPE 1977 ARMOURED DIVISION

2 tank regiments	7,000 men
2 mechanized infantry regiments	148 tanks
1 reconnaissance sqaudron	247 APCs
1 SP artillery regiment	24 155mm howitzers
1 anti-tank company	

FRENCH TYPE 1977 MOTORIZED INFANTRY DIVISION

1 armored recon regiment	6,900 personnel
3 motorized infantry regiments	36 armored recon vehicles
1 artillery regiment	370 wheeled APCs
1 antitank company	24 155mm howitzers
	18 120mm mortars
	72 Milan ATGMs

Note: French regiments are large battalion-sized formations.

In Germany II Corps controlled three armoured divisions; in France I Corps controlled four armoured divisions, with the eighth and last armoured division assigned to a new III Corps. The remaining seven divisions stayed in the general reserve and included five infantry divisions, 11th Parachute Division, 9th Marine Division and 27th Alpine Division, the latter two were formerly brigades.[16] As part of the intervention forces, most elements of 9th and 11th Divisions were professional troops with no conscripts.

4. Implementation of a new mobilization plan. Based on the 'derivation' principle, fourteen new divisions would be raised upon mobilization. Active divisions in

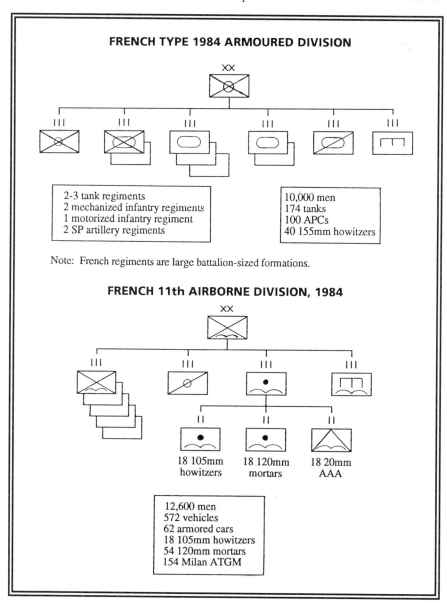

peacetime were required to prepare and train a reserve division at their own stations, made up of a 15 per cent active cadre and local reservists who had recently completed their service with that division. Although several of these divisions were successfully mobilized for exercises, the only available equipment for them was obsolete. Ultimately, this plan failed to meet its objectives for lack of resources.

As might be expected, cost-cutting was a major if not primary consideration. Most combat and service support was consolidated at division level. Nuclear artillery, additional field artillery, air-defence artillery, army aviation and military intelligence support was concentrated at corps level. The ratio of headquarters was reduced by assigning a fourth company to each battalion so that the ratio of supported to supporting units went from 3:1 to 4:1. Under this principle the armoured divisional commander had just four battalions (two mechanized, two armoured) for manoeuvre and one (artillery) for support. The infantry divisional commander had three infantry, one armoured and one artillery battalions. The exceptions were the airborne and alpine divisions which had six infantry battalions. These streamlining measures enabled the army to be cut from 337,000 to 312,000 men.

The 1983 Reorganization

In 1983 a further reorganization stepped closely on the heels of the barely completed and assimilated reorganization of 1977–82. It was again motivated by the government's cost-cutting priorities and provoked the resignation of the French Army Chief of Staff and another four-star general. The following were its chief features:[17]

1. In 1985, for the first time since the second restoration of the Bourbons after Napoleon's defeat at Waterloo in 1815, the French Army fell below 300,000 men (and women). The improved ratio of supported to supporting units at battalion level achieved in 1977 was lost. One company or battery in every combat or combat support battalion was reduced to inactive cadre status. In tandem with the desire to cut costs was the French demographic decline that was making it increasingly difficult to provide sufficient conscripts to man the force. Part of the problem was the short, 12-month conscription term that causes the French Army to expend so much of its energy in training. The army would have preferred a longer term, but the government was unwilling to expend the political capital to enact such an extension. As a compromise, the strength of the army was reduced, and attempts would be made to professionalize as much as possible of the remaining force.[18]

Table 4-4. French Army Strength 1639–1989

Year	Strength	Year	Strength	Year	Strength
1639	100,000	1967	331,867	1983	311,200
1763	135,000	1969	323,727	1984	304,500
1793	300,000	1971	322,169	1985	300,000
1812	600,000	1973	331,617	1986	296,480
1818	240,000	1975	331,522	1987	279,900
1869	444,191	1977	330,000	1989	280,900
1910	595,551	1979	326,800	1989	292,500
1938	665,000	1979	326,800		
1954	639,336	1981	321,320		
1959	731,489				
1963	497,213				
1965	344,727				

Sources: *The Military Balance* and Michel Martin, *Warriors to Managers, The French Military Establishment Since 1945.*

2. The eight 'Type 1977' armoured divisions were consolidated into six larger 'Type 1984' armoured divisions comparable to approximately half a US armoured division.

3. A Rapid Action Force (*Force d'Action Rapide* – FAR) of five divisions was created for power projection missions outside Europe, to act in support of First Army in central Europe, or independently.

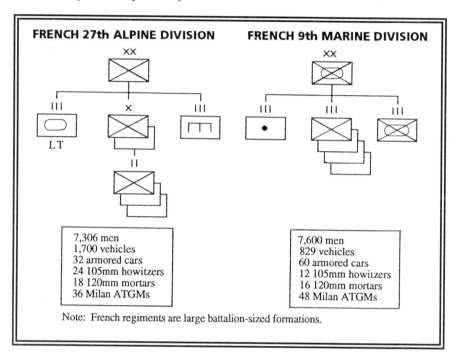

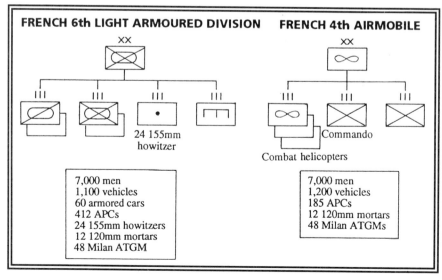

4. The *Défense Operationnelle du Territoire* (DOT) was re-created and the reserve divisions abolished to be replaced by cadre home-defence brigades and combined arms regiments.

The creation of FAR was one of the most positive changes of the 1983 reorganization. It was a recognition that the swift deployment of reserves would be necessary in a war in central Europe, and was symbolic of closer military ties and integration with NATO. Besides 9th Marine, 11th Parachute and 27th Alpine Divisions, two new divisional types had been created by 1985 – 4th Airmobile and 6th Light Armoured Cavalry.

LOW-INTENSITY CONFLICT

Since 1975 French forces have been committed in a number of small low-intensity conflict (LIC) operations around the world. The bad penny was Chad where chronic instability required the intervention of French forces in 1978 and 1983. A reinforced 2nd REP was committed in 1978 in what became essentially internal security operations as the Chadian leadership underwent yet another of its chronic fallings-out which lasted until 1980. In 1983 the commitment of French forces was prompted by the intervention of Libyan forces in Chadian squabbles. Four rotating contingents of troops known as the 'Manta' formed a defensive shield against further Libyan penetration south into Chad. A total of 2,800 men of the FAR, including for the third

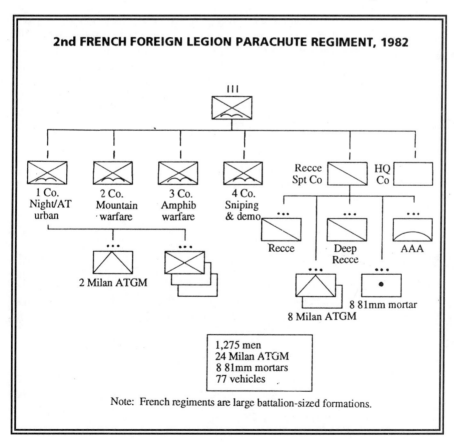

2nd FRENCH FOREIGN LEGION PARACHUTE REGIMENT, 1982

1 Co. Night/AT urban
2 Co. Mountain warfare
3 Co. Amphib warfare
4 Co. Sniping & demo
Recce Spt Co
HQ Co

2 Milan ATGM

Recce
Deep Recce
AAA

8 Milan ATGM
8 81mm mortar

1,275 men
24 Milan ATGM
8 81mm mortars
77 vehicles

Note: French regiments are large battalion-sized formations.

time 2nd REP, were dispatched; eight had been killed before French forces withdrew in 1984 under the terms of a ceasefire.[19]

In 1978 the 2nd REP was also committed to the bloodiest passage of French arms since the Algerian War, the rescue operation at Kolwezi in Zaire. On 13 May the mining town of Kolwezi in southern Zaire had been seized by as many as 4,000 Katangan rebels. Their occupation rapidly degenerated into a nightmare of murder and rape. At the request of the Zairean government, the French dispatched 2nd REP to rescue the remaining hostages. Within 24 hours of receipt of its orders, the regiment was in the air. By noon of the 19th, 405 Legionnaires had made a combat jump outside the town and fought their way in. The town was cleared by 21 May by which time the entire regiment had been brought in. By the 28th the region within a 300-kilometre radius had been cleared; by 4 June 2nd REP was back in Corsica having given a textbook demonstration of military excellence and daring at a cost of five dead and 25 wounded. The rebels suffered 250 killed and 167 captured.[20]

The most pacific albeit deadliest mission given to the French Army was that of peacekeeping in Lebanon in 1983. The army's 'Diodon' forces were made up of four successive contingents as part of a multinational security force in Beirut. About 60 men were killed when terrorists rammed their barracks with an explosive-filled truck.

The French Army has had considerable success with its LIC operations in the 1980s because it has applied two basic principles: (1) intervention in time to prevent a crisis (this has been facilitated by the location of support forces in French overseas dependencies) and (2) the maintenance of a retaliation capability, the 'rapid, long-range projection of forces' of the FAR. (The Kolwezi rescue was an anomaly in that it was outside the French sphere of influence, and French assistance had been requested.) Both efforts were dependent on close operational and planning co-operation of the French air force and navy. Both efforts demanded a rapid adaptability to local conditions, sensitivity to the military and diplomatic situation, an alertness to the terrorist environment, and a certain coolness and restraint in the face of provocation.[21]

WEST GERMANY

The fourth decade saw the West German Army become a powerful and mature organization, the central pillar of the Western Alliance and the most capable army on the continent.

GENERAL STAFF OFFICERS WITHOUT A GENERAL STAFF

The German general staff system was clearly the agent responsible for the brilliance of German arms in the modern era. It was based on the concept that military genius in individuals is too rare to be allowed to form the basis of a nation's defence. Instead, 'in striving to institutionalize excellence in military affairs, the general staff can be said to have institutionalized military genius itself.'[22] This striving for military excellence developed the first thorough concept of institutional military professionalism. The principles distilled by and infused throughout the army were initiative, the offensive-aggressive stance, mutual responsibility of all the troops, objectivity, and the famous concept of *Auftragstaktik* or mission-type orders. Such was the successful adoption of the spirit of these principles army-wide and the high uniform standard of training and performance among general staff officers that the Wehrmacht was able to out-perform its enemies long after Hitler had killed the general staff as an institution.

Although the general staff as a national military institution was officially destroyed by the Allies, the Bundeswehr was created by former general staff officers, it being obvious that only officers with such high professional qualifications would be able to forge a competent new army. Although the Federal Republic would not permit the re-establishment of the general staff itself, the Bundeswehr did retain the traditions of the general staff officer in order to occupy key positions within the Army and NATO. It can be argued that since the army will fight as corps level units within a coalition, a national general staff is not really necessary. It exists as an entity at corps level and below; rather than strategic direction, it functions at the operational and tactical level. Selection is rigorous and based on an appraisal of the 'total man' usually at the 12-year stage in an officer's service. Although there is no formal body known as the General Staff, graduates from 2-year course at the Führungsakademie der Bundeswehr in Hamburg retain a corporate sense of identity. With few exceptions no staff position can be occupied by other than a general staff officer graduate of the academy.[23] That corporate sense maintains the institutionalization of excellence that has distinguished the modern German army.

HEERSTRUKTUR IV – 1981–1992

The fourth major restructuring of the Bundesheer was begun as a series of experiments in the middle 1970s and was instituted comprehensively in 1981 to meet the changing threat represented by the rapid growth of the Warsaw Pact's combined arms forces. Heerstruktur IV addressed four main themes:

1 Emphasize capability to defeat enemy forces within a conventional environment;
2 Deploy ready units as far forward as possible to maximize terrain suited for the defence;
3 Improve flexibility and mobility by reducing the size of battalions and increasing the number equipped with new weapons;

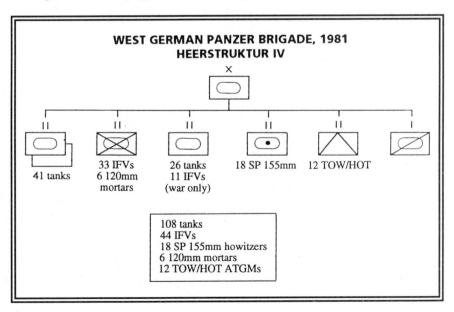

WEST GERMAN PANZER BRIGADE, 1981
HEERSTRUKTUR IV

41 tanks

33 IFVs
6 120mm
mortars

26 tanks
11 IFVs
(war only)

18 SP 155mm   12 TOW/HOT

108 tanks
44 IFVs
18 SP 155mm howitzers
6 120mm mortars
12 TOW/HOT ATGMs

4   Assume responsibility for integrated rear area support across NATO rear boundaries to release allied forces for forward defence missions.[24]

The Heerstruktur IV reforms were directed almost entirely at the battalion and brigade level in both the Field Army and Territorial Army. The Field Army's 33 brigades had already been increased to 36 by raising three new Panzer brigades in 1975 from the corps level Panzer regiments; an additional four Panzergrenadier brigades were created in 1980 by converting three Jäger brigades and one Gebirgs (mountain) brigade. The conversion left the Field Army with seventeen Panzer, fifteen Panzergrenadier, three Fallschirmjäger (airborne) and one Gebirgsjäger brigades. In the process 2nd and 4th Jäger Divisions were converted to Panzergrenadier divisions, and 1st and 7th Panzergrenadier Divisions were converted to Panzer divisions. By 1983 the Field Army's divisions consisted of six Panzer, four Panzergrenadier, one Gebirgsjäger and one Luftlande (airlanding).[25]

Table 4-5. The Feldheer 1973–1983

	Divisions:		Brigades:	
	1973	1983	1973	1983
Panzer	4	6	13	17
Panzergrenadier	4	4	12	15
Jäger	2	0	3	0
Gebirgsjäger	1	1	2	1
Luftlande	1	1	3	3
Total	12	12	33	36

Source: IISS *The Military Balance 1973–4, 1983–4*

In addition to creating a force that was more tank and mechanized infantry heavy, Heerstruktur IV increased the number of manoeuvre battalions in each brigade

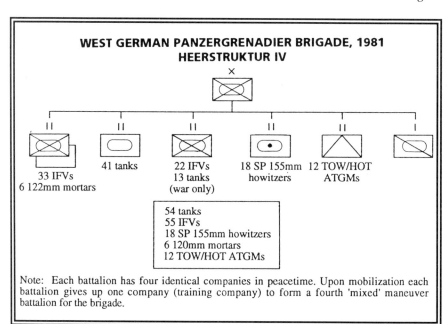

WEST GERMAN PANZERGRENADIER BRIGADE, 1981 HEERSTRUKTUR IV

×

33 IFVs
6 122mm mortars

41 tanks

22 IFVs
13 tanks
(war only)

18 SP 155mm howitzers

12 TOW/HOT ATGMs

54 tanks
55 IFVs
18 SP 155mm howitzers
6 120mm mortars
12 TOW/HOT ATGMs

Note: Each battalion has four identical companies in peacetime. Upon mobilization each battalion gives up one company (training company) to form a fourth 'mixed' maneuver battalion for the brigade.

from three to four. In peacetime this fourth battalion had an active headquarters company but was essentially an equipment holding unit.

Under Heerstruktur IV the Territorial Army was raised to be a powerful adjunct to the Feldheer and to allied armies. It was originally designed to provide purely national military requirements, such as replacement, medical and logistic support for German forces assigned to NATO. The new Territorial Army emerged from a radical reorganization based on the concept that the host country (West Germany) was best suited to provide a number of functions that in total would ensure NATO forces operational freedom throughout the depth of the combat zone. These functions included rear area security, movement control, logistic support, civil-military co-operation, medical support and information on local conditions. Upon mobilization the Territorial Army's personnel would be divided 11 per cent to logistics units, 26 to medical units, 27 per cent as replacements for the entire army, and 46 per cent to combat forces.[26]

Those combat forces emerged from the reorganization as the heart of NATO's rear area security. The six home-defence brigades (*Heimatschutzbrigade* – HSB) were reorganized and upgraded. An additional sixteen HSBs, fifteen home-defence regiments (HSR), 150 companies, and 300 platoons were organized. The six original HSBs were kept at between 52 and 85 per cent active-duty strength. The new units would be filled by reservists. The HSBs represented an important addition to the army's combat power. By 1985 each active HSB was the light equivalent of a Feldheer Panzergrenadier brigade with one Panzer, one Panzergrenadier, one Jäger and one towed artillery battalions. The six additional HSBs had one Panzer, two Jäger and one towed artillery battalion. The HSRs had three Jäger battalions. Although these units were armed with older equipment such as M48A2 tanks and the Jagdpanzer Kanone, they represented the wartime manoeuvre unit equivalent of two Panzer, two Jäger and five light infantry divisions (without divisional-level units). The separate companies and platoons were the similar equivalent of 27 light infantry brigades or nine divisions.[27] Clearly the Territorial Army have made any Soviet penetration into the NATO rear a dangerous and difficult undertaking.

Heerstruktur IV was a remarkable organizational effort to expand the combat power of the army in wartime without a significant increase in personnel or number of divisions. The Feldheer had become a more powerful conventional force with the addition of new tank and mechanized brigades. The light forces that had been upgraded to Panzer and Panzergrenadier in the Feldheer had been replaced by the new units of the Territorial Army. The result was an army with one of the highest 'tooth to tail' ratios in the world.

MANPOWER

By the end of this decade a manpower crisis could be discerned on the none too distant horizon. Germany's birth rate in the 1960s had gone into such steep decline that by the late 1980s it had fallen below its replacement rate. Projections by the German government in 1984 for the year 2000 foresaw a drop in the military age population from 6,000,000 to as little as 3,750,000. Conscript age males were expected to drop from 300,000 to 160,000. It was obvious that there would be serious difficulties in maintaining the Bundeswehr's minimum active duty strength of 472,000 men and a mobilization strength of 1,250,000. In 1984 the government announced, as an interim measure, that it would maintain the Bundeswehr at 495,000 men by extending conscription service from 15 to 18 months later in the decade.[28]

In 1985 the Bundesheer numbered 335,600, about 70 per cent of the Bundeswehr's 478,000 men. Within the army 188,300 or 56 per cent were conscripts, a reversal of the army's goal to have a force that was 55 per cent professional. The Feldheer numbered 266,000, the Territorial Army 44,200 and support elements 25,400.[29] Although the reforms of Helmut Schmidt had alleviated the worst NCO shortages of the 1970s, the army continued to suffer a chronic shortage of quality NCOs. The army needed 46,000 NCOs in 1982 and had barely 74 per cent (34,000). The recession of the early 1980s eventually eased the problem by increasing the NCO corps to 91 per cent of its requirement (42,000).[30]

The Tradition That Would Not Die

In 1980 another page in the contest over the valid military tradition of the Bundesheer was begun. The left wing of the SPD had begun a campaign against the concept and practice of tradition as laid down in the 1965 decree, finding even the minimal continuity that existed between the old armies and the Bundesheer intolerable. Passions were aroused just in time for the celebrations marking the 25th anniversary of West Germany's entry into NATO on 6 May which would include a combined grand tattoo (*Grosse Zapfenstreich*) and the swearing-in of recruits holding the colours. These ceremonies had deep roots in German history and had been reintroduced in 1956–7; they had become a popular pageant as local governments 'insisted that the townspeople wanted to see their Bundeswehr'. The ceremony of 6 May, however, was turned into a violent riot by the left. The ceremony in Bonn marking the 25th anniversary of the founding of the Bundeswehr was disrupted by demonstrators hurling paint bombs despite the presence of 9,000 police to protect 200 soldiers.[31]

In September 1982 the Decree of 1965 regarding traditions was replaced by a new set of guidelines. The new document was implemented as a final act of spite by the SPD left just as the liberal-social coaltion was disintegrating. The guidelines stressed that tradition should be based on the 'union of democratic values of liberty between the Federal Republic and its armed forces', and that 'all military deeds must be oriented to the norms of the state grounded in the law and international law ...'. So determined were the authors to sever any connection with the past that even the men of the 20th of July plot against Hitler were excluded from the pantheon of acceptable heroes. The guidelines further emphasized the unbridgeable break between the Wehrmacht and the Bundeswehr by stating that 'Traditions from units of former German armed forces will not be awarded to the Bundeswehr. The flags and standards of earlier German units will neither be trooped nor escorted.' The grand tattoo and swearing-in on the colours were retained, but were soon crippled as meaningful military symbols by regulations that restricted the former to retirements of senior officers, and forbade their combination.[32]

A counter-attack came from the new CDU government of Helmut Kohl in the form of a 1985 white paper. As the forerunner of a new regulation on tradition, it did much to re-establish the compromises of the 1965 Decree:

'There are many examples of human virtues and military achievement in German History which deserve to be passed on by tradition: the military reforms of the early nineteenth century, the gallantry and sufferings of German soldiers in times of war and captivity, the resistance against the national socialist rule of violence, and the example set by those soldiers of the Bundeswehr who laid down their lives to save those of others.'[33]

In 1985 the German Army reached its thirtieth year of existence; it had been a longer and happier period than the haunted years from 1919 to 1945. Despite the determination of the left to find a Nazi in every uniform, the attachment of the armed forces to the German democracy was in the bones of the German soldier. If he wished to be inspired by the genius, deeds and sacrifices of his forbears, that in no way detracted from his dedication to the service of that democracy. After all, he had sought to choose only the very best of his past, and in so doing had made the German Army, man for man, the most formidable on the continent

EAST GERMANY

IN THE SOVIET ARMY'S SHADOW

By 1981 the NVA had been integrated into the Warsaw Pact more fully than any other of the eastern European states. In that year 2,400 NVA officers were attending Soviet military academies, almost one-tenth of the entire officer corps, while 125 senior officers had attended the Voroshilov General Staff Academy. After thirty years of such close and exclusive association, it is small wonder that despite the Wehrmacht uniforms, discipline, drill and pageants, The NVA's organization, tactics, operational art and doctrine remained thoroughly Soviet.

At a time when the Western Allies had either officially given up their Second World War victors' rights of control in West Germany or allowed them to lapse, the Soviet Union maintained a tight grip not only on the DDR but also on the NVA. In sharp contrast to Poland and Hungary, the DDR had no say regarding the size of Soviet forces in country and had no control over their deployment. The commander of Soviet forces in East Germany had the right unilaterally to declare a state of emergency throughout the country, something excluded from similar status of forces agreements elsewhere in the Warsaw Pact. The NVA was also the only army wholly subordinated to the Warsaw Pact in peacetime which apparently gave the Soviets greater day-to-day control especially in matters of training. Soviet physical presence within the NVA was also much more extensive than in other countries with a permanent 80-man contingent permanently assigned to the ministry of defence. Joint training exercises on the regimental level between NVA and GSFG units became more common. NVA subservience was also based on the fact that the DDR's inability to support its own arms industry made it absolutely dependent on Soviet arms. Finally Soviet control effectively denied the NVA any independent wartime role. Unlike the Bundesheer, which would fight as self-contained corps under NATO command, the six NVA divisions would be individually integrated into various Soviet armies in GSFG. No NVA officer would command field forces above divisional level.[34]

The reaction within the NVA to close Soviet control and integration has been less positive than had been hoped. Paradoxically the experience of joint training led to a distancing of the armies to such an extent that both Soviet and NVA officers tended to discourage it. Contact between Soviet and East German units all too often had the opposite effect of the much trumpeted notion of 'Brotherhood in Arms'. German troops were appalled at the primitive and hard living conditions of the Soviets which did much to weaken their opinion of the Soviet Union. Soviet troops in turn were stunned by the far higher living conditions of the Germans. As explained by one former NVA political officer:

'... the political deputies of the Soviet army very often were reluctant to participate and not interested in meetings between Soviet soldiers and soldiers of the NVA, simply because the differences and contradictions would then come out in the open and that had negative consequences in the Soviet army.'[35]

THE RED AFRIKA KORPS

While a significant sector of West German and international opinion has continued to distrust the Bundeswehr as being the ghost of the Wehrmacht, it has been the NVA that acted in the spirit of Hitler's army around the world. The decade 1975–1985 saw the DDR's military involvement expand dramatically in the Third World and NVA contingents were dubbed 'The Red Afrika Korps'. The reason could not be found in German security concerns; after all what threat to East Germany could be found in the Ogaden or in the motives of Angola's UNITA? Rather it was found in the ideological motivations of the East German regime. The DDR had no reason to exist as a separate German state except as a unique German 'Communist' state. As such it had special obligations to the Soviet Union to assist in ensuring the success of fledgling Marxist states in the Third World.

The NVA's first foray began as early as 1973 with the dispatch of military advisers to Brazzaville in the Congo. By 1978 NVA involvement had spread rapidly with large contingents in Angola, Yemen and Ethiopia. More than 1,500 NVA personnel had been sent to Angola to solidify the MPLA's grasp on power. Although there were reports of NVA paratroops engaged against UNITA, East German troops were more visible as military and security instructors, technical specialists and advisers. At the same time, a contingent of 2,000 men was sent to South Yemen to take over the young Marxist state's security system and reportedly to build and run concentration camps.[36] In the same year, the German press reported that West German Leopard I tanks, built under licence in Italy and sold to Libya, had been re-exported to the Soviet Union which then sent them to Ethiopia to be combat tested with NVA crews in the Ogaden War.[37] The 1980s saw NVA involvement spread across the world when the DDR joined Cuba as a happy source of Moscow's Foreign Legions. The NVA not only sent troops to the new Marxist states but trained large numbers of their personnel in the DDR as well as aiding guerrilla movements in Rhodesia and Namibia. For most of the 1980s the NVA serviced a stable clientele, as shown below, until the Soviet Union lost interest in Third World adventures and allowed and encouraged its NVA assistants to return home.

Table 4-6 . NVA Contingents in the Third World 1981–1988

	1981	1982	1983	1984–8	1989
Algeria	250	250	250	250	–
Angola	500	450	450	500	–
Ethiopia	550	250	550	550	–
Guinea	125	125	125	125	–
Iraq	160	160	160	160	–
Libya	400	400	400	400	–
Mozambique	100	100	100	100	75
South Yemen	75	325	75	75	60
Syria	210	210	210	65	–
Total	2,370	2,270	2,320	2,370	200

Source: IISS *The Military Balance 1981–9*

POLAND

THE FOOD PRICE RIOTS, 1976

The Polish People's Army (PPA) entered the fourth decade of the post-war era and was immediately faced with another internal security crisis. In June 1976 riots broke out in Warsaw and Lodz following a recent government increase in food prices. Painfully, mindful of the trauma within the military caused by its involvement in the suppression of the 1970 demonstrations in the Baltic ports, General Jaruselski informed the Party leadership that this time, 'Polish soldiers will not fire on Polish workers.' The government caved in and immediately rescinded the price increases.

Nevertheless, the PPA's leadership were anxious about the army's reliability in the event of its becoming involved that the 'ideologically unfit' were winnowed out of their units and transferred to special holding units located in isolated forests, cut off from contact with the people, and disarmed; only officers were allowed to carry weapons.[38]

MARTIAL LAW, 1981

The rise of Solidarity at the end of the 1970s led to the nervous breakdown and eventual disintegration of the Polish Communist Party. By September 1980 the growing paralysis of government threatened both Communist rule and the alliance with the Soviet Union. General Jaruselski ordered immediate preparation of plans for the imposition of martial law. The planning and execution were directly controlled by General Florian Siwicki, the Chief of the General Staff. Because of widespread sympathy for Solidarity within the officer corps, he assembled a small staff of senior officers, all generals and colonels, assisted by Party and internal security elements. The plan called for the mobilization of 250,000 troops and up to 1,000,000 civil defence workers. Again mindful of the lessons of 1970, the planners gave the mission of physically suppressing Solidarity to the internal security forces, the much-hated ZOMOs. The army would act only in a support role and would not directly confront Polish workers. Its mission would be the 'maintenance of internal order in cities', with a show of force such as to terrify the population into passive acceptance.[39]

By late 1980 the Soviet Union had determined to intervene as it had in Czechoslovakia in 1968. The plan, shown to Jaruselski and the Polish Communist leadership, called for eighteen Soviet, Czech and East German divisions to move into Poland simultaneously with a Soviet and East German naval blockade. Jaruselski insisted that a role for the Polish forces be included. Accordingly four Polish divisions were assigned 'secondary tasks' as Jaruselski called them. Two Polish divisions were to support the Czech forces and two the East Germans. It was later argued that Jaruselski imposed martial law to save Poland from the worse fate of a Warsaw Pact invasion, but his willingness, even eagerness, to participate in the rape of his motherland damns that figleaf of an apology. Fortunately the invasion was short-circuited for a number of reasons, including strong warnings from the United States to the Soviet Union. In April 1981 the impetus for invasion built up again, but the Soviets again backed down in the face of continued US pressure and growing uncertainty as to the reaction of the Polish people and the PPA itself. Soviet analysis apparently concluded that not even Jaruselski's helpfulness could guarantee the conduct of the PPA.[40]

In December 1981 ZOMO efficiently imposed martial law throughout Poland. As planned, the PPA would take no direct action against the workers, but worries about the reliability of the troops even in their support role had caused the leadership to take preventive measures. General Leon Dubicki, who later defected to the West in protest, later stated:

> '... The soldiers are so stationed that the ideologically uncertain are always observed by the ideologically firm. Beyond that, one must always denounce others. In this way, uncertain people are easily eliminated ... a significant number of privates remain in the barracks, whole battalions and companies. Some soldiers refuse orders, are sentenced and arrested. In the Polish army there are now many (very) many officers and privates under arrest.'[41]

The success of the operation was also due to Jaruselski's carefully tuned use of the army. He was shrewdly aware of just how little stress the PPA could stand and tailored its involvement to minimize that stress. He knew that he could rely on a large element of the professional cadre and that the ranks could be finessed by not exposing them to emotionally charged conflict situations and by isolating the suspect. In this he was correct.

Jaruselski had every reason to worry about the reliability of the PPA. Although the army had achieved a high reputation within the Warsaw Pact for the professionalism and efficiency of its officers and men, there is solid evidence that the Polish sword would have turned in the Soviet hand in the event of war with NATO.

A survey taken among former Polish soldiers indicated that the PPA would have been fundamentally unreliable under coalition war conditions. There was a marked reluctance to fight NATO armies with the exception of West Germany. For example, 59 per cent stated that their units would not fight Americans, 29.5 per cent were unsure. Figures for the British and French were only slightly smaller. Only 7.6 per cent stated that their units would not fight Germans. The ideologically based motives were the most damning. Only 1 per cent said that they would have fought for Marxist Leninism. The responses to questions on the probable actions of Polish units would have thrown any Soviet plans involving the PPA into severe doubt.

Table 4-7. Possible Actions Impeding Soviet War Efforts

	Strongly Agree	Agree	Unsure	Disagree	Strongly Disagree
Your unit would have refused to move out of Poland	2.9	15.2	58.1	18.1	5.7
If possible, the men in your unit would seek to escape to NATO lines	22.6	41.5	26.4	4.7	4.7
Your unit would have revolted violently against the Soviets	40.4	35.6	16.3	6.7	1.0

Source: Edmund Walendowski, *Combat Motivations of the Polish Forces* (New York: St. Martin's Press, 1988), p. 97.

One former soldier commented that the Christmas wish among the troops was, 'Let there be war against the Americans so they can take us prisoners of war.' The only motivating factor of any significance was the threat of punishment or, as one soldier put it, that the Polish soldier's motivation would consist of not getting a bullet in the brain for refusing to fight.[42]

The imposition of martial law marked only the temporary eclipse of Solidarity. More importantly, it marked the permanent eclipse of the Communist Party as a governing élite outside the army. When the Party within the army tried to rule, it too failed.

SOVIET UNION

For the Ground Forces this was the apogee decade in which the post-war trends reached their culmination and the beginnings of exhaustion. The conventional war option was decisively embraced in response to the conclusions of the Party and

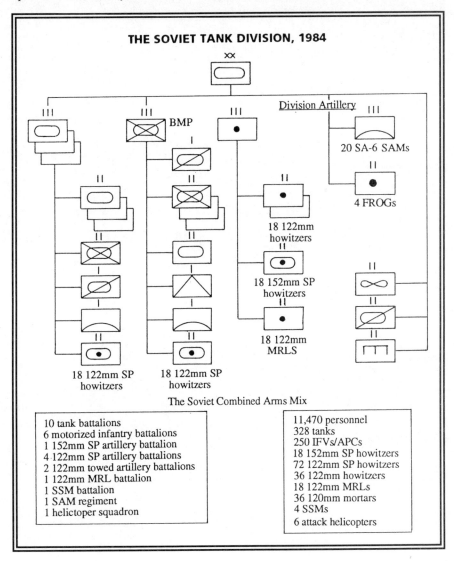

THE SOVIET TANK DIVISION, 1984

BMP

Division Artillery

20 SA-6 SAMs

4 FROGs

18 122mm howitzers

18 152mm SP howitzers

18 122mm MRLS

18 122mm SP howitzers

18 122mm SP howitzers

The Soviet Combined Arms Mix

10 tank battalions	11,470 personnel
6 motorized infantry battalions	328 tanks
1 152mm SP artillery battalion	250 IFVs/APCs
4 122mm SP artillery battalions	18 152mm SP howitzers
2 122mm towed artillery battalions	72 122mm SP howitzers
1 122mm MRL battalion	36 122mm howitzers
1 SSM battalion	18 122mm MRLs
1 SAM regiment	36 120mm mortars
1 helictoper squadron	4 SSMs
	6 attack helicopters

general staff that the use of nuclear weapons had lost all rational utility in light of their proliferation. As a result, industry continued at an even higher pace to produce lavish equipment inventories; conscription was tightened to drag in everyone possible, even the unfit, to fill the 33 new divisions and countless smaller units raised by 1985. While the Soviet Union was straining to meet the requirements of war in the West, the war in Afghanistan nailed the Ground Forces to one of the most vile campaigns of the twentieth century and its first protracted military opera-

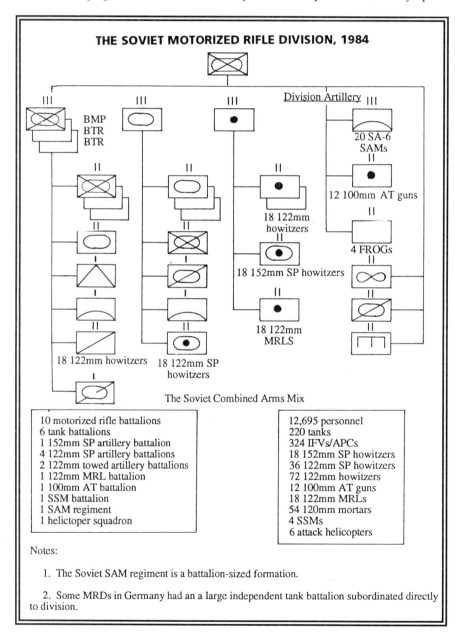

THE SOVIET MOTORIZED RIFLE DIVISION, 1984

Division Artillery

BMP
BTR
BTR

20 SA-6 SAMs

12 100mm AT guns

18 122mm howitzers

18 152mm SP howitzers

4 FROGs

18 122mm MRLS

18 122mm howitzers   18 122mm SP howitzers

The Soviet Combined Arms Mix

10 motorized rifle battalions	12,695 personnel
6 tank battalions	220 tanks
1 152mm SP artillery battalion	324 IFVs/APCs
4 122mm SP artillery battalions	18 152mm SP howitzers
2 122mm towed artillery battalions	36 122mm SP howitzers
1 122mm MRL battalion	72 122mm howitzers
1 100mm AT battalion	12 100mm AT guns
1 SSM battalion	18 122mm MRLs
1 SAM regiment	54 120mm mortars
1 helictoper squadron	4 SSMs
	6 attack helicopters

Notes:

1. The Soviet SAM regiment is a battalion-sized formation.

2. Some MRDs in Germany had an a large independent tank battalion subordinated directly to division.

tion since 1945. That war became a showcase, exposing the Soviet Army as a strange mix of First and Third World capabilities and attitudes.

NUCLEAR WAR RECONSIDERED

Two events in 1977 marked the Soviet Union's turning away from a belief in the utility of nuclear weapons. In January Brezhnev made a speech at Tula in which he stated that the Soviet Union was not aiming at a first strike capability. Essentially the Soviet Union was admitting that damage limitation from the retaliatory strike was technologically and financially impossible. Shortly after this Marshal N.V. Ogarkov was appointed Chief of the General Staff. Ogarkov was to become the outspoken proponent of the realization that nuclear weapons themselves by their very numbers and precision were the resort of suicides. The use of nuclear weapons would lock both sides in a death dance that would engulf 'all mankind' and 'the whole of civilization'. In this he was eventually supported by the senior spectrum of military policy makers.

The consequences for the Ground Forces were enormous. If nuclear weapons had lost their usefulness for anything other than deterrence, the only alternative method of armed conflict was the old-fashioned but still durable conventional form

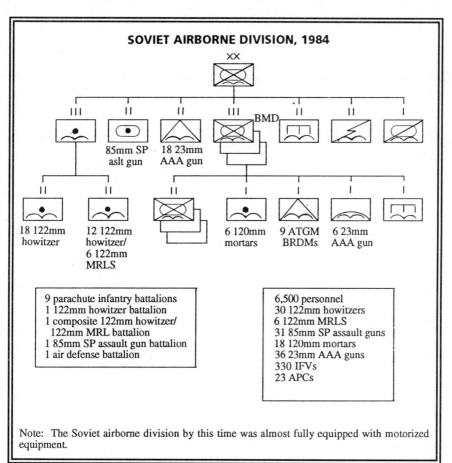

SOVIET AIRBORNE DIVISION, 1984

85mm SP aslt gun
18 23mm AAA gun

18 122mm howitzer
12 122mm howitzer/ 6 122mm MRLS
6 120mm mortars
9 ATGM BRDMs
6 23mm AAA gun

9 parachute infantry battalions
1 122mm howitzer battalion
1 composite 122mm howitzer/ 122mm MRL battalion
1 85mm SP assault gun battalion
1 air defense battalion

6,500 personnel
30 122mm howitzers
6 122mm MRLS
31 85mm SP assault guns
18 120mm mortars
36 23mm AAA guns
330 IFVs
23 APCs

Note: The Soviet airborne division by this time was almost fully equipped with motorized equipment.

of war. In fact technological advances had improved the 'classical' conventional arms and 'sharply increased their combat capabilities'.[43] In recognition of the shifting primacy of means, Ogorkov stated in 1982 that the Ground Troops 'are, in essence, the basic branch of our Armed Forces'.[44] In that same year the Chief of the Main Political Administration placed the Ground Troops ahead of the Strategic Rocket Forces in the military's order of precedence, which was the first time that the latter had been displaced since their inception in 1959.[45]

Much of this emphasis on conventional means centred on new technologies, but much also rested on mass and the general quality of equipment. Mass was represented by the sharp acceleration in the raising of 33 new manoeuvre divisions by 1985 and 47 by 1989, a 29 percent increase in the ground order-of-battle.

Table 4-8. Growth of the Soviet Ground Forces 1975 – 1989

	MRD	TD	AB	Total
1975	110	49	7	166
1976	111	50	7	168
1977	115	45	8	168
1978	115	46	8	169
1979	118	47	8	173
1980	119	46	8	173
1981	119	46	8	173
1982	126	46	8	180
1983	134	50	7	191
1984	136	50	7	193
1985	141	51	7	199
1986	142	51	7	200
1987	150	52	7	209
1988	150	52	7	209
1989	153	53	7	213

Source:IISS *The Military Balance 1975–90*

By 1985 there were also sixteen artillery divisions. In addition to the new divisions, a large number of non-divisional combat units such as air assault, attack helicopter, artillery, anti-tank, and air-defence battalions and brigades were created which were the equivalent of many more divisions in combat power. All these new units had to be manned, but according to the International Institute for Strategic Studies' *The Military Balance*, Ground Forces personnel strength rose only from 1,825,000 to 1,995,000. Economies were effected by having smaller crews on some combat equipment and by making many of the new units either mobilization base or low category readiness divisions with small personnel requirements. These units, with their equipment on hand in storage, would be fleshed out with reservists upon mobilization.

DEDOVSHCHINA: A CANCER WITHIN

Nevertheless the problems of manning such a force became acute during this decade. Whole categories of the heretofore medically and mentally unfit became eligible for conscription. University deferments to conscription were abolished. For the first time since 1945, the privileged sons of the upper and middle classes found themselves in the brutal environment of the army. Within that system of official harshness there existed another system of 'shadow regulations' that engendered even more hardship and cruelty for the conscript. Officially the Soviet military refer to it as 'non-regulation relations between troops'. The troops who have to live with it called it *dedovshchina, starikovstvo* or *starikovshchina* which can be translated literally as 'grandfatherism' or 'old-timerism'.[46] In reality these terms signified:

> 'an elaborate caste system based on a strict hierarchy in which every conscript (private and NCO alike) occupies a position entailing unofficial "duties". In the course of "assuming" the prescribed role, a soldier often either acts as a "bully" and abuses other soldiers, or is on the receiving end of such abuse.'[47]

The caste system is derived from the twice-yearly conscript cycles which divides the conscripts into four classes.

Table 4-9. The *Dedovshchina* Caste System

Time in Service	Nickname	Rights and Duties
1–6 months	*salaga* 'little fish'	Absolute subordination
	chizik 'finch'	to all above him
	synok 'sonny'	
6–12 months	*skvorets* 'starling'	Differs from a *salaga* only by his experience and 'hope for future
	rights'	
12–18 months	*limon* 'lemon'	A 'boss' of the 'little fishes/starlings'
	cherpak 'ladle'	but is subordinate to the *stariki*
18–21 months	*stariki* 'old-timer'	He has an 'ocean of rights' and is subordinate to the commander only nominally
From the day he receives his demobilization orders until day he leaves for home	*ded* or *dedushka*	He is a civilian and 'grandpa' or only by an ironic twist is he still in a military uniform

Source: Yuriy Plyakov, 'Sto dney do prikaza', in *Yunost*, no. 11, 1987; cited in Tyson, p. 28.

The system obviously stood good order and discipline on its head, and destroyed the already weak authority of the NCO corps which was promoted from the same classes of conscripts. Against seasoned bullies in an entrenched system the brand-new conscript NCO stood little chance, especially when the officer corps collectively looked the other way and does little to correct the problem. In fact, officers, while almost unanimously aware of the system, relied on it to control the unit without their having to become personally involved with the troops. They would even go to great lengths to suppress complaints arising from the system. Not surprisingly, one survey revealed that only 33 per cent of troops thought that they could take such a problem to an officer. It has even been suggested that it was tolerated as a control mechanism to divide and rule.[48] For ruling slaves it has a certain utility, but for building the cohesion and morale of the 'band of brothers' necessary to prevail in war, it was an appalling stupidity.

The origin of *dedovshchina* is unclear. It has been variously traced back to Tsarist times or to changes brought about by the 1967 Law on Universal Military Service which changed the length of conscript service from three to two years. The older, three-year conscripts felt cheated at having to fulfil their service terms while the newer men had to serve only two years. They took this animosity out on the two-year men by assigning them duties and fatigues. Another explanation came from Marshall Dmitrii Yazov, Minister of Defence under Gorbachev, who ascribed the phenomenon to the large number of conscripts with criminal records brought in by the tighter sweep of the 1967 Law.

THE WAR IN AFGHANISTAN

The opening phases of the invasion of Afghanistan were a close copy of the invasion of Czechoslovakia, but the similarity stopped there. Instead of a rational Middle European people with no tradition of romantic heroism, the army had picked a fight with a medieval, stiff-necked people who savour revenge as a national pastime. The ensuing nine-year struggle left both Afghanistan and the reputation of the army in ruins.

The invasion was preceded by mobilization of Ground Force divisions in the Turkestan and Central Asian Military Districts. The mobilization did not go all that well; there were reports that corrupt officials had sold off war reserve POL, parts, and even tank engines which required widespread cannibalization to put vehicles in working order.[49] These low-category readiness units were fleshed out with local Muslim reservists comprised of the same ethnic groups to be found in Afghanistan; the army chiefs thought that this would ease the occupation. Soviet advisers effectively sabotaged the Afghan Army by such ruses as calling in all armoured vehicle batteries ostensibly for maintenance. Airborne forces from three divisions began landing at Kabul airport and other airfields at major centres in a two-day airlift beginning on 24 December 1979. They quickly snuffed out isolated Afghan Army resistance. On 27 December two motorized rifle divisions entered Afghanistan and quickly occupied key points throughout the country. The Afghans were momentarily stunned; most of the Afghan Army either melted away or mutinied. It was then that the army discovered that this was not Middle Europe.

Resistance groups, already formed to fight the previous Afghan Communist regime, multiplied. The Soviets were forced to fight everywhere and learned they had made a major mistake with the mobilization of Muslim reservists who had little interest in combat and even less ability. They were extremely apprehensve, and viewed the prospect of operations against a Muslim country with the greatest reluctance. They showed more interest in obtaining copies of the Koran and in leaving caches of weapons, ammunition and fuel for the Afghan resistance. At best they were passive. Most of them were essentially useless as combat troops because their active duty service had been in construction (*stroibat*) or other support units.[50] That the mobilization plans called for them to man combat units and engage in operations betrayed a disturbing sense of unreality. Had the Afghan Army been able to offer organized resistance, the MRDs might have suffered serious reverses in the opening phases of the invasion.

The Soviet forces in Afghanistan, in one of the most awkward euphemisms in military history, were referred to as the Limited Contingent of Soviet Forces in Afghanistan (LCSFA). The Ground Forces were assigned to 40th Army whose headquarters were in Kabul. The first five years fighting from 1980 to 1984 represented a long and very slow learning curve for the Soviets.

1980 — The army had intended to garrison the country while the Afghan Army (DRA) conducted large sweeps against the Mujahedin. The DRA immediately diminished by desertion or mutiny from 100,000 to 20,000 men. The Soviets were

immediately faced not only with fighting the burgeoning resistance but in ruthlessly suppressing the demonstrations of the populations of Kabul and Khandahar.
Large sweeps were conducted by mechanized forces some of which were badly
mauled by the resistance. The army had uncritically applied the norms of a mechanized war in Europe to the mountains of Afghanistan and suffered severely. This
year saw the army's extensive application of scorched earth tactics to the countryside, in what was to become the Soviet trademark of the war. The Muslim reservists
had proven ineffective and after a few months were replaced by regular conscripts.
Soviet losses in 1980 have been estimated at 6,000 men.[51]

1981 — The army concentrated on securing major bases through a series of smaller-
sized operations into the countryside in order to avoid the heavy casualties of 1980.
But some of these operations were a signal failure because the Soviets continued to
use mechanized units instead of foot infantry to engage the Mujahedin in their own
environment.

1982 — This year the Soviet forces reverted to large ground sweeps to clear the
countryside. Now the mechanized forces were used in combination with heliborne
troops to encircle and trap the enemy. They were rewarded with considerable success, but the Mujahedin stepped up raids and ambushes that caused the Soviets
heavy losses on their extended lines of communication. The single greatest loss
involved the death of hundreds of troops trapped in the Salang Tunnel by fire and
or asphyxiation. By the end of 1982 Soviet casualties may have numbered as high as
5,000 dead with a further 10,000 wounded.[52]

1983 — A third and very effective element was added to the mechanized and heliborne combined arms forces: the massive deployment of fighter-bombers.

1984 — Combined arms operations were conducted even more aggressively and
with even greater air support, but a series of large, multi-division sweeps of which
'Panjshir VII' was the most notable, were depressing failures, as the Mujahedin
slipped out of the most carefully prepared nets. Casualties were heavy; 'Panjshir
VII' for example costing as many as 500 men killed and wounded. In that operation
a battalion-sized heliborne blocking force was almost wiped out.[53] The year saw the
LCSFA achieve the structure it would retain throughout the rest of the war, 40th
Army fielding one airborne and three three motorized rifle divisions, and one air
assault brigade giving a strength of 115,000 men.

By the end of the year it was apparent to even the most obtuse that the army
was bogged down in a war for which it had no strategy other than the steady and
ruthless destruction of the Afghan countryside and population. Entire provinces
were systematically ravaged. Villages were destroyed; their populations frequently
massacred. Crops, orchards and herds were destroyed. Wells and irrigation systems
that had taken centuries to create were diligently wrecked or poisoned. These
actions were the official policy of the army. It is not surprising that the Afghans
would repeat a Soviet statement with grim seriousness, 'We can still build a socialist Afghanistan if there are only one million Afghans left.'

OTHER CAMPAIGNS

Ground Force troops saw limited combat in a number of Third World countries
during the decade. Numbers involved were relatively small, and most troops were
employed in advisory, headquarters and training support capacities. The most dramatic involvement was in the crushing of the Somali offensive into the Ogaden in
1978. The 1,500-man contingent in Ethiopia was able to organize a number of effective combat units from the 17,000 Cuban troops supplied by Castro. The combined

Soviet-Cuban-Ethiopian force was a well-armed, well-supported and well-integrated team. The Soviet commander, General Vasily Petrov, broke the back of the Somali Army by his brilliant vertical envelopment of their strong positions in the Jiiga Pass, deploying Soviet helicopters and Cuban paratroopers.[54] It was one of the neater and more professional *coups de main* of the post-war period and represented a small but valuable facet of the army's battle honours.

Closer to home the army found itself conducting major manoeuvres in 1980 and 1981 in preparation for an invasion of Poland. That the invasion did not take place may have been partly due to a the fact that the mobilization of the key Carpathian Military District in the western Ukraine was a fiasco, so badly prepared that the local reservists simply deserted in their thousands and went home. So many 'voted with their feet' that no action could be taken. In the spirit of the period, the military district commander, a crony of Brezhnev's, did not fall from grace but was actually commended.

EQUIPMENT

As in every post-war decade, the army fielded a complete new generation of combat equipment. The T-80 tank was apparently a follow-on to the T-64 series produced in the previous decade and had the same 125mm gun and the ability to fire the AT-Songster missile. Two BTR wheeled armoured personnel carriers followed closely upon each another. The BTR-70 appeared in 1980, basically an improved BTR-60 with slightly more powerful gasoline engines, improved vision and greater armour protection. The BTR-80 appeared in the early 1980s and was an even further refinement of the BRT-60, with a single diesel engine, a side hatch for easier dismounting, and a 14.5mm turret machine-gun with a +60 degree elevation sufficient to engage low-flying aircraft or troops in surrounding hills. One of the first lessons learned in Afghanistan was that the BTR-60 could not elevate its turret machine-guns sufficiently to engage Mujahedin firing down from the hills. The same lesson was incorporated into the BMP-1 follow-on, the BMP-2 tracked infantry combat vehicle, introduced in 1982. In place of the 73mm short-barrelled AT gun it featured a long-barrelled 30mm cannon with a +74 degree elevation suitable for engaging low-flying aircraft or troops at higher elevations. It retained an anti-tank capability with the Spandrel ATGW.[55]

Artillery saw the introduction of the 203mm SPG (self-propelled gun) 2S7, the 152mm SPG 2S5, and the 240mm SPM (self-propelled mortar) 2S4 in the middle and late 1970s. The addition of these SPs to those fielded during the previous decade provided a full range of mobile artillery to the Ground Forces. Air defence saw the fielding of two replacement systems. The SA-13 Gopher low-altitude SAM, fielded in the late 1970s, was designed to replace the SA-9 Gaskin. The SA-11 Gadfly low- to medium-altitude SAM had been designed to replace and possibly complement the SA-6 system which had been in service for fifteen years. It was probably fielded in 1979.[56]

ISRAEL

The Yom Kippur War taught the Israelis that quantity as well as quality was essential if they were to win a future war; a war which the Israelis reckoned would be essentially a replay of the 1973 war. There began an immediate major expansion that within ten years would make the IDF a far larger, completely mechanized and more complex organization, as shown in table 4-10:

Table 4-10. IDF Ground Force Expansion 1973–1983

	1973	1983
Equipment		
Tanks	1,700	3,600
APCs	1,450	4,000
Order-of-Battle		
Armoured Brigades	10	33
Mechanized Brigades	9	10
Infantry Brigades	9	12
Parachute Brigades	5	*
Artillery Brigades	3	15
Personnel		
Regulars	11,500	25,000
Conscripts	83,000	110,000
Mobilization	275,000	450,000

* Five mechanized brigades were parachute trained. Source: IISS *The Military Balance 1973–4, 1983–4*

The goal of manpower policy was to raise as many brigades as the population of Israel could support. Beginning in 1974, the IDF began conscripting personnel from categories never before considered such as those with low education and personal problems such as minor police records. A greater proportion of women were inducted and placed in support units to free more men for combat. The conscript component of the active force was thereby increased by 33 per cent. Reserve unit rosters were strictly reviewed to transfer more men from support to combat. The strength of the regulars was also increased by 110 per cent. The result of these measures provided Israel upon mobilization with a force that was 64 per cent larger than in 1973.[57]

The expansion produced a drop in overall quality as the IDF tried to assimilate the less capable conscript categories. Expansion and the loss of 1,300 officers killed or wounded in 1973, caused an acceleration in promotions and a shortening of assignments to the point where inexperienced officers were put in command of units. The expansion in size and complexity was transforming the IDF inevitably into a mature bureaucracy, lessening the sense of intimacy within the regular officer corps.[58] Having reached its goals of numerical expansion by the early 1980s, efforts were refocused on raising the overall quality and professionalism of the army.

The order-of-battle expansion quickly absorbed the additional manpower. By 1983 the nineteen armoured and mechanized infantry brigades of 1973 had been increased to 43 by the mechanization of infantry and paratroop brigades and by the forming of many more tank units. The infantry brigades in the 1983 order-of-battle were territorial and border guard formations. The most dramatic expansion was in the artillery which grew by 500 per cent from three to fifteen brigades of five battalions each and numbering more than 2,000 guns. A great part of the increase was made up of US 155mm, 175mm and 203mm self-propelled guns. Israel's first domestically designed tank, the Merkava, went into production in 1979. Designed in the late 1960s, with emphasis on battlefield survivability, the heavy tank and personnel losses of the first few days of the war added urgency to its completion and deployment. This remarkable vehicle presented bold new design features devoted to crew survivability that included a forward engine compartment and numerous safety features such as armoured self-sealing fuel tanks, fireproof containers for ammunition, and the Spectronix fire-suppression system that detects an internal fire in three milliseconds and suppresses it in 200. The Merkava developed such a reputation for safety that it tended to depress the morale of the crews of other tank models. Another unique feature was the rear compartment for an infantry squad, thus producing the first tank/APC hybrid. In place of infantrymen the Merkava can carry additional ammunition to its 83-round basic load – up to 200 rounds – which gives it the truly phenomenal capability of remaining in combat without replenishment at least four times longer than any tank fielded by a potential enemy. The Merkava saw its first action in Lebanon in 1982 and gave an excellent account of itself.[59]

The IDF's increase in numerical strength was accompanied by a dramatic shift to a combined arms (*Shiluv Kohot*) approach to combat. The Yom Kippur War had proved that tanks were still the decisive weapon on the battlefield but could no longer be employed unaccompanied. The post-war army configured itself into tightly integrated but flexible tank, mechanized infantry, self-propelled artillery, engineer and tactical intelligence formations aided by ground-support aircraft.

OPERATION 'PEACE FOR GALILEE' – THE INVASION OF LEBANON, 1982

This decade saw the IDF's growing involvement in Lebanon as a counter to the PLO's establishment of bases in southern Lebanon from which they launched attacks on northern Israel. In 1978 the IDF launched 15,000 troops against these bases in a major punitive expedition, Operation 'Litani', in the first deployment of the reconfigured IDF. The new combined arms techniques were successful the mechanized infantry in particular gaining valuable new experience. The PLO lost 250 fighters but easily re-established its bases after the IDF's withdrawal and continued its raids despite a UN border patrol.[60]

By 1982 the raids were becoming serious enough to justify another punitive expedition. The initial goal was to establish a permanent 40-kilometre buffer zone inside Lebanon, but at the urging of Defence Minister Ariel Sharon, the decision was made to go for a killing blow at the PLO's military arm even if they had to be pursued into Beirut. On 6 June 1982 the IDF attacked into Lebanon with a larger force than in 1978, including 1,240 tanks. Within five days they had achieved the primary goal of the campaign and stood at the gates of Beirut. Despite determined resistance, the PLO had been overrun, losing 1,000 dead, 7,000 prisoners and enormous amounts of Soviet equipment stockpiled in their bases. The survivors had fled into the safety of Beirut. The IDF refused to be drawn into city fighting but pounded the PLO with artillery and air strikes. Eventually the remaining PLO were evacuated by sea under international agreement. In their operations in Beirut, Tyre and Sidon, the IDF had gone to great lengths to limit damage and avoid civilian casualties.

As a consequence of the operation against the PLO, the IDF was obliged to conduct a simultaneous campaign against the 30,000 Syrian troops garrisoned in Lebanon. From 9 to 11 June the IDF fought the Syrians in the Bekka Valley and its surrounding foothills, an area of about 30 by 25 miles. In the opening stage, the IDF obliterated the Syrian air-defence system by a combination of air and artillery strikes that destroyed nineteen SA2/3/6 SAM batteries and numerous SA 8/9 launchers for the loss of one aircraft. In the air, the IAF shot down 85 Syrian MiGs for no loss. On the ground the fighting was also intense but less one-sided. The Israelis had 130 tanks hit of which 30 were destroyed. The Syrians seem to have lost about three times as many including nine of the new and impressive Soviet-made

T-72s and numerous BMPs.[61] Although the tank losses on both sides were from all anti-tank systems, the Israeli tank gunnery reportedly accounted for 60 per cent of Syrian losses including all the T-72s at ranges as long as 3,500 metres.[62]

Despite the overall success of the operation in military terms, a number of problems were quickly evident. The IDF had been reconfigured to fight another Yom Kippur conventional war and had therefore been completely mechanized. There were no straight leg infantry left except the reserve home-defence territorial brigades, and they were inappropriate for offensive operations. In Lebanon, the IDF was operating for the first time in heavily built-up urban areas, thick citrus groves, narrow mountain roads and alpine conditions with steep terrain. In other words, ideal infantry country, and the IDF expeditionary force had no infantry and had not been trained in either mountain or urban warfare. It was also ideal defensive terrain for infantry such as were deployed by the PLO and especially the Syrians. Richard Gabriel makes the point that the IDF continued to adhere to the lesson of 1973 that infantry should support tanks when exactly the opposite relationship was needed in the difficult conditions of Lebanon. As a result advances were often reduced to the pace of a walking man and still suffered numerous ambushes at the hands of Syrian Army commandos and infantry usually supported effectively by one or two tanks.[63]

The cost of the war in southern Lebanon was 368 dead and 2,383 wounded; the subsequent year of occupation cost another 148 dead and 340 wounded for a total bill barely short of the June 1967 War. It is significant that the greatest losses were suffered during the siege of Beirut and the fight with the Syrians where the IDF was dealing with unfamiliar urban and mountainous environments.

Table 4-11. IDF Losses in Lebanon, 1982

Losses in action against:

	PLO/Beirut	Syrians	PLO/South	Total
KIA	88 (23.9%)	255 (69.2%)	25 (6.9%)	368
WIA	750 (31.4%)	1,537 (64.4%)	96 (4.2%)	2,383
Total	838 (30.5%)	1,792 (65.1%)	121 (4.4%)	2,751

A breakdown of the death toll showed that the IDF for all its organizational miscalculations was still maintaining its tradition of leadership from the front. The dead by rank included 49 privates, 90 corporals, 132 sergeants, 46 lieutenants, 28 captains, ten majors, two lieutenant-colonels and one major- general. Sergeants and company grade officers amounted to 206 dead or 56 per cent of all fatalities, an incredible proportion of leadership at the lowest unit levels. In what other army do the deaths of sergeants and junior officers outnumber privates 3 to 1 and 1.5 to 1 respectively?[64] However laudatory the sense of example and sacrifice, the resulting decapitation of junior leadership may be too high a price. General Patton once commented that you could always tell when a division was not fighting hard enough – not enough lieutenants were getting killed. It is doubtful, though, that even that hardened warrior intended to lose one lieutenant for every private.

The siege of Beirut and especially the occupation of southern Lebanon imposed severe strains on the training and morale of the IDF. The extended commitment of large numbers of troops required many reservists to serve 60 to 90 days on active duty in successive call-ups. Regular units were similarly committed on an extended basis. Training of both IDF components suffered as a result. The extended and open-ended presence of the IDF in Lebanon and the sense of purposelessness depressed morale; this was the first war that had not been fought on the 'no-alternative' basis. Reservists began to demonstrate against the war after demobilization. Some began to seek out billets in the rear services. More than 100 reservists were prosecuted and given prison sentences for refusing to serve in Lebanon.[65]

EGYPT

The 1973 War and the ensuing peace with Israel largely invalidated the central theme of Egypt's defence policy of the previous twenty-five years. Instead of massing heavy forces for a major clash with Israel, the army was realigned to provide a defensive force against Israel in the Sinai and a mobile interventionist force. Intervention was more and more seen to be in support of moderate and conservative governments, unlike the support provided under Nasser to socialist and other radical regimes. Egyptian military advisers were reported to be in Chad to assist in repelling Libyan invasion. President Sadat's repudiation of the radical elements of the Arab world provoked a Libyan campaign of subversion and sabotage in Egypt as well as series of assassination attempts on Sadat himself. Sadat finally delivered an object lesson on 23 July 1977 when a well-prepared Egyptian ground and air attack hit Libyan forces on the Egyptian-Libyan border. The ground attack was deliberately shallow, but it was but deep enough to catch and gut a Libyan tank battalion. Four days later a ceasefire was accepted by both sides, but Egypt continued to deploy 15 per cent of its combat power, including 200 tanks and 35,000 men, on that frontier.[66]

The government also committed the army to an anti-terrorist mission, sending commandos to Cyprus in 1978 to free an airliner hijacked by Palestinian terrorists. The Egyptians attempted an Entebbe-style rescue without the permission of the Cypriot government, and fifteen commandos were killed in the ensuing gun battle with the authorities. In response, a special anti-terrorist unit, Unit 777, was formed. Its first operation was equally disastrous. In 1985 the Abu Nidal faction of the PLO hijacked an Egyptian airliner and landed in Malta. This time the Egyptians secured the permission of the Maltese government to take action. The assault on the aircraft turned into a bloody battle in which 57 passengers were killed.

Although much of its organizational structure and equipment remained of Soviet origin, this decade saw a steady increase in Western influences. Egypt became a partner in regional stability with the United States and participated in a number of the joint Bright Star Exercises which saw Egyptian and US soldiers training together in Egypt. Western equipment began to displace older Soviet models in the army's inventory. By 1985 there were 659 US M-60A3 tanks (with another 250 on order) alongside 1,500 older Soviet models. Western firms were also modernizing much of that equipment.

SYRIA

The Syrian Army had been defeated on points in the 1973 War, but had sustained a moral victory that restored its pride and gave it a hardy self-esteem. Weaknesses revealed during the war were promptly addressed as qualitative improvements, particularly mobility and manoeuvre skills, were stressed. Training received even greater emphasis as Syria prepared for another slogging-match with Israeli armour, but found itself instead engaged with the Lebanese tar baby.

In June 1976, determined to prevent a Palestinian takeover of Lebanon while civil war was ripping that country apart, Assad dispatched 6,000 troops to support the losing Christians. Their initial advance was stopped by the PLO using anti-tank weapons originally supplied by the Syrians themselves. Morale sank badly as Arab fought Arab. The Syrians withdrew but returned with a new determination in September. Their 3rd Armoured Division led the way in well co-ordinated advance with commandos and engineers in the lead to clear the highways as more commandos leapfrogged the hills on the flanks. Nevertheless the advance eventually bogged down in the mountains. The massive use of firepower broke it free to move on Beirut. More savage fighting occurred in the PLO refugee camps in the south. '... the "Pax Syrica" was only imposed by close-quarter combat finally involving the use of ZSU-23 and -57 vehicles to root out snipers'.[67]

In February 1982 Sunni Muslim fundamentalists, opposed to Alawite domination of Syria under Assad, rose against the Syrian government in the city of Hama. Assad reacted to this threat to his regime by immediately sending a tank brigade and internal security troops of the Alawite *Saraya ad-Difa* (Defence Companies). The army's reluctance to become involved in fratricide forced Assad to rely mostly on the *Saraya ad-Difa* and the even more bloodthirsty *Saraya as-Sira* (Struggle Companies). Eventually 17,000 army troops held a cordon around Hama as the internal security troops and air force destroyed the city, killing an estimated 20–30,000 people at the cost of 1,500 military dead and wounded.

LEBANON, 1982
The Israeli invasion of Lebanon in June 1982 provoked the next round between the Syrian Army and the IDF. For the Israelis the re-match was to be a Pyrrhic victory. The Syrian experience in Lebanon had shown the usefulness of commando and paratroop forces which were increased to 30 battalions now organized in brigades. They were well equipped with both Soviet and European anti-tank weapons. Overall, the Syrians had 30,000 men in Lebanon.

The Israelis initially had the best of the ground combat, battering the Syrian brigades along the coast and near the Beirut-Damascus highway, and destroying numerous Syrian tanks with their attack helicopters. To the east the Israelis drove the 1st Armoured Division through the hills back toward the Bekka Valley. Now the tables turned as Syrian Gazelle and Hind attack helicopters joined the fighting, destroying dozens of Israeli tanks and APCs in stalled convoys along the mountain roads. Although Israeli tanks proved superior to even the T-72 deployed by the Syrians, it was the Syrian commandos that gave the best performance in two days of fighting. Teams of them armed with anti-tank weapons and supported by tanks harried and ambushed the Israeli armoured columns pushing through the hills toward the Bekka. The Syrians greatest triumph occurred when they cut off and destroyed an Israeli tank battalion, hauling off many intact M-60 tanks. Just before the ceasefire a Syrian unit stumbled into a similar trap, losing nine of the new T-72 tanks, although the Israelis were not able to recover them.

Although the army did suffer a defeat, it remained an effective and dangerous force. It had fought so stubbornly and skilfully that the Israelis hesitated to continue the fight. Two days of fighting cost the Syrians 350–400 tanks, 1,200 dead, 3,000 wounded and 296 prisoners against 130 Israeli tanks, 255 dead and 1,537 wounded, a scale proportionate to the 1973 War. In defence of the Syrian Army, it must be stated that a good proportion of Syrian personnel losses were in the air defence and air forces, which lost 85 aircraft and dozens of SAM units for no Israeli loss. All in all, the Syrian Army's performance was even more impressive than in 1973, especially since, save for attack helicopters, it fought well with no air support and little air defence.

IRAQ

The twentieth century has seen more than a few revolutionary armies assume the colours of traditional national antagonisms. The most antique re-enactment by far was the replay by Iraq and Iran of the endless wars of Assyria and Babylon against Elam. Tracks have replaced chariot wheels but the performance of the Iraqi Army in this fourth decade of the post-war era deserved a salute from the ghosts of Ashurbanipal's vanished hosts.

The year 1975 saw the army in the midst of a major expansion that would double its size and modernize its equipment by 1980. Its primary combat experience had been gained in three counter-insurgency campaigns against the Kurds and one short and painful conventional campaign against the Israelis in 1973. The gritty Kurdish campaigns engaged most of the army for long periods and provided a healthy dose of extended operational experience. The painful but brief encounter with the Israelis drove home the inadequacies of the army in a more modern and quickly lethal environment. The experience was both expensive and inglorious. Its losses were heavy and its most notable achievement was consistently to bring artillery fire on Jordanian armoured forces on the Golan Heights.[68]

The expansion, begun on the heels of the 1973 lesson, would build on both experiences and give the army the ability to sustain a 9-year mid-intensity war whose appetite for men and *matériel* was reminiscent of the First World War.

The Iraqi Army had been founded in 1921 and remained under British influence until 1958 when the Soviet Union supplanted Britain as Iraq's arms supplier and military model. By 1980 equipment and tactics were largely Soviet although many British organizational features, such as the brigade system, survived. The army's expansion filled it with T-62 tanks and BMP APCs; even the T-72 had begun to enter the inventory. The Iraqis had learned from the 1973 war and expanded its anti-tank arm with Soviet Sagger and French HOT and Milan anti-tank missiles, and added more than 1,000 tank transporters. Artillery, however, was seriously deficient; by 1980 Egypt and Syria had 200–300 per cent more than Iraq.[69] Table 4-12 shows the remarkable growth of the army from 1973.

Table 4-12 . Growth of the Iraqi Army 1973–1989

	1973	1977	1980	1986	1989
Personnel:	90,000	160,000	200,000	570,000	955,000
Divisions:	3	9⅔	13	18	53⅓
Tank	1	4⅓	4	5	3
Mechanized	0	2	4	3	7
Infantry	2	4	4	10	42
Pres. Guard	0	⅓	⅓	1	1
Special Forces	0	⅓	⅔	2	6⅔
Div Equiv	0	⅔	0	8	0
Equipment:					
Tanks	1,000	1,350	2,600	4,500	5,500
APCs1,300	1,800	2,400	4,000	8,100	
Artillery	700	790	1,050	5,500	4,000

Conscription filled the ranks, but prior to the war with Iran a large percentage of the enlisted men and almost all the NCOs were career soldiers. The expansion was thus based on a solid core of professionals. A Reserve College also produced 2,000 reserve officers each year which allowed for a rapid expansion during the war.[70]

THE INVASION OF IRAN, 1980

The war with Iran hammered the army into one of the best in the Third World and the one with the greatest operational experience in sustained mid-intensity warfare. Probably the most impressive achievements have been its resilient cohesion and its logistics and organizational capabilities.

The army maintained its sense of cohesion despite being on the defensive in all but the first and last phases of a 7½-year war. Despite the loss of approximately 500,000 dead and wounded, and more than 100,000 prisoners, the army continued to fight well and continuously improved its combat skills. Iranian appeals to the Shiite majority in the Iraqi ranks were not strong enough to overcome the Iraqi soldier's allegiance to his own Arab state, and the diligent efforts of the regime's security apparatus. Much of this allegiance was the result of the state's very real reluctance to squander the lives of its soldiers and risk the loss of domestic support. This prime consideration underlay the grim and determined reliance on the defensive throughout much of the war. To lessen casualties, Hussein oversaw the steady technological improvement of the army during the war and supplied it on a lavish scale with Soviet, Western and Chinese equipment. Another important factor in eventual Iraqi success was the steady improvement in leadership. The army had entered the war with much of its senior leadership chosen for their political loyalty to Iraq's strongman, Saddam Hussein. Chosen for politics, they failed in war. Saddam applied a more ruthless wartime standard of selection. Execution or dismissal for failure and rewards for success nurtured a new corps of capable officers who would see the war through to victory.

The conduct of mobile operations in the first phase of the war inside Iran was not impressive. Despite its greater resources, the army was never able to mount successful major, swift armoured attacks; the deepest penetration was barely 20 miles. The Iraqi Army's operational experience came from its frequent campaigns against the Kurds which dictated a very deliberate, tightly controlled offensive. Iraqi operations were inhibited further by Hussein's insistence that all major decisions be referred to him. Attacks seemed to bog down in city fighting for which the army was untrained and woefully lacking in infantry; co-operation was poor among the different arms and worse among the support services.[71] Armour was not used aggressively in the breakthrough and exploitation roles and was rarely supported by infantry. The initial attack on Khorramshahr was made by an unsupported tank division. Armour attacks were stopped by the determined resistance of Iranian infantry formations. Only in the last phase of the war, when the army resumed the offensive, were combined arms attacks effective and these were successful largely because of the massive use of chemical weapons which prepared the way.

The most surprising feature of the army's performance was the success of its logistics chain in sustained operations that stretched from the Kurdish mountains to the head of the Gulf. During the first year of the war 100,000 men in nine divisions were supported inside Iran with no apparent difficulties despite the wretched terrain.[72] Throughout the war the engineers' ability to build dykes, roads and defensive positions were crucial to Iraqi operations:

'The length of the campaign demanded that the Iraqis had to run an unexpectedly difficult, major logistic support operation firstly across long dry desert routes, then across long wet ones. Their learning curve, perforce, had to be a short one. Also, for the first time in its history, the Iraqi Army had to launch a major river- crossing operation in enemy territory, across a wide river whose water level rose and fell by 1.5m every few hours.'[73]

Iranian offensives of late 1981 and early 1982 drove the Iraqis out of southern Iran, leaving behind tens of thousands of prisoners. Back on its home ground, The battered army pulled itself together and dug itself into an increasingly complex system of defences. Hussein was now gambling that the army could survive a war of a attrition against an enemy with three times the population. Against Iranian manpower, he threw into the scales not only a more technologically sophisticated and well-equipped army but one that was rigidly on the defensive. For the next few years, the army stayed in its foxholes and engaged in no manoeuvre expect for counter-attacks against Iranian penetrations. Operationally, Hussein had surrendered the initiative to the Iranians who would pound the front incessantly. Strategically, he had committed the Iranians to a form of combat that even their numbers could not make work.

Nevertheless, it was a close-run thing. Hussein was operating on a delicate balance in this war of attrition. He had to inflict sufficient casualties on the Iranians eventually to exhaust them, while limiting his own casualties to avoid a plunge in military and civilian morale. The Iraqi government provided lavishly for the next of kin of the dead, offering enough money to buy a new home, a car and a plot of land. Less obtrusive measures were also employed. According to Anthony Cordesman, Baghdad, 'had to place increasing limits on the number of public funerals and has tried to conceal the number of military dead', in some cases, 'bodies were refrigerated and only slowly released to the next of kin'.[74] However, such was the unremitting ferocity of Iranian offensives, that an element of desperation soon crept into Iraqi calculations after Iran carried the war into Iraq. Field fortifications, artillery and the stoic endurance of the Iraqi soldier were still not enough. An equalizer was sought and found in chemical weapons. In late 1983 the Iranians reported to the UN that the Iraqis had used mustard, a skin agent, and tabun, a nerve agent, on its troops. Saddam Hussein had found his equalizer.[75]

IRAN

Few armies have undergone the roller-coaster ride suffered by the Iranians during the period 1975 to 1985. It began the decade as the Imperial Iranian Army in the throes of a major expansion and re-armament surge. At almost midpoint, it practically dissolved under the blows of the Iranian Revolution. Rescued from oblivion by the Iraqi invasion, it reconstituted itself and achieved a creditable battlefield record under extraordinary conditions.

THE IMPERIAL IRANIAN ARMY

By 1975 the Imperial Iranian Army was in the midst of a lavish process of re-equipment on a qualitative scale unequalled in the world. It was also to begin a major expansion in size as shown in table 4-13.

Table 4-13. The Imperial Iranian Army 1972–1979

	1972	1976	1977	1979
Manpower (000s)	160	200	220	285
Tanks	860	1,360	1,620	1,735
Chieftain	0	500	760	875
M-60A1	460	460	460	460
M-47/48	400	400	400	400

Note. Before his downfall, The Shah had on order 875 Chieftain Mk P5 and 1,200 Shir Iran (Persian Lion) now Challenger tanks.

The Shah's desire was to make the Iranian Army a major army. For a country with an illiteracy rate of 55 per cent, this was rather optimistic. There was an enormous shortfall in the numbers of technically qualified personnel such a force demanded. The air force was operating with less than 75 per cent of the necessary personnel. The army, five times its size, had a problem in proportion. The degree of technical change also had skipped several generations of equipment in a few years, progressing from Second World War levels to state of the art between 1969 and 1978, so much so that by 1978 50,000 US technicians were supporting the armed forces.[76] The strain was evident to the British commander of the Sultan of Oman's forces during the Dhofar Rebellion, who also commanded rotating Iranian brigades from 1972 to 1977. Major-General Ken Perkins observed that the army had:

> 'acquired as many Chieftain tanks as the British Army. The scale and variety of helicopter support was breath-taking; the helicopter park at Isfahan was the largest in the world ... It is doubtful if any army, no matter how well trained and experienced, could have coped with such a comprehensive and concurrent re-equipment ...' [77]

Not only was the army failing to cope with the technical complexities of expansion, but it was also failing to adjust to the social ramifications of a large influx of conscripts, poorly trained junior officers and NCOs. The army's professional cadre of officers and NCOs were spread too thinly to manage the expansion, and the continuing rigid, feudal disciplinary system did little to help the situatione. Recourse to a more 'enlightened attitude more suited to the new army' was never attempted. The performance of the Iranian brigades in Oman reflected the army's problems. A reliance was placed on the mass use of *matériel* rather than on the skill resulting from through training. Iranian Special Forces elements were attached to each company 'to undertake those tasks which, although within the capability of properly led infantry, required particular initiative, expertise or special skills'.[78] Nevertheless, 15,000 troops were rotated through Oman giving 7–10 per cent of the army valuable experience at no little cost; 210 Iranians were killed in 1976 alone.[79] Major-General Perkins' observations made in early 1980 of the brittleness of the Iranian Imperial Army were prophetic; the Islamic revolution would validate them, yet, in the harsher school of war, the army was to prove unexpectedly supple.

THE ISLAMIC REVOLUTION, 1979

The accelerating disturbances that led to the flight of the Shah and the victory of the Islamic Revolution in Iran also saw the army come apart at the seams. Progagandized constantly by the mullahs, conscripts and technicians deserted or absented themselves in droves. Remaining troops were considered unreliable. The revolutionary tide swamped many garrisons as troops joined the rioters to sack their own garrisons and armouries. Sixty per cent of the army disappeared in the chaos of revolution.

The Khomeini regime put a quick stop to the disintegration of the army; it intended to reform not destroy it. Key positions were filled by reliable officers. Only the Imperial Guard, the Javidan Guard and the military household of the Shah were abolished. The government had concluded that an Islamic army was necessary to defend it from radical parties on the left. The army was renamed the Islamic Iranian Ground Forces (IIGF). At the same time, the government determined to defend itself from disloyal elements in the officer corps. Within a year of the February 1979 revolution 9,000 officers and 1,000 NCOs had been purged from the army, large numbers having been shot. The officers represented 25 per cent of the 36,480 officers of the pre-1979 army. Counting the thousands of officers who fled the country, the loss was at least 35 per cent; the professional loss to the army was staggering.[80]

Concurrent with the purging and re-indoctrination of the army, the government raised a rival military force, the *Pasdaran* or *Sepah*. If the role of the army were defined as defence of the state, the role of the *Pasdaran* was defence of the revolution itself.[81] As a fanatic élite devoted to Khomeini, the *Pasdaran* played the role of the Waffen SS to the Iranian Army's Wehrmacht. It was not to be a happy rivalry. In 1980 the *Pasdaran* was also given the responsibility for creating a large popular militia, the *Basij*, recruited from the rural peasant population.

THE IRAN-IRAQ WAR

The massive Iraqi thrust into Khuzestan on 22 September 1980 was supposed to overrun a poorly defended province in two weeks, the few IIGF units and *Pasdaran* deployed there not being thought to present a serious obstacle. This turned out to be a miscalculation of historical importance. Only one division of the IIGF was deployed when the Iraqis attacked, defence of the province having been entrusted to the *Pasdaran*. Iranian resistance by both forces was ferocious, small groups of infantry repeatedly stopping tank formations dead. The Iraqi spearhead shattered against three stoutly defended Iranian cities – Khorramshahr, Dezful and Abadan. Although Khorramshahr fell on 10 November, the cost was Pyrrhic. Some 3,000 army and *Pasdaran* troops had inflicted casualties numbering 2,000 dead and 6,000 wounded on the Iraqi Army. Abadan was defended by 10,000 army and 5,000 Pasdaran and did not fall. By late November, the Iranians had sent 200,000 troops (army, *Pasdaraan* and *Basij*) to the front. By January 1981 the Iranians were strong enough to launch their first offensive, commanded by President Bani Sadr, who was to prove that not every revolutionary leader is a Trotsky, but the army's armoured forces, completely deprived of ground and air support, suffered a major defeat at Susangerd.

The defeat helped usher Bani Sadr off the stage and led to the structuring of a unified command for the army and *Pasdaran* under which the the quality of preparation, planning and co-ordination greatly improved. Mobilization breathed new life into the army. All reservists and deserters were ordered to return to the colours; many purged officers were reinstated. By the middle of 1983 the army had expanded to 21 divisions and reached its maximum wartime strength of 300,000. Bani Sadr had re-created the General Staff; in a short time its branches were functioning effectively. The promotion of young, foreign-trained officers to replace the older purged officers gave the army a fighting efficiency that did much to balance the loss of *matériel* support, a result not uncommon in the armies of revolutionary states.[82] The dividends were not long in coming.

The siege of Abadan was broken in September 1981, and, finally, in March 1982 Operation 'Undeniable Victory' tore open the Iraqi front at Susangerd, destroying in the process the greater part of three Iraqi armoured and mechanized divisions, killing and wounding 75,000 Iraqis and capturing 15,000 prisoners, 150 tanks, 670 APCs and other vehicles, and more than 300 guns. From this point, the Iranians seized the initiative and held it until the final phase seven years later.

Operation 'Undeniable Victory' illustrated the new mode of deployment of the Iranian forces which were becoming a triad of army, *Pasdaran*, and *Basij* ele-

ments. The 120,000 men were equally divided between army and *Pasdaran-Basij* elements. From September 1981 to June 1987 all the 26 major offensives were combined operations.[83] After 'Undeniable Victory', the ratio of army forces rarely
exceeded one-third of the total engaged. Army forces retained control of the traditional armoured, mechanized, artillery, air-defence and engineer missions, but its
proportion of infantry fell. A labour division also evolved. The Pasdaran remained
essentially an infantry force. Despite the division of work there was a basic difference between the two forces' approach to combat. The army reflected its Western
education and preferred careful selection of targets, the element of surprise, the
close co-ordination of supporting air and artillery, and the avoidance of unnecessary losses. The *Pasdaran*, true to its revolutionary origins, relished the close
infantry assault and looked on fanaticism and the nation's superior numbers as
assets to be expended.[84]

Until 1985 the *Pasdaran* largely had its way and added a new chapter in the
horrific ledger of twentieth-century warfare. With the full support of the government, it controlled the machinery of conscription and by late 1982 had begun to
sweep even the adolescent youth of Iran to the front. The human wave attacks of
the *Pasdaran* often cost as many as 30,000 dead in a single offensive. The *Pasdaran*
minister declared that children made up 57 per cent of the combat forces in the 1984
major Kheybar offensive. Ten thousand children are estimated to have been be
killed, wounded or captured. Iranian domestic propaganda glorified the image of
the empty classroom as the mirror of martyrdom. In the words of a leading Tehran
daily newspaper:

'Fifteen years old, 20, 25, 14 years old ... A desert of mines, and they –
like a garden in the morning ready to blossom, to scatter their petals on
the wind and take wing. They would pass over the mines, eyes no
longer seeing, ears no longer hearing.

'An instant, and when the dust settled, there was nothing. Pieces of
flesh and bone scattered across the desert, clinging to rocks.'[85]

As a consequence of Iran's political and economic isolation in the aftermath of the
seizure of the US Embassy, the ability to deploy sophisticated *matériel* in quantity
diminished, but the army was able to squeeze a great deal of use out of what it had
through technical and organizational innovation; for example it endeavoured to
refit the several thousand tanks captured from Iraq. As a consequence of US training, the army's use of artillery was far more effective, unit for unit, than Iraq's.
Engineer and artillery support for the operations on the island of Shatt al Arab in
1986 was particularly impressive. In a surprise attack the Iranians seized the port of
Fao across the Shatt, built ten bridges to the island and got 60–100,000 men across in
two weeks in the face of repeated counter-attacks. But nothing could redress the
matériel imbalance; slowly the quantity and quality of Iranian equipment diminished while Iraq's got better. By the end of the war Iran's impressive pre-Revolution
tank fleet of Chieftains and M60A1s had become mostly T-54/55s, T-59s, T-62s, a
few captured T-72s and a small remnant of the original fleet.[86]

Throughout the war the army and the *Pasdaran* were clearly superior in their
aggressive willingness to take the battle to the Iraqis, to seek and retain the initiative. The Iraqi front repeatedly shuddered under the weight of these assaults, and if
the Iraqis had not resorted in desperation to overwhelming use of chemical
weapons, the Iranians might well have won the war.

PAKISTAN

Following the trauma of defeat in the 1971 war with India, the Pakistan Army stayed out of politics and concentrated on repairing the professional shortcomings demonstrated in the war – until 1977. The widespread corruption and vote-rigging in the March elections for the national assembly led to violent rioting and civil disobedience in all Pakistan's major cities. Prime Minister Bhutto and the opposition were unable to resolve the issue, and to prevent civil war and supervise new elections, the Army Chief of Staff, General Zia ul-Haq, seized control of the government by *coup d'état* in July. Once in power, Zia arrested Bhutto, tried him for treason, and executed him. Zia postponed elections indefinitely and ruled through the Army as Chief Martial Law Administrator while retaining his position as Chief of Staff. Public opinion did not blame the army for its intervention but the politicians who had brought the country to such a sorry state that the military was forced, albeit reluctantly, to assume the civil power and save the nation.

Zia and his closest advisers concluded rather quickly that an immediate return to civilian rule would be impracticable for a number of reasons. Responsible politicians hesitated to come forward; the Baluchi rebels might rise again; and the army's morale would not stand another change in army leadership. Zia's solution was found in his own background as a representative of the increasingly middle class and orthodox Muslim officer corps. That solution was to Islamicize the nation and army to provide it with a stable governing ideology that would be proof against the divisiveness of party politics, a system that would combine religion and the military tradition of order and discipline. In the 1960s General Ayub had also tried to use Islam in a similar endeavour to find a social binder. Zia's system had one basic difference in its 'systematic attempt to control, intimidate or uproot all traces of independent centres of political power (including the press, the judiciary and Pakistan's already enfeebled intellectual class)'.[87]

After the 1971 war with India, Pakistan's security problems had shifted to its western and north-western borders where Baluchi and Pathan tribes rose in revolt. Although Bhutto has claimed that the revolt had been suppressed by late 1976, it continued to sputter. Zia effectively resolved the issue by granting amnesty to 50 Baluchi leaders. In September 1976 in the North-west Frontier Province the army reportedly committed two divisions to suppress rebellious Pathan tribesmen, killing 300–600 of them.

In December 1979 the Soviet invasion of Afghanistan suddenly presented Pakistan with an ominous new threat. Faced with India to the east and now Soviet forces to the north-west, the army was in the jaws of an enormous vice. The US arms embargo, in place since 1971, had been lifted in 1975. Now that Pakistan was the only base from which the United States could oppose the Soviets in Afghanistan, the old US-Pakistan military co-operation relationship was revived, especially under the Reagan Administration. One hundred M-48A5 tanks, 35 recovery vehicles, 60 155mm and 8in self-propelled howitzers, and 75 towed howitzers were quickly promised. By 1985 the United States had delivered about 200 tanks, 150 SP and 75 towed howitzers. The promise of 50 F-16 Hornet fighter-bombers to provide up-to-date ground support evoked considerable opposition from India.

Zia and the army actively supported the Mujahedin during the war in Afghanistan. US arms deliveries passed through army hands before being distributed to the Mujahedin, and some of was kept by the army. But the army's support was not limited to that of a middleman. They provided equipment, intelligence, training, secure bases and strategic planning skills. Without doubt army support kept resistance alive and provided a good deal of the organization that the congenitally undisciplined Afghans began to display.

INDIA

With the decisive defeat and dismemberment of Pakistan in 1971, the Indian Army could seemingly look forward to a diminished threat from that direction; but the Indians remained uneasy, especially after the completion in the early 1980s of the Karakorum highway linking Pakistan with China, and certain unpleasant consequences of the Chinese punitive attack on Vietnam and the Soviet invasion of Afghanistan in 1979. To the army planners, the completion of the highway prompted nightmares of the 1962 Chinese attack on India in the Himalayas, but now the 'hordes of Chinese infantry armed with burp guns' could be trucked along the highway into Pakistan to support any Pakistani attack on India from the northwest. The attack on Vietnam seemed to demonstrate Chinese ability and willingness to strike, and the Soviet invasion of Afghanistan had resulted in the renewal of US military support and aid to Pakistan.[88]

As a consequence of these factors the Indian Army grew steadily in size and quality of equipment during this decade.

Table 4-14 . The Indian Army 1975–1985

	1975	1985
Manpower	826,000	1,100,000
Divisions	27	32
Armour	2	2
Mechanized	0	1
Mountain	10	10
Infantry	15	19
Independent Brigades	22	30
Armour	5	7
Infantry	6	10
Parachute	2	1
Mountain	0	1
Artillery	9	8
Engineer	0	3
Tanks	1,800	2,500
T-72	0	300
T-54/55	1,000	700
Vijayanta	500	1,500
Centurion	180	0
PT-76	120	0
APCs	500	850

Source:IISS *The Military Balance 1975–6, 1985–6*

The Army continued to enjoy high prestige and the luxury of high selection standards for its enlisted ranks. The Indian *Jawan*, despite the government's continued attempts to integrate all the races of India, is still largely drawn from the traditionally martial races, especially in the infantry and the armoured corps, the latter home to Jats, Sikhs, Dorgras, Rajputs and Marathas. Up to 100,000 of the warlike Gurkhas, mostly infantry, serve in the army and paramilitary forces. The equally martial Sikhs, who represent a small proportion of the overall population, comprise at least

10–12 per cent of the army, and up to 20 per cent of the officer corps. The two large Sikh regiments, the Sikh Light Infantry and the Sikh Regiment, field twenty highly trained battalions that form the core of the army's striking power. The over-abundance of recruits also contributes to the martial races' composition of the army because preference is usually given to recruits whose fathers or other relatives have served with the regiments. Although some regiments have been integrated, more retain their traditional recruiting grounds. Most telling is the composition of the Brigade of Guards which has one battalion of Punjabis, one of Rajputs and one of other martial races. The Indian government does lay sufficient emphasis on integration to ensure that not only a number of the untouchable castes and non-martial races are included but also Indian Muslims and Christians.[89] The Muslims, however, are not entirely trusted.

The army's regiments are based on the British model and include a number of separate battalions which are assigned to various brigades. Despite attempts at integration, the following chart shows that most regiments are still composed of the martial races, even some of those listed as totally mixed.

Table 4-15 . Regiments of the Indian Army

Pure (Martial Races)

Maratha Light Infantry	High-caste Maratha Hindus
Jat Regiment	Middle-caste Hindus of Ragastan and Utar Pradesh
Sikh	High-caste Sikhs
Dogra Regiment	Dogras (high-caste northern Hindus)
Garwahl Rifles	Garwhalis of the Himalayan foothills
Kumaon Regiment	Kumaonis of the Himalayan foothills
Assam Regiment	Assamese (Gurkhas)
Gorkha Rifles	Gurkhas of Nepal

Mixed

Punjab Regiment	Sikhs and Punjabi Hindus, high-caste Maratha Hindus and Muslims
Rajputana Rifles	Jat, Hindu and Muslim companies
Rajput Regiment	High-caste Rajasthan Hindu and Bengali battalions
Jammu and Kashmir Regiments	Kashmiri Sikhs, Dogras and Muslims

Totally Mixed

Brigade of Guards	Separate battalions of Rajputs, Punjabis and other martial races
Parachute Regiment	Separate battalions of martial races
Madras Regiment	South Indians, completely mixed
Bihar Regiment	Eastern low-caste Hindus and Christians
Mahar Regiment	'Scheduled caste' northern Hindus

The Army remained fundamentally apolitical but was increasingly called out from 1975 to assist the civil authorities in keeping public order, a job universally detested the world over by professional soldiers. From 1980 to 1985 the army was called out on approximately 400 occasions. The most serious incident occurred when Sikh extremists seized their Golden Temple in June 1984. The army retook the temple with considerable bloodshed. A number of Sikh officers and men were disciplined for taking part in the seizure and for mutinies elsewhere, although the initial threat to hang deserters was not carried out after it was discovered that many had deserted because of misleading rumours spread by agitators. This first racial split in the army was traumatic and called into question the loyalty of the two large Sikh regiments.[90]

VIETNAM

With the defeat and absorption of South Vietnam in 1975, the People's Army of Vietnam (PAVN) shut the book on an extraordinary chapter of its history. In the First Indo-China War it had militarily and politically defeated the French and liberated Vietnam, albeit in two states of which it controlled only one. In the Second Indo-China War it had conquered the other Vietnamese state at enormous cost and politically defeated its foreign protector, the United States. PAVN expected a long-deserved rest, only to find itself trapped in a third major war.

ENDLESS WAR

No sooner had the last war ended, than the first tremors of another war were felt. Cambodia had fallen to PAVN's erstwhile protégé, the Khmer Rouge, which had proceeded to inflict a holocaust upon its own nation. In its blood-drunk hysteria, the Khmer Rouge began cross-border attacks on newly unified Vietnam within a month of the fall of Saigon. Border clashes continued throughout 1976 and increased in 1977. In May PAVN launched its first multi-division incursions into Cambodia followed by larger operations in September and finally major multi-corps attacks in November. By February of the next year, PAVN forces had withdrawn into Vietnam after decimating Khmer Rouge forces in 'no quarter' fighting.

But PAVN's leadership had not been entirely pleased with the performance of its forces. The diversion of many experienced units to economic activities in 1975 and their replacement by inexperienced Southern conscripts was partly to blame, but there was far more to PAVN's disquiet than sullen Southerners. PAVN had been exhausted by the second war and now faced problems that could no longer be solved by the skills of a light infantry army in a revolutionary environment.

In 1978 the Great Campaign was begun to modernize and professionalize PAVN into a regular army of a national state with the standard mission to defend its borders. One of the first reforms was the severe curtailment of the authority of the political officer which had even exceeded that of commanders since 1952. Now he would be clearly subordinate to the commander. The professionalization of the officer corps was one of the pillars of the reform, and for the first time a normal military hierarchy was officially defined. 'Previous emphasis on egalitarianism had led to virtual denial of even the concept of rank. Uniforms were devoid of insignia, and references to rank or title were avoided in conversation.' Now clear distinctions between officers and enlisted men were formalized and a thirteen-rank system for officers was introduced. A new Army Officers' Service Law set standards for selection and training, defined rights and duties, and established a regular system of promotions, assignments and ranks. Great emphasis was placed on technical training which was heavily supported by the Soviet Union.[91]

Before the positive effects of the Great Campaign could be felt, Khmer Rouge provocations escalated. By the autumn Hanoi had determined to solve 'the Pol Pot problem'. A total of 350,000 men was mobilized and ten divisions began preparations along the border for a tank-led *Blitzkrieg* operation recommended by Soviet advisers. The attack began in late November with tanks leading the way for the infantry in a fast-moving but bitterly contested advance. The advance was facilitated by PAVN engineer bridging units that were able to get heavy forces across the Mekong, one of the world's great rivers. On 7 January 1979 PAVN entered the deserted capital of Phnom Penh, its population long-since deported to be worked to death or murdered by the Khmer Rouge. By the 14th PAVN had reached the Thai border.They had lost 10,000 men in less than two months, but had achieved a decisive success in removing the threat of a hostile enemy. PAVN's success had also saved the Cambodian People from genocide, the least Hanoi could do for unleashing that horror on them to begin with. But the fighting was not over. The Khmer Rouge would not give up, and from bases PAVN could not subdue, they continued guerrilla operations in the west, north and north-east.

THE SINO-VIETNAMESE WAR, 1979

As PAVN attempted to cope with this new phase of the war, China had become incensed at the destruction of its Cambodian protégé, the the latest in a number of provocations it laid at Hanoi's doorstep. To teach the Vietnamese an imperial lesson, 85,000 Chinese troops attacked across their border in the pre-dawn darkness of 17 February 1979. Most of PAVN's regular divisions were in Cambodia, and the only bar to the Chinese were 100,000 paramilitary troops in economic construction divisions of about 3,500 men each, formed of veterans of the Second Indo-China War. As Douglas Pike, a long-time observer of the PAVN, noted:

'The Chinese apparently made the mistake of regarding these troops as mere militia ... But because most were veterans of the long war in the south, these soldiers proved to be cool under fire, battlewise and skilled in guerrilla warfare techniques. They were, in fact, exactly the kind of military force to throw against a tank-led enemy army slowly advancing down confining mountain passes. Probably these troops were more effective against the Chinese than would have been the so-called crack divisions from Hanoi made up of younger unblooded soldiers.'[92]

Forming a second line of defence were the few regular divisions and other economic construction units. They were quickly committed as the Chinese pushed towards Cao Bang and through Friendship Pass towards the provincial capital and regional hub of Long San along the traditional invasion route from the north. With Soviet assistance the Vietnamese airlifted four divisions from Cambodia to the North to defend Hanoi should the Chinese break through to the plain of the Red River delta and to reinforce the defences behind Long San. The Vietnamese employed classic Maoist tactics by conducting delaying actions while raiding and ambushing deep into the Chinese rear, even across the border into China itself. Soviet-supplied anti-tank weapons were used to deadly effect to destroy perhaps 100 Chinese tanks in the first few days. Vietnamese artillery was clearly superior in range and handling. They would pound PLA troop concentrations and then re-deploy to strike the slowly moving infantry columns. The climax of the war flared when 70,000 Chinese drove the 3rd 'Gold Star' Division into Long San, surrounded it and finally destroyed it after a desperate resistance by the Vietnamese with tanks and APCs. The city had fallen on 4 March; the next day the Chinese announced that the Vietnamese had been taught their lesson and were pulling out. Less than three weeks of fighting had tallied a butcher's bill of 28,000 killed and 43,000 wounded Chinese regulars against a similar or slightly higher loss for Vietnamese, mostly paramilitary troops. Despite being outgunned by Chinese tanks and artillery from the onset, PAVN's paramilitary forces, who bore the brunt of the fighting, had done well. In fact the Vietnamese consistently out-performed the Chinese, whose intense post-war reflection was a true indication test of who had received the better lesson.

THE OCCUPATION OF CAMBODIA

By late 1979 PAVN had consolidated its control of the cities and towns of Cambodia and saw little fighting for the next two years as the Khmer Rouge rebuilt their strength. Beginning in 1981, PAVN had to increase the tempo of the counter-insurgency operations of its 180,000-man garrison. In multi-division operations year after year, PAVN repeatedly tried to clean the Khmer Rouge out of their base in the Phnom Malai mountains near the Thai border, with frustrating results as the Khmer Rouge avoided decisive engagement and slipped across the Thai border. They finally captured the area in 1985 but it was a hollow victory as their enemies again slipped into Thailand. On several occasions PAVN units followed them into Thailand without success. PAVN's empty victory did not even provide temporary relief – the Khmer Rouge had infested the interior of Cambodia with guerrilla units by the year's end. In a bloody and frustrating irony, PAVN found itself in exactly the same situation that the United States had experienced in Vietnam. They were a fully conventional army fighting insurgents in a foreign country who had easy access to a cross-border sanctuary.

CHINA

THE RETURN TO PROFESSIONALISM

In 1976 the fall of the Gang of Four who favoured political loyalty above professionalization sparked the beginning of a fundamental reform of the People's Liberation Army (PLA). The excesses of the Cultural Revolution had played havoc with the PLA's ability to defend China from its primary enemy, the Soviet Union, and the military leadership knew it. The PLA was a generation out of date and woefully under-equipped for modern warfare. Under the firm guidance of China's new leader, the pragmatic old soldier politician, Deng Xiaoping, the PLA was firmly set on the path of professionalization. Within a month military and government leaders were calling for a new emphasis on training rather than indoctrination. Within a few years, as noted by the US government's handbook on China, the changes were dramatic:

> 'The most important aspect of the military training drive in progress in late 1980 was that it was remarkably depoliticized; troops were reportedly spending about 80 per cent of their time doing strictly military work. There was also a refreshing pragmatism about the way political training was to support the "four modernizations" ... performance in combat skills, training, military bearing and efficiency were seen as the best indicators of a soldier's correct ideological outlook.'[93]

The de-emphasis on indoctrination reduced the commissar's share of training time from 40 to 20 per cent. 'His missions ... were to look after his men, support the commanders, and aid in the "four modernizations".' It was not difficult to see the handwriting on the wall when Deng Xiaoping stated in 1979 that a soldier could not be 'red' if he were not 'expert'. Since then, the commissar class has taken a much greater interest in the technology of war.[94]

The PLA took a firm grip on the officer corps in 1978 by fundamentally reforming the promotion and assignment system, breaking the hold of the 'sponsor-protégé' system that concentrated too much power regionally or in a functional élite. Education and competence became the standards for promotion. In early 1978 the PLA began to raise its educational standards. By then most of its military academies, closed by the Cultural Revolution, had been re-opened and re-staffed with qualified instructors. Educational standards for both conscripts and new officers were also raised. At the same time China ended its military isolation from the rest of the world, exchanging numerous military delegations with other countries to study their institutions and experiences. As tension with Vietnam grew, the PLA was about to acquire a set of its own experiences to study.

THE SINO-VIETNAMESE WAR, 1979

After the Vietnamese victory in the Second Indo-China War, relations with China had badly deteriorated. Border clashes had become common since 1977. The Vietnamese invasion of Cambodia and its oppression of the Chinese minority were the final straws that decided Beijing to launch a 'self-defence counter-attack to teach the Vietnamese a lesson' on 17 February 1979. There is also a suspicion that Deng Xiaoping, faced with a hostile Soviet Union, wanted a blood test of the efficiency of the PLA.

The attack was timed carefully for maximum advantage on China's northern and southern borders. In the south it would take place in the Vietnamese-Chinese border area just before the beginning of the rainy season. In the north it would take place on the Chinese-Soviet border just before the spring thaw that would mire any Soviet movements in support of the Vietnamese. The Chinese had also cut off oil shipments to Vietnam whose oil reserves had fallen by half. A quick, sharp punitive beating followed by a quick withdrawal was the Chinese plan. Anything longer would allow the Soviets to reinforce and resupply the Vietnamese.

The PLA concentrated 300,000 men in eight army corps of 20 divisions drawn from ten of China's eleven military districts, although most came from neighbouring districts. In support were 700–1,000 aircraft, 1,000 tanks and 1,500 artillery pieces. But the PLA actively committed barely 85,000 troops, only some of its tanks and none of its air support because of the excellent Vietnamese air-defence system and the difficulty of such support in mountainous areas. The Vietnamese defenders were mostly paramilitary forces with a large number of experienced veterans.

The main attack was launched just before dawn. Thousands of PLA infantry and engineers had already infiltrated the border area to cut communications, destroy installations and secure crossing sites for follow-on echelons. Chinese main attacks penetrated the border in 26 places assisted by the infiltration across mountainous terrain of light Type 62 tanks. Priority was given to five provincial capitals. It was very much a conventional operation with the Chinese attacking down major roads, overrunning population centres and seizing the controlling high ground. The Chinese were engaged and severely handled by the Vietnamese paramilitary forces in a number of pitched battles.[95] The Chinese, who relied on human wave infantry attacks apparently lost 2,000 to 3,000 casualties in the first few days of the fighting. The Chinese artillery was clearly out-ranged by the enemy who would pound their troop concentrations and then fall back to strike their slow-moving columns. The Chinese also may have lost as many as 100 tanks to the more advanced anti-tank weapons, such as the Sagger ATGM, of the Vietnamese. As if the attacking Chinese did not have enough problems with outmoded tactics, doctrine, equipment and little grasp of modern war, they also suffered from the absence of a clearly identified rank structure.

The lack of rank insignia caused the PLA significant problems in command and control. The army believed that insignia were unnecessary because leaders were elected by their own units and were, therefore, easily recognized. But when leaders were killed in the initial assaults they were replaced by cadre members from other units. In subsequent battles units became disorganized because soldiers did not recognize the strangers as their leaders. The resulting confusion was a key factor in the high casualty rate suffered by the PLA.[96]

The PLA was paying the price for the ideological nonsense of the past typified by the slogan 'a red head can jolt a tank'. It was also learning 'the truth of the classic military maxim: Mass without mobility cannot easily or swiftly achieve war aims'.[97]

Initially held up in front of three objectives, the Chinese concentrated 70,000 men for the attack on Long San, a strategic city that controlled the traditional invasion route from the north and entry into the Red River delta and less than 100 miles from Hanoi. The PLA defeated the defending Vietnamese division in front of Long San and drove it back into the city which had been fortified for just such an eventuality. On 27 February in regimental strength, the PLA seized the high ground to the north of the city by a tank-infantry assault following a massive artillery preparation. Within a matter of days the city was surrounded. On 2 March the PLA attacked and reduced the city in three days of brutal house-to-house fighting. The capture of the high ground to the south of the city on 5 March opened the way for the invasion of the Red River delta, but within four hours Beijing announced that enough punishment had been administered and ordered a withdrawal that was completed in ten days.[98]

LESSONS LEARNED ACCELERATE REFORM

The Chinese had conducted a disciplined limited operation and realized that to go further would have escalated the war beyond their means and would have brought in the Soviet Union. As it was, in less than a month of fighting they had suffered 28,000 dead and 43,000 wounded against a similar loss to the enemy. In less than a month they had suffered half as many dead as the Americans had lost in ten years of fighting the Vietnamese. The limited nature of the attack was an acknowledgement that the PLA had about as much power projection capability as it had in 1950. The PLA was disappointed in its performance but very ready to examine the lessons learned in the war, and a great many of those lessons had been embarrassing.

Although morale and motivation had been high, there had been severe failures in C3I at higher levels, fire-support co-ordination, and junior officer tactical performance. Chinese junior officers seemed to have little more in their tactical repertoire than the suicidal frontal attack which caused heavy casualties. Senior officers seemed to have no better understanding of modern war. The poor preparedness of the officer cadres was in marked contrast to the skill of the individual soldier. The PLA had concentrated on producing excellent fighting men but had utterly neglected the development of leaders. The PLA did show a quick sense of improvisation, though, in developing techniques to winkle the Vietnamese out of their tunnels and caves. Supply trucks had broken down and this caused severe shortages of artillery ammunition and forced the PLA to use porters. Beyond the Chinese border the logistics system, which had relied on civilian support, was severely handicapped. The medical system was unable to cope with the number of casualties. Many senior commanders failed because of age – too many regimental commanders were 60- and even 70-year-old survivors of the revolutionary school of war. The PLA also learned that most of its equipment was not up to the standards of modern war either through design or poor quality construction. The greatest overall lesson learned, however, was one common to this era. Modern war is a war of rapid attrition in both personnel and costly modern equipment. Vietnamese Sagger anti-tank missiles had wrought dreadful execution among attacking Chinese tanks in the opening battles, a striking parallel with the Israeli experience in the 1973 War.[99]

Changes came quickly. The PLA's *Liberation Army Daily* reported, '... the recent border war with Vietnam has "helped clear away some erroneous ideas", apparently including the primacy Peking had long attached to Mao Ze-dong's doctrine of guerrilla war.'[100] A campaign of 'revolutionization, rejuvenation and intellectualization' rapidly began removing over-aged and incompetent senior officers; the recruitment of better-educated officers; and a great increase in the number of military schools and academies for the training of both officers and men. The PLA was also relieved of many non-military duties and encouraged in a more narrow military specialization and professionalization. Military ranks were authorized by law in 1984 as a direct result of the confusion during the war caused by the inability to identify officer replacements. The Chief of the PLA General Staff wrote:

'The new military service law also provides for the restoration of our Army's system of military ranks. Conferring military ranks on soldiers can raise the military and political quality of the Army, strengthen its sense of organization and discipline, and heighten its prestige, morale and combat strength. What is more important is that it makes it easier correctly to organize and command a large-scale and complicated joint operation of the various services, to meet the needs of a future war against aggression.'[101]

The experiences of the war placed a great emphasis on combined arms training up to and including army corps level. It also prompted the development of combined arms mobile units operating under a doctrinal innovation called 'active defence'. China's economic recovery programme did not permit the rapid re-equipment of the PLA, however. Despite the creation of mobile units and the emphasis on combined arms training, the force remained essentially an infantry army throughout the period. In 1975 the PLA consisted of 125 infantry divisions and seven tank divisions with 8,500 tanks. By 1985 it had 118 (some mechanized) infantry divisions and thirteen tank divisions with 11,450 tanks according to *The Military Balance* of those years. Its mechanization could in no way compare with that of the Soviet Army between 1945 and 1955.

In 1980 the military won one of the chief requirements of a modern professional institution when its leadership sought and obtained the conditions to achieve parity with the Soviet Union. The Party recognized the military's freedom from political interference in the allocation, organization and use of its resources and in the discussion and development of doctrine.

This decade had been one of reform that was both pragmatic and profound. With the fall of the Gang of Four, China and the PLA closed a major chapter in their history and marched into the twentieth century determined to compete on its own terms with its primary enemy, the Soviet Union.

NORTH KOREA

The latter half of the 1970s witnessed the continued expansion of the Korean People's Army's special operations forces to a strength of 41,000 in 1978 and to 81,000 in 1982 when the process seemed to stop. Kim Il Sung's obsession with such formations had created a force unprecedented in size for a conventional army, but in complete accord with his concepts, defined in 1972, of fighting a two-front war with a combination of guerrilla and conventional warfare. In 1984 the KPA began another series of reorganizations that converted infantry and motorized divisions to more capable combined arms brigades. In consonance with its knock-out punch structure, the KPA covertly acquired 87 Hughes MD 500D/E helicopters in 1983–5, civilian versions of the same helicopter used by the ROK Air Force. Painted in ROK colours, they became a blatant threat of surprise attack.[102]

Kim had not neglected the conventional side of his armed forces. He had made North Korea into one of the most industrialized states in Asia, primarily to feed the expansion of the conventional ground forces which had grown steadily since the late fifties. In 1965 the defence budget had been trebled. So well was this effort concealed that as late as 1978 western analysts estimated the strength of the KPA as no more than 440,000 men in two tank, three motorized infantry and 20 infantry divisions. President Carter's intention to withdraw US forces from South Korea triggered a major reassessment of KPA strength. *The Military Balance* for 1979 showed a massive increase to 600,000 men in two tank, three motorized and 35 infantry divisions. Equipment inventories showing 2,300 tanks (mostly T-54/55s) and 3,500 guns far outnumbered holdings of the ROK Army. By 1983 the manpower estimates had grown to 700,000. The KPA established a Strategic Forces Command (SFC) to accomplish special missions, approval for which could only be granted by Kim Il Sung. The SFC included all the tank and motorized infantry divisions, twenty brigades of VII Special Corps, five élite training regiments, five SAM and five AAA regiments, and ten free rocket over ground (FROG) battalions.[103]

The KPA was able to meet this manpower figure from a population of barely 17.5 million by universal military service and by service periods that averaged an incredible nine years. Conscripted between the ages of 17 and 21, the soldier was generally forced to serve until the age of 27. Numbers were stretched by recruiting women as anti-aircraft gunners, typists, hospital workers, signal communicators and psychological warfare personnel. North Korean society is the most Orwellian in the world; nowhere else does so little news of the outside world intrude to conflict with the intense indoctrination from birth. The result was a thoroughly convinced and well-motivated soldier. Training, especially physical training, was thorough and exhaustive. The KPA, much like the ROK Army, excels in unarmed combat. KPA soldiers were well trained in their combat skills, though the emphasis was on rote rather than understanding.[104]

SOUTH KOREA

With the sudden revelation of the well-concealed increases in the strength of the Korean People's Army (KPA), the Republic of Korea (ROK) Army suddenly found that its major advantage against the North, manpower, had been snatched away. The ROK Army's 520,000 men in 1979 were now shown to be actually outnumbered by the KPA's 600,000 men. The 20,000 men of the ROK Marine Corps still did not balance the equation. The loss of the manpower advantage made the ROK Army's existing disadvantage in equipment even more serious, especially given Kim Il Sung's preference for the single knock-out punch. The ROK Army's 1,100,000 reserves in 23 cadre divisions would not tip the balance in a short war. The ROK Army's 860 tanks and 2,000 guns were opposed by the KPA's 2,300 tanks and 3,500 guns. Increases in strength during the rest of the decade were slow and incremental, though within the ability of the army to train and prepare for them. Active duty manpower did not increase at the same rate.

Table 4-16. ROK Army Equipment Increases 1979–1985

	1979	1982	1983	1985
Tanks	860	1000	1200	1200
APCs	520	850	850	700
Artillery	2,000	2,000	2,500	3,000
Helicopters	25	25	125	150

Source: IISS *The Strategic Balance*

President Park was assassinated by his own Korean Central Intelligence Agency (KCIA) chief in 1979. Martial law restrictions and the imprisonment of the opposition's leader provoked widespread demonstrations in 1980 that were put down by the ROK Army's special forces, more than 200 civilians being killed in the southern city of Kwangju. General Chun Doo Hwan, chairman of the committee that had governed since Park's death, assumed *de facto* leadership of the state and instituted sweeping political controls. The military's role in society, which had seemed to be moderating during Park's last years as South Korean society had matured, was vastly increased.

The ROK military had been the engine of South Korea's modernization beginning in 1961. Well-developed ROK Army institutions provided the leaders and many entrepreneurs for South Korea's growth. The army had coped with the enormous job of building the country's infrastructure. Military rule had infused South Korean society with a drive and spirit it had heretofore lacked. Unfortunately the very advances encouraged by military rule had made that rule increasingly onerous and less necessary. The Chun government tragically failed to distinguish between this maturation and a threat to the state.[105]

JAPAN

With its first two decades behind it, Japan's new post-war army, the Ground Self-Defence Force (GSDF), was becoming an increasingly stable fixture of Japanese society. It was also becoming an increasingly mature and capable professional force. Although its numbers varied little from year to year, it maintained a steady growth in the sophistication of its weaponry and its tables of organization.

During this decade the structure of the army's combat forces was realized at thirteen divisions of three types. The Type A (or *Ko*) division, of which there were seven, was the strongest at a strength of 9,000 men and organized with four infantry regiments, one artillery regiment, one tank battalion, one anti-tank unit, one reconnaissance unit, one engineer battalion, one signal battalion and support units. The five Type B (or *Otsu*) divisions of 7,000 men were much the same as the Type A but with one less infantry regiment. The single Type C (or *Hei*) division was an armoured division of 7,000 men. In addition to the thirteen divisions, the GSDF formed independent tank, parachute and composite brigades. It should be noted that the Japanese division of any type is small by Western standards. Its combat power is really the equivalent of a NATO brigade. The infantry regiments, for example, are essentially battalions.[106]

Equipment was increasingly produced in Japan. For example, in 1975 600 of 750 tanks were Japanese models; in 1985 100 per cent of 1,070 tanks were domestically built. The artillery, however, remained largely US-produced models throughout the decade.

Operationally, the GSDF emphasized platoon, company and battalion operations. The few, small training areas in Japan coupled with a sensitive public precluded many large exercises. Although the post-war armed forces had been consciously modelled to avoid continuity with their imperial predecessors and had been remarkably successful, too successful some would claim. The individual services rediscovered a few of the more negative traditions of the past, the worst of them being the lack of inter-service co-ordination, co-operation and planning that made defence planning difficult. The services were run as separate fiefdoms that treated one another as rivals rather than partners. Critics also pointed out that ammunition and other stocks remained far too low for modern combat consumption rates to be sustained for more than a week. The GSDF voluntary reserve of barely 41,000 men in 1985 also added seriously to worries that wartime defence of the homeland could not be sustained for more than a week. The Japaanese did not see these as crippling and irrational failures to plan for the obvious exigencies of modern warfare. Rather, these weaknesses were masked by the firm assumption that any attack on the Japanese mainland, such as a Soviet attempt to seize the Island of Hokkaido, would find the Japanese defenders immediately reinforced by the armed forces of the United States.

AUSTRALIA

The Australian government's Defence White Paper of 1976 advocated a 'core force' concept for the army from which 'the structure, equipment and professional skills adequate for timely expansion against a range of contingencies of various types and timings' were to be developed. A task so vague that it seemed to say, 'plan for everything' would have been difficult even for a country of far greater population and wealth than Australia. For an army living on a shoestring it was impossible since the government refused to provide the funds to implement any of these plans. The previous Labour government had abandoned forward deployment as a strategy and encouraged the dissolution of SEATO in 1975. The Liberal-Country government that replaced it in 1975 continued its policies. As a consequence the armed forces were given no clear statement of the threat and the national strategy to meet it. By the early 1980s the army was incapable of meeting any but the most low-level threat at short notice.[107]

During this decade equipment purchases provided new tanks, SAMs and some new artillery, though in almost pathetic quantities. Most of the purchases were the result of initiatives of the previous decade.

Table 4-17. Australian Army Weapons Acquisitions 1976–1985

1976–1981	103 Leopard I tanks replaced equal number of Centurions
1979–1982	20 Rapier SAM systems acquired to supplement Redeyes
1984–1985	36 M198 155mm howitzers acquired
1984–1985	12 Milan AT systems acquired to supplement 106mm RR

Source: IISS, *The Military Balance*

To put these purchases in perspective, it should be noted that the Israelis lost more equipment in their first day's counter-attack against the Egyptians when they crossed the Canal in 1973.

THE ART OF STRATEGY

The seven most instructive military actions of this fourth post-war decade that illustrate the relation of military means to policy can be neatly divided into three successful and four failed operations. The successful oeprations included three short, sharp campaigns of a limited nature. The four failures were large, open-ended operations that bogged down in stalemate. The first trio included the Chinese punative expedition against Vietnam, the British Falklands campaign and the American liberation of Grenada. The second trio included the Vietnamese invasion of Cambodia, the Soviet invasion of Afghanistan, the Iraqi invasion of Iran, and the Israeli invasion of Lebanon.

Each of the first three operations had clear policy objectives that were limited in time and space and within the military grasp of the armies charged with their execution. The British in the Falklands and the Americans in Grenada were operationally as well as strategically successful. The overwhelming force applied by the Americans and their proximity to the area of operations left little doubt of the outcome. There was much room for error. The British, on the other hand, were operating at great distances where superiority was in quality of forces only. Their performance had to be as finely machined as any complex weapons componet, yet in the end, it was within British capabilities, even if just so. The Chinese essentially suffered a draw which in the context of the aims of policy translated into a strategic victory. The Vietnamese who had handled themselves well on the battlefield nevertheless heeded the political message of the operation, its real aim. The Chinese strategic performance was a model of a limited objective operation planned and conducted with careful restraint. Only a small part of the forces assembled actually entered Vietnam. Military objectives were only a series of regional capitals within easy reach of Chinese forces. The Chinese resisted the temptation to strike only a little further and threaten the approaches to Hanoi and thereby let the operation get out of hand.

Out of hand is exactly what the Vietnamese, Soviet, Iraqi and Isreali operations all became. They all foundered on poorly thought-out policy objectives that could not be translated into practicable military objectives. All four operations were based on poor estimates of the enemy's ability to resist and a disregard for the fact that the operations could not be geographically or politically contained. The enemy in all instances received critical foreign military and political support. The Vietnamese and Soviet counterinsurgency efforts ultimately had to be written off as military failures and the Israeli effort as politically unsustainable. The Soviet failure directly contributed to the undermining of the prestige of the Soviet Union, one of the proximate causes of its sudden collapse. While the Iraqis eventually achieved a formal victory, they won nothing but a merciful relief from a near decade of bloody attrition.

NOTES

1   Russell F. Weigley, *History of the Unites States Army*, (Bloomington: Indiana University Press, 1984), pp. 578–9.
2   *FM 100-5 Operations* (Washington, DC: Headquarters, Department of the Army, May 1986), pp. 14, 23.
3   The Army's overt identification of the anticipated enemy caused no end of complaint from the Soviet armed forces, a strange sensitivity for a system that had branded the United States as the *glavny vrag* (the main enemy), for three generations. The opposite also applied when the author visited the now Russian Tank Museum at Kubinka in July 1992 and saw a complete collection of US armour, some with holes, except for the M1 Tank.
4   Hans Hlberstadt, *NTC: A Primer of Modern Land Combat* (Novato: Presidio Press, 1989, pp. 22–3.
5   H. Norman Schwarzkopf, *It Doesn't Take a Hero* (New York: Bantam Books, 1992, p. 244.
6   Halberstadt, op. cit., pp. 118–9.
7   Schwarzkopf, op. cit., p. 254. Schwarzkopf relates how a Marine colonel refused pointblank Schwarzkopf's order to ferry Army troops in his empty helicopters even when his own Marines were not available to accomplish a pressing mission. Schwarzkopf explained the difference between

a major general and a colonel and then promised to court-martial him if he didn't comply. He did, gracelessly.

8   Dominick Graham, 'England', in Richard Gabriel, ed., *Fighting Armies, NATO and the Warsaw Pact: A Fighting Assessment* (Westport, CT: Greenwood Press, 1983), pp. 69–70.

9   Terry Gander, *Encyclopaedia of the Modern British Army* (2nd ed.), (Cambridge: Patrick Stephens, 1982), pp. 17–8.

10   Gander, *Encyclopaedia* (3rd ed.), (Wellingsborough: Patrick Stephens, 1986), pp. 20–22.

11   Max Hastings and Simon Jenkins, *The Battle for the Falklands* (New York: W. W. Norton & Co., 1983), pp. 267–69.

12   Ibid., pp. 268, 330.

13   In fairness a good part of the planned helicopter support for the expeditionary force was lost when the *Atlantic Conveyer* carrying six Wessex and five Chinook helicopters was sunk. Luckily one Chinook escaped the dying ship and remained the only heavy lift helicopter for the entire campaign.

14   Gary L. Guertner, 'The 74–Day War: New Technology and Old Tactics,' *Military Review*, November 1982, p. 72.

15   *The British Army in the Falklands – 1982* (Her Majesty's Stationary Office, 1983), p. 32.

16   Ruiz Palmer, 'France' in Jeffery Simon, ed., *NATO – Warsaw Pact Force Mobilization* (Washington, DC: National Defense University Press, 1988), p. 289–293.

17   Ibid., pp. 293–4,

18   Anthony H. Cordesman, *NATO's Central Region Forces: Capabilities, Challenges, Concepts* (London: Jane's, 1988), pp. 199–200.

19   J. J. Cox, 'Chad: France in Africa,' *The Army Quarterly and Defense Journal*, Volume 118, April 1988, pp. 161–5.

20   Martin Windrow and Wayne Braby, *French Foreign Legion Paratroops* (London: Osprey Publishing, 1985), pp. 29–31.

21   Michel L. Castillon, 'Low-Intensity Conflict in the 1980's: The French Experience,' *Military Review*, January 1986, pp. 69–70; translated from *Armees d'aujourd'hui*, May 1985.

22   T. N. Dupuy, *A Genius For War* (Englewood Cliffs, NJ: Prentice Hall, Inc., 1977), p. 299.

23   Norbert Majewski and John H. Peyton, 'German Army General Staff Officer Training, *Military Review*, December 1984, pp. 24–5.

24   Phillip A. Karber and John H. Milam, 'The Federal Republic of Germany', in Jeffery Simon, ed., *NATO – Warsaw Pact Force Mobilization* (Washington, DC: The National Defense University Press, 1988), pp. 253–4.

25   Karber and Milam, ibid. ; and *The Military Balance 1973–1974, 1975–1976, 1980–1981, 1983–1984* (London: The International Institute for Stategic Studies, 1973, 1975, 1980, 1983),.

26   J. A. English, 'The German Territorial Army,' in Ian V. Hogg, ed., *Jane's 1982–1983 Military Review* (London: Jane's Publishing Inc., 1982), pp. 96–101.

27   Karber and Milam, ibid. ; David Isby and Charles Kamps, Jr., *Armies of NATO's Central Front* (London: Jane's Publishing Co., 1985), pp. 197–8.

28   Anthony H. Cordesman, *NATO's Central Region Forces* (London: Jane's Publishing, 1988), p. 83. Although the extension to conscription was eventually passed by the *Bundestag* in 1988, it was never actually implemented due to widespread opposition.

29   *The Military Balance 1985–1986* (London: International Institute for Strategic Studies, 1985), p. 49.

30   Cordesman, ibid., p. 93.

31   Donald Abenheim, *Reforging the Iron Cross: The Search for Tradition in the West German Forces* (Princeton: The Princeton University Press, 1988), pp. 270–5.

32   Abenheim, ibid., pp. 280–2.

33   Abenheim, ibid., pp. 285–6.

34   A. Ross Johnson, Robert W. Dean, and Alexander Alexiev, *Eastern European Military Establishments: The Warsaw Pact Northern Tier* (New York: Crane Russak, 1982), pp. 69–72.

35   Johnson, et. al., ibid., pp. 72–5.

36   David Childs, *The GDR: Moscow's German Ally* (London: George Allen & Unwin, 1983), p. 290.

37   David C. Isby and Charles Kamps Jr., *Armies of NATO's Central Front* (London: Jane's Publishing Co., 1983), p. 214.

38   Edmund Walendowski, *Combat Motivation of the Polish Forces* (New York: St. Martin's Press, 1988), p. 103.

39   Les Griggs, 'The Polish People's Army,' in Jeffery Simon, ed., *NATO – Warsaw Pact Force Mobilization* (Washington, DC: The National Defense University Press, 1988), p. 365.

40   Griggs, ibid., pp. 365–6.

41   Leon Dubicki, 'Di UdSSR hat Angst vor dem polnichesn Volk' (The USSR is afraid of the Polish People,' interview with Polish general Leon Dubicki, *Der Spiegel*, no. 53 (December 26, 1981), cited in Walendoswki, op. cit., p. 104.

42   Walendowski, op. cit., pp. 95–100.

43   N. V. Ogarkov, 'Military Science and the Defense of the Socialist Fatherland,' *Kommunist*, No. 7, 1978, p. 115.

44   Ogarkov, *Always in Readiness to Defend the Homeland* (Moscow: Voenizdat, 1982), p. 49.

45   A. A. Yepishev, 'A Great Historical Mission,' *Krasnaya Zvezda*, 23 February 1982, p. 2.

46   The Russian ending *chinna* signifies 'the evil rule of or time of' as in Ivan the Terrible's secret police

Oprichniki giving rise to the name of a time of terror, *Oprichnina*.

47   David Tyson, 'Bullying in the Soviet Army,' *How They Fight*, US Army Intelligence and Threat Analysis Center, Oct–Dec 1988, p. 27.

48   Alexander Alexiev, *Inside the Soviet Army in Afghanistan*, R–627–A, The Rand Corp., May 1988, p. 42.

49   *Der Spiegel*, 16 June 1980, pp. 112–114.

50   Alexander Alexiev, *Inside the Soviet Army in Afghanistan* (Santa Monica, CA: The Rand Corp., 1988), p. 5.

51   David C. Isby, *War in a Distant Country – Afghanistan: Invasion and Resistance* (London: Arms and Armour Press, 1989), p. 24; Anthony R. Tucker, 'Armed Forces of the Afghan Conflict,' *Jane's Soviet Intelligence Review*, March 1990, pp. 114–118.

52   Tucker, ibid.

53   Isby, op. cit., p. 33.

54   Mark Urban, 'Soviet Intervention and the Ogaden Counteroffensive of 1978, *RUSI*, London, Vol 128, No. 2, 2 June 1983, pp. 43–5.

55   Christopher F. Foss, *Jane's AFV Recognition Handbook* (London: Jane's Publishing Co., 1987), pp. 65, 256–7, 282.

56   Ibid., pp. 370–1, 380, 445, 447.

57   Reuven Gal, *A Portrait of the Israeli Soldier* (New York: Greenwood Press, 1986), pp. 22–23.

58   Ibid., pp. 23–4.

59   Richard A. Gabriel, 'Lessons of War: The IDF in Lebanon,' *Military Review*, August 1984, pp. 50–51.

60   Sam Katz, *Israeli Defence Forces since 1973* (London: Osprey Publishing Ltd, 1989), p. 13.

61   Gabriel, op. cit., p. 52.

62   W. Seth Carus, 'Military Lessons of the 1982 Israel-Syria Conflict,' Robert E. Harkavy and Stephanie Neuman, eds., *The Lessons of Recent Wars in the Third World, Volume I* (Lexington, MA: Lexington Books, 1985), p. 270.

63   Gabriel, op. cit., pp. 48, 55–56.

64   Gabriel, op. cit., pp. 62–63, 65. The Syrians may have lost about 1,000 dead.

65   Mark Heller, ed., *The Middle East Military Balance 1984* (Tel Aviv: Tel Aviv University, 1984), pp. 117–8.

66   John Keegan, *World Armies*, 2nd Ed., (Detroit: Gale Research Company, 1983), pp. 166–7.

67   Samuel M. Katz, *Arab Armies of the Middle East Wars (2)*, (London: Osprey Publishing, 1988), p. 16.

68   Chaim Herzog, *The War of Atonement* (Boston: Little, Brown & Co., 1975), p. 140.

69   John S. Wagner, 'Iraq,' Richard A. Gabriel, ed., *Fighting Armies, Antagonists in the Middle East: A Combat Assessment*. (Westport, CT: Greenwood Press, 1983), pp. 72–3.

70   Gwynne Dyer, 'Iraq,' in John Keegan, ed., *Word Armies* (second edition), (Detroit, MI: Gale Research Co., 1983), p. 291.

71   Anthony R. Tucker, 'Armoured Warfare in the Gulf. ' *Armed Forces*, May 1988, p. 225

72   Wagner, op. cit., p. 78.

73   F. W. E. Furdson, 'The Iraq/Iran War,' in John Weeks, ed., *Jane's 1981–82 Military Annual* (London: Jane's Publishing Co., 1981), p. 124.

74   Fox Butterfield, '8-Year Gulf War: Victims but no Victors,' *The New York Times*, 25 July 1988.

75   Peter Dunn, 'The Chemical War: Iran Revisited–1986,' *NBC Defense & Technology International*, Vol I, No. 3, June 1986, pp. 32–3.

76   Sepher Zabih, *The Iranian Military in Revolution and War* (London: Routledge, 1988), p. 11.

77   Ken Perkins, 'The Death of an Army: A Short Analysis of the Imperial Iranian Armed Forces', *RUSI*, Volume 125 No. 2 June 1980, p. 22.

78   Ibid., p. 21.

79   Helen Chapin Metz, ed., *Iran: A Country Study* (Washington, DC: Federal Research Division, 1989), p. 243.

80   Zabih, op. cit., pp. 118, 123.

81   Metz, op. cit., p. 268.

82   Edgar O'Ballance. *The Gulf War* (London: Brassey's Defence Publishers, 1988), pp. 51, 121.

83   Zabih, op. cit., pp. 200–1.

84   Zabih, op. cit., pp. 212–213.

85   *Ettelaat* (Tehran), 7 May 1982, cited in Zabih, op. cit., pp. 218–220.

86   Zahib, op. cit.

87   Stephen P. Cohen, *The Pakistan Army*, (Berkeley, California: University of California Press, 1984), p. 128.

88   Edgar O'Ballance, 'The Armed Forces of India,' *Armed Forces*, September 1986, Vol 5, No. 9, pp. 404–6.

89   Ibid., p. 408.

90   Ibid., p. 409.

91   Roland J. Cima, ed., *Vietnam: A Country Study* (Washington: American University, 1989), p. 252.

92   Douglas Pike, 'Vietnam, a Modern Sparta,' *Pacific Defense Reporter*, April 1983.

93   Fredrica M. Bunge, ed., *China: A Country Study* (Washington, DC: The American University, 1981), p. 482.

94   Harlan W. Jencks, 'China's 'Punitive' War on Vietnam: A Military Assessment', *Asian Survey*, Vol

XIX, No. 8, August 1979, pp. 489–90.

95   Ibid.,p. 802.

96   Jer, Donald Get, 'PLA Lessons Learned in Vietnam,' *Military Review*, July 1987, p. 22, based on an interview with BG Bernard G. Loeffke, US attaché to the PRC 1982–84, at Fort Brag, NC, 16 Aug 1984.

97   Drew Middleton, 'How Chinese performed: Lack of Mobility Evident,' *The New York Times*, 6 March 1979, p. 10.

98   Jencks, ibid., pp. 810–11.

99   Harlan W. Jencks, 'Lessons of a 'Lesson': China–Vietnam, 1973,' in *The Lessons of Recent Wars in the Third World, volume I*, ed. Robert E. Harkavy (Lexington, MA: Lexington Books, 1985), pp. 148–53.

100   Fox Butterfield, 'Mao's Ideas on War Are Losing Ground, ' *The New York Times*, 26 March 1979, p. 7.

101   'A Fundamental Law for Modernizing Our Country's National Defense,' *Xinhua*, translated in FBIS, 8 June 1984, pp. K4–K5.

102   Joseph S., Jr., *North Korean Special Forces* (Surrey: Jane's Publishing Co., 1988), pp. 38–40.

103   US Army Field Manual 34–71, *Opposing Forces Training Module: North Korean Military Forces*, (Washington, DC: Department of the Army, 1982), p. 3–1.

104   Ibid., p. 4–1.

105   Edward A. Olsen, 'The Societal Role of the ROK Armed Forces,' in Olsen, ed., *The Armed Forces of Contemporary Asian Societies* (Boulder: Westview Press, 1986), p. 100.

106   John Keegan, *World Armies*, Detroit: (Gale Research Co., 1983), p. 327.

107   Jeffrey Grey, *A Military History of Australia* (Cambridge: Cambridge University Press, 1990), p. 252.

CHAPTER 5

THE END OF AN ERA
THE ABBREVIATED FIFTH POST-WAR DECADE
1985–1989

INTRODUCTION

At the beginning of the decade there was absolutely no indication that the post-Second World War era was at its last gasp. The old verities seemed secure. The NATO and Warsaw Pact alliances, with various clients around the world, were intact, and the Arabs and Israelis, Pakistanis and Indians, and Vietnamese and Chinese seemed to be locked securely in their special relationships of enmity as before. Development seemed to be on its predictable straight-line course as the United States and the Soviet Union continued arming and training for the envisaged great battle in Germany. Three long and brutal wars would exhaust themselves and come to an end in 1988 and 1989 – the Iran–Iraq War, the Soviet invasion of Afghanistan and the Vietnamese occupation of Cambodia. Nothing seemed to have changed much save there were now millions fewer people in the Middle East and South-east Asia.

Then the bottom fell out of the entire box of tricks. One of the two great pillars of the post-war order, the Soviet Union, suffered a nervous breakdown. The rise to power of Mikhail Gorbachev in 1985 and his series of hand-to-mouth reforms seemed to evaporate the fuel of post-war relationships. Those reforms led directly to the abandonment of the regime in East Germany. On 9 November the Berlin Wall fell, and the era came to an end. Nothing would ever be the same again after the Berliners swarmed over the hated *Mauer* as the Volksarmee stood aside, signing its own death warrant. By transforming the political environment of the bipolar world, the fall of the Berlin Wall challenged the mission and organization of almost every one of the world's armies.

UNITED STATES

The fifth decade of this era saw the fruition of the US Army's post-Vietnam reforms. All the post-Vietnam professional reforms, the Reagan Administration's lavishing of funds for new equipment, facilities and training had come together to produce the finest army the United States had ever fielded. It would be the army that would fight the first war of the next era, 'Desert Storm', and make a virtuoso performance look so easy.

By the late 1980s the army's order-of-battle included four armoured, seven mechanized infantry, one infantry, four light infantry, one air assault and one airborne divisions. Separate brigades added two more division equivalents, and the three armoured cavalry regiments (ACRs) were more powerful than the divisions of many armies. A further ten divisions (two armoured, two mechanized, five infantry and one light inantry) plus twenty independent brigades could be available from the Reserve Components upon mobilization.[1]

The careful use of manpower had added 79 combat battalions to the army without an increase in strength over the 1980 establishment. Much of this had been done by transferring support functions to the Reserve Components and by combing out non-essential functions. Nevertheless, an important fighting role ostensibly was left to the reserves. The active force supported 379 combat battalions compared to 391 in the Reserve Components. The Total Army Concept of a tight bond between Active and Reserve Components was advertised as a foundation of a balanced force. A new look was given to special operations with the establishment of the 1st Special Operations Command that combined Ranger, Special Forces, Psychological Operations and Civil Affairs missions. A third Ranger battalion and a fourth Special Forces Group were also activated.[2]

The quality of the 766,500 (including 82,700 women) personnel and their training had become twin engines driving the army's professionalization. In 1988 90.9 per cent of recruits had a high-school diploma and 70.8 per cent were in the higher intelligence categories. During this period the NCO corps had recovered much of the stature and role it had had before Vietnam ruined it, but this was a new NCO corps, one able to deal with far more sophisticated training, equipment and leadership skills. Criticized in 1981 for consistently failing to win major NATO training competitions, the army won all three major competitions in 1988. By the end of 1987, 143 battalions with nearly 250,000 troops had gone through the National Training Center at Fort Irwin in California at the rate of 28 battalions a year.[3] In 1987 an NTC-type training centre for low- to mid-intensity combat, the Joint Readiness Training Center (JRTC), was established at Fort Chafee, Arkansas. High standards of physical training and fitness also had become standard. So intent was the army on physical fitness that it instituted draconian measures to keep personnel at prescribed body weight limits. Personnel were variously immersed in water, pinched with calipers, or measured with tape measures to ensure that no unauthorized body fat went undetected. So unforgiving was the army that a tubby Alexander would have been dismissed while the slim Darius was retained. In all honesty, the army did energetically wage a war against the fat between its officers' ears – though without the same mindless intensity as the hunt for fat around their middles. The officer training and education reforms of the previous decade had been expanded and institutionalized. The average combat arms officer was now thoroughly grounded in the skills of his arm, and it was not unusual for him to be able to discuss intelligently Sun Tzu or Clausewitz and their relevance to warfare in the 1980s.

A whole generation of new equipment that had first appeared in the early 1980s was now flowing in great quantities into the increasingly skilled hands of the combat forces. By late 1988 thirty M1 Abrams tank battalions had been equipped as well as 20 battalions with Bradley M2 Fighting Vehicles. Aviation and artillery received more punch with 454 new AH-64A attack and 931 Blackhawk transport helicopters and the 416 Multiple-Launch Rocket Systems (MLRS). The emphasis on combat equipment for the armoured, infantry, artillery and aviation combat arms, however, meant a continuing lower priority for other types of equipment such as combat engineer vehicles.

The J-Series Table of Organization (TOE) was introduced in the mid-1980s for armoured and mechanized infantry divisions under the Army of Excellence reorganization. Although built upon the basic ROAD structure of the early 1960s, the J-Series, also called 'Division 86', was designed to meet the more demanding requirements of AirLand Battle. Artillery and aviation assets were especially strengthened. All divisions were basically indentical, differing only in the mix of armoured and mechanized battalions. The terms armoured and infantry (mechanized) retained only the lineages and numbers of the particular divisions. Light divisions, introduced in 1984–5, were increased to four with the activation of the 10th Mountain Division. They were designed for low-intensity conflict regions with the guiding principle that their TOE and manning (10,770) must be capable of being airlifted by no more than 500 C-141 aircraft sorties. Weaknesses appeared to be anti-tank and transporation capabilities that could put them at the mercy of the increasingly tank rich armies in the Third World. The armoured cavalry regiments came to be recognized as especially capable formations. Designed to be a corps covering force, they also conduct reconnaissance in force, screening, flank security and deep

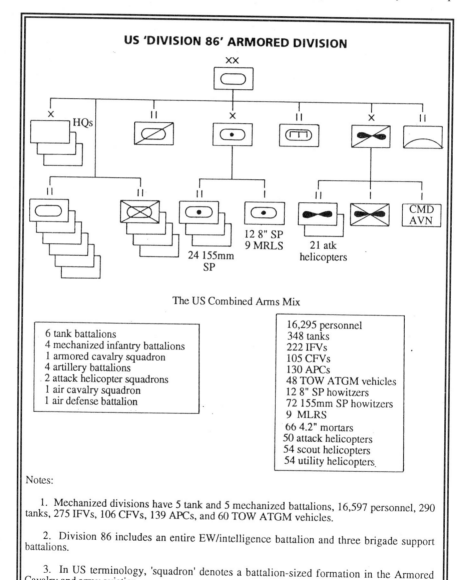

US 'DIVISION 86' ARMORED DIVISION

The US Combined Arms Mix

6 tank battalions
4 mechanized infantry battalions
1 armored cavalry squadron
4 artillery battalions
2 attack helicopter squadrons
1 air cavalry squadron
1 air defense battalion

16,295 personnel
348 tanks
222 IFVs
105 CFVs
130 APCs
48 TOW ATGM vehicles
12 8" SP howitzers
72 155mm SP howitzers
9 MLRS
66 4.2" mortars
50 attack helicopters
54 scout helicopters
54 utility helicopters

12 8" SP
9 MRLS
24 155mm SP
21 atk helicopters

Notes:

1. Mechanized divisions have 5 tank and 5 mechanized battalions, 16,597 personnel, 290 tanks, 275 IFVs, 106 CFVs, 139 APCs, and 60 TOW ATGM vehicles.

2. Division 86 includes an entire EW/intelligence battalion and three brigade support battalions.

3. In US terminology, 'squadron' denotes a battalion-sized formation in the Armored Cavalry and army aviation.

attack missions. Their 129 Abrams tanks, 111 Bradley IFVs, 24 155mm SP guns and 26 attack helicopters make these supple combined arms teams stronger than most divisions in the world's armies.

As the 1980s ended the army immediately leaped into a new era. Within a month of the fall of the Berlin Wall, the army played the major role in Operation 'Just Cause', the invasion of Panama in late December 1989. 'Desert Storm' lay just ahead, a graduate examination for the army of the 1980s.

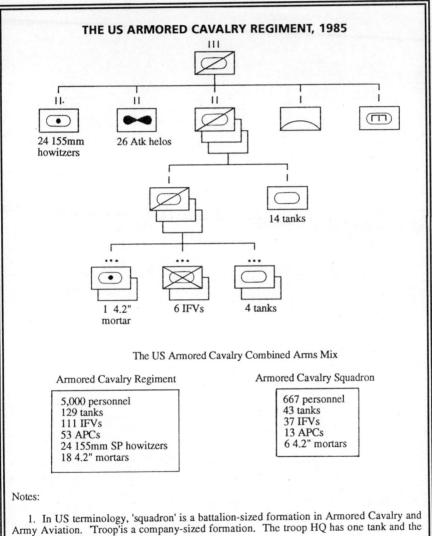

THE US ARMORED CAVALRY REGIMENT, 1985

24 155mm howitzers

26 Atk helos

14 tanks

1 4.2" mortar

6 IFVs

4 tanks

The US Armored Cavalry Combined Arms Mix

Armored Cavalry Regiment

| 5,000 personnel |
| 129 tanks |
| 111 IFVs |
| 53 APCs |
| 24 155mm SP howitzers |
| 18 4.2" mortars |

Armored Cavalry Squadron

| 667 personnel |
| 43 tanks |
| 37 IFVs |
| 13 APCs |
| 6 4.2" mortars |

Notes:

1. In US terminology, 'squadron' is a battalion-sized formation in Armored Cavalry and Army Aviation. 'Troop' is a company-sized formation. The troop HQ has one tank and the squadron HQ 2 tanks each.

2. The Armored Cavalry Regiment is served by an entire organic combat electronic warfare ˙nd intelligence company.

Table 5-1. Manoeuvre Order-of-Battle of the US. Army 1985–1989

Divisions	Honorifics
1st Infantry Division (Mechanized)	Big Red One
2nd Infantry Division	Indianhead
3rd Infantry Division (Mechanized)	Rock of the Marne
4th Infantry Division (Mechanized)	Ivy Division
5th Infantry Division (Mechanized)	Red Diamond Division
6th Infantry Division (Light)	Sightseeing Sixth
7th Infantry Division (Light)	Bayonet Division
8th Infantry Division (Mechanized)	Golden Arrow Division
9th Infantry Division (Motorized)	Old Reliables
10th Mountain Division (Light Infantry)	Mountaineers
24th Infantry Division (Mechanized)	Victory Division
25th Infantry Division (Light)	Tropical Lighting
82nd Airborne Division	All Americans
101st Airborne Division (Air Assault)	Screaming Eagles
1st Cavalry Division	First Team
1st Armored Division	Old Ironsides
2nd Armored Division	Hell on Wheels
3rd Armored Division	Spearhead Division

Separate Brigades/Regiments/Groups	
177th Armored Brigade (Separate)	None
193rd Infantry Brigade (Separate)	No Ground to Give
194th Armored Brigade (Separate)	Thunderbolts of Battle
197th Infantry Brigade (Mechanized)(Separate)	Follow Me
Berlin Brigade	None
2nd Armored Cavalry Regiment	Second Dragoons
3rd Armored Cavalry Regiment	Brave Rifles
11th Armored Cavalry Regiment	The Black Horse Regiment
1st Special Forces Group (Airborne)	
3rd Special Forces Group (Airborne)	
5th Special Forces Group (Airborne)	
7th Special Forces Group (Airborne)	
10th Special Forces Group (Airborne)	
75th Ranger Regiment	Merrill's Marauders

GREAT BRITAIN

In the late 1980s the British Army was the strongest NATO army after the US and German Armies, though it was smaller than many others, having barely 155,500 troops (6,500 women) in 1989.

Modernization of equipment proceeded though at a much slower pace than for the US and German armies which had more generous budgets. The production rate of the new Challenger main battle tank was excruciatingly slow. From 130 vehicles in 1985, the number in the field had inched up to barely 420 in 1989, with a seventh regiment on order that year. The Warrior IFV came into service even more slowly, from 150 in 1985 to 200 in 1989. Defence expenditures failed to increase during the final years of the post-war era and actually resulted in cuts – 7,500 personnel from 163,000 in 1985. Chronic under-funding further resulted in endemic weaknesses in the ability to sustain forces in combat to the point where BAOR, even when reinforced under mobilization, would still have had less than the combat power of three US or German armoured divisions. Artillery stocks were so low as to permit barely 8-12 days of sustained operations. Luckily, the era passed without subjecting this hollowness to the explosive pressure of war with the Warsaw Pact. The danger was only revealed during Operation 'Desert Shield'. In order to send one 2-brigade armoured division to Saudi Arabia, BAOR was obliged to strip the other three of personnel and equipment. Despite its small size and relative poverty, the professionalism and high training standards of the British Army continued to make up for its shortcomings, as 'Desert Storm' was to prove. It was a back-up system that British governments had come to rely upon, perhaps, far too much.

The years 1985-9 were relatively tranquil for the army. For the first time since 1945 there were no hot overseas commitments. The army still maintained almost 8 per cent of its strength (12,330 troops including all its Gurhka battalions) in peaceful garrisons in Cyprus (2,300), Brunei (900), Belize (1,200), Hong Kong (5,900), Gibraltar (700) and the Falkland Islands (1,600). The only danger continued to be close at hand in Northern Ireland. The army deployed ten major units with 9,200 men excluding nine Ulster Defence Regiment battalions (6,500), in support of the civil authority and the Ulster Constabulary against the terrorism of the IRA. These units actively patrolled, manned vehicle checkpoints, and undertook search operations to hunt down terrorists and lend a sense of security to local communities. An upsurge in terrorism in 1988 continued to provide the army with a certain realism in its operations.

The bulk of the fighting forces (55,000 men and all three of its armoured divisions) in the British Army of the Rhine (BAOR) continued to be stationed in northern Germany which, in almost fifty years, had become a second home. So permanent did this forward deployment seem that training areas and garrisons in the United Kingdom itself were sufficient only for the forces stationed at home. Most of the army's 74,000 reserves in the Territorial Army (TA) would also have found themselves in Germany had they been mobilized to meet a Soviet attack on NATO. The TA made up 40 per cent of the order-of-battle and would have provided vital unit and individual reinforcements for the understrength BAOR as well as taking responsibility for the defence of the United Kingdom itself. TA personnel were all volunteers. The fact that they were able to abandon their membership almost at a moment's notice, and yet maintained very high levels of commitment and performance demonstrated the value of these troops in wartime. They were the vital backstop that prevented the economies of decades from crippling the active force.

FRANCE

Much like the British Army, the French Army was obliged by budgetary constraints to reorganize existing assets into more effective structures. The most successful such effort was the Rapid Reaction Force or FAR, initiated during the previous period. By 1988 FAR, with 47,000 men, had grown into an impressively mobile, though lightly armed, reserve for the Central Front in any NATO-Warsaw Pact war.

Table 5-2. French Army Rapid Action Force (FAR) 1988

Division	Strength	Subordinate Regiments
4th Airmobile Division	7,100	one 1 infantry, three combat helicopter
6th Armoured Cavalry	7,500	two cavalry, two mechanized, one Division artillery, one engineer
Division	Strength	Subordinate Regiments

293

9th Marine Division	8,100	two light armoured, two infantry, one artillery, one engineer
11th Parachute Division	13,000	six para infantry, one cavalry, one artillery, one engineer
27th Alpine Division	8,700	six mountain infantry, one light armour, one engineer

Source: IISS *The Military Balance 1989–90*

The excellence of FAR, however, could not make up for the lack of modern equipment in quantity which the army was increasingly unable to afford. Introduction of a new tank, the LeClerc, was repeatedly delayed. Anthony Cordesman noted pointedly that:

> 'France, with twice the active military manpower of the UK, and cheaper conscript manpower, now has only 1,300 obsolescent AMX-30 medium tanks while the UK can field a total of 1,150 far more modern and capable Challenger and Chieftain medium tanks ... Another way of gauging the priority France gives to Central Region combat is the number of men in the army per main battle tank. Britain has 167 men per tank, the FRG has 79 and France has 276.'[4]

A comparison with a possible enemy was a more telling reproof of the inadequacy of French scales of equipment. To protect herself France could commit approximately 200,000 men – with 1,200 tanks, 400 guns and several thousand other armoured combat vehicles – from an army of 292,000 (6,700 women), this number having dropped from 311,200 in 1985. That equipment scale was equivalent to one Soviet combined arms army, the personnel complement of which numbered only some 60,000 men.

These last few years were peaceful. Garrisons continued to be maintained in the former French empire, chiefly by marine infantry and Foreign Legion troops. There was one minor interruption to this tranquil imperial sunset. In 1986 Ghaddafi blatantly seized northern Chad which prompted the fourth commitment of French troops since 1969. French training and advisers enabled the Chadians to deliver a brutally expensive drubbing to the Libyans.[5]

WEST GERMANY

The Bundesheer entered the decade in better shape than at any time since its founding, second only to the newly re-equipped US Army in the scale and quality of its equipment within NATO. In 1989 the large hard core of its armoured vehicle fleet consisted of 2,130 Leopard 1A1s and 2,000 Leopard 2s as well as 2,136 Marder A1 armoured fighting vehicles supported by more than 1,600 medium and heavy self-propelled guns.[6] Programmes were in place to modernize the older Leopard and the Marders. Yet the Bundesheer could see a severe manning problem looming as a consequence of the low birthrate since the 1960s. Already the number of conscripts and volunteers was on the decrease. At the same time, the Soviet threat was seen as still growing in size and quality.

HERESTRUKTUR 2000

Faced with these self-reinforcing problems, the Bundesheer initiated its fifth postwar restructuring programme, Heerestruktur 2000, on 23 February 1988. The personnel element of Heerestruktur 2000 called for an increase in the length of conscript service from 15 to 18 months, additional financial benefits for volunteers and regulars, and an increasing reliance on the reserves. These measures would allow the army to retain its strength by including reservists and troops of the stand-by readiness component in the active-duty establishment. The army's actual strength would fall by 17,000 which would have to be absorbed throughout the service and compensated by a greater use of reservists. The army's manpower goals called for a greater density of officers at company level, i.e., a third officer; more senior NCOs; a high effective strength at company level to provide the most effective training; and more active personnel assigned to reserve units.[7]

Under Heerestruktur 2000 the army would keep its 12-division structure but fall from 48 to 41–42 brigades largely as a consequence of lack of recruits. Readiness levels in the divisions would fall from 90 per cent to 50–70 per cent.[8] Four brigades were testing the new organization, when these plans suddenly became irrelevant as the threats upon which they were based were swept away after the Berlin Wall came down. Instead of fighting the East German Volksarmee, the Bundesheer suddenly realized it would have to absorb it.

EAST GERMANY

The fall of the Berlin Wall on 9 November 1989 was the decisive event in the history of the Nationale Volksarmee (NVA). In the moment of supreme national crisis, the NVA refused to obey its orders to close the Wall. This act of disobedience removed the last serious obstacle to reunification of the German states. For the NVA it was an unintentional self-immolation on the altar of its country.

Mikhail Gorbachev's announcement of a unilateral Soviet force reduction in December 1988 was loyally echoed by the East German government in early 1989. Reductions of 10,000 men and 600 tanks were made in the NVA's ground forces as the Soviet defensive doctrine was embraced. At the same time the DDR's leadership was bitterly opposed to the political liberalization also encouraged by Gorbachev. This recalcitrance in the face of history was evident on the reviewing stand that October in celebration of the 40th anniversary of the DDR. Erich Honecker and Gorbachev, the reluctant guest, took the salute of a first-rate, goose-stepping NVA parade. On his way home, Gorbachev slammed the political door shut, hard enough to bring the whole house of the DDR down.

The demonstrations that began in Saxony soon rippled through the rest of East Germany. The regime was daily loosing its nerve. Increasingly the NVA became a question mark. Would this coddled child of the Party protect the regime? West German television reporters asked an NVA staff officer leaving a hurried meeting of the Leipzig authorities whether military action were contemplated. He blurted out in frustration that the troops simply could not be trusted. Indeed the NVA had already received orders to support the Stassi internal security forces to suppress the demonstrations. The NVA hung back prudently and partly in response to the caution urged by senior Soviet generals in East Germany. A 'Chinese solution', to smash the revolution was ordered by the then defence minister, Heinze Kessler. The General Staff forced the withdrawal of the order to the 1st Motorized Infantry Division to close the Wall.[9] Ironically, the NVA had come full circle. In its first call to action, the NVA had refused to fire upon German workers during the Berlin riots of 1953; in the 1989 revolution it had also refused to do violence to its own people in what was its last call to action. Within a year the NVA would cease to exist, most of its personnel disbanded and its equipment sold off or junked. A relatively few professional NCOs and junior officers would don the uniform of the Bundesheer.

During its final year the Volksarmee was a powerful force. The best equipped army in the Warsaw Pact, it was at the peak of its development in the year before its dissolution. *In memoriam* it is perhaps worthwhile to list its assets, as shown in *The Military Balance*.

Table 5-3. Volksarmee Strength and Equipment 1988
Strength: 120,000 including 71,500 conscripts
Forces: four motorized rifle divisions and two tank divisions all in the highest readiness category one artillery brigade, one airborne battalion, two SCUD, two artillery, two SA-4, one AD artillery, five engineer and two anti-tank regiments
Reserves: five motorized rifle divisions
Tanks: 3,140: 2,100 T-54/55, 400 T-72, 640 T-34 (store)
Recce: 1,050 BRDM-1/2
AIFV: 1,000 BMP-1/2
APC   4,350: 2,500 BTR-60P, 1,000 BTR-70, 150 MTLB, 700 BTR-50P (store)
Artillery: 870 towed: 122mm: 400 D-30, 200 M-1938; 130mm: 90 M46; 152mm: 180 D-20 390
SP: 122mm: 300 2S1; 152mm: 90 2S3 220
MRL: 122mm: 200 Cz RM-70; 240mm: 20 BM-24
Mortars: 82mm: 100; 120mm: 550
SSM: Launchers: 44 FROG-7, eight SS-21, 28 SCUD B
ATGW: 620: AT-3 Sagger, AT-4 Spigot, AT-5 Spandrel
AT Guns   300: 85mm: 100 D-48; 100mm: 200 T-12
AD Guns   300: 23mm: ZU-23, 96 SZU-23-4; 57mm: ZSU-57-2
SAM: SA-7, 300: SA-4/6/8/9
Source: IISS *The Military Balance 1989–90*.

POLAND

The Communists' defeat in the summer 1989 elections was the first warning tremor heralding the end of an era, and it was felt quickly in the armed forces. As sop to the army, the new government left the ministry of defence in the hands of General Florian Siwicki, the Party general who had crushed Solidarity in 1981. His was a transitory appointment; by the following year he had been replaced. A transformation of the army was already under way as part of the new defensive doctrine that had been initiated by the Soviet Union. In 1989 the armed forces were reduced by 33,000 men of whom 7,000 were regulars. Total strength fell to 314,000 of whom 206,600 were in the army: 100,000 regulars and 206,000 conscripts. The regular officer component consisted of 54,341 officers, 29,058 warrant officers, and 24,600 NCOs. In 1989, 68 units were disbanded and 147 'structurally transformed'. Four hundred tanks, 600 APCs, 700 artillery pieces and 80 aircraft were withdrawn from service and slated for destruction. These cuts, according to General Siwicki, the officer who executed the imposition of martial law in 1981, were not only evidence of reform but proof of a commitment to 'defensive doctrine'. In one breath he had made a bow to his new Polish masters as well as to his Soviet patrons. The defensive posture served both equally well since it eliminated tensions the new Polish government had no interest in maintaining and reduced the military budget in a time of extreme austerity.[10]

A central point of the restructuring was the de-emphasis of the tank and the disappearance of the tank division. At the beginning of 1989 there were twelve divisions of which five were tank divisions. By the end of 1989 that number had been reduced to nine mechanized divisions, the tank division having been eliminated as a type.[11] Restructuring gave priority to the strengthening of anti-tank, engineering, air defence and anti-landing defence.[12]

The army's personnel structure was also the object of reform. A projected goal of 50 per cent regulars in the next few years was the subject of a draft law on military service to be introduced in September. Professional military service for the officer and NCO was to be made entirely voluntary and could be terminated at any time. Officer and NCO specialists were to be offered 'contracts' to encourage their retention. The army had realized that military service had to be 'competitive with civilian professions'. Western armies were seen as positive models for the professional cadres.[13] Conscription was to be retained but reduced from 18 to 12 months. The high military suicide rate, especially among first year conscripts, which amounted to 20 per cent of all non-combat military deaths, indicated that serious problems needed to be addressed.[14]

The beginning of the reforms anticipated all the massive changes that would rumble through the former Warsaw Pact in the next two years. Of all the world's armies, only the Polish Army did not wait for the Berlin Wall to come down in order to leap out of the post-war era.

SOVIET UNION

When Mikhail Gorbachev became General Secretary of the Communist Party of the Soviet Union in 1985, the army was at the apogee of its development since 1945. It had never been so powerful, well-equipped and pandered to with such uncritical praise and unstinted resources. Yet it was an army thrashing clumsily in a vile, protracted campaign against a fifth-rate Third World country. It was an army that could squeeze no more in manpower or production from an exhausted population and industry. It was also an army that realized it faced a major technological revolution. Finally, it was an army hanging in that brief moment of suspension between the exhaustion of momentum and descent.

PERESTROIKA AND GLASNOST

Shortly after his rise to power, Gorbachev informed the General Staff that they would have to defer future spending while the economy was restructured (Perestroika) to be able support vigorous high-technology military production. For the time being the army would have to forego quantity for the promise of future quality.[15] Two years later, Gorbachev informed the General Staff that Perestroika was not proceeding as quickly as he had hoped. But two of his initiatives, Glasnost and democratization, were doing quite well, and new concepts were seeping unobtrusively into the conservative minds of the army's chiefs.

ATTEMPTS AT REFORM

Stymied in the military competition with the West, Gorbachev decided to reduce the threat by political means. The first step was the adoption of the so-called 'Defensive Doctrine' announced in May 1987. In practical terms this meant changing the structure of the armed forces to impart a non-offensive and hence non-threatening character; reducing the size of the strike forces; re-deployment of the forces for defensive missions; and limiting military production. In a dramatic speech to the United Nations in December 1988, Gorbachev announced the doctrine's first instalment – reduction of 500,000 men, 10,000 tanks, 8,500 artillery pieces and 820 combat aircraft by January 1991. The Ground Forces were to take the brunt of the cuts. To demonstrate the lowering of Soviet offensive potential, non-divisional battlefield missile systems, Spetsnaz, engineer bridging, and attack helicopter units were withdrawn from the groups of forces in eastern Europe. The remaining forces were to suffer sharp cuts in offensive weapons systems. The order-of-battle of the Ground Forces, in general, was to be cut almost in half.[16]

At the same time, the Ground Forces made a radical departure from previous Russian/Soviet reliance upon mass and numbers. The decision was made to pursue a smaller but higher quality force. As the Minister of Defence, Marshal D.T. Yazov, admitted: 'Quantitative approaches towards accomplishing defence tasks have become obsolete ... and inefficient from a strictly military point of view.'[17] The Ground Forces initiated a major effort to re-orient training, tactical-operational planning and the tenets of military science to the requirements of a defensively oriented force. Manoeuvres were reduced in size and frequency and were generally defensive in nature. The pace, vigour and effectiveness of these efforts were immensely aided by the new freedoms to discuss openly previously taboo subjects. Coming at the end of the war in Afghanistan, these changes embodied many of the lessons learned. Especially important was the emphasis on less restrictive control of subordinate units. Training materials, manuals, regulations and the curricula in the military school system were redesigned as well. The training establishment went through a particularly thorough change of direction. Examinations that used to be based on 'the mindless memorization of military statutes, exhortations or numerical data', were changed to emphasize student knowledge, and ability to grasp principles and apply them creatively to changing situations.

The Ground Forces had discovered the validity of T.E. Lawrence's statement, 'Very few people will use skill if brute force will do the trick. The worst thing for a good general is to have superior numbers.' The previous Soviet reliance on numbers had created an atmosphere in which tactics had deteriorated abysmally. Lieutenant-General Khazikov, Chief of the Main Combat Training Directorate, noted in an inspection of a motorized rifle regiment in the Kiev Military District that not one company commander could put his company in line during an exercise. And this was not an exceptional case. Khazikov fumed, 'Today's generation of officers are used to beautiful show exercises in which the basic standard has been fire, speed and eyes right.' He went on to note that tactics had become fossilized by the early 1970s.[18]

The 1989 training year emphasized the theme that 'less, but better is preferable'. That year's session of the Ground Forces Military Council set the task of 'reviving tactics as the art of fighting'. For the first time, training was to be judged on 'qualitative indexes'. Exercises were conducted with opposing battalions of different units, and laser fire-and-hit systems, copied from the US Army were being phased into use. An opposed forces training centre was also established.[19]

AFGHANISTAN 1985–1989

1985 — When Gorbachev came to power, he placed military operations in Afghanistan under careful scrutiny, and major changes in the direction of the war were made. Commanders were replaced, and a General Staff Operations Group was assigned to monitor major operations. More Spetsnaz battalions were transferred to the 40th Army, signalling a shift to light infantry operations. Emphasis was placed on large-scale sweeps through rebel-held areas, strengthening of the lines of communications by the establishment of numerous posts, and a great increase in the deployment of artillery combined with air strikes to search out the enemy. Many operations, in a futile replay of US efforts in Vietnam, were aimed at sealing the porous border with Pakistan. Operations were marked by greater flexibility and the repeated use of tactical surprise. Nevertheless, the only Soviet gains were the continued devastation of the countryside at the cost of heavy casualties to both sides.

1986 — In this year, 40th Army made a sudden change in its approach. Large sweeps were discontinued, and most motorized rile units were assigned security duties. No less than 60 per cent of the manoeuvre units were devoted to this mission. The conduct of the war shifted to the élite, light specialized forces such as the Spetsnaz battalions, airborne and air assault regiments and brigades. They carried the war to the Mujahedin on their own terms for the first time with heliborne raids and ambushes. Combined with heavy artillery and air strikes, these operations were severely weakening the Mujahedin who were increasingly off balance.

1987 — Continued international support for the Mujahedin and the heavy commitment of US Stinger and British Blowpipe hand-held SAMs brought this successful approach to a halt. The SAMs ripped the air support off Soviet troops in the field. At one stroke 40th Army lost the single greatest weapon in its order of battle as air operations were drastically modified to avoid the SAMs. Close tactical air support and the use of helicopters for troop transport and attack in special operations were particularly hobbled.[20] To avoid the SAMs, Soviet fighter-bombers delivered their ordnance from such a high altitude that, as one Muhjahed said, they could be sure only of hitting the ground.

1988 — By now it had become clear to Gorbachev that the war could not be won at a price he was willing to pay and he made the political decision to withdraw. The two-phase withdrawal began in the summer and ended with the final departure of Soviet troops on 15 February 1989. In difficult circumstances the withdrawal was conducted with considerable efficiency by 40th Army's commander, General Boris Gromov. The youngest general officer in the Soviet Army, the dynamic Gromov had requested the command in Afghanistan even when the war was obviously lost. He earned the respect of the nation by his concern for the troops and by the conduct of the withdrawal, not least his final gesture; he waited on the Afghan side of the bridge on the border for the last Soviet vehicle to pass. Then he turned his back on Afghanistan and walked across the bridge.

THE LESSONS OF AFGHANISTAN

During almost a decade the army had been given an opportunity to demonstrate its abilities under the most difficult conditions. From the beginning it was evident that it was unprepared for this type of warfare. Equipment and training had been meticulously developed for central European conditions. Afghanistan could not have been a more contrary theatre of war; many conscripts said that they had never even seen mountains before, much less trained in them.

Probably the single most glaring deficiency was the poor quality of the motorized rifle units throughout the course of the war. 'Soviet infantry was poorly prepared for its assignments due to shortcomings in equipment, training and organization. This extended to even the smallest details', such as uniforms, load-bearing equipment and magazine carriers. The deficiencies were so pervasive that from 1985 across-the-board remedial measures were taken that radically transformed the appearance of the Soviet soldier. Sniping was so deadly that it led to the widespread use of flak jackets. The basic problem of the poor quality of motorized rifle units remained despite improved equipment and the additional six months of special training given to conscripts before their arrival in Afghanistan. As a result the élite light infantry forces carried the brunt of the war from 1986 when their numbers were significantly increased.[21] These units performed well and did great damage to the Mujahedin. The insoluble problem for 40th Army was the built-in limitation of élite forces. There were never of them enough to carry the whole load of any war or campaign. Even their effectiveness was later hamstrung when their air support was shot away by the SAMs.

In addition to the poor organization and training of rifle troops, another series of morale and discipline factors had corrosive effects on performance. For an army that prided itself on the thorough indoctrination of its troops, the psychological preparation was poor if not counter-productive. *Dedovshchina* became an even more acute problem under the stress of war, and poisoned unit cohesion and discipline. It was estimated that more than 50 per cent of the troops became regular drug users. Serious health and morale problems arose from extremely poor hygiene, miserable living conditions and extended isolation. Incredibly, the army seemed not to have grasped the essentials of field sanitation and proper food handling and the result was a sick rate from hepatitis, other intestinal diseases such as dysentery, and malaria, jaundice and such antiques as typhus, that may have reached more than 25 per cent of field strength; a level more appropriate to a pre-First World War army. Soviet soldiers feared disease more than Afghan bullets. Reprisals and brutality towards the civilian population were officially sanctioned and rewarded. Freelance looting and atrocities, however, were 'strongly discouraged', and punished. Finally, black-marketeering, smuggling and theft of military equipment and supplies were commonplace.[22]

According to the Ministry of Defence, Soviet losses in Afghanistan in May 1988 when the withdrawals began were 13,310 dead, 35,478 wounded and 310 missing. By the time Gromov walked alone over the bridge, the dead had risen to 13,833 of whom 697 had died of non-combat causes. These figures are suspect to say the least. The US State Department had been claiming for the last four years of the war that Soviet dead did not exceed 12,000. With such helpful and authoritative support, it was easy for the Soviets to arrive at a similar figure. Other estimates range as high as 30,000 dead. Overall, 500,000 troops, mostly conscripts, served in Afghanistan. Veterans of the war, known as *Afgantsy*, who remained on active duty, became the driving force for much of the military reform, particularly the rebirth of tactics and the need for greater flexibility and initiative at lower levels of command.

THE STRUGGLE AGAINST CONSCRIPTION

Glasnost brought more than a healthy climate for the reform of tactics and leadership – it shone a bright light on the darker side of military life and the army's place in society. Increasingly honest reporting on the war, *dedovshchina*, cruel and arbitrary military environment, and the enormous cost of military spending thoroughly destroyed societal support for the army. Public opinion of the armed forces swung abruptly from extreme and uncritical adulation to invective and outright scepticism. Feeding this growing revulsion were the horrific revelations that as many as 15,000 conscripts a year died from neglect, accident, disease and the brutalities of *dedovshchina*.

It did not take long for the conscript-based army to begin reflecting the changes in public perceptions as the prestige of miliary service crashed. 'The Army is a school of life, but let others attend it ...' and 'Serving in the Army means losing two years, during which they also turn you into a half-wit', represented an increasingly common attitude.[23] Resistance to conscription, which had been almost non-existent in 1985, began to rise. By the end of the autumn 1989 conscription period, the General Staff had to admit that it had only been 80 per cent fulfilled. Local prosecutors refused to press charges in most cases of evasion. One of the reformers of the Supreme Soviet, Major Vladimir Lopatin, revealed how low the quality of the conscript classes had sunk:

'According to last year's data (1989), 45 per cent of the conscripts in our 4-million man Army are people with various mental aberrations. Fifteen per cent have criminal records. This is to whom we entrust weapons in the drive for numerical strength. One-third of the conscripts almost have no command of the Russian language – the language of directives! This is twelve times more than in 1969. If we retain the former system of manpower acquisition, then by the 2000 ... half of all our soldiers will not understand Russian. How can an army like this be commanded?'[24]

Lapotin's term 'drive for numerical strength' described the conscription system's vacuuming up of every possible man to fill its bloated order-of-battle, a drive that became desperate in the 1980s as the decline in the Slavic conscript cohorts became increasingly serious. Whole categories of physically and mentally unfit were called up. The military's gorging on the nation's economic resources had starved the health care system of funds. As a result, when physical and mental standards were raised to normal limits in 1989, 40 per cent of the draft were rejected for poor health.

A CRISIS IN CONFIDENCE

Under the blows of one storm after another, the institutional confidence of the army's professional cadres began to disintegrate. The drumbeat of criticism from the public had badly devalued the worth of a military career. The army's reaction split badly along generational lines. The senior leadership reacted to any criticism with outrage bordering on hysteria. They had been isolated too long by the secrecy surrounding the army, by the uncritical *carte blanche* the Party had given them, and by the cushion of privilege.

Below them, the officer corps up to the rank of lieutenant-colonel was much more in tune with reality and much more in favour of reform. For this stratum of the officer corps, hardship and not privilege was the normal state. The army's squandering of resources had done them little good. Pay was poor and living conditions were often miserable if not intolerable:

'When the young lieutenants who have been assigned beyond the mountain ranges and mountain passes of the North ... find themselves in subhuman conditions, living in barracks with icy chandeliers hanging from the ceiling, under which their young wives and nursing children are freezing, they are no longer capable of executing their combat task or simply remaining in a normal state of mental ease and morale.'[25]

An open letter to Gorbachev by sixty helicopter pilots of the Transbaykal Military District in 1989 distilled the cadres' frustration at being blamed for society's ills while living so badly themselves. They complained of increased physical assaults on officers by civilians; heretofore unheard of officious treatment by the police; duty schedules that crippled family life ('People call officers' wives single mothers'); and poverty-level pay, isolated stations, no facilities or decent medical care for families. '... tell us, what kind of material advantages do we have over the civilian population?' They asked, at least, for the right to resign.[26]

Compounding this growing stress was the demobilization of 150,000 officers and warrant officers as part of Gorbachev's 500,000-man reduction. Despite pledges to ease passage into civilian life for these professionals, little effective help was forthcoming. The Ministry of Defence was short of 180,000 officer housing units for those remaining in the force and simply threw up its hands in despair. To facilitate demobilization, officers were finally given the right to resign. A flood of resignations from many of the best junior officers followed. In 1989, 91 per cent of those applying for discharge were thirty years old or younger, and more than 75 per cent were described as being among the best.

THE WRITING ON THE WALL

By late 1989 Gorbachev's promises to the armed forces had evaporated as it became clear that the economy, political system and society were in a shambles. By then the army found itself trapped in the growing revolutionary chaos that was spreading throughout the Soviet Union. As an institution and as a fighting force it was on the point of collapse. The fall of the Berlin Wall and the subsequent loss of eastern Europe signalled that there was no going back. The trends accelerated to a crisis that would erupt the very next year with the attempted coup. The words of one writer at the time were prophetic:

> 'We are witnesses to the way in which the world's second largest military formation is disintegrating and disappearing like smoke, as though it is evaporating in some enormous kettle, repeating the fate of its predecessor, the army of the Russian empire.'[27]

ISRAEL

By the late 1980s the ground element of the IDF had successfully been reorganized into a heavy combined arms force. Ground forces consisted of 104,000 active duty personnel (88,000 conscripts) and 598,000 reservists available upon mobilization. This force comprised three regular armoured divisions and five mechanized brigades, one parachute trained. There were three border defence infantry divisions as well. Upon mobilization, another nine armoured divisions and one airmobile/mechanized infantry division would be added to the ground order-of-battle. Of 3,794 tanks, only 253 were rebuilt Soviet T-54/55s and T-62s, the dwindling booty of its wars with the Egyptians and Syrians. The heart of the force was its 1,300 US M60A1/A3s and 600 Israeli-built Merkavas. As happens all too often, the type of conflict an army prepares for is often not the one it has to fight.

THE INTIFADA

In 1988 IDF found themselves engaged in a most thankless and difficult job, one uniformly detested by armies – the maintenance of civil order against an insurgent and defiant population. In December 1987 the Palestinian *Intifada* or uprising erupted in the West Bank and Gaza among the Arab population conquered in the 1967 War.

The demands of controlling the *Intifada* disrupted both the IDF's budget and regular and reserve training programmes as well as routine operations. The costs of paying for the repeated call-ups of reservists drained 3 per cent off procurement, training, etc. Reserve and regular troops engaged in maintaining order were not available for normal operational training. As noted in *The Middle East Balance*:

> 'The IDF had to provide on its own for the urgent development and manufacture of protective equipment and arms adapted to specific new

riot-control duties; and it dedicated significant intelligence efforts toward collecting and analysing data on the uprising. These duties caused serious disruptions in training and operations, and, no less important, focused a considerable part of planning, intelligence, staff and command efforts on the urgent – yet, from a military standpoint, strategically marginal – problems of dealing with the Intifada.'[28]

Regular forces can re-adjust in little time, but time spent in training reserves cannot be made good. In 1988 many reservists had served 60 days without training for their wartime missions. The effect on the readiness of the reserves for mobilization became serious. The effect on the individual soldier was even worse as he became increasingly involved in this 'ugly' business. Morale fell, and the unthinkable began to happen in Israel – reservists refusing to serve. Although the figure was quite low, only 60 by March 1989, it was another worry as increasing involvement pushed Israelis and Palestinians to extremes of violence and cruelty. As Field Marshal Montgomery had observed in the campaign against the Sinn Fein after the First World War, such war tends to lower standards of 'decency and chivalry'. IDF retaliation extended to destruction of homes and the bulldozing of ancient olive groves, the latter an act of especial hard-heartedness in the Mediterranean. Rather than having a deterrent effect, these measures goaded the Palestinians to increased resistance such as setting fire to an Israeli forest which sent a surge of outrage throughout the nation. Up to the end of 1989 the IDF suffered nine dead and 1,635 wounded, and killed nearly 600 Palestinians. The number of Israeli wounded is attributed to the Palestinian main weapon – stones.

By late 1989 the IDF seemed to have decreased the intensity of the Intifada's violence through its improvements in the tactics of security forces, the deployment of special forces to deal with the commandos of the uprising, and a refinement in the orders to fire upon youths throwing gasoline bombs. Although Palestinian youths continued to resist, much of the general population seemed to be cowed by the IDF's measures. The IDF became more confident and shed some of the panic engendered by a chaotic situation. The over-commitment of the reserves was cut back, and normal training cycles were resumed.

EGYPT

The army continued to benefit professionally from its unaccustomedly long period of peace with Israel. Lavish military assistance from the United States, a smaller force, and the absence of the burden of constant mobilization allowed the army to develop into a more professional and efficient force. The years of war provided the professional officer corps, the best in the Arab world, to take good advantage of these favourable opportunities. Equipment ccontinued to be US-supplied; 144 M-109A2 SP howitzers, 1,700 M-113A2 APCs and 850 M-60A3 tanks in the inventory and 700 more tanks on order in 1990. Egyptian order of battle had undergone few major changes since 1973, but changes of emphasis were significant. Although Second and Third Armies were still stationed along the Suez Canal, the deployment continued to be defensive. First Army continued to be the GHQ reserve and was deployed largely in the Delta, but this army consisted of a number of mobile units, many coming under Headquarters, Special Forces. Egypt maintained an increasingly capable intervention force to support its claim as a major regional power – demonsrated in 1990 when the army contributed a heavy corps to the defence of Saudi Arabia. Continued hostility with Libya also ensured that a force remained deployed in the Western Desert.

The army's strength levelled off at 320,000 men of whom 140,000 are professional, the rest conscripts, a ratio that corresponded favourably with the German and French armies. The Egyptian military school system was efficient and trained large numbers of foreign personnel under a number of Egyptian military assistance programmes with other African and Arab countries. The army also sent a number of instructors throughout the region; for example, the Somali war college was staffed entirely by Egyptian officers.

The professional strides made by the army since 1945 amply justified Egypt's standing as a major regional power. Tested repeatedly in war, it grew into an effective force with a large professional and increasingly well-educated cadre capable of mastering modern warfare. The increased emphasis placed on combat service support was one of the surer signs of institutional growth and modernization.

SYRIA

The short 1982 Israeli-Syrian combat in Lebanon sparked a major expansion in the size and equipment inventories of the army. In From 1982 to 1987 the following Soviet arms deliveries were made to Syria:[29]

Table 5-4. Soviet Arms Deliveries to Syria 1982–87

T-62 Tanks	400
T-72 Tanks	800
BMP-1/2 MICV	800
122mm SPG	500
152mm SPG	300
BM-27 MRL	50
SS-21 SSM	18 launchers
SS-23 SSM	23 launchers
SS-1 SCUD	9 launchers
SA-5 SAM	48 launchers

In addition there were large numbers of other modern SAMs and anti-tank weapons delivered. This new equipment allowed the army to grow from 5–6 armoured/mechanized divisions in 1982 to six armoured and two mechanized divisions in 1990. The aim was to be able to deploy large forces simultaneously on two fronts, e.g., the Golan Heights and Lebanon, and to achieve parity with Israel. By the late 1980s the modernization had slowed as the Syrian economy weakened and as the Soviet Union, more and more obsessed with its own growing economic problems, began cutting back on arms deliveries. Nevertheless the army had a large and effective force of some 300,000 men which included 130,000 conscripts and 50,000 reservists. In the latter part of the 1980s the army concentrated on qualitative improvements in training, especially for breakthroughs of fortified areas, such as the Israelis maintained on the Golan Heights.

IRAQ

The Iran-Iraq War 1986–1988

Driven back to its own territory by 1983, the army had its hands full in simply hanging on in the face of Iranian offensives. For the next three years the Iraqis seemed to be on the sinking end of the attrition game, but unobtrusively significant improvements were being made in the army's operational capabilities. Inefficient commanders had been removed, new, sophisticated equipment in large quantities had been integrated, and chemical warfare capabilities were becoming more and more effective with experience.

By 1986 the army had dug-in in a well-engineered network of defensive positions and carefully sited artillery fire traps. The Iraqis' skill in defence had been learned from Soviet military advisers. As might be expected, artillery lavishly supported the defence. Helicopter gunships added a flexible precision to the fire support available to the ground commanders which more than made up for the lack of fixed-wing aircraft to provide close air support on any targets smaller than a city. Helicopters functioned as airborne artillery and anti-tank platforms and became a favourite and valued asset to the ground commanders. Sustained by air superiority and abundant *matériel*, the Iraqi defences were impervious to the human-wave attacks of the Iranian Revolutionary Guards and the diminishing offensive power of the Iranian Army. The skilful use of armour and mechanized brigades as mobile reserves across the front provided the flexibility to counter-attack and hammer Iranian penetrations bought at great cost. One Iraqi tank brigade was kept loaded on tank transporters at all times so as to be able to respond quickly to an emergency.

By 1986 the Iraqis had also developed a high level of skill in the use of chemical weapons. Iranian attacks were met with nerve agents mixed with smoke-screens; mustard gas was concentrated on Iranian headquarters, logistics and reserves. Initially, the use of chemical weapons had required the personal approval of Hussein himself, but their use became increasingly routine and eventually could be ordered by corps commanders.[30] Over time the Iranians were to bleed to death enmeshed in the thick and poisonous Iraqi defences.

As the war progressed, the role and size of Hussein's praetorian guard, the Republican Guard (RG), increased enormously. These divisions received absolute priority on equipment and supplies and were committed in the most critical situations, much like the Waffen SS. Like the latter, they were the personal forces of the dictator who was hyper-sensitive to their survival. Although they had no operational control over Guard units, army corps commanders were held accountable for every RG casualty incurred in their areas of operation.

Danger of an Iranian victory peaked and receded in the latest of the Karbala offensives of late 1986 and early 1987, aimed at Basra. As the tight Iraqi defences ground the attack to a halt, it became obvious that Iranian resources were exhausted. The next offensive was mounted by Iraq south of Basra in the spring of 1988. Dubbed *Tawakalna ala Allah* (Trust in God), the offensive consisted of a series of well co-ordinated combined arms attacks heavily supported by chemical weapons. The Iraqis overran areas such as the Al Faw Peninsula, Fao and the Manjoon Islands which the Iranians had won with so much blood since the war shifted into Iraq six years before. The Battle of Al Faw was the first operation of the offensive, and the Iraqis expected to take five days to clear the Iranians out of the tip of the peninsula which was heavily fortified. A two-corps force of Republican Guards and VII Corps drove the Iranians out in 36 hours. They had massed 200,000 men against 15,000 defenders; delivered a short but crushingly intense bombardment; and massively employed attack helicopters. Initial Iranian resistance was stiff, then collapsed quickly under great pressure. The Iranians fled *en masse* across the single pontoon bridge. The Iraqis had carefully left them this 'golden bridge' so as to avoid cornering them and incurring heavy casualties in a fight to the death. In the event their losses were only a few hundred; the Iranians' lost more, but not significantly because of their precipitous flight.[31]

In this series of operations the Iraqis used chemical weapons offensively for the first time, and so heavily that panic, 'brother to blood-stained rout', swept through the Iranian defenders. The Iraqis recognized their limitations and did not engage in deep pursuit to destroy the Iranian Army or gain large amounts of territory. The secret of Iraqi success had been built on the following factors: limited objectives; tight control of forces in limited geographic areas; the assembly of overwhelming force; and the massive application of fire-power including chemical weapons. By July the Iranian Army was ruined and Iran sued for peace.

The use of chemical weapons had been the deciding factor. Used in increasing quantities as the war progressed, they, more than anything else, finally broke the back of Iranian morale and saved the Iraqis from the inevitable consequences of an endless war of attrition. The ruthless use of chemicals against the Iranians had the excuse of desperation; its concurrent use against Kurdish non-combatants had not. In both cases, however, the Iraqi Army was rewarded with success. There was a warning in this victory, though. It was won against an enemy shorn of air power, isolated from most of the armouries of the world, unable to manoeuvre on the battlefield, deprived of a unified and rational leadership, and unable to respond in kind to chemical warfare. It was a victory won over its enemy's only plentiful resource – manpower. The Fates dealt the Iraqi Army a hand of unique advantage, something they rarely do twice.

POSTWAR REORGANIZATION – PREPARING FOR NEW CONQUESTS

The success of Iraqi arms propelled the army into the front ranks of the major Third World armies and made it the largest and most lavishly equipped player in the Middle East. This arrival had been signalled by the production of an Iraqi version of the Soviet T-72 tank in late 1989. Ominously it was named *Assad Babil*, 'Lion of Babylon'.[32] Dictators' dreams of resurrecting ancient glories is not a new phenomenon; witness Mussolini, for example. Hussein seemed particularly obsessed by the idea; two of his Republican Guard divisions bore the honorifics Hammurabi and Nebuchadnezzar, and he had embarked on the reconstruction of the latter's palace and other royal structures in Babylon; each brick was stamped with Hussein's name, a practice of kingship that had begun in Sumerian times. The museum in Baghdad, dedicated to Nebuchadnezzar, has an imposing mural of the great Babylonian conqueror shaking hands with Hussein. Such imperial megalomania is jealous of its laurels. The victory over Iran was therefore Hussein's victory, and not the army's or the generals', despite 500,000 casualties.

The end of the war found Iraq's economy devastated by military spending that had devoured about 40 per cent of the country's gross national product. Many of the benefits promised to families of the war dead could not be provided. The officer corps did not receive the credit or material rewards it had been promised. Disaffection grew as evidenced by Hussein's renewed hunt for enemies that reportedly led to four generals being shot and four more arrested in April, all war heroes. But Islamic fundamentalist groups had not been eradicated from the army, and reportedly they tried to assassinate Hussein during an Army Day parade – as happened to Sadat in Egypt. During the parade a tank was found to be carrying ammunition in violation of standing orders. Reportedly, four officers were shot on the spot, and the village of the tank unit's commander was destroyed.[33]

If benefits to those who won the war were stinted, funds to re-equip the army were not. The cost contributed greatly to the failure of the Iraqi economy to recover after the war. The Institute of Strategic Studies listed the growing assets of the army in 1989; in one year tank strength increased by 1,000 vehicles. The inventory now included more than 500 T-72s, 1,000 T-62s, 2,500 T-54/55s and 1,500 Chinese T-59s. In almost every category the army had a greater equipment inventory than the British and French armies combined. Iraq also sought to emulate these powers in their strategic arsenals by 'making a massive effort to improve its ability to deliver weapons of mass destruction, with notable advances in its capability to deliver chemical warheads'. The range of the Soviet-supplied SCUD missile was improved from 250 to 350 miles enabling it to reach targets in Saudi Arabia and Israel.

Table 5-5. The Iraqi Army 1989

Manpower	955,000
Regulars	475,000
Retained Reservists	480,000
Order-of-Battle	
Republican Guard	
Armoured Divisions	3
Infantry Division	1
Commando Brigade	1
Regular Army	
Armoured/mechanized Divisions	7
Infantry Divisions	42
Special Forces Brigades	20+
SSM Brigades	2
Equipment	
Tanks	5,500
APCs	7,100
Artillery (towed)	3,000
(SP)	500
(MRL)	200
SSMs	66+
AD Artillery	4,000
SAM systems	330
Armed helicopters	160

Source: IISS *The Strategic Balance 1989–90.*

While the Iraqis had improved a great deal of the Soviet-provided arsenal, and developed an important military production base, they still depended on the outside world for repair or replacement of high-tech equipment. Much of their domestic maintenance and war production was actually carried out by a host of foreign contract personnel that included approximately 8,000 Soviets of whom about 1,000 were military. It was this experienced, well-equipped but tired army that would march into Kuwait the following year.

PAKISTAN

The 11-year rule of General Zia came to an end on 17 August 1988 when a bomb blew his C-130 aircraft out of the sky. A number of senior officers of the armed forces died with him, and thus a clean sweep seemed to have smoothed the way for the re-establishment of civilian rule.

The war in Afghanistan had provoked the resumption of foreign, particularly US, aid which helped modernize and expand the army.

Table 5-6. The Pakistan Army, 1972–1990

	1972	1990
Manpower	287,000	500,000
Divisions	12	21
Armour	2	2
Infantry	10	19
Brigades	2	22 (3 more forming)
Armour	1	7 (1 more forming)
Infantry	0	4
Artillery	0	7 (2 more forming)
AAA	1	4
Recce Regiments	0	3
Special Service Group	0	1
Tanks	350	1,850
APCs	250	800
Artillery	900	1,445
Towed	900	1,230
SP	0	215

Source: IISS *The Military Balance 1972–3, 1990–1*

The doubling of the size of the army did not result in a dilution of the domination of the martial races – the Punjabis (65 per cent) and Pathans. Punjabis were even more prevalent in the officer corps. Despite government efforts at integration, few Sindhi and Baluchis were in uniform and some regiments had no Pathans. The ethnic composition of the army may suggest that to designate a certain group as being 'martial' is as politically incorrect as it would be among certain Western societies. In fact, the army is remarkably like the Indian Army in its preservation of its 'martial races' content.

Unlike the long-serving troops of the Indian Army, the term of service – seven years – was relatively short for the Pakistani soldier, so the army was forced to maintain a large reserve of 500,000 men. These would be used largely as replacements and not as organized units. The 150,000-man paramilitary National Guard had a variety of units that could provide well-trained replacements in wartime, and there was another reserve organized into fixed formations. During this period some 30,000 Pakistani soldiers served in the armed forces of 22 countries, including Saudi Arabia, Jordan and Libya. Most of them (20,000) served in Saudi Arabia using Saudi equipment, to provide the hard professional muscle that the Saudi government could not create from its own population. A 3,000-man brigade also served in Jordan.[34]

Much though the army had improved, by 1990 it had been matched by even greater improvements in the Indian Army, and the Pakistanis recognized that, even to maintain their current ratio of inferiority, they would have to struggle and depend upon the same level of foreign aid in the future as they had done in the recent past. The army's adoption of a defensive strategy in case of war with India is evidence of that reality. An offensive strategy would make no headway against Indian superiority in numbers. On the other hand, a forward defence that emphasized mobility along the front could prove a serious obstacle to an Indian offensive. Given the Indian army's organization for short-war scenarios, the Pakistanis appeared to have chosen the best of a bad set of options.

INDIA

Despite its recent unpleasant experience in Sri Lanka, the Indian Army would look upon 1990 with a good deal of satisfaction. Its efforts in the last two wars had made India the pre-eminent power in south-west Asia. This half-decade was a period of continued training and modernization.

Increasing purchases of modern Soviet equipment such as T-72 tanks and BMP-1 infantry fighting vehicles proceeded together with a vigorously up-graded domestic programme for older equipment such as the *Vijayanta* and T-55 tanks. The army embarked on a systems approach for life-cycle management of equipment to wring the best out of increasingly expensive high-technology weaponry. India had begun assembling her own T-72s as well as starting the design of a domestically produced new main battle tank, the *Arjun*, with Chobham-type armour.

The steady growth of the army was increasingly leaving its most danger-ous rival, the Pakistan Army, behind. The sheer size, at 1,100,000 regulars, was rein-forced by the efficiency of a long-service (17 years) personnel system that created a deep professionalism. The Indian reserve system by contrast was puny at 200,000 men (counted in the total of regulars) and another 50,000 in the Territorials. But Indian experience had shown that her wars were likely to be short and that trained and efficient manpower had to be always instantly available. Pakistan's larger reserve would allow it to claim manpower parity in a long war. During this period the army concentrated on improving the tooth to tail ratio so as to absorb a larger and more modern equipment inventory. For example, the number of Soviet T-72s had increased from 300 in 1985 to 700 in 1990. By 1990 the army also had a superior-ity of 2.2 to 1 in manpower, 1.7 in tanks, 1.6 in APCs/IFVs and 2.8 in artillery. By 1987 the army had acquired sufficient modern Soviet SAMs to equip all their armoured and mechanized divisions and fourteen of nineteen infantry divisions to Warsaw Pact standards. By 1990 six air defence brigades had also been added to the order of battle. Only in modern, heavy self-propelled artillery did the army lag, with 100 modified 130mm D-46s compared to the Pakistan Army's 125 modern US 155mm M-109A2s and 40 203mm M-110A2s.[35]

PEACEKEEPING FAILURE IN SRI LANKA

The army's morale had been buoyed by its sharp performance in two wars with Pakistan. It was to receive an equally sharp setback by its well-intentioned but dis-astrous peacekeeping role in Sri Lanka. By 1987 the bloody Tamil 'Tiger' insurrec-tion in that country had proved beyond the power of the Sri Lankan armed forces to suppress. The Sri Lankan government and the Tamils requested India to send a peacekeeping force. The Indian Peacekeeping Force (IPKF), initially of 10,000 men, arrived in August, but the fighting continued because of Tamil intransigence which led to attacks on Indian personnel. Exasperated, in March the Indians launched an attack with 6,000 men of the 54th Infantry Division on the Tamil stronghold of Jaffna. The army quickly discovered that seeking out a guerrilla force in the midst of a large civilian population was frustratingly different from slugging it out with Pakistani regular forces. The army were unsuited to and not properly trained for such a role. Their heliborne operations were particularly inept. The operation was essentially an internal security mission which in India had largely been handled by Indian paramilitary forces. Although fighting continued, the Tamils were not bro-ken despite the expansion of the IPKF to three divisions and 40,000 men. By the fol-lowing June the army had lost 350 killed and 1,100 wounded for the loss of 607 Tamils.[36] Forces were finally withdrawn in 1990 with no significant change to the *status quo*. In an unfortunate way the army had indeed joined the big leagues. The good intentions of its government had thrown it into the same sort of quagmire that sucked the US Army into Vietnam and the Soviet Army into Afghanistan. The Indians, however, had the good sense to write-off a bad investment and promptly leave.

The period from 1985 to 1989 saw the army take its place as one of the Third World's best armies. Since 1945 it had fought four wars, grown to more than a million men, absorbed relatively high levels of technology, and maintained impressive levels of cohesion and professionalism. Its greatest achievement, perhaps, was its maintenance of the mature civil-military relationship that allowed Indian democracy to set deep roots in the country. If its army is any measure, India has outgrown its Third World status.

VIETNAM

WITHDRAWAL FROM CAMBODIA

As the counter-insurgency war against the Khmer Rouge dragged on, PAVN was reduced to retracing each painful US footstep of the previous war. In a bitter echo of the Americans' Vietnamization policy, PAVN attempted to bolster the forces of the client Cambodian government in order to take over more of the fighting. By 1988 these forces had taken over responsibility for border defence while the Vietnamese withdrew into the interior. The Khmer Rouge promptly retook their bases in Phnom Malai. Nevertheless, Hanoi had had enough and decided to cut its losses. Strength, already reduced to 120,000 in 1987, had fallen to 80,000 in 1988. Except for advisers, the last PAVN forces departed Cambodia in September 1989.

POST-WAR PAVN

The very term 'Post-war PAVN' seems strange when applied to a military organization that for its entire existence has been continuously engaged in one war or another. In 1989 this army, born of revolutionary guerrilla warfare, was very much a conventional army. Its strength stood at 1,100,000 men in 63 divisions of which two were training and 28 were cadre formations, much like the Soviet system, backed up by 3,500,000 paramilitary forces. Vietnam rivals North Korea as the most heavily militarized nation in the world, making Douglas Pike's descriptions of the Vietnamese as the Prussians and Spartans of Asia, an apt one. PAVN also boasted a respectable tank force of ten tank brigades with 1,600 Soviet T-34-54/-55s and 350 Chinese Type-59 copies of the T-55. There were also 1,500 Soviet, Chinese, and US (M113) APCs.

Despite the scale of its forces and the list of its victories, PAVN has been undergoing a number of changes. Revolutionary ardour has also ebbed as time increasingly separates the present generation from those early struggles. Attention has been concentrated on the skills of soldiering. The revolutionary image of selfless honesty has been replaced by endemic corruption that matches that of Vietnamese society in general. PAVN troops stationed in the South have been particularly susceptible to the 'yellow wind' – the seductions of the gentler attitudes towards life.

CHINA

By 1985 efforts had been made to repair the damage to the People's Liberation Army (PLA) wrought by Mao's Great Cultural Revolution, though the repairs had largely been patching holes in the ruined edifice of Mao's doctrines of People's War. The 1979 Sino-Vietnamese War had shown that the PLA was incapable of fighting a modern war, despite the individual skill of its soldiers. In operational technique and technological sophistication, they had clearly been outclassed.

DENG'S REFORMS

In May and June 1985 Deng Xiaoping took the bold step of initiating reforms that effectively demolished the ruins of Mao's doctrine. He initiated the construction of a modern, technologically competent force with a matching doctrine. He put the PLA back on the road to professionalization from which Mao had so disastrously detoured in 1960. These reforms, many of which remained only on paper until Deng won a major political struggle in 1987, were:

1. Cut the PLA's numbers from 4 to 2.5 million.
2. Reduce the military regions from 11 to 7.
3. Reduce 35 infantry armies to 24 combined arms armies.
4. Modernize and increase regional divisions from 73 to 93.
5. Merge old political, military and logistics academies into a single Univesity of National Defence.
6. Re-introduce a regular military hierarchy of rank.

The reduction in the size of the PLA was begun immediately with a 25 per cent cut of one million men, the intention being to return it to 2.5 million in 1966. The reduction was accomplished largely by reducing the conscript requirement, but several hundred thousand officers were retired. Their going was eased by generous retirement in terms of housing, job opportunities,and other benefits. The reduction meant the elimination of 4,000 units of regiment size or greater, and was intended to free funds for investment in the production of modern weapons. The second reform, reducing the number of military regions, was not implemented until after Deng's political victory. The reduction in the number of senior commands was meant to weaken regional autonomy and strengthen the power of the central government. The third reform began the transformation of an essentially light infantry army into a well-equipped combined arms force. The fourth reform expanded, modernized and reorganized the regional forces in order to lessen the importance of the militia, the central pillar of Mao's People's War. The fifth reform, the creation of the University of National Defence, was intended to shake up the military educational system and force-feed new ideas.[37]

Binding all these reforms together was a new doctrinal matrix, 'People's War Under Modern Conditions'. Described as a logical development of Mao's ideas, it was in effect a complete about face from Mao's teachings, despite the reluctance to abandon the term 'People's War'. The Party and PLA jettisoned Mao's notion that nuclear and conventional war were intertwined, that a nuclear attack would be followed by a land invasion. They would now rely on their nuclear forces to deter a nuclear attack and upon growing combined arms forces to wage limited conventional war in defence of China's territory and vital centres. The militia, to be reduced by at least half, was down-graded to an unimaginable last resort scenario featuring an aggressor's attempt to conquer the whole of China. In the future, China's strength would be her conventional ground forces, trained and equipped to fight modern, technological war.[38]

The investments in China's defence industry were meant to produce the equipment that would transform her mass of light infantry into a largely mechanized force. The result was a steady though slow mechanization. By 1989 all 80 infantry divisions, some of which were mechanized 'all arms' formations, ten tank divisions and 5–6 field and air-defence artillery divisions had been regrouped into the 24 Integrated Group Armies (43,500 men) which were about the size of a western corps. The Group Armies (GA) normally consisted of three infantry divisions, one tank, one artillery and one air-defence brigade.

The sixth reform, the award and wearing of insignia of rank approved in 1984, was delayed in late 1988 by rearguard opposition of the older conservative (in the PLA context, the 'radical') elements of the PLA. Deng hoped the measure would improve sagging morale together with the earlier introduction of non-commissioned ranks. Another delay was caused by the tense issue of deciding who got which rank. Prior to the awards of rank, the PLA civilianized 100,000 cadres who filled clerical, educational and other non-military specific positions. That still left 800,000 cadres to become officers, out of a 3,000,000-man force, described by a Chinese general as an 'irrational' officer-to-soldier ratio. Nevertheless, on 1 October the PLA emerged proudly wearing its new insignia of rank, 23 years after Mao had abolished the practice.[39]

THE TIANAMEN SQUARE MASSACRE, 1989

The peaceful revolution that bloomed in Beijing in May of 1989 was an epochal fork in the road for the PLA. Heretofore, the PLA had been considered inseparable from the people and had maintained great domestic respect and support. This connection had been probably the PLA's single greatest moral asset. It was wantonly squandered when the PLA, at the order of the Party's leadership, crushed the student movement on 4 June.

The initial reaction of the PLA to the student revolution was one of political detachment, having gladly abandoned its daily political role in the country after the rise of Deng Xiaoping. Realizing the danger to itself, the regime called upon the PLA to suppress the students. As in Petrograd in 1917, the regime made the mistake of calling out the capital's garrison, 38th Army. This group army was the most professional and best equipped in the PLA and was recruited from the capital's population. By all accounts, 38th Army's attempts to clear the Square were half-hearted. Basically the 38th refused to act with force against the people, and even its limited efforts stretched its loyalty to the breaking point. *The Times* reported on 8 June that many of the students in Tianamen Square had actually completed their military service in that group before going on to university.[40] The regime was as deaf to the changes within the PLA that favoured professionalization and wanted to shed political controls as it was to the growing liberalization of Chinese society. In desperation, President Yang Shangkun ordered other group armies to the capital that eventually numbered 300,000 men. Entire regiments from these GAs reportedly refused to obey their orders, such as elements of the 28th GA which burned their vehicles rather than march on Beijing. Units in other cities that were staging their own demonstrations were ignoring appeals from the Party to take action. In great secrecy at the end of May, Deng ordered the leaders of the seven military regions to a meeting in Beijing. To a man they opposed martial law. A few days later when Yang proposed that all military personnel who refused to obey orders be executed, he was summarily dressed-down by the military collective. A letter from a hundred senior active and retired officers sent to the *People's Daily* strongly opposed the use of force:

'The People's Liberation Army belongs to the people. It cannot confront the people, even more so it cannot suppress the people and will never shoot the people. To keep the situation from worsening, the Army cannot enter the city.'[41]

Yang, however, was not completely deterred. He turned to the 27th GA from Shijiazhuang Military District in the western Beijing Military Region. The 27th GA had much to recommend it. Recruited largely from delinquents who had enlisted to avoid prison, its personnel had not been infected by the heady political atmosphere of a large metropolitan area and did not speak the language of the capital. It had also been blooded ten years ago in the war with Vietnam. Most importantly, it was Yang's praetorian guard and may have been commanded by a brother or son. Yang's carefully placed relations in the PLA would form the cutting edge of the counter-revolution.[42] Deng also brought elements from another eight group armies as well as the 15th Airborne Corps to Beijing. Perhaps this was a demand for the military region and group army commanders to declare themselves. If so, Deng had gambled successfully on the fact that they were all his appointees.

Apparently the 27th GA was ordered to set an example to the whole of China. Ordered off the Square, the students were moving out when the troops opened fire, beginning the carnage that would claim 3–5,000 lives in the next few days. News reporting graphically depicted the 27th GA as being out of control as it chased the survivors from the Square and began randomly killing citizens of Beijing, including women, children and the aged. It was as if barbarians from beyond the Great Wall had been let loose. The killing was not all one-sided. Beijing residents lynched more than a few soldiers in revenge, and a number of troops were killed by friendly fire in the Square. However, the ludicrous figure of 1,000 PLA dead against unarmed opponents was released by the Chinese government.

With the revolution crushed, the 27th was sent home within a week. Rumours of fighting among PLA units that seemed to foretell civil war could not be confirmed. A purge did remove those officers whose loyalty seemed suspect in the uncertain days before the massacre. In retrospect, the PLA's role had been essentially passive, despite the massacre. As an institution, it appeared unwilling to use force against either pro-regime PLA forces or the students and may have stood aside to let the regime fall; however, Yang's control and ruthless employment of a single army, the 27th GA, was enough to suppress the democracy movement and save the regime, however temporarily.

The revulsion of the Chinese people severed much of the natural bond between people and army that had been the PLA's moral touchstone since its foundation. Although public opinion transferred much of the blame from the rank and file to the leadership, the reputation of the PLA had been irrevocably stained, a fact which profoundly demoralized the army. Perhaps one of the most telling stories about the PLA's loss of respect circulating after the massacre concerned a confrontation between Deng and Prime Minister Zhao Ziyang who supported the students. Deng laid his cards on the table and said brusquely that he had two million bayonets behind him. Asked what forces he was bringing to the struggle, Zhao replied simply, 'The Chinese people'. Deng sneered, 'You have nothing.'

NORTH KOREA

In this final period of the Cold War, Kim Il Sung continued to arm North Korea to the hilt for the war that seemed to have passed him by. By 1989 he had squeezed a total of 930,000 men for active service out of a population of 22,230,000, making North Korea the most heavily militarized state in the world.

By 1987 another reorganization of the Korean People's Army appeared to be under way, which would convert the old army corps system into one that would include one tank, three mechanized and eight all-arms corps consisting of two tank, five motorized and mechanized, and 25 infantry divisions, eight independent tank and 21 independent infantry brigades. The favoured special operations forces grew to a strength of 112,000 in a Special Purposes Corps of 25 brigades. By 1989, the IISS *Military Balance* reported more changes. The number of corps increased to fifteen: one tank, four mechanized, one infantry, eight all-arms and one artillery. The heavy divisions appear to have been broken up into fifteen tank and twenty motorized brigades. The infantry divisions had been increased to 31 and designated infantry/motorized infantry divisions.

KPA equipment inventories surged also during this period, as North Korea was able to build more and more of its own equipment. Kim's policy of self-sufficiency resulted in a domestic arms industry able to produce all but the most sophisticated ground equipment. Production of the SCUD missile began in about 1985. Sufficient food and ammunition were stockpiled in underground facilities to support several months of operations.[43] The tank fleet now numbered 3,500 vehicles including 1,200 T-62s. Two hundred BMP/BMP1s were added to 1,600 APCs of older types. According to *The Military Balance*, in 1989 multiple rocket- launchers numbered 2,500 and towed artillery 1,900, but the 2,800 SP artillery pieces were the real added punch to the force. The DIA estimates were much higher: 4,000 APCs, 3,000 towed and 5,400 SP guns. The unprecedented number of SP artillery pieces is due to the Korean ability to marry gun tubes with available chassis types.[44]

This massive host was deployed to strike quickly to destroy Allied defences before US reinforcements could arrive. The KPA concentrated troops, SP artillery and logistics in the forward area between Pyongyang and the DMZ. KPA reserves were provided with large numbers of artillery pieces and anti-tank weapons to defend the rear areas and so free all regular forces for offensive operations. Painfully aware that the US Air Force so savaged North Korea during the Korean War that it had finally to admit that there were no more targets, Kim ensured that all defence industry and other vital installations were built underground and were virtually invulnerable.

No nation has ever been so committed to preparation for war, yet so consistently stayed its hand. At the very moment in history when North Korean strength had surged in 1989, the world order upon which it rested began to shift. Everything seemed about to slip away.

SOUTH KOREA

General Chun's government continued President Park's policy of strengthening South Korea's economy and military. The booming economy allowed him to devote one-third of government spending on national defence and consistently outstrip North Korea's defence spending for the entire decade. In February 1988 free elections brought the first civil government to power in Seoul since 1961. The new government issued the first Korean Defence White Paper in 1988, reformed conscription abuses and tried to soften some of the more harsh aspects of military discipline.

The army had increased very little in manpower (520,000 to 550,000) in the 1980s, unlike the KPA which vacuumed up every available male for the most productive years of his life. The numbers of divisions had also stabilized at two mechanized infantry and nineteen infantry divisions for ten years. Increased combat power was provided by newer equipment in larger quantities. By 1989 the tank fleet had increased to 1,560 as some 200 Type 88, a domestically produced Korean version of the M1 Abrams tank modified to meet Korean conditions, entered service to augment the 1,350 M-47s and M48A5s, and 60 M60s. Two hundred domestically produced Korean Infantry Fighting Vehicles (KIFVs) also joined the force of 1,550 APCs. The bulk of the order-of-battle, its nineteen infantry divisions, were considered light by Western standards. Three infantry regiments of four battalions, an artillery regiment of four battalions, and single reconnaissance/ranger and tank battalions made up the fighting strength of a Korean division. Ten thousand of its strength of 14,716 men were in the three infantry regiments, providing a slim but adequate combat support and rear echelon element. Weak transportation and communications capabilities and too few anti-tank weapons remained liabilities. However, these problems are not as serious under expected Korean combat conditions. As one appraisal in *Military Review* describes possible future combat:

'The Korean War indicates that any conflict on the Korean peninsula probably would involve several battles running across a series of mountains and ridges. Armor and mechanized operations would be necessarily confined by the situation and immediate geography. The majority of the land battles would be with light infantry operating at night and in the mountains. Modest penetrations by foot are possible. These types of operations are extensively practiced and planned for by the ROKA infantry division.'[45]

The army has emphasized three types of tactical operations: night operations, mountain operations and infiltration – all of which are seen as ways to counter KPA advantages in numbers of tanks, artillery and aircraft.

As 1989 came to a close, the army could be described as one of the world's military success stories. Beginning in 1961, it had become the engine that had mobilized South Korean society to transform itself into a modern, industrialized nation with a drive and spirit that had not been noticeable in Korean society before. Despite 27 years of authoritarian military rule, the army had forged a sense of ROK nationhood. Seventy-five per cent of adult males had served in the regular army, the reserves or the Homeland Reserve Force in a shared experience of nation-building. Like all armies in power, it stayed too long, but finally, when the nation made it plain in 1988 that it had outgrown its military pedagogue, the army stood aside and assumed its appropriate role in a modern society.

JAPAN

The Japanese Ground Self-Defence Forces (GSDF) continued to grow, not in numbers, but in the quality and quantity of its equipment, facilities and training. Perhaps the greatest achievement was the re-orientation of the concept for the defence of Japan's most vulnerable main island, Hokkaido. The island's close proximity to the Soviet southern Kuriles and the great island of Sakhalin, offered a Soviet invasion a conveniently close staging area, well within supporting range of Soviet air forces stationed in the Far East.

Until the late 1980s Japanese defence plans for the island called for a withdrawal inland to defend the mountain-ringed Sapporo Plain and the island's major city of Sapporo in the south-west. The plan, perhaps, was based on painful lessons learned during the Second World War of the futility of defending islands on the beach. More likely, they were based on the unchallenged assumption that significant US ground and air forces would be on hand to relieve the Japanese at the critical moment. But by 1988 they had become convinced that a more aggressive defence was likely to succeed. The GSDF concluded that new technologies could cripple a Soviet air-sea-landing operation in the critical hours as it attempted to secure a foothold on the island. New weapons systems such as the US Multiple

Launch Rocket System (MLRS) and Japanese-built anti-ship missiles could wreak havoc with both shipping and initial landing forces and prevent the Soviets from establishing a foothold from which to build up ground combat power. Together with these innovations, the GSDF also continued to increase the combat power of the four divisions of the Northern Army already on the island. Japanese planning for 1986–1990 called for the replacement of older types of tanks, APCs and artillery pieces by newer Japanese models, many of them the second generation produced domestically.

Table 5-7. Japanese Ground Self-Defence Force Equipment Acquisitions

1986–1990	Goal	Delivered 1988
Tanks (T-71)	246	160
APCs (Type 74)	310	166
Artillery (SP)	277	178
SSM-1 Anti-ship	6	54
Transport helicopters	24	13
I-Hawk	4.5 groups	2.5 groups

Source: Reynolds, *Japan's Military Buildup: Goals and Accomplishments* (Washington, DC: Congressional Research Service, 1989), pp. 5–6.

The new defence concept marked a profound change in the GSDF. Heretofore, the inadequacies of the force's structure and equipment and ammunition policies had been mitigated by Japan's serene reliance on the United States coming to the rescue if need be. Now the Japanese had devised a strategy that made themselves the arbiters of their own fate. It was a sign of a new maturity and self-confidence.

AUSTRALIA

In the latter 1980s, new foreign policy objectives gave the army concrete guidance on its missions for the first time since the early 1970s. Missions included:

    1. National territorial defence.

    2. Regional projection of strategic forces in SW Pacific/SE Asia.

    3. Capability to conduct combined operations with allies.

    4. Capability to conduct UN peacekeeping operations.

For the first time, the army has been directed to fight alone if necessary rather than as part of a larger British or American force as in the past. To accomplish these missions and to respond to the only plausible threat to the Australian landmass, the new NORCOM or Northern Command was established at Darwin, on the northern coast of Australia. The most plausible future operations were expected to involve Low-Intensity Conflicts (LICs).[46]

But this low-level threat is about the only one that the army, after almost twenty years of neglect, would be able to counter. The expansion base in particular had been badly neglected as both the active forces and reserves gave priority to LIC operations for lack of resources to prepare for anything more. As described by Major-General D.J. Stevenson:

'Despite the current priority being given to low level operations in northern Australia, the Army has to maintain the "state of the art" for conduct of higher level operations in defence of Australian territory against a major lodgment of enemy forces and possibly for land operations beyond Australia.'

316

One improvement during this period was the creation of an Operational Deployment Force (ODF) of two fully manned and equipped infantry battalions with 180 days' stocks earmarked for logistics support.[47]

Despite an increase in funding for some new equipment, the army continued to be last in line behind the RAN and the RAAF. The new funding did enable the army to make up a good deal of lost time. Since 1985 it has received a major boost in its anti-ank capability with the acquisition of more than 500 84mm Carl Gustav antitank weapons. By early 1989 an ambitious new modernization programme was replacing most of the transport fleet of light vehicles, medium trucks, and semi-trailers and prime movers, as well as producing domestically 120 new 105mm light guns to replace older pieces, and 67,000 F88 rifles and 2,420 light machine-guns. The RBS 70 low-level air-defence weapons system also entered service during this period.

New equipment purchases made a skewed contrast with declining morale, growing dissatisfaction with conditions of service and failure to retain qualified personnel. Depressed pay levels for middle grade officers, part of a government-wide pay cap, and the exclusion of officers above the grade of major from service allowance, drove an inordinate number out of the service in their peak performance years. Senior NCOs and technicians also left in large numbers. Personnel-type problems continued to be the army's greatest challenge at the end of the post-war era.

THE ART OF WAR

By 1985 the post-war era's proclivity for war seemed to have exhausted itself. In the four years leading to 1989 and the end of the Cold War, no new conflicts erupted among the major armies of the world. To be sure, the carnage in the Gulf, Afghanistan, and Cambodia continued for awhile, but these wars, begun in the previous decade, played themselves out. It was as if the era had also played itself out and was waiting expectantly for the inevitable change.

As the change came with the rippling collapse of the Soviet Empire and its satellites, there was much nonsense written about the end of history with all of its dirty wars. A world that embraced liberal democracy would see warfare, armies and the military arts, chief among them, strategy, wither away. Communism had also promised at the beginning of the century that the state would wither away as well, so there was much hope for the art of strategy in these fairy tail predications.

The post-war era had indeed revalidated some rather enduring truths in the exercise of the art of strategy by the world's armies. All the successful as well as the unsuccessful applications of this art had reinforced these truths embodied in Liddell Hart's definition of strategy as 'the art of distributing and applying the military means to fulfill the ends of policy'. This definition rests on triple pillars: (1) that the ends of policy must be practicable which means they must be clear-cut and limited in time and space; (2) the military means available must be competent to execute these objectives which means a high degree of professionalism and technical expertise is vital; and (3) that the identification and pursuit of political and military objectives must show a cold-blooded sense of restraint not to overreach themselves.

All of these precepts would have been familiar to Sun Tzu over two thousand years before – with one difference. The experience of two world wars and especially the advent of nuclear weapons had precluded the exercise of strategy in that 'breaker of worlds', a third world war among the superpowers that would have dragged all other armies with them into the abyss.

NOTES

1   *The Military Balance 1989–1990* (London: The Institute for Strategic Studies, 1989), pp. 17–18.
2   John O. Marsh, 'Army Training: Ancient Roots, Future Benefit,' *Army: 1988–89 Greenbook*, October 1988, pp. 16, 18.
3   Ibid.
4   Anthony Cordesman, *NATO's Central Region Forces* (London: Jane's, 1988), p. 207.
5   J. J. Cox, 'Chad: France in Africa,' *The Army Quarterly and Defense Journal*, Volume 118, April 1988, pp. 161–5.
6   *The Military Balance 1989–1990* (London: The International Institute for Strategic Studies, 1989), p. 63.
7   Ruprecht Haasler, 'The German Army – The Present and the Future,' *NATO's Sixteen Nations*, October 1988, pp. 31–35.
8   Heinz Schulte, 'W German Army may lose up to 7 brigades,' *Jane's Defence Weekly*, 26 November 1988, p. 1327.
9   DPA, Hamburg, 1413 GMT, 9 July 1990.
10 'Polish reforms to disband 57 units,' *Jane's Defence Weekly*, 27 January 1990, p. 143; 'Update on the Polish Armed Forces,' *Jane's Soviet Intelligence Review*, March 1990, pp. 128–9; Janusz B. Grochowski, 'Who Is To Defend the Security of the Country?' *Zolnierz Rzeczypospolitej*, Warsaw, 9 May 1990, pp. 1,6 in JPRS-EER-90-080, 8 June 1990, p. 14.
11 'Update,' ibid.
12 Zbigniew Lewandowski, 'Structural Transformations in the Armed Forces,' *Zolnierz Rzeczypospolitej*, Warsaw, 10–13 May 1990, in JPRS-EER-90-099, 6 July 1990, p. 12.
13 Warsaw Domestic Service, 2005 GMT, 7 July 1990 in FBIS-EEU-90-133, 11 July 1990, p. 48.
14 Irean Baczynska, 'Suicides – What Is the True Picture,' *Zolnierz Rzeczypospolitej*, 20 June 1990, pp. 1, 3; FBIS-EEU-90-124, 27 June 1990, pp. 51–2; Suicides comprised 20 percent of all military accidental deaths – 71 in 1985, 63 in 1986, 59 in 1987, 58 in 1988; and 41 in 1989.
15 Richard Gasparre, '*Perestroika* and Soviet Military Power – Does Reform Equal Peace?' *Jane's Soviet Intelligence Review*, December 1989, pp. 550–551.
16 D. T. Yazov, 'A New Model of Security for the Armed Forces,' *Kommunist*, No. 18, Moscow, December 1989, pp. 61–72; M. A. Moiseyev, 'Once More About the Prestige of the Army,' *Kommunist Vooruzhennykh sil*, No. 13, Moscow, 1 July 1989, pp. 3–14.
17 Yazov, ibid.
18 Stepan Fedoseyev, 'The Guideline is Quality,' *Narodna Armiya*, Sofia, 13 October 1989 (FBIS-SOV-89-200, 18 October 1989, p. 119),.
19 Ibid.
20 V. G. Safronov, 'How It Was,' *Voyenno-Istoricheskiy Zhurnal*, No. 5, Moscow, 1990, pp. 61–71.
21 Steve Zaloga, 'Soviet Infantry: Lessons from the War in Afghanistan,' *Armed Forces Journal International*, Washington, October 1989, p. 25.
22 Alexander Alexiev, *Inside the Soviet Army in Afghanistan* (Santa Monica: The Rand Corporation, 1989), pp. vi–vii.
23 Chernyak, 'Topic for Reflection: Fall Draft,' *Komsomolskaya Pravada*, 28 November 1989, pp. 1,4.
24 S. Alexandrov, 'To Serve the People and not the Parties,' *Nedelya*, No. 22, 28 May 1990, pp. 1, 3.
25 Aleksandr Prokhanov, 'Notes of a Conservative,' *Nash Sovremennik*, No. 5, Moscow, May 1990, pp. 85–98.
26 *Izvestia TsK KPSS*, No. 12, December 1989, pp. 126–8.
27 Prokhanov, op. cit.
28 Shlomo Gazit, et al, *The Middle East Balance 1988–1989* (Tel Aviv: Tel Aviv University, 1989), p. 2.
29 Kassem M Ja'far, 'Syria's Military Build-up After June 1982: Implications For The Future of the Arab–Israeli Balance,' *Defence Yearbook 1988*, (London: Brassey's Defence Publishers, 1988), p. 185.
30 R. Jeffery Smith, 'Relying on Chemical Arms,' *The Washington Post*, 10 August 1990, p. 27.
31 Stephen C. Pelletiere, et al, *Iraqi Power and US Security in the Middle East* (Carlisle Barracks: Strategic Studies Institute, US Army War College, 1990), pp. 25–29.
32 Cairo, *Mena*, in Arabic, 13 Sep 89.
33 James Rupert, 'Iraq's Saddam Is Strapped for Cash, Obligated to Army,' *The Washington Post*, 4 August 1990, p. A15.
34 Anthony H. Cordesman, 'Western Strategic Interests and the India–Pakistan Military Balance,' *Armed Forces*, March 1988, p. 129.
35 IISS, *The Military Balance, 1990–1991* (London: Brassey's, 1990), pp. 161 and 173.
36 Anthony R. Tucker, 'The Indian Army in Sri Lanka,' *Armed Forces*, June 1988, pp. 280–1.
37 Marko Milivojevic, 'The People's Liberation Army of China – Part 2,' *Armed Forces*, September 1988, p. p. 413–14.
38 Ellis Joffre, 'The Chinese Army: A Decade of Reforms,' *Rusi and Brassey's Defense Yearbook 1988* (London: Brassey's Defence Publishers, 1988), p. 259.
39 Clare Hollingsworth, 'No 1 – Badges of rank reflect the changes,' *Pacific Defense 1989 Reporter Annual Reference Edition*, p. 48.
40 Paul Beaver and Bridget Harney, 'Role of the PLA in Tianamen Square,' *China in Crisis: The Role of the Military* (London: Jane's Defence Data, 1989), p. 23.
41 Howard Handleman, 'Some military opposed the slaughter,' *Pacific Defense Reporter*, July 1989, p. 17.

42   'China: The PLA is no longer a pillar of the regime,' *Defense & Armament – Heracles*, July/August 1989, pp. 24–5.

43   *North Korea: The Foundations of Military Strength* (Washington, DC: Defense Intelligence Agency, 1991), pp. 34–35.

44   Ibid. , p. 41.

45   James D. Marett, 'The Republic of Korea Army: The Light Infantry Division,' *Military Review*, Fort Leavenworth, November 1987, p. 68.

46   Edwin W. Besch, 'Oceania' in Chris Westhorp, ed. , *The World's Armies* (London: Salamander Books, Ltd. , 1991), p. 68.

47   J. D. Stevenson, 'No 1 – Is the defence force effective?' *Pacific Defense Reporter 1989 Annual Reference Edition*, p. 228.

CHAPTER 6

TRANSITION INTO A NEW ERA:
1989 AND BEYOND

As the Soviet Empire shrivelled and fell away after the fall of the Berlin Wall in late 1989, the Marxist ideological engine that had powered the post-war era finally broke down. The worlds' armies suddenly discovered that the old verities that had governed their existence since 1945 had suddenly become antiques. It seemed as if the two great alliance systems, the Warsaw Pact and NATO, should more appropriately take their place alongside such dusty relics as the Delian League and Triple Entente. The Warsaw Pact gave up the ghost and was dissolved in 1990.

PANAMA CITY AND BAKU – PREVIEWS OF THE NEW ERA

Less than two months after the fall of the Berlin Wall, the US Army launched Operation 'Just Cause' to depose a regional thug, Manuel Noriega, in Panama. The operation was greeted by little more than a shrug from the Soviet Union. In the New Year of 1990 the Soviet Ground Forces launched an armed assault on Baku, capital of Soviet Azerbaijan, when nationalists seized control of the city. Soviet power was collapsing even at home. The attempt to mobilize reservists was abandoned after a great public outcry of wives and mothers unwilling to underwrite the empire with one more life. The Western armies which once would have leaped for joy at such a diversion in the Soviet rear, could only shake their heads in sympathy at such a difficult mission.

DESERT STORM – FIRST ACT OF A NEW ERA

The NATO nations witnessed the nervous breakdown of their former enemies and began to prepare for the cutbacks that their political masters were eager to implement. US, British and French Armies were drawing-up plans for major reductions. The US Army had even begun to disband several heavy divisions. Then the world suddenly became a dangerous place again. In early August 1990 Saddam Hussein took the first bold step in the post-Cold War world and ordered the Iraqi army to invade Kuwait. Suddenly freed of the restraints of his former patron, he took the first bold step of the new era. Thus, he triggered the great, but brief, war that slammed the book shut on one era and opened a new book on another. Saddam's euphoria at finding himself freed from the constraints of his former patron had blinded him to the fact that the new situation allowed unparalleled freedom of action for the surviving superpower, the United States. All the skill, technology and training that the Western armies had expended in expectation of confronting a Soviet Theatre Strategic Operation (TSO) in Europe, was now lavished upon the hapless army of another regional thug.

The deployment of 532,000 US, 35,000 British and 13,500 French troops and their vast panoply of modern armour in Operation 'Desert Shield' was one of a whole series of virtuoso performances by these three old allies. The second was the rapid and undetected in-theatre lateral re-deployment of the US XVIII Airborne and VII Corps – a logistics masterpiece, the forte of the management and leadership skills inherent in the West. The third was the actual hundred-hour battle, Operation 'Desert Storm', that transformed one of the best regional armies in the world into

320

either corpses, POWs or terrified survivors fleeing through Basra. It all looked so easy to the world on CNN Television, but the epitome of skill is to make the difficult appear easy. 'Desert Storm' was a vindication of two of the major trends of the post-war era: the emphasis on professionalism and tactical and operational skill, and the integration of high-technology equipment in combat. Other trends seemed to count for much less: emphasis on masses of equipment and the integration of nuclear weapons. Numbers without skill merely provided targets. Only one side had nuclear weapons and forbore to use them. Nuclear weapons on the side of the allies actually provided insurance that Saddam would not use the other weapons of mass destruction at his disposal, chemical and biological weapons. The threat of the use of these so-called 'poor man's nukes' is probably a trend of the new era. They offer a psychological and political threat that huge tank inventories cannot match, and they are much cheaper, an attractive feature for Third World armies.

BORN AND PERISHED IN REVOLUTION – EPITAPH OF THE SOVIET ARMY

Even before 'Desert Storm', former Warsaw Pact satrapies in eastern Europe quickly began to restructure their armies, now freed of choking Soviet control. Poland made the most rapid transformation, beginning even before the Berlin Wall was torn down. The Volksarmee was simply swallowed in one gulp by the Bundeswehr in late 1990. The pride of the Warsaw Pact disappeared without protest, its officer corps for the most part dismissed and its inventory sold off, given away or cut up as scrap, a kinder fate than was meted out to the Army of the Republic of Vietnam, the only other major army to be dissolved since 1945.

The Soviet Army Ground Forces suffered the most traumatic fate of any of the armies. Save for the lack of war and death, it exhibited all the hallmarks of a badly defeated army. Withdrawn from its former forward bases, the spoils of the Great Patriotic War, it came home to economic chaos, massive demobilization, a painful loss of prestige, and poverty, as the value of army pay evaporated, and outright civil war in the Transcaucasus. Public support for conscription, the very basis of the doctrinal and organizational structure of the army collapsed. Soviet generals, not known to be selected for their sense of innovation, began heeding the rumble for reform from the junior and field grade ranks. They began speaking of a mix of volunteers and conscripts, though with a marked lack of enthusiasm and even less action.

As the dust settled from 'Desert Storm', the rotten edifice of the Soviet Union collapsed after the attempted August 1990 coup. The tottering structure received its final push because most of the Soviet Army simply stood aside and refused to lift a finger to save it. A more active minority of Soviet soldiers wholeheartedly supported Boris Yeltsin and the Russian democrats, and they made the difference. The most remarkable feature of the coup was the political unreliability of the Soviet officer and soldier. The previous five years had been an education for the military as well as civil society. Much of the army had watched with the rest of the world, the 'Chinese solution' in Tianamen Square the year before. To his eternal credit, the average Soviet soldier would not fire on his own people. A desperate Marshal Yazov rotated battalion after battalion to the White House, only to find that the arguments of their fellow citizens made them unreliable within fifty minutes. The coup finally collapsed when the various élite units that had been ordered to storm the Russian Parliament refused to do so. The deadly counter-terrorist Alfa Group refused to a man. The army had passed a profound test, the same one that the PLA had failed so miserably the previous summer in Tianamen Square.

Before the New Year, the Soviet Union had been abolished and fifteen republics proclaimed – all of which needed new armies. The bulk of the Soviet Army's Ground Forces transferred to the Russian Army and quickly began rediscovering old traditions of the Tsar's Army. A chaplain's corps was quickly established. The old Cossack bands were refounded and immediately established ties with the army. The major institutions of the Soviet Army remained in Russia, such as the General Staff, the major academies and most of the military industrial base. Russian troops saw their first combat in Moldova where the 14th Army defended ethnic Russians from the suddenly oppressive new Moldovan state.

THE WAVE OF CHANGE IN ASIA

The loss of the Soviet patron and arms supplier already has had major negative effects in India, Vietnam and North Korea. The Indian Army suddenly ran out of spare parts for its massive Soviet equipment inventories because its former Soviet suppliers went out of the weapons business or refused to be paid in tea or rupees. Vietnam found itself in the same boat but without even the tea and rupees to barter for Soviet aid. North Korea, much more self-sufficient, was given notice that the Russians would abrogate their defence treaty when President Yeltsin visited Seoul in November 1992. China, on the other hand, found itself in a much more enviable position, being relieved of its most dangerous threat by the collapse of the Soviet Union. The PLA had done without Soviet aid since the early sixties. China was actually able to barter food and consumer goods for Soviet equipment for the PLA. Deng's 1970s assessment that no major threat faced China before the next century proved prophetic. The PLA will continue to modernize in a much less serious national security environment. North Korea began making noises about nuclear weapons as its Soviet and Chinese patrons lost their reliability. North Korea faced a future without reliable patrons, a future haunted by the disappearance of another state contrived out of a split nation. South Korea's army remains vigilant, knowing that it is facing one of the world's few remaining high-potentials for war, a desperate dictator in the midst of his fantasies. Japan's quiet little army finally poked its head out into the sun in 1992 after the government won authority in parliament to send Japanese troops on a UN peacekeeping mission to Cambodia, the first time Japanese troops have been sent overseas since 1945.

THE MIDDLE EAST

Enough of Saddam Hussein's army survived 'Desert Storm' to put down Shia and Kurdish revolts with genocidal fury. The UN embargo will ensure for the next few years that the Iraqi Army continues to be a danger only to its own people. The Egyptian Army's two divisions put in the best performance of the non-Western elements of the 'Desert Storm' coalition, adding to its reputation gained in 1973. The Egyptians, Syrians and Israelis can all look forward to their region's loss of influence after the end of the Cold War world – and to the readiness of the United States and Russia continually to re-arm them at cut-rate prices. Iran, with oil to barter, took advantage of Russia's desperation to sell weaponry to earn hard currency with which to re-arm its battered ground forces.

THE US ARMY AND NO MORE TASK FORCE SMITHS

The post-'Desert Storm' US Army quickly resumed the cutbacks it had been undergoing before the great deployment to Saudi Arabia. Despite the participation of the two superb British and French divisions, 'Desert Storm' had been largely a US show, the last hurrah for that great post-Vietnam army rebuilt on the ashes of failure. This time the army insisted and was supported by the Administration, that the cutbacks should not be ruinous. The new Chief of Staff, General Gordon Sullivan, in a video shown to all the army's military and civilian personnel, stated repeatedly that there would be no more Task Force Smiths. The reduction in size to about 500,000 from 761,000 would be orderly and patient, designed to do as little damage as possible to the institution and its capabilities. As with the British Army, an inordinate cut was made in the armoured and mechanized forces, but special operations units were spared. Nevertheless, the ongoing reduction has been painful. The army released professionals, not conscripts and short-service reserve officers.

'Desert Storm' left a festering problem within the army. The failure of National Guard brigades to be deployed was seen by the Reserve Components as a deliberate act of sabotage by the highest levels of the army. Allegations were made that the army's leadership looked to the post-'Desert Storm' cuts and decided that a successful National Guard performance would result in more cuts of the Active Component and a larger role for the Reserve Components. The army contends that the National Guard brigades were simply not ready. The resulting bitterness in the Reserve Components will poison the Total Army concept for years to come.

THE BRITISH AND FRENCH ARMIES FALL BACK IN TIME

After 'Desert Storm' the major NATO armies resumed the reduction plans that had been so peremptorily announced the year before. If Saddam Hussein had waited until these cuts were under way none of the armies that helped crush him would have been in condition to do much at all – a vindication of the aphorism that timing is everything.

The British Army would be cut from 160,000 to 120,000; BAOR would lose two of its three armoured divisions in Germany and 30,000 men, which would leave the army with one armoured division in the remnant of BAOR and one infantry division based in the UK. The government's announcement acknowledged that a unified Germany might well ask for the total withdrawal of British forces in the foreseeable future. Like the other three war-time powers, the army had for fifty years had its garrisons there as part of its permanent structure. Every tenth married soldier in BAOR had a German wife. Now the army would be faced with the same problem as the other departing powers – there was no accommodation at home for re-deployed units. The defence ministry had concluded that there were no permanent facilities available in the UK 'capable of housing a major army unit and its families'; facilities for a battalion would cost as much as £55 million. Rather than re-deploy the battalions in the UK, they will most likely be disbanded. The defence review noted that it hoped to retain personnel from disbanded units to fill existing vacancies.

'It would be absurd to lose highly trained personnel when the services cannot recruit and retain enough of them.'[1]

The toughening German attitude towards land use for ground forces' training will also have serious implications for the future British Army. For almost 50 years the army has been able to use West Germany for its large-scale exercises and training operations, especially those deploying large numbers of armoured vehicles. The future restricted use or even loss of these areas will throw the army back on its rather limited domestic training areas, of which five exist. Only one of them, Salisbury Plain, is suitable for armour training, and even here limited use has resulted in a degree of ecological protection that could not be maintained if it were the sole centre for tank manoeuvres in the United Kingdom. The British public complained loudly about Exercise 'Brave Defender' in 1986 though it was smaller than exercises normally conducted in Germany.[2] The public is unlikely to be less exacting when the army is forced to rely on its UK training centres to a greater degree than ever before. The use of alternative training centres of other NATO allies in Europe might be feasible. Canadian and Australian training areas would be far too expensive for extended use. Given these restrictions and the diminishing prospect of high-intensity mechanized war in Europe, the Royal Armoured Corps will probably suffer the most grievous cuts.

The end of the post-war era will re-cast the British Army in entirely new form. It will be far more of an infantry army than at any time since 1940. Its even smaller size will have an adverse effect on the promotion system, a sensitive issue to the modern professional soldier. A more ominous prospect is reflected in the words of Major-General J. D. Lunt, 'There is too the danger that a much reduced regular army, tucked away in its cantonments and carrying out its major training exercises somewhere overseas, will lose touch with the Nation, which has happened before in our history.'[3]

The army's departure from its last major overseas garrison in Germany would mark not only the end of the post-war era, but an era cast much deeper into history. As the departure from its home in India in 1948 was the first step in the long withdrawal from empire, the departure from Germany will be the last. For two centuries India had been the emotional home of the army; for 45 years, the fighting strength of the army called northern Germany home. Current developments will probably deny it any but the most minor overseas garrisons, reducing it to the same geography of Elizabeth I – Great Britain and, of course, Ireland – as Correlli Barnett had predicted.

By early 1990 it was evident to the French Army that the loosening of the Soviet hold on eastern Europe and the success of the CFE negotiations would inevitably lead to major force reductions. The army was alarmed at the prospect of the concessions that the political leadership of France was about to make: '... all the signs indicate that we're going to be consigned to oblivion before the others have even disarmed', seemed to be the general consensus. There was great reluctance to see the already thinly equipped force fall below 350 helicopters or be decreased by as much as 15 per cent of its armoured vehicles. Such an agreement would be considered a negotiating defeat for France.[4] The French Army's new Hades nuclear missile was one weapon that the government was intent on protecting despite the awkward fact that its range from within French borders would not reach beyond a united Germany.

Another fear was that force reductions would be such as no longer to justify the conscription system upon which the French Army was based. Already the French armed forces can only place 75 per cent of the conscripts available. Arguments were already being heard in the army for a volunteer system that would abolish conscription altogether. Most military professionals were against such a change, putting greater value on the loyalty to the army generated by the involvement of the nation's youth in the national defence. Armies are socially conservative institutions, and such reservations are to be expected.

Their fears proved prophetic. The rapid evaporation of the Soviet threat was reflected in the government's announcement in July 1990 of the 'Armed Forces 2000' concept. Thirty-five thousand men were to be cut within four years, the greater slice coming out of the army. A threat to the conscription system was implied in the hint that the term of service might be reduced from 12 to 10 months if enough conscripts could be persuaded to extend their service to 18 to 24 months. The six AMX-30-equipped tank divisions would be reduced to four Le Clerc-equipped divisions. President Mitterand had already sounded the death knell of the French presence in Germany, 'Logic could dictate that the French army stationed in Germany will come home.' First Army in Germany would be eliminated, some of its units being transferred to Second and Third Armies garrisoned in metropolitan France. None of the divisions in FAR was scheduled for elimination.[5]

Should 'Armed Forces 2000' be implemented, the French Army will have reverted to much the same setting it occupied in 1940, garrisoned only in metropolitan France and its former colonies.

GERMANY – IN THE SINGULAR ONCE AGAIN

The collapse of East Germany and the inevitability of reunification posed a problem for the Bundesheer that none of the other NATO armies faced – the prospect of what to do with a second national army, the East German Nationale Volksarmee (NVA), when the DDR went out of business. West Germany was in the unique position of being able to call the shots since it held the purse strings that would finance reunification. The first reactions were adamant that it would be impossible to absorb an army marinated in Communist ideology and the harsh leadership style of the NVA. All the NVA's professional officers and NCOs would have to go. At most junior officers and conscripts with less than two years' service might be acceptable. This attitude was modified in the following months as it became apparent that 60,000 ruined and embittered NVA professionals looking for work would not be socially healthy for the new Germany. There were too many similarities with 1919. There was also the not inconsiderable aspect of equitable treatment. Almost every other profession in East Germany would be admitted on equal terms by its West German counterparts. It could not have been lost on the West German defence ministry that the absorption of East Germany would increase the conscript pool by 25 per cent; the absorption of a sizable number of NVA professionals would also alleviate junior officer and senior NCO shortages.

The Krasnodar summit between Germany and the Soviet Union fixed the size of the German armed forces after unification at 370,000 of which 50,000 would be NVA personnel of all services. Counting Territorial Army forces, the Bundesheer in 1990 amounted to 72 per cent of the Bundeswehr. A similar ratio would yield a unified German Army of almost 267,000.

While the Federal Republic and the Bundesheer were deciding what the future of the German Army would be, the other 'terminal' German army was suffering a prolonged death scene. The NVA discovered quickly that it was an army without a state and an army with enormous morale and disciplinary problems. Events soon overtook the NVA's leadership as the soldiers began to ask, 'Why do we need an army?' The first soldiers' protests were heard in Hagenau in early December but were hushed up. Another incident followed at Beelitz. In a typically petty act of discipline, soldiers were forbidden to toast the New Year with a glass of champagne. This time things could not be hushed up; soldiers, NCOs and even officers protested in their barracks and joined the people in the streets in support of the revolution.[6] Unofficial councils mushroomed representing the grievances of all ranks. The natural order of things was reversed as soldiers refused to obey their orders and intimidated their officers who in turn became reluctant to punish offences. Guards refused to stand their posts, soldiers were drunk on duty and desertion began to empty the barracks. The flea markets of West Germany began to hawk a growing display of NVA uniforms and medals. Even before the troops began voting with their feet, the NVA had begun to shrink rapidly with the reduction of military service from 18 to 12 months in December to alleviate the severe worker shortage. Twenty thousand conscripts were released in December and 25,000 in January, in addition to 15,000 NCOs. The officer corps abandoned the Communist Party in droves, and political officers were reduced to lower ranks and to teaching 'civics'. Over 2,000 officers and NCOs made inquiries about joining the Bundeswehr.[7]

The host of petty restrictions on soldiers' lives was quickly modified or abolished. The Communist term of military address, 'Comrade', was replaced with the traditional German 'Herr'. Soldiers were allowed to wear civilian clothes after duty and have unrestricted access to the Western media; military ceremonies were drastically cut back. The soldiers' councils were recognized as almost official bodies.[8] Military exercises were drastically reduced as the NVA officially declared its orientation to a defensive posture. Elite regiments decided not to participate in joint exercises with Soviet troops. The percentage of troops required to be on ready alert was dropped by almost a half. At the same time numerous contacts between personnel of the Bundeswehr and NVA were made. The first German–German military summit took place on 17 January in Vienna between the NVA chief of staff and the Bundeswehr's inspector-general as a sideline to a CSCE seminar on military doctrine.

The March elections removed the remnant of Communist control from the NVA. The defence ministry was renamed The Ministry of Disarmament and Defence; its first minister was Rainer Eppelmann, a 47-year-old bricklayer, pastor and pacifist. He was unequivocal in his aim, an 'NVA which is no longer capable of waging war'.[9] Shortly after assuming his duties, Eppelmann was confronted with a conspiracy of sorts. A newspaper reported that a group of NVA colonels had sent a letter to the West German defence minister offering immediately to dissolve the NVA and admit the Bundeswehr into the DDR. Eppelmann rushed to the ministry at midnight and called the office of the West German defence minister, Gerhard von Stollenberg, asking to confirm the letter. Von Stollenberg's aide denied knowledge of such a letter. The affair eventually died down but had highlighted the deteriorating morale within the NVA's officer corps at the prospect of professional ruin.[10] Von Stollenberg had probably done much to worsen this uncertainty in early March when it was reported that in his view, 'long-serving NVA members have no chance of joining the Bundeswehr because of the Communist orientation of the NVA up to last autumn'.[11] In response Eppelmann took the position that there must be a guarantee that at least certain parts of the NVA would be incorporated into a unified federal German army and that remaining reductions would be conducted in a socially acceptable manner. To bolster the army's self-image, he declared, 'The Army remains loyal to the people. It has not left this place, and remembered its role as people's army even in last autumn's most critical situation.'[12] The legitimacy arising from the March elections had already slowed down desertions; Eppelmann's actions now helped calm the panic among the regular cadre.

Eppelmann's goal throughout succeeding months was to retain at least a corps of the NVA as a separate entity within a unified German army. By late June the West German defence ministry had come to the conclusion that it would be politically impossible to discharge all the professionals of the NVA when almost every other profession in East Germany was to be accepted on equal footing in a united Germany. There would be a vetting commission to review the records of all personnel wishing to serve in the united army, similar to that endured by former Wehrmacht personnel when the Bundeswehr was established in 1956. NVA officers and NCOs could also expect intensive retraining in Bundeswehr leadership concepts. [13]

The movement to military unification moved inexorably on as these issues were decided. On 1 June full bilateral relations between the NVA and Bundeswehr at all levels were put into effect. At the same time, co-operation with the Warsaw Pact was being terminated; on 18 July the NVA announced also that it would no longer participate in Warsaw Pact exercises because, 'the great majority of the members in the Army no longer see any sense in participating in troop and staff exercises in this coalition framework'. The commander of the Soviet Western Group Forces (WGF) in East Germany was less than understanding but was bluntly told, 'There is no sense for NVA soldiers, who would in the foreseeable future be soldiers in a joint German Army, to still take part in such manoeuvrers now.'[14]

On 20 July the soldiers of the NVA took a new oath of allegiance to replace the one to the former Communist leadership, 'I swear, true to the laws of the German Democratic Republic, that I will always meet my military obligations in a disciplined and honourable way. I swear that I will devote all my strength to the preservation of peace and the protection of the German Democratic Republic.' The date was the anniversary of the 1944 military coup against Hitler, a moral signpost in German history of intense meaning to Germans east and west. To ensure that the meaning would not be lost, the honorifics of the NVA were changed to incorporate the names of the heroes of 20 July 1944. The NVA was doing more in these ceremonies than honouring a moral tradition; it was staking its claim to the legitimacy that comes from that tradition. To underscore that point, the NVA chief of staff, Admiral Theodor Hoffmann, stated that the NVA had earlier prepared a crisis plan to support the people if the civil authorities were to attempt a counter-revolution. The NVA had strengthened the transition to democracy and earned the right to enter a unified German army, 'not as losers but as equals'.[15] It was all in vain. When unification took place in late 1990 it was done thoroughly on the Bundeswehr's terms – as if the NVA had never been.

THE VICTIMS OF KATYN FOREST RETURN HOME
On 2 February 1990 the Polish Ministry of Defence ordered the depoliticization of the army much to the relief of the overwhelming majority of the officer corps whose careers had been burdened by the Communist Party's advice, 'If you do not join, you do not advance.' The Main Political Board, the Party's control mechanism, was hurriedly renamed and reduced in the military organization scale to the Education Department, and 1,300 political officers were released from service. That still left 5,300 former political officers who were now reduced to teaching 'civics'. As one suspicious Solidarity writer noted, that still left one 'political supervisor' to 55 soldiers. 'Obviously, somebody does not realize that in order to be an education officer one needs something more than a set of evening courses in Marxism-Leninism.' A further cut of 35 to 40 per cent was planned. Nevertheless, the turmoil surrounding the army's restructuring hid a great deal of manoeuvring by members of the former Nomenclatura to preserve their privileges and this provoked a number of protests by junior officers, NCOs and soldiers.[16]

With the collapse of Communist power, the actual condition of the Polish Army began to come to light. The Polish equipment inventory was revealed to be antiquated by General of Division Tadeusz Kasmierski, chief inspector of military technology. Between 35 and 38 per cent of the equipment inventories belongs to the latest generation whereas NATO countries generally had 50 per cent in this category. Sixty-four per cent of Polish equipment is produced domestically, but the number and type of critical items were dictated by the Soviet Union for security or political reasons resulting in severe distortions in Polish capabilities. The fielding of advanced C3I systems in particular had been badly retarded. More prosaic equipment was also of a mature vintage. Production of T-55s and even the ancient T-34 had only been discontinued in 1975. By 1989 the army had only acquired 360 T-72s. The skyrocketing cost of modern systems and maintenance and operations was putting a brake on the purchase of new equipment at the same time as exports to Czechoslovakia and East Germany had dried up. Until the Polish economy recovers, the army is in for an extended period of penury. The pinch was illustrated by the eager sale of withdrawn equipment to farmers, discharged regulars, and even to collectors in the West who have been known to pay $60,000 for the cachet of having a Warsaw Pact aircraft mounted in the front yard.[17]

While the economic recovery of the Polish Army will take some time, its spiritual recovery has leaped ahead. Chaplains had been barely tolerated by the previous regime as a concession to the indelible Catholic nature of Poland and were limited to saying Mass in the few available churches. New guidelines issued by the President Jaruselski on 1 March allowed spiritual instruction of the troops and the conducting of services inside the barracks where no churches were available. So dramatic were the changes that the Church found there were not enough padres in the army to implement them.[18]

On an equally spiritual note was the resolution of the issue of the Katyn Forest Massacre of 4,500 Polish officers by their Soviet captors in 1940; another 10,500 officers had been murdered at the same time in other unknown locations. With the collapse of Communist control, the army was the first Polish organization to set up a Katyn committee to collect funds for a monument. 'We feel we are the heirs of these men and are morally obliged to tackle this issue.'[19] In one of the strangest turnabouts in history, General Jaruzelksi, the man who crushed the Baltic demonstrations of 1970 and Solidarity in 1981, carried home from the Soviet Union the names of the 15,000 dead. As the elegantly precise Polish honour guard presented arms at the solemn memorial at Katyn Forest, the general saluted the monument, tears streaming down his face from under his dark glasses. After a harrowing journey through history, Poland's army was entirely her own again.

NOTES

1   Evans, 'How German unity leaves services' fate in the balance,' *The Times*, 26 July, 1990, p. 15.
2   Francis Tusa, 'Hands-on – but Where? Armed Forces Journal International, Washington, July 1990, p. 30.
3   J. D. Lunt, 'Swords into Ploughshares,' Army Defence Quarterly, Vol. 120, No. 1, January 1990, pp. 62–3.
4   Jean Guisnel, 'Army Feels Increasingly Disarmed,' Liberation, Paris, 6 February 1990, p. 6; FBIS-WEU-90-064, 3 April 1990, pp. 22–3.
5   'Army faces brunt of force cuts,' Jane's Defence Weekly, London, 21 July 1990, p. 72.
6   ADN International Service, East Berlin, 2253 GMT, 18 January 1990.
7   'The East German Army: High Speed Perestroika,' International Defense Review, 4/1990, p. 361.
8   Rainer Funke, 'Do We Still Need an Army?' Neues Deutschland, East Berlin, 28 December 1989, p. 3 in FBIS-EEU-90-007, 10 January 1990, pp. 47–8.
9   ADN International, East Berlin, 0205 GMT, 23 April 1990.
10 ADN International Service, East Berlin, 0205 GMT, 23 April 1990; FBIS-EEU-90-078, 23 April 1990, p. 28; Deutschlandfunk Network, Cologne, 1100 GMT, 23 April 1990 in FBIS-EEU-90-079, 24 April 1990, pp. 27–8.
11 DPA, Hamburg, 1610 GMT, 1 March 1990.
12 ADN International, East Berlin, 1301 GMT, 27 April 1990 in FBIS-EEU-90-082, 27 April 1990, p. 19.
13 ADN International, East Berlin, 1109 GMT, 5 July 1990 in FBIS-EEU-90-130, 6 July 1990, p. 35; Anne

McElvoy, 'Wrangle over Berlin's Soviet arsenal,' The Times, London, 20 July 1990.

14 DPA, Hamburg, 1818 GMT, 18 July 1990.
15 Ian Murray, 'Berlin in move to save army,' The Times, London, 18 July 1990.
16 Witold Paek, 'Before the Storm,' Tygodnik Solidarnosc, Warsaw, 20 April 1990, pp. 12–13 in FBIS-EEU-90-082, pp. 37–9.
17 Ewa Wilk, 'The State of the Army,' Tygodnik Solidarnosch, 22 June 1990, pp. 12–13; FBIS-EEU-90-124, 27 June 1990, pp. 48–51.
18 'Straight Facts About the Army,' Zolnierz Wolnosci, Warsaw, 26 March 1990, pp. 1,3 in FBIS-EEU-90-060, p. 46.
19 Ibid.

CHAPTER 7

INTO THE FUTURE

THE WESTERN ALLIES

That pillar of the Cold War era, the 1st (British) Corps was disbanded with great ceremony on 2 October 1992 at Catterick Barracks at Bielefeld in the newly united Germany. On that damp, overcast day, the massed British Cavalry Bands and the honour guard of the 1st Battalion the Argyll and Sutherland Highlanders put on that sort of splendid military show that no other army can better. They were not there, however, to put a brave face on another casualty of post-Cold War economics. They were celebrating the metamorphosis rather than the disappearance of the old 1st Corps.

The origin of this metamorphosis was the end of the Cold War and the old bipolar world, the political environment around which the armies had been built. Following the heels of this transition, Desert Storm and the breakup of multinational states, the Soviet Union and Yugoslavia, announced the nature of the post-Cold War military environment. The prospect of war among the traditional great powers of the twentieth century had evaporated. Rather, these powers were presented with seething chaos amid the debris of broken empires and in the ever unstable Third World. Massed coalition armies of which 1st (British) Corps was an example were suddenly ill prepared to deal with these conditions.

'Desert Storm' had been the harbinger of the new era. Rapid reaction and deployment of highly professional and well-equipped forces to an out-of-area crisis was the obvious lesson. The metamorphosis of 1st (British) Corps was a logical next step. Simultaneously with 1st Corps' disbandment, NATO established the Allied Command Europe Rapid Reaction Corps (ARRC), known informally as the 'Ark', the ground element of NATO's new Reaction Forces of ten divisions. Although thirteen nations are represented on the ARRC's staff, the British Army was given the lead role in staffing (60 percent) and command of the Ark in order to ensure operational effectiveness. Its mission: 'Be prepared to deploy ARRC forces of Corps troops and up to four divisions Allied Command Europe (ACE) wide on military operations in support of SACEUR's crisis management options'.[1]

The US Army's Chief of Staff, General Gordon Sullivan, defined the American vision of the new reality:

> The essence of the vision is imbedded in the concept of power projection, and credible power projection is dependent upon the Army being trained and equipped and postured to put the correct force where needed in a timely manner.... Crisis response is the centerpiece of our capabilities as a power projection force.[2]

General Sullivan was confident of this mission having seen the Army through its first post-war reconfiguration that did not result its near ruin. His emphasis on 'No More Task Force Smiths' had paid off to an important degree. Despite a four division and 200,000 man force reduction, he has maintained that operational readiness and training had not suffered appreciably. However, there are indications that Sullivan's optimism is only partially justified. The tactical proficiency of maneuver brigades at the NTC reportedly has slipped drastically to the the levels of the early

1980s when the army was beginning its long climb back from Vietnam. Training funds for the Reserve Components have been drastically reduced as well. In December 1993, an army study warned that a serious shortage of combat support equipment would endanger the army's 'ability to deploy and sustain combat forces in an extended crisis.' As one analyst described the situation, 'Sullivan is being asked to fit a five-pound force structure into a three-pound budget bag.'[3]

The initial instances for crisis response by NATO and the US, have not been encouraging either. The timidity of the Europeans to the next door blood bath in Yugoslavia, leads one to question whether it makes any difference how they reorganize their armies and strategies, if political will is absent. The French General Phillippe Morillon, commanding NATO forces in Bosnia, ascribed to the American hesitation to commit peacekeeping forces there to a lesson of Dersert Storm:

> 'Desert Storm left one awful legacy: It imposed the idea that you must
> be able to fight the wars of the future without suffering losses. The idea
> of zero-kill as an outcome has been imposed on American generals. But
> there is no such thing as a clean ro risk-free war. You condemn yourself
> to inactivity if you set that standard.'[4]

Yet, one must ask whether Morillon's complaint misses the point. The strategic lessons of the post-war era were clear. There must be a fine fit between military means and the aims of policy. This formula does not exist for any country that might consider imposing a military solution in Bosnia. Such a solution would be as open-ended as the quagmires that bogged down the Americans in Vietnam, the Soviets in Afghanistan, the Vietnamese in Cambodia, the Israelis in Lebanon and the Iraqis in Iran. If the American military leadership learned a lesson in Desert Storm, it was one that revalidated the successful operations of the post-war era. Military operations must be based on clear and achievable policy goals, and both policy goals and military objectives must be limited in time and space and demonstrate a cold-blooded self-restraint in their appetites. Unfortunately, Sullivan's dilemma in fitting a five-pound military structure into a three-pound budget bag is a warning that those responsible for policy do not understand the formula as well as their generals.

THE RUSSIANS

The fine touch in crisis response has been exhibited by the losers in the Cold War, the Russian Army. Russia is in the process of actively rebuilding its empire through the traditional means of its army. With great subtlety, the Russians have been successfully meddling in the fragments of the Soviet Union they term the 'near abroad'. All three Transcaucasian republics have been drawn back into the Russian orbit by a combination of pressure and protection. Both Georgia and Azerbaijan have been humbled on the battlefield by Russian proxies and in some cases troops. Armenians, for the second time in this century, have been protected from Turkish genocide by Russian support. The Russian Army tore the Slav-inhabited region of the Trans-Dniester from Moldova and intervened in the Tadzhik civil war to beat back the Afghan-assisted Muslim fundamentalist bid for power.

For an army that had just gone through a gut-wrenching ride in the fall of the Soviet Union, it has been a remarkable performance paralleled by the Russian Army's recovery of political influence. for the second time in two years, in September 1993, the Russian Army intervened in a coup attempt to support the current leadership and has not been shy to collect on the debt. The influence of the Russian Army has been seen to be behind the reversal of the Yeltsin government's initial

willingness to return the Northern Territories to Japan and to allow the incorporation of former Warsaw Pact allies into NATO. The army was also finding its way
back into the good opinion of the nation by its association with Russian national-
ism. Public opinion polls were finding in August 1993 that the army was the 'most
trustworthy institution' in the country.

Internal reorganization of the Russian Army has been advancing quickly on
both the doctrinal and institutional levels. The refusal of all but 25 percent of the
conscript cohort to report has been the defacto tool to shape a new volunteer force.
One recent observer noted the evidence of fundamental change:

> 'Mid-level officers clearly relish the opportunity to build a new,
> uniquely Russian military from the ground up. The obvious hardships
> notwithstanding, their morale appears high and their nationalism – not
> to mention their chauvinism – is unmistakable. These younger Russian
> officers also look and behave differently from the stereotypical Russian:
> they are fit and trim, taking obvious pride in their service and uniform.
> They treat their subordinates with care and respect. some of this is a
> legacy of Afghanistan, but the *esprit* is new. These officers have – and
> communicate – a clear sense of mission: holding the military together
> and leading it through the painful, but necessary, restructuring process.[5]

THE MIDDLE EAST AND SOUTHWEST ASIA

The closing of superpower checkbooks after the end of the Cold War and Desert
Storm took much of the steam out of the Arab-Israeli rivalry. With the humbling of
Iraq, Syria and Israel remained the only major players in a drama neither could
afford much longer. Israel's ground forces, especially its reserve structure, have
seen heavy cut backs as more and more Israelis question the need for a Fortress
Israel mentality. The current round of peace initiatives are evidence of these
changes. Nevertheless, future wars remain likely as Saddam Hussein continues to
make great efforts to rebuild the army shattered by Desert Storm and as Iran makes
similar efforts to rebuild the army shattered by Saddam. In the Indian subcontinent,
the Indian Army's fixation on Pakistan as a serious threat has become less and less
credible given India's lead in every sphere of competition.

EAST ASIA

The end of the Cold War also ushered in basic changes in the roles of the armies of
East Asia. Both the Chinese People's Liberation Army and the Japanese Ground
Self-Defence Forces find themselves taking more of a back seat to their respective
navies and air forces as each country attempts to build a power projection capability. The lessons of Desert Storm clearly have influenced the Japanese who have
been discussing seriously the acquisition of aircraft carriers as they cut back on
ground forces and the production of their equipment.

In one of the convolutions of Chinese politics, in 1992 Deng successfully
moved against the military clique of the Yang family that had executed the Tianamen Square massacre. A Deng loyalist was appointed to the critical position of vice
chairman of the Central Military Council, Liu Huaqing. Liu's background was
naval and as a disciple of Soviet Admiral Gorshkov, he has pushed a blue-water
capability for China at the expense of the PLA at the same time the service was losing sight of its basic mission.

Deng's direction to the PLA to engage in commerce and industry in the last
decade had been meant to relieve military demands for financial resources from the

central government. So successful has the effort been that some analysts believe the PLA generates revenues that equal the defence budget. After paying 30 percent to the central government the remainder of profits are meant to support training and support for military personnel. However, the ethics of the soldier and the entrepreneur have proven incompatible. Too many officers within the PLA have concentrated on money-making to the detriment of professionalism and cohesion. Profits often are directed to luxury goods or bonuses for officers and men. One foreign attache has noted, 'Military chiefs complain of inadequate military funds, but many units have Mercedes Benz or Toyota sedans that are not covered by the official military budget'. Corruption, unthinkable twenty years ago, has become a major problem within the PLA.[6]

The armies of Vietnam and North Korea remain huge but increasingly hollow as their national economies disintegrate, dinosaurs in the new world of mammals. If the Vietnamese at least recognize their problems but lack the resources to reform, the North Koreans lack both vision and means. As North Korea's economy implodes, its huge once coddled army is now being shorted of essential resources to include basic subsistence of officers and men. Growing unrest among the population, once unthinkable has broken out. As a result, the sense of being cornered for the North Koreans has become inescapable. This heightened sense of hysteria within the dual leadership of Kim il Sun and his son is the likeliest impending cause of a major war in the world today. Such a war among the large conscript armies of the two Koreas would be the belated and bloody closing chapter of the Cold War.

NEW THEMES

For the first time in more than one hundred years, the worlds' armies are not responding to the attraction of great alliance systems. Without the tension of these systems and especially the ideological hostilities that powered them, the prospects for more great wars to disfigure the world are almost non-existent (with the exception of the final act on the Korean Peninsula). The great hosts are shrinking, not only in the advanced world but in Asia and the Middle East. The twin lessons that emerged from the post-war era and were so dramatically demonstrated to the world, courtesy of CNN – high technology and professionalism – will be the dominant themes of this new unnamed era. Only a pernicious shortsighted sense of economy could cripple this winning combination in the advanced countries of the world. While high-quality armies do not have to rely on numbers alone, there is a floor of quantity beneath which even they cannot fall without becoming hollow shells.

Conscript armies will continue to have value as nation-building tools in more undeveloped parts of the world, but their military utility is rapidly declining. Conscripted peasants are a clumsy anachronism. Well-educated, motivated volunteers armed with the weapons of high technology are the future. Only such troops will be able to master the increasingly complex and expensive technologies that now are everywhere. It is only such armies in the future that will ride the Desert Storm.

NOTES

1 Edward Furdson, 'Farewell 1st (British) Corps – Welcome the "Ark"', *Army Quarterly and Defence Journal*, January 1993, pp. 45.
2 Gordon R. Sullivan, 'Ready for Action – The New United States Army', *Nato's Sixteen Nations*, Volume 38, No.1/1993, p. 64.

3 John Lancaster, 'Army Study Warns of Possible Equipment Shortages', *The Washinton Post*, 14 December 1993, p. A4.
4 Jim Hoagland, 'Even America Gets the Blues', *The Washington Post*, 14 December 1993, p. A25.
5 Ilana Kass, 'The Russian military: fractured not shattered', *International Defence Review*, 9/1993, p. 695.
6 Tai Ming Cheung, 'Serve the People', *Far East Economic Review*, 14 October 1993, pp. 64–66.

SELECT BIBLIOGRAPHY

AUSTRALIA

Grey, Jeffrey. *A Military History of Australia.* Cambridge: Cambridge University Press, 1990.

CHINA

Area Handbook for the People's Republic of China. Department of the Army Pamphlet 550-60. Washington, DC: US Government Printing Office, 1972.

Bunge, Frederica M. and Sinn, Rinn-Sup. *China: A Country Study.* Washington, DC: American University, 1981.

China in Crisis: The Role of the Military. Surrey: Jane's Information Group, Ltd., 1989.

The Chinese Armed Forces Today. Englewood Cliffs, NJ: Prentice-Hall, Inc., 1979.

Corr, Gerard H. *The Chinese Red Army.* New York: Schoken Books, 1974.

George, Alexander L. *The Chinese Communist Army in Action: The Korean War and its Aftermath.* New York: Columbia University Press, 1967.

Gittings, John. *The Role of the Chinese Army.* London: Oxford University Press, 1967.

Godwin, Paul H. B. *The Chinese Communist Armed Forces.* Maxwell Airforce Base, AL: Air University Press, 1988.

Griffith, Samuel B. II. *The Chinese People's Liberation Army.* New York: McGraw-Hill Book Co., 1967.

Jencks, Harlan W. *From Muskets to Missiles: Politics and Professionalism in the Chinese Army, 1945–1981.* Boulder: Westview Press, 1982.

O'Ballance, Edgar. *The Red Army of China: A Short History.* New York: Frederick A. Praeger, 1963.

GREAT BRITAIN

Barnett, Correlli. *Britain and Her Army 1500–1970.* New York: William Morrow & Co., 1970.

Blaxland, Gregory. *The Regiments Depart: A History of the British Army 1945–1970.* London: William Kimber, 1971.

Chappell, Mike. *The British Army in the 1980s.* London: Osprey Publishing Ltd., 1987.

Farwell, Bryon. *The Gurkhas.* London: W. W. Norton & Co., 1984.

Fowler, William. *Battle for the Falklands (I) Land Forces.* London: Osprey Publishing Ltd., 1982.

Gander, Terry. *Encyclopaedia of the Modern British Army.* 2nd ed. Cambridge: Patrick Stephens, 1982.

— *Encyclopaedia of the Modern British Army.* 3rd ed. Wellingborough: Patrick Stephens, 1986.

Geraghty, Tony. *This Is the SAS: A Pictorial History of the Special Air Service Regiment.* London: Arms & Armour Press; New York: Arco Publishing Inc., 1983.

Grey, Jeffrey. *The Commonwealth Armies and the Korean War.* Manchester University Press, 1988.

Griffin, David. *Encyclopedia of Modern British Army Regiments.* Wellingborough: Patrick Stephens, 1985.

Hamilton, Nigel. *Monty: Final Years of the Field Marshall 1944–1976.* New York: McGraw-Hill Book Co., 1987,

Hastings, Max and Simon Jenkins. *The Battle for the Falklands.* New York: W.W. Norton & Co., 1983.

Hogg, Ian V. *The British Army in the Twentieth Century.* London: Ian Allan Ltd, 1985.

Hallows, Ian S. *Regiments and Corps of the British Army.* London: Arms & Armour Press, 1991.

Messenger, Charles. *History of the British Army* Novato, CA: Presidio Press, 1986.

Montgomery, Bernard. *The Memoirs of Field Marshal Montgomery.* Cleveland: The World Publishing Co., 1958.

France

Bocca, Geoffrey. *La Légion.* New York: Thomas Y. Crowell Co., 1964.

Fall, Bernard. *Street Without Joy.* Harrisburg: The Stackpole Co., 1967.

Gorce, Paul-Marie de la. *The French Army: A Military and Political History.* New York: George Braziller, 1963.

Kelly, George Armstrong. *Lost Soldiers: The French Army and Empire in Crisis 1947–1962.* Cambridge: The M.I.T. Press, 1965.

Martin, Michel L. *Warriors to Managers: The French Military Establishment Since 1945.* Chapel Hill: The University of North Carolina Press, 1981.

Yost, David S. *France and Conventional Defense in Europe.* Boulder: Westview Press, 1985.

Windrow, Martin, and Braby, Wayne. *French Foreign Legion Paratroops.* London: Osprey Publishing Ltd., 1985.

Germany

Abenheim, Donald. *Reforging the Iron Cross: The Search for Tradition in the West German Armed Forces.* Princeton: Princeton University Press, 1988.

Burant, Stephan R. (ed.). *East Germany: A Country Study.* Washington, DC: American University Press, 1987.

Childs, David. *The GDR: Moscow's German Ally.* London: George Allen & Unwin, 1983.

Forster, Thomas M. *The East German Army: A Pattern of a Communist Military Establishment.* London: George Allen & Unwin, 1967.

— *The East German Army: The Second Power in the Warsaw Pact.* London: George Allen & Unwin, 1980.

Keefe, Eugene K., *et al. Area Handbook for the Federal Republic of Germany.* Washington, DC: American University, 1975.

— *East Germany: A Country Study.* Washington, DC: American University, 1981.

Nelson, Walter Henry. *Germany Rearmed.* New York: Simon and Schuster, 1972.

Nyrop, Richard F., *et al. Federal Republic of Germany: A Country Study.* Washington, DC: American University, 1982.

Reed, John A., Jr. *Germany and NATO.* Washington, DC: National Defense University Press, 1987.

Scheibert, Horst. *Panzer-Grenadier-Division Grossdeutschland und Ihre Schwesterverbaende.* Dorheim: Podzun-Verlag, 1970.

Simpson, Keith. *History of the German Army.* Greenwich, CT: The Military Press, 1985.

Walpole, Norman C., *et al. Area Handbook for Germany.* Washington, DC: US Government Printing Office, 1960.

GREECE

Averoff-Tossizza, Evangelos. *By Fire and Ax: The Communist Party and the Civil War in Greece, 1944–49.* New Rochelle, New York: Caratzas Brothers, 1978.

The History of the United Nations Forces in the Korean War. Vol III. Seoul: Ministry of National Defence, The Republic of Korea, 1974.

Kiriakopoulos, G.C. *Ten Days to Destiny 1941: The Battle for Crete.* New York: Franklin Watts, 1985.

O'Ballance, Edgar. *The Greek Civil War 1944–1949.* New York: Frederick A. Praeger, 1966.

Papagos, Alexandros. *The Battle of Greece 1940–1941.* Athens: The J.M. Scazikis 'Alpha' Editions, 1949.

INDIA

Baranwal, Sukhdeo Prasad. *Military Yearbook.* New Dehli: Guide Publications, 1988.

Longer, V. *Red Coats to Olive Green: A History of the Indian Army 1600–1974.* Bombay: Allied Publishers, 1974.

Nyrop, Richard F. (ed.). *India: A Country Study.* Washington, DC: American University, 1985.

Shinn, Rinn-Sup, *et al. Area Handbook for India.* Washington, DC: American University, 1970.

Walpole, Norman C., *et al. U.S. Army Area Handbook for India.* Department of the Army Pamphlet No. 550-21. Washington, DC: US Government Printing Office, 1964.

ISRAEL

Adan, Avraham. *On the Banks of the Suez.* Novato, CA: Presidio Press, 1980.

Allon, Yigal. *The Making of Israel's Army.* New York: Universe Books, 1971.

Collins, Larry. *Oh Jerusalem!.* New York: Simon and Schuster, 1972.

Herzog, Chaim. *The War of Atonement: October 1973.* Boston: Little, Brown and Co., 1975.

Katz, Sam. *Israeli Defence Forces Since 1973.* London: Osprey Publishing Ltd., 1986.

Luttwak, Edward, and Horowitz, Dan. *The Israeli Army.* New York: Harper & Row, 1983.

Nyrop, Richard F. *Israel: A Country Study.* Washington, DC: The American University, 1987.

Selected Readings in Tactics: The 1973 Middle East War. Fort Leavenworth, KS: The US Army Command and General Staff College, 1980.

Teveth, Shabtai. *The Tanks of Tammuz.* New York: The Viking Press, 1968.

JAPAN

Buck, James H. (ed.). *The Modern Japanese Military System.* Beverly Hills, CA: Sage Publications, 1975.

McIntosh, Malcolm. *Japan Rearmed.* London: Frances Pinter, 1986.

Reynolds, Gary K. *Japan's Military Buildup: Goals and Accomplishments.* Washington, DC: Congressional Research Service, Library of Congress, 1989.

Korea

Bermudez, Joseph S., Jr. *North Korean Special Forces*. Coulsden, Surrey, UK: Jane's Publishing Co., Ltd., 1988.

Bolger, Daniel P. *Scenes from an Unfinished War: Low-Intensity Conflict in Korea, 1966–1969*. Fort Leavenworth: Combat Studies Institute, 1991.

Bunge, Frederica M. *North Korea: A Country Study*. Washington, DC: American University, 1981.

— *South Korea: A Country Study*. Washington, DC: American University, 1981.

Clare, Kenneth G., *et al. Area Handbook for the Republic of Korea*. Washington, DC: US Government Printing Office, 1969.

North Korea: The Foundations of Military Strength. Washington, DC: The Defense Intelligence Agency, 1991.

North Korean Military Forces. Field Manual 34-71. Washington, DC: Department of the Army, 1982.

Ridgway, Mathew. *The Korean War*. Garden City, NY: Doubleday and Co., 1967.

Savada, Andreas Matlas. *South Korea: A Country Study*. Washington, DC: American University, 1992.

Sawyer, Robert K. *Military Advisors in Korea: KMAG in Peace and War*. Washington, DC: Office of the Chief of Military History, 1962.

Pakistan

Cohen, Stephen P. *The Pakistan Army*. Berkeley, California: University of California Press, 1984.

Hasan-Askari Rizvi. *The Military and Politics in Pakistan, 1947–1968*. Dehli: Konark Publishers Pvt Ltd, 1988.

Khan, Fazal Muqeem. *The Story of the Pakistan Army*. Karachi: Oxford University Press, 1963.

Nyrop, Richard F., *et al. Area Handbook for Pakistan*. Washington, DC: American University, 1975.

— *Pakistan: A Country Study*. Washington, DC: American University, 1983.

Poland

Keefe, Eugene, *et al. Poland: A Country Study*. Washington, DC: American University, 1972.

Walendowski, Edmund. *Combat Motivation of the Polish Forces*. New York: St. Martin's Press, 1988.

Soviet Union

Chaney, Otto Preston, Jr. *Zhukov*. Norman: University of Oklahoma Press, 1971.

Gander, Terry. *A History of the Soviet Army*. New York: Frederick A. Praeger, 1966.

Grechcko, A.A. *The Armed Forces of the Soviet State*. Moscow: Voenizdat, 1975. Translated and published under the auspices of the US Air Force. Washington, DC. US Government Printing Office, n.d.

Grigorenko, Petro. *Memoirs*. New York: W.W. Norton Co., 1982.

Isby, David C. *War in A Distant Country, Afghanistan: Invasion and Resistance*. London: Arms & Armour Press, 1989.

Kolkowicz, Roman. *The Soviet Military and the Communist Party*. Boulder: Westview Press, 1985.

Lee, William T., and Staar, Richard F. *Soviet Military Power since World War II*. Stanford, CA: Hoover Institution Press, 1986.

Liddell Hart, Basil H., ed. *The Red Army.* New York: Harcourt and Brace, 195 .

Milsom, John. *Russian Tanks 1900–1970.* Harrisburg, PA: Stackpole Books, 1971.

O'Ballance, Edgar. *The Red Army.* Faber and Faber, 1964.

Record, Jeffrey. *Sizing Up the Soviet Army.* Washington, DC: The Brookings Institute, 1972.

Scott, Harriet Fast, and Scott, William. *The Armed Forces of the USSR.* Boulder: Westview, 1979.

Seaton, Albert, and Seaton, Joan. *The Soviet Army: 1918 to Present.* New York: New American Library, 1986.

— *Stalin As Military Commander.* New York: Praeger, 1976.

Sodol, Petro R. *UPA: They Fought Against Hitler and Stalin.* New York: Committee for the World Convention and Reunion of Soldiers in the Ukrainian Insurgent Army, 1987.

Sokolovskiy, V.D. *Soviet Military Strategy.* 3rd ed., Harriet Fast Scott (ed.). New York: Crane, Russak & Co., 1975.

Tyushkevich, S.A. *The Soviet Armed Forces: A History of Their Organizational Development.* Moscow: Voenizdat, 1978.

 Translated and published under the auspices of the US Air Force. Washington, DC: US Government Printing Office, n.d.

Zaloga, Steven J. *Modern Soviet Armor.* Englewood Cliffs, NJ: Prentiss-Hall, Inc., 1979.

UNITED STATES

Appleton, Roy E. *United States Army in the Korean War: South to the Naktong, North to the Yalu.* Washington, DC: Office of the Chief of Military History, 1961.

Bacevich, A. J. *The Pentomic Era: The U.S. Army Between Korea and Vietnam.* Washington, DC: National Defense University Press, 1986.

Bradley, Omar. *A General's Life.* New York: Simon and Schuster, 1983.

Doughty, Robert A. *The Evolution of US Army Tactical Doctrine, 1946–76.* Leavenworth, KS: US Army Command and General Staff College, 1979.

Gugeler, Russell A. *Combat Actions in Korea.* Washington, DC: Office of the Chief of Military History, 1970.

Halberstadt, Hans. *NTC: A Primer of Modern Land Combat.* Novato: Presidio Press, 1989.

Heller, Charles E., and Storft, William A. (eds.). *America's First Battles 1776–1965.* Lawrence: University Press of Kansas, 1986.

Huston, James A. *The Sinews of War: Army Logistics 1775–1953.* Washington, DC: Office of the Chief of Military History, 1966.

Krepinevich, Andrew F., Jr. *The Army and Vietnam.* Baltimore: The Johns Hopkins University Press, 1986.

Marshall, S. L. A. *Bringing Up the Rear.* San Rafael, CA: Presidio Press, 1979.

— *Men Against Fire.* New York: William Morrow and Co., 1947.

Paddock, Alfred H., Jr. *US Army Special Warfare: Its Origins.* Washington, DC: National Defense University Press, 1982.

Palmer, Bruce, Jr. *The 25-Year War: America's Military Role in Vietnam.* New York: Simon and Schuster, 1984.

Ridgway, Mathew B. *The Korean War.* Garden City, NY: Doubleday and Co. Inc., 1967.

Rottman, Gordon L. *Inside the US Army Today.* London: Osprey Publishing Ltd., 1988.

— *US Army Airborne 1940–1990.* London: Osprey Publishing Ltd., 1990.

— *US Army Special Forces 1952–84.* London: Osprey Publishing Ltd., 1985.

Russell, Lee E., and Mendez, Albert M. *Grenada 1983.* London: Osprey Publishing Ltd., 1985.

Schnabel, James F. *United States Army in the Korean War, Policy and Direction: The First Year.* Washington, DC: Office of the Chief of Military History, 1972.

Schwarzkopf, H. Norman. *It Doesn't Take a Hero.* New York: Bantam Books, 1992.

Sheehan, Neil. *A Bright Shining Lie: John Paul Vann and America in Vietnam.* New York: Random House, 1988.

Sparrow, John C. *History of Personnel Demobilization in the United States Army.* Washington, DC: Department of the Army, 1952.

Stanton, Shelby L. *The Rise and Fall of an American Army: U.S. Ground Forces in Vietnam, 1965–1973.* Novato: Presidio Press, 1985.

Taylor, Maxwell. *The Uncertain Trumpet.* New York: Harper Brothers, 1960.

Turley, G. H. *The Easter Offensive: The Last American Advisors: Vietnam, 1972.* Novato, CA: Presidio Press, 1985.

Vetock, Dennis J. *Lessons Learned: A History of US Army Lesson Learning.* Carlisle Barracks, PA: US Army Military History Institute, 1988.

Weighley, Russell F. *The American Way of War.* New York: The Macmillan Publishing Co., 1973.

— *History of the United States Army.* Bloomington, IN: Indiana University Press, 1984.

Vietnam

Arnold, James R. *Tet Offensive 1968: Turning Point of the War.* London: Osprey Publishing Ltd., 1990.

Cima, Ronald J. (ed.). *Vietnam: A Country Study.* Washington, DC: American University, 1989.

Conboy, Ken, *et al. The NVA and Viet Cong.* London: Osprey Publishing Ltd., 1991.

Davidson, Phillip B. *Vietnam at War: The History 1946–1975.* Novato, CA: Presidio Press, 1988.

Fall, Bernard. *Street Without Joy.* Harrisburg, PA: The Stackpole Company, 1967.

— *The Two Vietnams: A Political and Military Analysis.* New York: Frederick A. Praeger, Publishers, 1967.

Hosmer, Stephen T., *et al. The Fall of South Vietnam: Statements by Vietnamese Military and Civilian Leaders.* New York: Crane, Russak & Co., Inc., 1980.

Pike, Douglas. *PAVN: People's Army of Vietnam.* Novato, CA: Presidio Press, 1986.

— *Viet Cong.* Cambridge, MA: The M.I.T. Press, 1966.

Sheehan, Neil. *A Bright Shining Lie: John Paul Vann and America in Vietnam.* New York: Random House, 1988.

Smith, Harvey H., *et al. Area Handbook for South Vietnam.* Washington, DC: US Government Printing Office, 1967.

— *North Vietnam: A Country Study.* Washington, DC: American University, 1966.

NATO And Tthe Warsaw Pact

Cordesman, Athony. *NATO's Central Region Forces.* London: Jane's, 1988.

Gabriel, Richard A. *Fighting Armies: NATO and the Warsaw Pact, A Combat Assessment.* Westport, CT: Greenwood Press, 1983.

Isby, David C., and Kamps, Charles, Jr. *Armies of NATO's Central Front.* London: Jane's Publishing Co., Ltd, 1983.

Johnson, A. Ross, *et al. East European Military Establishments: The Warsaw Pact Northern Tier*. New York: Crane Russak, 1980.

Lewis, William J. *Warsaw Pact: Arms, Doctrine, and Strategy*. New York: McGraw-Hill Publications Co., 1982.

Nelson, Daniel N. *Soviet Allies: The Warsaw Pact and the Issue of Reliability*. Boulder, CO: Westview Press, 1984.

Pivka, Otto von. *The Armies of Europe Today*. London: Osprey Publishing Ltd., 1974.

Rottman, Gordon L. *Warsaw Pact Ground Forces*. London: Osprey Publishing Ltd., 1987.

Simon, Jeffrey (ed.). *NATO – Warsaw Pact Force Mobilization*. Washington, DC: The National Defense University Press, 1988.

Woller, Rudolf. *Warsaw Pact Reserve Systems: A White Paper*. Munich: Bernard & Graefe Verlag, 1978.

THE MIDDLE EAST

Collelo, Thomas (ed.). *Syria: A Country Study*. Washington, DC: American University, 1988.

Gabriel, Richard A. *Fighting Armies: Antagonists in the Middle East, A Combat Assessment*. Westport, CT: Greenwood Press, 1983.

Heller, Mark, *et al* (eds.). *The Middle East Military Balance 1984*. Tel Aviv: Tel Aviv University, 1984.

Isby, David C. *War in a Distant Country, Afghanistan: Invasion and Resistance*. London: Arms & Armour Press, 1989.

Katz, Samuel. *Arab Armies of the Middle East Wars (2)*. London: Osprey Publishing Ltd., 1988.

— *Armies in Lebanon 1982–84*. London: Osprey Publishing Ltd., 1986.

Laffin, John. *Arab Armies of the Middle East Wars 1948–73*. London: Osprey Publishing Ltd., 1985.

Metz, Helen Chapin. *Iran: A Country Study*. Washington, DC: American University, 1989.

— *Iraq: A Country Study*. Washington, DC: American University, 1990.

Nyrop, Richard F. (ed.). *Egypt: A Country Study*. Washington, DC: American University, 1983.

— *Iran: A Country Study*. Washington, DC: American University, 1978.

O'Ballance, Edgar. *The Gulf War*. London: Brassey's Defence Publishers, 1988.

Zabih, Sepehr. *The Iranian Military in Revolution and War*. London: Routledge, 1988.

GENERAL WORKS

Carver, Michael. *Twentieth-Century Warriors: The Development of the Armed Forces of the Major Military Nations in the Twentieth Century*. New York: Weidenfeldt & Nicholson, 1987.

Foss, Christopher F. *Jane's AFV Recognition Handbook*. London: Jane's, 1987.

Foss, Christopher F. *Jane's World Armoured Fighting Vehicles*. New York: St. Martin's Press, 197 .

Gabriel, Richard A. *Fighting Armies: Non-aligned, Third World, and Other Ground Armies – A Combat Assessment*. Westport, CT: Greenwood Press, 1983.

Harkavy, Robert E., and Neumann, Stephanie G. *The Lessons of Recent Wars in the Third World*, vol.I. Lexington, MA: Lexington Books, 1985.

House, Jonathan M. *Toward Combined Arms Warfare: A Survey of 20th-Century Tactics, Doctrine, and Organization*. Fort Leavenworth, KS: US Army Command and

General Staff College, 1984.

Keegan, John. *World Armies*. Detroit: Gale Research Co., 1983.

McMichael, Scott R. *A Historical Perspective on Light Infantry*. Fort Leavenworth, KS: US Army Command and General Staff College, 1987.

Messenger, Charles. *The Blitzkrieg Story*. New York: Charles Scribner's Sons, 1976.

Olsen, Edward A., and Jurika, Stephen, Jr. *The Armed Forces of Contemporary Asian Societies*. Boulder: Westview Press, 1986.

INDEX